CULTURE

What makes *CULTURE* special?

What's Inside

Engaging pedagogy designed to be eye-catching and visually appealing can be found throughout the text.

Got IT?

Got It introduces the reading with important questions discussed in the chapter.

STUDY TIP

Study Tips call attention to important concepts and suggest effective strategies for learning and studying.

Pop Quiz

Pop Quiz helps students to master key chapter material.

CULTURE THINK

Culture Think questions throughout each chapter prompt students to think more deeply about a topic discussed in the text.

Did You Know

Did You Know provides short, engaging nuggets of information relevant to the chapter.

Get Involved sections push students to actively investigate anthropological issues that are relevant to them.

get involved!

ANTHROPOLOGY WORKS

Anthropology Works exposes students to the ways anthropology is useful in a variety of careers such as teaching, business, law enforcement and healthcare.

FOR REVIEW

For Review summarizes the key points of each chapter in an easy-to-read format.

POPCULTURE

Pop CULTURE teaches anthropological concepts through popular culture familiar to students.

Name: ..... Lisa Gezon ....

Education: ..... B.A. in Anthropology from Albion College; Ph.D. from the University of Michigan (Conrad Kottak was my advisor)

Occupation: ..... Professor and Department Chair at the University of West Georgia, Mother

Hobbies: ..... Hiking, yoga, swimming, singing in a chorus

Favorite places to travel: ..... I love exploring new places, but I enjoy going back to Madagascar, France, and Central America.

Family: ..... I have two boys (ages 14 and 15), two siblings, and four nephews.

Last books read: ..... The Gift by Hafiz; All Things Bright and Beautiful by James Herriot

Favorite films: ..... The Color of Paradise, Groundhog Day

Latest accomplishment: ..... My book was published in 2012. It is called Drug Effects: Khat in Biocultural and Socioeconomic Perspective (Left Coast Press)

Favorite quote: ..... "A little learning is a dangerous thing: Drink deep or taste not the Pierian spring" –Alexander Pope, 1711, from "An Essay in Criticism"

Name: ..... Conrad Kottak ....

Education: ..... Columbia College and Columbia University

Occupation: ..... Academic and Applied Anthropologist, Writer, Researcher

Hobbies: ..... Swimming laps, watching baseball, movies, theater, TV

Favorite places to travel: ..... Brazil, New York, San Francisco, London, Paris

Family: ..... Married with two adult children and three (expecting a fourth) grandchildren

Last books read: ..... The Hunger Games by Suzanne Collins

Favorite films: ..... Star Wars (the original one) and Casablanca

Latest accomplishment: ..... Chairing Section 51, Anthropology, at the National Academy of Sciences

Favorite quote: ..... "Never doubt that a small group of concerned citizens can change the world. Indeed, it's the only thing that ever has." —Margaret Mead

Ch. 4
LANGUAGE AND COMMUNICATION

Brief Contents

Ch. 7
FAMILIES, KINSHIP,
AND MARRIAGE

Ch. 11 >
ETHNICITY
AND RACE

Ch. 5 >
MAKING A LIVING

CULTURE, SECOND EDITION

Senior Vice President, Products & Markets **Kurt L. Strand**

Vice President, General Manager, Products & Markets **Michael Ryan**

Vice President, Content Production & Technology Services **Kimberly Meriwether David**

Managing Director **Gina Boedeker**

Director **Matthew Busbridge**

Brand Manager **Courtney Austermehle**

Senior Director of Development **Dawn Groundwater**

Content Development Editor **Craig Leonard**

Editorial Coordinator **Ryan Viviani**

Marketing Manager **Josh Zlatkus**

Director, Content Production **Terri Schiesl**

Content Project Manager **Jennifer Gehl**

Senior Buyer **Laura Fuller**

Designer **Margarite Reynolds**

Interior Designer **Linda Robertson**

Cover Designer **Preston Thomas**

Cover Images **front cover** © Hugh Sitton/Corbis;
**back cover © Comstock Images; inside front cover
(top) © Hugh Sitton/Corbis;
(bottom) © Robin Utrecht/Fotografie/HillCreek Pictures/Corbis;
inside back cover © Photodisc/Getty Images**

Content Licensing Specialist **Brenda Rolwes**

Photo Researcher **Toni Michaels / PhotoFind, LLC**

Media Project Manager **R. Mahalakshmi**

Compositor **Laserwords Private Limited**

Typeface **10/12 Times Roman**

Printer **LSC Communications**

2 3 4 5 6 7 8 9 LWI 21 20 19 18 17

ISBN 978-0-07-803504-3
MHID 0-07-803504-X

Library of Congress Control Number: 2010942152

www.mhhe.com

Table of Contents

What Is Anthropology? 1

2

Culture 16

3 Doing Anthropology 38

4 Language and Communication 56

Making a Living   76

6

Political Systems   98

Families, Kinship, and Marriage   122

10

The World System and Colonialism   188

Ethnicity and Race 212

12

Applying Anthropology 238

13

Anthropology's Role in a Globalizing World   258

WHAT IS ANTHROPOLOGY?

UNDERSTANDING OURSELVES

When you were young, your parents might have told you that drinking milk and eating vegetables would help you grow up "big and strong."

They probably didn't as readily recognize the role that *culture* plays in shaping bodies, personalities, and personal health. If nutrition matters in growth, so, too, do cultural guidelines. Our bodies are affected by the kinds of work we do, the homes we live in, the ways we play and relax, the gender roles of males and females, our religion, and the ways we relate to our family, friends, and neighbors. Culture is an environmental force that affects our development as much as do nutrition, heat, cold, and altitude.

Think about the phrases and sentences you would use to describe yourself in a personal ad or on a networking site—your likes and dislikes, hobbies, and habits. How many of these descriptors would be the same if you had been born in a different place or time? We usually think about "who we are" as a collection of set characteristics and tendencies, but this idea is as culturally determined as any of the traits we might put on an "about me" list. In other cultures, people might describe themselves by referencing their relationship to one or more gods, their success as a hunter, or their roles as family members.

Among scholarly disciplines, anthropology stands out as the field that provides the cross-cultural test. How much would we know about human behavior, thought, and feeling if we studied only our own kind? What if our entire understanding of human behavior were based on analysis of questionnaires filled out by college students in Oregon? One culture, age group, or gender can't tell us everything we need to know about what it means to be human. Often culture is "invisible," and thus unexamined, until it is placed in comparison to another culture. For example, to appreciate how watching television affects us as human beings, we need to study not just North America today but some other place—and perhaps also some other time (such as Brazil in the 1980s; see Kottak 1990b). The cross-cultural test is fundamental to the anthropological approach, which orients this textbook.

>> The Cross-Cultural Perspective

"That's just human nature." "People are pretty much the same all over the world." Such opinions, which we hear in conversations, in the mass media, and in a dozen scenes in daily life, promote the erroneous idea that people in other countries have the same desires, feelings, values, and aspirations that we do. Such statements proclaim that because people are essentially the same,

ethnography Fieldwork in a particular culture.

they are eager to receive the ideas, beliefs, values, institutions, practices, and products of an expansive North American culture. Often this assumption turns out to be wrong.

Anthropology offers a broader view—a distinctive comparative, cross-cultural perspective. Most people think that anthropologists study nonindustrial societies, and they do—but that's not all they do. Although Lisa Gezon has done some research on sustainable agriculture and water use in the state of Georgia, USA, she has spent most of her research time in Madagascar, a large island off the southeast coast of Africa. With Conrad Kottak as her graduate school adviser, she first studied how people in a local chiefdom responded to forest conservation. In her next study, she traced the drug *khat* as

it went from farmers' fields into the hands of traders, and finally into the mouths of urban consumers. Conrad Kottak's research also has taken him to remote villages in Brazil and Madagascar. In Brazil he sailed with fishers in simple sailboats on Atlantic waters. Among Madagascar's Betsileo people he worked in rice fields and took part in ceremonies in which he entered tombs to rewrap the corpses of decaying ancestors.

Anthropology, which originated as the study of nonindustrial peoples, is a comparative science that now extends to all societies, ancient and modern, simple and complex. Most of the other social sciences tend to focus on a single society, usually an industrial nation such as the United States or Canada. Anthropology offers a unique cross-cultural perspective, constantly comparing the customs of one society with those of others.

To become a cultural anthropologist, one normally does **ethnography** (the firsthand, personal study of local settings). Ethnographic fieldwork usually entails spending a year or more in another society, living with the local people and learning about their way of life. No matter how much the ethnographer discovers about the society, he or she remains an alien there. That experience of alienation has a profound impact. Having learned to respect other customs and beliefs, anthropologists can never forget that there is a wider world. There are normal ways of thinking and acting other than our own.

>> Human Adaptability

Anthropologists study human beings wherever and whenever they find them—in a Turkish café, a Mesopotamian tomb, or a North American shopping mall. Anthropology is the exploration of human diversity in time and space. Anthropology studies the whole of the human condition: past, present, and future; biology, society, language, and culture. Of particular interest is the diversity that comes through human adaptability.

In Mozambique's Gaza province, the Dutch ethnographer Janine van Vugt (red hair) sits on a mat near reed houses, talking to local women.

Two key assumptions of anthropology:

- Understanding human nature requires comparative, cross-cultural studies.

- People are best understood holistically, incorporating the whole of the human condition, including biological and cultural influences.

Humans are among the world's most adaptable animals. In the Andes of South America, people wake up in villages 16,000 feet above sea level and then trek 1,500 feet higher to work in tin mines. Tribes in the Australian desert worship animals and discuss philosophy. People survive malaria in the tropics. Men have walked on the moon. The model of the starship *Enterprise* in Washington's Smithsonian Institution symbolizes the desire to "seek out new life and civilizations, to boldly go where no one has gone before." Wishes to know the unknown, control the uncontrollable, and create order out of chaos find expression among all peoples. Creativity, adaptability, and flexibility are basic human attributes, and human diversity is the subject matter of anthropology.

Students often are surprised by the breadth of **anthropology,** which is the study of the human species and its immediate ancestors. Anthropology is a uniquely comparative and **holistic** science. *Holism* refers to the study of the whole of the human condition: past, present, and future; biology, society, language, and culture.

People share *society*—organized life in groups—with other animals, including baboons, wolves, mole rats, and even ants. Culture, however, is more distinctly human. **Cultures** are traditions and customs, transmitted through learning, that form and guide the beliefs and behavior of the people exposed to them. Children learn such a tradition by growing up in a particular society, through a process called enculturation. Cultural traditions include customs and opinions, developed over the generations, about proper and improper behavior. These traditions answer such questions as these: How should we do things? How do we make sense of the world? How do we tell right from wrong? What is right, and what is wrong? A culture produces a degree of consistency in behavior and thought among the people who live in a particular society.

anthropology The study of the human species and its immediate ancestors.

holistic Pertaining to the whole of the human condition, past, present, and future; biology, society, language, and culture.

culture Traditions and customs that govern behavior and beliefs; distinctly human; transmitted through learning.

The most critical element of cultural traditions is their transmission through learning rather than through biological inheritance. Culture is not itself biological, but it rests on certain features of human biology. For more than a million years, humans have had at least some of the biological capacities on which culture depends. These abilities are to learn, to think symbolically, to use language, and to employ tools and other products in organizing their lives and adapting to their environments.

A culture produces a degree of consistency among members of the same society. Cultural celebrations, such as this Chinese wedding, are patterned in particular ways based on cultural traditions.

Anthropology confronts and ponders major questions of human existence as it explores human biological and cultural diversity in time and space. By examining ancient bones and tools, we unravel the mysteries of human origins. When did our ancestors separate from those remote great-aunts and great-uncles whose descendants are the apes? Where and when did *Homo sapiens* originate? How has our species changed? What are we now, and where are we going? How have changes in culture and society influenced biological change? Our genus, *Homo,* has been changing for more than two million years. Humans continue to adapt and change both biologically and culturally.

adaptation The process by which organisms cope with environmental stresses.

food production Plant cultivation and animal domestication.

general anthropology The field of anthropology as a whole, consisting of cultural, archaeological, biological, and linguistic anthropology.

ADAPTATION, VARIATION, AND CHANGE

Adaptation refers to the processes by which organisms cope with environmental forces and stresses, such as those posed by climate and *topography,* or terrains, also called landforms. How do organisms change to fit their environments, such as dry climates or high mountain altitudes? Like other animals, humans use biological means of adaptation. But humans are unique in also having cultural means of adaptation. Table 1.1 summarizes the cultural and biological means that humans use to adapt to high altitudes.

CULTURE THINK

How have people adapted to changing economic conditions? Talk with people around you about what kinds of jobs they or people they know are finding. How do you think things were different at a previous time in history, say, at the time of the American Revolution or after World War II? What kinds of jobs were available then?

Mountainous terrains pose particular challenges, those associated with high altitude and oxygen deprivation. Consider four ways (one cultural and three biological) in which humans may cope with low oxygen pressure at high altitudes. Illustrating cultural (technological) adaptation would be a pressurized airplane cabin equipped with oxygen masks. There are three ways of adapting biologically to high altitudes: genetic adaptation, long-term physiological adaptation, and short-term physiological adaptation. First, native populations of high-altitude areas, such as the Andes of Peru and the Himalayas of Tibet and Nepal, seem to have acquired certain genetic advantages for life at very high altitudes. The Andean tendency to develop a voluminous chest and lungs probably has a genetic basis. Second, regardless of their genes, people who grow up at a high altitude become physiologically more efficient there than genetically similar people who have grown up at sea level would be. This illustrates long-term physiological adaptation during the body's growth and development. Third, humans also have the capacity

TABLE 1.1

Forms of Cultural and Biological Adaptation (to High Altitude)

Form of Adaptation	Type of Adaptation	Example
Technology	Cultural	Pressurized airplane cabin with oxygen masks
Genetic adaptation (occurs over generations)	Biological	Larger "barrel chests" native highlanders
Short-term physiological adaptation (occurs spontaneously when the individual organism enters a new environment)	Biological	Increased heart rate, hyperventilation
Long-term adaptation (occurs during growth and development of the individual organism)	Biological	More efficient respiratory system, to extract oxygen from "thin air"

for short-term or immediate physiological adaptation. Thus, when lowlanders arrive in the highlands, they immediately increase their breathing and heart rates. Hyperventilation increases the oxygen in their lungs and arteries. As the pulse also increases, blood reaches their tissues more rapidly. All these varied adaptive responses—cultural and biological—achieve a single goal: maintaining an adequate supply of oxygen to the body.

As human history has unfolded, the social and cultural means of adaptation have become increasingly important. In this process, humans have devised diverse ways of coping with the range of environments they have occupied in time and space. The rate of cultural adaptation and change has accelerated, particularly during the past ten thousand years. For millions of years, hunting and gathering of nature's bounty—*foraging*—was the sole basis of human subsistence. It took only a few thousand years, however, for **food production** (the cultivation of plants and domestication of animals), which originated some ten to twelve thousand years ago, to replace foraging in most areas. The first civilizations rose between 6000 and 5000 B.P. ("before the present"—years ago; in this case, five to six thousand years ago). These were large, powerful, and complex societies, such as ancient Egypt, that conquered and governed large geographic areas.

Much more recently, the spread of industrial production has profoundly affected human life. Throughout human history, major innovations have spread at the expense of earlier ones. Each economic revolution has had social and cultural repercussions. Today's global economy and communications link all contemporary people, directly or indirectly, in the modern world system. People must cope with forces generated by progressively larger systems—region, nation, and world. The study of such contemporary adaptations generates new challenges for anthropology: "The cultures of world peoples need to be constantly rediscovered as these people reinvent them in changing historical circumstances" (Marcus and Fischer 1986, p. 24).

Got IT? Can you define adaptation, identifying how humans adapt in both cultural and biological ways?

The Sherpas of Nepal, one of whom is shown here (on the right) with a female trekker, have adapted culturally and biologically to their high-altitude environment.

>> General Anthropology

The academic discipline of anthropology, also known as **general anthropology,** or "four-field" anthropology, includes four main subdisciplines or subfields. They are sociocultural, archaeological, biological, and linguistic anthropology. (From here on, the shorter term *cultural anthropology* will be used as a synonym for "sociocultural anthropology.") Of the subfields, cultural anthropology has the largest membership. Most departments of anthropology teach courses in all four subfields.

There are historical reasons for the inclusion of four subfields in a single discipline. The origin of anthropology

CULTURE THINK

What unites the four subdisciplines of anthropology into a single discipline? How might anthropology's diversity—as a discipline that includes biological as well as cultural perspectives, for example—be a strength? How might it be a weakness?

as a scientific field, and of American anthropology in particular, can be traced to the nineteenth century. Early American anthropologists were concerned especially with the history and cultures of the native peoples of North America. Interest in the origins and diversity of Native Americans brought together studies of customs, social life, language, and physical traits. Anthropologists still ponder such questions as these: Where did Native Americans come from? How many waves of migration brought them to the New World? What are the linguistic, cultural, and biological links among Native Americans and between them and Asia? (Note that a unified four-field anthropology did not develop in Europe, where the subfields tend to exist separately.)

There also are logical reasons for the unity of American anthropology. Each subfield considers variation in time and space (that is, in different geographic areas). Cultural and archaeological anthropologists study (among many other topics) changes in social life and customs. Archaeologists use studies of living societies to imagine what life might have been like in the past. Biological anthropologists examine evolutionary changes in physical form, for example, anatomical changes that might have been associated with the origin of tool use or language. Linguistic anthropologists may reconstruct the basics of ancient languages by studying modern ones.

Ely S. Parker, or Ha-sa-no-an-da, was a Seneca Indian who made significant contributions to early anthropology.

The subfields influence one another as anthropologists interact with one another, read books and journals, and meet in professional organizations. General anthropology explores the basics of human biology, society, and culture and considers their interrelations. Anthropologists share certain key assumptions. Perhaps the most fundamental is the idea that sound conclusions about "human nature" cannot be derived from studying a single population, nation, society, or cultural tradition. A comparative, cross-cultural approach is essential.

biocultural Combining biological and cultural approaches and perspectives.

Got IT? Can you list anthropology's four subdisciplines and explain both historical and logical reasons for their being united in a single discipline?

>> Cultural Forces Shape Human Biology

Anthropology's comparative, biocultural perspective recognizes that cultural forces constantly mold human biology. (**Biocultural** refers to the inclusion and combination of both biological and cultural perspectives and approaches to comment on or solve a particular issue or problem.) Culture is a key environmental force in determining how human bodies grow and develop. Cultural traditions promote certain activities and abilities, discourage others, and set standards of physical well-being and attractiveness. Physical activities, including sports, which are influenced by culture, help build the body. For example, North American girls are encouraged to pursue, and therefore do well in, competition involving figure skating, gymnastics, track and field, swimming, diving, and many other sports. Brazilian girls, although excelling in the team sports of basketball and volleyball, haven't fared nearly as well in individual sports as have their American and Canadian counterparts. Why are people encouraged to excel as athletes in some nations but not others? Why do people in some countries invest so much time and effort in competitive sports that their bodies change significantly as a result?

Cultural standards of attractiveness and propriety influence participation and achievement in sports. Americans run or swim not just to compete but to keep trim and fit. Brazil's beauty standards have traditionally accepted more fat, especially in female buttocks and hips. Brazilian men have had some international success in swimming and running, but Brazil rarely sends female swimmers or runners to the Olympics. One reason Brazilian women avoid competitive swimming in particular may be that sport's effects on the body. Years of swimming sculpt a distinctive physique: an enlarged upper torso, a massive neck, and powerful shoulders and back. Successful female swimmers tend to be big, strong, and bulky. The countries that produce them most consistently are the United States, Canada, Australia, Germany, the Scandinavian nations, the Netherlands, and the former Soviet Union, where this body type isn't as stigmatized as it is in Latin countries. Swimmers develop hard bodies, but Brazilian culture says that women should be soft, with big hips and buttocks, not big shoulders. Many young female swimmers in Brazil choose to abandon the sport rather than the "feminine" body ideal.

Although our genetic attributes provide a foundation for our growth and development, human biology is fairly plastic—that is, it is malleable. Culture is an environmental force that affects our development as much as do nutrition, heat, cold, and altitude. Culture also guides our emotional and cognitive growth and helps determine the kinds of personalities we have as adults.

>> The Subdisciplines of Anthropology

CULTURAL ANTHROPOLOGY

The study of human society and culture, known as **cultural anthropology,** is the subfield that describes, analyzes, interprets, and explains social and cultural similarities and differences. To study and interpret cultural diversity, cultural anthropologists engage in two kinds of activity: ethnography (based on fieldwork) and ethnology (based on cross-cultural comparison). Ethnography provides an account of a particular community, society, or culture. During ethnographic fieldwork, the ethnographer gathers data that he or she organizes, describes, analyzes, and interprets to build and present that account, which may be in the form of a book, article, or film. Traditionally, ethnographers have lived in small communities and studied local behavior, beliefs, customs, social life, economic activities, politics, and religion (see Wolcott 2008).

The anthropological perspective derived from ethnographic fieldwork often differs radically from that of economics or political science. Those fields focus on national and official organizations and policies and often on elites. The groups that anthropologists traditionally have studied usually have been relatively poor and powerless. Ethnographers often observe discriminatory practices directed toward such people, who experience food shortages, dietary deficiencies, and other aspects of poverty. Political scientists tend to study programs that national planners develop, while anthropologists discover how these programs work on the local level.

Cultures are not isolated. As noted by Franz Boas (1940/1966) many years ago, contact between neighboring tribes always has existed and has extended over enormous areas. Human populations construct their cultures in interaction with one another, and not in isolation (Wolf 1982, p. ix). Villagers increasingly participate in regional, national, and world events. Exposure to external forces comes through the mass media, migration, and modern transportation. City and nation increasingly invade local communities with the arrival of

President Barack Obama and his mother, Ann Dunham, who was a cultural and applied anthropologist, in an undated photo from the 1960s.

tourists, development agents, government and religious officials, and political candidates. Such linkages are prominent components of regional, national, and international systems of politics, economics, and information. These larger systems increasingly affect the people and places anthropology traditionally has studied. The study of such linkages and systems is part of the subject matter of modern anthropology.

Ethnology examines, interprets, analyzes, and compares the results of ethnography—the data gathered in different societies. It uses such data to compare and contrast and to make generalizations about society and culture. Looking beyond the particular to the more general, ethnologists attempt to identify and explain cultural differences and similarities, to test hypotheses, and to build theory to enhance our understanding of how social and cultural systems work. Ethnology gets its data for comparison not just from

> **cultural anthropology** The study of human society and culture; describes, analyzes, interprets, and explains social and cultural similarities and differences.
>
> **ethnology** The theoretical, comparative study of society and culture; compares cultures in time and space.

TABLE 1.2

Ethnography and Ethnology—Two Dimensions of Cultural Anthropology

Ethnography	Ethnology
Requires fieldwork to collect data	Uses data collected by a series of researchers
Often descriptive	Usually synthetic
Group/community specific	Comparative/cross-cultural

archaeological anthropology The branch of anthropology, commonly known as archaeology, that reconstructs, describes, and interprets human behavior and cultural patterns through material remains; best known for the study of prehistory.

ethnography but also from the other subfields, particularly from archaeological anthropology, which reconstructs social systems of the past. (Table 1.2 summarizes the main contrasts between ethnography and ethnology.)

ARCHAEOLOGICAL ANTHROPOLOGY

The subfield **archaeological anthropology** (more simply, "archaeology") reconstructs, describes, and interprets human behavior and cultural patterns through material remains. At sites where people live or have lived, archaeologists find *artifacts*—material items that humans have made, used, or modified, such as tools, weapons, campsites, buildings, and garbage. Plant and animal remains and ancient garbage tell stories about consumption and activities. Wild and domesticated grains have different characteristics, which allow archaeologists to distinguish between gathering and cultivation. Examination of animal bones reveals the ages of slaughtered animals and provides other information useful in determining whether species were wild or domesticated.

Analyzing such data, archaeologists answer several questions about ancient economies. Did the group get its meat from hunting, or did it domesticate and breed animals, killing only those of a certain age and sex? Did plant food come from wild plants or from sowing, tending, and harvesting crops? Did the residents make, trade for, or buy particular items? Were raw materials available locally? If not, where did they come from? From such information, archaeologists reconstruct patterns of production, trade, and consumption.

Archaeologists have spent much time studying potsherds, fragments of earthenware. Potsherds are more durable than many other artifacts, such as textiles and wood. The quantity of pottery fragments allows estimates of population size and density. The discovery that potters used materials that were not available locally suggests systems of trade. Similarities in manufacture and decoration at different sites may be proof of cultural connections. Groups with similar pots may be historically related. Perhaps they shared common cultural ancestors, traded with one another, or belonged to the same political system.

Many archaeologists examine paleoecology. *Ecology* is the study of interrelations among living things in an environment. The organisms and environment together constitute an *ecosystem,* a patterned arrangement of energy flows and exchanges. Human ecology studies ecosystems that include people, focusing on the ways in which human use "of nature influences and is influenced by social organization and cultural values" (Bennett 1969, pp. 10–11). *Paleoecology* looks at the ecosystems of the past.

In addition to reconstructing ecological patterns, archaeologists may infer cultural transformations, for example, by observing changes in the size and type of sites and the distance between them. A city develops in

An archaeological team works at Harappa, one site from an ancient Indus River civilization dating back some 4,800 years.

a region where only towns, villages, and hamlets existed a few centuries earlier. The number of settlement levels (city, town, village, hamlet) in a society is a measure of social complexity. Buildings offer clues about political and religious features. Temples and pyramids suggest that an ancient society had an authority structure capable of marshaling the labor needed to build such monuments. The presence or absence of certain structures, like the pyramids of ancient Egypt and Mexico, reveals differences in function between settlements. For example, some towns were places where people came to attend ceremonies. Others were burial sites; still others were farming communities.

Archaeologists also reconstruct behavior patterns and lifestyles of the past by excavating. This involves digging through a succession of levels at a particular site. In a given area, through time, settlements may change in form and purpose, as may the connections between settlements. Excavation can document changes in economic, social, and political activities.

Although archaeologists are best known for studying prehistory—that is, the period before the invention of writing—they also study the cultures of historical and even living peoples (see Sabloff 2008). Studying sunken ships off the Florida coast, archaeologists have been able to verify the living conditions on the vessels that brought ancestral African Americans to the New World as enslaved people. In a research project begun in 1973 in Tucson, Arizona, archaeologist William Rathje has learned about contemporary life by studying modern garbage. The value of "garbology," as Rathje calls it, is that it provides "evidence of what people did, not what they think they did, what they think they should have done, or what the interviewer thinks they should have done" (Harrison, Rathje, and Hughes 1994, p. 108). What people report may contrast strongly with their real behavior as revealed by garbology. For example, the garbologists discovered that the three Tucson neighborhoods that reported the lowest beer consumption actually had the highest number of discarded beer cans per household (Podolefsky and Brown 1992, p. 100)! Rathje's garbology also exposed misconceptions about what kinds of trash go into landfills: While most people thought that fast-food containers and disposable diapers were major waste problems, in fact they were relatively insignificant compared with paper, including environmentally friendly, recyclable paper (Rathje and Murphy 2001).

> **biological (physical) anthropology** The branch of anthropology that studies human biological diversity in time and space—for instance, hominid evolution, human genetics, human biological adaptation; also includes primatology (behavior and evolution of monkeys and apes).

BIOLOGICAL, OR PHYSICAL, ANTHROPOLOGY

The subject matter of **biological,** or **physical, anthropology** is human biological diversity in time and space. The

CULTURE THINK

Why do we find impressive civic architecture—for example, the Egyptian pyramids, Mayan temples, and modern skyscrapers—around the world and through history? What messages do these structures communicate about those who built them—or who had them built?

focus on biological variation unites five special interests within biological anthropology:

- Human evolution as revealed by the fossil record (paleoanthropology)

- Human genetics

- Human growth and development

- Human biological plasticity (the body's ability to change as it copes with stresses, such as heat, cold, and altitude)

- The biology, evolution, behavior, and social life of monkeys, apes, and other nonhuman primates

These interests link physical anthropology to other fields: biology, zoology, geology, anatomy, physiology, medicine, and public health. *Osteology*—the study of bones—helps paleoanthropologists, who examine skulls, teeth, and bones, to identify human ancestors and to chart changes in anatomy over time. A *paleontologist* is a scientist who studies fossils. A *paleoanthropologist* is one sort of paleontologist, one who studies the fossil record of human evolution. Paleoanthropologists often collaborate with archaeologists, who study artifacts, in reconstructing biological and cultural aspects of human evolution. Fossils and tools often are found together. Different types of tools provide information about the habits, customs, and lifestyles of the ancestral humans who used them.

primates Members of the zoological order that includes humans, apes, monkeys, and prosimians, such as lemurs.

More than a century ago, Charles Darwin noticed that the variety that exists within any population permits some individuals (those with the favored characteristics) to do better than others at surviving and reproducing. Genetics, which developed later, enlightens us about the causes and transmission of this variety. However, it isn't just genes that cause variety. During any individual's lifetime, the environment works along with heredity to determine biological features. For example, people with a genetic tendency to be tall will be shorter if they are poorly nourished during childhood. Thus, biological anthropology also investigates the influence of environment on the body as it grows and matures. Among the environmental factors that influence the body as it develops are nutrition, altitude, temperature, and disease, as well as cultural factors, such as standards of attractiveness we considered previously.

Biological anthropology (along with zoology) also includes primatology. The **primates** include our closest relatives—apes and monkeys. Primatologists study their biology, evolution, behavior, and social life, often in the primates' natural environments. Primatology assists paleoanthropology, because primate behavior may shed light on early human behavior and human nature.

LINGUISTIC ANTHROPOLOGY

We don't know (and probably never will) when our ancestors acquired the ability to speak, although

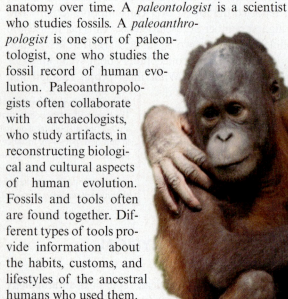

Primatologists study the evolution, biology, behavior, and social life of monkeys and apes, such as these young orangutans.

biological anthropologists have looked to the anatomy of the face and the skull to speculate about the origin of language. And primatologists have described the communication systems of monkeys and apes. We do know that well-developed, grammatically complex languages have existed for thousands of years. Linguistic anthropology offers further illustration of anthropology's interest in comparison, variation, and change. **Linguistic anthropology** studies language in its social and cultural context, across space and over time. Some linguistic anthropologists make inferences about universal features of language, linked perhaps to uniformities in the human brain. Others reconstruct ancient languages by comparing their contemporary descendants and in so doing make discoveries about history. Still others study linguistic differences to discover varied perceptions and patterns of thought in different cultures.

Historical linguistics considers variation in time, such as the changes in sounds, grammar, and vocabulary between Middle English (spoken from approximately 1050 to 1550 C.E.) and modern English. **Sociolinguistics** investigates relationships between social and linguistic variation. No language is a homogeneous system in which everyone speaks just like everyone else. How do different speakers use a given language? How do linguistic features correlate with social factors, including class and gender differences (Tannen 1990)? One reason for variation is geography, as in regional dialects and accents. Linguistic variation also is expressed in the bilingualism of ethnic groups. Linguistic and cultural anthropologists collaborate in studying links between language and many other aspects of culture, such as how people reckon kinship and how they perceive and classify colors.

Got IT? Can you describe the major characteristics of each of the subdisciplines of anthropology?

>> Anthropology and Other Academic Fields

As mentioned previously, one of the main differences between anthropology and the other fields that study people is holism, anthropology's unique blend of biological, social, cultural, linguistic, historical, and contemporary perspectives. Paradoxically, while distinguishing anthropology, this breadth is what also links it to many other disciplines. Techniques used to date fossils and artifacts have come to anthropology from physics, chemistry, and geology. Because plant and animal remains often are found with human bones and artifacts, anthropologists collaborate with botanists, zoologists, and paleontologists.

As a discipline that is both scientific and humanistic, anthropology has links with many other academic fields. Anthropology is a **science**—a "systematic field of study or body of knowledge that aims, through experiment, observation, and deduction, to produce reliable explanations of phenomena, with references to the material and physical world" (*Webster's New World Encyclopedia* 1993, p. 937). The following chapters present anthropology as a humanistic science devoted to discovering, describing, understanding, and explaining similarities and differences in time and space among humans and our ancestors. Clyde Kluckhohn (1944) described anthropology as "the science of human similarities and differences" (p. 9). His statement of the need for such a field still stands: "Anthropology provides a scientific basis for dealing with the crucial dilemma of the world today: how can peoples of different appearance, mutually unintelligible languages, and dissimilar ways of life get along peaceably together?" (p. 9). Anthropology has compiled an impressive body of knowledge that this textbook attempts to encapsulate.

linguistic anthropology The branch of anthropology that studies linguistic variation in time and space, including interrelations between language and culture; includes historical linguistics and sociolinguistics.

sociolinguistics Study of relationships between social and linguistic variation; study of language in its social context.

science A systematic field of study or body of knowledge that aims, through experiment, observation, and deduction, to produce reliable explanations of phenomena, with reference to the material and physical world.

Besides its links to the natural sciences (e.g., geology, zoology), and social sciences (e.g., sociology, psychology), anthropology also has strong links to the humanities. The humanities include English, comparative literature, classics, folklore, philosophy, and the arts. These fields study languages, texts, philosophies, arts, music, performances, and other forms of creative expression. Ethnomusicology, which studies forms of musical expression on a worldwide basis, is especially closely related to anthropology. Also linked is folklore, the systematic study of tales, myths, and legends from a variety of cultures. One might well argue that anthropology is among the most humanistic of all academic fields because of its fundamental respect for human diversity. *Humanism* refers to respect for human diversity and welfare. Anthropologists listen to, record, and represent voices from a multitude of nations and cultures. Anthropology values local knowledge, diverse worldviews, and alternative philosophies. Cultural anthropology and linguistic anthropology in particular bring a comparative and non-elitist perspective to forms of creative expression, including language, art, narratives, music, and dance, viewed in their social and cultural context.

[Got IT?] **Can you compare and contrast anthropology with other disciplines in the humanities and social sciences?**

>> Applied Anthropology

Anthropology is not a science of the exotic carried on by quaint scholars in ivory towers. Rather, anthropology has a lot to tell the public. Anthropology's foremost professional organization, the American Anthropological Association (AAA), has formally acknowledged a public service role by recognizing that anthropology has two dimensions: (1) academic or general anthropology and (2) practicing, or **applied anthropology.** The latter refers to the application of anthropological data, perspectives, theory, and methods to identify, assess, and solve contemporary social problems. As Erve Chambers (1987, p. 309) states it, applied anthropology is the "field of inquiry concerned with the relationships between anthropological knowledge and the uses of that knowledge in the world beyond anthropology." More and more anthropologists from the four subfields now work in such "applied" areas as public health, family planning, business, economic development, and cultural resource management.

applied anthropology The application of anthropological data, perspectives, theory, and methods to identify, assess, and solve contemporary social problems.

cultural resource management (CRM) The branch of applied archaeology aimed at preserving sites threatened by dams, highways, and other projects.

Bronislaw Malinowski is famous for his fieldwork among the matrilineal Trobriand Islanders of the South Pacific. Does this Trobriand market scene suggest anything about the status of Trobriand women?

Applied anthropology encompasses any use of the knowledge and/or techniques of the four subfields to identify, assess, and solve practical problems. Because of anthropology's breadth, it has many applications. For example, applied medical anthropologists consider both the sociocultural and the biological contexts and implications of disease and illness. Perceptions of good and bad health, along with actual health threats and problems, differ among societies. Various ethnic groups recognize different illnesses, symptoms, and causes and have developed different health care systems and treatment strategies.

Applied archaeology, usually called *public archaeology,* includes such activities as cultural resource management, contract archaeology, public education, and historic preservation. One key role for public archaeology has been created by legislation requiring evaluation of sites threatened by dams, highways, and other construction activities. To decide what needs saving, and to preserve significant information about the past when sites cannot be saved, is the work of **cultural resource management (CRM).** CRM involves not only preserving sites but also allowing their destruction if they are not significant. The

POPCULTURE

Consider any one of the four *Indiana Jones* movies directed by Steven Spielberg. Archaeologists often complain that these movies distort public perceptions of their field by portraying archaeologists as greedy, adventurous, amoral, unscientific looters. How, if at all, has Indiana Jones influenced your views about archaeology? More generally, do media portrayals of archaeologists make you think more favorably or less favorably about the field of archaeology?

"management" part of the term refers to the evaluation and decision-making process. Cultural resource managers work for federal, state, and county agencies and other clients. Applied cultural anthropologists sometimes work with the public archaeologists, assessing the human problems generated by a proposed change and determining how they can be reduced.

Got IT? Can you identify how applied anthropology is used to solve problems?

get**involved!**

Learn more about the breadth and unity of the four subfields of anthropology at americananthropological association.org, the website of American anthropologists' foremost professional society. Under "About AAA," click on "What Is Anthropology?" While you're there, also explore "What Do Anthropologists Do?"

FOR REVIEW

I. What is anthropology, and how does it differ from other fields that study human beings?

- Anthropology is the holistic, biocultural, and comparative study of humanity. Unlike other fields that study humans, anthropology explores the whole of the human condition: the origins of, and changes in, our biological and cultural adaptations, and the world's vast diversity of societies, languages, customs, and beliefs. Anthropology seeks to explain both the differences and the similarities among peoples everywhere, past, present, and future.

II. What are the four subfields of anthropology?

- The four subfields are cultural, archaeological, biological, and linguistic anthropology. Cultural anthropology explores human society and culture, describing and explaining cultural similarities and differences. Archaeology reconstructs, describes, and interprets cultural patterns, often of prehistoric populations, through material remains. Biological anthropology studies human biological diversity in time and space. Linguistic anthropology studies language in its social and cultural context across time and space. These subfields have a strong academic dimension, but anthropologists from each subfield are increasingly applying their knowledge to identify, assess, and solve contemporary social problems.

EXPERIENCING CULTURE

TO ACCESS THESE VIDEOS
ON YOUR COMPUTER, VISIT

www.mhhe.com/gezonqr

1-1

1-2

Pop Quiz

Multiple Choice:

1. Which of the following statements most completely characterizes anthropology as a unique field of study?
   a. It studies only ancient and nonindustrial societies.
   b. It includes biology.
   c. It deals with crucial world dilemmas.
   d. It is comparative and holistic.

2. What is the most critical element of cultural traditions?
   a. Their stability owing to the unchanging characteristics of human biology.
   b. Their tendency to change radically every generation.
   c. Their transmission through learning rather than through biological inheritance.
   d. Their tendency to remain unchanged despite changing historical circumstances.

3. How has human reliance on cultural means of adaptation changed?
   a. Humans are just beginning to depend on them.
   b. Humans have become increasingly dependent on them.
   c. Humans have become entirely reliant on biological means.
   d. Humans no longer use cultural means.

4. Four-field anthropology
   a. was shaped largely by early American anthropologists' interests in Native Americans.
   b. lacks unity, since only archaeology and biological anthropology consider variation in time and space.
   c. lacks unity because the four subfields do not share key assumptions.
   d. is weak in examining the relation between biology and culture.

5. Which of the following accurately distinguishes ethnography from ethnology?
   a. Ethnology focuses on the study of particular cultures, while ethnography looks at cultures comparatively.
   b. Traditionally, ethnography was done in large societies with wealth and power, while ethnology focused on small societies with little wealth.
   c. Ethnography studies cultures that are isolated from one another, while ethnology studies nations influenced by globalization.
   d. Ethnologists look beyond the particular cultural data that ethnographers describe and interpret to compare and contrast and make generalizations about society and culture.

6. Anthropology is a humanistic science most particularly because
   a. the techniques it uses come from a variety of sciences, including those that study humans' relations with other animals.
   b. it discovers, describes, and attempts to explain similarities and differences among humans, with concern for the full diversity of worldviews and voices.
   c. it is a systematic study that respects experiment, observation, and deduction as applied to both contemporary human life and human evolution.
   d. over the years it has compiled an impressive body of knowledge about human life.

7. All of the following are true about applied anthropology *except* that
   a. it uses the knowledge, perspectives, or methods of the four subfields to identify, assess, and solve practical human problems.
   b. it is a growing aspect of anthropology, with increasingly more anthropologists developing applied components of their work.
   c. it is less relevant for archaeology, since archaeology concerns the material culture of societies that no longer exist.
   d. it has many applications because of anthropology's breadth.

Fill in the Blank:
1. A _____ approach refers to the inclusion and combination of both biological and cultural perspectives and approaches to comment on or solve a particular issue or problem.

2. _____ provides an account of fieldwork in a particular community, society, or culture.

3. _____ encompasses any use of the knowledge and/or techniques of the four subfields of anthropology to identify, assess, and solve practical problems. More and more anthropologists increasingly work in this dimension of the discipline.

4. The _____ characterizes any anthropological endeavor that formulates research questions and gathers or uses systematic data to test hypotheses.

1. (d), 2. (c), 3. (b), 4. (a), 5. (d), 6. (b), 7. (c)

1. biocultural; 2. Ethnography; 3. Applied anthropology; 4. scientific method

2

CULTURE

UNDERSTANDING OURSELVES

How special are you? To what extent are you "your own person," and to what extent are you a product of your particular culture? Americans may not fully appreciate the power of culture because of the value their culture places on "the *individual*." Yet individualism itself is a distinctive *shared* value, a feature of American culture, transmitted constantly in our daily lives. From the late Mr. (Fred) Rogers of daytime TV to parents, grandparents, and teachers, our enculturative agents insist we are all "someone special." That we are individuals first and members of groups second is the opposite of this chapter's lesson about culture. Certainly we have distinctive features because we are individuals, but we have other distinct attributes because we belong to cultural groups.

For example, a comparison of the United States with Brazil, Italy, or virtually any Latin nation reveals striking contrasts between a national culture (American) that discourages physical affection and national cultures in which the opposite is true. Brazilians approach, touch, and kiss one another much more frequently than North Americans do. In personal encounters, the Brazilian characteristically moves closer, while the North American is apt to retreat. Such movements are products of years of exposure to particular cultural traditions. Middle-class Brazilians teach their kids—both boys and girls—to kiss every adult relative they see. Given the size of Brazilian extended families, this can mean hundreds of people. Women continue kissing all those people throughout their lives, while men typically continue to kiss female relatives and friends, as well as their fathers and uncles.

Do you kiss your father? Your uncle? Your grandfather? How about your mother, aunt, or grandmother? The answer to these questions may differ between men and women, and for male and female relatives. Culture can help us to make sense of these differences.

>> What Is Culture?

Humans share *society,* organized life in groups, with other animals—social animals, such as monkeys, wolves, and ants. Other animals, especially the great apes, have rudimentary cultural abilities, but only humans have fully elaborated cultures—distinctive traditions and customs transmitted over the generations through learning and through language.

The concept of culture has long been basic to anthropology. Well over a century ago, in his book *Primitive Culture,* the British anthropologist Edward Tylor proposed that cultures— systems of human behavior and thought—obey natural laws and therefore can be studied scientifically. Tylor's definition of culture still offers an overview of the subject matter of anthropology and is widely quoted.

enculturation The social process by which culture is learned and transmitted across the generations.

"Culture . . . is that complex whole which includes knowledge, belief, arts, morals, law, custom, and any other capabilities and habits acquired by man as a member of society" (Tylor 1871/1958, p. 1). The crucial phrase here is "acquired . . . as a member of society." Tylor's definition focuses on attributes that people acquire not through biological inheritance but by growing up in a particular society in which they are exposed to a specific cultural tradition. **Enculturation** is the process by which a child *learns* his or her culture.

CULTURE IS LEARNED

The ease with which children absorb any cultural tradition rests on the uniquely elaborated human capacity to learn. Other animals may learn from experience, so that, for example, they avoid fire after discovering that it hurts. Social animals also learn from other members of their group. Wolves, for instance, learn

People learn and share beliefs and behavior as members of cultural groups, for example, in this Muslim primary school in Marrakesh, Morocco.

hunting strategies from other pack members. Such social learning is particularly important among monkeys and apes, our closest biological relatives. But our own *cultural learning* depends on the uniquely developed human capacity to use **symbols,** signs that have no necessary or natural connection to the things they stand for or signify.

On the basis of cultural learning, people create, remember, and deal with ideas. They grasp and apply specific systems of symbolic meaning. Anthropologist Clifford Geertz defined culture as ideas based on cultural learning and symbols. Cultures have been characterized as sets of "control mechanisms—plans, recipes, rules, instructions, what computer engineers call programs for the governing of behavior" (Geertz 1973, p. 44). These programs are absorbed by people through enculturation in particular traditions. People gradually internalize a previously established system of meanings and symbols, which helps guide their behavior and perceptions throughout their lives.

Every person begins immediately, through a process of conscious and unconscious learning and interaction with others, to internalize, or incorporate, a cultural tradition through the process of enculturation. Sometimes culture is taught directly, as when parents tell their children to say "thank you" when someone gives them something or does them a favor.

Culture also is transmitted through observation. Children pay attention to the things that go on around them. They modify their behavior not just because other people tell them to do so but as a result of their own observations and growing awareness of what their culture considers right and wrong. Culture also is absorbed unconsciously. North Americans acquire their culture's notions about how far apart people should stand when they talk, not by being told directly to maintain a certain distance, but through a gradual process of observation, experience, and conscious and unconscious behavior modification. No one tells Latins to stand closer together than North Americans do; they learn to do so as part of their cultural tradition.

CULTURE IS SYMBOLIC

Symbolic thought is unique and crucial to humans and to cultural learning. A symbol is something

verbal or nonverbal, within a particular language or culture, that comes to stand for something else. Anthropologist Leslie White defined culture as

> dependent upon symbolling. . . . Culture consists of tools, implements, utensils, clothing, ornaments, customs, institutions, beliefs, rituals, games, works of art, language, etc. (White 1959, p. 3)

For White, culture originated when our ancestors acquired the ability to use symbols, that is, to originate and bestow meaning on a thing or event and, correspondingly, to grasp and appreciate such meanings (White 1959, p. 3).

There need be no obvious, natural, or necessary connection between the symbol and what it symbolizes. The familiar pet that barks is no more naturally a *dog* than it is a *chien, Hund,* or *mbwa,* the words for "dog" in French, German, and Swahili, respectively. Language is one of

symbol A verbal or nonverbal sign that arbitrarily and by convention stands for something else, with which it has no necessary or natural connection.

the distinctive possessions of *Homo sapiens*. No other animal has developed anything approaching the complexity of language, with its multitude of symbols.

Symbols often are linguistic. There also are myriad nonverbal symbols, such as flags, which stand for various countries, and the arches that symbolize a particular fast-food chain. Holy water is a potent symbol in Roman Catholicism. As is true of all symbols, the association between a symbol (water) and what is symbolized (holiness) is arbitrary and conventional. Water probably is not intrinsically holier than milk, blood, or other natural liquids. Nor is holy water chemically different from ordinary water. Holy water is a symbol within Roman Catholicism, which is part of an international cultural system. A natural thing has been associated arbitrarily with a particular meaning for Catholics, who share common beliefs and experiences that are based on learning and transmitted across the generations.

All humans possess the abilities on which culture rests—to learn, to think symbolically, to manipulate language, and to use tools and other cultural products in organizing their lives and coping with their environments. Every contemporary human population has the ability to use symbols and thus to create and maintain culture. Our nearest relatives—chimpanzees and gorillas—have rudimentary cultural abilities. However, no other animal has elaborated cultural abilities to the extent that *Homo* has.

CULTURE IS SHARED

Culture is an attribute not of individuals per se but of individuals as members of *groups*. Culture is transmitted in society. Don't we learn our culture by observing, listening, talking, and interacting with many other people? Shared beliefs, values, memories, and expectations link people who grow up in the same culture. Enculturation unifies people by providing us with common experiences.

Today's parents were yesterday's children. If they

grew up in North America, they absorbed certain values and beliefs transmitted over the generations. People become agents in the enculturation of their children, just as their parents were for them. Although a culture constantly changes, certain fundamental beliefs, values, worldviews, and child-rearing practices endure. Consider a simple American example of enduring shared enculturation. As children, when we didn't finish a meal, our parents may have reminded us to think of starving children in some foreign country, just as our grandparents might have done a generation earlier. The specific country changes (China, India, Bangladesh, Ethiopia, Somalia, Rwanda—what was it in your home?). Still, American culture goes on transmitting the idea that by eating all our brussels sprouts or broccoli, we can justify our own good fortune, compared to a hungry child in an impoverished or war-ravaged country.

CULTURE AND NATURE

Culture takes the natural biological urges we share with other animals and teaches us how to express them in particular ways. People have to eat, but culture teaches us what, when, and how. In many cultures people have their main meal at noon, but most North Americans prefer a large dinner in the evening. English people eat fish for breakfast, but North Americans prefer hotcakes and cold cereals. Brazilians put hot milk into strong coffee, whereas many North Americans pour cold milk into a weaker brew. Midwesterners dine at five or six, Spaniards at ten.

Cultural habits, perceptions, and inventions mold "human nature" into many forms. People have to eliminate wastes from their bodies. But some cultures teach people to defecate standing, while others tell them to do it sitting down. Peasant women in the Andean highlands squat in the streets and urinate, getting all the privacy they need from their massive skirts. All these habits are parts of cultural traditions that have converted natural acts into cultural customs.

Our culture—and cultural changes—affect how we perceive nature, human nature, and "the natural." Through science, invention, and discovery, cultural advances have overcome many "natural" limitations. We prevent and cure diseases such as polio and smallpox, which felled our ancestors. We use Viagra to enhance or restore sexual potency. Through cloning, scientists have challenged the way we think about biological identity and the meaning of life itself. Culture, of course, does not always protect us from natural threats. Hurricanes, floods, earthquakes, and other natural forces regularly overthrow our wishes to modify the environment through building, development, and expansion. Can you think of other ways in which nature strikes back at culture?

Culture is all encompassing. Lady Gaga is part of American culture as well as American popular culture.

CULTURE IS ALL-ENCOMPASSING

For anthropologists, culture includes much more than refinement, good taste, sophistication, education, and appreciation of the fine arts. Not only college graduates but all people are "cultured." The most interesting and significant cultural forces are those that affect people every day of their lives, particularly those that influence children during enculturation.

Culture, as defined anthropologically, encompasses features that are sometimes regarded as trivial or unworthy of serious study, such as those of "popular" culture. To understand contemporary North American culture, we must consider television, fast-food restaurants, sports, and games. As a cultural manifestation, a rock star may be as interesting as a symphony conductor (or vice versa); a comic book may be as significant as a book-award winner.

CULTURE IS INTEGRATED

Cultures are not haphazard collections of customs and beliefs. Cultures are integrated, patterned systems. If one part of the system (the overall economy, for instance) changes, other parts change as well. For example, during the 1950s most American women planned domestic

> **core values** Key, basic, or central values that integrate a culture and help distinguish it from others.

careers as homemakers and mothers. Most of today's college women, by contrast, hope to find paying jobs when they graduate.

What are some of the social repercussions of this particular economic change? Attitudes and behavior regarding marriage, family, and children have altered. Late marriage, "living together," and divorce have become more common. Work competes with marriage and family responsibilities and reduces the time available to invest in child care.

Cultures are integrated not simply by their dominant economic activities and related social patterns but also by sets of values, ideas, symbols, and judgments. Cultures train their individual members to share certain personality traits. A set of characteristic **core values** (key, basic, central values) integrates each culture and

POP CULTURE

We can learn a lot about a culture by analyzing the ideas, images, and themes reflected in its popular songs. See what you can learn about contemporary American culture by studying the lyrics of a few of the current top-ten songs or last year's top songs. (Top song lists are available at "The Billboard Hot 100" and www.top10songs.com, which gives top ten songs by week and year. For lyrics see www.lyrics.com.)

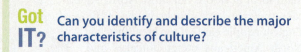

Got IT? Can you identify and describe the major characteristics of culture?

CULTURETHINK

Many cultural patterns such as overconsumption and pollution appear to be maladaptive in the long run. Do you agree? Can you think of others?

helps distinguish it from others. For instance, the work ethic and individualism are core values that have integrated American culture for generations. Different sets of dominant values influence the patterns of other cultures.

CULTURE IS INSTRUMENTAL, ADAPTIVE, AND MALADAPTIVE

Culture is the main reason for human adaptability and success. Other animals rely on biological means of adaptation (such as fur or blubber, which are adaptations to cold). Humans also adapt biologically—for example, by shivering when we get cold or sweating when we get hot. But in addition to biological responses, people also have cultural ways of adapting. To cope with environmental stresses we habitually use technology, or tools. We hunt cold-adapted animals and use their fur coats as our own. We turn the thermostat up in the winter and down in the summer. Or we plan action to increase our comfort. We have a cold drink, jump in a pool, or travel to someplace cooler in the summer or warmer in the winter. People use culture *instrumentally*, that is, to fulfill their basic biological needs for food, drink, shelter, comfort, and reproduction.

hominids Members of the zoological family that includes fossil and living humans, chimps, and gorillas.

hominins Members of the evolutionary line leading to and including modern humans, as distinct from chimps and gorillas.

People also use culture to fulfill psychological and emotional needs, such as friendship, companionship, approval, and being desired sexually. People seek informal support—help from people who care about them—as well as formal support from associations and institutions. To these ends, individuals cultivate ties with others on the basis of common experiences, political interests, aesthetic sensibilities, or personal attraction.

On one level, cultural traits (e.g., air conditioning) may be called *adaptive* if they help individuals cope with environmental stresses. But, on a different level, such traits can also be *maladaptive*. That is, they may threaten a group's continued existence. Thus chlorofluorocarbons from air conditioners deplete the ozone layer and, by doing so, can harm humans and other life. Many modern cultural patterns may be maladaptive in the long run. Some examples of maladaptive aspects of culture are policies that encourage overpopulation, poor food-distribution systems, overconsumption, and industrial pollution of the environment.

>> Culture's Evolutionary Basis

The human capacity for culture has an evolutionary basis that extends back at least two and a half million years to early toolmakers. Evidence for these toolmakers exists in the archaeological record. Based on observation of tool use and manufacture by apes, however, scientists believe the evolutionary basis for culture may extend even farther back.

Similarities between humans and apes, our closest relatives, are evident in anatomy, brain structure, genetics, and biochemistry. Most closely related to us are the African great apes: chimpanzees and gorillas. *Hominidae* is the zoological family that includes fossil and living humans, as well as chimps and gorillas. We refer to members of this family as **hominids.** We use the term **hominins** for the group that leads to humans but not to chimps and gorillas and that encompasses all the human species that have ever existed.

Many human traits reflect the fact that our primate ancestors lived in the trees. These traits include grasping ability and manual dexterity (especially opposable thumbs), depth and color vision, learning ability based on a large brain, substantial parental investment in a limited number of offspring, and tendencies toward sociality and cooperation. Like other primates, humans have flexible, five-fingered hands and *opposable thumbs:* Each thumb can touch all the other fingers on the same hand. Like monkeys and apes, humans also have excellent depth and color vision. Our eyes are placed forward in the skull and look directly ahead, so that their fields of

Hominins have hunted (and gathered) for millions of years. This Hadza man uses a bow and arrow to hunt near Lake Eyasi, Tanzania.

vision overlap. Depth perception, impossible without overlapping visual fields, proved adaptive—for judging distance, for example—in the trees. Having color and depth vision also facilitates the identification of various food sources, as well as mutual grooming—picking out burrs, insects, and other small objects from hair. Such grooming is one way of forming and maintaining social bonds.

The combination of manual dexterity and depth perception allows monkeys, apes, and humans to pick up small objects, hold them in front of their eyes, and appraise them. Our ability to thread a needle reflects an intricate interplay of hands and eyes that took millions of years of primate evolution to achieve. Such dexterity, including the opposable thumb, confers a tremendous advantage in manipulating objects and is essential to a major human adaptive capacity: toolmaking.

In primates, and especially in humans, the ratio of brain size to body size exceeds that of most mammals. Even more important, the brain's outer layer—concerned with memory, association, and integration—is relatively larger. Monkeys, apes, and humans store an array of images in their memories, which permits them to learn more. Such a capacity for learning is another tremendous adaptive advantage. Like most other primates, humans usually give birth to a single offspring. Receiving more parental attention, that one infant has enhanced learning opportunities. The need for longer and more attentive care of offspring places a selective value on support by a social group. Humans have developed considerably the primate tendency to be social animals, living and interacting regularly with other members of their species.

WHAT WE SHARE WITH OTHER PRIMATES

There is a substantial gap between primate *society* (organized life in groups) and fully developed human *culture,* which is based on symbolic thought. Nevertheless, studies of nonhuman primates reveal many similarities with humans, such as the ability to learn from experience and change

behavior as a result. Apes and monkeys, like humans, learn throughout their lives. For example, in one group of Japanese macaques (land-dwelling monkeys), a three-year-old female started washing sweet potatoes before she ate them. First her mother, then her age peers, and finally the entire troop began washing sweet potatoes as well. The ability to benefit from experience confers a tremendous adaptive advantage, permitting the avoidance of fatal mistakes. Faced with environmental change, humans and other primates don't have to wait for a genetic or physiological response. They can modify learned behavior and social patterns instead.

Although humans employ tools much more than any other animal does, tool use also turns up among several nonhuman species, including birds, beavers, sea otters, and especially apes (see Mayell 2003). Humans are not the only animals that make tools with a specific purpose in mind. Chimpanzees living in the Tai forest of Ivory Coast make and use stone tools to break open hard, golf-ball-sized nuts (Mercader, Panger, and Boesch 2002; Wilford 2007). At specific sites, the chimps gather nuts, place them on stumps or flat rocks, which are used as anvils, and pound the nuts

Tool use by chimps. These chimps in Liberia are using stone tools to crack palm nuts, as described in the text.

with heavy stones. The chimps must select hammer stones suited to smashing the nuts and carry them to where the nut trees grow. Nut cracking is a learned skill, with mothers showing their young how to do it.

In 1960, Jane Goodall (1996) began observing wild chimps—including their tool use and hunting behavior—at Gombe Stream National Park in Tanzania, East Africa. The most studied form of ape toolmaking involves "termiting," in which chimps make tools to probe termite hills. They choose twigs, which they modify by removing leaves and peeling off bark to expose the sticky surface beneath. They carry the twigs to termite hills, dig holes with their fingers, and insert the twigs. Finally, they pull out the twigs and dine on termites that were attracted to the sticky surface. Given what is known about ape tool use and manufacture, it is almost certain that early hominins shared this ability, although the first evidence for hominin stone toolmaking dates back only 2.6 million years. In addition, *bipedalism* (moving around upright on two legs) would have permitted the carrying and use of tools and weapons against predators and competitors in an open grassland habitat.

The apes have other abilities essential to culture. Wild chimps and orangs aim and throw objects. Gorillas build nests, and they throw branches, grass, vines, and other objects. Hominins have elaborated the capacity to aim and throw, without which we never would have developed projectile technology and weaponry—or baseball.

Like toolmaking, hunting once was cited as a distinctive human activity not shared with the apes. Again, however, primate research shows that other primates, especially chimpanzees, are habitual hunters. For example, in Uganda's Kibale National Park, chimps form large hunting parties, including an average of twenty-six individuals (almost always adult and adolescent males). Most hunts (78 percent) result in at least one prey item being caught—a much higher success rate than that among lions (26 percent), hyenas (34 percent), or cheetahs (30 percent). Chimps' favored prey in Kibale Park is the red colobus monkey (Mitani and Watts 1999).

Archaeological evidence suggests that humans hunted by at least 2.6 million years ago, based on stone tools found in Ethiopia and Tanzania. Given our current understanding of hunting and toolmaking by chimps, we can infer that hominids may have been hunting much earlier than the first archaeological evidence attests. However, because chimps typically devour the

TABLE 2.1

Cultural Features of Chimpanzees (Rudimentary) and Humans (Fully Developed)		
	Chimpanzees	**Humans**
Cultural Learning	Rudimentary	Fully developed
Tool Use	Occasional	Habitual
Tool Manufacture	Occasional: hammer stones, termiting	Habitual and sophisticated
Aimed Throwing	Occasional objects, not tools	Projectile technology
Hunting	Significant, but no tools	Basic hominin subsistence strategy, with tools
Food Sharing	Meat sharing after hunt	Basic to human life
Cooperation	Occasional in hunting	Basic to human life
Mating and Marriage	Female estrus cycle, limited pair bonds	Year-round mating, marriage, and exogamy
Kin Ties	Limited by dispersal at adolescence	Maintained through sons and daughters

monkeys they kill, leaving few remains, we may never find archaeological evidence for the first hominin hunt, especially if it was done without stone tools.

HOW WE DIFFER FROM OTHER PRIMATES

Although chimps often share meat from a hunt, apes and monkeys (except for nursing infants) tend to feed themselves individually. Cooperation and sharing are much more developed among humans. Until fairly recently (twelve thousand to ten thousand years ago), all humans were hunter-gatherers living in small social groups called bands. In some world areas, the hunter-gatherer way of life persisted into recent times, permitting study by ethnographers. In such societies, men and women bring resources back to the camp and share them. Everyone shares the meat from a large animal. Nourished and protected by younger band members, elders live past reproductive age and are respected for their knowledge and experience. Humans are among the most cooperative of the primates—in the food quest and other social activities. In addition, the amount of information stored in a human band is far greater than that in any other primate group.

Another difference between humans and other primates involves mating. Among baboons and chimps, most mating occurs when females enter estrus, during which they ovulate. In estrus, the vaginal area swells and reddens, and receptive females form temporary bonds with, and mate with, males. Human females, by contrast, lack a visible estrus cycle, and their ovulation is concealed. Not knowing when ovulation is occurring, humans maximize their reproductive success by mating throughout the year. Human pair bonds for mating are more exclusive and more durable than are those of chimps. Related to our more constant sexuality, all human societies have some form of marriage. Marriage gives mating a reliable basis and grants to each spouse special, though not always exclusive, sexual rights in the other.

Marriage creates another major contrast between humans and nonhuman primates: exogamy and kinship systems. Most cultures have rules of *exogamy* requiring marriage outside one's kin or local group. Coupled with the recognition of kinship, exogamy confers adaptive advantages because it creates ties between the spouses' different kin groups. Their children have relatives, and therefore allies, in two kin groups rather than just one. The key point here is that ties of affection and mutual support between members of different local groups tend to be absent among primates other than *Homo.* Other primates tend to disperse at adolescence. Among chimps and gorillas, females tend to migrate, seeking mates in other groups. Humans also choose mates from outside the natal group, and usually at least one spouse moves. However, *humans maintain lifelong ties with sons and daughters.* The systems of kinship and marriage that preserve these links provide a major contrast between humans and other primates. Table 2.1 lists differences in the cultural abilities of humans and chimpanzees, our nearest relatives.

Got IT? Can you explain the evolutionary basis of culture, demonstrating how humans are similar to and different from other primates?

>> Universality, Generality, and Particularity

Anthropologists agree that cultural learning is uniquely elaborated among humans and that all humans have culture. Anthropologists also accept a doctrine termed in the nineteenth century "the psychic unity of man." This means that although *individuals* differ in their emotional and intellectual tendencies and capacities, all human *populations* have equivalent capacities for culture. Regardless of their genes or their physical appearance, people can learn *any* cultural tradition.

To understand this point, consider that contemporary Americans and Canadians are the genetically mixed descendants of people from all over the world. Our ancestors were biologically varied, lived in different countries and continents, and participated in hundreds of cultural traditions. However, early colonists, later immigrants, and their descendants all have become active participants in American and Canadian life. All now share a common national culture.

To recognize biopsychological equality is not to deny differences among populations. In studying human diversity in time and space, anthropologists distinguish among the universal, the generalized, and the particular. Certain biological, psychological, social, and cultural features are **universal,** found in every culture. Others are merely **generalities,** common to several but

universal Something that exists in every culture.

generality Culture pattern or trait that exists in some but not all societies.

not all human groups. Still other traits are **particularities,** unique to certain cultural traditions.

UNIVERSALS AND GENERALITIES

Biologically based universals include a long period of infant dependency, year-round (rather than seasonal) sexuality, and a complex brain that enables us to use symbols, languages, and tools. Among the social universals is life in groups and in some kind of family (see Brown 1991). Generalities occur in certain times and places but not in all cultures. They may be widespread, but they are not universal. One cultural generality that is present in many but not all societies is the *nuclear family,* a kinship group consisting of parents and children. Although many middle-class Americans ethnocentrically view the nuclear family as a proper and "natural" group, it is not universal. It was absent, for example, among the Nayar, located on India's Malabar Coast. Traditionally, the Nayar lived in female-headed households, and husbands and wives did not live together. In many other societies, the nuclear family is submerged in larger kin groups, such as extended families, lineages, and clans.

Societies can share the same beliefs and customs because of borrowing or through (cultural) inheritance from a common cultural ancestor. Speaking English is a generality shared by North Americans and Australians because both countries had

particularity Distinctive or unique culture trait, pattern, or integration.

English settlers. Another reason for generalities is domination, as in colonial rule, when a more powerful culture imposes customs and procedures on another one. In many countries, use of the English language reflects colonial history. More recently, English has spread through *diffusion* (cultural borrowing) to many other countries, as it has become the world's foremost language for business and travel.

PARTICULARITY: PATTERNS OF CULTURE

A cultural particularity is a trait or feature of culture that is not generalized or widespread; rather it is confined to a single place, culture, or society. Yet because of cultural borrowing, which has accelerated through modern transportation and communication systems, traits that once were limited in their distribution have become more widespread. Traits that are useful, that have the capacity to please large audiences, and that don't clash with the cultural values of potential adopters are more likely to be borrowed than others are. Still, certain cultural particularities persist. One example is a particular food dish (e.g., pork barbeque with a mustard-based sauce available only in South Carolina, or the pastie—beef

Cultures use rituals to mark such universal life-cycle events as birth, puberty, marriage, parenthood, and death. But particular cultures differ as to which events merit special celebration and in the emotions expressed during their rituals. Compare the wedding party (left) in Bali, Indonesia, with the funeral (right) among the Tanala of eastern Madagascar. How would you describe the emotions suggested by the photos?

stew baked in pie dough—characteristic of Michigan's upper peninsula). McDonald's food outlets, on the other hand, once confined to San Bernardino, California, have spread across the globe through diffusion. But there are other reasons why cultural particularities are increasingly rare. Many cultural traits are shared as cultural universals and as a result of independent invention. When facing similar problems, people in different places have come up with similar solutions. Again and again, similar cultural causes have produced similar cultural results.

At the level of the individual cultural trait or element (e.g., bow and arrow, hot dog, MTV), particularities may be getting rarer. But at a higher level, particularity is more obvious. Different cultures emphasize different things. Cultures are integrated and patterned differently and display tremendous variation and diversity. When cultural traits are borrowed, they are modified to fit the culture that adopts them. They are reintegrated—patterned anew—to fit their new setting. MTV in Germany or Brazil isn't at all the same thing as MTV in the United States. As stated in the earlier section "Culture Is Integrated," patterned beliefs, customs, and practices lend distinctiveness to particular cultural traditions.

Consider universal life-cycle events, such as birth, puberty, marriage, parenthood, and death, that many cultures observe and celebrate. The occasions (e.g., marriage, death) may be the same and universal, but the patterns of ceremonial observance may be dramatically different. Cultures vary in just which events merit special celebration. Americans, for example, regard expensive weddings as more socially appropriate than lavish funerals. The Betsileo of Madagascar take the opposite view. The marriage ceremony is a minor event that brings together just the couple and a few close relatives. A funeral is a measure of the deceased person's social position and lifetime achievement, and it may attract a thousand people. Why use money on a house, the Betsileo say, when one can use it on the tomb where one will spend eternity in the company of dead relatives? How unlike contemporary Americans' dreams of home ownership and preference for quick and inexpensive funerals. Cremation, an increasingly common option in the United States, would horrify the Betsileo, for whom ancestral bones and relics are important ritual objects.

Cultures vary tremendously in their beliefs, practices, integration, and patterning. By focusing on and trying to explain alternative customs, anthropology forces us to reappraise our familiar ways of thinking. In a world full of cultural diversity, contemporary American culture is just one cultural variant, more powerful perhaps, but no more natural, than the others.

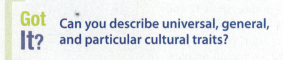

Got It? Can you describe universal, general, and particular cultural traits?

Generations of anthropologists have theorized about the relationship between the "system," on one hand, and the "person" or "individual" on the other. The system can refer to various concepts, including culture, society, social relations, or social structure. Individual human beings always make up, or constitute, the system. But, living within that system, humans also are constrained (to some extent, at least) by its rules and by the actions of other individuals. Cultural rules provide guidance about what to do and how to do it, but people don't always do what the rules say should be done. People use their culture actively and creatively, rather than blindly following its dictates (see Handwerker 2009). Humans aren't passive beings doomed to follow their cultural traditions like programmed robots. Cultures are dynamic and constantly changing. People learn, interpret, and manipulate the same rule in different ways—or they emphasize different rules that better suit their interests. Culture is *contested:* Different groups in society struggle with one another over whose ideas, values, goals, and beliefs will prevail. Even common symbols may have radically different meanings to different individuals and groups in the same culture. Golden arches may cause one person to salivate while another plots a vegetarian protest. The same flag may be waved to support or oppose a given war.

Even when they agree about what should be done, people don't always do as their culture directs or as other people expect. Many rules are violated, some very often (for example, automobile speed limits). Some anthropologists find it useful to distinguish between ideal and real culture. The *ideal culture* consists of what people say they should do and what they say they do. *Real culture* refers to their actual behavior as observed by the anthropologist.

Culture is both public and individual, both in the world and in people's minds. Anthropologists are interested not only in public and collective behavior but also in how individuals think, feel, and act. The individual and culture are linked because human social life is a process in which individuals internalize the meanings of public (i.e., cultural) messages. Then, alone and in groups, people influence culture by converting their private (and often divergent) understandings into public expressions (D'Andrade 1984).

Conventionally, culture has been seen as social glue transmitted across the generations, binding people through their common past, rather than as something being continually created and reworked in the present. The tendency to view culture as an entity rather than as a process is changing. Contemporary anthropologists now emphasize how day-to-day action, practice, or

resistance can make and remake culture (Gupta and Ferguson 1997b). *Agency* refers to the actions that individuals take, both alone and in groups, in forming and transforming cultural identities.

The approach to culture known as *practice theory* (Ortner 1984) recognizes that individuals within a society or culture have diverse motives and intentions and different degrees of power and influence. Such contrasts may be associated with gender, age, ethnicity, class, and other social variables. Practice theory focuses on how such varied individuals—through their ordinary and extraordinary actions and practices—manage to influence, create, and transform the world they live in. Practice theory appropriately recognizes a reciprocal relation between culture (the system—see above) and the individual. The system shapes how individuals experience and respond to external events, but individuals also play an active role in how society functions and changes. Practice theory recognizes both constraints on individuals and the flexibility and changeability of cultures and social systems.

Got it? Can you explain how individuals can make and remake culture through day-to-day actions?

>> Popular, Civic, and Public Culture

In the contemporary world, the systems in which we participate as individuals are not merely local or regional; they have national and international scope. The next section distinguishes between systems that are larger and smaller than nations. Here we focus on domains of national culture, which include popular, civic, and public culture. Any contemporary nation, such as the United States, Canada, Italy, Brazil, India, or Japan, has its national cultural traditions, its own media and popular culture; its own civic culture consisting of laws, institutions, and associations; and its own ways of doing things in public. To be sure, there are international spillovers. For example, the civic cultures of the United States, Canada, and India have been influenced by British law. The spillover is even greater in popular culture: American movies are watched worldwide; Simon Cowell is a powerful media figure in both England and the United States; you can take yoga or Bollywood classes in Los Angeles; Godzilla has visited New York. Despite its international spread, popular culture still varies and is patterned differently from country to country.

Today's consumption patterns both reflect and fuel *popular culture,* supplying widely shared images, information, narratives, products, events, and celebrations that have meaning for many or most people within the same national culture. American examples include Thanksgiving, Halloween, homecoming dances, reality shows, dinner-and-a-movie dates, and retirement parties. Although popular culture is available to us all, we use it selectively, and its meaning varies from one person to the next. In his book *Understanding Popular Culture* (1989), John Fiske argues that each individual's use of popular culture is a creative act. For example, *Glee,* Lady Gaga, the World Cup, the Superbowl, or *The Hunger Games* mean something different to each of their fans. As Fiske puts it, "the meanings I make . . . [from popular culture] are pleasurable when I feel that they are my meanings and that they relate to my everyday life in a practical, direct way" (1989, p. 57). All of us creatively consume and interpret print media, music, television, films, theme parks, celebrities, politicians, and other popular culture products.

A nation's *civic culture* includes its citizens' compliance with the legal system, participation in formal elections, and membership in voluntary and faith-based associations. Fellow countrymen and -women also share a public culture: generally accepted social behaviors, dress codes, speech, and other forms of expression that citizens enact in public spaces, including bars,

parks, malls, and even grieving sites, such as Ground Zero (see Morrill, Snow, and White 2005; Shaffer 2008).

>> Levels of Culture

Anthropologists also recognize cultural systems—levels of culture—that are larger and smaller than nation-states. **National culture,** examined in the previous section, embodies those beliefs, learned behavior patterns, values, and institutions that are shared by citizens of the same nation. **International culture** extends beyond and across national boundaries. Because culture is transmitted through learning rather than genetically, cultural traits can spread through borrowing or diffusion from one group to another.

Illustrating the 2011 Occupy movement, labor and community activists in Boston rally to demand investments in infrastructure and employment opportunities to benefit most (99 percent of) Americans.

Because of diffusion, migration, colonialism, and globalization, many cultural traits and patterns have acquired international scope. The contemporary United States, Canada, Great Britain, and Australia share cultural traits they have inherited from their common linguistic and cultural ancestors in Great Britain. Roman Catholics in many different countries share beliefs, symbols, experiences, and values transmitted by their church. The World Cup has become an international cultural event, as people in many countries know the rules of, play, and follow soccer.

Cultures also can be smaller than nations (see Jenks 2005). Although people who live in the same country share a national cultural tradition, all cultures also contain diversity. Individuals, families, communities, regions, classes, and other groups within a culture have different learning experiences as well as shared ones. **Subcultures** are different symbol-based patterns and traditions associated with particular groups in the same complex society. In large or diverse nations such as the United States or Canada, a variety of subcultures originate in region, ethnicity, language, class, and religion. The religious backgrounds of Jews, Baptists, and Roman Catholics create subcultural differences between them. While sharing a common national culture, U.S. northerners and southerners also differ in their beliefs, values, and customary behavior as a result of national and regional history. French-speaking Canadians sometimes pointedly contrast with English-speaking people in the same country. Italian Americans have ethnic traditions different from those of Irish, Polish, and African Americans. Table 2.2 lists sports and food examples illustrating levels of culture.

national culture Cultural experiences, beliefs, learned behavior patterns, and values shared by citizens of the same nation.

international culture Cultural traditions that extend beyond national boundaries.

subcultures Different cultural symbol-based traditions associated with subgroups in the same complex society.

TABLE 2.2 — Levels of Culture, with Examples from Sports and Food

Levels of Culture	Sports Examples	Food Examples
International	Soccer, basketball	Pizza
National	Monster truck rallies	Apple pie
Subculture	Bocce	Big Joe Pork Barbecue (South Carolina)

Nowadays, many anthropologists are reluctant to use the term *subculture.* They feel that the prefix *sub-* is offensive because it means "below." Subcultures thus may be perceived as "less than" or somehow inferior to a dominant, elite, or national culture. In this discussion of levels of culture, we intend no such implication. Our point is simply that nations may contain many different culturally defined groups. As mentioned earlier, culture is contested. Various groups may strive to promote the correctness and value of their own practices, values, and beliefs in comparison with those of other groups or the nation as a whole.

ethnocentrism The tendency to view one's own culture as best and to judge the behavior and beliefs of culturally different people by one's own standards.

cultural relativism The position that the values and standards of cultures differ and deserve respect. Anthropology is characterized by methodological rather than moral relativism: In order to understand another culture fully, anthropologists try to understand its members' beliefs and motivations. Methodological relativism does not preclude making moral judgments or taking action.

 Got it? Can you describe levels of culture that are larger and smaller than nation-states?

Would you say you have an ethnocentric position on eating grasshoppers?

>> Ethnocentrism, Cultural Relativism, and Human Rights

The tendency to view one's own culture as superior and to apply one's own cultural values in judging the behavior and beliefs of people raised in other cultures is known as **ethnocentrism.** We hear ethnocentric statements all the time. Ethnocentrism contributes to social solidarity, a sense of value and community, among people who share a cultural tradition. People everywhere think that the familiar explanations, opinions, and customs are true, right, proper, and moral. They regard different behavior as strange, immoral, or savage. Often other societies are not considered fully human. Their members may be castigated as cannibals, thieves, or people who do not bury their dead.

Among several tribes in the Trans-Fly region of Papua New Guinea, homosexuality was valued over heterosexuality (see Chapter 9). Men who grew up in the Etoro tribe (Kelly 1976) favored oral sex between men, while their neighbors the Marind-anim encouraged men to engage in anal sex. (In both groups heterosexual coitus was stigmatized and allowed only for reproduction.) Etoro men considered Marind-anim anal sex to be disgusting, while seeing nothing abnormal about their own oral homosexual practices.

Opposing ethnocentrism is **cultural relativism,** the viewpoint that behavior in one culture should not be judged by the standards of another culture. This position also presents problems. At its most extreme, cultural relativism argues that there is no superior, international, or universal morality, that the moral and ethical rules of all cultures deserve equal respect. In the extreme relativist view, Nazi Germany would be evaluated as nonjudgmentally as Athenian Greece.

In today's world, human rights advocates challenge many tenets of cultural relativism. For example, several societies in Africa and the Middle East have traditions of female genital modification (FGM). *Clitoridectomy* is the removal of a girl's clitoris. Infibulation involves sewing the lips (labia) of the vagina, to constrict the vaginal opening. Both procedures reduce female sexual pleasure, and, it is believed in some cultures, the likelihood of adultery. Human rights advocates, especially women's rights groups, oppose such practices. The idea is that the tradition infringes on a basic human right—control over one's body and one's sexuality. Some African countries have banned or otherwise discouraged the procedures, as have Western nations that receive immigrants from such cultures.

CULTURETHINK

Cite one or more examples of ethnocentrism you have encountered.

Similar issues arise with circumcision and other male genital operations. Is it right for a baby boy to be circumcised without his permission, as has been done routinely in the United States? Is it proper to require adolescent boys to undergo collective circumcision to fulfill cultural tradition, as has been done in parts of Africa and Australia?

Some argue that the problems with relativism can be solved by distinguishing between methodological and moral relativism (see Kellenberger 2008). In anthropology, cultural relativism is not a moral position, but a methodological one: To understand another culture fully, you must try to see how the people in that culture see things. What motivates them—what are they thinking—when they do those things? Such an approach does not preclude making moral judgments or taking action. When faced with Nazi atrocities, a methodological relativist would have a moral obligation to stop doing anthropology and take action to intervene. In the FGM example, one can understand the *motivations* for the practice by looking at the situation from the point of view of those who engage in it. Having done this, one then faces the moral question of whether to intervene to stop it. We should recognize as well that different people and groups living in the same society—for example, women and men, old and young, the more and less powerful—can have widely different views about what is proper, necessary, and moral (see Hunt 2007).

The idea of **human rights** invokes a realm of justice and morality beyond and superior to the laws and customs of particular countries, cultures, and religions (see R. Wilson 1996). Human rights include the right to speak freely, to hold religious beliefs without persecution, and not to be murdered, injured, or enslaved or imprisoned without charge. Such rights are seen as *inalienable* (nations cannot abridge or terminate them) and international (larger than and superior to individual nations and cultures). Four United Nations documents describe nearly all the human rights that have been internationally recognized. Those documents are the U.N. Charter; the Universal Declaration of Human Rights; the Covenant on Economic, Social and Cultural Rights; and the Covenant on Civil and Political Rights.

Alongside the human rights movement has arisen an awareness of the need to preserve cultural rights. Unlike human rights, **cultural rights** are vested not in individuals but in groups, such as religious and ethnic minorities and indigenous societies. Cultural rights include a group's ability to preserve its culture, to raise its children in the ways of its forebears, to continue its language, and not to be deprived of its economic base by the nation in which it is located (Greaves 1995). The related notion of indigenous **intellectual property rights (IPR)** has arisen in an attempt to conserve each society's cultural base—its core beliefs, knowledge, and practices (see Merry 2006). Much traditional cultural knowledge has commercial value. Examples include ethnomedicine (traditional medical knowledge and techniques), cosmetics, cultivated plants, foods, folklore, arts, crafts, songs, dances, costumes, and rituals (see Nazarea 2006). According to the IPR concept, a particular group may determine how indigenous knowledge and its products may be used and distributed and the level of compensation required.

The notion of cultural rights is related to the idea of cultural relativism, and the problem discussed previously arises again. What does one do about cultural rights that interfere with human rights? We believe that anthropology's main job is to present accurate accounts and explanations of cultural phenomena. The anthropologist doesn't have to approve infanticide, cannibalism, or torture to record their existence and determine their causes and the motivations behind them. However, each anthropologist has a choice about where he or she will do fieldwork. Some anthropologists choose not to study a particular culture because they discover in advance or early in fieldwork that behavior they consider morally repugnant is practiced there. Anthropologists respect human diversity. Most ethnographers try to be objective, accurate, and

human rights Doctrine that invokes a realm of justice and morality beyond and superior to particular countries, cultures, and religions. Human rights, usually seen as vested in individuals, include the rights to speak freely, to hold religious beliefs without persecution, and not to be enslaved.

cultural rights Doctrine that certain rights are vested not in individuals but in identifiable groups, such as religious and ethnic minorities and indigenous societies.

intellectual property rights (IPR) Each society's cultural base—its core beliefs and principles. IPR is claimed as a group right—a cultural right, allowing indigenous groups to control who may know and use their collective knowledge and its applications.

diffusion Borrowing between cultures either directly or through intermediaries.

sensitive in their accounts of other cultures. However, objectivity, sensitivity, and a cross-cultural perspective don't mean that anthropologists have to ignore international standards of justice and morality. What do you think?

Got it? Can you provide an example of how anthropologists respect diversity while valuing human rights, using the terms *ethnocentrism, cultural relativism,* and *human rights?*

war on one another. Diffusion is *forced* when one culture subjugates another and imposes its customs on the dominated group. Diffusion is *indirect* when items or traits move from group A to group C via group B without any firsthand contact between A and C. In this case, group B might consist of traders or merchants who take products from a variety of places to new markets. Or group B might be geographically situated between A and C, so that what it gets from A eventually winds up in C, and vice versa. In today's world, much international diffusion is indirect—culture spread by the mass media and advanced information technology.

>> Mechanisms of Cultural Change

Why and how do cultures change? We gave some examples earlier of **diffusion,** or borrowing of traits between cultures. Such exchange of information and products has gone on throughout human history because cultures have never been truly isolated. Contact between neighboring groups has always existed and has extended over vast areas (Boas 1940/1966). Diffusion is *direct* when two cultures trade with, intermarry among, or wage

CULTURE THINK

White Americans took Native American children from their families and placed them in boarding schools where they were not allowed to speak their own language or wear local clothing and adornments. What mechanism of cultural change did they experience? Think of other examples of cultural change (for example, food, technology, entertainment) and identify the mechanism at work.

Illustrating acculturation is this sign in pidgin English at a landing on Efate Island, Vanuatu, South Pacific. It reads, "If you want the ferry to come, strike the gong."

Acculturation, a second mechanism of cultural change, is the ongoing exchange of cultural features that results when groups have continuous firsthand contact. The cultures of either or both groups may be changed by this contact (Redfield, Linton, and Herskovits 1936). With acculturation, parts of the cultures change, but each group remains distinct. One example of acculturation is a *pidgin,* a mixed language that develops to ease communication between members of different cultures in contact. This usually happens in situations of trade or colonialism. Pidgin English, for example, is a simplified form of English. It blends English grammar with the grammar of a native language. Pidgin English was first used for commerce in Chinese ports. Similar pidgins developed later in Papua New Guinea and West Africa. In situations of continuous contact, cultures have also exchanged and blended foods, recipes, music, dances, clothing, tools, and technologies.

Independent invention—the process by which humans innovate, creatively finding solutions to problems—is a third mechanism of cultural change. Faced with comparable problems and challenges, people in different societies have innovated and changed in similar ways, which is one reason cultural generalities exist. One example is the independent invention of agriculture in the Middle East and Mexico. Over the course of human history, major innovations have spread at the expense of earlier ones. Often a major invention, such as agriculture, triggers a series of subsequent interrelated changes. These economic revolutions have social and cultural repercussions. Thus in both Mexico and the Middle East, agriculture led to many social, political, and legal changes, including notions of property and distinctions in wealth, class, and power (see Naylor 1996).

>> Globalization

The term **globalization** encompasses a series of processes that work transnationally to promote change in a world in which nations and people are increasingly interlinked and mutually dependent. Promoting globalization are economic and political forces, along with modern systems of transportation and communication. The forces of globalization include international commerce and finance, travel and tourism, transnational migration, and the media—including the Internet and other high-tech information flows (see Appadurai, ed. 2001; Friedman and Friedman 2008; Kjaerulff 2010; Scholte 2000). New economic unions (which have met considerable resistance in their member nations) have been created through the World Trade Organization (WTO), the International Monetary Fund (IMF), and the European Union (EU).

The media, including the Internet, play a key role in globalization. Long-distance communication is faster and easier than ever, and now covers most of the globe. I can now e-mail or call families in Arembepe, Brazil, which lacked phones and even postal service when I first began to study the community. Information about Arembepe is now available to anyone, including potential tourists, on hundreds of websites. Anything can be Googled. The media help propel a transnational culture of consumption, as they spread information about products, services, rights, institutions, lifestyles, and the perceived costs and benefits of globalization. Emigrants transmit information and resources

acculturation The exchange of cultural features that results when groups come into continuous firsthand contact; the original cultural patterns of either or both groups may be altered, but the groups remain distinct.

independent invention Development of the same culture trait or pattern in separate cultures as a result of comparable needs and circumstances.

globalization A set of processes, including diffusion, migration, and acculturation, that promote change in today's interlinked world.

STUDY **TIP**

Globalization is a complex set of processes. It helps to think of it as having three main characteristics:

- Increasing global political and economic interdependence.

- Increased mobility of people (migration and travel).

- Fast and efficient communications technologies that link people across the globe.

In our interlinked, twenty-first-century world, even men in remote villages may have access to computers and the Internet. Shown here, two men with a laptop in the village of Bhaktapur, Nepal.

transnationally, as they maintain their ties with home (phoning, texting, e-mailing, visiting, sending money). In a sense such people live multilocally—in different places and cultures at once. They learn to play various social roles and to change behavior and identity depending on the situation (see Cresswell 2006).

The effects of globalization are broad and not always welcome. Local people must cope increasingly with forces generated by progressively larger systems—region, nation, and world. An army of outsiders and potential change agents now intrudes on people everywhere. Tourism has become the world's number one industry (see Holden 2005). Economic development agents and the media promote the idea that work should be for cash rather than mainly for subsistence. Indigenous peoples and traditional societies have devised various strategies to deal with threats to their autonomy, identity, and livelihood (Maybury-Lewis 2002). New forms of cultural expression and political mobilization, including the rights movements discussed previously,

are emerging from the interplay of local, regional, national, and international cultural forces (see Ong and Collier, eds. 2005).

Illustrating political mobilization against globalization are regular protests at the meetings of the main

get involved!

Interview a friend, a classmate, or a relative who is from a different country. If you don't know anyone, perhaps a friend can recommend someone who does. Ask about particular beliefs, traditions, values, or symbols. Which of these views or traditions might other Americans see as strange or improper? Can you determine what the person you interview finds odd in America's national culture? Note any ethnocentric statements you hear from this person and any ethnocentrism you experience yourself during the interview.

agencies concerned with international trade. One of the largest protests took place in December 1999 in Seattle, which witnessed a massive and violent demonstration against the WTO, which was meeting there. Protesters continue to show their disapproval of policies of the WTO, the IMF, and the World Bank. In November 2009 there were clashes with police during a march by demonstrators protesting the opening of a WTO meeting in Geneva. The WTO had called that meeting of its 153 members to find ways to revive world trade and get the global economy out of recession (*Huffington Post* 2009).

WTO opponents claim the agreements it produces foster the growth of wealth among corporations at the expense of farmers, workers, and others at the low end of the economy. Environmentalists seek tougher environmental impact assessments. Human rights groups contend that international development policies help only big business, not poor countries and their citizens. Trade unionists advocate for global labor standards. Are such protests valid, and are they likely to halt globalization? What's your opinion of globalization?

 Got it? Can you list and define mechanisms of culture change, analyzing globalization as a specific example?

"I learned much more about acting from philosophy courses, psychology courses, history and anthropology than I ever learned in acting class."

Tim Robbins

FOR REVIEW

EXPERIENCING CULTURE

TO ACCESS THESE VIDEOS ON YOUR COMPUTER, VISIT

www.mhhe.com/gezonqr

2-1

2-2

I. What is culture, and why do we study it?

-   Culture, which is distinctly human, refers to customary behavior and beliefs that are passed on through learning and symbols. We study culture to understand the human condition: our origins in our primate ancestors' evolving capacity for culture, our shared human capacity for culture, culture's unique and universal forms, how we think and act as members of groups, and how we organize and change our lives and our relations with others. The study of culture also teaches us about our unique relation to nature, the significance of understanding ourselves as biocultural creatures, and our interactions, both adaptive and maladaptive, with our environments.

II. What is the relation between culture and the individual?

-   Cultural rules constrain individuals but do not dictate their behavior. People use culture actively and creatively. They interpret and manipulate the rules in different ways, emphasize rules that best suit their needs, and contest the rules. People play an active role in how society functions and changes. Having internalized the meanings of cultural messages, individuals then influence their culture by converting their private (often divergent) understandings into public expressions.

III. How does culture change?

-   Culture changes through three chief mechanisms: diffusion, acculturation, and independent invention. Diffusion is the spread of cultural traits as groups borrow from one another. Acculturation involves the exchange of cultural features that results when groups have continuous firsthand contact. Independent invention is the development of the same cultural trait in separate cultures as a result of comparable circumstances. In addition, globalization—a series of processes that includes diffusion, acculturation, and migration—promotes change in our contemporary world, where nations and peoples are increasingly linked and interdependent.

Pop Quiz

Multiple Choice:

1. Which of the following is *not* one of the ways in which individuals acquire culture?
   a. Genetic transmission
   b. Conscious and unconscious learning
   c. Observation
   d. Direct instruction

2. Which of the following statements about culture is false?
   a. Despite increased reliance on cultural means of adaptation, humans still adapt biologically.
   b. Cultural traditions are transmitted through learning.
   c. Cultural patterns might offer short-term benefits to a particular group but nevertheless threaten that group's long-term survival.
   d. If certain cultural patterns offer short-term benefits, they usually are adaptive in the long run as well.

3. The chapter's discussion of the similarities and differences between humans and apes
   a. states that all hominids have evolved the same capacities for culture.
   b. emphasizes culture's evolutionary basis, stressing the interaction between biology and culture.
   c. states that genetics has been more important than culture in determining our particular evolutionary path.
   d. illustrates how human females' lack of a visible estrus cycle determined our unique capacity for culture.

4. The "psychic unity" of humans, a doctrine that most anthropologists accept, means that
   a. psychology is the exclusive domain of the academic discipline of psychology.
   b. genetically mixed descendants of people from around the world will not be capable of acquiring the common national culture of the country they now live in.
   c. although individuals differ in their emotional and intellectual tendencies, all human populations have equivalent capacities for culture.
   d. psychological attributes are determined by our genes.

5. Anthropologists have found that certain biological, psychological, social, and cultural features are universal, i.e., found in every society. All the following are examples of universal features *except*
   a. a long period of infant dependency.
   b. seasonal (rather than year-round) sexuality.
   c. life in groups and in some kind of family.
   d. capacity to use symbols, languages, and tools.

6. Anthropologists have noted that culture is often contested. This means that
   a. different groups in a society struggle over whose ideas, values, goals, and beliefs will prevail.
   b. certain symbols may have different meanings to specific individuals and groups, even though most common symbols are agreed upon by everyone in a culture.
   c. humans are passive beings who must follow their cultural traditions.
   d. "real" culture (the actual behavior of individuals in a society) is of primary importance to anthropological study, while "ideal" culture has no significance.

7. In anthropology, cultural relativism
   a. is primarily a methodological position rather than a moral one.
   b. is equally a moral and a methodological stance toward other cultures.
   c. is synonymous with moral relativism.
   d. is a political position that argues for the defense of human rights, regardless of culture.

8. The series of processes that are making nations and people increasingly interlinked and mutually dependent is known as
   a. acculturation.
   b. independent invention.
   c. diffusion.
   d. globalization.

Fill in the Blank:

1. Cultural traits, patterns, and inventions also can be _____, threatening the group's continued existence (survival and reproduction).

2. According to Leslie White, culture, and therefore humanity, came into existence when humans began to use _____.

3. The term _____ refers to any fossil or living human, chimp, or gorilla, while the term _____ refers only to any fossil or living human.

4. Unlike human rights, _____ are vested not in individuals but in groups, including indigenous peoples and religious and ethnic minorities.

1. (a), 2. (d), 3. (b), 4. (c), 5. (b), 6. (a), 7. (a), 8. (d)
1. maladaptive; 2. symbols; 3. hominid, hominin; 4. cultural rights

3

DOING ANTHROPOLOGY

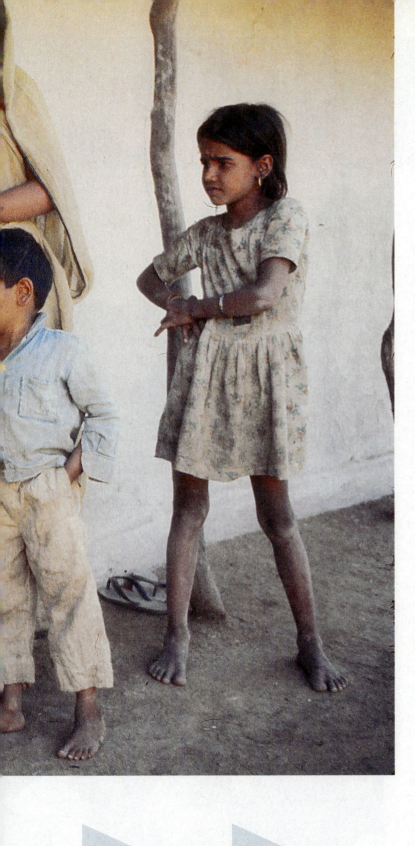

UNDERSTANDING OURSELVES

"Been on any digs lately?" Ask your instructor if she or he has been asked this question. Then ask how often he or she actually has been on a dig. Remember that anthropology has four subfields, only two of which (archaeology and biological anthropology) require much digging—in the ground at least. To be sure, cultural anthropologists "dig out" information about varied lifestyles. Traditionally, cultural anthropologists have done a variant on the *Star Trek* mission of seeking out, if not new, at least different "life" and "civilizations."

Despite globalization, the cultural diversity under anthropological scrutiny right now may be as great as ever, because anthropologists now study modern nations. Today's cultural anthropologists are as likely to be studying artists in Miami or bankers in Beirut as Trobriand sailors in the South Pacific. Still, we can't forget that anthropology did originate in non-Western, nonindustrial societies. Its research techniques were developed to deal with small populations. Even when working in modern nations, anthropologists still consider ethnography with small groups to be an excellent way of learning about how people live their lives and make decisions.

Before this course, did you know the names of any anthropologists? If so, which ones? For the general public, biological anthropologists tend to be better known than cultural anthropologists because of what they study. You're more likely to have seen film of Jane Goodall with chimps or a paleoanthropologist holding a skull than an ethnographer at work. One particularly wise and charismatic cultural anthropologist and an important public figure through her death in 1978 was Margaret Mead. Famed for her work on teen sexuality in Samoa and gender roles in New Guinea, Mead may well be the most famous anthropologist who ever lived. She appeared regularly on NBC's *Tonight Show*. In all her ventures—including teaching, museum work, TV, anthropological films, popular books, and magazines—Mead helped Americans appreciate the relevance of anthropology to understanding their daily lives. Her work is featured here and elsewhere in this book.

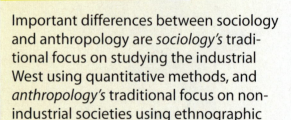

>> Research Methods in Cultural Anthropology

Cultural anthropology and sociology share an interest in social relations, organization, and behavior. Early students of society, such as the French scholar Émile Durkheim, were among the founders of both sociology and anthropology. Durkheim studied the religions of Native Australians (Durkheim 1912/2001), as well as mass phenomena, such as suicide rates, in modern nations (Durkheim 1897/1951). Key differences between anthropology and sociology eventually emerged from the kinds of societies each studied. Sociologists focused on the industrial West; anthropologists, on nonindustrial societies. Different methods of data collection and analysis were developed to deal with those different kinds of societies. To study large-scale, complex nations, sociologists came to rely on questionnaires and other means of gathering masses of quantifiable data. For many years sampling and statistical techniques have been basic to sociology, whereas statistical training has been less common in anthropology (although this is changing somewhat as anthropologists increasingly work in modern nations).

Traditional ethnographers studied small, nonliterate (without writing) populations and relied on ethnographic methods appropriate to that context. "Ethnography is a research process in which the anthropologist closely observes, records, and engages in the daily life of another

participant observation
A characteristic ethnographic technique; taking part in the events one is observing, describing, and analyzing.

STUDY TIP

Important differences between sociology and anthropology are *sociology's* traditional focus on studying the industrial West using quantitative methods, and *anthropology's* traditional focus on nonindustrial societies using ethnographic techniques during fieldwork.

culture—an experience labeled as the fieldwork method—and then writes accounts of this culture, emphasizing descriptive detail" (Marcus and Fischer 1986, p. 18). One key method described in this quote is **participant observation**—taking part in the events one is observing, describing, and analyzing.

World-famous anthropologist Margaret Mead (1901–1978) in the field in Bali, Indonesia, in 1957.

Anthropologists such as the late Marjorie Shostak (center left) typically form personal relationships with their cultural consultants. Shostak worked with the !Kung San in the Dobe region of southwest Africa, on the border between Botswana and South Africa.

>> Ethnography: Anthropology's Distinctive Strategy

Anthropology developed into a separate field as early scholars worked on Indian (Native American) reservations and traveled to distant lands to study small groups of foragers (hunters and gatherers) and cultivators. Traditionally, the process of becoming a cultural anthropologist has required a field experience in another society. Early ethnographers lived in small-scale, relatively isolated societies, with simple technologies and economies.

Ethnography thus emerged as a research strategy in societies with greater cultural uniformity and less social differentiation than are found in large, modern, industrial nations. Traditionally, ethnographers have tried to understand the whole of a particular culture (or, more realistically, as much as they can, given limitations of time and perception). To pursue this goal, ethnographers adopt a free-ranging strategy for gathering information. In a given society or community, the ethnographer moves from setting to setting, place to place, and subject to subject to discover the totality and interconnectedness of social life. By expanding our knowledge of the range of human diversity, ethnography provides a foundation for generalizations about human behavior and social life. Ethnographers draw on varied techniques to piece together a picture of otherwise alien lifestyles. Anthropologists usually employ several (but rarely all) of the techniques discussed here (see also Bernard 2006; Wolcott 2008).

>> Ethnographic Techniques

The characteristic *field techniques* of the ethnographer include the following:

- Direct, firsthand observation of behavior, including *participant observation*
- Conversation with varying degrees of formality, from the daily chitchat, which helps maintain rapport and provides knowledge about what is going on, to prolonged *interviews,* which can be unstructured or structured
- The *genealogical method*

Raoni Metuktire, a Kayapó Native American from Brazil (center), being interviewed in France. Raoni has become an internationally recognized key consultant on, and a strong advocate for preserving, the Amazon rainforest, indigenous peoples, and their cultures.

- Detailed work with *key consultants,* or *informants,* about particular areas of community life
- In-depth interviewing, often leading to the collection of *life histories* of particular people (narrators)
- Discovery of local (native) beliefs and perceptions, which may be compared with the ethnographer's own observations and conclusions
- Problem-oriented research of many sorts
- Longitudinal research—the continuous long-term study of an area or site
- Team research—coordinated research by multiple ethnographers
- Multisited research that studies the various sites and systems in which people participate

CULTURE THINK

A conversation with someone can be like an informal interview and a way to get to know more about them. What kinds of information might you learn about someone standing next to you in a long, slow line by engaging in a natural, informal conversation? Try it out, thinking of yourself as an anthropologist.

OBSERVATION AND PARTICIPANT OBSERVATION

Ethnographers must pay attention to hundreds of details of daily life, seasonal events, and unusual happenings. They should record what they see as they see it. Things never will seem quite as strange again as they do during the first few weeks in the field. The ethnographer eventually gets used to, and accepts as normal, cultural patterns that initially were alien. Staying a bit more than a year in the field allows the ethnographer to repeat the season of his or her arrival, when certain events and processes may have been missed because of initial unfamiliarity and culture shock.

Many ethnographers record their impressions in a personal *diary,* which is kept separate from more formal *field notes.* Later, this record of early impressions will help point out some of the most basic aspects of cultural diversity. Such aspects include distinctive smells, noises people make, how they cover their mouths when they eat, and how they gaze at others. These patterns, which are so basic as to seem almost trivial, are part of what Bronislaw Malinowski called "the imponderabilia of native life and of typical behavior" (Malinowski 1922/1961, p. 20). These features of culture are so fundamental that natives take them for granted. They are too basic even to talk about, but the unaccustomed eye of the fledgling ethnographer picks them up. Thereafter, becoming familiar, they fade to the edge of consciousness. Initial impressions are valuable and should be recorded. First and foremost, ethnographers should try to be accurate observers, recorders, and reporters of what they see in the field.

Ethnographers strive to establish *rapport,* a good, friendly working relationship based on personal contact, with our hosts. One of ethnography's most characteristic procedures is participant observation, which means that we take part in community life as we study it. As human beings living among others, we cannot be totally impartial and detached observers. We take part in many events and processes we are observing and trying to comprehend. By participating, we learn why local people find such events meaningful, as we see how they are organized and conducted.

In Arembepe, Brazil, Conrad Kottak learned about fishing by sailing on the Atlantic with local fishers. He gave Jeep rides to malnourished babies, to pregnant mothers, and once to a teenage girl possessed by a spirit. All of those people needed to consult specialists outside the village. He danced at Arembepe's festive

Lisa Gezon in Diego Suarez, Madagascar, sitting with her friend (right) who is selling khat, a leafy plant that people chew for a stimulant effect. On the left are Lisa Gezon's Malagasy daughter and sister.

1964, Kottak and his fellow field-workers attempted to complete an interview schedule in each of Arembepe's 160 households. They entered almost every household (fewer than 5 percent refused to participate) to ask a set of questions on a printed form. Their results provided them with a census and basic information about the village. They wrote down the name, age, and gender of each household member. They gathered data on family type, religion, present and previous jobs, income, expenditures, diet, possessions, and many other items on their eight-page form.

Although they were doing a survey, their approach differed from the survey research design routinely used by sociologists and other social scientists working in large, industrial nations. That survey research, discussed below, involves sampling (choosing a small, manageable study group from a larger population). Kottak and his colleagues did not select a partial sample from the total population. Instead, they tried to interview in all households in the community (that is, to have a total sample). They used an interview schedule rather than a questionnaire. With the **interview schedule,** the ethnographer talks face to face with people, asks the questions, and writes down the answers. *Questionnaire* procedures tend to be more indirect and impersonal; often the respondent fills in the form.

Kottak's goal of getting a total sample allowed him to meet almost everyone in the village and helped establish rapport. Decades later, Arembepeiros still talk warmly about how these ethnographers were interested enough in them to visit their homes and ask them questions. This stood in sharp contrast to the other outsiders the villagers had known, who considered them too poor and backward to be taken seriously.

Like other survey research, however, Kottak's interview schedule did gather comparable quantifiable information. It gave his group of researchers a basis for assessing patterns and exceptions in village life. Their schedules included a core set of questions that were posed to everyone. Interesting side issues often came up during the interview, which they would pursue then or later.

> **interview schedule** Ethnographic tool for structuring a formal interview. A prepared form guides interviews, with households or individuals being compared systematically. This contrasts with a questionnaire because the researcher has personal contact and records people's answers.

occasions, drank libations commemorating new births, and became a godfather to a village girl. Lisa Gezon was considered a family member in a village in northern Madagascar. Early in her fieldwork, she tutored her Malagasy "daughter" and attended the funeral of her "father." Years later, her own children (from the United States) went to the village to participate in an important ritual that marked their membership in the community: They symbolically got their hair cut, received silver necklaces, and were blessed by the elders and ancestors. Most anthropologists have similar field experiences. The common humanity of the student and the studied, the ethnographer and the research community, makes participant observation inevitable.

CONVERSATION, INTERVIEWING, AND INTERVIEW SCHEDULES

Participating in local life means that ethnographers constantly talk to people and ask questions. As our knowledge of the native language and culture increases, we understand more. There are several stages in learning a field language. First is the naming phase—asking for name after name of the objects around us. Later we are able to pose more complex questions and understand the replies. We begin to understand simple conversations between two villagers. If our language expertise proceeds far enough, we eventually become able to comprehend rapid-fire public discussions and group conversations.

One data-gathering technique Kottak has used in both Arembepe and Madagascar involves an ethnographic survey that includes an interview schedule. In

Village meetings may be part of anthropological fieldwork, as is illustrated by this scene in Kenya.

Kottak and his colleagues followed such leads into many dimensions of village life. One woman, for instance—a midwife—became the key cultural consultant they sought out later when they wanted detailed information about local childbirth. Another woman had done an internship in an Afro-Brazilian cult (*candomblé*) in the city. She still went there regularly to study, dance, and get possessed. She became their candomblé expert.

Thus, their interview schedule provided a structure that *directed but did not confine* them as researchers. It enabled their ethnography to be both quantitative and qualitative. The quantitative part consisted of the basic information gathered and later analyzed statistically. The qualitative dimension came from follow-up questions, open-ended discussions, pauses for gossip, and work with key consultants.

genealogical method Procedures by which ethnographers discover and record connections of kinship, descent, and marriage, using diagrams and symbols.

key cultural consultant An expert on a particular aspect of local life who helps the ethnographer understand that aspect.

THE GENEALOGICAL METHOD

As ordinary people, many of us learn about our kin connections by tracing our genealogies. Various computer programs and websites like ancestry.com allow us to trace our "family trees" and degrees of relationship.

The **genealogical method** is a well-established ethnographic technique. Early ethnographers developed notation and symbols to deal with kinship, descent, and marriage. Genealogy is a prominent building block in the social organization of nonindustrial societies, where people live and work each day with their close kin. Anthropologists need to collect genealogical data to understand current social relations and to reconstruct history. In many nonindustrial societies, kin links are basic to social life. Anthropologists even call such cultures "kin-based societies." Everyone is related, and each person spends most of his or her time with relatives. Rules of behavior attached to particular kin relations are basic to everyday life (see Carsten 2004). Marriage also is crucial in organizing nonindustrial societies because strategic marriages between villages, tribes, and clans create political alliances.

KEY CULTURAL CONSULTANTS

Every community has people who by accident, experience, talent, or training can provide the most complete or useful information about particular aspects of life. These people are **key cultural consultants,** also called *key informants*. In Ivato, the Betsileo village in Madagascar where Kottak spent most of his time, a man named Rakoto was particularly knowledgeable about village history. When asked to work on a genealogy of the fifty to sixty people buried in the village tomb, however, he called in his cousin Tuesdaysfather, who knew more about that subject. Tuesdaysfather had survived an epidemic of influenza that ravaged Madagascar, along with much of the world, around 1919. Immune to the disease himself, Tuesdaysfather had the grim job of burying his kin as they died. He kept track of everyone buried in the tomb. Tuesdaysfather helped Kottak with the tomb genealogy. Rakoto joined him in providing personal details about the deceased villagers.

LIFE HISTORIES

In nonindustrial societies as in our own society, individual personalities, interests, and abilities vary. Some villagers prove to be more interested in the ethnographer's work and are more helpful, interesting, and pleasant than others are. Anthropologists develop likes and dislikes in the field as we do at home. Often, when we find someone unusually interesting, we collect his or her **life history.** This recollection of a lifetime of experiences provides a more intimate and personal cultural portrait than would be possible otherwise. Life histories, which may be recorded or videotaped for later review and analysis, reveal how specific people perceive, react to, and contribute to changes that affect their lives. Such accounts can illustrate diversity, which exists within any community, since the focus is on how different people interpret and deal with some of the same problems. Many ethnographers include the collection of life histories as an important part of their research strategy.

LOCAL BELIEFS AND PERCEPTIONS, AND THE ETHNOGRAPHER'S

One goal of ethnography is to discover local (native) views, beliefs, and perceptions, which may be compared with the ethnographer's own observations and conclusions. In the field, ethnographers typically combine two research strategies, the *emic* (native-oriented) and the *etic* (scientist-oriented). These terms, derived from linguistics, have been applied to ethnography by various anthropologists. Marvin Harris (1968/2001) popularized the following meanings of the terms: An **emic** approach investigates how local people think. How do they perceive and categorize the world? What are their rules for behavior? What has meaning for them? How do they imagine and explain things? Operating emically, the ethnographer seeks the "native viewpoint," relying on local people to explain things and to say whether something is significant or not. The term **cultural consultant,** or *informant,* refers to individuals the ethnographer gets to know in the field, the people who teach him or her about their culture, who provide the emic perspective.

The **etic** (scientist-oriented) approach shifts the focus from local observations, categories, explanations, and interpretations to those of the anthropologist. The etic approach recognizes that members of a culture often are too involved in what they are doing to interpret their cultures impartially. Operating etically, the ethnographer emphasizes what he or she (the observer) notices and considers important. As a trained scientist, the ethnographer should try to bring an objective and comprehensive viewpoint to the study of other cultures. Of course, like any other scientist, the ethnographer is also a human being with cultural blinders that prevent complete objectivity. As in other sciences, proper training can reduce, but not totally eliminate, the observer's bias. But anthropologists do have special training to compare behavior between different societies.

life history Of a cultural consultant; provides a personal cultural portrait of existence or change in a culture.

emic The research strategy that focuses on native explanations and criteria of significance.

cultural consultant Someone the ethnographer gets to know in the field, who teaches him or her about their society and culture (also called *informant*).

etic The research strategy that emphasizes the observer's rather than the natives' explanations, categories, and criteria of significance.

What are some examples of emic versus etic perspectives? Consider our holidays. For North Americans, Thanksgiving Day has special significance. In our view (emically), it is a unique cultural celebration that commemorates particular historical themes. But a wider, etic perspective sees Thanksgiving as just one more example of the postharvest festivals held in many societies. Another example: Local people (including many Americans) may believe that chills and drafts cause colds, which scientists know are caused by germs. In cultures that lack the germ theory of disease, illnesses are emically explained by various causes, ranging from spirits to ancestors to witches. *Illness* refers to a culture's (emic) perception and explanation of bad health, whereas *disease* refers to the scientific—etic—explanation of poor health, involving known pathogens.

Ethnographers typically combine emic and etic strategies in their fieldwork. The statements, perceptions, categories, and opinions of local people help ethnographers understand how cultures work. Local beliefs are also interesting and valuable in themselves. However, people often fail to admit, or even recognize, certain causes and consequences of their behavior. This is as true of North Americans as it is of people in other societies.

Got IT? Can you define ethnography and identify its characteristic field techniques?

THE EVOLUTION OF ETHNOGRAPHY

The Polish anthropologist Bronislaw Malinowski (1884–1942), who spent most of his professional life in England, is generally considered the founder of ethnography. Like most anthropologists of his time, Malinowski did *salvage ethnography,* in the belief that the ethnographer's job is to study and record cultural diversity threatened by Westernization. Early ethnographic accounts (ethnographies), such as Malinowski's classic *Argonauts of the Western Pacific* (1922/1961), were similar to earlier traveler and explorer accounts in describing the writer's discovery of unknown people and places. However, the *scientific* aims of ethnographies set them apart from books by explorers and amateurs.

The style that dominated "classic" ethnographies was *ethnographic realism.* The writer's goal was to present an accurate, objective, scientific account of a different way of life, written by someone who knew it firsthand. This knowledge came from an "ethnographic adventure" involving immersion in an alien language and culture. Ethnographers derived their authority—both as scientists and as voices of "the native" or "the other"—from this personal research experience.

Malinowski's ethnographies were guided by the assumption that aspects of culture are linked and intertwined. Beginning by describing a Trobriand sailing

Bronislaw Malinowski (1884–1942), who was born in Poland but spent most of his professional life in England, did fieldwork in the Trobriand Islands from 1914 to 1918. Malinowski is generally considered to be the father of ethnography. Does this photo suggest anything about his relationship with Trobriand villagers?

expedition, the ethnographer then follows the links between that entry point and other areas of the culture, such as magic, religion, myths, kinship, and trade. Compared with Malinowski, today's ethnographies tend to be less inclusive and holistic, focusing on particular topics, such as kinship or religion.

According to Malinowski, a primary task of the ethnographer is "to grasp the native's point of view, his relation to life, to realize *his* vision of *his* world" (1922/1961, p. 25—Malinowski's italics). This is a good statement of the need for the emic perspective, as discussed earlier. Since the 1970s, *interpretive anthropology* has considered the task of describing and interpreting that which is meaningful to natives. Interpretivists such as Clifford Geertz (1973) view cultures as meaningful texts that natives constantly "read" and ethnographers

CULTURE THINK

Why do people practice religion? Think of a specific religious practice. What would be an emic answer to this question? In other words, how would the people themselves answer?

must decipher. According to Geertz, anthropologists may choose anything in a culture that interests them, fill in details, and elaborate to inform their readers about meanings in that culture. Meanings are carried by public symbolic forms, including words, rituals, and customs.

A recent trend in ethnographic writing has been to question traditional goals, methods, and styles, including ethnographic realism and salvage ethnography (Clifford 1982, 1988; Marcus and Cushman 1982). Marcus and Fischer argue that experimentation in ethnographic writing is necessary because all peoples and cultures have already been "discovered" and must now be "rediscovered . . . in changing historical circumstances" (1986, p. 24).

Some contemporary cultural anthropologists see ethnographic writing as an art as much as a science. Such a view might regard an ethnographic account as a literary creation in which the ethnographer, as mediator, communicates information from the "natives" to readers. Some experimental ethnographies are "dialogic," presenting ethnography as a dialogue between the anthropologist and one or more key consultants (e.g., Behar 1993; Dwyer 1982). These works draw attention to ways in which ethnographers, and by extension their readers, communicate with other cultures. Some ethnographies of this type have been criticized for spending too much time talking about the anthropologist and too little time describing the local people and their culture.

The dialogic ethnography is one genre within a larger experimental category—*reflexive ethnography*. Here the ethnographer puts his or her personal feelings and reactions to the field situation right in the text. Experimental writing strategies are prominent in reflexive accounts. The ethnographer may adopt some of the conventions of the novel, including first-person narration, conversations, dialogues, and humor. Experimental ethnographies, using new ways of showing what it means to be a Samoan or a Brazilian, may convey to the reader a richer and more complex understanding of human experience.

Linked to Malinowski's salvage ethnography was the idea of the *ethnographic present*—the period before Westernization, when the "true" native culture flourished. This notion often gives classic ethnographies an unrealistic timeless quality. Providing the only jarring note in this idealized picture are occasional comments by the author about traders or missionaries, suggesting that in actuality the natives were already part of the world system.

Anthropologists now recognize that the ethnographic present is a rather unrealistic construct. Cultures have been in contact—and have been changing—throughout history. Most native cultures had at least one major foreign encounter before any anthropologist ever came their way. Most of them already had been incorporated in some fashion into nation-states or colonial systems.

Contemporary ethnographies usually recognize that cultures constantly change and that an ethnographic account applies to a particular moment. A current trend in ethnography is to focus on the ways in which cultural ideas serve political and economic interests. A related trend is the anthropology of globalization, which describes how various particular "natives" participate in broader historical, political, and economic processes (Shostak 1981).

PROBLEM-ORIENTED ETHNOGRAPHY

Although anthropologists are interested in the whole context of human behavior, it is impossible to study everything. Most ethnographers now enter the field with a specific problem to investigate, and they collect data relevant to that problem (see Chiseri-Strater and Sunstein 2001; Kutsche 1998). Local people's answers to questions are not the only data source. Anthropologists also gather information on factors such as population density, environmental quality, climate, physical geography, diet, and land use. Sometimes this involves direct measurement—of rainfall, temperature, fields, yields, dietary quantities, or time allocation (Bailey 1990; Johnson 1978). Often it means that we consult government records or archives.

The information of interest to ethnographers is not limited to what local people can and do tell us. In an increasingly interconnected and complicated world, local people lack knowledge about many factors that affect their lives. Our local consultants may be as mystified as we are by the exercise of power from regional, national, and international centers.

LONGITUDINAL RESEARCH, TEAM RESEARCH, AND MULTISITED ETHNOGRAPHY

Geography limits anthropologists less now than in the past, when it could take months to reach a field site, and return visits were rare. New systems of transportation allow anthropologists to widen the area of their research and to return repeatedly. Ethnographic reports now routinely include data from two or more field stays. **Longitudinal research** is the long-term study of a community, region, society, culture, or other unit, usually based on repeated visits.

One example of such research is the longitudinal study of Gwembe District, Zambia. This study, planned in 1956 as a longitudinal project by Elizabeth Colson and Thayer Scudder, continues with Colson, Scudder, and their associates of various nationalities. Thus, as is often the case with longitudinal research, the Gwembe study also illustrates team research—coordinated research by multiple ethnographers (Colson and Scudder 1975; Scudder and Colson 1980). In this study, four villages in different areas have been followed for five decades. Periodic village censuses provide basic data on population, economy, kinship, and religious behavior. Censused people who have moved are traced and interviewed to see how their lives compare with those of people who have stayed in the villages.

A series of different research questions have emerged, while basic data on communities and individuals continue to be collected. The first focus of study was the impact of a large hydroelectric dam, which subjected the Gwembe people to forced resettlement. The dam also spurred road building and other activities that brought the people of Gwembe more closely in touch with the rest of Zambia. In subsequent research Scudder and Colson (1980) examined how education provided access to new opportunities as it also widened a social gap between people with different educational levels. A third study then examined a change in brewing and drinking patterns, including a rise in alcoholism, in

longitudinal research Long-term study of a community, society, culture, or other unit, usually based on repeated visits.

Conrad Kottak with his Brazilian nephew, Gui Roxo, in the field in Arembepe, Bahia, Brazil.

relation to changing markets, transportation, and exposure to town values (Colson and Scudder 1988).

As mentioned, longitudinal research often is team research. Kottak's field site of Arembepe, Brazil, for example, first entered the world of anthropology as a field-team village in the 1960s. It was one of four sites for the now defunct Columbia-Cornell-Harvard-Illinois Summer Field Studies Program in Anthropology. For at least three years, that program sent a total of about twenty undergraduates annually, the author included, to do brief summer research abroad. They were stationed in rural communities in four countries: Brazil, Ecuador, Mexico, and Peru. Since Kottak's wife, Isabel Wagley Kottak, and he began studying it in 1962, Arembepe has become a longitudinal field site. Three generations of researchers have monitored various aspects of change and development. The community has changed from a village into a town and illustrates the process of globalization at the local level. Its economy, religion, and social life have been transformed (Kottak 2006).

Brazilian and American researchers worked with Kottak on team research projects during the 1980s (on

STUDY TIP

Approaches that enhance traditional ethnography include study of government and archival documents, longitudinal research, multisited research, and team research.

television's impact) and the 1990s (on ecological awareness and environmental risk perception). Graduate students from the University of Michigan have drawn on baseline information from the 1960s as they have studied various topics in Arembepe. In 1990 Doug Jones, a Michigan student doing biocultural research, used Arembepe as a field site to investigate standards of physical attractiveness. In 1996–1997, Janet Dunn studied family planning and changing female reproductive strategies. Chris O'Leary, who first visited Arembepe in summer 1997, investigated a striking aspect of religious change there—the arrival of Protestantism; his dissertation research then examined changing food habits and nutrition in relation to globalization (O'Leary 2002). Arembepe is thus a site where various field-workers have worked as members of a longitudinal team. The more recent researchers have built on prior contacts and findings to increase knowledge about how local people meet and manage new circumstances.

Traditional ethnographic research focused on a single community or "culture," treated as more or less isolated and unique in time and space. In recent years ethnography has shifted toward studies of change and of contemporary flows of people, technology, images, and information. Reflecting today's world, fieldwork must be more flexible and on a larger scale. Ethnography increasingly is multitimed and multisited. That is, it studies people through time and in multiple places. Malinowski could focus on Trobriand culture and spend most of his field time in a particular community. Nowadays we cannot afford to ignore, as Malinowski did, the outside forces that increasingly impinge on the places we study. Integral to our analyses now are the external entities (e.g., governments, corporations, nongovernmental organizations, new social movements) now laying claim to land, people, and resources throughout the world. Also important in contemporary ethnography is increased recognition of power differentials and how they affect cultures, and of the importance of diversity within cultures and societies.

Anthropologists increasingly study people in motion. Examples include people living on or near national borders, nomads, seasonal migrants, homeless and displaced people, immigrants, and refugees. As fieldwork changes, with less and less of a spatially set field, what can we take from traditional ethnography? Gupta and Ferguson correctly cite the "characteristically anthropological emphasis on daily routine and lived experience" (1997a, p. 5). The treatment of communities as discrete entities may be a thing of the past. However, "anthropology's traditional attention to the close observation of particular lives in particular places" has an enduring importance (Gupta and Ferguson 1997b, p. 25). The method of close observation helps distinguish cultural anthropology from sociology and survey research, to which we now turn.

Got IT? Can you explain the history of ethnography, identifying how it has differed from traditional sociological approaches?

>> Survey Research

Working increasingly in large-scale societies, anthropologists have developed innovative ways of blending ethnography and survey research (Fricke 1994). Before examining such combinations of field methods, let's consider survey research and the main differences between survey research and ethnography (see Table 3.1). Working mainly in large, populous nations, sociologists, political scientists, and economists have developed and refined the **survey research** design, which involves sampling, impersonal data collection, and statistical analysis. Survey research usually draws a **sample** (a manageable study group) from a much larger population. By studying a properly selected and representative sample, social scientists can make accurate inferences about the larger population.

> **survey research** Characteristic research procedure among social scientists other than anthropologists, which studies society through sampling, statistical analysis, and impersonal data collection.

> **sample** A smaller study group chosen to represent a larger population.

Ethnography and Survey Research Contrasted

Ethnography (Traditional)

Survey Research

TABLE 3.1

Ethnography (Traditional)	Survey Research
Studies whole, functioning communities	Studies a small sample of a larger population
Usually is based on firsthand fieldwork, during which information is collected after rapport, based on personal contact, is established between researcher and hosts	Often is conducted with little or no personal contact between study subjects and researchers, as interviews are frequently conducted by assistants over the phone or in printed form
Traditionally is interested in all aspects of local life (holistic)	Usually focuses on small number of variables (e.g., factors that influence voting) rather than on the totality of people's lives
Traditionally has been conducted in nonindustrial, small-scale societies, where people often do not read and write	Normally is carried out in modern nations, where most people are literate, permitting respondents to fill in their own questionnaires
Makes little use of statistics, because the communities being studied tend to be small, with little diversity besides that based on age, gender, and individual personality variation	Depends heavily on statistical analyses to make inferences regarding a large and diverse population, based on data collected from a small subset of that population

Canadians of Japanese descent fill out a survey at an alternative energy conference at the University of Calgary.

In small communities, ethnographers can get to know almost everyone. Given the greater size and complexity of nations, survey research can't help being more impersonal. Survey researchers call the people they study *respondents.* These are people who respond to questions during a survey. Sometimes survey researchers personally interview them. Sometimes, they ask a sample of respondents to fill out a questionnaire, nowadays often online.

Probably the most familiar example of sampling is the polling used to predict political races. The media hire agencies to estimate outcomes and do exit polls to find out what kinds of people voted for which candidates. During sampling, researchers gather information about age, gender, religion, occupation, income, and political party preference. These characteristics (**variables**—attributes that vary among members of a sample or population) are known to influence political decisions.

Many more variables affect social identities, experiences, and activities in a modern nation than in the small communities where ethnography grew up. In contemporary North America hundreds of factors influence our behavior and attitudes. These social predictors include our religion; the region of the country we grew up in; whether we come from a town, suburb, or city; and our parents' professions, ethnic origins, and income levels.

Ethnography can be used to supplement and fine-tune survey research. Anthropologists can transfer the personal, firsthand techniques of ethnography to virtually any setting that includes human beings. A combination of survey research and ethnography can provide new perspectives on life in **complex societies** (large and populous societies with social stratification and central governments). Preliminary ethnography also can help develop culturally appropriate questions for inclusion in surveys.

In any complex society, many predictor variables (*social indicators*) influence behavior and opinions. Because we must be able to detect, measure, and compare the influence of social indicators, many contemporary anthropological studies have a statistical foundation. Even in rural fieldwork, more anthropologists now draw samples, gather quantitative data, and use statistics to interpret them (see Bernard 1998, 2006). Quantifiable information may permit a more precise assessment of similarities and differences among communities. Statistical analysis can support and round out an ethnographic account of local social life.

In the best studies, the hallmark of ethnography remains: Anthropologists enter the community and get to know the people. They participate in local activities, networks, and associations in the city, town, or countryside. They observe and experience social conditions and problems. They watch the effects of national and international policies and programs on local life. The ethnographic method and the emphasis on personal relationships in social research are valuable gifts that cultural anthropology brings to the study of any society.

> "The way to do fieldwork is never to come up for air until it is all over."
>
> Margaret Mead

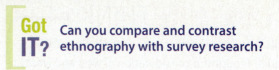

Got IT? Can you compare and contrast ethnography with survey research?

>> Doing Anthropology Right and Wrong: Ethical Issues

Science exists in society and in the context of law and ethics. Anthropologists can't study things simply because they happen to be interesting or of value to science. Ethical issues must be considered as well. Anthropologists typically have worked abroad, outside their own society. In the context of international contacts and cultural diversity, different ethical codes and value systems will meet, and sometimes challenge one another.

Anthropologists must be sensitive to cultural differences and aware of procedures and standards in the host country (the place where the research takes place). The researcher must inform officials and colleagues in the host country about the purpose, funding, and likely results, products, and impacts of their research. **Informed consent**

variables Attributes (e.g., sex, age, height, weight) that differ from one person or case to the next.

complex societies Nations; large and populous, with social stratification and central governments.

informed consent An agreement sought by ethnographers from community members to take part in research.

CULTURE THINK

During the 1980s, anthropologist Nancy Scheper-Hughes studied survival strategies in a poverty-stricken Brazilian shantytown. Because they lacked the resources needed to ensure the survival of their children, women often neglected sickly babies who seemed doomed to die. Dr. Scheper-Hughes treated and fed one of those babies, who then lived to be a healthy adult. Did she do the right thing? What are the costs and benefits of the decision she made?

CULTURE THINK

What are the advantages and disadvantages of doing survey research? What about participant observation and other ethnographic techniques?

(agreement to take part in the research—after having been informed about its nature, procedures, and possible impacts) should be obtained from anyone who provides information or who might be affected by the research.

It is appropriate for North American anthropologists working in another country to (1) include host country colleagues in their research planning; (2) establish truly collaborative relationships with those colleagues and their institutions before, during, and after fieldwork; (3) include host country colleagues in dissemination, including publication, of the research results; and (4) ensure that something is "given back" to host country colleagues. For example, research equipment is allowed to remain in the host country. Or funding is sought for host country colleagues to do research, attend international meetings, or visit foreign institutions—especially those where their international collaborators work.

THE CODE OF ETHICS

To guide its members in making decisions involving ethics and values, the American Anthropological Association (AAA) offers a Code of Ethics. The most recent code, approved in 2009, points out that anthropologists have obligations to their scholarly field, to the wider society and culture, and to the human species, other species, and the environment. Like physicians who take the Hippocratic oath, the anthropologist's first concern should be to do no harm to the people being studied. The stated aim of the AAA code is to offer guidelines and to promote discussion and education, rather than to investigate possible misconduct. The code addresses several contexts in which anthropologists work. Some of its main points are highlighted here.

Anthropologists should be open and honest about their research projects with all parties affected by the research. These parties should be informed about the nature, procedures, purpose(s), potential impacts, and source(s) of support for the research. Researchers should pay attention to proper relations between themselves as guests and the host nations and communities where they work. The AAA does not advise anthropologists to avoid taking stands on issues. Indeed, seeking to shape actions and policies may be as ethically justifiable as inaction. The full Code of Ethics is available at the AAA website http://www.aaanet.org/issues/policy-advocacy/Code-of-Ethics.cfm.

ANTHROPOLOGISTS AND TERRORISM

The AAA has deemed it of "paramount importance" that anthropologists study the roots of terrorism and violence. How should such studies be conducted? What ethical issues might arise?

Consider a Pentagon program, Project Minerva, initiated late in the George W. Bush administration, designed to draw on social science expertise to combat national security threats. Project Minerva sought scholars to translate original documents captured in Iraq, study China's shift to a more open political

POPCULTURE

Set on another globe, *Avatar*, the most popular film ever made to date, is about what it means to be human and not human, while still cultured in the anthropological sense. *Avatar* also raises ethical questions involving humanoid rights and proper loyalties for humans—to nature, indigenous "peoples," science, and commerce. *Avatar* portrays the struggle that local cultures face in resisting and surviving the powerful forces and threats they face from outside.

The movie also features a quasi-anthropologist, Dr. Grace Augustine, played by Sigourney Weaver. As you watch *Avatar*, pay attention to how Grace's attitudes, beliefs, and opinions differ from those of other members of the cast. What are her main similarities to and differences from the anthropologists discussed in this chapter?

system, and explain the resurgence of the Taliban in Afghanistan (Cohen 2008). Project Minerva and related programs have raised serious concerns among anthropologists. Scholars worry that governments will use anthropological knowledge for goals, and in ways, that are ethically problematic. Government policies and military operations have the potential to harm the people anthropologists study.

Social scientists also object to the notion that the military should determine which research projects are worthy of funding. Rather, scholars favor a (peer review) system in which panels of their professional peers (other social scientists) judge the value and propriety of proposed research, including research that might help identify and deter threats to national security. One proposal was to have the National Science Foundation (because of its long experience with social science research), rather than the Pentagon, distribute Minerva money.

Anthropologists have been especially outspoken about the Pentagon's Human Terrain System (HTS) program. Launched in February 2007, HTS embeds anthropologists and other social scientists in military teams in Iraq and Afghanistan. The multimillion-dollar project planned to operate as many as 26 teams in those countries.

On October 31, 2007, the AAA Executive Board issued a statement of disapproval of HTS—outlining how HTS violates the AAA Code of Ethics (see http://www.aaanet.org/about/Policies/statements/Human-Terrain-System-Statement.cfm). The board noted that HTS places anthropologists, as contractors with the U.S. military, in war zones, where they are charged with collecting cultural and social data for use by the military. The ethical concerns raised by these activities include the following:

1. It may be impossible for anthropologists in war zones to identify themselves as anthropologists, as distinct from military personnel. This constrains their ethical responsibility as anthropologists to disclose who they are and what they are doing.

2. HTS anthropologists are asked to negotiate relations among several groups, including local populations and the military units in which they are embedded. Their responsibilities to their units may conflict with their obligations to the local people they study or consult. This may interfere with the obligation, stipulated in the AAA Code of Ethics, to do no harm.

3. In an active war zone, it is difficult for local people to give "informed consent" without feeling coerced to provide information. As a result, "voluntary

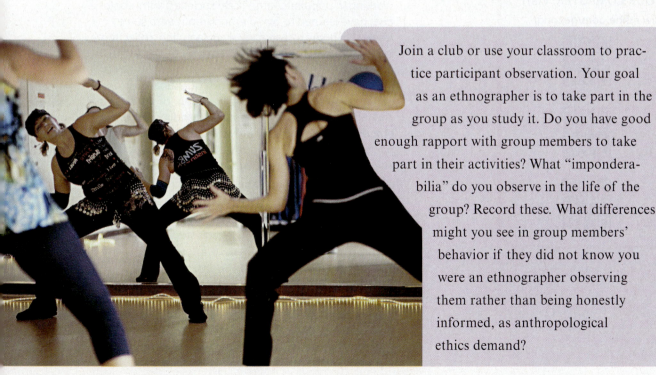

informed consent" (as stipulated by the AAA Code of Ethics, section III, A, 4) is compromised.

4. Information supplied by HTS anthropologists to military field commanders could help target specific groups for military action. Such use of fieldwork-derived information would violate the AAA Code of Ethics stipulation to do no harm to people.

5. The identification of anthropology and anthropologists with the U.S. military may indirectly (through suspicion of "guilt by association") endanger the research, and even the personal safety, of other anthropologists and their consultants throughout the world.

How should anthropologists study terrorism? What do you think about anthropologists' role in war?

 Got IT? Can you identify ethical issues faced by anthropologists and apply them to particular case studies?

FOR REVIEW

EXPERIENCING CULTURE

TO ACCESS THESE VIDEOS ON YOUR COMPUTER, VISIT

www.mhhe.com/gezonqr

3-1

3-2

3-3

I. Where and how do cultural anthropologists do fieldwork?

- Early anthropologists worked in small, relatively isolated societies with a certain cultural uniformity. Ethnographers sought to create a holistic account, revealing a culture's totality and interconnectedness. Ethnographers have developed a variety of techniques. A key method is participant observation, taking part in community life as it is studied. Ethnographers also gather data from conversations and interviews, and by tracing genealogies, working with key cultural consultants, and collecting life histories. Ethnography seeks also to discover the native viewpoint.

- In today's interlinked world, anthropologists increasingly study people on the move. Ethnographers now tend to enter the field with a particular problem to investigate. Enabled by modern systems of transportation, ethnographers often return for multiple stays to monitor change. Such longitudinal research may entail coordinated team research.

II. What are some ways of studying complex societies in modern nations?

- Working in populous, large-scale societies, anthropologists have learned to blend ethnography with survey research. Survey research involves sampling, collecting impersonal data, and statistical analysis. Social scientists make inferences about the larger population by surveying a sample of "respondents." Such quantifiable information allows a more precise assessment of similarities and differences among communities and rounds out the ethnographic account. By providing data acquired by personal, firsthand techniques, ethnography supplements and fine-tunes survey research.

III. What ethical concerns and issues must anthropologists consider?

- Because science exists in society, and in the context of law and ethics, anthropologists can't study things simply because they happen to be interesting or of scientific value. Anthropologists have obligations to their scholarly field, to the wider society and culture (including that of the host country), and to the human species, other species, and the environment. The AAA Code of Ethics offers ethical guidelines for anthropologists. Ethical problems often arise when anthropologists work for governments, especially the military.

Pop Quiz

Multiple Choice:

1. Which of the following statements about ethnography is false?

   a. Early ethnographers tried to understand the culture they studied as a whole (that is, sought to make a holistic account).

   b. Ethnographers see little value in collecting quantitative data.

   c. Bronislaw Malinowski, considered the founder of ethnography, sought to grasp the natives' points of view and visions of their world.

   d. Ethnographers today recognize that the culture they study is described only in a moment of time.

2. All the following are true about ethnography *except* this statement:

   a. It was used traditionally to study whole communities.

   b. It is based on firsthand fieldwork.

   c. It is more personal than survey research.

   d. It privileges ethnographers' observations and conclusions over the local people's views and beliefs.

3. Trends in doing ethnography include the following *except*

   a. a move away from holistic accounts toward investigations of specific problems.

   b. the inclusion of field-gathered data from two or more stays in the field (longitudinal research).

   c. doing more work for colonial governments.

   d. giving increased attention to contacts from outside the communities being studied.

4. In a modern world in which people, images, and information move around as never before, ethnography

   a. is becoming increasingly challenging for those wishing to focus on a spatially set culture.

   b. is becoming a less useful and less valuable tool for understanding culture.

   c. has become more traditional.

   d. now requires that researchers stay in the same site for more than three years.

5. Which of the following most completely characterizes the ethnographic approach?

   a. It relies on firsthand contact with the community being studied, including participation in its cultural life and observation of its social conditions.

   b. It takes into consideration people in motion and may require the anthropologist to follow the people being studied.

   c. It involves team research projects.

   d. Sources of data for ethnography include answers to questions, measurement of environmental conditions, and consultation of government records

6. Which of the following is *not* a part of the AAA Code of Ethics?

   a. The recognition that anthropologists are obligated to their scholarly field, to the wider society and culture, and to the human species.

   b. The recommendation that anthropologists avoid taking stands on issues that arise in their dealings with another culture.

   c. The requirement that all parties involved in doing anthropological research be informed about the nature, procedures, purpose, and potential impacts of the research.

   d. The recommendation that the people anthropologists work with in the field be respected, acknowledged, and compensated in appropriate ways.

Fill in the Blank:

1. As one of the ethnographer's characteristic field research methods, the _____ method focuses on kin connections.

2. _____ is the research method typically used by sociologists; it involves sampling, impersonal data collection, and statistical analysis.

3. _____ is agreement by an informant, consultant, or community to take part in anthropological research after having been told about its nature, procedures, and possible impacts.

4. The Pentagon's _____, which embeds anthropologists and other social scientists in military teams in Iraq and Afghanistan, has been criticized by the American Anthropological Association.

1. (b), 2. (d), 3. (c), 4. (a), 5. (a), 6. (b)

1. genealogical; 2. Survey research; 3. Informed consent; 4. Human Terrain System

4

LANGUAGE AND COMMUNICATION

UNDERSTANDING OURSELVES

Can you identify anything distinctive or unusual about the way you talk? If you're from Canada, Virginia, or Savannah, you may say "oot" instead of "out." A southerner may request a "soft drink" rather than the New Yorker's "soda." How might a "Valley Girl" or "surfer dude" talk? Usually when we pay attention to the way we talk, it's because someone else comments on our speech. It may be only when you move from one state or region to another that you realize how much of a regional accent you have.

Unlike grammarians, linguistic anthropologists are interested in what people actually say, rather than what they should say. Speech differences are associated with, and tell us a lot about, social variation, such as region, education, ethnic background, and gender. Men and women talk differently. We're sure you can think of examples based on your own experience, although you probably never realized that women tend to peripheralize their vowels (think of the sounds in "weasel" and "whee"), whereas men tend to centralize them (think of "rough" and "ugh"). Men are more likely to speak "ungrammatically" than women are.

Men and women also show differences in their sports and color terminologies. Men typically know more terms related to sports, make more distinctions among them (e.g., *runs* versus *points*), and try to use the terms more precisely than women do. Correspondingly, influenced more by the fashion and cosmetics industries, women use more color terms and attempt to use them more precisely than men do. For example, women are much more likely than men to distinguish between various shades of purple, such as mauve, lilac, lavender, and wisteria. Rare is the man who on the spur of the moment can imagine the difference between fuchsia and magenta or grape and aubergine.

>> Language

Linguistic anthropology illustrates anthropology's characteristic interests in diversity, comparison, and change—but here the focus is on language. Language, spoken (*speech*) and written (*writing,* which has existed for about six thousand years), is our primary means of communication. Like culture in general, of which language is a part, language is transmitted through learning. Language is based on arbitrary, learned associations between words and the things they stand for. Unlike the communication systems of other animals, language allows us to discuss the past and future, share our experiences with others, and benefit from their experiences.

call systems Systems of communication among nonhuman primates, composed of a limited number of sounds that vary in intensity and duration; tied to environmental stimuli.

Anthropologists study language in its social and cultural context (see Bonvillain 2012; Salzmann, Stanlaw, and Adachi 2011). Some linguistic anthropologists reconstruct ancient languages by comparing their contemporary descendants and, in doing so, make discoveries about history. Others study linguistic differences to discover the varied worldviews and patterns of thought in a multitude of cultures. Sociolinguists examine dialects and styles in a single language to show how speech reflects social differences, as in the discussion in "Understanding Ourselves" of regional speech contrasts. Linguistic anthropologists also explore the role of language in colonization and globalization (Blommaert 2010; Trudgill 2010).

>> Nonhuman Primate Communication

CALL SYSTEMS

Only humans speak. No other animal has anything approaching the complexity of language. The natural communication systems of other primates (monkeys and apes) are **call systems.** These vocal systems consist of a limited number of sounds—*calls*—that are produced only when particular environmental stimuli are encountered. Such calls may be varied in intensity and duration, but they are much less flexible than language because they are automatic and can't be combined. When primates encounter food and danger simultaneously, they can make only one call. They can't combine the calls for food and danger into a single utterance, indicating that both are present. At some point in human evolution, however, our ancestors began to combine calls and to understand the combinations. The number of calls also expanded, eventually becoming too great to be transmitted even partly through the genes. Communication came to rely almost totally on learning.

Although wild primates use call systems, the vocal tract of apes is not suitable for speech. Until the 1960s, attempts to teach spoken language to apes suggested that they lack linguistic abilities. In the 1950s, a couple raised a chimpanzee, Viki, as a member of their family and systematically tried to teach her to speak. Viki learned only four words: "mama," "papa," "up," and "cup."

SIGN LANGUAGE

More recent experiments have shown that apes can learn to use language, if not speak it (Fouts 1997; Miles 1983). Several apes have learned to converse with people through means other than speech. One such communication system is American Sign Language (ASL), which is widely used by hearing-impaired people in the United States, Canada, and several other nations. British Sign Language (BSL), used in the United Kingdom, differs significantly from ASL, and the two are not mutually intelligible. Sign languages employ a limited number of basic gesture units that are analogous to sounds in spoken language. These units combine to form words and larger units of meaning.

The first chimpanzee to learn ASL was Washoe, a female, who died in 2007 at the age of forty-two.

歡迎
Welcome
Bienvenue
Bienvenido
Willkommen
Benvenuto
Boas-Vindas
환영
ようこそ

Call systems, used in animal communication, have three features:

- They have a limited number of sounds.

- They are used only when certain stimuli are present.

- They cannot be combined to produce more complex messages.

Hearing-impaired dancers in China's Disabled People's Performing Art Troupe communicate through sign language while undergoing physical conditioning.

Captured in West Africa, R. Allen Gardner and Beatrice Gardner, scientists at the University of Nevada in Reno, acquired Washoe in 1966, when she was a year old. Four years later, she moved to Norman, Oklahoma, to a converted farm that had become the

Apes, such as these Congo chimpanzees, use call systems to communicate in the wild. Their vocal systems consist of a limited number of sounds—calls—that are produced only when they encounter particular environmental stimuli.

Institute for Primate Studies. Washoe revolutionized the discussion of the language-learning abilities of apes (Carey 2007). At first she lived in a trailer and heard no spoken language. The researchers always used ASL to communicate with each other in her presence. The chimp gradually acquired a vocabulary of more than one hundred signs representing English words (Gardner, Gardner, and Van Cantfort 1989). At the age of two, Washoe began to combine as many as five signs into rudimentary sentences, such as "You, me, go out, hurry."

The second chimp to learn ASL was Lucy, Washoe's junior by one year. Lucy died, or was murdered by poachers, in 1986, after having been introduced to "the wild" in Africa in 1979 (Carter 1988). From her second day of life until her move to Africa, Lucy lived with a family in Norman, Oklahoma. Roger Fouts, a researcher from the nearby Institute for Primate Studies, came two days a week to test and improve Lucy's knowledge of ASL. During the rest of the week, Lucy used ASL to converse with her foster parents. After acquiring language, Washoe and Lucy exhibited several human traits: swearing, joking, telling lies, and trying to teach language to others (Fouts 1997).

Did You Know?

Kanzi is a bonobo, a great ape similar to a chimpanzee but genetically and behaviorally closer to humans. He learned to communicate using symbols, or lexigrams, when he was very young. His primary mentor, Sue Savage-Rumbaugh, reported that eight-year-old Kanzi could communicate with grammatical complexity similar to that of a two-year-old child.

When irritated, Washoe called her monkey neighbors at the institute "dirty monkeys." Lucy insulted her "dirty cat." On arrival at Lucy's place, Fouts once found a pile of excrement on the floor. When he asked the chimp what it was, she replied, "dirty, dirty," her expression for feces. Asked whose "dirty, dirty" it was, Lucy named Fouts's coworker, Sue. When Fouts refused to believe her about Sue, the chimp blamed the excrement on Fouts himself.

Cultural transmission of a communication system through learning is a fundamental attribute of language. Washoe, Lucy, and other chimps have tried to teach ASL to other animals, including their own offspring. Washoe taught gestures to other institute chimps, including her son Sequoia, who died in infancy (Fouts, Fouts, and Van Cantfort 1989).

Because of their size and strength as adults, gorillas are less likely subjects than chimps for such experiments. Lean adult male gorillas in the wild weigh 400 pounds (180 kilograms), and full-grown females can easily reach 250 pounds (110 kilograms). Because of this, psychologist Penny Patterson's work with gorillas at Stanford University seems more daring than the chimp experiments. Patterson raised her now full-grown female gorilla, Koko, in a trailer next to a Stanford museum. Koko's vocabulary surpasses that of any chimp. She regularly employs four hundred ASL signs and has used about seven hundred at least once.

Koko and the chimps also show that apes share still another linguistic ability with humans: **productivity.** Speakers routinely use the rules of their language to produce entirely new expressions that are comprehensible to other native speakers. A human speaker could, for example, create "baboonlet" to refer to a baboon infant. This is done through analogy with English words in which the suffix -*let* designates the young of a species. Anyone who speaks English immediately understands the meaning of the new word. Koko, Washoe, Lucy, and others have shown that apes also are able to use language productively. Lucy used gestures she already knew to create "drinkfruit" for watermelon. Washoe, seeing a swan for the first time, coined "waterbird." Koko, who knew the gestures for "finger" and "bracelet," formed "finger bracelet" when she was given a ring.

Chimps and gorillas have a rudimentary capacity for language. They may never have invented a meaningful

cultural transmission A basic feature of language; transmission through learning.

productivity The ability to use the rules of one's language to create new expressions comprehensible to other speakers; a basic feature of language.

displacement A linguistic capacity that allows humans to talk about things and events that are not present.

"What is important, is that not only has Koko been taught basic sign language, but that she can use that knowledge to communicate meaningful and complex ideas."

Source: © Tom Chalkey, The New Yorker Collection, www.cartoonstock.com

gesture system in the wild. Given such a system, however, they show many humanlike abilities in learning and using it. Of course, language use by apes is a product of human intervention and teaching. The experiments mentioned here do not suggest that apes can invent language (nor are human children ever faced with that task). However, young apes have managed to learn the basics of gestural language. They can employ it productively and creatively, although not with the sophistication of human ASL users.

Apes also have demonstrated linguistic **displacement.** Absent in call systems, this is a key ingredient in language. Normally, each call is tied to an environmental stimulus, such as food. Calls are uttered only when that stimulus is present. Displacement means that humans can talk about things that are not present. We don't have to see the objects before we say the words. Human conversations are not limited by place. We can discuss the past and future, share our experiences with others, and benefit from theirs.

Patterson has described several examples of Koko's capacity for displacement (Patterson 1978). The gorilla once expressed sorrow about having bitten Penny three days earlier. Koko has used the sign "later" to postpone doing things she doesn't want to do. Table 4.1 summarizes the contrasts between language, whether sign or spoken, and call systems.

Certain scholars doubt the linguistic abilities of chimps and gorillas (Sebeok and Umiker-Sebeok 1980; Terrace 1979). They contend that Koko and the chimps are comparable to trained circus animals and don't really have linguistic ability. In defense of Patterson and the other researchers (Hill 1978; Van Cantfort and Rimpau 1982), only one of their critics has worked with an ape. This was Herbert Terrace, whose experience teaching a chimp sign language lacked the continuity and personal involvement that have contributed so much to Patterson's success with Koko.

No one denies the huge difference between human language and gorilla signs. There is a major gap between the ability to write a book or say a prayer and the few hundred gestures employed by a well-trained chimp. Apes aren't people, but they aren't just animals either. Let Koko express it: When asked by a reporter whether she was a person or an animal, Koko chose neither. Instead, she signed "fine animal gorilla" (Patterson 1978). For the latest on Koko, see http://koko.org.

THE ORIGIN OF LANGUAGE

Although the capacity to remember and combine linguistic symbols may be latent in the apes (Miles 1983), human evolution was needed for this seed to flower

Language Contrasted with Call Systems

Human Language	Primate Call Systems
Has the capacity to speak of things and events that are not present (displacement).	Are stimuli-dependent; the food call will be made in the presence of food; it cannot be faked.
Has the capacity to generate new expressions by combining other expressions (productivity).	Consist of a limited number of calls that cannot be combined to produce new calls.
Is group specific in that all humans have the capacity for language, but each linguistic community has its own language, which is culturally transmitted.	Tend to be species specific, with little variation among communities of the same species for each call.

TABLE 4.1

into language. A mutated gene known as FOXP2 helps explain why humans speak and chimps don't (Paulson 2005). The key role of FOXP2 in speech came to light in a study of a British family, identified only as KE, half of whose members had an inherited, severe deficit in speech (Trivedi 2001). The same variant form of FOXP2 that is found in chimpanzees causes this disorder. Those who have the non-speech version of the gene cannot make the fine tongue and lip movements necessary for clear speech, and their speech is unintelligible—even to other members of the KE family (Trivedi 2001). Chimps have the same (genetic) sequence as the KE family members with the speech deficit. Comparing chimp and human genomes, it appears that the speech-friendly form of FOXP2 took hold in humans around 150,000 years ago. This mutation conferred selective advantages (linguistic and cultural abilities) that allowed those who had it to spread at the expense of those who did not (Paulson 2005).

Language offered a tremendous adaptive advantage to *Homo sapiens*. Language permits the information stored by a human society to exceed by far that of any nonhuman group. Language is a uniquely effective vehicle for learning. Because we can speak of things we have never experienced, we can anticipate responses before we encounter the stimuli. Adaptation can occur

Got IT? Can you compare and contrast language with call systems, evaluating the ability of apes to communicate with language?

Hieroglyphics from an Egyptian tomb illustrate this early form of writing. Language has been around a lot longer than writing. How much longer, do you think?

CULTURETHINK

How does language provide an adaptive advantage? In other words, how do you think it has helped humans survive?

more rapidly in *Homo* than in the other primates because our adaptive means are more flexible.

>> Nonverbal Communication

Language is our principal means of communicating, but it isn't the only one we use. We *communicate* when we transmit information about ourselves to others and receive such information from them. Our expressions, stances, gestures, and movements, even if unconscious, convey information and are part of our communication styles. Deborah Tannen (1990) discusses differences in

the communication styles of American men and women, and her comments go beyond language. She notes that American girls and women tend to look directly at each other when they talk, whereas American boys and men do not. Males are more likely to look straight ahead rather than turn and make eye contact with someone, especially another man, seated beside them. Also, in conversational groups, American men tend to relax and sprawl out. American women may adopt a similar relaxed posture in all-female groups, but when they are with men, they tend to draw in their limbs and adopt a tighter stance.

Kinesics is the study of communication through body movements, stances, gestures, and expressions. Linguists pay attention not only to what is said but to how it is said, and to features besides language itself that convey meaning. A speaker's enthusiasm is conveyed not only through words, but also through facial expressions, gestures, and other signs of animation. We use gestures, such as a jab of the hand, for emphasis. We vary our intonation and the pitch or loudness of our voices. We communicate through strategic pauses, and even by being silent. An effective communication strategy may be to alter pitch, voice level, and grammatical forms, such as declaratives ("I am . . ."), imperatives ("Go forth . . ."), and questions ("Are you . . . ?"). Culture teaches us that certain manners and styles should accompany certain kinds of speech. Our demeanor, verbal and nonverbal, when our favorite team is winning would be out of place at a funeral or when a somber subject is being discussed.

Culture always plays a role in shaping the "natural." Cross-culturally, nodding does not always mean affirmative, nor does head shaking from side to side always

kinesics The study of communication through body movements, stances, gestures, and facial expressions.

mean negative. Brazilians wag a finger to mean no. Americans say "uh huh" to affirm, whereas in Madagascar a similar sound is made to deny. Americans point with their fingers; the people of Madagascar point with their lips.

Body movements communicate social differences. In Japan, bowing is a regular part of social interaction, but different bows are used depending on the social status of the people who are interacting. In Madagascar and Polynesia, people of lower status should not hold their heads above those of people of higher status. When one approaches someone older or of higher status, one bends one's knees and lowers one's head as a sign of respect. In Madagascar, one always does this, for politeness, when passing between two people. Although our gestures, facial expressions, and body stances have roots in our primate heritage, and can be seen in the monkeys

Men and women have different communication styles, as illustrated in these two photos. Men, for example, are less likely to engage in face-to-face conversation than women are. What differences do you notice in the gender-based communication styles shown here?

and the apes, they have not escaped cultural shaping. Language, which is so highly dependent on the use of symbols, is the domain of communication in which culture plays the strongest role.

Got IT? Can you describe forms of nonverbal communication, noting how they are different cross-culturally?

>> The Structure of Language

The scientific study of a spoken language, called **descriptive linguistics,** involves several interrelated areas of analysis: phonology, morphology, lexicon, and syntax. **Phonology,** the study of speech sounds, considers which sounds are present and significant in a given language. **Morphology** studies the way sounds combine to form *morphemes*—words and their meaningful parts. Thus, the word *cats* would be analyzed as containing two morphemes—*cat,* the name for a kind of animal, and *-s,* a morpheme indicating plurality. A language's **lexicon** is a dictionary containing all its morphemes and their meanings. **Syntax** refers to the arrangement and order of words in phrases and sentences. For example, do nouns usually come before or after verbs? Do adjectives normally precede or follow the nouns they modify?

Got IT? Can you identify areas of analysis in descriptive linguistics?

SPEECH SOUNDS

From the movies and TV, and from meeting foreigners, we know something about foreign accents and mispronunciations. We know that someone with a marked French accent doesn't pronounce *r* like an American does. But at least someone from France can distinguish between "craw" and "claw," which someone from Japan may not be able to do. The difference between *r* and *l* makes a difference in English and in French, but it doesn't in Japanese. In linguistics we say that the difference between *r* and *l* is *phonemic* in English and French but not in Japanese. In English and French, *r* and *l* are phonemes, but not in Japanese. A **phoneme** is a sound contrast that makes a difference, that differentiates meaning.

CULTURETHINK

Sometimes the meaning of headlines is unclear due to confusion about parts of speech and word order. This is technically referred to as *syntactic* (from syntax) *ambiguity*. What, specifically, makes these headlines confusing—and humorous? Squad Helps Dog Bite Victim; Drunk Gets Nine Months in Violin Case; Iraqi Head Seeks Arms.

We find the phonemes in a given language by comparing *minimal pairs*—words that resemble each other in all but one sound. The words have different meanings, but they differ in just one sound. The contrasting sounds are therefore phonemes in that language. An example in English is the minimal pair *pit/bit*. These two words are distinguished by a single sound contrast between /p/ and /b/ (we enclose phonemes in slashes). Thus /p/ and /b/ are phonemes in English. Another example is the different vowel sound of *bit* and *beat* (see "Vowel Phonemes in Standard American English," on p. 64). This contrast serves to distinguish these two words and the two vowel phonemes written /I/ and /i/ in English.

Standard (American) English (SE), the "region-free" dialect of TV network newscasters, has about thirty-five phonemes—at least eleven vowels and twenty-four consonants. The number of phonemes varies from language to language— from fifteen to sixty, averaging between thirty and forty. The number of phonemes also varies between dialects of a given language. In North American English, for example, vowel phonemes vary noticeably from dialect to dialect. Try pronouncing the words in the figure on page 64, paying attention to (or asking someone else) whether you (or your partner) can distinguish each of the vowel sounds. Most North Americans don't pronounce them all.

Phonetics is the study of speech sounds in general, what people actually say in various

descriptive linguistics The scientific study of a spoken language, including its phonology, morphology, lexicon, and syntax.

phonology The study of sounds used in speech.

morphology The study of form; used in linguistics (the study of morphemes and word construction) and for form in general—for example, biomorphology relates to physical form.

lexicon Vocabulary; a dictionary containing all the morphemes in a language and their meaning.

syntax The arrangement and order of words in phrases and sentences.

phoneme Significant sound contrast in a language that serves to distinguish meaning, as in minimal pairs.

phonetics The study of speech sounds in general; what people actually say in various languages.

Source: From Aspects of Language, 3rd ed. by Bolinger, Fig. 2.1. Copyright © 1981 Heinle/Arts & Sciences, a part of Cengage Learning, Inc. Reprinted by permission.

Vowel Phonemes in Standard American English

Tongue high				
	i		u	
	ɪ		ʊ	
Mid	e	ə	o	
	ɛ		ɔ	
Tongue low	æ	a		
	Tongue front	Central	Tongue back	

High front (spread)	[i]	as in *beat*
Lower high front (spread)	[ɪ]	as in *bit*
Mid front (spread)	[e]	as in *bait*
Lower mid front (spread)	[ɛ]	as in *bet*
Low front	[æ]	as in *bat*
Central	[ə]	as in *butt*
Low back	[a]	as in *pot*
Lower mid back (rounded)	[ɔ]	as in *bought*
Mid back (rounded)	[o]	as in *boat*
Lower high back (rounded)	[ʊ]	as in *put*
High back (rounded)	[u]	as in *boot*

Vocal phonemes are shown according to height of tongue and tongue position at front, center, or back of mouth. Phonetic symbols are identified by English words that include them; note that most are minimal pairs.

languages. **Phonemics** studies only the *significant* sound contrasts (phonemes) of a given language. In English, like /r/ and /l/ (remember *craw* and *claw*), /b/ and /v/ also are phonemes, occurring in minimal pairs like *bat*

phonemics The study of significant sound contrasts (phonemes) of a particular language.

and *vat*. In Spanish, however, the contrast between [b] and [v] doesn't distinguish meaning, and they therefore are not phonemes (we enclose sounds that are not phonemic in brackets). Spanish speakers normally use the [b] sound to pronounce words spelled with either *b* or *v*.

In any language, a given phoneme extends over a phonetic range. In English the phoneme /p/ ignores the phonetic contrast between the [pʰ] in *pin* and the [p] in *spin*. Most English speakers don't even notice that there is a phonetic difference. The [pʰ] is aspirated, so that a puff of air follows the [p]. The [p] in *spin* is not.

CULTURE THINK

Say the following words casually, with an informal but acceptable pronunciation: top, stop, little, kitten, Atlanta. Are the *t*'s all pronounced the same? How many variants can you count? (Note: One of them is aspirated.) The sound we think of as *t* can be pronounced in several ways.

(To see the difference, light a match, hold it in front of your mouth, and watch the flame as you pronounce the two words.) The contrast between [pʰ] and [p] is phonemic in some languages, such as Hindi (spoken in India). That is, there are words whose meaning is distinguished only by the contrast between an aspirated and an unaspirated [p].

Native speakers vary in their pronunciation of certain phonemes, such as the /e/ phoneme in the midwestern United States. This variation is important in the evolution of language. Without shifts in pronunciation, there could be no linguistic change. The section on sociolinguistics later in the chapter considers phonetic variation and its relationship to social divisions and the evolution of language.

Got IT? Can you demonstrate how the study of phonemics and phonetics helps us understand why people speak with accents?

>> Language, Thought, and Culture

The well-known linguist Noam Chomsky (1957) has argued that the human brain contains a limited set of rules for organizing language, so that all languages have a common structural basis. (Chomsky calls this set of rules *universal grammar.*) The fact that people can learn foreign languages and that words and ideas translate from one language to another supports Chomsky's position that all humans have similar linguistic abilities and thought processes. Another line of support comes from creole languages. Such languages develop from *pidgins*—languages that form in situations of acculturation, when different societies come into contact and must devise a system of communication. Pidgins based on English and native languages developed through trade and colonialism in many world areas, including China, Papua New Guinea, and West Africa. Eventually, after generations of being spoken, pidgins may develop into *creole languages.* These are more mature languages, with developed grammatical rules and native speakers (people who learn the language as their primary one during enculturation).

Creoles are spoken in several Caribbean societies. Gullah, which is spoken by African Americans on coastal islands in South Carolina and Georgia, is a creole language. Supporting the idea that creoles are based

Shown here (in 1995) is Leigh Jenkins, who was or is director of cultural preservation for the Hopi council. The Hopi language would not distinguish between *was* and *is* in the previous sentence. For the Hopi, present and past are real and are expressed grammatically in the same way, while the future remains hypothetical and has a different grammatical expression.

speakers to think about time and reality in different ways than English speakers do.

A similar example comes from Portuguese, which employs a future subjunctive verb form, introducing a degree of uncertainty into discussions of the future. In English we routinely use the future tense to talk about something we think will happen. We don't feel the need to qualify "The sun'll come out tomorrow," by adding "if it doesn't go supernova." We don't hesitate to proclaim, "I'll see you next year," even when we can't be absolutely sure we will. The Portuguese future subjunctive qualifies the future event, recognizing that the future can't be certain. Our way of expressing the future as certain is so ingrained that we don't even think about it, just as the Hopi don't see the need to distinguish between present and past, both of which are real, while the future remains hypothetical. It seems, however, that language does not tightly restrict thought, because cultural changes can produce changes in thought and in language, as we'll see in the next section (see also Gumperz and Levinson 1996).

FOCAL VOCABULARY

As mentioned earlier, a lexicon (or vocabulary) is a language's dictionary, its set of names for things, events, and ideas. Lexicon influences perception. Thus,

on universal grammar is the fact that such languages all share certain features. Syntactically, all use particles (e.g., will, was) to form future and past tenses and multiple negation to deny or negate (e.g., he don't got none). Also, all form questions by changing inflection rather than by changing word order. For example, "You're going home for the holidays?" (with a rising tone at the end) rather than "Are you going home for the holidays?"

THE SAPIR-WHORF HYPOTHESIS

Other linguists and anthropologists take a different approach to the relation between language and thought. Rather than seeking universal linguistic structures and processes, they believe that different languages produce different ways of thinking. This position sometimes is known as the **Sapir-Whorf hypothesis,** after Edward Sapir (1931) and his student Benjamin Lee Whorf (1956), its prominent early advocates. Sapir and Whorf argued that the grammatical categories of particular languages lead their speakers to think about things in different ways. For example, English divides time into past, present, and future. Hopi, a language of the Pueblo region of the Native American Southwest, does not. Rather, Hopi distinguishes between events that exist or have existed (what we use present and past to discuss) and those that don't or don't yet (our future events, along with imaginary and hypothetical events). Whorf argued that this difference leads Hopi

POPCULTURE

Playing video games is a popular pastime among college students. Gamers have developed their own Internet-based subculture and gamer lingo (a focal vocabulary) to go along with it. The terms express gaming-specific concepts and experiences, such as "pwning," which, as legend has it, is derived from a misspelling of "own." If someone says, "I pwned [pronounced "poned"] you!" it means that you have been beaten badly. To be on a "kill streak" is to kill many opponents in a row before being killed yourself. A "camper" hides out in one place, waiting for the chance to kill someone unsuspecting. "Hax" (hacks) and cheat codes refer to ways of gaining an unfair advantage in a game, such as being able to see through walls or automatic aiming. Some terms express social judgment: A "noob" is someone who is either inexperienced or just not very good at gaming. Calling someone a "noob" can be an insult, and is an important way of policing acceptable behavior through peer pressure. Are you familiar with this or any other focal vocabularies associated with your own interests? What nonstandard words do you and your friends use?

Eskimos (or Inuit) have several distinct words for different types of snow that in English are all called *snow*. Most English speakers never notice the differences between these types of snow and might have trouble seeing them even if someone pointed them out. Eskimos recognize and think about differences in snow that English speakers don't see because our language gives us just one word.

focal vocabulary A set of words and distinctions that are particularly important to certain groups (those with particular foci of experience or activity), such as types of snow to Eskimos or skiers.

Similarly, the Nuer of Sudan have an elaborate vocabulary to describe cattle. Eskimos have several words for snow, and Nuer have dozens for cattle, because of their particular histories, economies, and environments (Brown 1958; Eastman 1975). When the need arises, English speakers can also elaborate their snow and cattle vocabularies. For example, skiers name varieties of snow with words that are missing from the lexicons of Florida retirees. Similarly, the cattle vocabulary of a Texas rancher is much more ample than that of a salesperson in a New York City department store. Such specialized sets of terms

Illustrating focal vocabulary, Eskimos, or Inuit, have several distinct words for different types of snow that in English are all called "snow."

and distinctions that are particularly important to certain groups (those with particular *foci* of experience or activity) are known as **focal vocabulary.**

Vocabulary is the area of language that changes most readily. New words and distinctions, when needed, appear and spread. For example, who would have "texted" or sent a "tweet" a generation ago? Names for items get simpler as they become common and important. A television has become a *TV,* an automobile a *car,* a digital video disc a *DVD,* and smartphone applications *apps.*

Language, culture, and thought are interrelated. Opposing the Sapir-Whorf hypothesis, however, it might be more accurate to say that changes in culture produce changes in language and thought than to say the reverse. Consider differences between female and male Americans regarding the color terms they use (Lakoff 2004). Distinctions implied by such terms as *salmon, rust, peach, beige, teal, mauve, cranberry,* and *dusky orange* aren't in the vocabularies of most American men. Many of them weren't even in American women's lexicons fifty years ago. These changes reflect changes in American economy, society, and culture. Color terms and distinctions have increased with the growth of the fashion and cosmetic industries. A similar contrast (and growth) in Americans' lexicons shows up in football, basketball, and hockey vocabularies. Sports fans, more often males

Elements of Hockey	Insiders' Term
Puck	Biscuit
Goal/net	Pipes
Penalty box	Sin bin
Hockey stick	Twig
Helmet	Bucket
Space between the goalie's leg pads	Five hole

Focal Vocabulary for Hockey

than females, use more terms concerning, and make more elaborate distinctions between, the games they watch, such as hockey. Thus, cultural contrasts and changes affect lexical distinctions (for instance, *peach* versus *salmon*) within semantic domains (for instance, color terminology). **Semantics** refers to a language's meaning system.

The ways in which people divide the world—the lexical contrasts they perceive as meaningful or significant—reflect their experiences (see Bicker, Sillitoe, and Pottier 2004). Anthropologists have discovered that certain sets of vocabulary items evolve in a determined order. For example, after studying more than a hundred languages, Berlin and Kay (1969/1992) discovered ten basic color terms: *white, black, red, yellow, blue, green, brown, pink, orange,* and *purple* (they evolved in more or less that order). The number of terms varied with cultural complexity. Representing one extreme were Papua New Guinea cultivators and Australian hunters and gatherers, who used only two basic terms, which translate as *black* and *white* or *dark* and *light.* At the other end of the continuum were European and Asian languages with all the color terms. Color terminology

was most developed in areas with a history of using dyes and artificial coloring.

 Got IT? Can you discuss how language, thought, and culture influence one another, making reference to the Sapir-Whorf hypothesis?

>> Sociolinguistics

No language is a uniform system in which everyone talks just like everyone else. The field of **sociolinguistics** investigates relationships between social and linguistic variation (Romaine 2000; Spencer 2010; Trudgill 2000). How do different speakers use a given language? How do linguistic features correlate with social diversity and stratification, including class, ethnic, and gender differences (Tannen 1990, 1993)? How is language used to express, reinforce, or resist power (Geis 1987; G. Lakoff 2008; Mooney 2011)?

Sociolinguists focus on features that vary systematically with social position and situation. To study variation, sociolinguists observe, define, and measure variable use of language in real-world situations. To show that linguistic features correlate with social, economic, and political differences, social attributes of speakers must be measured and related to speech (Fasold 1990; Labov 1972a).

Variation within a language at a given time is historical change in progress. The same forces that, working

> **semantics** A language's meaning system.
>
> **sociolinguistics** Study of relationships between social and linguistic variation; study of language in its social context.

How might social variation show up in texting?

After graduation, Amber Griffith joined AmeriCorps and was assigned to work at a medical center in Atlanta, Georgia. She works as a counselor, educating patients about HIV and helping patients with limited means find housing, jobs, and the medical assistance they need. Amber uses her anthropology background when she talks to people about HIV. When she converses with patients in their teens or early 20s, her language is not too technical and may even include profanity. With all ages, she has learned that successful outreach requires getting to know patients as individuals. She asks open-ended questions, for example, about how they meet partners and what they themselves might do to prevent the spread of sexually transmitted diseases. Amber plans to attend graduate school to study public health.

style shifts Variations in speech in different contexts.

diglossia The existence of "high" (formal) and "low" (familial) dialects of a single language, such as German.

LINGUISTIC DIVERSITY WITHIN NATIONS

As an illustration of the linguistic variation encountered in all nations, consider the contemporary United States. Ethnic diversity is revealed by the fact that millions of Americans learn first languages other than English. Spanish is the most common. Most of those people eventually become bilinguals, adding English as a second language. In many multilingual (including colonized) nations, people use two languages on different occasions—one in the home, for example, and the other on the job or in public.

Whether bilingual or not, we all vary our speech in different contexts; we engage in **style shifts.** In certain parts of Europe, people regularly switch dialects. This phenomenon, known as **diglossia,** applies to "high" and "low" variants of the same language, for example, in German and Flemish (spoken in Belgium). People employ the high variant at universities and in writing, professions, and the mass media. They use the low variant for ordinary conversation with family members and friends. (See Tannen, Kendall, and Gordon [2007] and Tannen [2005] for analyses of communication among American families and friends.)

Just as social situations influence our speech, so do geographical, cultural, and socioeconomic differences. Many dialects coexist in the United States with Standard (American) English (SE). SE itself is a dialect that differs, say, from "BBC English," which is the preferred dialect in Great Britain. Different dialects are equally effective as systems of communication, which is language's main job. Our tendency to think of particular dialects as cruder or more sophisticated than others is a social rather than a linguistic judgment. We rank certain speech patterns as better or worse because we recognize that they are used by groups that we also rank. People who say *dese, dem,* and *dere* instead of *these, them,* and *there* communicate perfectly well with anyone who recognizes that the *d* sound systematically replaces the *th* sound in their speech. However, this form of speech has become an indicator of low social rank. We call it, like the use of *ain't,* "uneducated speech." The use of *dese, dem,* and *dere* is one of many phonological differences that Americans recognize and look down on.

GENDER SPEECH CONTRASTS

Comparing men and women, there are differences in phonology, grammar, and vocabulary, and in the body stances and movements that accompany speech (Eckert and McConnell-Ginet 2003; R. Lakoff 2004; McConnell-Ginet 2010; Tannen 1990). In phonology, American women tend to pronounce their vowels more

gradually, have produced large-scale linguistic change over the centuries are still at work today. Linguistic change occurs not in a vacuum but in society. When new ways of speaking are associated with social factors, they are imitated, and they spread (see Blommaert 2010). In this way, a language changes.

CULTURETHINK

The text identifies several factors that make the speech of men and women different, including pronunciation, types of words and expressions, and overall linguistic styles. Pay attention to the conversations around you: Do you notice these differences? What other differences do you notice? Do you agree with Tannen that men tend to value hierarchy, while women focus on building relationships?

peripherally ("rant," "rint" when saying "rent"), whereas men tend to pronounce theirs more centrally ("runt"). In public contexts, Japanese women tend to adopt an artificially high voice, for the sake of politeness, according to their traditional culture. Women tend to be more careful about uneducated speech. This trend shows up in both the United States and England. Men may adopt working-class speech because they associate it with masculinity. Perhaps women pay more attention to the media, in which standard dialects are employed.

According to Robin Lakoff (2004), the use of certain types of words and expressions has been associated with women's traditional lesser power in American society (see also Coates 1986; Romaine 1999; Tannen 1990, 1993). For example, "Oh dear," "Oh fudge," and "Goodness!" are less forceful than "Hell" and "Damn." Watch the lips of a disgruntled male athlete in a televised competition, such as a football game. What's the likelihood he's saying "Phooey on you"? Women also are more likely to use such adjectives as *adorable, charming, sweet, cute, lovely,* and *divine* than men are.

Differences in the linguistic strategies and behavior of men and women are examined in several books by the well-known sociolinguist Deborah Tannen (1990, 1993). Tannen uses the terms "rapport" and "report" to contrast women's and men's overall linguistic styles. Women, says Tannen, typically use language and the body movements that accompany it to build rapport—social connections with others. Men, on the other hand, tend to make reports, reciting information that serves to establish a place for themselves in a hierarchy, as they also attempt to determine the relative ranks of their conversation mates.

STRATIFICATION AND SYMBOLIC DOMINATION

We use and evaluate speech in the context of *extralinguistic* forces—social, political, and economic. Mainstream Americans evaluate the speech of low-status groups negatively, calling it "uneducated." This is not because these ways of speaking are bad in themselves but because they have come to symbolize low status. Consider variation in the pronunciation of *r.* In some parts of the United States, *r* is regularly pronounced, and in other (*r*less) areas, it is not. Originally, American *r*less speech was modeled on the fashionable speech of

Pronunciation of *r* in New York City Department Stores

Percentage *r* pronunciation

England. Because of its prestige, *r*lessness was adopted in many areas and continues as the norm around Boston and in the South.

New Yorkers sought prestige by dropping their *r*'s in the nineteenth century, after having pronounced them in the eighteenth. Contemporary New Yorkers are going back to the eighteenth-century pattern of pronouncing *r*'s. What matters, and what governs linguistic change, is not the reverberation of a strong midwestern *r* but social evaluation, whether *r*'s happen to be "in" or "out."

Studies of *r* pronunciation in New York City have clarified the mechanisms of phonological change. William Labov (1972b) focused on whether *r* was pronounced after vowels in such words as *car, floor, card,* and *fourth.* To get data on how this linguistic variation correlated with social class, he used a series of rapid encounters with employees in three New York City department stores, each of whose prices and locations attracted a different socioeconomic group. Saks Fifth Avenue (68 encounters) catered to the upper middle class, Macy's (125) attracted middle-class shoppers, and S. Klein's (71) had predominantly lower-middle-class and working-class customers. The class origins of store personnel reflected those of their customers.

Having already determined that a certain department was on the fourth floor, Labov approached ground-floor salespeople and asked where that department was. After the salesperson had answered, "Fourth floor," Labov repeated his "Where?" in order to get a second response. The second reply was more formal and emphatic, the salesperson presumably thinking that Labov hadn't heard or understood the first answer. For each salesperson, therefore, Labov had two samples of /r/ pronunciation in two words.

Labov calculated the percentages of workers who pronounced /r/ at least once during the interview. These were 62 percent at Saks, 51 percent at Macy's, but only 20 percent at S. Klein's. He also found that on upper floors, where he asked, "What floor is this?" (and where more expensive items were sold), personnel pronounced *r* more often than ground-floor salespeople did.

Yesterday was: Tuesday
Nag hmo yog:

Today is: Wednesday
Hnub no yog:

Tomorrow is: Thursday
Tagkis yog:

The weather is: Sunny
Huab cua yog:

In Labov's study, *r* pronunciation was clearly associated with prestige. Certainly the job interviewers who had hired the salespeople never counted *r*'s before offering employment. However, they did use speech evaluations to make judgments about how effective certain people would be in selling particular kinds of merchandise. In other words, they practiced sociolinguistic discrimination, using linguistic features in deciding who got certain jobs.

Americans have stereotypes about how people from certain regions talk, and some stereotypes are more widespread than others. Most Americans think they can imitate a "southern accent," and southern speech tends to be devalued outside the South. Americans also stereotype, without necessarily stigmatizing, speech in New York City (the pronunciation of coffee, for example), Boston ("I pahked the kah in Hahvahd Yahd"), and Canada ("oot" for "out").

It's sometimes asserted that midwestern Americans don't have accents. This belief stems from the fact that midwestern dialects don't have many stigmatized linguistic variants—speech patterns that people in other regions recognize and look down on, such as *r*lessness and *dem*, *dese*, and *dere* (instead of *them*, *these*, and *there*).

Far from having no accents, midwesterners, even in the same high school, exhibit linguistic diversity (see Eckert 1989, 2000). One of the best examples of variable midwestern speech, involving vowels, is pronunciation of the *e* sound (the /e/ phoneme), in such words as *ten*, *rent*, *section*, *lecture*, *effect*, *best*, and *test*. In southeastern Michigan, there are four different ways of pronouncing this *e* sound. Speakers of Black English (see the next section) and immigrants

Although never a native speaker of BEV, President Barack Obama, speaking here in 2012 at the University of North Carolina, exemplifies an upwardly mobile person with an effective mastery of SE.

from Appalachia often pronounce ten as "tin," just as Southerners habitually do. Some Michiganders say "ten," the correct pronunciation in Standard English. However, two other pronunciations also are common. Instead of "ten," many Michiganders say "tan," or "tun" (as though they were using the word ton, a unit of weight).

One day Kottak encountered a Michigan-raised graduate student instructor in the hall. She was deliriously happy. When he asked her why, she replied, "I've just had the best suction."

"What?" he questioned.

She finally spoke more precisely. "I've just had the best saction." She considered this a clearer pronunciation of the word "section."

In another example of such speech, a Michigan undergraduate lamented, after an exam, that she had not done her "bust on the tust" (i.e., best on the test). The truth is, regional patterns affect the way we all speak.

Our speech habits help determine our access to employment and other material resources. Because of this, "proper language" itself becomes a strategic resource—and a path to wealth, prestige, and power (Gal 1989; Thomas and Wareing, eds., 2004). Illustrating this, many ethnographers have described the importance of verbal skill and oratory in politics (Beeman 1986; Bloch 1975; Brenneis 1988; Geis 1987; G. Lakoff 2008). Ronald Reagan, known as a "great communicator," dominated American society in the 1980s as a two-term president. Another twice-elected president, Bill Clinton, despite his southern accent, was known for his verbal skills in certain contexts (e.g., televised debates and town-hall meetings). Communications flaws may have helped doom the presidencies of Gerald Ford, Jimmy Carter, and George Bush the elder. How would you rate the linguistic skills of the current leader of your nation?

The French anthropologist Pierre Bourdieu views linguistic practices as *symbolic capital* that properly trained people may convert into economic and social capital. The value of a dialect—its standing in a "linguistic market"—depends on the extent to which it provides access to desired positions in the labor market. In turn, this reflects its legitimation by formal institutions—educational institutions, state, church, and prestige media. Even people who don't use the prestige dialect accept its authority and correctness, its "symbolic domination" (Bourdieu 1982, 1984). Thus, linguistic forms, which lack power in themselves, take on the power of the groups they symbolize. The education system, however (defending its own worth), denies linguistic relativity. It misrepresents prestige speech as being inherently better. The linguistic insecurity often felt by lower-class and minority speakers is a result of this symbolic domination.

BLACK ENGLISH VERNACULAR (BEV)

The sociolinguist William Labov and several associates, both white and black, have conducted detailed studies of what they call **Black English Vernacular (BEV).** (*Vernacular* means ordinary, casual speech.) BEV is the "relatively uniform dialect spoken by the majority of black youth in most parts of the United States today, especially in the inner-city areas of New York, Boston, Detroit, Philadelphia, Washington, Cleveland, . . . and other urban centers. It is also spoken in most rural areas and used in the casual, intimate speech of many adults" (Labov 1972a, p. xiii). This does not imply that all, or even most, African Americans speak BEV.

BEV is a complex linguistic system with its own rules, which linguists have described. Consider some of the phonological and grammatical differences between BEV and SE. One phonological difference is that BEV speakers are less likely to pronounce *r* than SE speakers are. Actually, many SE speakers don't pronounce *r*'s that come right before a consonant (card) or at the end of a word (car). But SE speakers usually do pronounce an *r* that comes right before a vowel, either at the end of a word (four o'clock) or within a word (Carol). BEV speakers, by contrast, are much more likely to omit such intervocalic (between vowels) *r*'s. The result is that speakers of the two dialects have different *homonyms* (words that sound the same but have different meanings). BEV speakers who don't pronounce intervocalic *r*'s have the following homonyms: Carol/Cal; Paris/pass.

Observing different phonological rules, BEV speakers pronounce certain words differently than SE speakers do. Particularly in the elementary school context, the homonyms of BEV-speaking students typically differ from those of their SE-speaking teachers. To evaluate reading accuracy, teachers should determine whether students are recognizing the different meanings of such BEV homonyms as *passed, past,* and *pass.* Teachers need to make sure students understand what they are reading, which is probably more important than whether they are pronouncing words correctly according to the SE norm.

Phonological rules may lead BEV speakers to omit *-ed* as a past-tense marker and *-s* as a marker of plurality. However, other speech contexts demonstrate that BEV speakers do understand the difference between past and present verbs, and between singular and plural nouns. Confirming this are irregular verbs (e.g., *tell, told*) and irregular plurals (e.g., *child, children*), in which BEV works the same as SE.

SE is not superior to BEV as a linguistic system, but it does happen to be the prestige dialect—the one used in the mass media, in writing, and in most public and professional contexts. SE is the dialect that has the most "symbolic capital." In areas of Germany where there is diglossia, speakers of Plattdeusch (Low German) learn the High German dialect to communicate appropriately in the national context. Similarly, upwardly mobile BEV-speaking students learn SE.

> **Black English Vernacular (BEV)** A rule-governed dialect of American English (sometimes called ebonics) with roots in southern English. African-American youth and many adults speak BEV in their casual, intimate speech.

Got IT? Can you identify how speech differences are associated with social variation according to national region, ethnicity, gender, and class in the study of sociolinguistics?

Rap and hip-hop weave BEV into musical expression. Here we see DJ Khaled, Rick Ross, and Ace Hood performing at the 2011 BET Hip-Hop Awards in Los Angeles.

>> Historical Linguistics

Sociolinguists study contemporary variation in speech, which is language change in progress. **Historical linguistics** deals with longer-term change. Historical linguists can reconstruct many features of past languages by studying contemporary **daughter languages.** These are languages that descend from the same parent language and that have been changing separately for hundreds or even thousands of years. We call the original language from which they diverge the **protolanguage.** Romance languages such as French and Spanish, for example, are daughter languages of Latin, their common protolanguage. German, English, Dutch, and the Scandinavian languages are daughter languages of proto-Germanic. The Romance languages and the Germanic languages all belong to the Indo-European

historical linguistics Subdivision of linguistics that studies languages over time.

daughter languages Languages developing out of the same parent language; for example, French and Spanish are daughter languages of Latin.

protolanguage Language ancestral to several daughter languages.

language subgroups Languages within a taxonomy of related languages that are most closely related.

language family. Their common protolanguage is called Proto-Indo-European (PIE). Historical linguists classify languages according to their degree of relationship (see "PIE Family Tree" on this page).

Language changes over time. It evolves—varies, spreads, divides into **language subgroups** (those within a taxonomy of related languages that are most closely related). Dialects of a single parent language become distinct daughter languages, especially if they are isolated from one another. Some of them split, and new "granddaughter" languages develop. If people remain in the ancestral homeland, their speech patterns also change. The evolving speech in the ancestral homeland should be considered a daughter language like the others.

A close relationship between languages doesn't necessarily mean that their speakers are closely related biologically or culturally, because people can adopt new languages. In the equatorial forests of Africa, "pygmy" hunters have discarded their ancestral languages and now speak those of the cultivators who have migrated to the area. Immigrants to the United States spoke many different languages on arrival, but their descendants now speak fluent English.

Knowledge of linguistic relationships often is valuable to anthropologists interested in history, particularly events during the past 5,000 years. Cultural features may (or may not) correlate with the distribution of language families. Groups that speak related languages may (or may not) be more culturally similar to each other than they are to groups whose speech derives from different linguistic ancestors. Of course, cultural similarities aren't limited to speakers of related languages. Even groups whose members speak unrelated languages have contact through trade, intermarriage, and warfare. Ideas and inventions diffuse widely among human groups. Many items of vocabulary in contemporary English, particularly food items, such as "beef" and "pork," come from French. Even without written documentation of France's influence after the Norman Conquest of England in 1066, linguistic evidence in contemporary English would reveal a long period of important firsthand contact with France. Similarly, linguistic evidence may confirm cultural

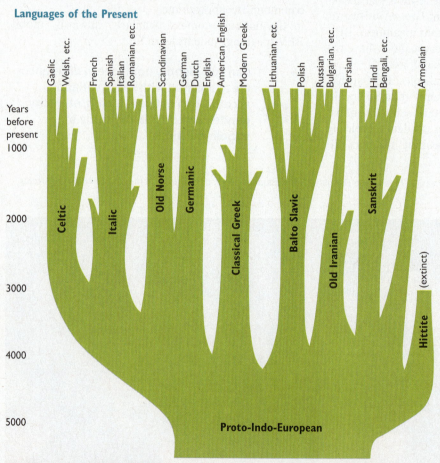

Languages of the Present

PIE Family Tree

Main languages and subgroups of the Indo-European language stock, showing approximate time to their divergence.

contact and borrowing when written history is lacking. By considering which words have been borrowed, we also can make inferences about the nature of the contact.

LANGUAGE LOSS

One aspect of linguistic history is language loss. When languages disappear, cultural diversity is reduced as well. According to linguist K. David Harrison, "When we lose a language, we lose centuries of thinking about time, seasons, sea creatures, reindeer, edible flowers, mathematics, landscapes, myths, music, the unknown and the everyday" (quoted in Maugh 2007). Harrison's book *When Languages Die* (2007) notes that an indigenous language goes extinct every two weeks, as its last speakers die. The world's linguistic diversity has been cut in half (measured by number of distinct languages) in the past 500 years, and half of the remaining languages are predicted to disappear during this century. Colonial languages (e.g., English, Spanish, Portuguese, French, Dutch, Russian) have expanded at the expense of indigenous ones. Of approximately 7,000 remaining languages, about 20 percent are endangered, compared with 18 percent of mammals, 8 percent of plants, and 5 percent of birds (Maugh 2007).

Harrison, who teaches at Swarthmore College in Pennsylvania, is director of research for the Living Tongues Institute for Endangered Languages (http://www.livingtongues.org), which works to maintain, preserve, and revitalize endangered languages through multimedia documentation projects. Researchers from the institute use digital audio and video equipment to record the last speakers of the most endangered languages. *National Geographic*'s Enduring Voices Project (http://www.nationalgeographic.com/mission/enduringvoices/) has as its mission the preservation of endangered languages by identifying the geographic areas with unique, poorly understood, or threatened languages and by documenting those languages and cultures.

get involved!

Sociolinguists have studied the ways that speech patterns differ between American men and American women. Save emails from your male and female friends and family members to see if there are comparable differences in electronic communication styles. Are there different ratios of what sociolinguist Deborah Tannen calls "rapport" (building social connections) and "report" (reciting information)? How about differences in kinds of words used, size and completeness of sentences, and typography? Does the use of emoticons vary, both in type (joking or serious, reassuring or negative) and in number? Keep a table of your findings: women's style on one side, men's on the other.

Did You Know?

Papua New Guinea, an island with just over six million people, once had at least 841 spoken languages. Many of those languages are endangered, and some have no living speakers.

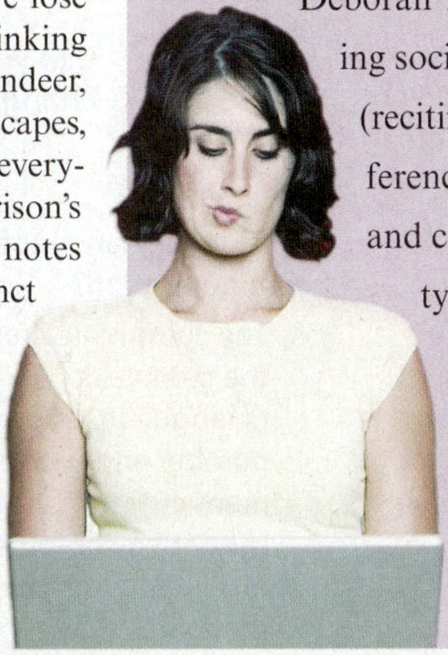

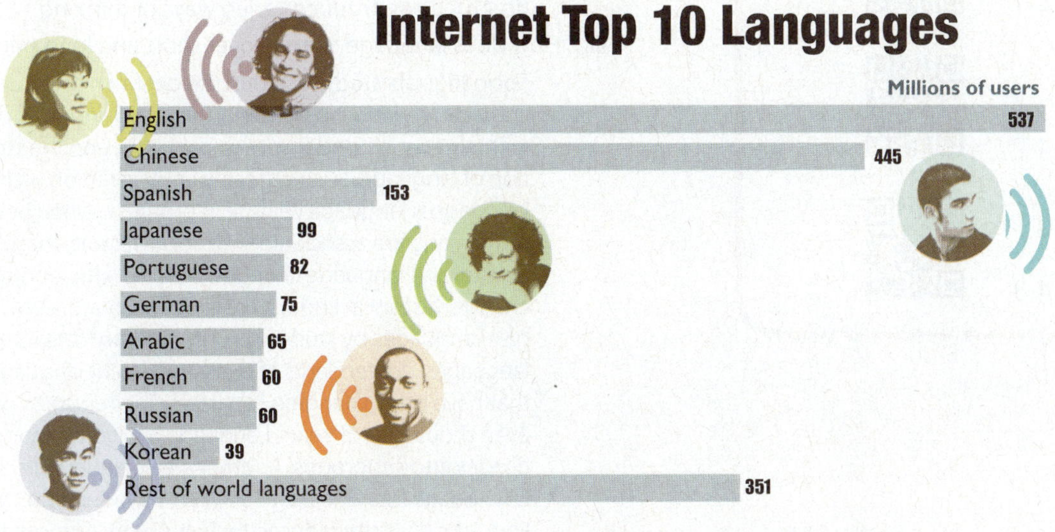

Internet Top 10 Languages
Millions of users
English 537
Chinese 445
Spanish 153
Japanese 99
Portuguese 82
German 75
Arabic 65
French 60
Russian 60
Korean 39
Rest of world languages 351

The website shows various language hot spots where the endangerment rate ranges from low to severe. In the United States, the rate is high in an area encompassing Oklahoma, Texas, and New Mexico, where 40 Native American languages are at risk. The top hot spot is northern Australia, where 153 Aboriginal languages are endangered (Maugh 2007). Other hot spots are in central South America, the Pacific Northwest of North America, and eastern Siberia. In all these areas, indigenous tongues have yielded, either voluntarily or through coercion, to a colonial language.

Despite language loss, linguistic diversity is alive and well in many countries, including India. Despite that nation's colonial history, only about a tenth of the Indian population speaks English. Even many of those English speakers prefer to read, and to seek Internet content, in their own regional languages. Local entrepreneurs and international companies such as Google, Yahoo, and Microsoft are rushing to meet the demand for Web content in local languages. This example illustrates one of the main lessons of applied anthropology, that external inputs fit in best when they are tailored properly to local settings.

Got IT? Can you explain ways in which languages change over time?

FOR REVIEW

I. **What makes language different from other forms of communication?**

- The communication systems used by other animals lack the complexity and adaptive advantages characteristic of language. Wild primates use calls—sounds limited in number and produced only when particular environmental stimuli are encountered. Calls are automatic and cannot be combined. Language, by contrast, is based on arbitrary, learned associations between words and the things they represent. The fundamental attributes of language are (1) cultural transmission through learning; (2) productivity—the ability to produce new expressions by combining other expressions; and (3) displacement—the ability to talk about things not present.

II. **How do anthropologists and linguists study language in general and specific languages in particular?**

- Anthropologists and linguists study a specific spoken language by describing its significant sounds and how they combine to form words and their meaningful parts. These scientists also compile a lexicon of the language's morphemes and their meanings, and they study syntax, the order and arrangement of words in phrases and sentences. Phonetics is the study of speech sounds in general. Some linguists seek universal linguistic structures and processes. Still others examine how different linguistic structures produce varied ways of thinking.

III. **How does language change over short and long periods?**

- Sociolinguists study relationships between social and linguistic variation in a society, including linguistic diversity within nations, gender speech contrasts, and the stratification of language. Such contemporary variation within a language is language change in progress. When new ways of speaking are associated with social factors, these ways spread, and language changes. Dealing with long-term change, historical linguists reconstruct features of past languages by studying contemporary daughter languages, descendants of the same parent language that have been changing separately for hundreds or even thousands of years. Language evolves, spreads, and divides into subgroups. Another area of language change is language loss. The past 500 years have seen the world's linguistic diversity reduced by half. Colonial languages have expanded at the expense of indigenous languages.

Pop Quiz

Multiple Choice:

1. Recent research on the origin of language suggests that
   a. The capacity to remember and combine linguistic symbols is latent in all mammals.
   b. A mutation in humans that occurred around 150,000 years ago may have conferred selective advantages (linguistic and cultural abilities) to those who had it.
   c. Fine tongue and lip movements that are necessary for clear speech are passed on through enculturation.
   d. The earliest forms of language slowed human adaptation because they were less effective for information storage and learning than were call systems.

2. The area of analysis of a spoken language that refers to all of a language's morphemes and their meanings is
   a. syntax
   b. semantics
   c. phonology
   d. lexicon

3. The Sapir-Whorf hypothesis states that
   a. the Hopi do not divide time into past, present, and future; the Hopi have no concept of time.
   b. different languages produce different ways of thinking.
   c. changes in culture produce changes in language and thought.
   d. all languages share the same grammatical categories.

4. Studies of the differences in the use of color terms between female and male Americans suggest that
   a. changes in culture produce changes in language and thought.
   b. changes in the American economy, society, and culture have no impact on the use of color terms.
   c. women and men are equally susceptible to the marketing tactics of the cosmetic industry.
   d. different languages produce different ways of thinking.

5. Which of the following statements about sociolinguistics is false?
   a. It investigates the relationships between social and linguistic variation.
   b. It has found that speakers retain their speech patterns even as the social context changes.
   c. It has found that men's and women's speech varies in all these ways: phonology, grammar, vocabulary, body stances, and movements accompanying speech.
   d. It considers the different social standings of a society's dialects, which include a prestige language that provides greater access to desirable jobs and is legitimized by the society's formal institutions.

6. Which of the following statements about Black English Vernacular (BEV) is true?
   a. BEV is a simple linguistic system with its own rules.
   b. All African Americans speak BEV.
   c. As a linguistic system, Standard English is superior to BEV.
   d. Upwardly mobile BEV-speaking students typically consider Standard English to be society's prestige dialect and learn it.

Fill in the Blank:

1. _____ refers to the ability to create new expressions by combining other expressions, while _____ is the ability to describe things and events that are not present.
2. Variation in speech in different contexts or situations is known as _____.
3. _____ refers to the existence of "high" and "low" dialects within a single language.
4. In a stratified society, even people who don't speak the prestige dialect tend to accept it as "standard" or superior. In Pierre Bourdieu's term, this is an instance of _____.

1. (b), 2. (d), 3. (b), 4. (a), 5. (b), 6. (d)

1. Productivity, displacement; 2. style shifting; 3. Diglossia; 4. symbolic domination

MAKING A LIVING

UNDERSTANDING OURSELVES

In the non-Western societies where ethnography originated, the need to balance work (making a living) and family wasn't as stark as it is for us. In traditional societies, one's workmates usually were also one's kin. There was no need for a "take your child to work" day because most women did that every day. People didn't work with strangers. Home and office, society and economy, were intertwined.

The fact that subsistence and sociality are both basic human needs creates conflicts in modern society. People have to make choices about allocating their time and energy between work and family. Think about the choices your parents have made in terms of economic versus social goals. Have their decisions maximized their incomes, their lifestyles, their individual happiness, family benefits, or what? What about you? What factors motivated you when you chose to apply to and attend college? Did you want to stay close to home, to attend college with friends, or to maintain a romantic attachment (all social reasons)? Did you seek the lowest tuition and college costs— or get a generous scholarship (economic decisions)? Did you choose prestige, or perhaps the likelihood that one day you would earn more money because of the reputation of your alma mater (maximizing prestige and future wealth)? Economists tend to assume that the profit motive rules in contemporary society. However, different individuals, like different cultures, may choose to pursue goals other than monetary gain.

Studies show that most American women now expect to join the paid labor force, just as men do. But the family remains attractive. Most young women and some men also plan to stay home with small children and return to work once their children enter school. How about you? If you have definite career plans, how do you imagine your work will fit in with your future family life—if you have one planned? What do your parents want most for you—a successful career or a happy family life, with children? Probably both. Will it be easy to fulfill such expectations?

>> Adaptive Strategies

In today's globalizing world, communities and societies are being incorporated, at an accelerating rate, into larger systems. The origin (around ten thousand years ago) and spread of food production (plant cultivation and animal domestication) led to the formation of larger and more powerful social and political systems. Food production led to major changes in human life. The pace of cultural transformation increased enormously. This chapter provides a framework for understanding a variety of human adaptive strategies and economic systems.

The anthropologist Yehudi Cohen (1974) used the term *adaptive strategy* to describe a society's system of economic production. Cohen argued that the most important reason for similarities between two (or more) unrelated societies is their possession of a similar adaptive strategy. In other words, similar economic causes have similar sociocultural effects. For example, there are clear similarities among societies that have a foraging (hunting and gathering) strategy. Cohen developed a typology of societies based on correlations between their economies and their social features. His typology includes these five adaptive strategies: foraging, horticulture, agriculture, pastoralism, and industrialism. Industrialism is discussed in the chapter "The World System and Colonialism." This chapter focuses on the first four adaptive strategies.

FORAGING

Until ten thousand years ago all humans were foragers (see Barnard 2004). However, environmental differences created substantial contrasts among the world's foragers. Some, like the people who lived in Europe during the ice ages, were big-game hunters. Today, hunters in the Arctic still focus on large animals and herd animals; they have much less vegetation and variety in their diets than do tropical foragers. Moving from colder to hotter areas, the number of species increases. The tropics contain tremendous biodiversity, and tropical foragers typically hunt and gather a wide range of plant and animal species. The same may be true in temperate areas. For

example, on the North Pacific Coast of North America, foragers could draw on varied sea, river, and land species, such as salmon and other fish, sea mammals, berries, and mountain goats. Despite differences caused by such environmental variation, all foraging economies have shared one essential feature: People rely on nature to make their living.

Animal domestication (initially of sheep and goats) and plant cultivation (of wheat and barley) began ten to twelve thousand years ago in the Middle East. Cultivation based on different crops, such as corn (maize), manioc (cassava), and potatoes, arose independently in the Americas. In both hemispheres most foragers eventually turned to food production. Today most foragers have at least some dependence on food production or on food producers (Kent 1992; 2002).

The foraging way of life survived into modern times in certain forests, deserts, islands, and very cold areas—places where food production was not practicable with simple technology (see Lee and Daly 1999). In many areas, foragers were exposed to the "idea" of food production but never adopted it because their own economies provided a perfectly adequate and nutritious diet—with

Drag net fishing at Benaulim beach, in the state of Goa, India. Fishing is a form of foraging.

Foraging has several characteristics:

- People rely on nature to make a living, with little management of natural resources.

- It requires less work than farming.

- Foraging traditionally correlates with the band social unit and with a mobile lifestyle.

- Modern foragers live on marginal lands (lands not good for agricultural production) and do not survive solely by foraging.

a lot less work. In some places, people reverted to foraging after trying food production and abandoning it. In most areas where hunter-gatherers did survive, foraging should be described as "recent" rather than "contemporary." *All modern foragers live in nation-states and depend to some extent on government assistance.* They are in contact with food-producing neighbors as well as with missionaries and other outsiders. We should not view contemporary foragers as isolated or pristine survivors of the Stone Age. Modern foragers are influenced by national and international policies and political and economic events in the world system.

Although foraging is disappearing rapidly as a way of life, we can trace the outlines of Africa's two broad belts of recent foraging. One is the Kalahari Desert of southern Africa. This is the home of the San ("Bushmen"), who include the Ju/'hoansi (see Kent 1996; Lee 2003). The other main African foraging area is the equatorial forest of central and eastern Africa, home of the Mbuti, Efe, and other "pygmies" (Bailey et al. 1989; Turnbull 1965).

People still do, or until recently did, subsistence foraging in certain remote forests in Madagascar, Southeast Asia, Malaysia, and the Philippines, and on certain islands off the Indian coast. Some of the best-known recent foragers are the aborigines of Australia. Those Native Australians lived on their island continent for more than sixty thousand years without developing food production.

The Western Hemisphere also had recent foragers. The Eskimos, or Inuit, of Alaska and Canada are well-known hunters. These (and other) northern foragers now use modern technology, including rifles and snowmobiles, in their subsistence activities (Pelto 1973). The native populations of California, Oregon, Washington, and British Columbia all were foragers, as were those of inland subarctic Canada and the Great Lakes. For many Native Americans, fishing, hunting, and gathering remain important subsistence (and sometimes commercial) activities.

Coastal foragers also lived near the southern tip of South America, in Patagonia. On the grassy plains of Argentina, southern Brazil, Uruguay, and Paraguay, there were other hunter-gatherers. The contemporary Aché of Paraguay usually are called hunter-gatherers, although they now get just a third of their livelihood from foraging. The Aché also grow crops, have domesticated animals, and live in or near mission posts, where they receive food from missionaries (Hawkes, O'Connell, and Hill 1982; Hill et al. 1987).

Throughout the world, foraging survived in environments that posed major obstacles to food production. (Some foragers took refuge in such areas after the rise of food production, the state, colonialism, or the modern world system.) The difficulties of cultivating at the North Pole are obvious. In southern Africa, the Dobe Ju/'hoansi San area studied by Richard Lee and others is surrounded by a waterless belt 43 to 124 miles (70 to 200 kilometers) in breadth (Solway and Lee 1990).

Environmental obstacles to food production aren't the only reason foragers survived. As shown in "Worldwide Distribution of Recent Hunter-Gatherers," their niches had one thing in common—their marginality. Their environments were not of immediate interest to farmers, herders, or colonialists. The foraging way of life persisted in a few areas that could be cultivated, even after contact with farmers. Those tenacious foragers, like the indigenous peoples of what is now California and the Pacific Northwest, did not adopt food production, because they were supporting themselves adequately by hunting and gathering. As the modern world system spreads, the number of foragers continues to decline.

Most of the estimated one hundred thousand San who survive today live in poverty on society's fringes. Each year more and more foragers come under the control of nation-states and are influenced by forces of globalization. As described by Motseta (2006), between 1997 and 2002, the government of Botswana in southern Africa relocated about three thousand Basarwa San Bushmen outside their ancestral territory, which was converted into a reserve for wildlife protection. The Basarwa received some compensation for their land, along with access to schools, medical facilities, and job training in resettlement centers. Critics claim this resettlement turned a society of free hunter-gatherers into communities dependent on food aid and government handouts (Motseta 2006).

In 2006 Botswana's High Court ruled that the Basarwa had been wrongly evicted from the "Central Kalahari Game Reserve." In the context of global political action for cultural rights, this verdict was hailed as a victory for indigenous peoples around the world (Motseta 2006). In December 2006, Botswana's attorney general recognized the court order to allow the Basarwa to return to their ancestral lands, while imposing conditions likely to prevent most of them from doing so. Only the 189 people who filed the lawsuit would have automatic right of return with their children, compared

Historically Known Foragers (Hunter-gatherers)

1 Eskimos or Inuit
2 Subarctic Indians
3 Northwest Coast Indians
4 Plateau Indians
5 California Indians
6 Great Basin Indians
7 Plains Indians
8 Amazon Basin Hunter-gatherers
9 Gran Chaco Indians
10 Tehuelche
11 Fuegians
12 "Pygmies"
13 Okiek
14 Hadza
15 San
16 Native Australians
17 Maori
18 Toala
19 Agta
20 Punan
21 Kubu
22 Semang
23 Andaman Islanders
24 Mlabri
25 Vedda
26 Kadar
27 Chenchu
28 Birhor
29 Ainu
30 Chukchi

Worldwide Distribution of Recent Hunter-Gatherers

Source: Adaptation from map by Ray Sim, in Göran Burenhult, ed. *Encyclopedia of Humankind: People of the Stone Age*, p. 193. © 1933. Reprinted by permission of Weldon Owen Pty. Ltd.

correlation An association between two or more variables such that when one changes (varies), the other(s) also change(s) (covaries); for example, temperature and sweating.

band Basic unit of social organization among foragers. A band includes fewer than 100 people; it often splits up seasonally.

with some 2,000 Basarwa wishing to return. The others would have to apply for special permits. Returning Basarwa would be allowed to build only temporary structures and to use enough water for subsistence needs. Water would be a major obstacle because the government shut the main well in 2002, and water is scarce in the Kalahari. Furthermore, anyone wishing to hunt would have to apply for a permit. So goes the foraging way of life in the world today.

Correlates of Foraging Typologies, such as Cohen's adaptive strategies, are useful because they suggest **correlations**—association or covariation between two or more variables. (Correlated variables are factors that are linked and interrelated, such as food intake and body weight, such that when one increases or decreases, the other changes too.) Ethnographic studies in hundreds of societies have revealed many correlations between the economy and social life. Associated (correlated) with each adaptive strategy is a bundle of particular sociocultural features. Correlations, however, rarely are perfect. Some foragers lack cultural features usually associated with foraging, and some of those features are found in groups with other adaptive strategies.

What, then, are some correlates of foraging? People who subsisted by hunting and gathering often, but not always (see the section "Potlatching" at the end of the chapter), lived in band-organized societies. Their basic social unit, the **band,** was a small group of fewer than a hundred people, all related by kinship or marriage. Among some foragers, band size stayed about the same year-round. In others, the band split up for part of the year. Families left to gather resources that were better exploited by just a few people. Later, they regrouped for cooperative work and ceremonies.

One typical characteristic of the foraging life was mobility. In many San groups, as among the Mbuti of Congo, people shifted band membership several times in a lifetime. One might be born, for example, in a band in which one's mother had kin. Later, one's family might move to a band in which the father had relatives. Because bands were exogamous (people married outside their own band), one's parents came from two different bands, and one's grandparents might have come from four. People could join any band to which they had kin or marital links. A couple could live in, or shift between, the husband's and the wife's band.

CULTURE THINK

The case of the Botswana Basarwa San is typical of global indigenous rights issues. Why do you think the government of Botswana removed the San from their ancestral territory? What were the costs and potential benefits for the San people of moving out? After they won the lawsuit, was moving back to the territory an attractive option for the San? Why or why not?

All human societies have some kind of division of labor based on gender. (See the chapter "Gender" for more on this.) Among foragers, men typically hunt and fish while women gather and collect, but the specific nature of the work varies among cultures. Sometimes women's work contributes most to the diet. Sometimes male hunting and fishing predominate. Among foragers in tropical and semitropical areas, gathering tends to contribute more to the diet than hunting and fishing do.

All foragers make social distinctions based on age. Old people often receive great respect as guardians of myths, legends, stories, and traditions. Younger people value the elders' special knowledge of ritual and practical matters. Most foraging societies are *egalitarian.* This means that contrasts in prestige are minor and are based on age and gender.

When considering issues of "human nature," we should remember that the egalitarian band was a basic form of human social life for most of our history. Food production has existed less than 1 percent of the time *Homo* has spent on Earth. However, it has produced huge social differences. We now consider the main economic features of food-producing strategies.

>> Adaptive Strategies Based on Food Production

In Cohen's typology, the three adaptive strategies based on food production in nonindustrial societies are horticulture, agriculture, and pastoralism. Just as they do in the United States and Canada, people in nonindustrial societies carry out a variety of economic activities. Each adaptive strategy refers to the main economic activity. Pastoralists (herders), for example, consume milk, butter, blood, and meat from their animals as mainstays of their diet. However, they also add grain to their diet by doing some cultivating or by trading with neighbors.

HORTICULTURE

Two types of cultivation found in nonindustrial societies are horticulture and agriculture. Both differ from the farming systems of industrial nations such as the United States and Canada, which use large land areas, machinery, and petrochemicals. According to Cohen, **horticulture** is cultivation that makes intensive use of *none* of the factors of production: land, labor, capital, and machinery. Horticulturalists use simple tools such as hoes and digging sticks to grow their crops. Their fields lie fallow for varying lengths of time. Horticulture often involves *slash-and-burn*

CULTURE THINK

In slash-and-burn horticulture, the land is cleared by cutting down (slashing) and burning trees and bush, using simple technology. What are the likely environmental effects of this kind of cultivation with low population numbers? What if the population increases?

techniques. Here, horticulturalists clear land by cutting down (slashing) and burning forest or bush or by setting fire to the grass covering the plot. The vegetation is broken down, pests are killed, and the ashes remain to fertilize the soil. Crops then are sown, tended, and harvested. Use of the plot is not continuous. Often it is cultivated only for a year or two.

When horticulturalists abandon a plot because of soil exhaustion or a thick weed cover, they clear another piece of land, and the original plot reverts to forest. After several years of fallowing, the cultivator returns to farm the original plot again. Because the relationship between people and land is not permanent, horticulture also is called *shifting cultivation.* Shifting cultivation does not mean that whole villages must

> **horticulture** Nonindustrial system of plant cultivation in which plots lie fallow for varying lengths of time.

move when plots are abandoned. Among the Kuikuru of the South American tropical forest, one village of 150 people remained in the same place for ninety years (Carneiro 1956). Kuikuru houses were large and well made. Because the work involved in building them was substantial, the Kuikuru preferred to walk farther to

Horticulture systems typically use simple technology. Here, a woman of the Toposa ethnic group uses a digging stick in a field in South Sudan.

Agriculture requires more labor than horticulture does and uses land intensively and continuously. Labor demands associated with agriculture reflect its use of domesticated animals, irrigation, and terracing. Shown here, rice farmers in Saramsa, Sikkim, India, work in flooded terraces.

their fields than to construct a new village. They shifted their plots rather than their settlements. On the other hand, horticulturalists in the montaña (Andean foothills) of Peru lived in small villages of about thirty people (Carneiro 1961/1968). Their houses were small and simple. After a few years in one place, these people built new villages near virgin land. Because their houses were so simple, they preferred rebuilding to walking even a half mile to their fields.

AGRICULTURE

The intensive and continuous use of land in **agriculture** requires more labor than horticulture does. The greater labor demands associated with agriculture reflect its use of domesticated animals, irrigation, or terracing.

Domesticated Animals Many agriculturists use animals as means of production—for transport, as cultivating machines, and for their manure. Asian farmers typically incorporate cattle and/or water buffalo into their agricultural economies. Those rice farmers may use cattle to trample pre-tilled flooded fields, thus mixing soil and water, before transplanting. Many agriculturists attach animals to plows and harrows for field preparation before planting or transplanting. Also, agriculturists typically collect manure from their animals, using it to fertilize their plots, thus increasing yields. Animals are attached to carts for transport and also to implements of cultivation.

agriculture Nonindustrial system of plant cultivation characterized by continuous and intensive use of land and labor.

Irrigation While horticulturalists must await the rainy season, agriculturists can schedule their planting in advance because they control water. Like other irrigation experts in the Philippines, the Ifugao water their fields with canals from rivers, streams, springs, and ponds. Irrigation makes it possible to cultivate a plot year after year. Irrigation enriches the soil because the irrigated field is a unique ecosystem with several species of plants and animals, many of them minute organisms, whose wastes fertilize the land.

An irrigated field is a capital investment that usually increases in value. It takes time for a field to start yielding; it reaches full productivity only after several years of cultivation. The Ifugao, like other irrigators, have farmed the same fields for generations. In some agricultural areas, including the Middle East, however, salts carried in the irrigation water can make fields unusable after fifty or sixty years.

Terracing The Ifugao also have mastered the agricultural technique of terracing. Their homeland has small valleys separated by steep hillsides. Because the population is dense, people need to farm the hills. If they simply planted on the steep hillsides, fertile soil and crops would be washed away during the rainy season. To prevent this, the Ifugao cut into the hillside and build stage after stage of terraced fields rising above the valley floor. Springs located above the terraces supply their irrigation water. The labor necessary to build and maintain a system of terraces is great. Terrace walls crumble each year and must be partially rebuilt. The canals that bring water down through the terraces also demand attention.

Costs and Benefits of Agriculture Agriculture requires human labor to build and maintain irrigation systems, terraces, and other works. People must feed, water, and care for their animals. But agricultural land can yield one or two crops annually for years, or even generations. An agricultural field does not necessarily produce a higher single-year yield than does a horticultural plot. The first crop grown by horticulturalists on long-idle land may be larger than that from an agricultural plot of the same size. Furthermore, because agriculturists work harder than horticulturalists do, agriculture's yield relative to the labor invested also is lower. Agriculture's main advantage is that the long-term yield per area is far greater and more dependable. Because a single field sustains its owners year after year, there is no need to maintain a reserve of uncultivated land as horticulturalists do. This is why agricultural societies tend to be more densely populated than horticultural ones.

AGRICULTURAL INTENSIFICATION: PEOPLE AND THE ENVIRONMENT

The range of environments available for food production has widened as people have increased their control over nature. For example, in arid areas of California, where Native Americans once foraged, modern irrigation technology now sustains rich

agricultural estates. Agriculturists live in many areas that are too arid for nonirrigators or too hilly for non-terracers. Increasing labor intensity and permanent land use have major demographic, social, political, and environmental consequences.

Thus, because of their permanent fields, agriculturists are sedentary. People live in larger and more permanent communities located closer to other settlements. Growth in population size and density increases contact between individuals and groups. There is more need to regulate interpersonal relations, including conflicts of interest. Economies that support more people usually require more coordination in the use of land, labor, and other resources (see the next chapter, "Political Systems").

Intensive agriculture has significant environmental effects. Irrigation ditches and paddies (fields with irrigated rice) become repositories for organic wastes, chemicals (such as salts), and disease microorganisms. Intensive agriculture typically spreads at the expense of trees and forests, which are cut down to be replaced by fields. Accompanying such deforestation is loss of environmental diversity (see Srivastava, Smith, and Forno 1999; Dove and Carpenter 2008). Agricultural economies grow increasingly specialized. They focus on one or a few caloric staples, such as rice, and on the animals that aid the agricultural economy. Because tropical horticulturalists typically cultivate dozens of plant species simultaneously, a horticultural plot mirrors the botanical diversity found in a tropical forest. Agricultural plots, by contrast, reduce ecological diversity by cutting down trees and concentrating on a few staple foods. Such crop specialization is true of agriculturists both in the tropics (e.g., Indonesian paddy farmers) and outside the tropics (e.g., Middle Eastern irrigation farmers).

Agriculturists attempt to reduce risk in production by favoring stability in the form of a reliable annual harvest and long-term production. Tropical foragers and horticulturalists, by contrast, attempt to reduce risk by relying on multiple species and benefiting from ecological diversity. The agricultural strategy is to put all one's eggs in one big and very dependable basket. The strategy of tropical foragers

and horticulturalists is to have several smaller baskets, a few of which may fail without endangering subsistence. The agricultural strategy makes sense when there are lots of children to raise and adults to be fed. Foraging and horticulture, of course, are associated with smaller, sparser, and more mobile populations.

Agricultural economies also pose a series of regulatory problems. How is water to be managed? How are disputes about access to and distribution of water to be resolved? With more people living closer together on more valuable land, agriculturists are more likely to come into conflict than are foragers and horticulturalists. The social and political implications of food production and intensification are examined more fully in the next chapter.

PASTORALISM

Herders, or **pastoralists,** are people whose activities focus on such domesticated animals as cattle, sheep, goats, camels, yak, and reindeer. They live in North and sub-Saharan Africa, the Middle East, Europe, and Asia. East African pastoralists, like many others, live in symbiosis with their herds. (*Symbiosis* is an obligatory interaction between groups—here, humans and animals—that is beneficial to each.) Herders attempt to protect their animals and to ensure their reproduction in return for food and other products, such as leather. Herds provide dairy products and meat.

People use livestock in various ways. Natives of North America's Great Plains, for example, didn't eat, but only rode, their horses. (Europeans reintroduced horses to the Western Hemisphere; the native American horse had become extinct thousands of years earlier.) For Plains Indians, horses served as "tools of the trade," means of production used to hunt buffalo, a main target of their economies. So the Plains Indians were not true pastoralists but hunters who used horses—as many agriculturists use animals—as means of production.

Pastoralists, by contrast, typically use their herds for food. They consume their meat, blood, and milk, from which they make yogurt, butter, and cheese. Although some pastoralists rely on their herds more completely than others do, it is impossible to base subsistence solely on animals. Most pastoralists therefore supplement their diet by hunting, gathering, fishing, cultivating, or trading.

In the sixteenth century, the Samis (also known as Lapps or Laplanders) of Norway, Sweden, and Finland domesticated the reindeer, which their ancestors used to hunt. Like other herders, they follow their animals in an annual trek, in this case from coast to interior. Nowadays, Samis use snowmobiles and four-wheel-drive vehicles to accompany their herds. Although their environment is harsher, the Samis, like other herders, live in nation-states and must deal with outsiders, including government officials, as they follow their herds and make their living through animal husbandry, trade, and sales (Hoge 2001; Paine 2009).

Unlike foraging and cultivation, which existed throughout the world before the Industrial Revolution, pastoralism was confined almost totally to the Old World. Before European conquest, the only pastoralists in the Americas lived in the Andean region of South America. They used their llamas and alpacas for food and wool and in agriculture and transport. Much more recently, Navajo of the southwestern United States developed a pastoral economy based on sheep, which were brought to North America by Europeans. The populous Navajo became the major pastoral population in the Western Hemisphere.

Two patterns of movement occur with pastoralism: *nomadism* and *transhumance.* Both are based on the fact that herds must move to use pasture available in particular places in different seasons. In pastoral **nomadism,** the entire group—women, men, and children—moves with the animals throughout the year. The Middle East and North Africa provide numerous examples of pastoral nomads. In Iran, for example, the Basseri and the Qashqai ethnic groups traditionally followed a nomadic route more than 300 miles (480 kilometers) long (see Salzman 2008).

CULTURETHINK

Pastoralists and agriculturalists live side by side in many parts of the world. The Fulani, for example, are nomadic herders who exchange dairy products for farm goods throughout West Africa. Many agree that pastoral nomadism could have emerged only after the rise of agriculture. Why would this be true?

With **transhumance,** part of the group moves with the herds, but most people stay in the home village. There are examples from Europe and Africa. In Europe's Alps only the shepherds and goatherds—not the whole village—accompany the flocks to highland

Yehudi Cohen's Adaptive Strategies (Economic Typology) Summarized

TABLE 5.1

Adaptive Strategy	Also Known As	Key Features/Varieties
Foraging	Hunting-gathering	Mobility, use of nature's resources
Horticulture	Slash-and-burn, shifting cultivation, dry farming	Fallow period
Agriculture	Intensive farming	Continuous use of land, intensive use of labor
Pastoralism	Herding	Nomadism and transhumance
Industrialism	Industrial production	Factory production, capitalism, socialist production

meadows in summer. Among the Turkana of Uganda, men and boys accompany the herds to distant pastures, while much of the village stays put and does some horticultural farming. During their annual trek, pastoral nomads trade for crops and other products with more sedentary people. Transhumants don't have to trade for crops. Because only part of the population accompanies the herds, transhumants can maintain year-round villages and grow their own crops. Table 5.1 summarizes Cohen's adaptive strategies discussed in this chapter.

Got IT? Can you compare and contrast distinguishing features of each major adaptive strategy identified by Cohen?

STUDY TIP

The four adaptive strategies discussed in this chapter are

- Foraging
- Horticulture
- Agriculture
- Pastoralism

>> Economic Systems

An **economy** is a system of production, distribution, and consumption of resources; *economics* is the study of such systems. Economists focus on modern nations and capitalist systems. Anthropologists have broadened understanding of economic principles by gathering data on nonindustrial economies. Economic anthropology studies economics from a comparative perspective (see Gudeman 1999; Plattner 1989; Sahlins 2004; Wilk and Cliggett 2007).

A **mode of production** is a way of organizing production—"a set of social relations through which labor is deployed to wrest energy from nature by means of tools, skills, organization, and knowledge" (Wolf 1982, p. 75). In the capitalist mode of production, money buys labor, creating a social gap in the production process between bosses and workers. By contrast, in nonindustrial societies, labor usually is not bought but is given as a social obligation. In such a *kin-based* mode of production, mutual aid in production is one among many expressions of a larger web of social relations (see Marshall 2011).

Societies representing each of the adaptive strategies just discussed (e.g., foraging) tend to have similar modes of production. Differences in the mode of

economy A population's system of production, distribution, and consumption of resources.

mode of production Way of organizing production—a set of social relations through which labor is deployed to wrest energy from nature by means of tools, skills, and knowledge.

Women hull rice in a Betsileo village. In the village of Ivato, farmers who traditionally grew only rice in their fields now use the same land for commercial crops, such as carrots, after the annual rice harvest.

production within a given strategy may reflect differences in environments, target resources, or cultural traditions (Kelly 1995). Thus a foraging mode of production may be based on individual hunters or teams, depending on whether the game is a solitary or a herd animal. Gathering usually is more individualistic than hunting, although teams of collectors may assemble when abundant resources ripen and must be harvested quickly. Fishing may be done alone (as in ice or spear fishing) or in crews (as with open-sea fishing and hunting of sea mammals).

DIVISION OF LABOR

Although some kind of division of economic labor related to age and gender is a cultural universal, the specific tasks assigned to each sex and to people of different ages vary (see the chapter "Gender"). Many horticultural societies assign a major productive role to women, but some make men's work primary. Similarly, among pastoralists, men generally tend large animals, but in some societies women do the milking. Jobs accomplished through teamwork in some cultivating societies are done in other societies by smaller groups or by individuals working over a longer period.

The Betsileo of Madagascar have two stages of teamwork in rice cultivation: transplanting and harvesting.

Both feature a traditional division of labor by age and gender that is well known and repeated across the generations. The first job in transplanting is the trampling of a flooded, previously tilled field by young men driving cattle in order to mix earth and water. They bring cattle to the fields just before transplanting. The young men yell at and beat the cattle, striving to drive them into a frenzy so they will trample the fields properly. Trampling breaks up clumps of earth and mixes irrigation water with soil to form a smooth mud. Once the tramplers leave the field, older men arrive. With their spades they break up the clumps the cattle missed. Meanwhile, the owner and other adults uproot rice seedlings and bring them to the field. Women plant the seedlings.

At harvest time, four or five months later, young men cut the rice off the stalks. Young women carry it to the clearing above the field. Older women arrange and stack it. The oldest men and women then stand on the stack, stomping and compacting it. Three days later, young men thresh the rice, beating the stalks against a rock to remove the grain. Older men then beat the stalks with sticks to make sure all the grains have fallen off.

MEANS OF PRODUCTION

In nonindustrial societies the relationship between the worker and the means of production is more intimate than it is in industrial nations. **Means, or factors, of production** include land, labor, and technology.

Land as a Means of Production Among foragers, ties between people and land were less permanent than among food producers. Although many bands had territories, the boundaries usually were not marked, and there was no way they could be enforced. The hunter's stake in an animal was more important than where the animal finally died. A person acquired the rights to use a band's territory by being born in the band or by joining it through a tie of kinship or marriage. In Botswana in southern Africa, Ju/'hoansi San women habitually used specific tracts of berry-bearing trees. When a woman changed bands, she immediately acquired a new gathering area.

Among food producers, rights to the means of production also come through kinship and marriage. Descent groups (groups whose members claim common ancestry) are common among nonindustrial food producers. Those who descend from the founder share the group's territory and resources. If the adaptive strategy is horticulture, the estate includes gardens and fallow land for shifting cultivation. As members of a descent group, pastoralists have access to animals to start their own herds, to grazing land, to garden land, and to other means of production.

Labor, Tools, and Specialization Like land, labor is a means of production. In nonindustrial societies, access to both land and labor comes through social links such as kinship, marriage, and descent. Mutual aid in production is merely one aspect of ongoing social relations that are expressed on many other occasions.

Nonindustrial societies contrast with industrial nations regarding another means of production—technology. Manufacturing often is linked to age and gender. Women may weave and men may make pottery, or vice versa. Most people of a particular age and gender share the technical knowledge associated with that age and gender. If married women customarily make baskets, most married women know how to make baskets. Neither technology nor technical knowledge is very specialized.

Some tribal societies, however, do promote specialization. Among the Yanomami of Venezuela and Brazil, for instance, certain villages manufacture clay pots and others make hammocks. They don't specialize, as one might suppose, because certain raw materials happen to be available near particular villages. Clay suitable for pots is widely available. Everyone knows how to make pots, but not everybody does so. Craft specialization reflects the social and political environment rather than the natural environment. Such specialization promotes trade, which is the first step in creating an alliance with enemy villages (Chagnon 1997).

ALIENATION IN INDUSTRIAL ECONOMIES

There are significant contrasts between nonindustrial economies and industrial ones. In the former, economic relations are just one part of a larger, multidimensional, social matrix. People don't just work for and with others; they live with those same people; they pray with, feast with, and care about them. One works for and with people with whom one has long-term personal and social bonds (e.g., kin or in-laws).

means (or factors) of production Land, labor, technology, and capital—major productive resources.

In industrial societies, by contrast, workers sell their labor to bosses who can fire them. Work and the workplace are separated—alienated—from one's social essence. Rather than expressing an ongoing, mutual social relationship, labor becomes a thing (commodity) to be paid for, bought, and sold—and from which the boss can generate an individual profit. Furthermore, industrial workers usually don't work with their relatives and neighbors. If coworkers are friends, the personal relationship often develops out of their common employment rather than being based on a previous social tie.

In nonindustrial societies, an individual who makes something can use or dispose of it as he or she sees fit. The maker may feel pride in such a personal product, and, if it is given away, a renewed commitment to the social relationship that is reinforced by the gift. On the other hand, when factory workers produce for their employer's profit, their products as well as their labor are alienated. Their bosses have use or disposal rights.

Human labor and its products belong to someone other than the individual producer. Unlike assembly-line workers, producers in nonindustrial societies typically see their work through from start to finish and feel a sense of accomplishment.

Thus, industrial workers have impersonal relations with their employers, coworkers, and products. People sell their labor for cash in a market economy, and work stands apart from family life. In nonindustrial societies, by contrast, the relations of production, distribution, and consumption are social relations with economic aspects. Economy is not a separate entity but is embedded in the society.

A Case of Industrial Alienation For decades, the government of Malaysia has promoted export-oriented industry, allowing transnational companies to install manufacturing operations in rural Malaysia. In search of cheaper labor, corporations headquartered in Japan, Western Europe, and the United States have moved labor-intensive factories to developing countries. Malaysia has hundreds of Japanese and American subsidiaries, which produce garments, foodstuffs, and electronics components. Thousands of young Malaysian women from peasant families now assemble microchips and microcomponents for transistors and capacitors. Aihwa Ong (1987) studied electronics assembly workers in an area where 85 percent of the workers were young unmarried females from nearby villages.

Ong found that, unlike village women, female factory workers had to cope with a rigid work routine and constant supervision by men. The discipline that factories value was being taught in local schools, where uniforms helped prepare girls for the factory dress code. Village women wear loose, flowing tunics, sarongs, and sandals, but factory workers had to don tight overalls and heavy rubber gloves, in which they felt constrained. Assembling electronics components requires precise, concentrated labor. Labor in these factories illustrates the separation of intellectual and manual activity—the alienation that Karl Marx considered the defining feature of industrial work. One woman said about her bosses, "They exhaust us very much, as if they do not think that we too are human beings" (Ong 1987, p. 202). Nor does factory work bring women a substantial financial reward, given low wages, job uncertainty, and family claims on wages. Although young women typically work just a few years, production quotas, three daily shifts, overtime, and surveillance take their toll in mental and physical exhaustion.

One response to factory relations of production has been spirit possession (factory women are possessed by spirits). Ong interprets this phenomenon as the women's unconscious protest against labor discipline and male control of the industrial setting. Sometimes possession takes the form of mass hysteria. Spirits have simultaneously invaded as many as 120 factory workers.

Female factory workers make toy lions in Qingdao City, Shandong province, East China. How might factory work create alienation?

Weretigers (the Malay equivalent of the werewolf) arrive to avenge the construction of a factory on aboriginal burial grounds. Disturbed earth and grave spirits swarm on the shop floor. First the women see the spirits; then their bodies are invaded. The weretigers send the women into sobbing, laughing, and shrieking fits. To deal with possession, factories employ local medicine men, who sacrifice chickens and goats to fend off the spirits. This solution works only some of the time; possession still goes on. Ong argues that spirit possession expresses anguish at, and resistance to, capitalist relations of production. By engaging in this form of rebellion, however, factory women avoid a direct confrontation with the source of their distress. Ong concludes that spirit possession, while expressing repressed resentment, doesn't do much to modify factory conditions. (Other tactics, such as unionization, would do more.) Spirit possession may even help maintain the current system by operating as a safety valve for accumulated tensions.

Got IT? Can you use the concepts of means and mode of production to compare and contrast economic systems in both industrial and nonindustrial societies?

>> Economizing and Maximization

Economic anthropologists have been concerned with two main questions:

- How are production, distribution, and consumption organized in different societies? This question focuses on *systems* of human behavior and their organization.

- What motivates people in different societies to produce, distribute or exchange, and consume? Here the focus is not on systems of behavior but on the *individuals* who participate in those systems.

Anthropologists view economic systems and motivations in a cross-cultural perspective. Motivation is a concern of psychologists, but it also has been a concern of economists and anthropologists. American economists assume that producers and distributors make decisions rationally, using the *profit motive,* as do consumers when they shop around for the best value. Although anthropologists know that the profit motive is not universal, the assumption that individuals try to maximize profits is basic to capitalism and to Western economic theory. In fact, the subject matter of economics often is defined as *economizing,* or the rational allocation of scarce means (or resources) to alternative ends (or uses).

What does that mean? Classical economic theory assumes that our wants are infinite, while our means are limited. People must make choices about how to use

CULTURE THINK

Think of examples of how you and your family set money aside for various purposes in subsistence, replacement, social, ceremonial, and rent funds.

their scarce resources—their time, labor, money, and capital. Western economists assume that when confronted with choices and decisions, people tend to make the one that maximizes profit. This is assumed to be the most rational choice.

The idea that individuals choose to maximize profits was a basic assumption of the classical economists of the nineteenth century and one

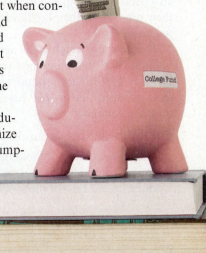

peasant Small-scale agriculturist living in a state, with rent fund obligations.

market principle Profit-oriented principle of exchange that dominates in states, particularly industrial states. Goods and services are bought and sold, and values are determined by supply and demand.

held by many contemporary economists. Certain economists now recognize that individuals may be motivated by many other goals. Depending on the society and the situation, people may try to maximize profit, wealth, prestige, pleasure, comfort, or social harmony. Individuals may want to realize their personal or family ambitions or those of another group to which they belong (see Sahlins 2004).

ALTERNATIVE ENDS

To what uses do people put their scarce resources? Throughout the world, people devote some of their time and energy to building up a *subsistence fund* (Wolf 1966). In other words, they have to work to eat, to replace the calories they use in daily activity. People also must invest in a *replacement fund.* They must maintain their technology and other items essential to production. If a hoe or plow breaks, they must repair or replace it. They also must obtain and replace items that are essential not to production but to everyday life, such as clothing and shelter.

People everywhere also have to invest in a *social fund.* They must help their friends, relatives, in-laws, and neighbors. It is useful to distinguish between a social fund and a *ceremonial fund.* The latter term refers to expenditures on ceremonies or rituals. To prepare a festival honoring one's ancestors, for example, requires time and the outlay of wealth.

Citizens of nonindustrial states also must allocate scarce resources to a *rent fund.* We think of rent as payment for the use of property. Rent fund, however, has a wider meaning. It refers to resources that people must render to an individual or agency that is superior politically or economically. Tenant farmers and sharecroppers, for example, either pay rent or give some of their produce to their landlords, as peasants did under feudalism.

Peasants are small-scale agriculturists who live in nonindustrial states and have rent fund obligations (see Kearney 1996). They produce to feed themselves, to sell their produce, and to pay rent. All peasants have two things in common:

- They live in state-organized societies;
- They produce food without the elaborate technology—chemical fertilizers, tractors, airplanes to spray crops, and so on—of modern farming or agribusiness.

Besides paying rent to landlords, peasants must satisfy government obligations, paying taxes in the form of money, produce, or labor. The rent fund is not simply an *additional* obligation for peasants. Often it becomes their foremost and unavoidable duty. Sometimes their own diets suffer as a result. The demands of social superiors may divert resources from subsistence, replacement, social, and ceremonial funds.

Motivations vary from society to society, and people often lack freedom of choice in allocating their resources. Because of obligations to pay rent, peasants may allocate their scarce means toward ends that are not their own but those of government officials. Thus, even in societies in which there is a profit motive, people often are prevented from rationally maximizing self-interest by factors beyond their control.

>> Distribution, Exchange

The economist Karl Polanyi (1968) stimulated the comparative study of exchange, and several anthropologists followed his lead. Polanyi defined three principles that guide exchanges: the market principle, redistribution, and reciprocity. These principles all can be present in the same society, but in that case they govern different kinds of transactions. In any society, one of them usually dominates. The principle of exchange that dominates in a given society is the one that allocates the means of production.

THE MARKET PRINCIPLE

In today's world capitalist economy, the **market principle** dominates. It governs the distribution of the means of production—land, labor, natural resources, technology, and capital. With market exchange, items are bought and sold, using money, with an eye to maximizing profit, and value is determined by the *law of supply and demand* (things cost more the scarcer they are and the

STUDY TIP

Three principles of exchange are

- The market principle
- Redistribution
- Reciprocity

more people want them). Bargaining is characteristic of market-principle exchanges. The buyer and seller strive to maximize—to get their "money's worth." Bargaining doesn't require that the buyer and seller meet. Consumers bargain whenever they shop around or use advertisements or the Internet in their decision making (see Madra 2004).

REDISTRIBUTION

The movement of goods, services, or their equivalent from the local level to a center is known as **redistribution.** The center may be a capital, a regional collection point, or a storehouse near a chief's residence. Products often move through a hierarchy of officials for storage at the center. Along the way, officials and their dependents may consume some of the products, but the exchange principle here is *re*distribution. The flow of goods eventually reverses direction—out from the center, down through the hierarchy, and back to the common people.

One example of a redistributive system comes from the Cherokee (the original owners of the Tennessee Valley), productive farmers who subsisted on maize, beans, and squash, supplemented by hunting and fishing. The Cherokee had chiefs, and each of their main villages had a central plaza, where meetings of the chief's council took place and where redistributive feasts were held. According to Cherokee custom, each family farm had an area where the family could set aside part of their annual harvest for the chief. This supply of corn was used to feed the needy, as well as travelers and warriors journeying through friendly territory. This store of food was available to all who needed it, with the understanding that it "belonged"

to the chief and was available through his generosity. The chief also hosted the redistributive feasts held in the main settlements (Harris 1978).

RECIPROCITY

The exchange between social equals, who normally are related by kinship, marriage, or another close personal tie, is known as **reciprocity.** Because it occurs between social equals, it is dominant in the more egalitarian societies—among foragers, cultivators, and pastoralists. There are three degrees of reciprocity: *generalized, balanced,* and *negative* (Sahlins 1968, 2004; Service 1966). These may be imagined as areas of a continuum defined by these questions:

- How closely related are the parties to the exchange?
- How quickly and unselfishly are gifts reciprocated?

Generalized reciprocity, the purest form of reciprocity, is characteristic of exchanges between closely related people. In *balanced reciprocity,* social distance increases, as does the need to reciprocate. In *negative reciprocity,* social distance is greatest and reciprocation is most calculated. This range, from generalized to negative, is called the **reciprocity continuum.**

With generalized reciprocity, someone gives to another person and expects nothing immediate in return. Such exchanges are not primarily economic transactions but expressions of personal relationships. Most parents don't keep accounts of every penny they spend on their children. They merely hope their children will respect their culture's customs involving obligations to parents.

Among foragers, generalized reciprocity usually has governed exchanges. People routinely have shared with other band members (Bird-David 1992; Kent 1992). So strong is the ethic of sharing that most foragers have lacked an expression for "thank you." To offer thanks would be impolite because it

redistribution Major exchange mode of chiefdoms, many archaic states, and some states with managed economies.

reciprocity One of the three principles of exchange. Governs exchange between social equals; major exchange mode in band and tribal societies.

reciprocity continuum Regarding exchanges, a range running from generalized reciprocity (closely related/deferred return) through balanced reciprocity, to negative reciprocity (strangers/immediate return).

Most food travels about 1,500 miles to get to grocery stores in the United States. Food transportation is responsible for the emission of almost 31,000 tons of greenhouse gases per year.

Did You Know?

This historic photo shows Tlingit clan members attending a potlatch at Sitka, Alaska, in 1904. Such ancestral headdresses have been repatriated recently from museums back to Tlingit clans. Have you ever partaken in anything like a potlatch?

North Pacific Coast is favorable, resources do fluctuate from year to year and place to place. Salmon and herring aren't equally abundant every year in a given locality. One village can have a good year while another is experiencing a bad one. Later their fortunes reverse. In this context, the potlatch cycle had adaptive value, and the potlatch was not a competitive display that brought no material benefit.

A village enjoying an especially good year had a surplus of subsistence items, which it could trade for more durable wealth items, such as blankets, canoes, or pieces of copper. Wealth, in turn, by being distributed, could be converted into prestige. Members of several villages were invited to any potlatch and took home the resources that were given away. In this way, potlatching linked villages together in a regional economy—an exchange system that distributed food and wealth from wealthy to needy communities. In return, the potlatch sponsors and their villages got prestige. The decision to potlatch was determined by

economist and social commentator Thorstein Veblen cited potlatching as an example of conspicuous consumption, claiming that potlatching was based on an economically irrational drive for prestige. This interpretation stressed the lavishness and supposed wastefulness, especially of the Kwakiutl displays, to support the contention that in some societies people strive to maximize prestige at the expense of their material well-being. This interpretation has been challenged.

Ecological anthropology, also known as *cultural ecology,* is a theoretical school that attempts to interpret cultural practices, such as the potlatch, in terms of their long-term role in helping humans adapt to their environments. Wayne Suttles (1960) and Andrew Vayda (1961/1968) saw potlatching not in terms of its immediate wastefulness, but in terms of its long-term role as a cultural adaptive mechanism. This view also helps us understand similar patterns of lavish feasting throughout the world. Here is the ecological interpretation: *Customs such as the potlatch are cultural adaptations to alternating periods of local abundance and shortage.*

How does this work? Although the natural environment of the

more people want them). Bargaining is characteristic of market-principle exchanges. The buyer and seller strive to maximize—to get their "money's worth." Bargaining doesn't require that the buyer and seller meet. Consumers bargain whenever they shop around or use advertisements or the Internet in their decision making (see Madra 2004).

REDISTRIBUTION

The movement of goods, services, or their equivalent from the local level to a center is known as **redistribution.** The center may be a capital, a regional collection point, or a storehouse near a chief's residence. Products often move through a hierarchy of officials for storage at the center. Along the way, officials and their dependents may consume some of the products, but the exchange principle here is *re*distribution. The flow of goods eventually reverses direction—out from the center, down through the hierarchy, and back to the common people.

One example of a redistributive system comes from the Cherokee (the original owners of the Tennessee Valley), productive farmers who subsisted on maize, beans, and squash, supplemented by hunting and fishing. The Cherokee had chiefs, and each of their main villages had a central plaza, where meetings of the chief's council took place and where redistributive feasts were held. According to Cherokee custom, each family farm had an area where the family could set aside part of their annual harvest for the chief. This supply of corn was used to feed the needy, as well as travelers and warriors journeying through friendly territory. This store of food was available to all who needed it, with the understanding that it "belonged"

to the chief and was available through his generosity. The chief also hosted the redistributive feasts held in the main settlements (Harris 1978).

RECIPROCITY

The exchange between social equals, who normally are related by kinship, marriage, or another close personal tie, is known as **reciprocity.** Because it occurs between social equals, it is dominant in the more egalitarian societies—among foragers, cultivators, and pastoralists. There are three degrees of reciprocity: *generalized, balanced,* and *negative* (Sahlins 1968, 2004; Service 1966). These may be imagined as areas of a continuum defined by these questions:

- How closely related are the parties to the exchange?
- How quickly and unselfishly are gifts reciprocated?

Generalized reciprocity, the purest form of reciprocity, is characteristic of exchanges between closely related people. In *balanced reciprocity,* social distance increases, as does the need to reciprocate. In *negative reciprocity,* social distance is greatest and reciprocation is most calculated. This range, from generalized to negative, is called the **reciprocity continuum.**

With generalized reciprocity, someone gives to another person and expects nothing immediate in return. Such exchanges are not primarily economic transactions but expressions of personal relationships. Most parents don't keep accounts of every penny they spend on their children. They merely hope their children will respect their culture's customs involving obligations to parents.

Among foragers, generalized reciprocity usually has governed exchanges. People routinely have shared with other band members (Bird-David 1992; Kent 1992). So strong is the ethic of sharing that most foragers have lacked an expression for "thank you." To offer thanks would be impolite because it

redistribution Major exchange mode of chiefdoms, many archaic states, and some states with managed economies.

reciprocity One of the three principles of exchange. Governs exchange between social equals; major exchange mode in band and tribal societies.

reciprocity continuum Regarding exchanges, a range running from generalized reciprocity (closely related/deferred return) through balanced reciprocity, to negative reciprocity (strangers/immediate return).

Did You Know?
Most food travels about 1,500 miles to get to grocery stores in the United States. Food transportation is responsible for the emission of almost 31,000 tons of greenhouse gases per year.

Sharing the fruits of production, a keystone of many nonindustrial societies, also has been a goal of socialist nations, such as China. These workers in Yunnan province strive for an equal distribution of meat.

live in a world of close personal relations, exchanges with outsiders are full of ambiguity and distrust. Exchange is one way of establishing friendly relations, but when trade begins, the relationship is still tentative. Often the initial exchange is close to being purely economic; people want to get something back immediately. Just as in market economies, but without using money, they try to get the best possible immediate return for their investment.

Generalized reciprocity and balanced reciprocity are based on trust and a social tie. Negative reciprocity involves the attempt to get something for as little as possible, even if it means being cagey or deceitful or cheating. Among the most extreme and "negative" examples of negative reciprocity was nineteenth-century horse thievery by North American Plains Indians. Men would sneak into camps and villages of neighboring tribes to steal horses. A similar pattern of livestock (cattle)

would imply that a particular act of sharing, which is the keystone of egalitarian society, was unusual. Among the Semai, foragers of central Malaysia (Dentan 1979), to express gratitude would suggest surprise at the hunter's success (Harris 1974).

Balanced reciprocity applies to exchanges between people who are more distantly related than are members of the same band or household. In a horticultural society, for example, a man presents a gift to someone in another village. The recipient may be a cousin, a trading partner, or a brother's fictive kinsman. The giver expects something in return. This may not come immediately, but the social relationship will be strained if there is no reciprocation.

Exchanges in nonindustrial societies also may illustrate negative reciprocity, mainly in dealing with people on the fringes of or outside their social systems. To people who

POP CULTURE

Supply and demand are key forces in our market economy. Advertising is a powerful industry based on the belief that its messages can stimulate demand for all sorts of products beyond our basic subsistence needs. Ads suggest choices about how we allocate our scarce means: "Choose our product," they say. Where better to stimulate demand than during televised events with huge mass audiences, such as the Super Bowl, the two NFL championship games, and the Oscars (Academy Awards)? Drawing the largest audience, the Super Bowl has become famous for its array of ads, many of them aimed at men. The Oscar telecast, by contrast, typically offers softer, more female- and family-oriented ads, because women constitute 70 percent of its audience (Dicker 2012). Viewers of the 2012 Oscar telecast, for example, could see Ellen de Generes promoting JC Penney, along with ads for McDonald's and Coca Cola. Hyundai's Oscar commercial used a softer tone to hawk its Azera luxury car, compared with the combat-themed ads it used during the Super Bowl that same year. Advertising is more successful when it uses knowledge of sociocultural diversity, such as gender differences, to target its spots at particular groups or audience segments. Compared with an NFL game, how many Viagra or Cialis ads do you see on *The View*?

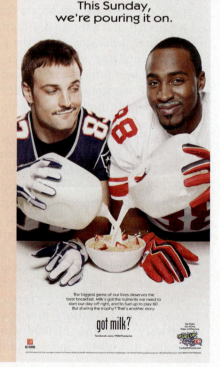

Location of Potlatching Groups

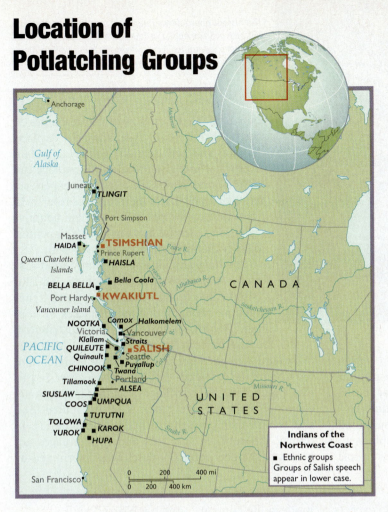

Indians of the Northwest Coast
■ Ethnic groups
Groups of Salish speech
appear in lower case.

production to the sale of consumer goods. We also have redistribution. Some of our tax money goes to support the government, but some of it also comes back to us in the form of social services, education, health care, and road building. We also have reciprocal exchanges. Generalized reciprocity characterizes the relationship between parents and children. However, even here the dominant market mentality surfaces in comments about the high cost of raising children and in the stereotypical statement of the disappointed parent: "We gave you everything money could buy."

Exchanges of gifts, cards, and invitations exemplify reciprocity, usually balanced. Everyone has heard remarks like "They invited us to their daughter's wedding, so when ours gets married, we'll have to invite them" and "They've been here for dinner three times and haven't invited us yet. I don't think we should ask them back until they do." Such precise balancing of reciprocity would be out of place in a foraging band, where resources are communal (common to all) and daily sharing based on generalized reciprocity is an essential ingredient of social life and survival.

POTLATCHING

One of the most famous cultural practices studied by ethnographers is the **potlatch.** This is a festive event within a regional exchange system among tribes of the North Pacific Coast of North America, including the Salish and Kwakiutl of Washington and British Columbia. Some tribes still practice the potlatch, sometimes as a memorial to the dead (Kan 1986, 1989). At each such event, assisted by members of their communities, potlatch sponsors traditionally gave away food, blankets, pieces of copper, or other items. In return for this, they got prestige. To give a potlatch enhanced one's reputation. Prestige increased with the lavishness of the potlatch—the value of the goods given away in it.

The potlatching tribes were foragers, but atypical ones for relatively recent times. They were sedentary and had chiefs. They had access to a wide variety of land and sea resources. Among their most important foods were salmon, herring, candlefish, berries, mountain goats, seals, and porpoises (Piddocke 1969).

According to classical economic theory, the profit motive is universal, with the goal of maximizing material benefits. How then does one explain the potlatch, in which substantial wealth is given away? In his influential book *Theory of the Leisure Class* (1899/1992),

> **potlatch** Competitive feast among Indians on the North Pacific Coast of North America.

raiding continues today in East Africa, among tribes such as the Kuria (Fleisher 2000). In these cases, the party that starts the raiding can expect reciprocity—a raid on their own village—or worse. The Kuria hunt down cattle thieves and kill them. It's still reciprocity, governed by "Do unto others as they have done unto you."

One way of reducing the tension in situations of potential negative reciprocity is to engage in "silent trade." One example was the silent trade of the Mbuti pygmy foragers of the African equatorial forest and their neighboring horticultural villagers. There was no personal contact during their exchanges. A Mbuti hunter left game, honey, or another forest product at a customary site. Villagers collected it and left crops in exchange. Often the parties bargained silently. If one felt the return was insufficient, he or she simply left it at the trading site. If the other party wanted to continue trade, it was increased.

COEXISTENCE OF EXCHANGE PRINCIPLES

In today's North America, the market principle governs most exchanges, from the sale of the means of

North Pacific Coast is favorable, resources do fluctuate from year to year and place to place. Salmon and herring aren't equally abundant every year in a given locality. One village can have a good year while another is experiencing a bad one. Later their fortunes reverse. In this context, the potlatch cycle had adaptive value, and the potlatch was not a competitive display that brought no material benefit.

A village enjoying an especially good year had a surplus of subsistence items, which it could trade for more durable wealth items, such as blankets, canoes, or pieces of copper. Wealth, in turn, by being distributed, could be converted into prestige. Members of several villages were invited to any potlatch and took home the resources that were given away. In this way, potlatching linked villages together in a regional economy—an exchange system that distributed food and wealth from wealthy to needy communities. In return, the potlatch sponsors and their villages got prestige. The decision to potlatch was determined by

economist and social commentator Thorstein Veblen cited potlatching as an example of conspicuous consumption, claiming that potlatching was based on an economically irrational drive for prestige. This interpretation stressed the lavishness and supposed wastefulness, especially of the Kwakiutl displays, to support the contention that in some societies people strive to maximize prestige at the expense of their material well-being. This interpretation has been challenged.

Ecological anthropology, also known as *cultural ecology,* is a theoretical school that attempts to interpret cultural practices, such as the potlatch, in terms of their long-term role in helping humans adapt to their environments. Wayne Suttles (1960) and Andrew Vayda (1961/1968) saw potlatching not in terms of its immediate wastefulness, but in terms of its long-term role as a cultural adaptive mechanism. This view also helps us understand similar patterns of lavish feasting throughout the world. Here is the ecological interpretation: *Customs such as the potlatch are cultural adaptations to alternating periods of local abundance and shortage.*

How does this work? Although the natural environment of the

How do aspects of modern life compare to tribal North Pacific Coast potlatching? Observe and talk with people about lifestyles and consumption behavior, paying particular attention to conspicuous consumption. What roles might huge mansions, lavish parties, and private jets, for example, play? Why do people spend so much on wedding celebrations, home theatres, and showy vehicles? Can you think of ways in which such expenditures might help connect people (within or between families, social clubs, or large political or economic networks)? Stoke the larger economy? Help distribute wealth to the needy? Do any of the practices you see suggest that Americans may favor competition and social prestige at the expense of society's overall social and environmental well-being?

get involved!

Got IT!

Can you compare and contrast the three systems of exchange: the market principle, redistribution, and reciprocity, assessing what motivates people to produce, exchange, and consume in different societies?

the health of the local economy. If there had been subsistence surpluses, and thus a buildup of wealth over several good years, a village could afford a potlatch to convert its surplus food and wealth into prestige.

The long-term adaptive value of intercommunity feasting becomes clear when a formerly prosperous village had a run of bad luck. Its people started accepting invitations to potlatches in villages that were doing better. The tables were turned as the temporarily rich became temporarily poor and vice versa. The newly needy accepted food and wealth items. They were willing to receive rather than bestow gifts and thus to relinquish some of their stored-up prestige. They hoped their luck would eventually improve so that resources could be recouped and prestige regained.

The potlatch linked local groups along the North Pacific Coast into a regional alliance and exchange network. Potlatching and intervillage exchange had adaptive functions, regardless of the motivations of the individual participants. The anthropologists who stressed rivalry for prestige were not wrong. They were merely emphasizing *motivations* at the expense of an analysis of economic and ecological *systems*.

The use of feasts to enhance individual and community reputations and to redistribute wealth is not peculiar to populations of the North Pacific Coast. Competitive feasting is widely characteristic of nonindustrial food producers. But among most surviving foragers, who live in marginal areas, resources are too meager to support feasting on such a level. In such societies, sharing rather than competition prevails.

FOR REVIEW

EXPERIENCING CULTURE

TO ACCESS THESE VIDEOS
ON YOUR COMPUTER, VISIT

www.mhhe.com/gezonqr

5-1

5-2

I. What are the major adaptive strategies found in nonindustrial societies?

- Foraging, or hunting and gathering, was the only human adaptive strategy until the advent of food production. Modern foragers depend in part on food production or food producers. Horticulture is cultivation that does not make intensive use of land, labor, capital, or machinery. After cultivating a plot for one or two years, horticulturalists abandon it, seek other land to cultivate, then return to the original plot after a fallow period. Agriculture is cultivation characterized by continuous, intensive use of land and labor. Agriculturalists may use irrigation, terracing, or domesticated animals for production. Pastoralism is the herding of domesticated animals used for food and other products. In pastoral nomadism, the entire group moves with the animals to pasturage throughout the year, often trading for crops with sedentary people. With transhumance, part of the group moves with the herds; the other part stays in the village and grows crops.

II. What is an economy, and what is economizing behavior?

- An economy is a system of production, distribution, and consumption of resources. Western economists assume that when confronted with choices, people tend to make the one that maximizes profit. These theorists focus on economizing, the rational allocation of scarce resources to alternative uses. However, in nonindustrial societies, indeed even in our own society, people often maximize alternative values, such as pleasure or social harmony. Even in societies where there is a profit motive, factors beyond their control may prevent people from rationally maximizing self-interest.

III. What principles regulate the exchange of goods and services in various societies?

- The market principle dominates in the world capitalist economy. It involves buying and selling items, using money, with the goal of maximizing profit; the law of supply and demand determines value. The redistribution principle operates when goods or services move from the local level to a center. The flow of goods eventually moves out of the center and back to the people. In reciprocity, exchange occurs between social equals related by kinship, marriage, or other close ties. With generalized reciprocity, someone gives to another person and expects nothing immediate in return. As social distance increases, reciprocity becomes balanced and, finally, negative. The potlatch was a North Pacific Coast tribal feast in which sponsors gave away goods in return for prestige. The exchange served to distribute wealth from wealthy to needy communities.

Pop Quiz

Multiple Choice:

1. Which of the following statements about foraging is false?
   a. All modern foragers have contacts with nonforaging societies.
   b. Some foragers have incorporated modern technology, such as rifles and snowmobiles, into their subsistence activities.
   c. All modern foragers live in nation-states and are influenced by national and international policies and by events in the world system.
   d. Foraging societies have all changed in similar ways because they have faced similar circumstances that encourage their adoption of food production.

2. Which of the following is associated with horticulture?
   a. Intensive use of land and human labor
   b. Use of irrigation and terracing
   c. Use of draft animals
   d. Periodic cycles of cultivation and fallowing

3. The key factor that distinguishes agriculturists from horticulturalists is that agriculturalists
   a. can produce one or two crops annually but only for a very few years.
   b. clear a tract of land they wish to use by cutting down trees and setting fire to the forest or bush.
   c. use land intensively and continuously.
   d. generally have much more leisure time at their disposal than do horticulturalists.

4. Which of the following is *not* a consequence of agriculture?
   a. Agriculture promotes nomadism to allow farmers to take full advantage of their land.
   b. Agriculture often spreads at the expense of trees and forests, which are cut down to make room for fields, thus reducing ecological diversity.
   c. By favoring dependability and size of the long-term yield, agricultural societies tend to be more densely populated than horticultural societies.
   d. Agriculture poses regulatory problems, such as resolving disputes about access to water and coordinating the use of land, labor, and other resources.

5. Most generally, economic alienation in industrial societies comes about as a result of
   a. separation of workers from the products they make.
   b. loss of land.
   c. negative reciprocity.
   d. discontent due to low pay.

6. Which of these statements about generalized reciprocity is true?
   a. It involves the immediate return of the object exchanged.
   b. It usually develops after the evolution of redistribution but before the market principle.
   c. It is the characteristic form of exchange in egalitarian societies.
   d. It disappears with the origin of the state.

Fill in the Blank:

1. In nonindustrial societies, a _____ mode of production prevails.

2. Economists tend to assume that producers and distributors make decisions rationally by using the _____ motive. Anthropologists, however, know that this motive is not universal.

3. When a farmer gives 20 percent of his crop to a landlord, he is contributing to a _____ fund.

4. The _____ is a festive event within a regional exchange system among tribes of the North Pacific Coast of North America. _____ anthropologists interpret this event as a cultural adaptation to alternating periods of local abundance and shortage, rejecting the belief that it illustrates economically wasteful and irrational behavior.

1. (d), 2. (d), 3. (c), 4. (a), 5. (a), 6. (c)
1. kin-based; 2. profit; 3. rent; 4. potlatch, Ecological

6

POLITICAL SYSTEMS

UNDERSTANDING OURSELVES

A "big man on campus" is a collegian who is very well known and/or popular. Useful in becoming a BMOC (see http://www.ehow.com/how_2112834_be-big-man-campus.html) are lots of friends, a cool car, a hip wardrobe, a nice smile, a sports connection, and a sense of humor. "Big man" has a related meaning in anthropology. Many indigenous cultures had a political figure that anthropologists call the "big man." Such a leader achieved his status through hard work, amassing wealth in the form of pigs and other native riches. The personality characteristics that enabled the big man to attract loyal supporters (aka lots of friends) included wealth, generosity, eloquence, physical fitness, bravery, and supernatural powers.

Do any of these factors contribute to political success today? Although contemporary politicians may use their own wealth to finance their campaigns, they also solicit labor and money (rather than pigs) from supporters. And, like big men, successful American politicians try to be generous with their supporters. Payback may take the form of largesse (e.g., earmarks) to a particular area. Tribal big men amass wealth and then give away pigs. Successful American politicians dish out "pork."

As with the big man, eloquence and communication skills contribute to political success (e.g., Barack Obama, Bill Clinton, and Ronald Reagan), although lack of such skills isn't necessarily fatal (e.g., either President Bush). What about physical fitness? Hair, height, health (and even a nice smile) are certainly political advantages. Bravery, as demonstrated through military service, can help political careers, but it certainly isn't required. Nor does it guarantee success. Just ask John McCain or John Kerry. Supernatural powers? Candidates who proclaim themselves atheists are as rare as self-identified witches (or non-witches).

Contemporary politics isn't just about personality, however, as it is in big man systems. We live in a state-organized, stratified society with inherited wealth, power, and privilege, all of which have political implications. As is typical of states, inheritance and kin connections play a role in political success. Just think of Kennedys, Bushes, and Clintons.

>> What Is "The Political"?

Anthropologists share an interest in political systems and organization with political scientists. Here again, however, the anthropological approach is global and comparative and includes nonstates, while political scientists tend to focus on contemporary and recent nation-states. Anthropological studies have revealed substantial variation in power, authority, and legal systems in different societies. (*Power* is the ability to exercise one's will over others; *authority* is the socially approved use of power.) (See Gledhill 2000; Kurtz 2001; Lewellen 2003; Nugent and Vincent 2004; Wolf with Silverman 2001.)

Morton Fried offered the following definition of political organization:

> Political organization comprises those portions of social organization that specifically relate to the individuals or groups that manage the affairs of public policy or seek to control the appointment or activities of those individuals or groups. (Fried 1967, pp. 20–21)

This definition certainly fits contemporary North America. Under "individuals or groups that manage the affairs of public policy" come various agencies and levels of government. Those who seek to influence public policy include political parties, unions, corporations, consumers, activists, action committees, religious groups, and nongovernmental organizations (NGOs).

Fried's definition is much less applicable to nonstates, where it's often difficult to detect any "public policy." For this reason, we prefer to speak of *sociopolitical organization* in discussing the exercise of power and the regulation of relations among groups and their representatives. Political regulation includes such processes as decision making, dispute management, and conflict resolution. The study of political regulation draws our attention to those who make decisions and resolve conflicts—whether or not there are formal leaders.

Through public action, citizens influence government policy. Here, citizens in Madrid, Spain, proclaim "no bread, no peace" as they protest austerity measures announced by the Spanish government in July, 2012.

>> Types and Trends

Ethnographic and archaeological studies in hundreds of places have revealed many correlations between economy and social and political organization. Decades ago, the anthropologist Elman Service (1962) listed four types, or levels, of political organization: band, tribe, chiefdom, and state. Today, none of the first three types can be studied as a self-contained form of political organization, since all exist within the context of nation-states and are subject to state control (see Ferguson 2002). There is archaeological evidence for early bands, tribes, and chiefdoms that existed before the first states appeared. However, because anthropology came into being long after the origin of the state, anthropologists never have been able to observe "in the flesh" a band, tribe, or chiefdom outside the influence of some state. There still may be local political leaders (e.g., village heads) and regional figures (e.g., chiefs) of the sort discussed in this chapter, but all now exist and function within the context of state organization.

A *band* is a small *kin-based* group (all its members are related by kinship or marriage) found among foragers. **Tribes** have economies based on nonintensive food production (horticulture and pastoralism). Living in villages and organized into kin groups based on common descent (clans and lineages—see the next chapter), tribes have no formal government and no reliable means of enforcing political decisions. **Chiefdom** refers to a form of sociopolitical organization intermediate between the tribe and the state. In chiefdoms, social relations were based mainly on kinship, marriage, descent, age, generation, and gender—just as in bands and tribes. However, although chiefdoms were kin-based, they featured differential access to resources (some people had more wealth, prestige, and power than others did) and a permanent political structure. The **state** is a form of sociopolitical organization based on a formal government structure and socioeconomic stratification.

The four labels in Service's typology are much too simple to account for the full range of political diversity and complexity known to archaeology and ethnography. We'll see, for instance, that tribes have varied widely in their political systems and institutions. Nevertheless, Service's typology does highlight some significant contrasts in political organization, especially those between states and nonstates. For example, in bands and tribes—unlike states, which have clearly visible governments—political organization did not stand out as separate and distinct from the total social order. In bands and tribes, it was difficult to characterize an act or event as political rather than merely social.

Service's labels "band," "tribe," "chiefdom," and "state" are categories or types within a **sociopolitical typology.** These types are correlated with the adaptive strategies (economic typology) discussed in the previous chapter. Thus, foragers (an economic type) tended to have band organization (a sociopolitical type). Similarly, many horticulturalists and pastoralists lived in tribes. Although most chiefdoms had farming economies, herding was important in some Middle Eastern chiefdoms. Nonindustrial states usually had an agricultural base.

With food production came larger, denser populations and more complex economies than was the case among foragers. These features posed new regulatory problems, which gave rise to more complex relations and linkages. Many sociopolitical trends reflect

tribe Form of sociopolitical organization usually based on horticulture or pastoralism. Socioeconomic stratification and centralized rule are absent in tribes, and there is no means of enforcing political decisions.

chiefdom Form of sociopolitical organization intermediate between the tribe and the state; kin-based with differential access to resources and a permanent political structure.

state (nation-state) Complex sociopolitical system that administers a territory and populace with substantial contrasts in occupation, wealth, prestige, and power. An independent, centrally organized political unit, a government.

sociopolitical typology Classification scheme based on the scale and complexity of social organization and the effectiveness of political regulation; includes band, tribe, chiefdom, and state.

CULTURETHINK

Why do you think food production, as opposed to foraging, leads to increasing demands for maintaining order and ultimately to more complex political systems?

the increased regulatory demands associated with food production. Archaeologists have studied these trends through time, and cultural anthropologists have observed them among more contemporary groups.

> **Got IT?** Can you identify Service's sociopolitical types, comparing and contrasting their social groups, means of conflict resolution, and forms of political leadership?

>> Bands and Tribes

This chapter examines a series of societies with different political systems. We address a common set of questions for each one: What kinds of social groups does the society have? How do the groups represent themselves to each other? How are their internal and external relations regulated? To answer these questions, we begin with bands and tribes and then consider chiefdoms and states.

FORAGING BANDS

Modern hunter-gatherers are today's remnants of foraging band societies. The strong ties they maintain with sociopolitical groups outside the band make them markedly different from Stone Age hunter-gatherers. Modern foragers live in nation-states and an interlinked world. The pygmies of Congo, for example, have for generations shared a social world and economic exchanges with their neighbors who are cultivators. All foragers now trade with food producers. In addition, most contemporary hunter-gatherers rely on governments and on missionaries for at least part of what they consume.

The San In the previous chapter, we saw how the Basarwa San have been affected by the policies of the government of Botswana, which relocated them after converting their ancestral lands into a wildlife reserve (Motseta 2006). More generally, San speakers ("Bushmen") of southern Africa have been influenced by Bantu speakers (farmers and herders) for two thousand years and by Europeans for centuries. Edwin Wilmsen (1989) argues that many San descend from herders who were pushed into the desert by poverty or oppression. He sees the San today as a rural underclass in a larger political and economic system dominated by Europeans and Bantu food producers. Within this system, many San now tend cattle for wealthier Bantu rather than foraging independently. San also have their own domesticated animals, further illustrating their movement away from a foraging lifestyle.

Susan Kent (1992, 1996) noted a tendency to stereotype foragers, to treat them all as alike. They used to be stereotyped as isolated, primitive survivors of the Stone Age. A new, and probably more accurate, view of contemporary foragers sees them as groups forced into marginal environments by states, colonialism, and world events.

CULTURE THINK

What were some characteristics of traditional bands—ones that had foraging as the basis of the economy? What has changed for foraging bands in contemporary times?

Kent (1996) stresses variation among foragers, focusing on diversity in time and space among the San. The nature of San life has changed considerably since the 1950s and 1960s, when a series of anthropologists from Harvard University, including Richard Borshay Lee, embarked on a systematic study of their lives. Studying the San over time, Lee and others have documented many changes (Lee 1979, 1984, 2003; Silberbauer 1981; Tanaka 1980). Such longitudinal research monitors variation in time, and fieldwork in many San areas has revealed variation in space. One of the most important contrasts was found to be that between settled (sedentary) and nomadic groups (Kent and Vierich 1989). Although sedentism has increased substantially in recent years, some San groups (along rivers) have been sedentary for generations. Others, including the Dobe Ju/'hoansi San studied by Lee (1984, 2003) and the Kutse San that Kent studied, have retained more of the hunter-gatherer lifestyle.

To the extent that foraging continues to be their subsistence base, groups like the San can illustrate links between a foraging economy and other aspects of band society and culture. For example, San groups that still are mobile, or that were so until recently, emphasize social, political, and gender equality, which are traditional band characteristics. A social system based on kinship, reciprocity, and sharing is appropriate for an economy with few people and limited resources. People have to share meat when they get it; otherwise it rots. The nomadic pursuit of wild plants and animals tends to discourage permanent settlement, wealth accumulation, and status distinctions.

Among tropical foragers, women make an important economic contribution through gathering, as is true among the San shown here in Namibia. What evidence do you see in this photo that contemporary foragers participate in the modern world system?

In the past, foraging bands—small, nomadic or seminomadic social units—formed seasonally when component nuclear families got together. The particular families in a band varied from year to year. Marriage and kinship created ties between members of different bands. Trade and visiting also linked them. Band leaders were leaders in name only. In such an egalitarian society, they were first among equals. Sometimes they gave advice or made decisions, but they had no way to enforce their decisions. Given the spread of states and the modern world system, it is increasingly difficult for ethnographers to find and observe such patterns of band organization.

The Inuit The aboriginal Inuit (Hoebel 1954, 1954/1968), another group of foragers, provide a good example of methods of settling disputes—**conflict resolution**—in stateless societies. All societies have ways of settling disputes (of variable effectiveness) along with cultural rules or norms about proper and improper behavior. *Norms* are cultural standards or guidelines that enable individuals to distinguish between appropriate and inappropriate behavior in a given society (N. Kottak 2002). While rules and norms are cultural universals, only state societies, those with established governments, have formal laws that are formulated, proclaimed, and enforced.

Foragers lacked formal **law** in the sense of a legal code with trial and enforcement, but they did have methods of social control and dispute settlement. The absence of law did not mean total anarchy. As described by E. A. Hoebel (1954) in a classic ethnographic study of conflict resolution, a sparse population of some twenty thousand Inuit spanned 6,000 miles (9,500 kilometers) of the Arctic region (see "Location of the Inuit"). The most significant social groups were the nuclear family and the band. Personal relationships linked the families and bands. Some bands had headmen. There were also shamans (part-time religious specialists). However, these positions conferred little power on those who occupied them.

Hunting and fishing by men were the primary Inuit subsistence activities. The diverse and abundant plant foods available in warmer areas, where female labor in gathering is important, were absent in the Arctic. Traveling on land and sea in a bitter environment, Inuit men faced more dangers than women did. The traditional male role took its toll in lives, so that adult women outnumbered men. This permitted some men to have two or three wives. The ability to support more than one wife conferred a certain amount of prestige, but it also encouraged envy. (*Prestige* is esteem, respect, or approval for culturally valued acts or qualities.) If a man seemed to be taking additional wives just to enhance his reputation, a rival was likely to steal one of them. Most disputes were between men and originated over women, caused by wife stealing or adultery.

> **conflict resolution** The means by which disputes are socially regulated and settled; found in all societies, but the resolution methods tend to be more formal and effective in states than in nonstates.
>
> **law** A legal code, including trial and enforcement; characteristic of state-organized societies.

Location of the Inuit

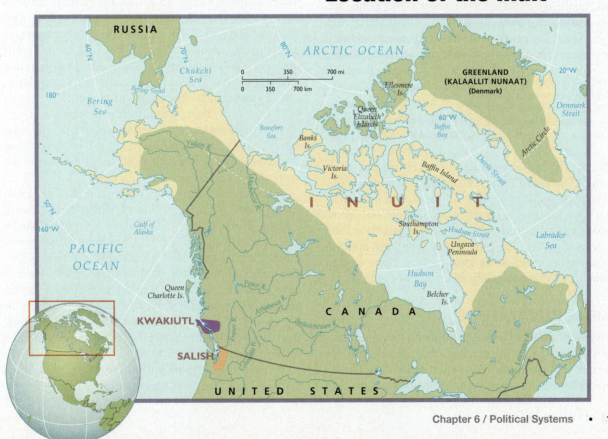

A jilted husband had several options. He could try to kill the wife stealer. If he succeeded, however, one of his rival's kinsmen surely would try to kill him in retaliation. One dispute could escalate into several deaths as relatives avenged a succession of murders. No government existed to intervene and stop such a *blood feud* (a murderous feud between families). However, one also could challenge a rival to a song battle. In a public setting, contestants made up insulting songs about each other. At the end of the match, the audience proclaimed the winner. If a man whose wife had been stolen won, there was no guarantee she would return. Often she stayed with her abductor.

Thefts are common in societies with marked property differentials, like our own, but thefts are uncommon among foragers. Each Inuit had access to the resources needed to sustain life. Every man could hunt, fish, and make the tools necessary for subsistence. Every woman could obtain the materials needed to make clothing, prepare food, and do domestic work. Inuit men could even hunt and fish in the territories of other local groups. There was no notion of private ownership of territory or animals.

village head Leadership position in a village (as among the Yanomami, where the head is always a man); has limited authority; leads by example and persuasion.

TRIBAL CULTIVATORS

As is true of foraging bands, there are no totally autonomous tribes in today's world. Still, there are societies, for example, in Papua New Guinea and in South America's tropical forests, in which tribal principles continue to operate. Tribes typically have a horticultural or pastoral economy and are organized by village life or membership in *descent groups* (kin groups whose members trace descent from a common ancestor). Tribes lack socioeconomic stratification (i.e., a class structure) and a formal government of their own. A few tribes still conduct small-scale warfare, in the form of intervillage raiding. Tribes have more effective regulatory mechanisms than foragers do, but tribal societies have no sure means of enforcing political decisions. The main regulatory officials are village heads, big men, descent-group leaders, village councils, and leaders of pantribal associations (discussed later in the chapter). All these figures and groups have limited authority.

Like foragers, horticulturalists tend to be egalitarian, although some have marked *gender stratification:* an unequal distribution of resources, power, prestige, and personal freedom between men and women (see the chapter "Gender"). Horticultural villages usually are small, with low population density and open access to strategic resources. Age, gender, and personal traits determine how much respect people receive and how much support they get from others. Egalitarianism diminishes, however, as village size and population density increase. Horticultural villages usually have headmen—rarely, if ever, headwomen.

THE VILLAGE HEAD

The Yanomami (Chagnon 1997; Ferguson 1995; Ramos 1995) are Native Americans who live in southern Venezuela and the adjacent part of Brazil. Their tribal society has about 26,000 people living in 200 to 250 widely scattered villages, each with a population between 40 and 250. The Yanomami are horticulturalists who also hunt and gather. Their staple crops are bananas and plantains (a bananalike crop). There are more significant social groups among the Yanomami than exist in a foraging society. The Yanomami have families, villages, and descent groups. Their descent groups, which span more than one village, are patrilineal (ancestry is traced back through males only) and exogamous (people must marry outside their own descent group). However, local branches of two different descent groups may live in the same village and intermarry.

Traditionally among the Yanomami the only leadership position has been that of **village head** (always a man). His authority, like that of a foraging band's leader, is severely limited. If a headman wants something done, he must lead by example and persuasion. The headman lacks the right to issue orders. He can only persuade, harangue, and try to influence public opinion. For example, if he wants people to clean up the central plaza in preparation for a feast, he must start sweeping it himself, hoping his covillagers will take the hint and relieve him.

When conflict erupts within the village, the headman may be called on as a mediator who listens to both sides. He will give an opinion and advice. If a disputant is unsatisfied, the headman has no power to back his decisions and no way to impose punishments. Like the band leader, he is first among equals.

A Yanomami village headman also must lead in generosity. Because he must be more generous than any other villager, he cultivates more land. His garden provides much of the food consumed when his village holds a feast for another village. The headman represents the village in its dealings with outsiders, including agents of the governments of Venezuela and Brazil.

The way someone acts as headman depends on his personal traits and the number of supporters he can muster. Napoleon Chagnon (1983/1992) describes how one village headman, Kaobawa, guaranteed safety to a delegation from a village with which a covillager of his wanted to start a war. Kaobawa was a particularly effective headman. He had demonstrated his fierceness in battle, but he also knew how to use diplomacy to avoid offending other villagers. No one in the village had a better personality for the headmanship. Nor (because Kaobawa had many brothers) did anyone have more supporters. Among the Yanomami, when a group is dissatisfied with a village headman, its members can leave and found a new village; this is done from time to time and is called *village fissioning*.

With its many villages and descent groups, Yanomami sociopolitical organization is more complex than that of a band-organized society. The Yanomami face more problems in regulating relations among groups and individuals. Although a headman sometimes can prevent a specific violent act, intervillage raiding has been a feature of some areas

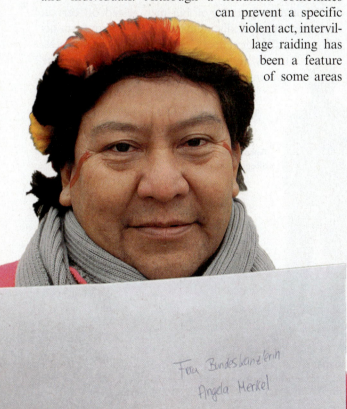

of Yanomami territory, particularly those studied by Chagnon (1997).

It's important to recognize as well that the Yanomami are not isolated from outside events, including missionization. They live in two nation-states, Venezuela and Brazil, and external warfare waged by Brazilian ranchers and miners has plagued them (Chagnon 1997; *Cultural Survival Quarterly* 1989; Ferguson 1995). During a Brazilian gold rush between 1987 and 1991, one Yanomami died each day, on average, from external attacks. By 1991, there were some forty thousand Brazilian miners in the Brazilian Yanomami homeland. Some Yanomami were killed outright. The miners introduced new diseases, and the swollen population ensured that old diseases became epidemic. In 1991, a commission of the American Anthropological Association reported on the plight of the Yanomami (American Anthropological Association 1991). Brazilian Yanomami were dying at a rate of 10 percent annually, and their fertility rate had dropped to zero. Since then, one Brazilian president declared a huge Yanomami territory off-limits to outsiders. Unfortunately, local politicians, miners, and ranchers have increasingly evaded the ban. The future of the Yanomami remains uncertain.

THE "BIG MAN"

Many societies of the South Pacific, particularly in the Melanesian Islands and Papua New Guinea, had a kind of political leader that we call the big man. The **big man** (almost always a male) was an elaborate version of the village head, but with one significant difference. The village head's leadership is within one village; the big man had supporters in several villages. The big man therefore was a regulator of *regional* political organization.

Consider the Kapauku Papuans, who live in Irian Jaya, Indonesia (which is on the island of New Guinea). Anthropologist Leopold Pospisil (1963) studied the Kapauku (then forty-five thousand people), who grow crops (with the sweet potato as their staple) and raise pigs. Their economy is too complex to be described as simple horticulture. Kapauku cultivation has used varied techniques for specific kinds of land. Labor-intensive cultivation in valleys involves mutual aid in turning the soil before planting. The digging of long drainage ditches, which a big man often helped organize, is even more complex. Kapauku plant cultivation supports a larger and denser population than does the simpler horticulture of the Yanomami. Kapauku society could not survive in

big man Figure often found among tribal horticulturalists and pastoralists. The big man occupies no office but creates his reputation through entrepreneurship and generosity to others. Neither his wealth nor his position passes to his heirs.

A Yanomami leader today—no longer just a village head. Kopenawa Yanomami, claiming to represent his people, holds a letter for German Chancellor Angela Merkel.

its current form without collective cultivation and political regulation of the more complex economic tasks.

The key political figure among the Kapauku was the big man, known as a *tonowi.* A tonowi achieved his status through hard work, amassing wealth in the form of pigs and other native riches.

Consider the term *status,* which often is used as a synonym for prestige. Thus, "She's got a lot of status" means she's got a lot of prestige; people look up to her. Among social scientists, that's not the primary meaning of status. Social scientists use *status* more neutrally—for any social position, no matter what the prestige. In this sense, **status** encompasses the various positions that people occupy in society, such as spouse, parent, trading partner, teacher, student, salesperson, big man, and many others. People always occupy multiple statuses (e.g., son, brother, father, big man). Among the statuses we occupy, particular ones dominate in particular settings, such as son or daughter at home and student in the classroom.

Some statuses are **ascribed:** People have little or no choice about occupying them. Age is an ascribed status; we can't choose not to age. One's status as a member of the nobility, or as a male or a female, usually is ascribed; people are born members of a certain social category and remain so all their lives. **Achieved statuses,** by contrast, aren't automatic; they come through choices, actions, efforts, talents, or accomplishments, and may be positive or negative. Examples of achieved statuses include big man, healer, senator, convicted felon, terrorist, salesperson, union member, father, and college student.

The achieved status of big men rested on certain characteristics that distinguished the big man from his fellows: wealth, generosity, eloquence, physical fitness, bravery, and supernatural powers. Men became big men because they had certain personalities.

The big man persuades people to organize feasts, which distribute pork and wealth. Shown here is such a regional event, drawing on several villages, in Papua New Guinea. Big men owe their status to their individual personalities rather than to inherited wealth or position. Does our society have equivalents of big men?

High School Popularity

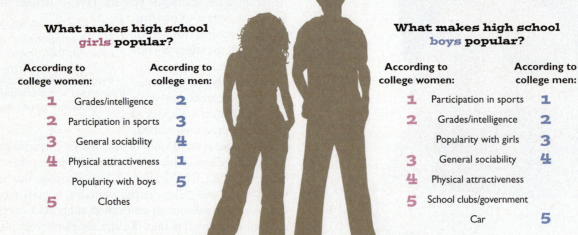

What makes high school girls popular?

According to college women:		According to college men:
1	Grades/intelligence	2
2	Participation in sports	3
3	General sociability	4
4	Physical attractiveness	1
	Popularity with boys	5
5	Clothes	

What makes high school boys popular?

According to college women:		According to college men:
1	Participation in sports	1
2	Grades/intelligence	2
	Popularity with girls	3
3	General sociability	4
4	Physical attractiveness	
5	School clubs/government	
	Car	5

How does this big man on campus compare with the Melanesian big man?

Note: Students at the following universities were asked in which ways adolescents in their high schools had gained prestige with their peers: Cornell University, Louisiana State University, Southeastern Louisiana University, State University of New York at Albany, State University of New York at Stony Brook, the University of Georgia, and the University of New Hampshire.

Source: Suitor et al. 2001:445.

Social Statuses

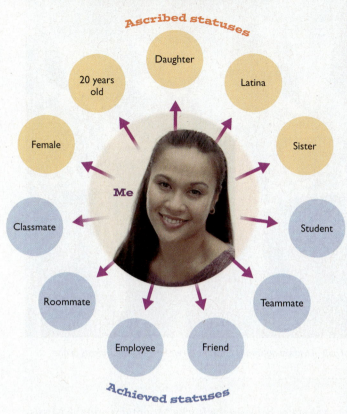

Ascribed statuses

20 years old · Daughter · Latina · Female · Me · Sister · Classmate · Student · Roommate · Teammate · Employee · Friend

Achieved statuses

CULTURE THINK

Sodalities, or nonkin-based groups, exist in industrial societies as well as in tribes. Do you or your family belong to any kind of sodality, or nonkin group, such as a club or a religious organization?

Unlike that of the Yanomami village head, a big man's wealth exceeded that of his fellows. His supporters, recognizing his past favors and anticipating future rewards, recognized him as a leader and accepted his decisions as binding. The big man was an important regulator of regional events in Kapauku life. He helped determine the dates for feasts and markets. He persuaded people to sponsor feasts, which distributed pork and wealth. He initiated economic projects requiring the cooperation of a regional community.

The Kapauku big man again exemplifies a generalization about leadership in tribal societies: If someone achieves wealth and widespread respect and support, he or she must be generous. The big man worked hard not to hoard wealth but to give away the fruits of his labor, to convert wealth into prestige and gratitude. A stingy big man would lose his support, his reputation plummeting. Selfish and greedy big men sometimes were murdered by their fellows (Zimmer-Tamakoshi 1997).

PANTRIBAL SODALITIES

Big men could forge regional political organization, albeit temporarily, by mobilizing people from several villages. Other social and political mechanisms in tribal societies—such as a belief in common ancestry, kinship, or descent—could be used to link local groups within a region. The same descent group might span several villages, and its dispersed members might follow a descent group leader.

Principles other than kinship also can link local groups, especially in modern societies. People who live in different parts of the same nation may belong to the same labor union, sorority or fraternity, political party, or religious denomination. In tribes, nonkin groups called *associations,* or *sodalities,* may serve a similar linking function. Often, sodalities are based on common age or gender, with all-male sodalities more common than all-female ones.

Pantribal sodalities are groups that extend across the whole tribe, spanning several villages. Such sodalities were especially likely to develop in situations

status Any position that determines where someone fits in society; may be ascribed or achieved.

ascribed status Social status that people have little or no choice about occupying (e.g., race or gender).

achieved status Social status that comes through talents, actions, efforts, activities, and accomplishments (e.g., big man or convicted felon).

pantribal sodality A nonkin-based group that exists throughout a tribe, spanning several villages.

They amassed resources during their own lifetime; they did not inherit their wealth or position. A determined man could become a big man, creating wealth through hard work and good judgment. Wealth resulted from successful pig breeding and trading. As a man's pig herd and prestige grew, he attracted supporters. He sponsored ceremonial pig feasts in which pigs were slaughtered and their meat distributed to guests.

To what extent has the political success of the Clinton family been achieved, or ascribed?

Here we see the Masai warrior (ilmurran) age grade dancing with a group of girls of a lower age grade (intoyie). Do we have any equivalents of age grades in our own society?

of warfare with a neighboring tribe. Mobilizing their members from multiple villages within the same tribe, pantribal sodalities could assemble a force to attack or retaliate against another tribe.

The best examples of pantribal sodalities come from the Central Plains of North America and from tropical Africa. During the eighteenth and nineteenth centuries, Native American societies of the Great Plains of the United States and Canada experienced a rapid growth of pantribal sodalities. This development reflected an economic change that followed the spread of horses, which had been reintroduced to the Americas by the Spanish, to the states between the Rocky Mountains and the Mississippi River. Many Plains Indian societies changed their adaptive strategies because of the horse. At first they had been foragers who hunted bison (buffalo) on foot. Later they adopted a mixed economy based on hunting, gathering, and horticulture. Finally they changed to a much more specialized economy based on horseback hunting of bison (eventually with rifles).

As the Plains tribes were undergoing these changes, other Indians also adopted horseback hunting and moved into the Plains. Attempting to occupy the same area, groups came into conflict. A pattern of warfare developed in which the members of one tribe raided another, usually for horses. The new economy demanded that people follow the movement of the bison herds. During the winter, when the bison dispersed, a tribe fragmented into small bands and families. In the summer, as huge herds assembled on the Plains, members of the tribe reunited. They camped together for social, political, and religious activities, but mainly for communal bison hunting.

Two activities demanded strong leadership: organizing and carrying out raids on enemy camps (to capture horses) and managing the summer bison hunt. All the Plains societies developed pantribal sodalities, and leadership roles within them, to police the summer hunt. Leaders coordinated hunting efforts, making sure that people did not cause a stampede with an early shot or an ill-advised action. Leaders imposed severe penalties, including seizure of a culprit's wealth, for disobedience.

Many tribes that adopted this Plains strategy of adaptation had once been foragers for whom hunting and gathering had been individual or small-group affairs. They never had come together previously as a single social unit. Age and gender were available as social principles that could quickly and efficiently forge unrelated people into pantribal sodalities.

Raiding of one tribe by another, this time for cattle rather than horses, also was common in eastern and southeastern Africa, where pantribal sodalities, based on age and gender, also developed. Among the pastoral Masai of Kenya, men born during the same four-year period were circumcised together and belonged to the same named group, an age set, throughout their lives. The sets moved through *age grades,* the most important of which was the warrior grade. Members of a set felt a strong allegiance to one another. Masai women lacked comparable set organization, but they also passed through culturally recognized age grades: the initiate, the married woman, and the female elder.

In certain parts of West and Central Africa, the pantribal sodalities are *secret societies,* made up exclusively of men or women. Like our college fraternities and sororities, these associations have secret initiation ceremonies. Among the Mende of Sierra Leone, men's and women's secret societies were very influential. The men's group, the Poro, trained boys in social conduct, ethics, and religion and supervised political and economic activities. Leadership roles in the Poro often overshadowed village headship and played an important part in social control, dispute management, and tribal political regulation. Age, gender, and ritual can link members of different local groups into a single social collectivity in a tribe and thus create a sense of ethnic identity, of belonging to the same cultural tradition.

NOMADIC POLITICS

Herders have varied political systems. Unlike the Masai (just discussed) and other tribal herders, some pastoralists have chiefs and live in nation-states. The scope of political authority among pastoralists expands considerably as regulatory problems increase in densely populated regions. Consider two Iranian pastoral nomadic tribes—the Basseri and the Qashqai (Salzman 1974). Starting each year from a plateau near the coast, these groups took their animals to grazing land 17,000 feet (5,400 meters) above sea level. The Basseri and the Qashqai shared this route with one another and with several other ethnic groups (see "Location of the Basseri and Qashqai" below).

Location of the Basseri and Qashqai

Use of the same pasture land at different times was carefully scheduled. Ethnic-group movements were tightly coordinated. Expressing this schedule is *il-rah*, a concept common to all Iranian nomads. A group's il-rah is its customary path in time and space. It is the schedule, different for each group, of when specific areas can be used in the annual trek.

Each tribe had its own leader, known as the *khan* or *il-khan*. The Basseri khan, because he dealt with a smaller population, faced fewer problems in coordinating its movements than did the leaders of the Qashqai. Correspondingly, his rights, privileges, duties, and authority were weaker. Nevertheless, his authority exceeded that of any political figure discussed so far. The khan's authority still came from his personal traits rather than from his office. That is, the Basseri followed a particular khan not because of a political position he happened to fill but because of their personal allegiance and loyalty to him as a man. The khan relied on the support of the heads of the descent groups into which Basseri society was divided.

Among the Qashqai, however, allegiance shifted from the person to the office. The Qashqai had multiple levels of authority and more powerful chiefs, or khans. Managing four hundred thousand people required a complex hierarchy. Heading it was the il-khan, helped by a deputy, under whom were the heads of constituent tribes, under each of whom were descent-group heads.

A case illustrates just how developed the Qashqai authority structure was. A hailstorm prevented some nomads from joining the annual migration at the appointed time. Although everyone recognized that they were not responsible for their delay, the il-khan assigned them less favorable grazing land, for that year only, in place of their usual pasture. The tardy herders and other Qashqai considered the judgment fair and didn't question it. Thus, Qashqai authorities regulated the annual migration. They also adjudicated disputes between people, tribes, and descent groups.

These Iranian cases illustrate the fact that pastoralism often is just one among many specialized economic activities within complex nation-states and regional systems. As part of a larger whole, pastoral tribes are constantly pitted against other ethnic groups. In these nations, the state becomes a final authority, a higher-level regulator that attempts to limit conflict between ethnic groups. State organization arose not just to manage agricultural economies but also to regulate the activities of ethnic groups within expanding social and economic systems (see Das and Poole, eds., 2004).

 Got IT? Can you compare and contrast different types of tribal leadership?

>> Chiefdoms

The first states emerged in the Old World about fifty-five hundred years ago. The first chiefdoms developed perhaps a thousand years earlier, but few survive today. In many parts of the world, the chiefdom was a transitional form of organization that emerged during the evolution of tribes into states. State formation began in Mesopotamia (currently Iran and Iraq). It next occurred in Egypt, the Indus Valley of Pakistan and India, and northern China. A few thousand years later states arose in two parts of the Western Hemisphere—Mesoamerica (Mexico, Guatemala, Belize) and the central Andes (Peru and Bolivia). Early states are known as *archaic states,* or nonindustrial states, in contrast to modern industrial nation-states. Robert Carneiro defines the state as "an autonomous political unit encompassing many communities within its territory, having a centralized government with the power to collect taxes, draft men for work or war, and decree and enforce laws" (Carneiro 1970, p. 733).

The chiefdom and the state, like many categories used by social scientists, are *ideal types.* That is, they are labels that make social contrasts seem sharper than they really are. In reality there is a continuum from tribe to chiefdom to state. Some societies had many attributes of chiefdoms but retained tribal features. Some advanced chiefdoms had many attributes of archaic states and thus are difficult to assign to either category. Recognizing this "continuous change" (Johnson and Earle 2000), some anthropologists speak of "complex chiefdoms" (Earle 1987, 1997), which are almost states.

POLITICAL AND ECONOMIC SYSTEMS

Geographic areas with chiefdoms included the circum-Caribbean (e.g., Caribbean islands, Panama, Colombia), lowland Amazonia, what is now the southeastern United States, and Polynesia. Chiefdoms created the megalithic cultures of Europe, such as the one that built Stonehenge. Bear in mind that chiefdoms and states can fall (disintegrate) as well as rise. Before Rome's expansion, much of Europe was organized at the chiefdom level, to which it reverted for centuries after the fall of Rome in the fifth century C.E.

Much of our ethnographic knowledge about chiefdoms comes from Polynesia, where they were common

CULTURETHINK

Consider the pros and cons of ideal types. Is such a typology a valuable way of presenting information, or is it an oversimplification? Do the categories of band, tribe, chiefdom, and state help you understand cross-cultural politics?

STUDY TIP

Neither band nor tribal leaders have permanent positions or can enforce decisions, unlike chiefs and state leaders, who hold offices and have clear-cut authority.

at the time of European exploration. In chiefdoms, social relations are based mainly on kinship, marriage, descent, age, generation, and gender—just as they are in bands and tribes. This is a fundamental difference between chiefdoms and states. States bring nonrelatives together and oblige them all to pledge allegiance to a government.

Unlike bands and tribes, however, chiefdoms administer a clear-cut and enduring regional political system. Chiefdoms may include thousands of people living in many villages or hamlets. Regulation is carried out by the chief and his or her assistants, who occupy political offices. An **office** is a permanent position, which must be refilled when it is vacated by death or retirement. Because offices are refilled systematically, the structure of a chiefdom endures across the generations, ensuring permanent political regulation.

Polynesian chiefs were full-time specialists whose duties included managing the economy. They regulated production by commanding or prohibiting (using religious taboos) the cultivation of certain lands and crops. Chiefs also regulated distribution and consumption. At certain seasons—often on a ritual occasion such as a first-fruit ceremony—people would offer part of their harvest to the chief through his or her representatives. Products moved up the hierarchy, eventually reaching the chief. Conversely, illustrating obligatory sharing with

kin, chiefs sponsored feasts at which they gave back much of what they had received. Unlike big men, chiefs were exempt from ordinary work and had rights and privileges unavailable to the masses. Like big men, however, they still returned a portion of the wealth they took in.

Such a flow of resources to and then from a central office is known as *chiefly redistribution.* Redistribution offers economic advantages. If the different areas specialized in particular crops, goods, or services, chiefly redistribution made those products available to the entire society. Chiefly redistribution also played a role in risk management. It stimulated production beyond the immediate subsistence level and provided a central storehouse for goods that might become scarce at times of famine (Earle 1987, 1997).

> **office** Permanent political position.

STATUS SYSTEMS

Social status in chiefdoms was based on seniority of descent. Because rank, power, prestige, and resources came through kinship and descent, Polynesian chiefs kept extremely long genealogies. Some chiefs (without writing) managed to trace their ancestry back fifty generations. All the people in the chiefdom were thought to be related to each other. Presumably, all were descended from a group of founding ancestors.

The status of chief was ascribed, based on seniority of descent. The chief would be the oldest child (usually son) of the oldest child of the oldest child, and so on.

Did You Know?

Indigenous leaders remain politically relevant. In Madagascar, for example, national presidents have routinely consulted local chiefs, realizing that the chiefs have a strong influence on their followers.

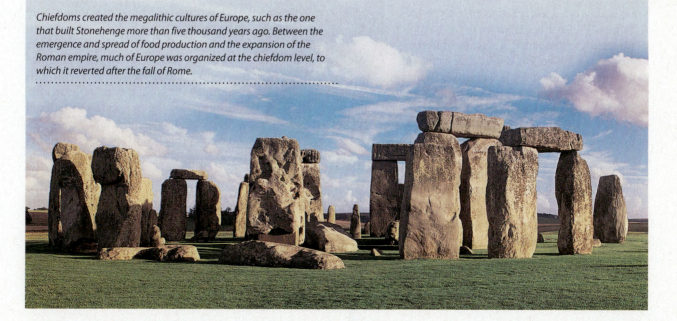

Chiefdoms created the megalithic cultures of Europe, such as the one that built Stonehenge more than five thousand years ago. Between the emergence and spread of food production and the expansion of the Roman empire, much of Europe was organized at the chiefdom level, to which it reverted after the fall of Rome.

These 2011 anti-government protesters in Sanaa, Yemen, call for the ouster of former President Ali Abdullah Saleh.

to resources. Some men and women had privileged access to power, prestige, and wealth. They controlled strategic resources such as land and water. Earle characterizes chiefs as "an incipient aristocracy with advantages in wealth and lifestyle" (1987, p. 290).

Compared with chiefdoms, archaic states drew a much firmer line between elites and masses, distinguishing at least between nobles and commoners. Kinship ties did not extend from the nobles to the commoners because of *stratum endogamy*—marriage within one's own group. Commoners married commoners; elites married elites.

differential access Unequal access to resources; basic attribute of chiefdoms and states. Superordinates have favored access to such resources, while the access of subordinates is limited by superordinates.

stratification Characteristic of a system with socioeconomic strata.

wealth All a person's material assets, including income, land, and other types of property; the basis of economic status.

power The ability to exercise one's will over others—to do what one wants; the basis of political status.

prestige Esteem, respect, or approval for acts, deeds, or qualities considered exemplary.

Degrees of seniority were calculated so intricately on some islands that there were as many ranks as people. For example, the third son would rank below the second, who in turn would rank below the first. The children of an eldest brother, however, would all rank above the children of the next brother, whose children would in turn outrank those of younger brothers. However, even the lowest-ranking person in a chiefdom was still the chief's relative. In such a kin-based context, everyone, even a chief, had to share with his or her relatives.

Because everyone had a slightly different status, it was difficult to draw a line between elites and common people. Other chiefdoms calculated seniority differently and had shorter genealogies than did those in Polynesia. Still, the concern for seniority and the lack of sharp gaps between elites and commoners are features of all chiefdoms.

The status systems of chiefdoms and states are similar in that both are based on **differential access**

This photo, taken in 1981 in Neiafu, Savaii, Western Samoa, shows an orator chief, or tulafale. His speaking staff and the fly whisk over his shoulder symbolize his status as a tulafale. Traditional Samoa provides one example of a Polynesian chiefdom. How do chiefs differ from ordinary people?

THE EMERGENCE OF STRATIFICATION

The status system of a chiefdom differed from that of a state because of the chiefdom's kinship basis. In the context of differential wealth and power, the chiefly type of status system didn't last very long. Chiefs would start acting like kings and try to erode the kinship basis of the chiefdom. In Madagascar they would do this by demoting their more distant relatives to commoner status and banning marriage between nobles and commoners (Kottak 1980). Such moves, if accepted by the society, created separate *social strata*—unrelated groups that differ in their access to wealth, prestige, and power. (A *stratum* is one of two or more groups that contrast in social status and access to strategic resources. Each stratum includes people of both sexes and all ages.) The creation of separate social strata is called **stratification,** and its emergence signified the transition from chiefdom to state. *The presence of stratification* is one of the key distinguishing features of a state.

The influential sociologist Max Weber (1922/1968) defined three related dimensions of social stratification: (1) Economic status, or **wealth,** encompasses all a person's material assets, including income, land, and other types of property; (2) **power,** the ability to exercise one's will over others—to do and get what one wants—is the basis of political status; (3) **prestige**—the basis of social status—refers to esteem, respect, or approval for acts, deeds, or qualities considered exemplary. Prestige, or "cultural capital" (Bourdieu 1984), gives people a sense of worth and respect, which they often may convert into economic advantage.

Max Weber's Three Dimensions of Stratification

Wealth = Economic status   Power = Political status   Prestige = Social status

In archaic states—for the first time in human evolution—there were contrasts in wealth, power, and prestige between entire groups (social strata) of men and women. Each stratum included people of both genders and all ages. The **superordinate** (the higher, or elite) stratum had privileged access to valued resources. Access to those resources by members of the **subordinate** (lower, or underprivileged) stratum was limited by the privileged group.

 Got IT? Can you compare and contrast status systems in chiefdoms and states?

>> State Systems

Table 6.1 summarizes the information presented so far on bands, tribes, chiefdoms, and states. States, remember, are autonomous political units with social classes and a formal government. States tend to be large and populous, and certain statuses, systems, and subsystems with specialized functions are found in all states (see Sharma and Gupta, eds, 2006). They include the following:

- Population control: fixing of boundaries, establishing citizenship categories, and censusing
- Judiciary: laws, legal procedure, and judges
- Enforcement: permanent military and police forces
- Fiscal: taxation

In archaic states, these subsystems were integrated by a ruling system or government composed of civil, military, and religious officials (Fried 1960). Let's look at the four subsystems one by one.

POPULATION CONTROL

To keep track of whom they govern, states conduct censuses. Each state demarcates boundaries that separate that state from other societies. Customs agents, immigration officers, navies, and coast guards patrol frontiers. States also regulate population through administrative subdivision: provinces, districts, "states," counties, subcounties, and parishes. Lower-level officials manage the populations and territories of the subdivisions.

superordinate The higher, or privileged, group in a stratified system.

subordinate The lower, or underprivileged, group in a stratified system.

CULTURETHINK

Compare and contrast leadership characteristics among bands, tribes, chiefdoms, and states. Are they permanent or temporary positions? Do they have the authority to enforce decisions? How much territory or how many people do they govern? Try drawing a chart or some other visual representation of this information.

TABLE 6.1

Economic Basis of and Political Regulation in Bands, Tribes, Chiefdoms, and States

Sociopolitical Type	Economic Type	Examples	Type of Regulation
Band	Foraging	Inuit, San	Local
Tribe	Horticulture, pastoralism	Yanomami, Kapauku, Masai	Local, temporary regional
Chiefdom	Productive horticulture, pastoral nomadism, agriculture	Qashqai, Polynesia, Cherokee	Permanent regional
State	Agriculture, industrialism	Ancient Mesopotamia, contemporary United States, Canada	Permanent regional

States often promote geographic mobility and resettlement, severing longstanding ties among people, land, and kin (Smith 2003). Population displacements have increased with globalization and as war, famine, and job seeking churn up migratory currents. People in states come to identify themselves by new statuses, both ascribed and achieved—including residence, ethnicity, occupation, political party, religion, and team or club affiliation—rather than only as members of a descent group or extended family.

States also manage their populations by granting different rights and obligations to citizens and noncitizens. Status distinctions among citizens also are common. Archaic states granted different rights to nobles, commoners, and slaves. In American history before the Emancipation Proclamation, there were different laws for enslaved and free people. In European colonies, separate courts judged cases involving only natives and cases involving Europeans. In contemporary America, a military judiciary coexists alongside the civil system.

> ### "Treat all men alike. Give them the same law. Give them an even chance to live and grow."
>
> Chief Joseph

JUDICIARY

All states have *laws* based on precedent and legislative proclamations. Without writing, laws may be preserved in oral tradition. *Crimes* are violations of the legal code ("breaking the law"), with specified types of punishment. To handle crimes and disputes, all states have courts and judges.

A striking contrast between states and nonstates is intervention in family affairs. Governments step in to halt blood feuds and regulate previously private disputes. States attempt to curb *internal* conflict, but they aren't always successful. About 85 percent of the world's armed conflicts since 1945 have begun within states—in efforts to overthrow a ruling regime or as disputes over ethnic, religious, and human rights issues (see Barnaby 1984; Chatterjee 2004; Nordstrom 2004; Tishkov 2004).

ENFORCEMENT

All states have agents to enforce judicial decisions, for example, to mete out punishment and collect fines. Confinement requires jailers. If there is a death penalty, executioners are needed. Government officials have the power to collect fines and confiscate property. The government attempts to suppress internal disorder (with police) and to guard against external threats (with the military and border officials).

Armies help states subdue and conquer neighboring nonstates, but this isn't the only reason why state organization has spread. Although states impose hardships, they also offer advantages. They have formal mechanisms designed to protect against external threats and to preserve internal order. When they are successful in promoting internal peace, states enhance production. Their economies can support massive, dense populations, which supply armies and colonists to promote expansion.

FISCAL SYSTEMS

States need financial, or **fiscal,** mechanisms (e.g., taxation) to support government officials and numerous other specialists. As in the chiefdom, the state intervenes in production, distribution, and consumption. The state may require a certain area to produce specific things or ban certain activities in particular places. Although, like chiefdoms, states have redistribution (aka "spreading the wealth around"), less of what comes in from the people actually goes back to the people.

In nonstates, people customarily share with their relatives, but citizens also have to turn over a substantial portion of what they produce to the state. Markets and trade usually are under at least some state oversight, with officials overseeing distribution and exchange, standardizing weights and measures, and collecting taxes on goods passing into or through the state. Of the revenues the state collects, it reallocates part for the general good and keeps another part (often larger) for itself—its agents and agencies. State organization doesn't bring more freedom or leisure to the common people, who may be conscripted to build monumental public works. Some projects, such as dams and irrigation systems, may be economically necessary, but residents of archaic states also had to build temples, palaces, and tombs for the elites. Those elites reveled in the consumption of sumptuary goods—jewelry, exotic food and drink, and stylish clothing reserved for, or affordable only by, the rich. Peasants' diets suffered as they struggled to meet government demands. Commoners perished in territorial wars that had little relevance to their own needs. Are any of these observations true of contemporary states?

Got IT? Can you list and describe specialized functions found in all states?

>> Social Control

In studying political systems, anthropologists pay attention not only to the formal institutions but to other forms of social control as well. The concept of social control is broader than "the political." **Social control** refers to "those fields of the social system (beliefs, practices, and institutions) that are most actively involved in the maintenance of any norms and the regulation of any conflict" (N. Kottak 2002, p. 290). Norms, as defined earlier in this chapter, are cultural standards or guidelines that enable individuals to distinguish between appropriate and inappropriate behavior.

> **fiscal** Pertaining to finances and taxation.
>
> **social control** Fields of the social system that maintain norms and resolve conflict.

Previous sections of this chapter have focused more on formal political organization than on sociopolitical process. We've seen how the scale and strength of political systems have expanded in relation to economic changes. We've examined means of conflict resolution, or their absence, in various types of society. We've looked at political decision making, including leaders and their limits. We've also recognized that all contemporary humans have been affected by states, colonialism, and the spread of the modern world system.

"Sociopolitical" was introduced as a key concept at the beginning of this chapter. So far, we've

CULTURE THINK

Many argue that taxes are necessary to the functioning of a state. Do you agree? What kinds of goods and services do taxes pay for in your community?

VOTE "NO" STOP SALES TAX INCREASE

focused mainly on the political part of "sociopolitical"; now we focus on the social part. In this section we'll see that political systems have their informal, social, and subtle aspects along with their formal, governmental, and public dimensions.

HEGEMONY AND RESISTANCE

Antonio Gramsci (1971) developed the concept of **hegemony** for a stratified social order in which subordinates comply with domination by internalizing their rulers' values and accepting the "naturalness" of domination (this is the way things were meant to be). According to Pierre Bourdieu (1977, p. 164), every social order tries to make its own arbitrariness (including its mechanisms of control and domination) seem natural and in everyone's interest. Often promises are made (things will get better if you're patient).

Both Bourdieu (1977) and Michel Foucault (1979) argue that it is easier and more effective to dominate people in their minds than to try to control their bodies. Nonphysical forms of social control include various techniques of persuading and managing people and of monitoring and recording their beliefs, activities, and contacts.

hegemony The internalization of a dominant ideology.

Hegemony, the internalization of a dominant ideology, is one way in which elites curb resistance and maintain power. Another way is to make subordinates believe they eventually will gain power—as young people usually foresee when they let their elders dominate them. Another way of curbing resistance is to separate or isolate people while supervising them closely, as is done in prisons (Foucault 1979).

Carnaval, Rio de Janeiro, 2012. How might such public celebrations allow for expressions of discontent?

Popular resistance is most likely to be expressed openly when people are allowed to assemble. The oppressed may draw courage from their common sentiments and the anonymity of the crowd. Sensing danger, the elites often discourage public gatherings. They try to limit and control holidays, funerals, dances, festivals, and other occasions that might unite the oppressed. For example, in the American South before the Civil War, gatherings of five or more slaves were prohibited unless a white person was present.

Factors that interfere with community formation—such as geographic, linguistic, and ethnic separation—also work to curb resistance. Consequently, southern U.S. plantation owners sought slaves with diverse cultural and linguistic backgrounds. Despite the measures used to divide them, the slaves resisted, developing their own popular culture, linguistic codes, and religious vision. The masters stressed portions of the Bible that stressed compliance, such as the book of Job. The slaves, however, preferred the story of Moses and deliverance. The cornerstone of slave religion became the idea of a reversal in the conditions of whites and blacks. Slaves also resisted directly, through sabotage and flight. In many New World areas, slaves managed to establish free communities in the hills and other isolated areas (Price, ed. 1973).

WEAPONS OF THE WEAK

The study of sociopolitical systems also should consider the sentiments and activity that may lurk beneath the surface of evident, public behavior. In public, the oppressed may seem to accept their own domination, even as they question it in private. James Scott (1990) uses "public transcript" to describe the open, public interactions between

CULTURE THINK

What forms of social control influence your behavior? How important are the informal ones (e.g., shame, gossip, fear of being humiliated) versus the formal ones (e.g., fear of punishment for breaking the law)?

superordinates and subordinates—the outer shell of power relations. He uses "hidden transcript" to describe the critique of power that proceeds out of sight of the power holders. In public, the elites and the oppressed may observe the etiquette of power relations. The dominants act like masters while their subordinates show humility and defer.

Often, situations that seem to be hegemonic do have active resistance, but it is individual and disguised rather than collective and defiant. James Scott (1985) uses Malay peasants, among whom he did fieldwork, to illustrate small-scale acts of resistance—which he calls "weapons of the weak." The Malay peasants used an indirect strategy to resist an Islamic tithe (religious tax). Peasants were expected to pay the tithe, usually in the form of rice, which was sent to the provincial capital. In theory, the tithe would come back as charity, but it never did. Peasants didn't resist the tithe by rioting, demonstrating, or protesting. Instead they used a "nibbling" strategy, based on small acts of resistance. For example, they failed to declare their land or lied about the amount they farmed. They underpaid, or delivered rice contaminated with water, rocks, or mud, to add weight. Because of this resistance, only 15 percent of what was due actually was paid (Scott 1990, p. 89).

Hidden transcripts tend to be expressed publicly at certain times (festivals and Carnavals) and in certain places (such as markets). Because of its costumed anonymity, Carnaval (aka Mardi Gras in New Orleans) is an excellent arena for expressing normally suppressed feelings. Carnavals celebrate freedom through immodesty, dancing, gluttony, and sexuality (DaMatta 1991). Carnaval may begin as a playful outlet for frustrations built up during the year. Over time, it may evolve into a powerful annual critique of stratification and domination and thus a threat to the established order (Gilmore 1987). (Recognizing that ceremonial license could turn into political defiance, the Spanish dictator Francisco Franco outlawed Carnaval.)

SHAME AND GOSSIP

Many anthropologists have cited the importance of "informal" processes of social control, such as stigma, shame, and gossip, especially in small-scale societies (see Freilich, Raybeck, and Savishinsky 1991). Gossip, which can lead to shame, sometimes is used when a direct or formal sanction is risky or impossible (Herskovits 1937). Margaret Mead (1937) and Ruth Benedict (1946) distinguished between shame as an external sanction (i.e., forces set in motion by others) and guilt as an internal sanction, psychologically generated by the individual. They regarded shame as a more prominent form of social control in non-Western societies and guilt as a more dominant emotional sanction in Western societies. Of course, to be effective as a sanction, the prospect of being shamed

or of shaming oneself must be internalized by the individual. In small-scale societies, in a social environment where everyone knows everyone else, most people try to avoid behavior that might spoil their reputations and alienate them from their social network (N. Kottak 2002).

Bronislaw Malinowski (1927) described how Trobriand Islanders might climb to the top of a palm tree and dive to their deaths because they couldn't tolerate the shame associated with public knowledge of some stigmatizing action. Nicholas Kottak (2002) heard Makua villagers in northern Mozambique tell the story of a man rumored to have fathered a child with his stepdaughter. The political authorities imposed no formal sanctions (e.g., a fine or jail time) on this man, but gossip about the affair circulated widely. The gossip crystallized in the lyrics of a song that groups of young women would perform. After the man heard his name and alleged incestuous behavior mentioned in that song, he hanged himself by the neck from a tree. (Previously we saw the role of song in the social control system of the Inuit. We'll see it again in the case of the Igbo women's war, discussed below.)

Although it isn't part of any formal or official authority structure, shame can be a powerful social sanction. People aren't just citizens of governments, they are members of society, and social sanctions exist alongside governmental ones. Such sanctions exemplify other "weapons of the weak," because they often are wielded most effectively by people, such as women or young people, who have limited access to the formal authority structure.

THE IGBO WOMEN'S WAR

Shame and ridicule—used by women against men—played a key role in a decisive protest movement that took place in southeastern Nigeria in late 1929. This is remembered as the "Aba Women's Riots of 1929" in British colonial history, and as the "Women's War" in Igbo history (see Dorward, ed. 1983; Martin 1988; Mba 1982; Oriji 2000; Van Allen 1971). During this two-month "war," at least 25,000 Igbo women joined protests against British officials, their agents, and their colonial policies. This massive revolt touched off the most serious challenge to British rule in the history of what was then the British colony of Nigeria.

In 1914, the British had implemented a policy of indirect rule by appointing local Nigerian men as their agents—known as "warrant chiefs." These chiefs became increasingly oppressive, seizing property, imposing arbitrary regulations, and imprisoning people who criticized them. Colonial administrators further stoked local outrage when they announced plans to impose taxes on Igbo market women. These women were key suppliers of food for Nigeria's growing urban population; they feared being forced out

Nigerian women, like these Muslim women taking part in a nationwide strike, have played key roles in Nigeria's political history.

of business by the new tax. Market women were key organizers of the protests.

After hearing about the tax in November 1929, thousands of Igbo women assembled in various towns to protest both the warrant chiefs and the taxes on market women. They used a traditional practice of censoring and shaming men through all-night song and dance ridicule (often called "sitting on a man"). This process entailed constant singing and dancing around the houses and offices of the warrant chiefs. The women also would follow the chiefs' every move, forcing the men to pay attention by invading their space. Disturbed by the whole process, wives of the warrant chiefs also pressured their husbands to listen to the protesters' demands.

The protests were remarkably effective. The tax was abandoned, and many of the warrant chiefs resigned, some to be replaced by women. Other women were appointed to the Native courts as judges. The position of women improved in Nigeria, where market women especially remain a powerful political force to this day. Many Nigerian political events in the 1930s, 1940s, and 1950s were inspired by the Women's War, including additional tax protests. This women's war inspired many other protests in regions all over Africa. The Igbo uprising is seen as the first major challenge to British authority in Nigeria and West Africa during the colonial period.

At the beginning of this chapter, *power* was defined as the ability to exercise one's will over others. It was contrasted with *authority*—the formal, socially approved use of power by government officials and others. The case of the Igbo women's war shows how women effectively used their social power (through song, dance, noise, and "in-your-face" behavior) to subvert the formal authority structure and, in so doing, gained greater influence within that structure. Can you think of other, perhaps recent, examples?

Got IT? Can you explain how informal social aspects of political systems (such as hegemony and gossip) work to maintain social control?

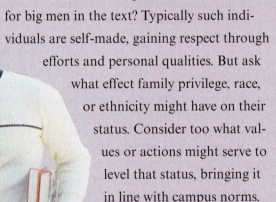

get involved!

Can you find parallels to the Melanesian "big man" on your campus? Talk with dorm residents or members of Greek houses or other social circles to see which students tend to take charge and acquire prestige. Or think back to high school. Who were the big men and women in your graduating class? How did their achievements compare with those described for big men in the text? Typically such individuals are self-made, gaining respect through efforts and personal qualities. But ask what effect family privilege, race, or ethnicity might have on their status. Consider too what values or actions might serve to level that status, bringing it in line with campus norms. Think of a campus big man or woman you know. Would you want to level or support his or her status? Why?

For REVIEW

I. **What kinds of political systems have existed worldwide, and what are their social and economic correlates?**

- Bands are small groups of foragers related by kinship or marriage. Foraging encourages equality, reciprocity, and sharing as well as mobility. Band leaders are first among equals; they lack sure ways to enforce decisions and have only local influence. Tribes, which have horticultural or pastoral economies, are organized around village life and descent groups. The village headman and the "big man," a regional leader, have limited authority. Chiefdoms have horticultural, pastoral nomadic, or agricultural economies. While kin-based, they feature differential access to resources and permanent political regulation of a territory. Chiefs, whose status is based on seniority of descent, receive products that come upward through the hierarchy, then redistribute them to the people. The state is an independent, centrally organized political unit with marked socioeconomic stratification. The economy is typically agricultural or industrial. Political regulation is permanent and regional.

II. **How does the state differ from other forms of political organization?**

- Marked social stratification distinguishes states from other forms of political organization. Whereas chiefdoms allowed differential access to resources, it was closely tied to kinship seniority; in states, each social stratum comprises unrelated groups. Inequalities are built into states and tend to persist across generations. Also distinctive of states is formal government. Government fixes boundaries, establishes citizenship, and conducts censuses; decrees and enforces laws; handles disputes through courts; guards the nation and promotes expansion with a military; and collects taxes. States tend to be large and populous and to foster geographic mobility, severing longstanding ties among people, land, and kin.

III. **How is social control accomplished informally?**

- Broader than the political is the concept of social control—those fields of the social system that work to maintain norms and regulate conflict. Hegemony describes a stratified social order in which subordinates comply with domination by internalizing its values. "Public transcript" refers to the open, public interactions between the dominators and the oppressed. "Hidden transcript" describes the critique of power that goes on where the power holders can't see it. Discontent also may be expressed in public rituals such as Carnaval. Shame and gossip can be effective social sanctions. In the Igbo women's war, women effectively used their social power (through song, dance, noise, and "in-your-face" behavior) to subvert the formal authority structure and, in so doing, gained greater influence within that structure.

Pop Quiz

Multiple Choice:

1. Band societies
   a. lack developed political systems that encourage equality.
   b. are isolated survivors of the Stone Age.
   c. have cultural rules that help members to distinguish between proper and improper behavior.
   d. lack means for conflict resolution since bands do not have established governments or formal laws.

2. Which of the following factors is responsible for the recent changes in Yanomami tribal society?
   a. Big men have amassed so much wealth that the Yanomami have begun to regard them as chiefs.
   b. The Brazilian and Venezuelan governments have relocated Yanomami to other territories to protect them from big business enterprises.
   c. Intervillage trade and cooperation have led to the expansion of Yanomami tribal society.
   d. Gold miners and cattle ranchers have encroached on Yanomami territory and attacked its people; the miners have introduced new diseases.

3. The comparison between the Basseri and the Qashqai, two Iranian nomadic tribes, illustrates that
   a. among tribal sociopolitical organizations, pastoralists are the least likely to interact with other populations in the same space and time.
   b. as regulatory problems increase, political hierarchies become more complex.
   c. as regulatory problems decrease, political hierarchies become more complex.
   d. state organization arises to manage agricultural economies.

4. In what kind of society does differential access to strategic resources based on social stratification occur?
   a. Chiefdoms
   b. Bands
   c. States
   d. Tribes

5. Which of the following would not constitute a status or specialized function that is found in all states?
   a. Control of populations
   b. Agents to enforce judicial decisions, police the society, and guard the nation against external threats
   c. Elimination of different rights granted to different social classes
   d. Taxation

6. Antonio Gramsci developed the concept of hegemony to describe
   a. a stratified social order in which subordinates comply with domination by internalizing their rulers' values and accepting the "naturalness" of domination.
   b. overt sociopolitical strategies.
   c. social controls that induce guilt and shame in the population.
   d. the critique of power by the oppressed that goes on offstage—in private—where the power holders can't see it.

Fill in the Blank:

1. _____ is the socially approved use of power.
2. Among the different types of sociopolitical systems, _____ lack socioeconomic stratification and stratum endogamy, but they do have inequality and a permanent political structure.
3. _____ is esteem, respect, or approval for culturally valued acts or qualities.
4. Broader than political control, the concept of _____ refers to those fields of the social system (beliefs, practices, and institutions) that are most actively involved in the maintenance of any norms and the regulation of any conflict.

1. (c), 2. (d), 3. (b), 4. (c), 5. (c), 6. (a)

1. Authority; 2. chiefdoms; 3. Prestige; 4. social control

7

FAMILIES, KINSHIP, AND MARRIAGE

UNDERSTANDING OURSELVES

Although it remains something of an ideal in our culture, the nuclear family (mom, dad, and kids) now accounts for barely more than one-fifth of all American households. What kind of family raised you? According to the radio talk show psychologist (and undergraduate anthropology major) Dr. Joy Browne, the dual job of parents is to give their kids "roots and wings." Roots, she says, are the easier part. In other words, it's easier to raise children than to let them go. Has that been true of those who raised you? We've heard comments about today's "helicopter parents" hovering over even their college-aged kids, using cell phones to follow their progeny more closely than in previous generations.

It can be difficult to make the transition between the family that raised us (our family of orientation) and the family we create when (or if) we form a long-term romantic partnership and have children (our family of procreation). Contemporary Americans usually get a head start by "leaving home" long before we marry. We go off to college or try to get a job that enables us to support ourselves so that we can live independently, or with roommates. In nonindustrial societies a woman often must leave her home village and her own kin and move in with her husband and his relatives. Many such women complain about feeling isolated in their husband's village, where they may be mistreated by their husband or in-laws.

Even in contemporary North America, conflicts with in-laws aren't at all uncommon. Just read "Dear Abby" or listen to Dr. Joy Browne (cited above) for a week. Even more of a challenge is learning to live with our spouse or domestic partner. Cohabitation always raises issues of accommodation and adjustment. Initially the couple is just that, unless there are children from a previous marriage. If there are, adjustment issues will involve stepparenthood and likely a prior spouse or partner. Once a couple has its own child, family loyalty shifts, but not completely, from the family of orientation to the family that includes spouse and child(ren). The cycle of "marriage and the family" begins anew.

>> Families

The societies anthropologists traditionally have studied have stimulated a strong interest in families, along with larger systems of kinship and marriage. The wide web of kinship—as vital in daily life in nonindustrial societies as work outside the home is in our own—has become an essential part of anthropology because of its importance to the people we study. We are ready to take a closer look at the systems of kinship and marriage that have organized human life for much of our history.

Ethnographers quickly recognize social divisions, or groups, within any society they study. They learn about significant groups by observing their activities and membership. Often people live in the same village or neighborhood, or

family A group of people (e.g., parents, children, siblings, grandparents, grandchildren, uncles, aunts, nephews, nieces, cousins, spouses, siblings-in-law, parents-in-law, children-in-law) who are considered to be related in some way, such as by "blood" (common ancestry or descent) or marriage.

work, socialize, or celebrate together because they are related in some way. A significant kin group might consist of descendants of the same grandfather. These people live in neighboring houses, farm adjoining fields, and help one another in daily tasks. Groups based on other kin links get together less often in that society (see Strathern and Stewart 2010).

The nuclear family is one kind of kin group that is widespread in human societies. Other kin groups include extended families (families consisting of three or more generations) and descent groups—lineages and clans. Much of kinship is *culturally constructed,* that is, based on learning and variable from culture to culture (McKinnon 2005; Schneider 1967). Different societies have different kinds of families, households, kin groups, marriage customs, and living arrangements.

Consider the term *family,* which is basic, *familiar* (so much so it even shares its root with *familiar*), and difficult to define in a way that applies to all cultures. A **family** is a group of people (e.g., parents, children, siblings, grandparents, grandchildren, uncles, aunts, nephews, nieces, cousins, spouses, siblings-in-law, parents-in-law, children-in-law) who are considered to be related in some way, such as by "blood" (common ancestry or descent) or marriage. Some families, such as the nuclear family,

This polygynous family (a man with multiple wives) in Mali, West Africa, displays their normal weekly diet on the roof of their mud-brick home. Ethnographers have studied many family types besides the nuclear family—the traditional American ideal.

CULTURE THINK

How strong is your extended family support system, compared with that of your best friend, roommate, or romantic partner? Write down the names of people in your extended family that you consider to be in your support system. How are they related to you? Are there any nonkin who play the role of kin in your life?

are residentially based; its members live together. Others are not; they live apart but come together for family reunions of various sorts from time to time.

Consider a striking contrast between the United States and Brazil, the two most populous countries of the Western Hemisphere, in the meaning and role of family. American adults usually define their family as consisting of their spouse and children. When middle-class Brazilians talk about their family *(família)*, they mean their parents, siblings, aunts, uncles, grandparents, and cousins. Later they add their children, but rarely the husband or wife, who has his or her own family. The children are shared by the two families. Because middle-class Americans typically lack an extended family support system, marriage assumes more importance. The husband–wife relationship is supposed to take precedence over either spouse's relationship with his or her own parents. This places a significant strain on North American marriages.

Living in a less mobile society, Brazilians stay in closer face-to-face contact with their relatives, including members of the extended family, than North Americans do. Residents of Rio de Janeiro and São Paulo, two of South America's largest cities, are reluctant to leave those urban centers to live away from family and friends. Brazilians find it hard to imagine, and unpleasant to live in, social worlds without relatives. Contrast this with a characteristic American theme: learning to live with strangers.

NUCLEAR AND EXTENDED FAMILIES

A nuclear family is *impermanent;* it lasts only as long as the parents and children remain together. Most people belong to at least two nuclear families at different times in their lives. They are born into a family consisting of their parents and siblings. When they reach adulthood, they may marry and establish a nuclear family that includes the spouse and eventually children. Since most societies permit divorce, some people establish more than one family through marriage.

Anthropologists distinguish between the **family of orientation** (the family in which one is born and grows up) and the **family of procreation** (formed when one marries and has children). From the individual's point of view, the critical relationships are with parents and siblings in the family of orientation and with spouse and children in the family of procreation. In Brazil, as we just saw, the family of orientation predominates, whereas in the United States it is the family of procreation.

In most societies, relations with nuclear family members (parents, siblings, and children) take precedence over relations with other kin. Nuclear family organization is very widespread but not universal, and its significance in society differs greatly from one place to another. In a few societies, such as the classic Nayar case described a little later in the chapter, nuclear families are rare or nonexistent. In others, the nuclear family plays no special role in social life. Other social units—most notably descent groups and extended families—can assume many of the functions otherwise associated with the nuclear family.

> **family of orientation** Nuclear family in which one is born and grows up.
>
> **family of procreation** Nuclear family established when one marries and has children.

Consider an example from the former Yugoslavia. Traditionally, among the Muslims of western Bosnia, nuclear families lacked autonomy (Lockwood 1975). Several such families lived in an extended family household called a *zadruga*. The zadruga was headed by a male household head and his wife, the senior woman. It included married sons and their wives and children, and unmarried sons and daughters. Each nuclear family had a sleeping room, decorated and partly furnished from the bride's trousseau. Zadruga members shared possessions, however—even clothing and trousseau items. Such a residential unit is known as a *patrilocal* extended family because each couple resides in the husband's father's household after marriage.

The zadruga took precedence over its component units. There were three successive meal settings—for men, women, and children, respectively. Traditionally, all children over the age of twelve slept together in boys' or girls' rooms. When a woman wished to visit another village, she sought the permission of the male zadruga head. Although men usually felt closer to their own children than to those of their brothers, they were obliged to treat them equally. Children were disciplined by any adult in the household. When a nuclear family broke up, children under age seven went with the mother. Older children could choose between their parents. Children were considered part of the household where they were born even if their mother left. One widow who remarried had to leave her five children, all over the age of seven, in their father's zadruga, now headed by his brother.

neolocality Postmarital residence pattern in which a couple establishes a new place of residence rather than living with or near either set of parents.

extended family household Expanded household including three or more generations.

Another example of an alternative to the nuclear family is provided by the Nayar (or Nair), a large and powerful caste on the Malabar Coast of southern India (Gough 1959; Shivaram 1996). Their traditional kinship system was matrilineal (descent traced only through females). Nayar lived in matrilineal extended family compounds called *tarawads*—a residential complex with several buildings, its own temple, granary, water well, orchards, gardens, and land holdings. Headed by a senior woman, assisted by her brother, the tarawad housed her siblings, sisters' children, and other *matrikin*—matrilineal relatives.

Traditional Nayar marriage seems to have been hardly more than a formality: a kind of coming-of-age ritual. A young woman would go through a marriage ceremony with a man, after which they might spend a few days together at her tarawad. Then the man would return to his own tarawad, where he lived with his sisters, aunts, and other matrikin. Nayar men belonged to a warrior class, who left home regularly for military expeditions, returning permanently to their tarawad on retirement. Nayar women could have multiple sexual partners. Children became members of the mother's tarawad; they were not considered to be relatives of their biological father. Indeed, many Nayar children didn't even know who their biological father (genitor) was. Child care was the responsibility of the tarawad. Nayar society therefore reproduced itself biologically without the nuclear family.

INDUSTRIALISM AND FAMILY ORGANIZATION

For many Americans and Canadians, the nuclear family is the only well-defined kin group. Family isolation arises from geographic mobility, which is associated with industrialism, so that a nuclear family focus is characteristic of many modern nations. Born into a family of orientation, North Americans leave home for college or work, and the break with parents is under way. Selling our labor on the market, we often move to places where jobs are available. Eventually most North Americans marry and start a family of procreation.

Many married couples live hundreds of miles from their parents. Their jobs have determined where they live. Such a postmarital residence pattern is **neolocality:** Married couples are expected to establish a new place of residence—a "home of their own." Among middle-class North Americans, neolocal residence is both a cultural preference and a statistical norm. Most middle-class Americans eventually establish households and nuclear families of their own.

There are significant differences between middle-class and poorer North Americans. For example, in the lower class, the incidence of expanded family households (those that include nonnuclear relatives) is greater than it is in the middle class. When an *expanded family household* includes three or more generations, it is an **extended family household,** such as the zadruga. Another type of expanded family is the *collateral household,* which includes siblings and their spouses and children.

The higher proportion of expanded family households among poorer Americans has been explained as an adaptation to poverty (Stack 1975). Unable to survive economically as nuclear family units, relatives band together in an expanded household and pool their resources. Adaptation to poverty causes kinship values and attitudes to diverge from middle-class norms. Thus, when North Americans raised in poverty achieve financial success, they often feel

Unable to survive economically as nuclear family units, relatives may band together in an expanded family household and pool their resources. This photo, taken in 2002 in Munich, Germany, shows German Roma, or Gypsies. Together with her children and grandchildren, this grandmother resides in an expanded family household.

In their book *Media and Middle-Class Moms: Images and Realities of Work and Family,* Lara Descartes and Conrad Kottak point out that, contrary to popular belief, it is the 1980s—not the 1950s—that best qualifies as the golden decade of the TV family. Not only did such family-oriented programs as *The Cosby Show* and *Family Ties* dominate Nielsen's top ten, there also was a revival of interest in earlier family shows. The now iconic series *Leave It to Beaver,* for example, never made it into even the Nielsen top thirty shows during its original broadcast years, 1957–1963. In the mid-1980s, *Beaver* reappeared in syndication, in a reunion telemovie, and in a sequel series. Idealized media representations of traditional nuclear families increased in tandem with the subversion of that structure by socioeconomic fact, as the divorce rate rose and more and more women joined the workforce. Watch an episode of the contemporary family-oriented sitcom *Modern Family* (above). Use the kinship symbols (e.g., triangles and circles) introduced in this chapter to diagram the links between the main characters in *Modern Family.*

joining men in the cash workforce. This often removes them from their family of orientation while making it more economically feasible to delay marriage. Furthermore, job demands compete with romantic attachments. The median age at first marriage for American women rose from twenty-one years in 1970 to twenty-six in 2011. For men the comparable ages were twenty-three and twenty-nine (U.S. Census Bureau 2012).

Also, the U.S. divorce rate has risen, so that divorced Americans are much more common today than they were in 1970. Between 1970 and 2010 the number of divorced Americans more than quintupled—23.7 million in 2010 versus 4.3 million in 1970. (Note, however, that each divorce creates two divorced people.) The illustration on page 129 shows the ratio of divorces to marriages in the United States for selected years between 1950 and 2010. A major jump in the divorce rate took place between 1960 and 1980. Over those two decades the ratio of divorces to marriage doubled. Then, between 1980 and 2000, the ratio hovered around 50 percent. That is, each year there were about half as many new divorces as there were new marriages. Since 2000 the rate has drifted up, to 55 percent in 2010.

The rate of growth in single-parent households also has outstripped population growth, almost tripling from fewer than 4 million in 1970 to 10.5 million in 2010. (The overall American population in 2010 was 1.5 times its size in 1970.) The percentage (23.1 percent) of children living in fatherless (mother-headed, no resident dad) households in 2010 was more than twice the 1970 rate, while the percentage (3.4 percent) in motherless (father-headed, no resident mom) homes increased fourfold (*Statistical Abstract of the United States 2012*). Census data also reveal that ever since 2005, more American women are now living without a husband than with one. Compare the 51 percent of American women living without a spouse in 2005 with 49 percent in 2000 and a mere 35 percent in 1950 (Roberts et al. 2007). To be sure, contemporary Americans maintain social

obligated to provide financial help to a wide circle of less fortunate relatives (see Willie 2003).

CHANGES IN NORTH AMERICAN KINSHIP

Although the nuclear family remains a cultural ideal for many Americans, the "Changes in Family and Household Organization" chart on page 128 shows that nuclear families accounted for only 21 percent of American households in 2010 (see also "Households by Type," also on page 128). Other domestic arrangements now outnumber the "traditional" American household almost five to one. There are several reasons for this changing household composition. Women increasingly are

CULTURETHINK

The average age of first marriage in 2011 was 26.5 for women and 28.7 for men. Consider recently married people you know: How much (if at all) do they vary from these figures?

Changes in Family and Household Organization in the United States, 1970 vs. 2010

	1970 Total households 63 million 3.1 people per household	**2010** Total households 118 million 2.6 people per household
Married couples living with children	40%	21%
Family households	81%	67%
Households with five or more people	21%	10%
People living alone	17%	27%
Percentage of single-mother families	5%	11%
Percentage of single-father families	0%	3%
Households with own children under 18	45%	30%

Sources: From U.S. Census data in J. M. Fields, "America's Families and Living Arrangements: 2003," *Current Population Reports*, p.20–553, November 2004, http://www.census.gov/prod/2004pubs/p20-553.pdf, p. 4; J. M. Fields and L. M. Casper, "America's Families and Living Arrangements: Population Characteristics, 2000," *Current Population Reports*, p.20–537, June 2001, http://www.census.gov/prod/2001pubs/p20-537.pdf; *Statistical Abstract of the United States 2012*, Tables 59, 62, http://www.census.gov/prod/2011pubs/12statab/pop.pdf.

Households by Type: Selected Years, 1970–2010

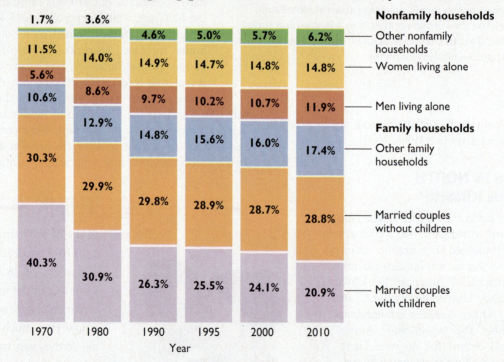

Nonfamily households
- Other nonfamily households
- Women living alone
- Men living alone

Family households
- Other family households
- Married couples without children
- Married couples with children

Year	1970	1980	1990	1995	2000	2010
Other nonfamily households	1.7%	3.6%	4.6%	5.0%	5.7%	6.2%
Women living alone	11.5%	14.0%	14.9%	14.7%	14.8%	14.8%
Men living alone	5.6% / 10.6%	8.6%	9.7%	10.2%	10.7%	11.9%
Other family households		12.9%	14.8%	15.6%	16.0%	17.4%
Married couples without children	30.3%	29.9%	29.8%	28.9%	28.7%	28.8%
Married couples with children	40.3%	30.9%	26.3%	25.5%	24.1%	20.9%

Sources: J. M. Fields, "America's Families and Living Arrangements: 2003," *Current Population Reports*, P20–553. November 2004, http://www.census.gov/prod2004pubs/p20-553.pdf, p. 4; *Statistical Abstract of the United States 2012*, Tables 59, 62, http://www.census.gov/prod/2011pubs/12statab/pop.pdf.

Ratio of Divorces to Marriages per 1,000 U.S. Population, Selected Years, 1950–2010

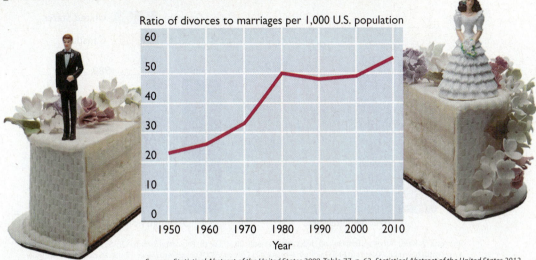

Ratio of divorces to marriages per 1,000 U.S. population

	1950	1960	1970	1980	1990	2000	2010

Year

Source: *Statistical Abstract of the United States 2009*, Table 77, p. 63, *Statistical Abstract of the United States 2012*, Table 132, http://www.census.gov/prod/2011pubs/12statab/pop.pdf.

lives through work, friendship, sports, clubs, religion, and organized social activities. However, the growing isolation from kin that these figures suggest may well be unprecedented in human history.

The "Households and Family Size" chart on page 130 documents similar changes in family and household size in the United States and Canada between 1980 and 2010. Those figures confirm a general trend toward smaller families and living units in North America. This trend is also detectable in Western Europe and other industrial nations.

Immigrants often are shocked by what they perceive as weak kinship bonds and lack of proper respect for

The American family has many forms. Here, a single mother (by choice) bakes cupcakes with her twin daughters in Brooklyn, New York.

family in contemporary North America. In fact, most of the people whom middle-class North Americans see every day are either nonrelatives or members of the nuclear family. On the other hand, Stack's (1975) study of welfare-dependent families in a ghetto area of a midwestern city shows that regular sharing with nonnuclear relatives is an important strategy that the urban poor use to adapt to poverty.

THE FAMILY AMONG FORAGERS

Foraging societies are far removed from industrial nations in terms of social complexity, but they feature geographic mobility, which is associated with nomadic or seminomadic hunting and gathering. Here again, the nuclear family often is the most significant kin group, although in no foraging society is it the only group based on kinship. The two basic social units of traditional foraging societies are the nuclear family and the band.

Unlike middle-class couples in industrial nations, foragers don't usually reside neolocally. Instead, they join a band in which either the husband or the wife has relatives. However, couples and families may move from one band to another several times. Although nuclear families are ultimately as impermanent among foragers

CULTURETHINK

Think of the nuclear family as an economic adaptation. What features do foragers and people living in industrial nations have in common that make the nuclear family practical? How is this different from nonindustrial food-producing societies?

Household and Family Size in the United States and Canada, 1980 vs. 2010

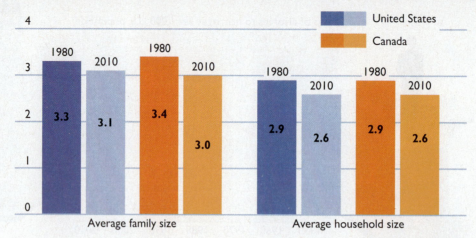

Sources: J. M. Fields, "America's Families and Living Arrangements: 2003," *Current Population Reports,* P20–553. November 2004, http://www.census.gov/prod2004pubs/p20-553.pdf, pp. 3–4; *Statistics Canada,* 2006 Census, http://www12.statcan.ca/english/census06/data/topics/, http://www40.statcan.ca/101/cst01/famil532. U.S. Census Bureau, *Statistical Abstract of the United States 2012,* Table 62.

as they are in any other society, they usually are more stable than bands.

Many foraging societies lacked year-round band organization. The Native American Shoshone of Utah and Nevada provide an example. The resources available to the Shoshone were so meager that for most of the year families traveled alone through the countryside hunting and gathering. In certain seasons families assembled to hunt cooperatively as a band, but after just a few months together they dispersed.

In neither industrial nor foraging economies are people permanently tied to the land. The mobility and the emphasis on small, economically self-sufficient family units promote the nuclear family as a basic kin group in both types of societies.

> **descent group** A permanent social unit whose members claim common ancestry; fundamental to tribal society.
>
> **patrilineal descent** Unilineal descent rule in which people join the father's group automatically at birth and stay members throughout life.

Got IT? Can you explain key features of nuclear families, considering both industrial and foraging societies?

>> Descent

We've seen that the nuclear family is important in industrial nations and among foragers. The analogous group among nonindustrial food producers is the descent group. A **descent group** is a *permanent* social unit whose members claim common ancestry. Descent group members believe they all descend from those common ancestors. The group endures even though its membership changes, as members are born and die, move in and move

out. Often, descent-group membership is determined at birth and is lifelong. In this case, it is an ascribed status.

CHARACTERISTICS OF DESCENT GROUPS

Descent groups frequently are exogamous (members seek their mates from other descent groups). Two common rules serve to admit certain people as descent-group members while excluding others. With a rule of **patrilineal descent,**

A Patrilineage Five Generations Deep

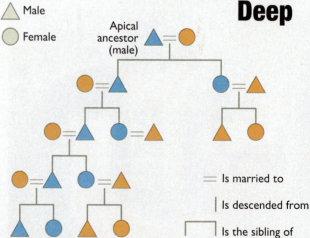

△ Male
○ Female

Apical ancestor (male)

═ Is married to
│ Is descended from
⎿ Is the sibling of

Lineages are based on demonstrated descent from an apical ancestor. With patrilineal descent, children of the group's men (blue) are included as descent-group members. Children of the group's women are excluded; they belong to their father's patrilineage.

A Matrilineage Five Generations Deep

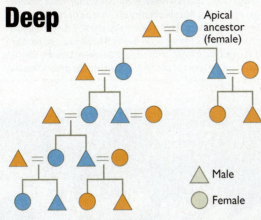

Apical ancestor (female)

△ Male

○ Female

Matrilineages are based on demonstrated descent from a female ancestor. Only the children of the group's women (blue) belong to the matrilineage. The children of the group's men are excluded; they belong to their mother's matrilineage.

STUDY TIP

Two important ways of organizing kin are the nuclear family and the descent group. The *nuclear family* is impermanent, includes only parents and children, and is common in foraging and industrial societies. The *descent group,* which is common among nonindustrial food producers (horticulturalists, agriculturalists, and pastoralists), is permanent and includes multiple generations.

people automatically have lifetime membership in their father's group. The children of the group's men join the group, but the children of the group's women are excluded. With **matrilineal descent,** people join the mother's group automatically at birth and stay members throughout life. Matrilineal descent groups therefore include only the children of the group's women.

Matrilineal and patrilineal descent are types of **unilineal descent.** This means the descent rule uses one line only, either the male or the female line. Patrilineal descent is much more common than matrilineal descent. In a sample of 564 societies (Murdock 1957), about three times as many were found to be patrilineal (247 to 84).

Descent groups may be **lineages** or **clans.** Common to both is the belief that members descend from the same *apical ancestor,* the person who stands at the apex, or top, of the common genealogy. For example, Adam and Eve are the apical ancestors of the biblical Jews, and, according to the Bible, of all humanity. Since Eve is said to have come from Adam's rib, Adam stands as the original apical ancestor for the patrilineal genealogy laid out in the Bible.

How do lineages and clans differ? A lineage uses *demonstrated descent.* Members recite the names of their forebears from the apical ancestor through the present. (This doesn't mean their recitations are accurate, only that lineage members think they are.) In the Bible the litany of men who "begat" other men is a demonstration of genealogical descent for a large patrilineage that ultimately includes Jews and Arabs (who share Abraham as their last common apical ancestor).

Unlike lineages, clans use *stipulated descent.* Clan members merely say they descend from the apical ancestor, without trying to trace the actual genealogical links. The Betsileo of Madagascar have both clans

and lineages. Descent may be demonstrated for the most recent eight to ten generations, then stipulated for the more remote past—sometimes with mermaids and vaguely defined foreign royalty mentioned among the founders (Kottak 1980). Like the Betsileo, many societies have both lineages and clans. In such a case, clans have more members and cover a larger geographical area than lineages do. Sometimes a clan's apical ancestor is not a human at all but an animal or plant (called a *totem*).

The economic types that usually have descent group organization are horticulture, pastoralism, and agriculture. Such societies tend to have several descent groups. Any one of them may be confined to a single village, but usually they span more than one village. Two or more local branches of different descent groups may live in the same village. Descent groups in the same village or different villages may establish alliances through frequent intermarriage.

matrilineal descent Unilineal descent rule in which people join the mother's group automatically at birth and stay members throughout life.

unilineal descent Matrilineal or patrilineal descent.

lineage Unilineal descent group based on demonstrated descent.

clan Unilineal descent group based on stipulated descent.

LINEAGES, CLANS, AND RESIDENCE RULES

As we've seen, descent groups, unlike families, are permanent and enduring units, with new members added in every generation. Members have access to the lineage estate, where some of them must live, in order to benefit from and manage that estate across the generations. An easy way to keep members at home is to have a rule about who belongs to the descent group and where they should live after they get married. Patrilineal and matrilineal descent, and the postmarital residence rules that usually accompany them, ensure that about half the people born in each generation will spend their lives on the ancestral estate.

Most societies have a prevailing opinion about where couples should live after they marry; this is called a postmarital residence rule. A common rule is patrilocality: The couple lives with the husband's relatives, so that the children grow up in their father's community. The image at left shows a twelve-year-old Muslim bride (veiled in pink) in the West African country of Guinea Bissau. On the last day of her three-day wedding ceremony, she will collect laundry from her husband's family, wash it with her friends, and be taken to his village on a bicycle. In the image below, in Lendak, Slovakia, women transport part of the bride's dowry to the groom's house.

patrilocality Customary residence with the husband's relatives after marriage, so that children grow up in their father's community.

matrilocality Customary residence with the wife's relatives after marriage, so that children grow up in their mother's community.

Patrilocality is the rule that when a couple marries, it moves to the husband's community, so that their children will grow up in their father's village. Patrilocality is associated with patrilineal descent. This makes sense. If the group's male members are expected to exercise their rights in the ancestral estate, it's a good idea to raise them on that estate and to keep them there after they marry. This can be done by having wives move to the husband's village, rather than vice versa.

A less common postmarital residence rule, often associated with matrilineal descent, is **matrilocality:** Married couples live in the wife's community, and their children grow up in their mother's village. This rule keeps related women together (see Stone 2010). Together, patrilocality and matrilocality are known as *unilocal* rules of postmarital residence.

Got IT? Can you identify key features of descent groups, noting how they contrast with nuclear families?

>> Marriage

"Love and marriage," "marriage and the family": These familiar phrases show how we link the romantic love of two individuals to marriage, and how we link marriage to reproduction and family creation. But marriage is an institution with significant roles and functions in addition to reproduction. What is marriage, anyway?

No definition of marriage is broad enough to apply easily to all societies and situations. A commonly quoted definition comes from *Notes and Queries on Anthropology:*

> Marriage is a union between a man and a woman such that the children born to the woman are recognized as legitimate offspring of both partners. (Royal Anthropological Institute 1951, p. 111)

This definition isn't valid universally for several reasons. In many societies, marriages unite more than two spouses. Here we speak of *plural marriages,* as when a man weds two (or more) women, or a woman weds a group of brothers—an arrangement called *fraternal polyandry* that is characteristic of certain Himalayan cultures. In the Brazilian community of Arembepe, people can choose among various forms of marital union. Most people live in long-term "common-law" domestic partnerships that are not legally sanctioned. Some have civil marriages, which

Is the *pater* (socially recognized father) always the *genitor* (biological father) in your experience? Is the *mater* (socially recognized mother) always the biological mother? What difference does this make socially?

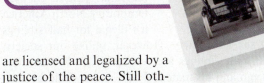

are licensed and legalized by a justice of the peace. Still others go through religious ceremonies, so they are united in "holy matrimony," although not legally. And some have both civil and religious ties. The different forms of union permit someone to have multiple spouses (e.g., one common-law, one civil, one religious) without ever getting divorced.

Some societies recognize various kinds of same-sex marriages. In Sudan, a Nuer woman could marry a woman if her father had only daughters but no male heirs, who are necessary if his patrilineage is to survive. He might ask his daughter to stand as a son in order to take a bride. This daughter would become the socially recognized husband of another woman (the wife). This was a symbolic and social relationship rather than a sexual one. The "wife" had sex with a man or men (whom her female "husband" had to approve) until she got pregnant. The children born to the wife were accepted as the offspring of both the female husband and the wife. Although the female husband was not the actual *genitor* (the biological father) of the children, she was their *pater*, or socially recognized father. What's important in this Nuer case is *social* rather than *biological paternity*. We see again how kinship is socially constructed. The bride's children were considered the legitimate offspring of her female husband, who was biologically a woman but socially a man, and the descent line continued.

EXOGAMY AND INCEST

In nonindustrial societies, a person's social world includes two main categories—friends and strangers. Strangers are potential or actual enemies. Marriage is one of the primary ways of converting strangers into friends, of creating and maintaining personal and political alliances, relationships of affinity. **Exogamy,** the custom and practice of seeking a mate outside one's own group, has adaptive value because it links people into a wider social network that nurtures, helps,

and protects them in times of need. Incest restrictions (prohibitions on sex with relatives) reinforce exogamy by pushing people to seek their mates outside the local group. Most societies discourage sexual contact involving close relatives, especially members of the same nuclear family.

exogamy Mating or marriage outside one's kin group; a cultural universal.

incest Sexual relations with a close relative.

Incest refers to sexual contact with a relative, but cultures define their kin, and thus incest, differently. In other words, incest, like kinship, is socially constructed. Marriage entails sex, so one can marry only someone with whom sex is permitted. Besides kinship, other factors that restrict sexual access include age and the range of sexual acts that are socially tolerated. In the United States the age of consent for sexual activity varies by state between 16 and 18. It is 16 in Canada and 14 in Italy. Cultures and governments routinely try to regulate sexual activity. Until 2003, when the Supreme Court struck down sodomy laws, several states used them mainly against gay men who engaged in nonreproductive sex. Most people probably don't know what is legal and what isn't in a given state or country and can get in trouble as a result (e.g., when an 18-year-old has sex with a 17-year-old).

A German bride and African groom marry in Copenhagen, Denmark, in 2010. International marriages are a form of exogamy.

Sex is contested. That is, people in the same culture can disagree and argue about the definition and propriety of particular sexual acts. President Bill Clinton famously asserted, "I did not have sexual relations with that woman." Should sexual practices other than heterosexual coitus (oral sex, for example) be considered "sexual relations"? With respect to incest restrictions, what, if any, kind of sexual contact is permissible between a teenager and his or her same-sex or opposite-sex cousin of comparable age? How about step siblings, half siblings, and siblings? Some U.S. states permit marriage, and therefore sex, with first cousins, while others ban it. The social construction of kinship, and of incest, is far from simple.

Let's turn from the United States to nonindustrial societies. When unilineal descent is very strongly developed, the parent who belongs to a different descent group than your own isn't considered a relative. Thus, with strict patrilineality, the mother is not a relative but a kind of in-law who has married a member of your own group—your father. With strict matrilineality, the father isn't a relative because he belongs to a different descent group.

> ## "An ounce of blood is worth more than a pound of friendship."
>
> Spanish proverb

The Lakher of Southeast Asia are strictly patrilineal (Leach 1961). Using the male ego (the reference point, the person in question) in the figure below, let's suppose that ego's father and mother get divorced. Each remarries and has a daughter by a second marriage. A Lakher always belongs to his or her father's group, all of whose members (one's agnates, or patrikin) are considered relatives, because they belong to the same descent group. Ego can't have sex with or marry his father's daughter by the second marriage, just as in contemporary North America it's illegal for half siblings to have sex and marry. However, unlike our society, where all half siblings are restricted, sex between our Lakher ego and his maternal half sister would be nonincestuous. She isn't ego's relative because she belongs to her own father's descent group rather than ego's. The Lakher illustrate very well that definitions of relatives, and therefore of incest, vary from culture to culture.

Incest Happens We know from primate research that adolescent males (among monkeys) or females (among apes) often move away from the group in which they were born (Rodseth et al. 1991). This emigration reduces the frequency of incestuous unions, but it doesn't eliminate them. DNA testing of wild chimps has confirmed incestuous unions between adult sons and their mothers, who reside in the same group. Human behavior with respect to mating with close relatives may express a generalized primate tendency, in which we see both urges and avoidance.

A cross-cultural study of 87 societies (Meigs and Barlow 2002) suggested that incest occurred in several of them. It's not clear, however, whether the authors of the study controlled for the social construction of incest. They report, for example, that incest occurs among the Yanomami, but they may be considering cross-cousin marriage to be incestuous, when it is not so considered by the Yanomami. Indeed it is the preferred form of marriage, not just for the Yanomami but in many tribal societies. Another society in their sample is the Ashanti, for whom the ethnographer Meyer Fortes reports "In the old days it [incest] was punished by death.

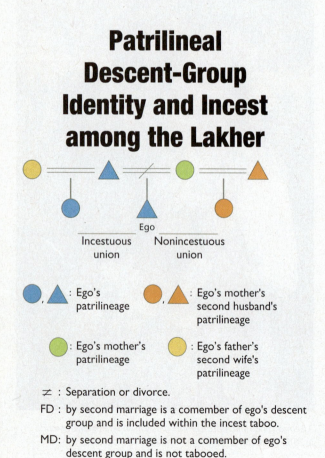

Patrilineal Descent-Group Identity and Incest among the Lakher

Ego

Incestuous union

Nonincestuous union

●, ▲ : Ego's patrilineage

●, ▲ : Ego's mother's second husband's patrilineage

● : Ego's mother's patrilineage

● : Ego's father's second wife's patrilineage

≠ : Separation or divorce.

FD : by second marriage is a comember of ego's descent group and is included within the incest taboo.

MD : by second marriage is not a comember of ego's descent group and is not tabooed.

CULTURE THINK

We tend to think of incest as wrong because of the potential for genetic defects due to inbreeding. Many states, however, consider it incestuous to have sexual relations with categories of relatives who are not biologically related, such as stepparents and siblings by adoption. Why are these considered wrong?

Nowadays the culprits are heavily fined" (Fortes 1950, p. 257). This suggests that there really were violations of Ashanti incest restrictions, and that such violations were, and still are, punished. More strikingly, among 24 Ojibwa individuals from whom he obtained information about incest, A. Irving Hallowell found 8 cases of parent-child incest and 10 cases of brother-sister incest (Hallowell 1955, pp. 294–95). Because reported cases of actual parent-child and sibling incest are rare in the ethnographic literature, questions about the possibility of social construction arise here, too. In many cultures, including the Ojibwa, people use the same terms for their mother and their aunt, their father and their uncle, and their cousins and siblings. Could the siblings in the Ojibwa case actually have been cousins; and the parents and children, uncles and nieces?

In ancient Egypt, sibling marriage apparently was allowed both for royalty and commoners, in some districts at least. Based on official census records from Roman Egypt (first to third centuries C.E.), 24 percent of all documented marriages in the Arsinoites district were between "brothers" and "sisters." The rates were 37 percent for the city of Arsinoe and 19 percent for the surrounding villages. These figures are much higher than any other documented levels of inbreeding among humans (Scheidel 1997). Again one wonders if the relatives involved were actually as close biologically as the kin terms would imply.

According to Anna Meigs and Kathleen Barlow (2002), for Western societies with nuclear family organization, "father-daughter incest" is much more common with stepfathers than with biological fathers. But is it really incest if they aren't biological relatives? American culture is unclear on this matter. Incest also happens with biological fathers, especially those who were absent or did little caretaking of their daughters in childhood (Williams and Finkelhor 1995). In a carefully designed study, Linda M. Williams and David Finkelhor (1995) found father-daughter incest to be least likely when there was substantial paternal parenting of daughters. This experience enhanced the father's parenting skills and his feelings of nurturance, protectiveness, and identification with his daughter, thus reducing the chance of incest.

A century ago, early anthropologists speculated that incest restrictions reflect an instinctive horror of mating with close relatives (Hobhouse 1915; Lowie 1920/1961). But why, one wonders, if humans really do have an instinctive aversion to incest, would formal restrictions be necessary? No one would want to have sexual contact with a relative. Yet, as social workers, judges, psychiatrists, and psychologists are well aware, incest is more common than we might suppose.

> **endogamy** Marriage between people of the same social group.

ENDOGAMY

The practice of exogamy pushes social organization outward, establishing and preserving alliances among groups. In contrast, rules of **endogamy** dictate mating or marriage within a group to which one belongs. Endogamic rules are less common but are still familiar to anthropologists. Indeed, most cultures are endogamous units, although they usually do not need a formal rule requiring people to marry someone from their own society. In our own society, classes and ethnic groups are quasi-endogamous groups. Members of an ethnic or religious group often want their children to marry within that group, although many of them do not do so. The outmarriage rate varies among such groups, with some more committed to endogamy than others.

Caste An extreme example of endogamy is India's caste system, which was formally abolished in 1949, although its structure and effects linger. Castes are stratified groups in which membership is ascribed at birth and is lifelong. Indian castes are grouped into five major categories, or *varna.* Each is ranked relative to the other four, and these categories extend throughout India. Each varna includes a large number of castes *(jati),* each of which includes people within a region who may intermarry. All the jati in a single varna in a given region are ranked, just as the varna themselves are ranked.

Occupational specialization often sets off one caste from another. A community may include castes of agricultural workers, merchants, artisans, priests, and sweepers. The untouchable varna, found throughout India, includes castes whose ancestry, ritual status, and occupations are considered so impure that higher-caste people hold even casual contact with untouchables to be defiling.

The belief that intercaste sexual unions lead to ritual impurity for the higher-caste partner has been important in maintaining endogamy. A man who has sex with a lower-caste woman can restore his purity with a bath and a prayer. A woman who has intercourse with a man of a lower caste has no such recourse. Her

> "Of all the peoples whom I have studied, from city dwellers to cliff dwellers, I always find that at least 50 percent would prefer to have at least one jungle between themselves and their mothers-in-law."
>
> Margaret Mead

This 2008 San Francisco wedding immediately followed a state supreme court ruling allowing same-sex marriage. Then came California Proposition 8, a state constitutional amendment banning the practice. Proposition 8 was voided by an Appeals Court judge in 2010.

defilement cannot be undone. Because the women have the babies, these differences protect the purity of the caste line, ensuring the pure ancestry of high-caste children. Although Indian castes are endogamous groups, many of them are internally subdivided into exogamous lineages. Traditionally this meant that Indians had to marry a member of another descent group from the same caste. This shows that rules of exogamy and endogamy can coexist in the same society.

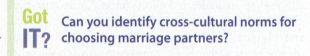

Got IT? Can you identify cross-cultural norms for choosing marriage partners?

>> Marital Rights and Same-Sex Marriage

The British anthropologist Edmund Leach (1955) observed that, depending on the society, several kinds of rights are allocated by marriage. According to Leach, marriage can, but doesn't always, accomplish the following:

- Establish the legal father of a woman's children and the legal mother of a man's
- Give either or both spouses a monopoly in the sexuality of the other
- Give either or both spouses rights to the labor of the other
- Give either or both spouses rights over the other's property

- Establish a joint fund of property—a partnership—for the benefit of the children
- Establish a socially significant "relationship of affinity" between spouses and their relatives

The discussion of same-sex marriage that follows will serve to illustrate the six rights just listed by seeing what happens in their absence (see also Stone 2004). What if same-sex marriages, which by and large remain illegal in the United States, were legal? Could a same-sex marriage establish legal parentage of children born to one or both partners after the partnership is formed? In the case of a different-sex marriage, children born to the wife after the marriage takes place usually are defined legally as her husband's regardless of whether he is the genitor.

Nowadays, DNA testing makes it possible to establish paternity, just as modern reproductive technology makes it possible for a lesbian couple to have one or both partners artificially inseminated (see Levine 2008 and the 2010 movie *The Kids Are All Right*). When same-sex marriage is legal, the social construction of kinship easily can make both partners parents. If a Nuer woman married to a woman can be the pater of a child she did not give birth to, why can't two lesbians be the *maters* (socially recognized mothers) of a child one of them did not father? And if a married different-sex couple can adopt a child and have it be theirs through the social and legal construction of kinship, the same logic could be applied to a gay male or lesbian couple.

Continuing with Leach's list of the rights transmitted by marriage, same-sex marriage certainly could give each spouse rights to the sexuality of the other. Same-sex marriages, as forms of monogamous commitment, have been

endorsed by representatives of many religions, including Unitarians, Quakers (the Society of Friends), and reform Jewish synagogues (Eskridge 1996). In June 2003 a court ruling established same-sex marriages as legal in the province of Ontario, Canada. On June 28, 2005, Canada's House of Commons voted to guarantee full marriage rights to same-sex couples throughout that nation. On May 9, 2012, President Barack Obama (like British Prime Minister David Cameron before him) announced his support of same-sex marriage. As of this writing, six U.S. states and the District of Columbia allow same-sex marriage. Those states are Massachusetts, Connecticut, Iowa, Vermont, New Hampshire, and New York. In 2012 Washington and Maryland passed laws legalizing same-sex marriage, subject to later voter approval. As of May 2012, with the passage of North Carolina's gay marriage ban, 12 U.S. states prohibit same-sex marriage by statute; and 30 states, by the state's constitution.

Legal same-sex marriages can easily give each spouse rights to the other spouse's labor and its products. Some societies allow marriage between members of the same biological sex. Several Native American groups had figures known as *berdaches*. These were biological men who assumed many of the mannerisms, behavior patterns, and tasks of women. Sometimes berdaches married men, who shared the products of their labor from hunting and traditional male roles, as the berdache fulfilled the traditional wifely role. Also, in some Native American cultures, a marriage of a "manly-hearted woman" to another woman brought the traditional male–female division of labor to their household. The manly woman hunted and did other male tasks, while the wife filled the traditional female role.

There's no logical reason why same-sex marriage cannot give spouses rights over the other's property. But in the United States, the same inheritance rights that apply to male–female couples usually do not apply to same-sex couples. For instance, even in the absence of a will, property can pass to a widow or a widower without going through probate. The wife or husband pays no inheritance tax. This benefit is not available to gay men and lesbians (Weston 1991).

What about Leach's fifth right—to establish a joint fund of property—to benefit the children? Here again, gay and lesbian couples are at a disadvantage. If there are children, property is separately, rather than jointly, transmitted. Some organizations do make staff benefits, such as health and dental insurance, available to same-sex domestic partners.

Finally, there is the matter of establishing a socially significant "relationship of affinity" between spouses and their relatives. In many societies, one of the main roles of marriage is to establish an alliance between groups, in addition to the individual bond. *Affinals* are relatives through marriage, such as a brother-in-law or mother-in-law. For same-sex couples in contemporary North America, affinal relations are problematic. In an unofficial union, terms like "daughter-in-law" and "mother-in-law" may sound strange. Many parents are suspicious of their children's sexuality and lifestyle choices and may not recognize a relationship of affinity with a child's partner of the same sex.

This discussion of same-sex marriage is intended to illustrate the different kinds of rights that typically accompany marriage, by seeing what may happen when there is a permanent pair bond without legal sanction. In just six of the United States are such unions fully legal. As we have seen, same-sex unions have been recognized in different historical and cultural settings. In certain African cultures, including the Igbo of Nigeria and the Lovedu of South Africa, women could marry other women. In situations in which women, such as prominent market women in West Africa, are able to amass property and other forms of wealth, they may take a wife. Such marriage allows the prominent woman to strengthen her social status and the economic importance of her household (Amadiume 1987).

Got IT? Can you describe social rights and functions associated with marriage cross-culturally?

>> Marriage Across Cultures

Outside industrial societies, marriage often is more a relationship between groups than one between individuals. We think of marriage as an individual matter. Although the bride and groom usually seek their parents' approval, the final choice (to live together, to marry, to divorce) lies with the couple. The idea of romantic love symbolizes this individual relationship.

In nonindustrial societies, although there can be romantic love (Goleman 1992), marriage is a group concern. People don't just take a spouse; they assume obligations to a group of in-laws. When residence is patrilocal, for example, a woman must leave the community where she was born. She faces the prospect of spending the rest of her life in her husband's village, with his relatives.

GIFTS AT MARRIAGE

In societies with descent groups, people enter marriage not alone but with the help of the descent group. Often it is customary for a substantial gift to be given before, at, or after the marriage by the husband and his kin to the wife and her kin. The BaThonga of Mozambique call such a gift **lobola,** and the custom of giving something like lobola is very widespread in patrilineal societies (Radcliffe-Brown 1952). This gift compensates the bride's group for the loss of her companionship and labor. More important, it makes the children born to the woman full members of her husband's descent group. In matrilineal societies, children are members of the mother's group, and there is no reason for a lobola-like gift.

lobola A customary gift before, at, or after marriage from the husband and his kin to the wife and her kin.

dowry Substantial gifts to husband's family from wife's group.

Another kind of marital gift, **dowry,** occurs when the bride's family or kin group provides substantial gifts when their daughter marries. For rural Greece, Ernestine Friedl (1962) has described a form of dowry in which the bride gets a wealth transfer from her mother, to serve as a kind of trust fund during her marriage. Usually, however, the dowry goes to the husband's family, and the custom is correlated with low female status. In this form of dowry, best known from India, women are perceived as burdens. When a man and his family take a wife, they expect to be compensated for the added responsibility.

Lobola-like gifts exist in many more cultures than dowry does, but the nature and quantity of transferred items differ. Among the BaThonga of Mozambique, whose name—*lobola*—I am using for this widespread custom, the gift consists of cattle. Use of livestock (usually cattle in Africa, pigs in Papua New Guinea) for lobola is common, but the number of animals given varies from society to society. We can generalize, however, that the larger the gift, the more stable the marriage. Lobola is insurance against divorce.

Imagine a patrilineal society in which a marriage requires the transfer of about twenty-five cattle from the groom's descent group to the bride's. Michael, a member of descent group A, marries Sarah from group B. His relatives help him assemble the lobola. He gets the most help from his close agnates (patrilineal relatives): his older brother, father, father's brother, and closest patrilineal cousins.

The distribution of the cattle once they reach Sarah's group mirrors the manner in which they were assembled. Sarah's father, or her oldest brother if the father is dead, receives her lobola. He keeps most of the cattle to use as lobola for his sons' marriages. However, a share also goes to everyone who will be expected to help when Sarah's brothers marry.

When Sarah's brother David gets married, many of the cattle go to a third group: C, which is David's wife's group. Thereafter, they may serve as lobola to still other groups. Men constantly use their sisters' lobola cattle to acquire their own wives. In a decade, the cattle given when Michael married Sarah will have been exchanged widely.

In such societies, marriage entails an agreement between descent groups. If Sarah and Michael try to make their marriage succeed but fail to do so, both groups may conclude that the marriage can't last. Here it becomes especially obvious that such marriages are relationships between groups as well as between individuals. If Sarah has a younger sister or niece (her older brother's daughter, for example), the concerned parties may agree to Sarah's replacement by a kinswoman.

However, incompatibility isn't the main problem that threatens marriage in societies with lobola customs. Infertility is a more important concern. If Sarah has no children, she and her group have not fulfilled their part of the marriage agreement. If the relationship is to endure, Sarah's group must furnish another woman, perhaps her younger sister, who can have children. If this happens, Sarah may choose to stay with her husband. Perhaps she will someday have a child. If she does stay on, her husband will have established a plural marriage.

Most nonindustrial food-producing societies, unlike most foraging societies and industrial nations, allow **plural marriages**, or **polygamy** (see Zeitzen 2008). There are two varieties; one is common, and the other is very rare. The more common variant is **polygyny,** in which a man has more than one wife. The rare variant is **polyandry,** in which a woman has more than one husband. If the infertile wife remains married to her husband after he has taken a substitute wife provided by her descent group, this is polygyny.

DURABLE ALLIANCES

It is possible to exemplify the group-alliance nature of marriage by examining still another common practice—continuation of marital alliances when one spouse dies.

Sororate What happens if Sarah dies young? Michael's group will ask Sarah's group for a substitute, often her sister. This custom is known as the **sororate.** If Sarah has no sister, or if all her sisters already are married, another woman from her group may be available. Michael marries her, there is no need to return the lobola, and the alliance continues.

The sororate exists in both matrilineal and patrilineal societies. In a matrilineal society with matrilocal postmarital residence, a widower may remain with his wife's group by marrying her sister or another female member of her matrilineage.

Levirate What happens if the husband dies? In many societies, the widow may marry his brother. This custom is known as the **levirate.** Like the sororate, it is a continuation marriage that maintains the alliance between descent groups, in this case by replacing the husband with another member of his group. The implications of the levirate vary with age. One study found that in African societies the levirate, although widely permitted, rarely involves cohabitation of the widow and her new husband. Furthermore, widows don't automatically marry the husband's brother just because they are allowed to. Often they prefer to make other arrangements (Potash 1986).

sororate Custom by which a widower marries the sister of the deceased wife.

levirate Custom by which a widow marries the brother of her deceased husband.

Got IT? Can you explain how customs and practices associated with marriage organize social relations cross-culturally?

Examples of the Sororate and Levirate

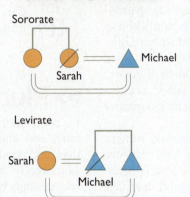

Sororate

Levirate

🟠 : Sarah's descent group

🔺 : Michael's descent group

>> Divorce

In some societies marriages may seem to go on forever, but in our own they are fairly brittle. Ease of divorce varies across cultures. What factors work for and against divorce? As we've seen, marriages that are political alliances between groups are more difficult to dissolve than are marriages that are more individual affairs, of concern mainly to the married couple and their children. A substantial lobola gift may decrease the divorce rate for individuals; replacement marriages (levirate and sororate) also work to preserve group alliances. Divorce tends to be more common in matrilineal than in patrilineal societies. When residence is matrilocal (in the wife's home village), the wife may simply send off a man with whom she's incompatible.

Among the Hopi of the American Southwest, houses were owned by matrilineal clans, with matrilocal postmarital residence. The household head was the senior woman of that household, which also included her daughters and their husbands and children. A son-in-law had no important role there; he returned to his own mother's home for his clan's social and religious activities. In this matrilineal society, women were socially and economically secure, and the divorce rate was high. Consider the Hopi of Oraibi (Orayvi) pueblo, northeastern Arizona (Levy 1992; Titiev 1992). In a study of the marital histories of 423 Oraibi women, Mischa Titiev found 35 percent to have been divorced at least once. Jerome Levy found that 31 percent of 147 adult women had been divorced and remarried at least once. For comparison, of all ever-married women in the United States, only 4 percent had been divorced in 1960, 10.7 percent in 1980, and 11.5 percent in 2004. Titiev characterizes Hopi marriages as unstable. Part

CULTURE THINK

Traditionally among the Nuer, marriages are arranged, and the groom and his group provide lobola. The Nuer also practice the levirate and sororate when one spouse dies. How does each of these illustrate the importance of marriage as an alliance between groups?

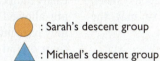

Did You Know?

One sociologist has found what he calls a "divorce divide": People with college degrees are less likely to get a divorce than those without degrees. Since the 1980s, the divorce rate has dropped for those with a college degree and risen for those without one. http://www.mercatornet.com/articles/view/the_new_divorce_divide

of this brittleness was due to conflicting loyalties to matrikin versus spouse. Most Hopi divorces appear to have been matters of personal choice. Levy generalizes that, cross-culturally, high divorce rates are correlated with a secure female economic position. In Hopi society women were secure in their home and land ownership and in the custody of their children. In addition, there were no formal barriers to divorce.

Divorce is harder in a patrilineal society, especially when substantial lobola would have to be reassembled and repaid if the marriage failed. A woman residing patrilocally (in her husband's household and community) might be reluctant to leave him. Unlike the Hopi, where the kids stay with the mother, in patrilineal, patrilocal societies the children of divorce would be expected to remain with their father, as members of his patrilineage. From the women's perspective this is a strong impediment to divorce.

plural marriage Also called **polygamy**. Marriage of a man to two or more women (**polygyny**) or marriage of a woman to two or more men (**polyandry**)—at the same time.

In contemporary Western societies, we have the idea that romantic love is necessary for a good marriage (see Ingraham 2008). When romance fails, so may the

STUDY TIP

Divorce is less common (1) when marriage involves political alliances; (2) where there is a lobola gift; (3) in patrilineal societies; (4) when women have a low economic position.

marriage. Or it may not fail, if the other rights associated with marriage, as discussed previously in this chapter, are compelling. Economic ties and obligations to children, along with other factors, such as concern about public opinion, or simple inertia, may keep marriages intact after sex, romance, or companionship fade.

Got IT? Can you assess factors that work for and against divorce in a given society?

>> Plural Marriages

In contemporary North America, where divorce is fairly easy and common, **polygamy** (marriage to more than one spouse at the same time) is against the law. Marriage in industrial nations joins individuals, and relationships between individuals can be severed more easily than can those between groups. North Americans are allowed to practice *serial monogamy:* Individuals may have more than one spouse but never, legally, more than one at the same time. As stated earlier, the two forms of polygamy are polygyny and polyandry. Polyandry is practiced in only a few societies, notably among certain groups in Tibet, Nepal, and India. Polygyny is much more common.

POLYGYNY

We must distinguish between the social approval of plural marriage and its actual frequency in a particular society. Many cultures approve of a man's having more than one wife. But even when polygyny is encouraged, most people are monogamous, and polygyny characterizes only a fraction of the marriages. Why?

One reason is equal sex ratios. In the United States, about 105 males are born for every 100 females. In adulthood the ratio of men to women equalizes, and eventually it reverses. The average

South African President Jacob Zuma and his three wives in Cape Town, following his State of the Nation address.

In the United States, as in South Africa (p. 140), powerful men often have multiple wives, but, legally, not at the same time. The three marriages of former Speaker of the House Newt Gingrich illustrate serial monogamy.

Plural wives can play important political roles in nonindustrial states. The king of the Merina, a populous society in the highlands of Madagascar, had palaces for each of his twelve wives in different provinces. He stayed with them when he traveled through the kingdom. They were his local agents, overseeing and reporting on provincial matters. The king of Buganda, the major precolonial state of Uganda, took hundreds of wives, representing all the clans in his nation. Everyone in the kingdom became the king's in-law, and all the clans had a chance to provide the next ruler. This was a way of giving the common people a stake in the government.

These examples show there is no single explanation for polygyny. Its context and function vary from society to society and even within the same society. Some men are polygynous because they have inherited a widow from a brother. Others have plural wives because they seek prestige or want to increase household productivity. Men and women with political and economic ambitions cultivate marital alliances that serve their aims. In many societies, including the Betsileo of Madagascar and the Igbo of Nigeria, women arrange the marriages.

POLYANDRY

Most of the world's polyandrous peoples live in South Asia—Tibet, Nepal, India, and Sri Lanka. Polyandry is rare and practiced under very specific conditions. In some of these areas, polyandry seems to be a cultural adaptation to mobility associated with customary male travel for trade, commerce, and military

North American woman outlives the average man. In many nonindustrial societies as well, the male-biased sex ratio among children reverses in adulthood.

The custom of men marrying later than women also promotes polygyny. Among Nigeria's Kanuri people (Cohen 1967), men got married between the ages of eighteen and thirty; women, between twelve and fourteen. The age difference between spouses meant there were more widows than widowers. Most of the widows remarried, some in polygynous unions. Among the Kanuri and in other polygynous societies, such as the Tiwi of northern Australia, widows made up a large number of the women involved in plural marriages (Hart, Pilling, and Goodale 1988).

In certain societies, the first wife requests a second wife to help with household chores. The second wife's status is lower than that of the first; they are senior and junior wives. The senior wife sometimes chooses the junior one from among her close kinswomen. Among the Betsileo of Madagascar, the different wives always lived in different villages. A man's first and senior wife, called "Big Wife," lived in the village where he cultivated his best rice field and spent most of his time. High-status men with several rice fields and multiple wives had households near each field. They spent most of their time with the senior wife but visited the others throughout the year.

Explore your family's history like an anthropologist. Search on one of the free genealogy websites, such as familysearch.org or the family history or public archives sites of a particular state or country. On either your mother's or your father's side (or both), look for changes across generations: Who got married to whom (from which towns, of which nationalities) and at what ages? Where did the couple reside relative to their parents? Were there divorces? Obtaining this information online may be difficult, but look at any kinship data you do uncover with an eye for investigating social change. If you can't trace your own family history online, choose some well-known person and investigate his or her family history.

get involved!

operations. Polyandry ensures there will be at least one man at home to accomplish male activities within a gender-based division of labor. Fraternal polyandry is also an effective strategy when resources are scarce. Brothers with limited resources (in land) pool their resources in expanded (polyandrous) households. They take just one wife. Polyandry restricts the number of wives and heirs. Less competition among heirs means that land can be transmitted with minimal fragmentation.

Got IT? Can you explain reasons for the practice and social approval of serial monogamy, polygyny, and polyandry?

FOR REVIEW

EXPERIENCING CULTURE

TO ACCESS THESE VIDEOS ON YOUR COMPUTER, VISIT

www.mhhe.com/gezonqr

7-1

7-2

7-3

I. What forms of kinship exist cross-culturally, and what are their social correlates?
- The nuclear family consists of a married couple and their children. It assumes importance in societies with geographic mobility, which promotes small, economically self-sufficient family units. In industrial societies, a couple typically starts its own nuclear family in a new home. The forager family usually joins a band in which either the husband or the wife has relatives. Extended families include three or more generations. Extended family households occur more frequently where kinspeople need to pool resources. The descent group is a basic kin group among nonindustrial food producers. This perpetual kin group manages an estate across generations.

II. How do families and descent groups differ?
- The descent group is a larger system of kinship and marriage than the family. It is important in nonindustrial food-producing societies. The descent group endures even though its membership changes. Descent group members are admitted into their group based on whether they belong to the father's (patrilineal) or the mother's (matrilineal) side. Descent groups take the form of a lineage or a clan. Members of lineages trace genealogical links, while clan members merely say they descend from the same ancestor. The rules of descent and postmarital residence ensure that at least some members spend their lives on the descent group's estate.

III. How is marriage defined and regulated, and what rights does it convey?
- Worldwide, marriage has various forms, roles, and functions. In many societies, marriage unites more than two spouses: A man may wed two or more women; a woman may wed a group of brothers. Some societies also recognize same-sex marriage. Generally, marriage establishes the legal parents of children, gives spouses the rights to the sexuality, labor, and property of the other, and establishes a socially significant "relationship of affinity." In societies with descent groups, a lobola gift from the groom and his kin to the bride and her kin creates and maintains group alliances. Marital alliances can continue when a man marries the sister of his deceased wife or a woman marries the brother of her deceased husband.

Pop Quiz

Multiple Choice:

1. Which of the following is a reason for the primacy of the nuclear family in modern North America?
   a. The nuclear family typifies North Americans of all ethnicities and social classes.
   b. Geographic mobility separates North Americans from their extended families.
   c. Households tend to be smaller among the urban poor.
   d. The North American family life has developed in parallel with families worldwide, with the nuclear family emerging as the most evolved form of domestic arrangement.

2. Which of the following is *not* true about the nuclear family?
   a. It is present in all human societies.
   b. Functions associated with nuclear families may be assumed by other social units.
   c. Nuclear families have no special adaptive advantage in conditions associated with poverty.
   d. The geographic mobility of foraging societies encourages the development of the nuclear family.

3. A lineage is distinguished from a clan by this particular characteristic:
   a. The lineage uses stipulated descent.
   b. The lineage believes all its members descend from the same apical ancestor.
   c. Lineage members can name their forebears from the apical ancestor through the present.
   d. Lineages establish alliances with other descent groups.

4. The rule of endogamy in India's caste system is an extreme example of that practice. All of the following are true of endogamy in India *except* this one:
   a. The untouchable *varna* is considered so impure by higher-caste people that even casual contact with untouchables is believed to be defiling.
   b. Although the caste system was formally abolished in 1949, its endogamous practices continue to affect Indian society.
   c. Castes are never subdivided into exogamous lineages.
   d. A woman cannot undo the attribution of defilement she suffers by having sexual intercourse with a man of a lower caste.

5. Which of the following statements about divorce is *false*?
   a. Divorce is less common in matrilineal societies than in patrilineal societies.
   b. Marriage is harder to dissolve when it creates political alliances.
   c. Divorce is rarer in societies in which the husband and his kin group provide a substantial lobola gift.
   d. The Western idea of romantic love is not necessarily a strong cement between spouses.

6. Polygamy includes all of these cases *except* this:
   a. A man who has three unrelated wives
   b. A woman who has three husbands, all of whom are brothers
   c. A man who marries, then divorces, then marries again, then divorces again
   d. A man who has three related wives

Fill in the Blank:

1. The family of _____ is the family in which a child is raised, while the family of _____ is established when one marries and has children.

2. _____ refers to the custom of marrying someone outside the group to which one belongs.

3. _____ is a marital exchange in which the bride's family or kin group provides substantial gifts when their daughter marries. This custom tends to be correlated with _____ female status.

4. When a widower marries a sister of his deceased wife, this is called _____ .

8

GENDER

UNDERSTANDING OURSELVES

Did you have chores when you were growing up? Was there any gender bias in what you were asked to do compared with your siblings? If you were raised by two parents, did any tension arise over their division of labor? Based on cross-cultural data from societies worldwide, a table in this chapter lists activities that are generally male, generally female, or swing (either male or female). Before you look at that table, see if you can assign the following to one gender or the other (M or F):

hunting large animals ____   cooking ____

gathering wild vegetable foods ____   fetching water ____

tending crops ____   making baskets ____

fishing ____   making drinks ____

Now consult Table 8.1 on page 148 and see how you did. Reflect on your results.

Ideas about gender have changed along with the employment patterns of men and women. Still, the lingering American expectation that proper female behavior should be polite, restrained, and/or meek poses a challenge for women, because American culture also values decisiveness. A man's assertiveness may be admired, but a woman's similar behavior may be labeled "aggressive"—or worse.

Both men and women are constrained by their cultural training. For example, American culture stigmatizes male crying. Becoming a man typically means stifling this natural expression of joy and sadness. American men also are trained to make decisions and stick to them. Our stereotypes associate changing one's mind more with women than with men. What a strange idea—that people shouldn't change their positions if they find a better way. Males, females, and humanity may be equally victimized by aspects of cultural training.

>> Sex and Gender

Because anthropologists study biology, society, and culture, they are in a unique position to comment on nature (biological predispositions) and nurture (environment) as determinants of human behavior. Human attitudes, values, and behavior are limited not only by our genetic predispositions—which often are difficult to identify—but also by our experiences during enculturation. Our attributes as adults are determined both by our genes and by our environment during growth and development.

Questions about nature and nurture emerge in the discussion of human sex/gender roles and sexuality. Men and women differ genetically. Women have two X chromosomes, and men have an X and a Y. The father determines a baby's sex because only he has the Y chromosome to transmit. The mother always provides an X chromosome.

The chromosomal difference is expressed in hormonal and physiological contrasts. Humans are sexually dimorphic, more so than some primates, such as gibbons (small tree-living Asiatic apes) and less so than others, such as gorillas and orangutans. **Sexual dimorphism** refers to differences in male and female biology besides the contrasts in breasts and genitals. Women and men differ not just in primary (genitalia and reproductive organs) and secondary (breasts, voice, hair distribution) sexual characteristics, but in average weight, height, strength, and longevity. Women tend to live longer than men and have excellent endurance capabilities. In a given population, men tend to be taller and to weigh more than women do. Of course, there is a considerable overlap between the sexes in terms of height, weight, and physical strength, and there has been a pronounced reduction in sexual dimorphism during human biological evolution.

Just how far, however, do such genetically and physiologically determined differences go? What effects do they have on the way men and women act and are treated in different societies? Anthropologists have discovered both similarities and differences in the roles of men and women in different cultures. The predominant anthropological position on sex–gender roles and biology may be stated as follows:

> The biological nature of men and women [should be seen] not as a narrow enclosure limiting the human organism, but rather as a broad base upon which a variety of structures can be built. (Friedl 1975, p. 6)

Although in most societies men tend to be somewhat more aggressive than women are, many behavioral and attitudinal differences between the sexes emerge from culture rather than biology. Sex differences are biological, but gender encompasses all the traits that a culture assigns to and inculcates in males and females. *Gender,* in other words, refers to the cultural construction of whether one is female, male, or something else.

Given the "rich and various constructions of gender within the realm of cultural diversity," Susan Bourque and Kay Warren (1987) note that the same images of masculinity and femininity do not always apply. Anthropologists have gathered systematic ethnographic data about similarities and differences involving gender in many cultural settings (Bonvillain 2008; Brettell and Sargent 2009; Gilmore 2001; Kimmel 2007; Mascia-Lees and Black 2000; Nanda 2000; Ward and Edelstein 2009). Before we examine the cross-cultural data, some definitions are in order.

Gender roles are the tasks and activities a culture assigns to the sexes. Related to gender roles are **gender stereotypes,** which are oversimplified but strongly held ideas about the characteristics of males and females. **Gender stratification** describes an unequal distribution of rewards (socially valued resources, power, prestige,

sexual dimorphism Marked differences, such as in height and weight, in male and female biology besides the contrasts in breasts and genitals.

gender roles The tasks and activities that a culture assigns to each sex.

gender stereotypes Oversimplified but strongly held ideas about the characteristics of males and females.

gender stratification Unequal distribution of rewards (socially valued resources, power, prestige, and personal freedom) between men and women, reflecting their different positions in a social hierarchy.

STUDY TIP

Sex refers to biological differences, and *gender* to cultural constructions of sex differences. There may be more than two recognized genders in a given society.

In stateless societies, gender stratification often is more obvious in regard to prestige than it is in regard to wealth. In her study of the Ilongots of northern Luzon in the Philippines, Michelle Rosaldo (1980a) described gender differences related to the positive cultural value placed on adventure, travel, and knowledge of the external world. More often than women, Ilongot men, as headhunters, visited distant places. They acquired knowledge of the external world, amassed experiences there, and returned to express their knowledge, adventures, and feelings in public oratory. They received acclaim as a result. Ilongot women had inferior prestige because they lacked external experiences on which to base knowledge and dramatic expression. On the basis of Rosaldo's study and findings in other stateless societies, Ong (1989) argues that we must distinguish between prestige systems and actual power in a given society. High male prestige may not entail economic or political power held by men over their families.

human rights, and personal freedom) between men and women, reflecting their different positions in a social hierarchy. According to Ann Stoler (1977), the economic determinants of gender status include freedom or autonomy (in disposing of one's labor and its fruits) and social power (control over the lives, labor, and produce of others).

Got IT? Can you explain the difference between the terms *sex* and *gender*, using specific examples?

>> Recurrent Gender Patterns

Data relevant to the cross-cultural study of gender can be drawn from the domains of economics, politics, domestic activity, kinship, and marriage. Table 8.1 shows cross-cultural data from 185 randomly selected societies on the division of labor by gender.

Remembering the discussion of universals, generalities, and particularities in the chapter "Culture," the findings in Table 8.1 about the division of labor by gender illustrate generalities rather than universals. That is, among the societies known to ethnography, there is a very strong tendency for men to build boats, but there are exceptions. One was the Hidatsa, a Native American group in which the women made the boats used to cross the Missouri River. (Traditionally, the Hidatsa were village farmers and bison hunters on the North American Plains; they now live in North Dakota.) Another exception: Pawnee women worked wood; this is the only Native American group that assigned this activity to women. (The Pawnee, also traditionally Plains farmers and bison hunters, originally lived in what is now central Nebraska and central Kansas; they now live on a reservation in north central Oklahoma.)

TABLE 8.1

Generalities in the Division of Labor by Gender, Based on Data from 185 Societies

Generally Male Activities	Swing (Male or Female) Activities	Generally Female Activities
Hunting of large aquatic animals (e.g., whales, walrus)	Making fire	Gathering fuel (e.g., firewood)
Smelting of ores	Body mutilation	Making drinks
Metalworking	Preparing skins	Gathering wild vegetal foods
Lumbering	Gathering small land animals	Dairy production (e.g., churning)
Hunting large land animals	Planting crops	Spinning
Working wood	Making leather products	Doing the laundry
Hunting fowl	Harvesting	Fetching water
Making musical instruments	Tending crops	Cooking
Trapping	Milking	Preparing vegetal foods (e.g., processing cereal grains)
Building boats	Making baskets	
Working stone	Carrying burdens	
Working bone, horn, and shell	Making mats	
Mining and quarrying	Caring for small animals	
Setting bones	Preserving meat and fish	
Butchering*	Loom weaving	
Collecting wild honey	Gathering small aquatic animals	
Clearing land	Clothing manufacture	
Fishing	Making pottery	
Tending large herd animals		
Building houses		
Preparing the soil		
Making nets		
Making rope		

*All the activities above "butchering" are almost always done by men; those from "butchering" through "making rope" usually are done by men.

Exceptions to cross-cultural generalizations may involve societies or individuals. A society like the Hidatsa can contradict the cross-cultural generalization that men build boats by assigning that task to women. Or, in a society where the cultural expectation is that only men build boats, a particular woman or women can contradict that expectation by doing the male activity. Table 8.1 shows that in a sample of 185 societies, certain activities ("swing activities") are assigned to either men or women or both. Among the most important of such

Time and Effort Expended on Subsistence Activities by Men and Women*

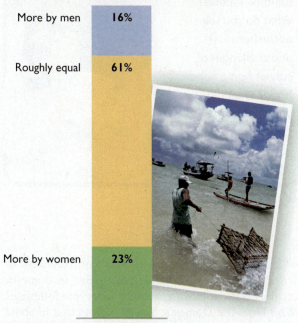

More by men 16%

Roughly equal 61%

More by women 23%

*Percentage of 88 randomly selected societies for which information was available on this variable.

Who Has the Final Authority over the Care, Handling, and Discipline of Infant Children (under Four Years Old)?*

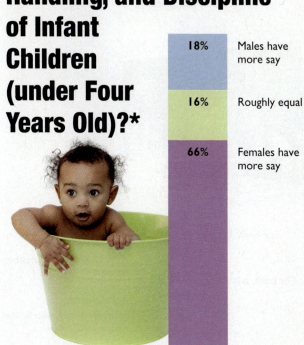

18% Males have more say

16% Roughly equal

66% Females have more say

*Percentage of 67 randomly selected societies for which information was available on this variable.

Who Does the Domestic Work?*

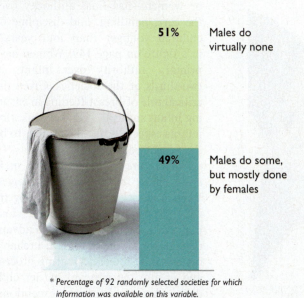

51% Males do virtually none

49% Males do some, but mostly done by females

*Percentage of 92 randomly selected societies for which information was available on this variable.

activities are planting, tending, and harvesting crops. Some societies customarily assign more farming chores to women, whereas others call on men to be the main farm laborers. Among the tasks almost always assigned to men (Table 8.1), some (e.g., hunting large animals on land and sea) seem clearly related to the greater average size and strength of males. Others, such as working wood and making musical instruments, seem more culturally arbitrary. And women, of course, are not exempt from arduous and time-consuming physical labor, such as gathering firewood and fetching water. In Arembepe, Bahia, Brazil, women routinely transported water in five-gallon tins, balanced on their heads, from wells and lagoons located long distances from their homes.

Both women and men have to fit their activities into twenty-four-hour days. Based on cross-cultural data, the figure showing "Time and Effort Expended on Subsistence Activities by Men and Women" indicates that these investments tend to be about equal. If anything, men do slightly less subsistence work than women do. Think about how female domestic activities could have been specified in greater detail in Table 8.1. The original coding of the data in Table 8.1 probably illustrates a male bias, because extradomestic activities received much more prominence than domestic activities did. For example, is collecting wild honey (listed in Table 8.1) more necessary or time-consuming than cleaning a baby's bottom (absent from Table 8.1)? Also, notice that Table 8.1 does not mention trade and market activity, in which either men or women or both are active.

Does the Society Allow Multiple Spouses?*

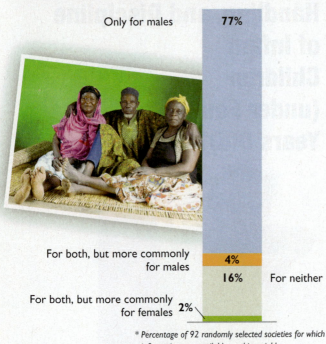

Only for males — **77%**

For both, but more commonly for males — **4%**

16% For neither

For both, but more commonly for females — **2%**

* Percentage of 92 randomly selected societies for which information was available on this variable.

Is There a Double Standard with Respect to Premarital Sex?*

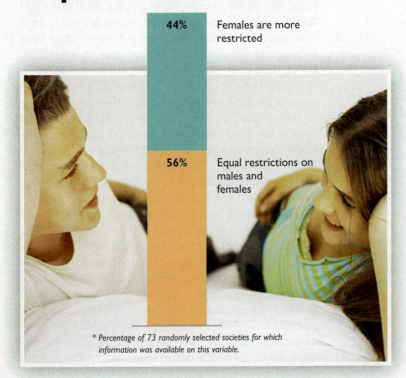

44% Females are more restricted

56% Equal restrictions on males and females

* Percentage of 73 randomly selected societies for which information was available on this variable.

Cross-culturally the subsistence contributions of men and women are roughly equal. But in domestic activities and child care, female labor predominates. "Who Does the Domestic Work?" shows that in about half the societies studied, men did virtually no domestic work. Even in societies where men did some domestic chores, the bulk of such work was done by women. Adding together their subsistence activities and their domestic work, women tend to work more hours than men do. Has this changed in the contemporary world?

What about child care? Women tend to be the main caregivers in most societies, but men often play a role. Cross-cultural data is used to answer the question, "Who—men or women—has final authority over the care, handling, and discipline of children younger than four years?" in a figure on page 149. Women have primary authority over infants in two-thirds of the societies. Given the critical role of breast-feeding in ensuring infant survival, it makes sense, for infants especially, for the mother to be the primary caregiver.

There are differences in male and female reproductive strategies. Women work to ensure their progeny will survive by establishing a close bond with each baby. It's also advantageous for a woman to have a reliable mate to ease the child-rearing process and ensure the survival of her children. (Again, there are exceptions,

Is There a Double Standard with Respect to Extramarital Sex?*

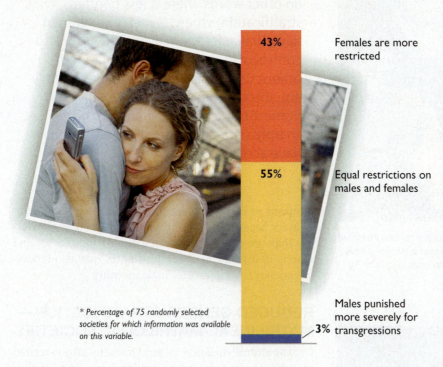

43% — Females are more restricted

55% — Equal restrictions on males and females

3% — Males punished more severely for transgressions

* Percentage of 75 randomly selected societies for which information was available on this variable.

>> Gender Roles and Gender Stratification

Several studies have shown that economic roles affect gender stratification. In one cross-cultural study, Sanday (1974) found that gender stratification decreased when men and women made roughly equal contributions to subsistence. She found that gender stratification was greatest when the women contributed either much more or much less than the men did.

In foraging societies gender stratification was most marked when men contributed much *more* to the diet than women did. This was true among the Inuit and other northern hunters and fishers. Among tropical and semitropical foragers, by contrast, gathering usually supplies more food than hunting and fishing do. Gathering generally is women's work. Men usually hunt and fish, but women also do some fishing and may hunt small animals. When gathering is prominent, gender status tends to be more equal than it is when hunting and fishing are the main subsistence activities.

Gender status also is more equal when the domestic and public spheres aren't sharply separated. (*Domestic* means within or pertaining to the home.) Strong differentiation between the home and the outside world is called the **domestic-public dichotomy** or the *private-public contrast*. The outside world can include politics, trade, warfare, or work. Often when domestic and public spheres are clearly separated, public activities have greater prestige than domestic ones

> **domestic-public dichotomy** Contrast between women's role in the home and men's role in public life, with a corresponding social devaluation of women's work and worth.

such as the matrilineal Nayar discussed in the previous chapter.) Women can have only so many babies during their reproductive years, which begin after menarche (the advent of first menstruation) and end with menopause (cessation of menstruation). Men, in contrast, have a longer reproductive period, which can last into the elder years. If they choose to do so, men can enhance their reproductive success by impregnating several women over a longer time. Although men do not always have multiple mates, they have a greater tendency to do so than women do, as the next three figures show. Among the societies known to ethnography, polygyny is much more common than polyandry, as is shown on the previous page.

Men mate, within and outside marriage, more than women do. The first "Double Standard" figure on the previous page shows cross-cultural data on premarital sex, and the figure above summarizes the data on extramarital sex. In both cases men are less restricted than women are, although the restrictions are equal in about half the societies studied. Double standards that restrict women more than men illustrate gender stratification, which we now examine more systematically.

[Got IT?] Can you describe variation in gender norms and patterns of behavior cross-culturally?

CULTURETHINK

Among the hunter-gatherer Agta of the Philippines, women's and men's roles overlap more than they do in some places. Women hunt alongside men, for example, and men help take care of children. In your society, how strong is the difference between men's and women's traditional roles?

In many societies women routinely do hard physical labor, as is illustrated by these villagers in India's Bihar state, where women and children work at a brick kiln for income during the summer, after crops have been harvested and before the monsoon rains arrive.

Among foragers, gender stratification tends to increase when men contribute much more to the diet than women do—as has been true among the Inuit and other northern hunters and fishers. Shown here, Mikile, an Inuit hunter, opens up a narwhal he hunted and killed near Qeqertat in northwestern Greenland.

do. This can promote gender stratification, because men are more likely to be active in the public domain than women are. Cross-culturally, women's activities tend to be closer to home than men's are. Thus, another reason hunter-gatherers have less gender stratification than food producers do is that the domestic-public dichotomy is less developed among foragers.

Certain roles tend to be more sex-linked than others. Men are the usual hunters and warriors. Given such

weapons as spears, knives, and bows, men make better fighters because they are bigger and stronger on average than are women in the same population (Divale and Harris 1976). The male hunter-fighter role also reflects a tendency toward greater male mobility.

REDUCED GENDER STRATIFICATION— MATRILINEAL-MATRILOCAL SOCIETIES

Cross-cultural variation in gender status also is related to rules of descent and postmarital residence (Friedl 1975; Martin and Voorhies 1975). With matrilineal descent and *matrilocality* (residence after marriage with the wife's relatives), female status tends to be high. Matriliny and matrilocality disperse related males, rather than consolidating them. By contrast, patriliny and *patrilocality* (residence after marriage with the husband's kin) keep male relatives together. Matrilineal-matrilocal systems tend to occur in societies where population pressure on strategic resources is minimal and warfare is infrequent.

Women tend to have high status in matrilineal, matrilocal societies for several reasons. Descent-group membership, succession to political positions, allocation of land, and overall social identity all come through female links. Among the matrilineal Malays of Negeri Sembilan, Malaysia (Peletz 1988), matriliny gave women sole inheritance of ancestral rice fields. Matrilocality created solidary clusters of female kin. These Malay women had considerable influence beyond the household (Swift 1963). In such matrilineal contexts, women are the basis of the entire social structure. Although public authority nominally may be assigned to the men, much of the power and decision making actually may belong to the senior women.

MATRIARCHY

Cross-culturally, anthropologists have described tremendous variation in the roles of men and women, and the power differentials between them. If a patriarchy is a political system ruled by men, what would a matriarchy be? Would a **matriarchy** be a political system ruled by women, or a political system in which women play a much more prominent role than men do in social and political organization? Anthropologist Peggy Sanday (2002) has concluded that matriarchies exist, but not as mirror images of patriarchies. The superior power that men typically have in a patriarchy isn't matched by women's equally disproportionate power in a matriarchy. Many societies, including the Minangkabau of West Sumatra, Indonesia, whom Sanday has studied for decades, lack the substantial power differentials that typify patriarchal systems. Minangkabau women play a central role in social, economic, and ceremonial life and as key symbols. The primacy of matriliny and matriarchy is evident at the village level, as well as regionally,

A Minangkabau bride and groom in West Sumatra, Indonesia, where anthropologist Peggy Reeves Sanday has conducted several years of ethnographic fieldwork.

ANTHROPOLOGY WORKS

People working on international development projects need to be aware of the role women play in family households and economy and to be attentive to issues of social equity. Rick Schroeder studied in the Gambia, West Africa, where women had developed profitable gardens on communal patrilineal lands. A new development project promoted male-controlled tree farms, which they planted on the very land that the women had been farming. The women lost their income and were encouraged to work for the men. This case reveals that development personnel often ignore women's economic contributions and overlook how new projects will affect gendered economic relations. People with anthropological training are important in international economic development projects to ensure that all members of communities are consulted and that benefits are equitably distributed.

where seniority of matrilineal descent serves as a way to rank villages.

The four million Minangkabau constitute one of Indonesia's largest ethnic groups. Located in the highlands of West Sumatra, they have a culture based on the coexistence of matrilineal custom and a nature-based philosophy called *adat*, complemented by Islam, a more recent (sixteenth-century) arrival. The Minangkabau view men and women as cooperative partners for the common good rather than

> **matriarchy** A political system in which women play a much more prominent role than men do in social and political organization.

competitors ruled by self-interest. People gain prestige when they promote social harmony rather than by vying for power.

Sanday considers the Minangkabau a matriarchy because women are the center, origin, and foundation of the social order. Senior women are associated with the central pillar of the traditional house, the oldest one in the village. The oldest village in a cluster is called the "mother village." In ceremonies, women are addressed by the term used for their mythical Queen Mother. Women control land inheritance, and couples reside matrilocally. In the wedding ceremony, the wife collects her husband from his household and, with her female kin, escorts him to hers. If there is a divorce, the husband simply takes his things and leaves. Yet despite the special position of women, the Minangkabau matriarchy is not the equivalent of female rule, given the Minangkabau belief that all decision making should be by consensus.

INCREASED GENDER STRATIFICATION—PATRILINEAL-PATRILOCAL SOCIETIES

Martin and Voorhies (1975) link the decline of matriliny and the spread of the **patrilineal-patrilocal complex** (consisting of patrilineality, patrilocality, warfare, and male supremacy) to pressure on resources. Faced with scarce resources, patrilineal-patrilocal cultivators such as the Yanomami often wage warfare against other villages. This favors patrilocality and patriliny, customs that keep related men together in the same village, where they make strong allies in battle. Such societies tend to have a sharp domestic-public dichotomy, and men tend to dominate the prestige hierarchy. Men may use their public roles in warfare and trade and their greater prestige to symbolize and reinforce the devaluation or oppression of women.

patrilineal-patrilocal complex An interrelated constellation of patrilineality, patrilocality, warfare, and male supremacy.

patriarchy Political system ruled by men in which women have inferior social and political status, including fewer basic human rights.

In some parts of Papua New Guinea, the patrilineal–patrilocal complex has extreme social repercussions. Regarding females as dangerous and polluting, men may segregate themselves in men's houses (such as this one, located near the Sepik River), where they hide their precious ritual objects from women. Are there places like this in your society?

The patrilineal-patrilocal complex characterizes many societies in highland Papua New Guinea. Women work hard growing and processing subsistence crops, raising and tending pigs (the main domesticated animal and a favorite food), and doing domestic cooking, but they are isolated from the public domain, which men control. Men grow and distribute prestige crops, prepare food for feasts, and arrange marriages. The men even get to trade the pigs and control their use in ritual.

In densely populated areas of the Papua New Guinea highlands, male-female avoidance is associated with strong pressure on resources (Lindenbaum 1972). Men fear all female contacts, including sex. They think that sexual contact with women will weaken them. Indeed, men see everything female as dangerous and polluting. They segregate themselves in men's houses and hide their precious ritual objects from women. They delay marriage, and some never marry.

By contrast, the sparsely populated areas of Papua New Guinea, such as recently settled areas, lack taboos on male-female contacts. The image of woman as polluter fades, heterosexual intercourse is valued, men and women live together, and reproductive rates are high.

PATRIARCHY AND VIOLENCE

A political system ruled by men in which women have inferior social and political status, including fewer basic human rights, is known as **patriarchy.** Barbara Miller (1997),

Women fish merchants in Seoul, South Korea. How likely is it that these women caught the items they are selling? Gender stratification typically is reduced in societies in which women have prominent roles in the economy (including marketing) and social life.

in a study of systematic neglect of females, describes women in rural northern India as "the endangered sex." Societies that feature a full-fledged patrilineal-patrilocal complex, replete with warfare and intervillage raiding, also typify patriarchy. Such practices as dowry murders, female infanticide, and clitoridectomy exemplify patriarchy, which extends from tribal societies such as the Yanomami to state societies such as India and Pakistan.

Although more prevalent in certain social settings than in others, family violence and domestic abuse of women are worldwide problems. Domestic violence certainly occurs in nuclear family settings, such as Canada and the United States. Cities, with their impersonality

and isolation from extended kin networks, are breeding grounds for domestic violence.

We've seen that gender stratification typically is reduced in societies in which women have prominent roles in the economy and social life. When a woman lives in her own village, she has kin nearby to look after and protect her interests. Even in patrilocal polygynous settings, women often count on the support of their cowives and sons in disputes with potentially abusive husbands. Such settings, which tend to provide a safe haven for women, are retracting rather than expanding in today's world, however. Isolated families and patrilineal social forms have spread at the expense of matrilineality. Many nations have declared polygyny illegal. More and more women, and men, find themselves cut off from extended kin and families of orientation.

With the spread of the women's rights movement and the human rights movement, attention to domestic violence and abuse of women has increased. Laws have been passed and mediating institutions established. Brazil's female-run police stations for battered women provide an example, as do shelters for victims of domestic abuse in the United States and Canada. But patriarchal institutions do persist in what should be a more enlightened world.

CULTURE THINK

Although some women now earn more than men do, because of the feminization of poverty, many more women now earn less than men do. Why do you think increasing numbers of women across the globe are falling below the poverty line? What can be done to counteract this trend?

Got IT? Can you identify social, political, and economic factors that affect women's status cross-culturally?

>> Gender in Industrial Societies

The domestic-public dichotomy also influences patterns of gender stratification in industrial societies, including the United States and Canada. Gender roles have been changing rapidly in North America. The "traditional" idea that "a woman's place is in the home" actually emerged in the United States as industrialism spread after 1900. Earlier, pioneer women in the Midwest and West had been recognized as fully productive workers in farming and home industry. Under industrialism, attitudes about gendered work came to vary with class and region. In early industrial Europe, men, women, and children had flocked to factories as wage laborers. Enslaved Americans of both sexes had done grueling work in cotton fields. With abolition, southern African-American women continued working as field hands and domestics. Poor white women labored in the South's early cotton mills. In the 1890s more than one million American women held menial and repetitive unskilled factory positions (Margolis 1984; Martin and Voorhies 1975).

After 1900, European immigration produced a male labor force willing to work for wages lower than those of American-born men. Those immigrant men moved into factory jobs that previously had gone to women. As machine tools and mass production further reduced the need for female labor, the notion that women were biologically unfit for factory work began to gain ground (Martin and Voorhies 1975).

Maxine Margolis (1984, 2000) has shown how gendered work, attitudes, and beliefs have varied in response to American economic needs. For example, wartime shortages of men have promoted the idea that work outside the home is women's patriotic duty. During the world wars the notion that women are unfit for hard physical labor faded. Inflation and the culture of consumption also have spurred female employment. When prices or demand rise, multiple paychecks help maintain family living standards.

The steady increase in female paid employment since World War II also reflects the baby boom and industrial expansion. American culture traditionally has defined clerical work, teaching, and nursing as female occupations. With rapid population growth and business expansion after World War II, the demand for women to fill such jobs grew steadily. Employers also found they could increase their profits by paying women lower wages than they would have to pay returning male war veterans.

Margolis (1984, 2000) contends that changes in the economy lead to changes in attitudes toward and about women. Economic changes paved the way for the contemporary women's movement, which also was spurred by the publication of Betty Friedan's book *The Feminine Mystique* in 1963 and the founding of the National Organization of Women (NOW) in 1966. The

During the world wars the notion that women were biologically unfit for hard physical labor faded. Shown here is World War II's famous Rosie the Riveter. Is there a comparable poster woman today? What does her image say about modern gender roles?

We Can Do It!

POST FEB. 15 TO FEB. 28

WAR PRODUCTION CO-ORDINATING COMMITTEE

Cash Employment of American Mothers, Wives, and Husbands, 1960–2010*

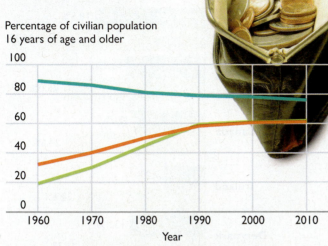

Percentage of civilian population 16 years of age and older

— Percentage of all married men (wife present)

— Percentage of all married women (husband present)

— Percentage of all married women (husband present, with children under six)

Trends in U.S. Women's Participation in the Paid Labor Force, 1890–2010

Source: Statistical Abstract of the United States 2010, Table 1330; Huffington Post, http://www.huffingtonpost .com/2010/07/03/worlds-happiest-countries_n_633814.

men. Women fill more than half (52 percent) of all management/professional jobs (*Statistical Abstract of the United States 2012,* Table 616). And it's not mainly single women working, as once was the case. The ever-increasing cash employment of American wives and mothers, including those with children under six years old, is shown in the figure "Cash Employment of American Mothers, Wives, and Husbands."

Note in the figure that the cash employment of American married men has been falling while that of American married women has been rising. There has been a dramatic change in behavior and attitudes since 1960, when 89 percent of all married men worked, compared with just 32 percent of married women. The comparable figures in 2010 were 76 percent and 61 percent. The ratio of female to male earnings rose from 68 percent in 1989 to 77 percent in 2006, then fell to 72 percent in 2010.

Ideas about the gender roles of males and females have changed. Compare your grandparents and your parents. Chances are you have a working mother, but your grandmother was more likely a stay-at-home mom. Your grandfather is more likely than your father to have worked in manufacturing and to have belonged to a union. Your father is more likely than your grandfather to have shared child care and domestic responsibilities. Age at marriage has been delayed for both men and women. College educations and professional degrees have increased. What other changes do you associate with the increase in female employment outside the home?

THE FEMINIZATION OF POVERTY

Alongside the economic gains of many American women stands an opposite extreme: the feminization of poverty, or the increasing representation of women

movement in turn promoted expanded work opportunities for women, including the goal of equal pay for equal work. Between 1970 and 2010, the female percentage of the American workforce rose from 38 to 47 percent. Almost half of all Americans who work outside the home are women. Over 65 million women now have paid employment, compared with 73 million

(and their children) among America's poorest people. Women head over half of U.S. households with incomes below the poverty line, more than double the number in 1959. Married couples are much more secure economically than single mothers are. The average income for married-couple families is more than twice that of families maintained by a woman. The average one-earner family maintained by a woman had an annual income of $32,597 in 2009. This was less than one-half the mean income ($71,830) of a married-couple household.

The feminization of poverty isn't just a North American phenomenon. The percentage of single-parent (usually female-headed) households has been increasing worldwide. The figure ranges from about 10 percent in Japan, to below 20 percent in certain South Asian and Southeast Asian countries, to almost 50 percent in certain African countries and the Caribbean (Buvinic 1995, *Statistical Abstract of the United States 2012,* Table 1337.). As we see in "Single-Parent Households in Various Countries," the percentage of single-parent households rose in every nation listed between 1980–81 and 2009. Of those countries studied, the United States maintained the largest percentage of single-parent households (29.5 percent), followed by the United Kingdom (25 percent), Canada (24.6 percent), Ireland (22.6 percent), and Denmark (21.7 percent). The rate of increase in single-parent households over the past 30 years has been highest in Ireland, where it tripled, from 7.2 to 22.6 percent.

Globally, households headed by women tend to be poorer than are those headed by men. In one study, the percentage of single-parent families considered poor was 18 percent in Britain, 20 percent in Italy,

Single-Parent Households in Various Countries, 1980 versus 2009

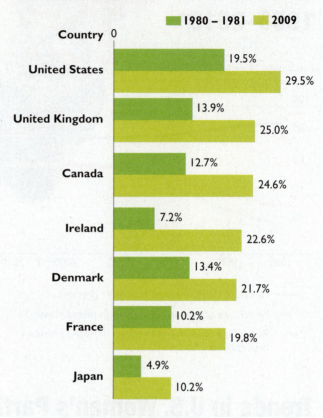

25 percent in Switzerland, 40 percent in Ireland, 52 percent in Canada, and 63 percent in the United States (Buvinic 1995).

Domestic violence isn't limited to tribal societies. It also occurs in nuclear family settings including the United States, Canada, and the United Kingdom. Shown here, women rally in London, England, on International Women's Day, March 3, 2012.

It is widely believed that one way to improve the situation of poor women is to encourage them to organize. New women's groups can in some cases revive or replace traditional forms of social organization that have been disrupted. Membership in a group can help women to mobilize resources, to rationalize production, and to reduce the risks and costs associated with credit (Dunham 2009). Organization also allows women to develop self-confidence and to decrease dependence on others. Through such organization, poor women throughout the world are working to determine their own needs and priorities, and to change things so as to improve their social and economic situation (Buvinic 1995).

WORK AND HAPPINESS

Look at the graphic "Women in Labor Force and Happiness," which is condensed from 30 countries for which data were available in 2008. The United States, with 69.3 percent of its women employed, ranked 13th, while Canada (74.4 percent) ranked 6th. Iceland topped the list, with 82.5 percent of its women in the workforce. Turkey was lowest; only 26.7 percent of its women were employed.

In 2010, Gallup conducted a survey of the world's 132 happiest countries, based on various measures, including the percentages of people in that country who were thriving—and suffering. Respondents also were asked to rate their own lives on a scale from zero (worst possible) to 10 (best possible). Denmark was the world's happiest nation; Canada came in 6th; the United States, 12th.

Interestingly, we can detect a correlation between the two rankings—of happiness and of women's work outside the home. Of the 13 countries with greatest female labor force participation, 10 ranked among the world's happiest (see Levy 2010). What factors might explain this correlation? Why, as more women work outside the home, might a country's population achieve a greater sense of well-being? More money? More taxes? More social services? More personal freedom? We report; you decide!

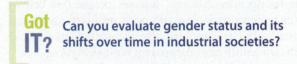

Got IT? Can you evaluate gender status and its shifts over time in industrial societies?

Women in Labor Force and Happiness

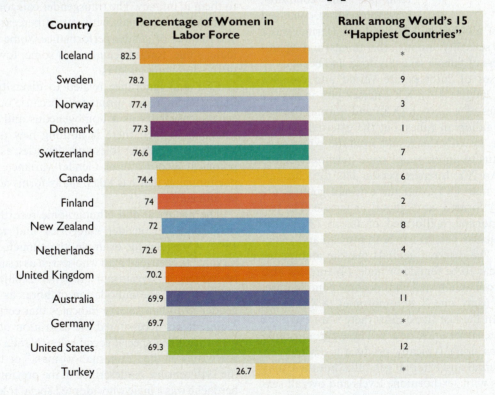

Country	Percentage of Women in Labor Force	Rank among World's 15 "Happiest Countries"
Iceland	82.5	*
Sweden	78.2	9
Norway	77.4	3
Denmark	77.3	1
Switzerland	76.6	7
Canada	74.4	6
Finland	74	2
New Zealand	72	8
Netherlands	72.6	4
United Kingdom	70.2	*
Australia	69.9	11
Germany	69.7	*
United States	69.3	12
Turkey	26.7	*

*These countries were not among the 15 "happiest countries"

Source: Statistical Abstract of the United States 2010, Table 1330; Huffington Post, http://www.huffingtonpost.com/2010/07/03/worlds-happiest-countries_n_633814.

>> Beyond Male and Female

Gender is socially constructed, and societies may recognize more than two genders. The contemporary United States, for example, includes individuals who self-identify using such labels as "transgender," "intersex," "third gender," and "transsexual." Such persons contradict dominant male/female gender distinctions by being part male and female, or neither male nor female. Because people who self-identify as "transgender" are increasingly visible, we must be careful about seeing "masculine " and "feminine" as absolute and binary categories.

Sex, we have seen, is biological, whereas gender is socially constructed. Transgender is a social category that includes individuals who may or may not contrast biologically with ordinary males and females. Within the transgender category, intersex people (see below) usually contrast biologically with ordinary males and females, but transgender also includes people whose gender identity has no apparent biological roots.

The term **intersex** encompasses a group of conditions involving a discrepancy between the external genitals (penis, vagina, etc.) and the internal genitals (testes, ovaries, etc.). The older term for this condition, hermaphroditism, combined the names of a Greek god and goddess. Hermes was a god of male sexuality (among other things) and Aphrodite a goddess of female sexuality, love, and beauty.

intersex Pertaining to a group of conditions reflecting a discrepancy between the external and the internal genitals.

The causes of intersex are varied and complex (Kaneshiro 2009): (1) An XX Intersex person has the chromosomes of a woman (XX) and normal ovaries, uterus, and fallopian tubes, but the external genitals appear male. Usually this results from the exposure of a female fetus to an excess of male hormones before birth. (2) An XY Intersex person has the chromosomes of a man (XY), but the external genitals are incompletely formed, ambiguous, or female. The testes may be normal, malformed, or absent. (3) A True Gonadal Intersex person has both ovarian and testicular tissue. The external genitals may be ambiguous or may appear to be female or male. (4) Intersex also can result from an unusual chromosome combination, such as X0 (only one X chromosome), XXY, XYY, and XXX. In the last three cases there is an extra sex chromosome, either an X or a Y. These chromosomal combinations don't typically produce a discrepancy between internal and external genitalia, but there may be problems with sex hormone levels and overall sexual development.

The XXY configuration, known as Klinefelter's syndrome, is the most common unusual sex chromosome combination and the second most common condition (after Down syndrome) caused by the presence of extra chromosomes in humans. Effects of Klinefelter's occur in about 1 of every 1,000 males. One in every 500 males has an extra X chromosome but lacks the main symptoms—small testicles and reduced fertility. With XXX, aka triple X syndrome, there is an extra X chromosome in each cell of a human female. Triple X occurs in about 1 of every 1,000 female births. There usually is no physically distinguishable difference between triple X women and other women. The same is true of XYY compared with other males.

Turner syndrome encompasses several conditions, of which X0 (absence of one sex chromosome) is most common. In this case, all or part of one of the sex chromosomes is absent. Typical females have two X chromosomes, but in Turner syndrome, one of those chromosomes is missing or abnormal. Girls with Turner syndrome typically are sterile because of nonworking ovaries and amenorrhea (absence of a menstrual cycle).

Biology isn't destiny; people construct their identities in society. Many individuals affected by one of the biological conditions just described see themselves simply as male or female, rather than transgender. Self-identified transgender people tend to be individuals whose gender identity contradicts their biological sex at birth and the gender identity that society assigned to them in infancy. The transgender category is diverse; it includes individuals with varied perceptions of self and manner of gender performance. Some lean toward male; some, toward female; and some, toward neither of the dominant genders.

Fear and ignorance related to diversity in gender fuels discrimination, principally because outsiders perceive transgender as a homogeneous and stigmatized category. In fact, there is nothing new or abnormal about diverse gender roles and identities, as the anthropological record attests. Gender variance is a human phenomenon that has taken many forms across societies and cultures.

The historical and ethnographic records reveal the malleability of gender categories and roles (Herdt 1994). Consider, for example, the eunuch, or "perfect servant" (a castrated man who served as a safe attendant to harems in Byzantium [Tougher 2008]). Acknowledgment and accommodation of hijras as a third sex/gender in Indian society indicates that certain societal requirements necessitated the castration of some men who then filled special social roles (Nanda 1998). Roscoe writes of the "Zuni man-woman," or berdache, in the 19th century. As described in the previous chapter, a berdache was a male who adopted social roles traditionally assigned to women, and through performance of a third gender role, contributed to the social and spiritual well-being of the community as a whole (1991; 1998).

Some Balkan societies included "sworn virgins," born females who assumed male gender roles and activities to meet societal needs when there was a shortage of men (Gremaux 1993).

Among the Gheg tribes of North Albania, "virginal transvestites" were biologically female, but locals considered them "honorary men" (Shryock 1988). Albanian adolescent girls have chosen to become men, remain celibate, and live among men, with the support of their families and villagers (Young 2000). And consider Polynesia. In Tonga the term *fakaleiti* describes males who behave like women, thereby contrasting with mainstream Tongan men who display masculine characteristics. Similar to the fakaleitis of Tonga, Samoan *fa'afafine* and Hawaiian *mahu* refer to men who adopt feminine attributes, behaviors, and visual markers.

In the contemporary West, the umbrella category **transgender** encompasses a similar variety of persons whose gender performance and identity contradict or defy a binary gender structure. Transgender people are productive and contributing members of society, at least in those sectors to which they have access and relative protection to live as who they are. In recent years, the gay and lesbian rights movement has achieved many successes, including the legalization of same-sex marriage in a few states and the repeal of the "Don't Ask Don't Tell" (DADT) policy of the U. S. armed services. The gay and lesbian rights movement has expanded to include the lesbian, gay, bisexual, and transgender community (LGBT), which works to promote government policies and social practices that protect its members' civil and human rights.

> ## Got IT?
> Can you explain and provide examples of how some societies recognize more than two genders?

>> Sexual Orientation

A person's habitual sexual attraction to, and sexual activities with, persons of the opposite sex (*heterosexuality*), the same sex (*homosexuality*), or both sexes (*bisexuality*) is termed their **sexual orientation.** *Asexuality*—indifference toward, or lack of attraction to, either sex—also is a sexual orientation. All four of these forms are found in contemporary North America and throughout the world. But each type of desire and experience holds different meanings for individuals and

groups. For example, an asexual disposition may be acceptable in some places but perceived as a character flaw in others. Male-male sexual activity may be a private affair in Mexico, rather than public, socially sanctioned, and encouraged as among the Etoro (see p. 163) of Papua New Guinea (see also Blackwood and Wieringa 1999; Boellstorff 2007; Kimmel and Messner 2013; Kottak and Kozaitis 2012; Nanda 2000).

> **transgender** A category of varied individuals whose gender identity contradicts their biological sex at birth and the gender identity that society assigned to them in infancy.

> **sexual orientation** A person's habitual sexual attraction to, and activities with, persons of the opposite sex (heterosexuality), the same sex (homosexuality), or both sexes (bisexuality); also, the lack of attraction (asexuality).

Recently in the United States the tendency has been to see sexual orientation as fixed and biologically based. There is not enough information at this time to determine the exact extent to which sexual orientation is based on biology. What we can say is that all human activities and preferences, including erotic expression, are at least partially culturally constructed.

> ### "As far as I'm concerned, being any gender is a drag."
>
> Patti Smith

In any society, individuals will differ in the nature, range, and intensity of their sexual interests and urges. No one knows for sure why such individual sexual differences exist. Part of the answer probably is biological, reflecting genes or hormones (Wade 2005). Another part may have to do with experiences during growth and development. But whatever the reasons for individual variation, culture always plays a role in molding individual sexual urges toward a collective norm. And such sexual norms vary from culture to culture.

What do we know about variation in sexual norms from society to society, and over time? A classic cross-cultural study (Ford and Beach 1951) found wide variation in attitudes about masturbation, bestiality (sex with animals), and homosexuality. In a single society, such as the United States, attitudes about sex differ over time and with socioeconomic status, region, and rural versus urban residence. However, even in the 1950s, prior to the "age of sexual permissiveness" (the pre-HIV period from the mid-1960s through the 1970s), research showed that almost all American men (92 percent) and more than half of American women (54 percent) admitted to masturbation. In the famous Kinsey report (Kinsey, Pomeroy, and Martin 1948), 37 percent of the men surveyed admitted having had at least one sexual experience leading to orgasm with another male. In a later study of twelve hundred unmarried women, 26 percent reported same-sex sexual activities. (Because Kinsey's research relied on nonrandom samples, it should be

Shown above, hijras (neither man nor woman) constitute India's third gender. Shown below, Roberta Close, a transgender (male to female) celebrity in Brazil. After her sex reassignment surgery (10 years before this photo), Close was voted the "Most Beautiful Woman in Brazil."

considered merely illustrative, rather than a statistically accurate representation, of sexual behavior at the time.)

Sex acts with people of the same sex were absent, rare, or secret in 37 percent of seventy-six societies for which data were available in the Ford and Beach study (1951). In the other societies, various forms of same-sex sexual activity were acceptable. Sometimes sexual relations between people of the same sex involved transvestism on the part of one of the partners (see Kulick 1998). Transvestism did not characterize male-male sex among the Sudanese Azande, who valued the warrior role (Evans-Pritchard 1970). Prospective warriors—young men aged twelve to twenty—left their families and shared quarters with adult fighting men, who paid lobola for them and had sex with them. During this apprenticeship, the young men performed the domestic duties of women. Upon reaching warrior status, these young men took their own younger male brides. Later, retiring from the warrior role, Azande men married women. Flexible in their sexual expression, Azande males had no difficulty shifting from sex with older men (as male brides), to sex with younger men (as warriors), to sex with women (as husbands) (see Murray and Roscoe 1998).

Consider also the Etoro (Kelly 1976), a group of four hundred people who subsist by hunting and horticulture in the Trans-Fly region of Papua New Guinea. The Etoro illustrate the power of culture in molding human sexuality. The following account, based on ethnographic fieldwork by Raymond C. Kelly in the late 1960s, applies only to Etoro males and their beliefs. Etoro cultural norms prevented the male anthropologist who studied them from gathering comparable information about female attitudes. Note, also, that the activities described have been discouraged by missionaries. Since there has been no restudy of the Etoro specifically focusing on these activities, the extent to which these practices continue today is unknown. For this reason, we'll use the past tense in describing them.

Etoro opinions about sexuality were linked to their beliefs about the cycle of birth, physical growth, maturity, old age, and death. Etoro men believed that semen was necessary to give life force to a fetus, which was, they believed, implanted in a woman by an ancestral spirit. Sexual intercourse during pregnancy nourished the growing fetus. The Etoro believed that men had a limited lifetime supply of semen. Any sex act leading to ejaculation was seen as draining that supply, and as sapping a man's virility and vitality. The birth of children, nurtured by semen, symbolized a necessary sacrifice that would lead to the husband's eventual death. Heterosexual intercourse—required only for reproduction—was otherwise discouraged. Women who wanted too much sex were viewed as witches, hazardous to their husbands' health. Etoro culture allowed heterosexual intercourse only about one hundred days a year. The rest of the time it was tabooed. Seasonal birth clustering shows the taboo was respected.

So objectionable was male-female sex that it was removed from community life. It could occur neither in sleeping quarters nor in the fields. Coitus could happen only in the woods, where it was risky because poisonous snakes, the Etoro claimed, were attracted by the sounds and smells of male-female sex.

Although coitus was discouraged, sex acts between men were viewed as essential. Etoro believed that boys could not produce semen on their own. To grow into men and eventually give life force to their children, boys had to acquire semen orally from older men. From the age of ten until adulthood, boys were inseminated by older men. No taboos were attached to this. Such oral insemination could proceed in the sleeping area or garden. Every three years, a group of boys around the age of twenty were formally initiated into manhood. They went to a secluded mountain lodge, where they were visited and inseminated by several older men.

Male-male sex among the Etoro was governed by a code of propriety. Although sexual relations between older and younger males were considered culturally essential, those between boys of the same age were discouraged. A boy who took semen from other youths was believed to be sapping their life force and stunting their growth. A boy's rapid physical development might suggest he was getting semen from other boys. Like a sex-hungry wife, he might be shunned as a witch.

> "Society as a whole benefits immeasurably from a climate in which all persons, regardless of race or gender, may have the opportunity to earn respect, responsibility, advancement and remuneration based on ability."
>
> Former Supreme Court Justice Sandra Day O'Connor

Did You Know?

For the first time in U.S. history, the 2010 census counted gay couples as married, even if they were not legally married. In 2000, they could only designate themselves as "unmarried partners" living in the same household.

CULTURE THINK

Compare and contrast Azande and Etoro sexual practices and identities with those you are familiar with. How do ideas about homosexuality differ cross-culturally?

These sexual practices among the Etoro rested not on hormones or genes but on cultural beliefs and traditions. The Etoro shared a cultural pattern, which Gilbert Herdt (1984) calls "ritualized homosexuality," with some fifty other tribes in Papua New Guinea, especially in that country's Trans-Fly region. These societies illustrate one extreme of a male-female avoidance pattern that is widespread in Papua New Guinea and indeed in many patrilineal-patrilocal societies.

Flexibility in sexual expression seems to be an aspect of our primate heritage. Both masturbation and same-sex sexual activity exist among chimpanzees and other primates. Male bonobos (pygmy chimps) regularly engage in a form of mutual masturbation known as "penis fencing." Females get sexual pleasure from rubbing their genitals against those of other females (de Waal 1997). Our primate sexual potential is molded by culture, the environment, and reproductive necessity. Heterosexual coitus is practiced in all human societies—which, after all, must reproduce themselves—but alternatives also are widespread (Rathus, Nevid, and Fichner-Rathus 2013). Like gender roles and attitudes more generally, the sexual component of human personality and identity—just how we express our "natural" sexual urges—is a matter that culture and environment determine and limit.

Got IT? Can you summarize and evaluate cross-cultural research that suggests that sexual orientation is not fixed and biologically based?

You may have known or heard about a woman in a violent marital or dating relationship. To learn about how a woman and her children might find temporary refuge from violent situations, visit the website of Safe Horizon (http://www.safehorizon.org), a New York City support agency. Take the "Domestic Violence Shelter Tour." Listen to the stories of women who have been battered by spouses or boyfriends. Although the women come from different situations, what common circumstances do you find running throughout their lives? How can urban life or immigrant status in a big city weaken women's position? How might the varied services the shelter provides help free women from their economic dependence on the men who batter them and from the feelings these women often have that *they* are to blame for the abuse?

FOR REVIEW

I. How are biology and culture expressed in human sex/gender systems?

- Although sexual dimorphism has decreased during human evolution, males and females still differ physiologically and anatomically.

  The roles of men and women both differ and resemble one another in different cultures. "The biological nature of men and women [should be seen] not as a narrow enclosure limiting the human organism, but rather as a broad base upon which a variety of structures can be built." Sex differences are biological, but gender encompasses the traits that a culture assigns to males and females. Gender refers to the cultural construction of whether one is female, male, or something else. Societies may recognize more than two genders. The term *intersex* describes a group of conditions, including chromosomal configurations, that may produce a discrepancy between external and internal genitals. Transgender individuals may or may not contrast biologically with ordinary males and females. Self-identified transgender people tend to be individuals whose gender identity contradicts their biological sex at birth and the gender identity that society assigned to them in infancy.

II. How do gender, gender roles, and gender stratification correlate with other social, economic, and political variables?

- In foraging societies both the domestic-public dichotomy and gender stratification are limited, and male and female activities tend to overlap. Female status tends to be high with matrilineal descent and matrilocality. Competition for resources favors the patrilineal-patrilocal complex. The superior power that men typically have in a patriarchy isn't matched by women's power in a matriarchy. Industrialization in the United States initially contributed to the notion that women were unfit for factory work, but industrial expansion after World War II increased female paid employment. The rise in poverty of women is a global phenomenon.

III. What is sexual orientation, and how do sexual practices vary cross-culturally?

- Sexual orientation refers to a person's habitual sexual attraction to, and sexual activities with, persons of the opposite sex (heterosexuality), the same sex (homosexuality), or both sexes (bisexuality). Asexuality is indifference toward, or lack of attraction to, either sex. All four forms of orientation occur worldwide but hold different meanings for individuals and groups. Anthropologists generally see sexual orientation as at least partially culturally constructed. In the United States, attitudes about sex have differed over time and with socioeconomic status, region, and rural versus urban residence. Flexibility in sexual expression seems to be an aspect of our primate heritage.

Pop Quiz

Multiple Choice:

1. Consider this quote: "The biological nature of men and women [should be seen] not as a narrow enclosure limiting the human organism, but rather as a broad base upon which a variety of structures can be built." Which of the following best describes this quote's significance?

   a. The quote reflects a cultural generality, rather than a cultural universal.

   b. The quote reflects the predominant anthropological position on sex/gender roles and biology.

   c. This quote summarizes how biological determinists think.

   d. This quote ignores considerable evidence.

2. Hidatsa women made boats, and Pawnee women worked wood. These two cases suggest that

   a. biology has nothing to do with gender roles.

   b. anthropologists are too optimistic about finding a society with gender equality.

   c. there are exceptions to cross-cultural generalizations about the kinds of work men and women usually do in different societies.

   d. a Hidatsa or Pawnee man would never do the female task.

3. Among foragers,

   a. warfare and trade make men dominant over women.

   b. female status falls when gathering is more important than hunting.

   c. the lack of a clear domestic-public dichotomy is related to relatively weak gender stratification.

   d. men and women are completely equal.

4. Transgender individuals

   a. do not necessarily contrast biologically with ordinary males and females.

   b. are the same as intersex individuals.

   c. exist mainly as the result of modern surgical techniques.

   d. are effective spiritual leaders in most societies.

5. "The feminization of poverty" means that

   a. poverty has been dressed up to seem more bearable.

   b. single mothers tend to be happier than married women are.

   c. women and their children are increasingly represented among the world's poorest people.

   d. an increasing percentage of female-headed households shows the growing power and independence of women.

6. All the following are key ideas to take away from this chapter's discussion of sexual orientation *except* this one:

   a. Different types of sexual desires and experiences hold different meanings for individuals and groups.

   b. In any society, individuals will differ in the nature, range, and intensity of sexual interests and urges.

   c. Culture always plays a role in molding individual sexual urges toward a collective norm.

   d. There is conclusive scientific evidence that sexual orientation is genetically determined.

Fill in the Blank:

1. _____ refer to the tasks and activities that a culture assigns to the sexes.

2. In general, the status of women is higher in societies with _____ descent than in those with _____ descent.

3. _____ refers to an unequal distribution of socially valued resources, power, prestige, and personal freedom between men and women.

4. _____ refers to a group of conditions involving a discrepancy between the external genitals (penis, vagina, etc.) and the internal genitals (testes, ovaries, etc.).

1. (b), 2. (c), 3. (c), 4. (a), 5. (c), 6. (d)

1. Gender roles; 2. matrilineal, patrilineal; 3. Gender stratification; 4. Intersex

9

RELIGION

UNDERSTANDING OURSELVES

Ever notice how much baseball players spit? Football players, with their customary headgear, don't spit, nor do basketball players, who might slip on the court. No spitting by tennis players, golfers, gymnasts, or swimmers. But watch any baseball game, and you'll see spitting galore. The custom likely originated on the mound and continues today as a carryover from the days when pitchers routinely chewed tobacco, believing that nicotine enhanced their concentration. The spitting custom spread to other players, who unabashedly spew saliva from the outfield to the dugout steps.

For the student of custom, ritual, and magic, baseball is an especially interesting game, to which lessons from anthropology are easily applied. The pioneering anthropologist Bronislaw Malinowski, writing about Pacific islanders, noted their use of all sorts of magic in sailing, a hazardous activity. He proposed that people turn to magic when they face uncertainty and conditions they can't control (e.g., wind and weather). Like sailing magic, baseball magic, in the form of rituals, taboos, and sacred objects, serves to reduce psychological stress, creating an illusion of control when real control is lacking.

All sorts of magical behaviors surround pitching and batting, which are full of uncertainty. There are fewer rituals for fielding, over which players have more control (see Gmelch 2006). Especially obvious are the rituals (like the spitting) of pitchers, who may tug their cap between pitches, spit in a particular direction, magically manipulate the resin bag, talk to the ball, or wash their hands after giving up a run. Batters have their rituals, too. One major leaguer routinely would spit, then ritually touch his gob with his bat to enhance his success at the plate.

To keep hope alive in situations of uncertainty, and for outcomes we can't control, all societies draw on magic and religion as sources of nonmaterial comfort, explanation, and control. What are your rituals?

>> Defining Religion

Given the varied and worldwide scope of beliefs and behavior labeled "religious," anthropologists know how difficult it is to define **religion.** In his book *Religion: An Anthropological View*, Anthony F. C. Wallace offered this definition: "belief and ritual concerned with supernatural beings, powers, and forces" (1966, p. 5). By "supernatural" he referred to a nonmaterial realm beyond (but believed to impinge on) the observable world. This realm cannot be verified or falsified empirically and is inexplicable in ordinary terms. It must be accepted "on faith." Supernatural beings—deities, ghosts, demons, souls, and spirits—make their homes outside our material world, although they may visit it from time to time. There also are supernatural or sacred forces, some of them wielded by deities and spirits, others that simply exist. In many societies, people believe they can benefit from, become imbued with, or manipulate supernatural forces (see Bowie 2006; Bowen 2008; Crapo 2003; Lambek 2008; Stein and Stein 2011; Warms, Garber, and McGee, eds. 2009).

religion Beliefs and rituals concerned with supernatural beings, powers, and forces.

communitas Intense community spirit, a feeling of great social solidarity, equality, and togetherness; characteristic of people experiencing liminality together.

Wallace's definition of religion focuses on presumably universal categories (beings, powers, and forces) within the supernatural realm. For Emile Durkheim (1912/2001), one of the founders of the anthropology of religion, the key distinction was between the sacred and the profane. Like the supernatural for Wallace, Durkheim's "sacred" was the domain set off from the ordinary or the mundane (he used the word "profane"). For Durkheim, every society had its sacred, but that domain was socially constructed; it varied from society to society. Durkheim focused on Native Australian societies, which he believed had preserved the most elementary or basic forms of religion. He noted that their most sacred objects, including plants and animals that served as totems, were not supernatural at all. Rather they were "real world" entities (e.g., kangaroos, grubs) that, over the generations, had acquired special meaning for the social groups that had made them sacred and continued to "worship" them.

Many definitions of religion focus on groups of people who gather together regularly for worship (see Reese 1999). These congregants or adherents internalize common beliefs and a shared system of meaning. They accept a set of doctrines involving the relationship between the individual and divinity, the sacred, or whatever is taken to be the ultimate nature of reality. Anthropologists like Durkheim have stressed the collective, social, shared, and enacted nature of religion, the emotions it generates, and the meanings it embodies. As Michael Lambek (2008, p. 5) remarks, "good anthropology understands that religious worlds are real, vivid, and significant to those who construct and inhabit them." Durkheim (1912/2001) highlighted religious effervescence, the bubbling up of collective emotional intensity generated by worship. Victor Turner (1969/1995) updated Durkheim's notion, using the term **communitas,** an intense community spirit, a feeling of great social solidarity, equality, and togetherness.

The word *religion* derives from the Latin *religare*—"to tie, to bind," but it is not necessary for all members of a given religion to meet together as a common body. Subgroups meet regularly at local congregation sites. They may attend occasional meetings with adherents representing a wider region. And they may form an imagined community with people of similar faith throughout the world.

In studying religion cross-culturally, anthropologists pay attention to religion as a social phenomenon as well as to the meanings of religious doctrines, settings, acts, and events. Verbal manifestations of religious beliefs include prayers, chants, myths, texts, and statements about, including rules of, ethics and morality (see Cunningham 1999; Klass 2003; Moro and Myers 2010; Stein and Stein 2011). The anthropological study of religion also encompasses notions about purity and pollution (including taboos involving diet and physical contact), sacrifice, initiation, rites of passage, vision quests, pilgrimages, spirit possession, prophecy, study, devotion, and moral actions (Lambek 2008, p. 9).

CULTURE THINK

Have you ever felt the intense community spirit of *communitas?* What are some secular settings where people might experience *communitas,* or collective effervescence?

Like ethnicity and language, religion is associated with social divisions within and between societies and nations. Religion both unites and divides. Participation in common rites may affirm, and thus maintain, the solidarity of a group of adherents. As we know from daily headlines, however, religious difference also may be associated with bitter enmity. In today's world, contacts and confrontations have increased between so-called world religions, such as Christianity and Islam, and the more localized forms of religion that missionaries typically lump together under the disparaging term "paganism." Increasingly, world religions compete for adherents and global power, and ethnic, regional, and class conflicts come to be framed in religious terms. Recent and contemporary examples of religion as a social and political force include the Iranian revolution, the rise of the religious right in the United States, and the spread of Pentecostalism in Korea, Africa, and Latin America.

Long ago, Edward Sapir (1928/1956) argued for a distinction between "a religion" and "religion." The former term would apply only to a formally organized religion, such as the world religions just mentioned. The latter—religion—is universal; it refers to religious beliefs and behavior, which exist in all societies, even if they don't stand out as a separate and clearly demarcated sphere. Indeed, many anthropologists (e.g., Asad 1983/2008) argue that such categories as "religion," "politics," and "the economy" are arbitrary constructs that apply best, and perhaps only, to Western, Christian, and modern societies. In such contexts religion can be seen as a specific domain, separate from politics and the economy. By contrast, in nonindustrial societies, religion typically is more embedded in society. Religious beliefs may help regulate the economy (e.g., astrologers determine when to plant) or permeate politics (e.g., divine right of kings). (Although religion also spills over into politics in the contemporary United States, it isn't supposed to. That is, the legal system views religion and politics as spheres that should be kept separate.)

Anthropologists agree that religion exists in all human societies; it is a cultural universal. However, we'll see that it isn't always easy to distinguish the sacred from the profane and that different societies conceptualize divinity, the sacred, the supernatural, and ultimate realities very differently.

STUDY TIP

Religion has several characteristics:
(1) It is concerned with the supernatural;
(2) it serves emotional needs; (3) it is a collective system of meaning; (4) it explains the unexplainable; (5) it is social in nature, based on religious roles.

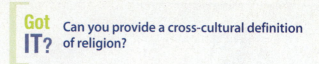

Got IT? Can you provide a cross-cultural definition of religion?

>> Expressions of Religion

When did religion begin? No one knows for sure. There are suggestions of religion in Neandertal burials and on European cave walls, where painted stick figures may represent shamans—early religious specialists. Nevertheless, any statement about when, where, why, and how religion arose, or any description of its original nature, can be only speculative. Although inconclusive, many such speculations have revealed important functions and effects of religious behavior. Several theories will be examined now.

SPIRITUAL BEINGS

Another founder of the anthropology of religion was the Englishman Sir Edward Burnett Tylor (1871/1958). Religion was born, Tylor thought, as people tried to understand conditions and events they could not explain by reference to daily experience. Tylor believed that our ancestors—and contemporary non-industrial peoples—were particularly intrigued with death, dreaming, and trance. People see images they may remember when they wake up or come out of the trance state. Tylor concluded that attempts to explain dreams and trances led early humans to believe that two entities inhabit the body, one active during the day and the other—a double or soul—active during sleep and trance states. Although they never meet, they are vital to each other. When the double permanently leaves the body, the person dies. Death is departure of the soul. From the Latin for soul, *anima,* Tylor named this belief animism. The soul was one sort of spiritual entity; people remembered various images from their dreams and trances—other spirits. For Tylor, **animism,** the earliest form of religion, was a belief in spiritual beings.

animism Belief in souls or doubles.

Tylor proposed that religion evolved through stages, beginning with animism. *Polytheism* (the belief in multiple gods) and then *monotheism* (the belief in a single, all-powerful deity) developed later. Because religion originated to explain things people didn't understand, Tylor thought it would decline as science offered better explanations. To an extent, he was right. We now have scientific explanations for many things that religion once explained. Nevertheless, because religion persists, it must do something more than explain the mysterious. It must, and does, have other functions and meanings.

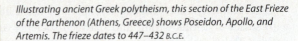

Illustrating ancient Greek polytheism, this section of the East Frieze of the Parthenon (Athens, Greece) shows Poseidon, Apollo, and Artemis. The frieze dates to 447–432 B.C.E.

Beliefs in manalike forces are widespread, although the specifics of the religious doctrines vary. Consider the contrast between mana in Melanesia and Polynesia (the islands included in a triangular area marked by Hawaii to the north, Easter Island to the east, and New Zealand to the southwest). In Melanesia, one could acquire mana by chance, or by working hard to get it. In Polynesia, mana wasn't potentially available to everyone but was attached to political offices. Chiefs and nobles had more mana than ordinary people did.

So charged with mana were the highest chiefs that contact with them was dangerous to the commoners. The mana of chiefs flowed out of their bodies wherever they went. It could infect the ground, making it dangerous for others to walk in the chief's footsteps. It could permeate the containers and utensils chiefs used in eating. Contact between chief and commoners was dangerous because mana could have an effect like an electric shock. Because high chiefs had so much mana, their bodies and possessions were **taboo** (set apart as sacred and off-limits to ordinary people). Contact between a high chief and commoners was forbidden. Because ordinary people couldn't bear as much sacred current as royalty could, when commoners were accidentally exposed, purification rites were necessary.

One function of religion is to explain. A belief in souls explains what happens in sleep, trance, and death. Melanesian mana explains differential success that people can't understand in ordinary, natural terms. People fail at hunting, war, or gardening not because they are lazy, stupid, or inept but because success comes—or doesn't come—from the supernatural world.

POWERS AND FORCES

Besides animism—and sometimes coexisting with it in the same society—is a view of the supernatural as a domain of impersonal power, or *force,* which people can control under certain conditions. (You'd be right to think of *Star Wars.*) Such a conception of the supernatural is particularly prominent in Melanesia, the area of the South Pacific that includes Papua New Guinea and adjacent islands. Melanesians believed in **mana,** a sacred impersonal force existing in the universe. Mana can reside in people, animals, plants, and objects.

mana Sacred impersonal force in Melanesian and Polynesian religions.

taboo Prohibition backed by supernatural sanctions.

Melanesian mana was similar to our notion of efficacy or luck. Melanesians attributed success to mana, which people could acquire or manipulate in different ways, such as through magic. Objects with mana could change someone's luck. For example, a charm or amulet belonging to a successful hunter might transmit the hunter's mana to the next person who held or wore it. A woman might put a rock in her garden, see her yields improve dramatically, and attribute the change to the force contained in the rock.

The beliefs in spiritual beings (e.g., animism) and supernatural forces (e.g., mana) fit within the definition of religion given at the beginning of this chapter. Most religions include both spirits and impersonal forces. Likewise the supernatural beliefs of contemporary North Americans include beings (gods, saints, souls, demons) and forces (charms, talismans, crystals, and sacred objects).

MAGIC AND RELIGION

Magic refers to supernatural techniques intended to accomplish specific aims. These techniques include spells, formulas, and incantations used with deities or with impersonal forces. Magicians use *imitative magic* to produce a desired effect by imitating it. If magicians wish to injure or kill someone, they may imitate that effect on an image of the victim. Sticking pins in "voodoo dolls" is an example. With *contagious magic,* whatever is done to an object is believed to affect a person who once had contact with it. Sometimes practitioners of contagious magic use body products from prospective victims—their nails or hair, for example. The spell

Trobriand Islanders prepare a traditional trading canoe for use in the Kula, a regional exchange system. The woman brings trade goods in a basket, while the men prepare the long boat to set sail. Magic is often associated with uncertainty, such as sailing in unpredictable waters.

performed on the body product is believed to reach the person eventually and work the desired result (see Stein and Stein 2011). Magic exists in societies with diverse religious beliefs, including animism, mana, polytheism, and monotheism.

UNCERTAINTY, ANXIETY, SOLACE

Religion and magic don't just explain things. They serve emotional needs as well as cognitive (e.g., explanatory) ones. Religion helps people face death and endure life crises. Magical techniques can dispel doubts that arise when outcomes are beyond human control. According to Malinowski, when people face uncertainty and danger, they often turn to magic. As mentioned in "Understanding Ourselves" at the beginning of this chapter, Malinowski found that the Trobriand Islanders used magic when sailing, a hazardous activity. He proposed that because people can't control matters such as wind, weather, and the fish supply, they turn to magic (Malinowski 1931/1978). Gmelch's research on baseball and magic, also discussed in "Understanding Ourselves," confirms Malinowski's conclusion that magic is most prevalent in situations of chance or uncertainty, especially pitching and batting (see Gmelch 2006).

> **magic** Use of supernatural techniques to accomplish specific aims.

Malinowski noted that it was only when confronted by situations they could not control that Trobrianders,

CULTURE THINK

Think about superstitions, such as knocking on wood to prevent an unwanted outcome. Think of three additional superstitious behaviors. How many of them are used, like magic, to produce an illusion of control in an uncertain situation?

ritual Behavior that is formal, stylized, repetitive, and stereotyped, performed earnestly as a social act; rituals are held at set times and places and have liturgical orders.

rites of passage Culturally defined activities associated with the transition from one place or stage of life to another.

Did You Know?

Mardi Gras exemplifies a ritual of rebellion, in which people are temporarily allowed to reject the dominant social order. Pre-Civil War Mardi Gras clubs originated in Alabama's wealthy, white, Catholic plantation society and eventually moved to Louisiana. The clubs' activities formed part of their winter festivities. The first ball held by a black Mardi Gras club was in 1894.

out of psychological stress, turned from technology to magic. Despite our improving technical skills, we still can't control every outcome, and magic persists in contemporary societies.

>> Rituals and Rites

Several features distinguish **rituals** from other kinds of behavior (Rappaport 1974, 1999). Rituals are formal—stylized, repetitive, and stereotyped. People perform them in special (sacred) places and at set times. Rituals include *liturgical orders*—sequences of words and actions invented prior to the current performance of the ritual in which they occur.

These features link rituals to plays, but there are important differences. Plays have audiences rather than participants. Actors merely *portray* something, but ritual performers—who make up congregations—are in *earnest*. Rituals convey information about the participants and their traditions. Repeated year after year, generation after generation, rituals translate enduring messages, values, and sentiments into action.

Rituals are *social* acts. Inevitably, some participants are more committed than others to the beliefs that lie behind the rites. However, just by taking part in a joint public act, the performers signal that they accept a common social and moral order, one that transcends their status as individuals.

RITES OF PASSAGE

Magic and religion, as Malinowski noted, can reduce anxiety and allay fears. Ironically, beliefs and rituals also can *create* anxiety and a sense of insecurity and danger (Radcliffe-Brown 1962/1965). Anxiety may arise *because* a rite exists. Indeed, participation in a collective ritual may build up stress, whose common reduction, through the completion of the ritual, enhances the solidarity of the participants.

Rites of passage can be individual or collective. The traditional vision quests of Native Americans, particularly the Plains Indians, illustrate **rites of passage** (customs associated with the transition from one place or stage of life to another). To move from boyhood to manhood, a youth was separated temporarily from his community. After a period of isolation in the wilderness, often featuring fasting and drug consumption, the young man would see a vision, which would become his guardian spirit. He would then return to his community as an adult.

Contemporary rites of passage include confirmations, baptisms, bar and bat mitzvahs, initiations, weddings, and applying for Medicare. Passage rites involve changes in social status, such as from boyhood to manhood and from nonmember to sorority sister. More generally, a rite of passage may mark any change in place, condition, social position, or age.

All rites of passage have three phases: separation, liminality, and incorporation. In the first phase, people withdraw from ordinary society. In the third phase, they reenter society, having completed a rite that changes their status. The second or *liminal* phase is the most interesting. It is the limbo or "time out" during which people have left one status but haven't yet entered or joined the next (Turner 1967/1974).

STUDY TIP

Rituals serve two purposes:

- They convey messages, values, and sentiments.
- They encourage a common social order.

Oppositions Between Liminality and Normal Social Life

Liminality	Normal Social Structure
Transition	State
Homogeneity	Heterogeneity
Communitas	Structure
Equality	Inequality
Anonymity	Names
Absence of property	Property
Absence of status	Status
Absence of rank	Rank
Humility	Pride
Nakedness or uniform dress	Dress distinctions
Sexual continence or excess	Sexuality
Minimization of sex distinctions	Maximization of sex distinctions
Disregard of personal appearance	Care for personal appearance
Unselfishness	Selfishness
Total obedience	Obedience only to superior rank
Sacredness	Secularity
Sacred instruction	Technical Knowledge
Silence	Speech
Simplicity	Complexity
Acceptance of pain and suffering	Avoidance of pain and suffering

TABLE 9.1

Source: From *The Ritual Process* by Victor Turner. Copyright © 1969 by Aldine Publishers. Reprinted by permission of Aldine Transaction, a division of Transaction Publishers.

Liminality always has certain characteristics. Liminal people exist apart from ordinary distinctions and expectations, living in a time out of time. A series of contrasts demarcate liminality from normal social life. For example, among the Ndembu of Zambia, a chief underwent a rite of passage before taking office. During the liminal period, his past and future positions in society were ignored, even reversed. He was subjected to a variety of insults, orders, and humiliations.

Passage rites often are collective. Several individuals—boys being circumcised, fraternity or sorority initiates, men at military boot camps, football players in summer training camps, women becoming nuns—pass through the rites together as a group. Table 9.1 summarizes the contrasts, or oppositions, between liminality and normal social life. Most notable is the social aspect of *collective liminality* we have mentioned previously, which Durkheim called communitas (Turner 1967/1974), an intense community spirit, a feeling of great solidarity,

liminality The critically important marginal or in-between phase of a rite of passage.

CULTURETHINK

Rites of passage into adulthood are formal rituals in many cultural contexts. What kinds of rituals or other events mark passage to adulthood in your society? Do any of these have characteristics of liminality?

Passage rites often are collective. A group, whether initiates in Togo or Marine Corps recruits on Parris Island, South Carolina, passes through the rites as a unit. Such liminal people, required to dress and act alike, experience communitas, an intense community spirit, a feeling of great social solidarity or togetherness.

equality, and togetherness. Liminal people experience the same treatment and conditions and must act alike. Liminality may be marked by *reversals* of ordinary behavior. For example, sexual taboos may be intensified, or conversely, sexual excess may be encouraged. Liminal symbols, such as special clothing or body paint, mark entities and circumstances as extraordinary—outside and beyond ordinary society and everyday life.

Liminality is basic to every passage rite. Furthermore, in certain societies, including our own, liminal symbols may be used to set off one (religious) group from another, and from society as a whole. Such "permanent liminal groups" (e.g., sects, brotherhoods, and cults) are found most characteristically in nation-states. Such liminal features as humility, poverty, equality, obedience, sexual abstinence, and silence may be required for all sect or cult members. Those who join such a group agree to its rules. As if they were undergoing a passage rite—but in this case a never-ending one—they may rid themselves of their previous possessions and cut themselves off from former social links, including those with family members. Is liminality compatible with Facebook?

Members of a sect or cult often wear uniform clothing. Often they adopt a common hairstyle (shaved head, short hair, or long hair). Liminal groups submerge the individual in the collective. This may be one reason why Americans, whose core values include individuality and individualism, are so fearful and suspicious of "cults."

Not all collective rites are rites of passage. Most societies observe occasions on which people come together to worship or celebrate and, in doing so, affirm and reinforce their solidarity. Rituals such as the totemic ceremonies described in the next section are *rites of intensification:* They intensify social solidarity. The

ritual creates communitas and promotes emotions (the collective spiritual effervescence described by Durkheim 1912/2001) that enhance social solidarity.

Got IT? Can you identify features of rituals in general and of rites of passage in particular?

TOTEMISM

Totemism was a key ingredient in the religions of the Native Australians. *Totems* could be animals, plants, or geographical features. In each tribe, groups of people had particular totems. Members of each totemic group believed themselves to be descendants of their totem. They customarily neither killed nor ate it, but this taboo was lifted once a year, when people assembled for ceremonies and rituals dedicated to the totem. These annual rites were believed to be necessary for the totem's survival and reproduction.

CULTURETHINK

What totems marking common identity are meaningful to people you know? What rituals maintain this sense of social oneness?

Totemism uses nature as a model for society. The totems usually are animals and plants, which are part of nature. People relate to nature through their totemic association with natural species. Because each group has a different totem, social differences mirror natural contrasts. Diversity in the natural order becomes a model for diversity in the social order. However, although totemic plants and animals occupy different niches in nature, on another level they are united because they all are part of nature. The unity of the human social order is enhanced by symbolic association with and imitation of the natural order (Durkheim 1912/2001; Lévi-Strauss 1963; Radcliffe-Brown 1962/1965).

Totemic principles continue to demarcate groups, including clubs, teams, and universities, in modern societies. Badgers and Wolverines are animals, and (it is said in Michigan) Buckeyes are some kind of nut (more precisely, buckeye nuts come from the buckeye tree). Differences between natural species (e.g., lions, and tigers, and bears) serve to distinguish sports teams, and even political parties (donkeys and elephants). Although the modern context is secular, one can still witness, in intense college football rivalries, some of the effervescence Durkheim noted in Australian totemic religion and other rites of intensification.

Totems are sacred emblems symbolizing common identity. This is true not just among Native Australians, but also among Native American groups of the North Pacific Coast of North America, whose totem poles are well known. Their totemic carvings, which commemorated, and told visual stories about, ancestors, animals, and spirits, were also associated with ceremonies. In totemic rites, people gather together to honor their totem. In so doing, they use ritual to maintain the social oneness that the totem symbolizes.

[**Got IT?** Can you explain characteristics and functions of religion?

Shaman Gray Squirrel blends the sands of a sand painting, as part of a four day Navajo ritual to bring rain, in Farmington, New Mexico.

>> Social Control

Religion means a lot to people. It helps them cope with uncertainty, adversity, fear, and tragedy. It offers hope that things will get better. Lives can be transformed through spiritual healing. Sinners can repent and be saved—or they can go on sinning and be damned. If the faithful truly internalize a system of religious rewards and punishments, their religion becomes a powerful influence on their attitudes and behavior, and what they teach their children.

Many people engage in religious activity because it works for them. Prayers get answered. Faith healers heal. Many American Indian people in southwestern Oklahoma use faith healers at high monetary costs, not just because it makes them feel better about the uncertain, but because it works (Lassiter 1998). Each year legions of Brazilians visit a church, Nosso Senhor do Bomfim, in the city of Salvador, Bahia. They vow to repay "Our Lord" (Nosso Senhor) if healing happens. Showing that the vows work, and are repaid, are the thousands of ex votos, plastic impressions of every conceivable body part, that adorn the church, along with photos of people who have been cured.

Religion can work by getting inside people and mobilizing their emotions—their joy, their wrath, their certainty, their righteousness. People can feel a deep sense of shared joy, meaning, experience, communion, belonging, and commitment

to their religion. The power of religion affects action. When religions meet, they can coexist peacefully, or their differences can be a basis for enmity and disharmony, even battle. Religious fervor has inspired Christians on crusades against the infidel and has led Muslims to wage holy wars against non-Islamic peoples. Throughout history, political leaders have used religion to promote and justify their views and policies.

How may leaders mobilize communities and, in so doing, gain support for their own policies? One way is by persuasion; another is by instilling hatred or fear. Consider witchcraft accusations. Witch hunts can be powerful means of social control by creating a climate of danger and insecurity that affects everyone, not just the people who are likely targets. No one wants to seem deviant, to be accused of being a witch. Witch hunts often take aim at people who can be accused and punished with least chance of retaliation. During the great European witch craze of the 15th, 16th, and 17th centuries (Harris 1974), most accusations and convictions were against poor women with little social support.

leveling mechanisms Customs and social actions that operate to reduce differences in wealth and thus to bring standouts in line with community norms.

Witchcraft accusations often are directed at socially marginal or anomalous individuals. Consider the Betsileo of Madagascar, who believe that married men should live in their father's village. Marcel contradicts this rule by residing in his mother's village. People like Marcel who violate cultural norms have to be particularly careful about how they act. Just a bit of unusual behavior (e.g., staying up late at night) can fuel suspicion that they are engaging in witchcraft; they may be avoided or ostracized as a result. In peasant communities, people who stand out economically, especially if they seem to be benefiting at the expense of others, often face witchcraft

accusations, leading to social ostracism or punishment. In this case witchcraft accusation becomes a **leveling mechanism,** a custom or social action that operates to reduce status differences and thus to bring standouts in line with community norms—another form of social control.

To ensure proper behavior, religions offer rewards (e.g., the fellowship of the religious community) and punishments (e.g., the threat of being cast out or excommunicated). Religions, especially the formal, organized ones typically found in state societies, often prescribe a code of ethics and morality to guide behavior. The Judaic Ten Commandments laid down a set of prohibitions against killing, stealing, adultery, and other misdeeds. Crimes are breaches of secular laws, as sins are breaches of religious strictures. Some rules (e.g., the Ten Commandments) proscribe or prohibit behavior; others prescribe behavior. The Golden Rule, for instance, is a religious guide to do unto others as you would have them do unto you. Moral codes are ways of maintaining order and stability. Codes of morality and ethics are constantly reinforced in religious sermons, catechisms, and the like. They become internalized psychologically. They guide behavior and produce regret, guilt, shame, and the need for forgiveness, expiation, and absolution when they are not followed.

"God has no religion."

Mahatma Gandhi

 Got IT? Can you evaluate how religion operates as a form of social control?

>> Kinds of Religion

Religion is a cultural universal. But religions exist in particular societies, and cultural differences show up systematically in religious beliefs and practices. For example, the religions of stratified, state societies differ from those of societies with less marked social contrasts—societies without kings, lords, and subjects. What can a given society afford in terms of religion? Churches, temples, and other full-time religious establishments, with their monumental structures and hierarchies of officials, must be supported in some consistent way, such as by tithes and taxes. What kinds of societies can support such hierarchies and architecture?

All societies have religious figures—those believed capable of mediating between humans and the supernatural. More generally, all societies have medico-magico-religious specialists. Modern societies can support both priesthoods and health care professionals.

The Right Reverend Kay Goldsworthy during her consecration service and Ordination as Australia's first female Anglican bishop at St George's Cathedral in Perth, Australia.

Lacking the resources for such specialization, foraging societies typically have only part-time specialists, who often have both religious and healing roles. *Shaman* is the general term encompassing curers ("witch doctors"), mediums, spiritualists, astrologers, palm readers, and other independent diviners. In foraging societies, shamans are usually part-time; that is, they also hunt or gather.

The annual totemic ceremonies of Native Australians temporarily brought together foragers who had to disperse most of the year to hunt and gather for subsistence. Given seasonal harvests of fish and other resources in a rich natural environment, foraging tribes on the North Pacific Coast of North America could host ceremonies like the potlatch described in the chapter "Making a Living." However, community rituals including harvest ceremonies and collective rites of passage are much more common in farming and herding societies than among foragers.

Societies with productive economies (based on agriculture and trade) and large, dense populations (nation-states) can support full-time religious specialists—professional priesthoods. Like the state itself, priesthoods are hierarchically and bureaucratically

organized. Anthony Wallace (1966) describes the religions of such stratified societies as "ecclesiastical" (pertaining to an established church and its hierarchy of officials) and "Olympian," after Mount Olympus, home of the classical Greek gods. In such religions, powerful anthropomorphic gods have specialized functions, for example, gods of love, war, the sea, and death. Such pantheons (collections of deities) were prominent in the religions of many nonindustrial nation-states, including the Aztecs of Mexico, several African and Asian kingdoms, and classical Greece and Rome.

Greco-Roman religions were polytheistic, featuring many deities. In monotheism, all supernatural phenomena are believed to be manifestations of, or under the control of, a single eternal, omniscient, omnipotent, and omnipresent being. In the ecclesiastical monotheistic religion known as Christianity, a single supreme being is manifest in a trinity. Robert Bellah (1978) viewed most forms of Christianity as examples of "world-rejecting religion." According to Bellah, the first world-rejecting religions arose in ancient civilizations, along with literacy and a specialized priesthood. These religions are so named because of their tendency to reject the natural (mundane, ordinary, material, secular) world and to focus instead on a higher (sacred, transcendent) realm of reality. The divine is a domain of exalted morality to which humans can only aspire. Salvation through fusion with the supernatural is the main goal of such religions.

>> World Religions

Information on the world's major religions today is shown graphically in "Religions of the World" on the next page. Based on people's claimed religions, Christianity is the world's largest, with some 2.1 billion adherents. Islam, with some 1.5 billion practitioners, is next, followed by Hinduism, then Chinese traditional religion (also known as Chinese folk religion or Confucianism), and Buddhism. More than a billion people claim no official religion, but only about a fifth of them are self-proclaimed atheists. Worldwide, Islam is growing at a rate of about 2.9 percent annually, versus 2.3 percent for Christianity, whose overall growth rate is the same as the rate of world population increase (Adherents. com 2002; Ontario Consultants 2001).

Within Christianity, the growth rate varies. There were an estimated 680 million "born-again" Christians (e.g., Pentecostals and Evangelicals) in the world in 2001, with an annual worldwide growth rate of 7 percent, versus just 2.3 percent for Christianity overall. (This would translate into 1.4 billion Pentecostals/Evangelicals by 2012.) The global growth rate of Roman Catholics has been estimated at only 1.3 percent, compared with a Protestant growth rate of 3.3 percent per year (Winter 2001). Much of this explosive growth, especially in Africa, is of a type

Religions of the World*

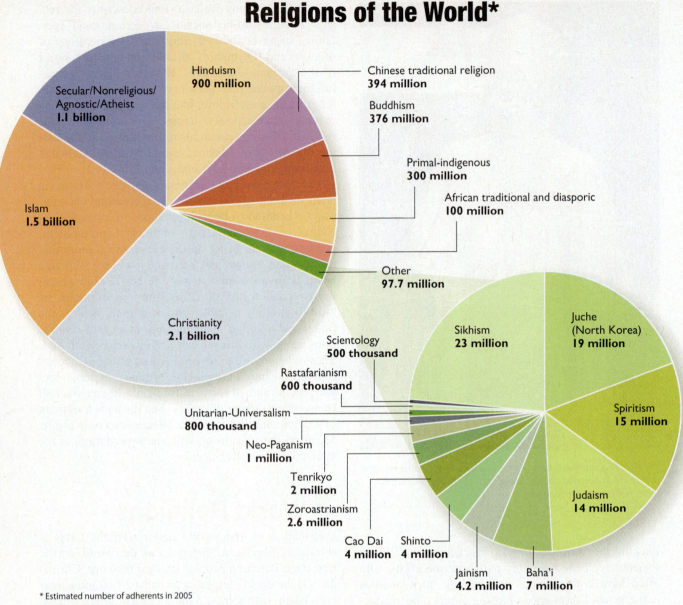

Hinduism
900 million

Secular/Nonreligious/
Agnostic/Atheist
1.1 billion

Islam
1.5 billion

Christianity
2.1 billion

Chinese traditional religion
394 million

Buddhism
376 million

Primal-indigenous
300 million

African traditional and diasporic
100 million

Other
97.7 million

Scientology
500 thousand

Rastafarianism
600 thousand

Unitarian-Universalism
800 thousand

Neo-Paganism
1 million

Tenrikyo
2 million

Zoroastrianism
2.6 million

Cao Dai
4 million

Shinto
4 million

Jainism
4.2 million

Baha'i
7 million

Sikhism
23 million

Juche
(North Korea)
19 million

Spiritism
15 million

Judaism
14 million

* Estimated number of adherents in 2005

Source: B.A. Robinson, "Religions of the World, "Ontario Consultants on Religious Tolerance, www.religioustolerance.org/worldrel.html. Reprinted by permission.

of Protestantism that would be scarcely recognizable to most Americans, given its incorporation of many animistic elements.

 Can you describe how religions in stratified, state societies differ from those with less marked social contrasts?

>> Religion and Change

Religious fundamentalists seek order based on strict adherence to purportedly traditional standards, beliefs, rules, and customs. Christian and Islamic fundamentalists recognize, decry, and attempt to redress change, yet they also contribute to change (Antoun 2008). In

a worldwide process, new religions challenge established churches. In the United States, for example, conservative Christian TV hosts have become influential broadcasters and opinion shapers. In Latin America, evangelical Protestantism is winning millions of converts from Roman Catholicism.

Like political organization, religion helps maintain social order. And like political mobilization, religious energy can be harnessed not just for change but also for revolution. Reacting to conquest or to actual or perceived foreign domination, for instance, religious leaders may seek to alter or revitalize their society. In an "Islamic Revolution," for example, Iranian ayatollahs marshaled religious fervor to create national solidarity and radical change. We call such movements *nativistic movements* (Linton 1943) or *revitalization movements* (Wallace 1956).

REVITALIZATION MOVEMENTS

Social movements that occur in times of change, in which religious leaders emerge and undertake to alter or revitalize a society, are termed **revitalization movements.** Christianity originated as a revitalization movement. Jesus was one of several prophets who preached new religious doctrines while the Middle East was under Roman rule. It was a time of social unrest, when a foreign power ruled the land. Jesus inspired a new, enduring, and major religion. His contemporaries were not so successful.

The Handsome Lake religion arose around 1800 among the Iroquois of New York State (Wallace 1969). Handsome Lake, the founder of this revitalization movement, was a leader of one of the Iroquois tribes. The Iroquois had suffered because of their support of the British against the American colonials. After the colonial victory and a wave of immigration to their homeland, the Iroquois were dispersed on small reservations. Unable to pursue traditional horticulture and hunting in their homeland, the Iroquois became heavy drinkers and quarreled among themselves.

Handsome Lake was a heavy drinker who started having visions from heavenly messengers. The spirits warned him that unless the Iroquois changed their ways, they would be destroyed. His visions offered a plan for coping with the new order. Witchcraft, quarreling, and drinking would end. The Iroquois would copy European farming techniques, which, unlike traditional Iroquois horticulture, stressed male rather than female labor. Handsome Lake preached that the Iroquois should also abandon their communal longhouses and matrilineal descent groups for more permanent marriages and individual family households. The teachings of Handsome Lake produced a new church and religion, one that still has members in New York and Ontario. This revitalization movement helped the Iroquois adapt to and survive in a modified environment. They eventually gained a reputation among their non-Indian neighbors as sober family farmers.

revitalization movements Movements that occur in times of change, in which religious leaders emerge and undertake to alter or revitalize a society.

cargo cults Postcolonial, acculturative, religious movements common in Melanesia that attempt to explain European domination and wealth and to achieve similar success magically by mimicking European behavior.

CARGO CULTS

Like the Handsome Lake religion just discussed, **cargo cults** are revitalization movements. Such movements

ANTHROPOLOGY WORKS

Sonja Traylor has been a flight attendant for fifteen years and has continued that work while getting her bachelor's degree as a nontraditional student. When she began studying anthropology, she felt she began to excel professionally. She now has a better sense of how to interact with passengers of different cultural and religious backgrounds. She also realizes that accommodating diverse religious practices—by providing space for prayer and alternative meal choices, for example—is critical to an airline's success in the global market.

STUDY TIP

Two religious responses to the expansion of the world capitalist economy are fundamentalisms (Christian and Islamic) and revitalization movements (Handsome Lake religion and cargo cults).

may emerge when natives have regular contact with industrial societies but lack their wealth, technology, and living standards. Some cargo cults attempt to explain European domination and wealth, and to achieve similar success magically by mimicking European behavior and manipulating symbols of the desired lifestyle. The cargo cults of Melanesia and Papua New Guinea weave Christian doctrine with aboriginal beliefs. They take their name from their focus on cargo—European goods of the sort natives have seen unloaded from the cargo holds of ships and airplanes.

In one early cult, members believed that the spirits of the dead would arrive in a ship. These ghosts would bring manufactured goods for the natives and would kill all the whites. More recent cults replaced ships with airplanes (Worsley 1959/1985). Many cults have used elements of European culture as sacred objects. The rationale is that Europeans use these objects, have wealth, and therefore must know the "secret of cargo." By mimicking how Europeans use or treat objects, natives hope also to come upon the secret knowledge needed to gain cargo.

For example, having seen Europeans' reverent treatment of flags and flagpoles, the members of one cult began to worship flagpoles. They believed the flagpoles were sacred towers that could transmit messages between the living and the dead. Other natives built airstrips to entice planes bearing canned goods, portable radios, clothing, wristwatches, and motorcycles. Near the airstrips they made effigies of towers, airplanes, and radios. They talked into the cans in a magical attempt to establish radio contact with the gods. Can you think of anything in your own society (including the media) that features similar behavior?

A cargo cult in Vanuatu, a country in Melanesia. Boys and men march with spears, imitating British colonial soldiers. Does anything in your own society remind you of a cargo cult?

Some cargo cult prophets proclaimed that success would come through a reversal of European domination and native subjugation. The day was near, they preached, when natives, aided by God, Jesus, or native ancestors, would turn the tables. Native skins would turn white, and those of Europeans would turn brown; Europeans would die or be killed.

Cargo cults blend aboriginal and Christian beliefs. Melanesian myths told of ancestors shedding their skins and changing into powerful beings and of dead people returning to life. Christian missionaries, who had been in Melanesia since the late nineteenth century, also spoke of resurrection. The cults' preoccupation with cargo is related to traditional Melanesian big man systems. In the chapter "Political Systems," we saw that a Melanesian big man had to be generous. People worked for the big man, helping him amass wealth, but eventually he had to give a feast and give away all that wealth.

Because of their experience with big man systems, Melanesians believed that all wealthy people eventually had to give away their wealth. For decades they had attended Christian missions and worked on plantations. All the while they expected Europeans to return the fruits of their labor as their own big men did. When the Europeans refused to distribute the wealth or even to let natives know the secret of its production and distribution, cargo cults developed.

Like arrogant big men, Europeans would be leveled, by death if necessary. However, natives lacked the physical means of doing what their traditions said they should do. Thwarted by well-armed colonial forces, natives resorted to magical leveling. They called on supernatural beings to intercede, to kill or otherwise deflate the European big men and redistribute their wealth.

Cargo cults are religious responses to the expansion of the world capitalist economy. However, this religious mobilization had political and economic results. Cult participation gave Melanesians a basis for common interests and activities and thus helped pave the way for political parties and economic interest organizations. Previously separated by geography, language, and customs, Melanesians started forming larger groups as members of the same cults and followers of the same prophets. The cargo cults paved the way for political action through which the indigenous peoples eventually regained their autonomy.

NEW AND ALTERNATIVE RELIGIOUS MOVEMENTS

The New Age movement, which emerged in the 1980s, draws on and blends cultural elements from multiple traditions. It advocates change through individual personal transformation.

Candomblé celebrants observe the day honoring Iemanjá (sea goddess) in Salvador, Bahia, Brazil.

In the United States and Australia, respectively, some people who are not Native Americans or Native Australians have appropriated the symbols, settings, and purported religious practices of Native Americans and Native Australians, for New Age religions. Native American activists decry the appropriation and commercialization of their spiritual beliefs and rituals, as when "sweat lodge" ceremonies are held on cruise ships, with wine and cheese served. They see the appropriation of their ceremonies and traditions as theft.

New religious movements have varied origins. Some have been influenced by Christianity; others, by Eastern (Asian) religions; still others, by mysticism and spiritualism. Religion also evolves in tandem with science and technology. For example, the Raelian movement, a religious group centered in Switzerland and Montreal, promotes cloning as a way of achieving eternal life (Palmer 2001).

Many contemporary nations contain unofficial religions. One example is "Yoruba religion," a term applied to perhaps 15 million adherents in Africa, as well as to millions of practitioners of *syncretic,* or blended, religions (with elements of Catholicism and spiritism) in the Western Hemisphere. Forms of Yoruba religion include *santeria* (in the Spanish Caribbean and the United States), *candomblé* (in Brazil), and *vodoun* (in

the French Caribbean). Yoruba religion, with roots in precolonial nation-states of West Africa, has spread far beyond its religion of origin, as part of the African diaspora. It remains an influential, identifiable religion today, despite suppression, such as by Cuba's communist government. There are perhaps 3 million practitioners of santeria in Cuba, plus another 800,000 in the United States. At least 1 million Brazilians participate in candomblé, also known as macumba. Voodoo (or *vodoun*) has between 2.8 and 3.2 million practitioners (Ontario Consultants 2002), many (perhaps most) of whom would name something else, such as Catholicism, as their religion.

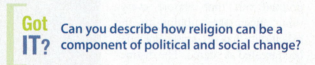

Got IT? Can you describe how religion can be a component of political and social change?

>> Secular Rituals

In concluding this discussion of religion, we may recognize some problems with the definitions of religion given at the beginning of this chapter. The first problem: If we define religion with reference to the sacred and/or to supernatural beings, powers, and forces, how do we classify ritual-like behaviors that occur in secular contexts? Some anthropologists believe there are both sacred and secular rituals. Secular rituals include formal, invariant, stereotyped, earnest, repetitive behavior and rites of passage that take place in nonreligious settings.

A second problem: If the distinction between the supernatural and the natural is not consistently made in a society, how can we tell what is religion and what isn't? The Betsileo of Madagascar, for example, view witches and dead ancestors as real people who play roles in ordinary life. However, their occult powers are not empirically demonstrable.

A third problem: The behavior considered appropriate for religious occasions varies tremendously from culture to culture. One society may consider drunken frenzy the surest sign of faith, whereas another may inculcate quiet reverence. Who is to say which is "more religious"?

It is possible for apparently secular settings, things, and events to acquire intense meaning for individuals who have grown up in their presence. For example, identities and loyalties based on fandom, football, baseball, and soccer can be powerful indeed. Rock stars and bands can mobilize many. A World Series win led to celebrations across a "Red Sox nation." Italians and Brazilians are rarely, if ever, as nationally focused and emotionally unified as they are when their teams are competing in the World Cup. The collective effervescence that Durkheim found so characteristic of religion can equally well describe what Brazilians experience when their country wins a World Cup.

In the context of comparative religion, the idea that the secular can become sacred isn't surprising. Long ago, Durkheim (1912/2001) pointed out that almost everything, from the sublime to the ridiculous, has in some societies been treated as sacred. The distinction between sacred and profane doesn't depend on the intrinsic qualities of the sacred symbol. In Australian totemic religion, for example, sacred beings include such humble creatures as ducks, frogs, rabbits, and grubs, whose inherent qualities could hardly have given rise to the religious sentiment they inspire.

Madagascar's tomb-centered ceremonies are times when the living and the dead are joyously reunited, when people get drunk, gorge themselves, and have sexual license. Perhaps the gray, sober, ascetic, and moralistic aspects of many official religious events, in taking the fun out of religion, force us to find religion (i.e., truth, beauty, meaning, passionate involvement) in fun.

Got IT? Can you explain how secular phenomena can be experienced as sacred?

Try to find a group on campus or in town that might be considered a "permanent liminal group." Examples of such groups include monks, nuns, cadets, and other established groups whose members display liminal features, such as uniform dress and/or sexual restrictions. If you can't find one, read about cults and sects and choose one in the United States or another society you may know well. Learn something about the group's practices and beliefs. Using Table 9.1, list liminal features that seem to fit this group. For example, do you see an absence of rank and a sharing of communitas? Note how such features are revealed in behavior patterns. How would the contrasts between liminality and "normal" social life help explain why outsiders might consider this group strange or even threatening?

FOR REVIEW

I. What is religion, and what are its various forms, social correlates, and functions?

- Given the varied and worldwide scope of beliefs and behavior labeled "religious," anthropologists recognize the difficulty of defining religion. Religion, a cultural universal, describes beliefs and behavior concerned with supernatural beings, powers, and forces. Religion also encompasses the feelings, meanings, and congregations associated with such beliefs and behavior. Anthropological studies have revealed many forms, expressions, and functions of religion. These belief systems include animism (spiritual beings), mana (a sacred impersonal force), and totemism, which uses nature as a model for society. Magic employs supernatural techniques to accomplish specific aims. Magic and religion help to explain the world and serve emotional needs, such as helping people cope with adversity and reducing anxiety, although rites also can create anxiety. Religion can divide as well as unite.

II. What is ritual, and what are its various forms and expressions?

- Rituals consist of behavior that is formal—stylized, repetitive, and stereotyped. People perform rituals in sacred places and at set times. Rituals convey information about the participants and translate enduring messages and values into action. Through ritual people subordinate their particular beliefs to a social collectivity. Rites of passage mark changes in place, condition, age, or social position. These rites have three stages: separation, liminality, and incorporation. In separation, people withdraw from the group; incorporation involves reentering it. Liminality is the limbo in between. In communitas, a liminal characteristic, participants experience social solidarity and equality. Rituals may be secular as well as religious.

III. What role does religion play in maintaining and changing societies?

- Religion establishes and maintains social control through moral and ethical beliefs and real and imagined rewards and punishments. Religion also can mobilize communities for collective action; leaders may use religious rhetoric to gain support for their policies. Religion can promote change through revitalization movements led by religious figures trying to help people adapt to change. Cargo cults blend aboriginal and Christian beliefs to explain European domination and wealth and achieve similar success magically. Among contemporary, "new" religious movements, some have been influenced by Christianity; others, by Eastern (Asian) religions; still others, by mysticism and spiritualism, or by science and technology. There are secular as well as religious rituals. It is possible for apparently secular settings, things, and events to acquire intense meaning for individuals who have grown up in their presence.

Pop Quiz

Multiple Choice:

1. According to Tylor, through what sequence did religion evolve?
   a. Animism, polytheism, monotheism
   b. Imitative magic, polytheism, monotheism
   c. Mana, polytheism, monotheism
   d. Olympianism, animism, monotheism

2. Which of the following describes the concept of mana in Polynesian and Melanesian cultures?
   a. Things charged with mana were taboo.
   b. In Melanesia, mana was similar to the notion of luck (anyone could get it); in Polynesia, mana was attached to political elites.
   c. Most anthropologists agree that mana was the most primitive religious doctrine in both areas.
   d. In both Polynesia and Melanesia, mana was concerned with supernatural beings rather than with powers or forces.

3. What is typically observed during the liminal phase of a rite of passage?
   a. Intensification of social hierarchy
   b. Symbolic reversals of ordinary behavior
   c. Formation of a ranking system
   d. No change in the social norms

4. Which of the following points is *not* consistent with the chapter's discussion of world religions?
   a. Christianity is the world's largest major religion.
   b. Islam is growing at a faster rate than Christianity.
   c. There is no variation in the growth rate of different groups of Christians.
   d. More than a billion people claim no religion.

5. Which statement most accurately defines a revitalization movement?
   a. It seeks to maintain order through strict adherence to purportedly traditional standards, customs, and beliefs.
   b. More correctly known as a nativistic movement, a revitalization movement seeks to maintain the old native ways of life.
   c. It is a colonial religious movement that lacked adaptive value for the people involved.
   d. It is a social movement that occurs in times of change in which religious leaders undertake to revitalize a society.

6. Cargo cults, which mix Melanesian and Christian beliefs, are
   a. Religious responses to the expansion of the world capitalistic economy, often with political and economic consequences.
   b. Cultural acts that mock the widespread but erroneous belief of European cultural supremacy.
   c. Movements that arise when natives begin to acquire and benefit from the wealth, technology, and living standards of industrial societies.
   d. Attempts to explain European domination without actually trying to achieve similar successes.

Fill in the Blank:

1. According to Tylor, _____, a belief in spiritual beings, was the earliest form of religion.

2. The term _____ refers to an intense feeling of solidarity that characterizes collective liminality.

3. A _____ is a custom or social action that operates to reduce differences in wealth and bring standouts in line with community norms.

4. Voodoo and santeria are examples of _____ religions, which blend beliefs and practices from various religious traditions and result from acculturation.

1. (a), 2. (b), 3. (b), 4. (c), 5. (d), 6. (a)

1. animism; 2. *communitas*; 3. leveling mechanism; 4. syncretic

10

THE WORLD SYSTEM AND COLONIALISM

UNDERSTANDING OURSELVES

In today's world system, people are linked as never before, and descendants of villagers who hosted ethnographers a generation ago now live transnational lives. Conrad Kottak (2010) reports on how transnationalism has affected a village in Madagascar, Ivato, that he first studied in 1966 and 1967.

When Kottak was not "in the field" in Ivato, he rented a small house in Ambalavao, a town whose residents included Indian cloth merchants, Chinese grocers, and a few French people, including two young men in the French equivalent of the Peace Corps. (Madagascar had been a French colony.) One of them, Noel, was courting Lenore, a young woman from a prominent local family originally from Ivato.

On Kottak's next trip to Madagascar, in 1981, he discovered that an active exchange program, including study abroad, had been established between Madagascar and the Soviet Union. One result of this program was that Kottak missed one of his best friends from Ivato who was spending three months studying in Moscow.

When Kottak next visited Madagascar, in 1990, he met Emily, the twenty-two-year-old daughter of Noel and Lenore, whose courtship he had witnessed in 1967. Emily was about to travel to the United States to study marketing. When Kottak saw her again a few months later in Gainesville, Florida, she inquired about her father, whom she had never met. She had sent several letters to France, but Noel never responded.

Descendants of Ambalavao now live all over the world. Emily, a child of colonialism, has two aunts in France and another in Germany. Members of her family, which is not especially wealthy, have traveled to Russia, Canada, the United States, France, Germany, and West Africa. How many of your classmates, including perhaps you, yourself, have recent transnational roots? The son of a man from a rural Kenyan village has even been elected president of the United States.

>> The World System

Although fieldwork in small communities has been anthropology's hallmark, isolated groups are impossible to find today. Truly isolated societies probably never have existed. For thousands of years, human groups have been in contact with one another. Local societies always have participated in a larger system, which today has global dimensions—we call it the *modern world system,* by which we mean a world in which nations are economically and politically interdependent.

The world system and the relations among the countries within it are shaped by the capitalist world economy. A huge increase in international trade during and after the fifteenth century led to the **capitalist world economy** (Wallerstein 1982, 2004b), a single world system committed to production for sale or exchange, with the object of maximizing profits, rather than supplying domestic needs. **Capital** refers to wealth or resources invested in business, with the intent of using the means of production to make a profit.

World-system theory can be traced to the French social historian Fernand Braudel. In his three-volume work *Civilization and Capitalism, 15th–18th Century* (1981, 1982, 1992), Braudel argued that society consists of interrelated parts assembled into a system. Societies are subsystems of larger systems, with the world system the largest. The key claim of **world-system theory** is that an identifiable social system, based on wealth and power differentials, extends beyond individual countries. That system is formed by a set of economic and political relations that has characterized much of the globe since the sixteenth century, when the Old World established regular contact with the New World (see Bodley 2008).

According to Wallerstein (1982, 2004b), countries within the world system occupy three different positions of economic and political power: core, semiperiphery, and periphery. The geographic center, or **core,** which is the dominant position in the world system, includes the strongest and most powerful nations, such as the United States, Germany, and Japan. In core nations, "the complexity of economic activities and the level of capital accumulation is the greatest" (Thompson 1983, p. 12). With its sophisticated technologies and mechanized production, the core churns out products that flow mainly to other core countries. Some also go to the periphery and semiperiphery.

capitalist world economy The single world system, which emerged in the sixteenth century, committed to production for sale, with the object of maximizing profits, rather than supplying domestic needs.

capital Wealth or resources invested in business, with the intent of producing a profit.

world-system theory Argument for the historic and contemporary social, political, and economic significance of an identifiable global system, based on wealth and power differentials, that extends beyond individual countries.

core Dominant structural position in the world system; consists of the strongest and most powerful states with advanced systems of production.

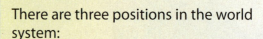

STUDY TIP

There are three positions in the world system:

- Core (most powerful nations, largest capital accumulation, sophisticated technologies, control over finance).

- Semiperiphery (intermediate between core and periphery, industrialized, export to core and periphery nations, source of cheap labor).

- Periphery (least powerful nations, less mechanized industries, export raw materials and agricultural commodities, source of cheap labor).

CULTURETHINK

Look at the labels on your clothing: Where was it made? Where do those nations fit into today's world system?
(See p. 206 for a map.)

MADE IN BANGLADESH

According to Arrighi (1994), the core monopolizes the most profitable activities, especially the control of world finance.

Semiperiphery and periphery countries have less power, wealth, and influence than the core does. The **semiperiphery** is intermediate between the core and the periphery. Contemporary nations of the semiperiphery, including Brazil, India, and China, are industrialized. Like core nations, they export both industrial goods and commodities, but they lack the power and economic dominance of core nations, although their power and influence are growing rapidly. Brazil, a semiperiphery nation, exports automobiles to Nigeria (a periphery nation) and auto engines, orange juice extract, coffee, and shrimp to the United States (a core nation). The **periphery** includes the world's least privileged and powerful countries, including Bangladesh, Guatemala, Haiti, and Madagascar, among many others. Economic activities there are less mechanized than are those in the core and semiperiphery, although some degree of industrialization has reached even peripheral nations. The periphery produces raw materials, agricultural commodities, and, increasingly, human labor for export to the core and the semiperiphery (Shannon 1996).

In the United States and Western Europe today, immigration—legal and illegal—from the periphery and semiperiphery supplies cheap labor, especially for agriculture, construction, and paid domestic labor in core countries. U.S. states as distant as California, Michigan, and South Carolina make significant use of farm labor from Mexico. The availability of relatively cheap workers from noncore nations such as Mexico (in the United States) and Turkey (in Germany) benefits farmers and business owners in core countries, while also supplying remittances to families in the semiperiphery and periphery. As a result of twenty-first-century telecommunications technology, cheap labor doesn't even need to migrate to the United States. Thousands of families in India are being supported as American companies outsource jobs—in fields from telephone assistance to software engineering—to nations outside the core (Nadeem 2011).

THE EMERGENCE OF THE WORLD SYSTEM

By the 15th century, Europeans were profiting from a transoceanic trade-oriented economy, and people worldwide entered Europe's sphere of influence. What was new was the transatlantic component of a long history of Old World sailing and commerce. As early as 600 B.C.E., the Phoenicians/Carthaginians sailed around Britain on regular trade routes and circumnavigated Africa. Likewise, Indonesia and Africa have been linked in Indian Ocean trade for at least two thousand years.

In the fifteenth century, Europe established regular contact with Asia, Africa, and eventually the New World (the Caribbean and the Americas). Christopher Columbus' first voyage from Spain to the Bahamas and the Caribbean in 1492 was soon followed by additional voyages. These journeys opened the way for a major exchange of people, resources, products, ideas, and diseases, as the Old and New Worlds were forever linked (Crosby 2003; Diamond 1997; Fagan 1998). Led by Spain and Portugal, Europeans extracted silver and gold, conquered the natives (taking some as slaves), and colonized their lands.

> **semiperiphery** Structural position in the world system intermediate between core and periphery; exporters of goods and commodities, but lacking the power of core nations.
>
> **periphery** Weakest structural position in the world system; less mechanized producers of raw materials, agricultural commodities, and human labor.

Previously in Europe as throughout the world, rural people had produced mainly for their own needs, growing their own food and making clothing, furniture, and tools from local products. Production beyond immediate needs was undertaken to pay taxes and to purchase trade items such as salt and iron. As late as 1650 the English diet was based on locally grown starches (Mintz 1985). In the two hundred years that followed, however, the English became extraordinary consumers of imported goods. One of the earliest and most popular of those goods was sugar (Mintz 1985).

Sugarcane originally was domesticated in Papua New Guinea, and sugar was first processed in India. Reaching Europe via the Middle East and the eastern Mediterranean, it was carried to the New World by Columbus (Mintz 1985). The climate of Brazil and the Caribbean proved ideal for growing sugarcane, and Europeans built plantations there to supply the growing demand for sugar. This led to the development in the seventeenth century of a plantation economy based on a single cash crop—a system known as *monocrop* production.

The demand for sugar in a growing international market spurred the development of the transatlantic

>> Industrialization

By the eighteenth century the stage had been set for the **Industrial Revolution**—the historical transformation (in Europe, after 1750) of "traditional" into "modern" societies through industrialization of the economy. The seeds of industrial society were planted well before the 18th century (Gimpel 1988). For example, a knitting machine invented in England in 1589 was so far ahead of its time that it played a profitable role in factories two and three centuries later. The appearance of cloth mills late in the Middle Ages foreshadowed the search for new sources of wind and water power that characterized the Industrial Revolution.

Industrialization required capital for investment. The established system of transoceanic trade and commerce supplied this capital from the profits it generated. Wealthy people sought investment opportunities and eventually found them in machines and engines to drive machines. Capital and scientific innovation fueled invention. Industrialization increased production in both farming and manufacturing.

European industrialization developed from (and eventually replaced) the *domestic system* of manufacture (or home-handicraft system). In this system, an organizer-entrepreneur supplied the raw materials to workers in their homes and collected the finished products from them. The entrepreneur, whose sphere of operations might span several villages, owned the materials, paid for the work, and arranged the marketing.

From producer to consumer in the modern world system. The top photo shows a worker harvesting bananas for the Tagum Agricultural Development Company in Davao del Norte province, on the southern Philippine island of Mindanao. Below, little Timmy enjoys an imported banana in Dubuque, Iowa. Which of the ingredients in your breakfast today were imported?

CAUSES OF THE INDUSTRIAL REVOLUTION

The Industrial Revolution began with cotton products, iron, and pottery. These were widely used goods whose manufacture could be broken into simple routine motions that machines could perform. When manufacturing moved from homes to factories, where machinery replaced handwork, agrarian societies evolved into industrial ones. As factories produced cheap staple goods, the Industrial Revolution led to a dramatic increase in production. Industrialization fueled urban growth

slave trade and New World plantation economies based on slave labor. By the eighteenth century, an increased English demand for raw cotton led to rapid settlement of what is now the southeastern United States and the emergence there of another slave-based monocrop production system. Like sugar, cotton was a key trade item that fueled the growth of the world system.

Industrial Revolution The historical transformation (in Europe, after 1750) of "traditional" into "modern" societies through industrialization of the economy.

 Got IT? Can you define the modern world system and explain its emergence?

STUDY TIP

Industrialism drew workers to a central production site (e.g., a factory), while people worked in their homes in the domestic system of manufacture. Why might our contemporary economy be called "postindustrial"?

The Art of Stocking-Frame-Work-Knitting.

Engravd for the Universal Magazine 17 50. for J. Hinton at the Kings. Arms in S.t Pauls Church Yard LONDON.

In the home-handicraft, or domestic, system of production, an organizer supplied raw materials to workers in their homes and collected their products. Family life and work were intertwined, as in this English scene. Is there a modern equivalent to the domestic system of production?

and created a new kind of city, with factories crowded together in places where coal and labor were cheap.

The Industrial Revolution began in England, and as its industrialization proceeded, Britain's population

began to increase dramatically. It doubled during the eighteenth century (especially after 1750) and did so again between 1800 and 1850. This demographic explosion fueled consumption, but British entrepreneurs couldn't meet the increased demand with the traditional production methods. This spurred further experimentation, innovation, and rapid technological change.

English industrialization drew on national advantages in natural resources. Britain was rich in coal and iron ore, and had navigable waterways and easily negotiated coasts. It was a seafaring island-nation located at the crossroads of international trade. These features gave Britain a favored position for importing raw materials and exporting manufactured goods. Another factor in England's industrial growth was the fact that much of its eighteenth-century colonial empire was occupied by English settler families who looked to the mother country as they tried to replicate European civilization in the New World. These colonies bought large quantities of English staples.

POP CULTURE

McDonald's is a global chain, and the ingredients in its products illustrate the historical world system in miniature. Consider just the Big Mac. Its two all-beef patties come from cattle, an Old World domesticate. Its special sauce is similar to mayonnaise, invented in France. Lettuce comes from Egypt, cheese from cow's milk (Old World), pickles from India, onions from Iran and West Pakistan. It comes on a sesame seed (India) bun (wheat—Middle East). The Egg McMuffin includes eggs, from chickens (Southeast Asia), and Canadian bacon, from pork (western Asia). The breakfast burrito is based on maize, or corn, a New World product—like the chocolate you might have in your milk or shake. Keep a food diary for two days. Then Google "food origins" or consult a site like http://www.foodtimeline.org/ to see how your own diet illustrates the diverse origins of the foods we eat every day.

bourgeoisie One of Karl Marx's opposed classes; owners of the means of production (factories, mines, large farms, and other sources of subsistence).

working class (proletariat) Those who must sell their labor to survive; the antithesis of the bourgeoisie in Marx's class analysis.

It also has been argued that particular cultural values and religion contributed to industrialization. Many members of the emerging English middle class were Protestant nonconformists. Their beliefs and values encouraged industry, thrift, the dissemination of new knowledge, inventiveness, and willingness to accept change (Weber 1904/1958).

Got IT? Can you explain the causes of the industrial revolution in England?

>> Socioeconomic Effects of Industrialization

The socioeconomic effects of industrialization were mixed. English national income tripled between 1700 and 1815 and increased thirty times more by 1939. Standards of comfort rose, but prosperity was uneven. At first, factory workers' wages were higher than those available in the domestic system. Later, owners started recruiting labor in places where living standards were low and labor (including that of women and children) was cheap.

Social ills worsened with the growth of factory towns and industrial cities, amid conditions like those Charles Dickens described in *Hard Times*. Filth and smoke polluted the nineteenth-century cities. Housing was crowded and unsanitary, with insufficient water and sewage disposal facilities. People experienced rampant disease and rising death rates. This was the world of Ebenezer Scrooge, Bob Cratchit, Tiny Tim—and Karl Marx.

"Such is the Old Town of Manchester, and on re-reading my description, I am forced to admit that instead of being exaggerated, it is far from black enough to convey a true impression of the filth, ruin and uninhabitableness, the defiance of all consideration of cleanliness, ventilation, and health which characterise the construction of this single district. . . . Everything which here arouses horror and indignation is of recent origin, belongs to the industrial epoch."

Friedrich Engels, *The Condition of the Working-Class in England*

INDUSTRIAL STRATIFICATION SYSTEMS

Social theorists Karl Marx and Max Weber focused on the stratification systems associated with industrialization. From his observations in England and his analysis of nineteenth-century industrial capitalism, Marx (Marx and Engels 1848/1976) saw socioeconomic stratification as a sharp and simple division between two opposed classes: the bourgeoisie (capitalists) and the proletariat (propertyless workers). The bourgeoisie traced its origins to overseas ventures and the world capitalist economy, which had created a wealthy commercial class.

Industrialization shifted production from farms and cottages to mills and factories, where mechanical power was available and where workers could be assembled to operate heavy machinery. The **bourgeoisie** were the owners of the factories, mines, large farms, and other means of production. The **working class,** or **proletariat,** were people who had to sell their labor to survive. With the decline of subsistence production, the rise of urban migration, and the possibility of unemployment, the bourgeoisie came to stand between workers and the means of production.

Industrialization hastened the process of *proletarianization*—the separation of workers from the means of production. The bourgeoisie also came to dominate the means of communication, the schools, and other key institutions. *Class consciousness* (recognition of collective interests and personal identification with one's economic group) was a vital part of Marx's view of class. He saw bourgeoisie and proletariat as socioeconomic divisions with radically opposed interests. Marx viewed classes as powerful collective forces that could mobilize human energies to influence the course of history. On the basis of their common experience, workers would develop class consciousness, which could lead to revolutionary change. Although no proletarian revolution was to occur in England, workers did develop organizations to protect their interests and increase their share of industrial profits. During the nineteenth century, trade unions and socialist parties emerged to express a rising

During the nineteenth and early twentieth centuries, women and children often worked long hours in factories, as in this Macon, Georgia, textile mill in 1909.

anticapitalist spirit. The concerns of the English labor movement were to remove young children from factories and limit the hours during which women and children could work. The profile of stratification in industrial core nations gradually took shape. Capitalists controlled production, but labor was organizing for better wages and working conditions. By 1900 many governments had factory legislation and social-welfare programs. Mass living standards in core nations improved as population grew.

In today's capitalist world system the class division between owners and workers is now worldwide. However, publicly traded companies complicate the division between capitalists and workers in industrial nations. Through pension plans and personal investments, some American workers now have a proprietary interest in the means of production. They are part owners rather than property-less workers. The key difference is that the wealthy have *control* over these means. The key capitalist now is not the factory owner, who may have been replaced by thousands of stockholders, but the CEO or the chair of the board of directors, neither of whom may actually own the corporation.

MODERN STRATIFICATION SYSTEMS

Modern stratification systems aren't simple and dichotomous. They include (particularly

Karl Marx observed and analyzed nineteenth-century industrial capitalism. He saw socioeconomic stratification in terms of two opposed classes: bourgeoisie and proletariat.

The Ratio of the Wealthiest 1% to Median Wealth in the United States, 2009

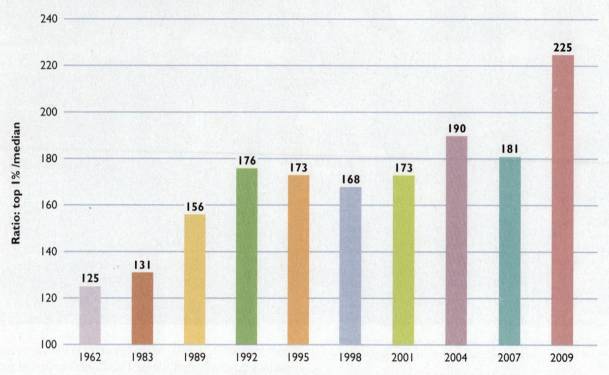

The ratio of the wealthiest 1% to median wealth in the United States

Source: Allegretto, S. A. 2011. The State of Working America's Wealth, Briefing Paper no. 292, Economic Policy Institute, March 23. http://www.epi.org/page/_/Briefingpaper292.pdf.

in core and semiperiphery nations) a middle class of skilled and professional workers. Gerhard Lenski (1966) argued that social equality tends to increase in advanced industrial societies. The masses improve their access to economic benefits and political power. In Lenski's scheme, the shift of political power to the masses reflects the growth of the middle class, which reduces the polarization between owning and working classes. The proliferation of middle-class occupations creates opportunities for social mobility. The stratification system grows more complex (Giddens 1981).

The complexity of their stratification system has gone largely unnoticed by many Americans, who think of themselves as middle class. The perception of the American middle class as a vast undifferentiated group helps mask the substantial differences in income and wealth that set off the richest from the poorest Americans. That gap has been widening.

According to U.S. Census data from 1970 to 2009, the top (richest) quintile (fifth) of American households increased its share of national income by 16 percent, while all other quintiles fell. The percentage share of the lowest fifth fell most dramatically—17 percent. In 2009 the top fifth got 50 percent of all national income, while the lowest fifth got only 3 percent. Comparable figures in 1970 were 43 percent and 4 percent. The 2009 ratio was 15:1, versus 14:1 in 2000 and 11:1 in 1970. In other words, the richest fifth of American households, with a mean annual income of $170,844 in 2009, had become 15 times wealthier than the poorest fifth, with a mean annual income of $11,552 (DeNavas-Walt, Proctor, and Smith 2010).

When we consider wealth (investments, property, possessions, etc.) rather than income, the contrast is even more striking: The top 1 percent of American households hold almost 36 percent of the nation's wealth (Allegretto 2011). Their net worth was 225 times greater than the median or typical household's net worth in 2009 (see "The Ratio of the Wealthiest 1% to Median Wealth in the United States, 2009"). This is the highest ratio on record. The top 1 percent owns more than the bottom 90 percent combined (Witt 2011, p. 229).

The Great Recession of December 2007–June 2009 increased inequality. While all Americans were affected,

CULTURETHINK

Ask some of the people you know what social class they think they belong to. How about you—in which social class do you place yourself? Why do you think so many Americans identify with the middle class? What are some cultural values associated with being middle class?

STUDY TIP

Three dimensions of social stratification, according to Weber, are power, prestige, and wealth.

the poor suffered more than the rich did. The percentage of households with zero or negative net worth shot up from 19 percent in 2007 to about 25 percent two years later. Between 2007 and 2009, household wealth shrank by 16 percent for the richest fifth of Americans but by 25 percent for the bottom 80 percent. Because of this disparity, the share of household wealth owned by the richest fifth rose 2 percentage points to 87 percent. The bottom 80 percent gave up those 2 percentage points, keeping just 13 percent of all wealth. Recognition of such disparities, and that the rich were getting richer, and the poor, poorer, led to the Occupy movement of 2011. That movement began on Wall Street and quickly spread to many other cities in the United States and Canada.

Max Weber faulted Karl Marx for an overly simple and exclusively economic view of stratification. As we saw in the chapter "Political Systems," Weber (1922/1968) defined three dimensions of social stratification: wealth, power, and prestige. Although, as Weber showed, wealth, power, and prestige are separate components of social ranking, they tend to be correlated. Weber also believed that social identities based on ethnicity, religion, race, nationality, and other attributes could take priority over class (social identity based on economic status). In addition to class contrasts, the modern world system is cross-cut by collective identities based on ethnicity, religion, and nationality (Shannon 1996). Class conflicts tend to occur within nations, and nationalism has prevented global class solidarity, particularly of proletarians. Although the capitalist class dominates politically in most countries, growing wealth has made it easier for core nations to grant higher wages (Hopkins and Wallerstein 1982). However, the improvement in core workers' living standards wouldn't have occurred without the world system. The wealth that flows from periphery and semiperiphery to core has helped core capitalists maintain their profits while satisfying the demands of core workers. In the periphery and semiperiphery, wages and living standards are lower. The current *world stratification system* features a substantial contrast between both capitalists and workers in the core nations and workers on the periphery.

Max Weber (1864–1920). Did Weber improve on Marx's view of stratification?

>> Colonialism

World-system theory stresses the existence of a global culture and economy. It emphasizes historical contacts, linkages, and power differentials between local people and international forces. The major forces influencing cultural interaction during the past five hundred years have been commercial expansion, industrial capitalism, and the dominance of colonial and core nations (Wallerstein 1982, 2004b; Wolf 1982). As state formation had done previously, industrialization accelerated local participation in larger networks. According to Bodley (2007), perpetual expansion is a distinguishing feature of industrial economic systems. Bands and tribes were small, self-sufficient, subsistence-based systems. Industrial economies, by contrast, are large, highly specialized systems in which market exchanges occur with profit as the primary motive (Bodley 2007).

During the nineteenth century, European business interests initiated a concerted search for markets. This process led to European imperialism in Africa, Asia, and Oceania. **Imperialism** refers to a policy of extending the rule of a country or empire over foreign nations and of taking and holding foreign colonies. Imperialism goes back to early states, including Egypt in the Old World and the Incas in the New. Alexander the Great forged a Greek empire, and Julius Caesar and his successors spread the Roman empire. More recent examples include the British, French, and Soviet empires (Scheinman 1980).

> **imperialism** A policy of extending the rule of a nation or empire over foreign nations and of taking and holding foreign colonies.

After 1850, European imperial expansion was aided by improved transportation, which facilitated the colonization of vast areas of sparsely settled lands in the interior of North and South America and Australia. The new colonies purchased masses of goods from the industrial centers and shipped back wheat, cotton, wool, mutton, beef, and leather. The first phase of European colonialism had been the exploration and exploitation of the Americas and the Caribbean after Columbus. A new second phase began as European nations competed for colonies between 1875 and 1914, setting the stage for World War I.

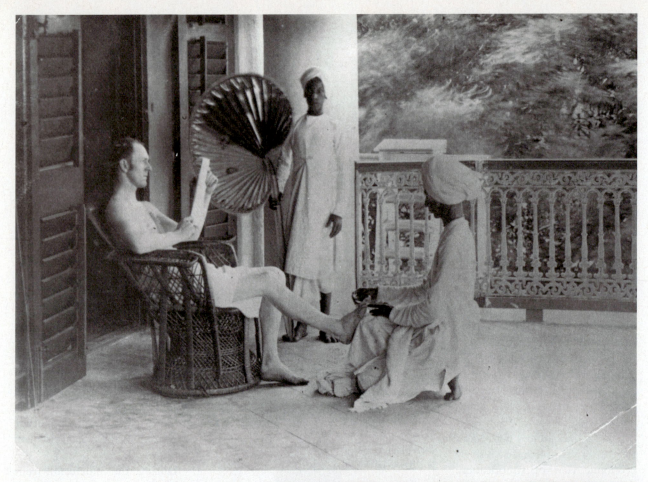

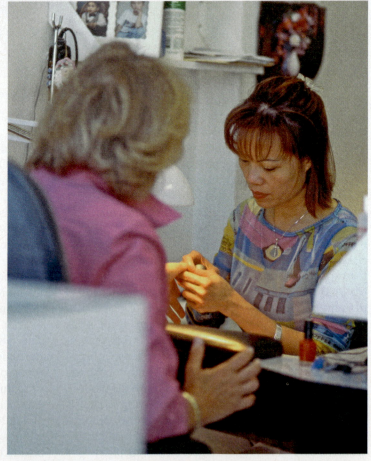

Above, in 1900, a British officer in India receives a pedicure. Below, a Vietnamese manicurist works at a beauty salon in San Rafael, California. How might a knowledge of colonialism help us understand the two photos?

Colonialism is the political, social, economic, and cultural domination of a territory and its people by a foreign power for an extended time (see Bremen and Shimizu 1999; Cooper and Stoler 1997). If imperialism is almost as old as the state, colonialism can be traced back to the Phoenicians, who established colonies along the eastern Mediterranean three thousand years ago. The ancient Greeks and Romans were avid colonizers, as well as empire builders.

colonialism The political, social, economic, and cultural domination of a territory and its people by a foreign power for an extended time.

The first phase of modern colonialism began with the European "Age of Discovery"—of the Americas and of a sea route to the Far East. After 1492, the Spanish, the original conquerors of the Aztecs and Incas, explored and colonized widely in the New World—the Caribbean, Mexico, the southern portions of what was to become the United States, and Central and South America. In South America, Portugal ruled over Brazil. Rebellions and wars

The two phases of European colonialism include (1) the exploration and exploitation of the New World after Columbus; and (2) the competition for colonies, ending with World War I.

aimed at independence ended the first phase of European colonialism by the early nineteenth century. Brazil declared independence from Portugal in 1822. By 1825 most of Spain's colonies were politically independent. Spain held onto Cuba and the Philippines until 1898, but otherwise withdrew from the colonial field. During the first phase of colonialism, Spain and Portugal, along with Britain and France, were major colonizing nations. Britain and France dominated the second phase.

BRITISH COLONIALISM

At its peak about 1914, the British empire covered a fifth of the world's land surface and ruled a fourth of its population (see "Map of British Empire in 1765 and 1914" below). Like several other European nations,

Britain had two stages of colonialism. The first began with the Elizabethan voyages of the sixteenth century. During the seventeenth century, Britain acquired most of the eastern coast of North America, Canada's St. Lawrence basin, islands in the Caribbean, slave stations in Africa, and interests in India.

The British shared the exploration of the New World with the Spanish, Portuguese, French, and Dutch. The British by and large left Mexico, along with Central and South America, to the Spanish and the Portuguese. The end of the Seven Years' War in 1763 forced a French retreat from most of Canada and India, where France previously had competed with Britain (Cody 1998; Farr 1980).

The American Revolution ended the first stage of British colonialism. A second colonial empire, on which the "sun never set," rose from the ashes of the first. Beginning in 1788, but intensifying after 1815, the British settled Australia. Britain had acquired Dutch South Africa by 1815. The establishment of Singapore in 1819 provided a base for a British trade network that extended to much of South Asia and along the coast of China. By this time, the empires of Britain's traditional rivals, particularly Spain, had been severely diminished in scope. Britain's position as imperial power and the world's leading industrial nation was unchallenged (Cody 1998; Farr 1980).

Map of British Empire in 1765 and 1914

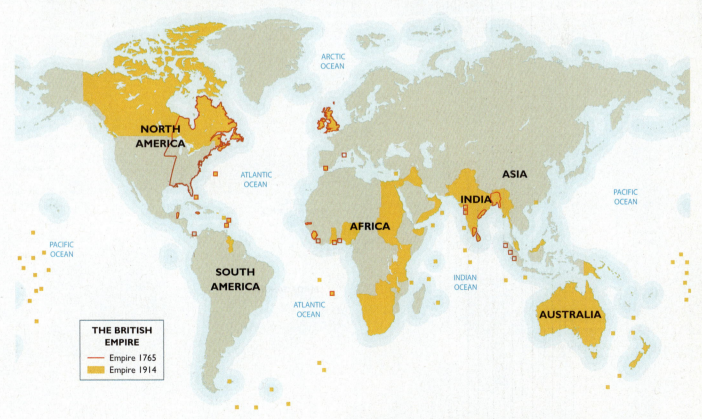

THE BRITISH EMPIRE
— Empire 1765
Empire 1914

Source: From the *Academic American Encyclopedia,* Vol. 3, p. 496. 1998 Edition. Copyright 1998 by Grolier Incorporated. Reprinted with permission.

During the Victorian Era (1837–1901), as Britain's acquisition of territory and of further trading concessions continued, Prime Minister Benjamin Disraeli implemented a foreign policy justified by a view of imperialism as shouldering "the white man's burden"— a phrase coined by the poet Rudyard Kipling. People in the empire were seen as unable to govern themselves, so that British guidance was needed to civilize and Christianize them. This paternalistic and racist doctrine served to legitimize Britain's acquisition and control of parts of central Africa and Asia (Cody 1998).

After World War II, the British empire began to fall apart, with nationalist movements for independence. India became independent in 1947, as did the Republic of Ireland in 1949. Decolonization in Africa and Asia accelerated during the late 1950s. Today, the ties that remain between Britain and its former colonies are mainly linguistic or cultural rather than political (Cody 1998).

FRENCH COLONIALISM

Two phases also characterized French colonialism. The first began with the explorations of the early 1600s. Before the French revolution in 1789, missionaries, explorers, and traders had carved out niches for France in Canada, the Louisiana territory, several Caribbean islands, and parts of India (Harvey 1980). The Treaty of Paris of 1763 ended the Seven Years' War, the American counterpart of which was the French and Indian War. That treaty awarded Canada to Great Britain, while France retained the prosperous West Indian sugar islands of Guadeloupe and Martinique.

The foundations of the second French empire were established between 1830 and 1870. In Great Britain the sheer drive for profit led expansion, but French colonialism was spurred more by the state, church, and armed forces than by pure business interests. France acquired Algeria and part of what eventually became Indochina (Cambodia, Laos, and Vietnam). By 1914 the French empire covered four million square miles and included some sixty million people (see "Map of the French

Map of the French Empire at Its Height Around 1914

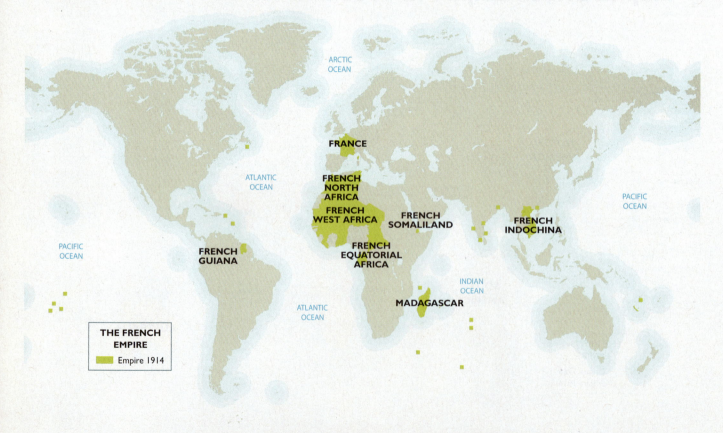

Source: From the *Academic American Encyclopedia*, Vol 3, p. 309. 1998 Edition. Copyright 1998 by Grolier Incorporated. Reprinted with permission.

Empire at Its Height Around 1914"). By 1893 French rule had been fully established in Indochina. Tunisia and Morocco became French protectorates in 1883 and 1912, respectively (Harvey 1980).

To be sure, the French, like the British, had substantial business interests in their colonies, but they also sought, again like the British, international glory and prestige. The French promulgated a *mission civilisatrice,* their equivalent of Britain's "white man's burden." The goal was to implant French culture, language, and religion, Roman Catholicism, throughout the colonies (Harvey 1980).

The French used two forms of colonial rule: *indirect rule,* governing through native leaders and established political structures, in areas with long histories of state organization, such as Morocco and Tunisia; and *direct rule* by French officials in many areas of Africa, where the French imposed new government structures to control diverse societies, many of them previously stateless. Like the British empire, the French empire began to disintegrate after World War II. France fought long—and ultimately futile—wars to keep its empire intact in Indochina and Algeria (Harvey 1980).

COLONIALISM AND IDENTITY

Many geopolitical labels in the news today had no equivalent meaning before colonialism. Whole countries, along with social groups and divisions within them, were colonial inventions. In West Africa, for example, by geographic logic, several adjacent countries could be one (Togo, Ghana, Ivory Coast, Guinea, Guinea-Bissau, Sierra Leone, Liberia). Instead, they are separated by linguistic, political, and economic contrasts promoted under colonialism.

Hundreds of ethnic groups and "tribes" are colonial constructions (see Ranger 1996). The Sukuma of Tanzania, for instance, were first registered as a single tribe by the colonial administration. Then missionaries standardized a series of dialects into a single Sukuma language into which they translated the Bible and other religious texts. Thereafter, those texts were taught in missionary schools and to European foreigners and other non-Sukuma speakers. Over time this standardized the Sukuma language and ethnicity (Finnstrom 1997).

As in most of East Africa, in Rwanda and Burundi farmers and herders live in the same areas and speak the same language. Historically they have shared the same social world, although their social organization is "extremely hierarchical," almost "castelike" (Malkki 1995, p. 24). There has been a tendency to see the pastoral Tutsis as superior to the agricultural Hutus. Tutsis have been presented as nobles, Hutus as commoners. Yet when distributing identity cards in Rwanda, the Belgian colonizers simply identified all people with more than ten head of cattle as Tutsi. Owners of fewer cattle were registered as Hutus (Bjuremalm 1997). Years later, these arbitrary colonial registers were used systematically for "ethnic" identification during the mass killings (genocide) that took place in Rwanda in 1994 (as portrayed vividly in the film *Hotel Rwanda*).

POSTCOLONIAL STUDIES

In anthropology, history, and literature, the field of postcolonial studies has gained prominence since the 1970s (see Ashcroft, Griffiths, and Tiffin 1989; Chakrabarty 2007; Cooper and Stoler 1997).

Tutsi and Hutu originated as arbitrary colonial categories. They became "ethnic" groups subject to mass killings (genocide) in Rwanda in 1994, as portrayed in the film Hotel Rwanda, *shown here.*

postcolonial Referring to interactions between European nations and the societies they colonized (mainly after 1800); more generally, it may be used to signify a position against imperialism and Eurocentrism.

intervention philosophy Guiding principle of colonialism, conquest, missionization, or development; an ideological justification for outsiders to guide native peoples in specific directions.

Postcolonial refers to the interactions between European nations and the societies they colonized (mainly after 1800). In 1914, European empires, which broke up after World War II, ruled more than 85 percent of the world (Petraglia-Bahri 1996). The term "postcolonial" also has been used to describe the second half of the twentieth century in general, the period succeeding colonialism. Even more generically, postcolonial may be used to signify a position against imperialism and Eurocentrism (Petraglia-Bahri 1996).

The former colonies (postcolonies) can be divided into settler, nonsettler, and mixed (Petraglia-Bahri 1996). The settler countries, with large numbers of European colonists and sparser native populations, include Australia and Canada. Examples of nonsettler countries include India, Pakistan, Bangladesh, Sri Lanka, Malaysia, Indonesia, Nigeria, Senegal, Madagascar, and Jamaica. All these had substantial native populations and relatively few European settlers. Mixed countries include South Africa, Zimbabwe, Kenya, and Algeria. Such countries had significant European settlement despite having sizable native populations.

Given the varied experiences of such countries, postcolonial has to be a loose term. The United States, for instance, was colonized by Europeans and fought a war for independence from Britain. Is the United States a postcolony? It usually isn't perceived as such, given its current world power position, its treatment of native Americans (sometimes called internal colonization), and its annexation of other parts of the world (Petraglia-Bahri 1996). Research in postcolonial studies is growing, permitting a wide-ranging investigation of power relations in varied contexts. Broad topics in the field include the formation of an empire, the impact of colonization, and the state of the postcolony today.

Got IT? Can you evaluate how the history of colonialism has affected contemporary world system relationships between nations?

ANTHROPOLOGY WORKS

Patricia Ensworth has a master's degree in anthropology along with training in financial services and software testing. She has helped companies develop culturally compatible software processes. For example, she identified distinct cultural differences in software use practices between North America and Asia. American sales representatives felt comfortable entering data directly into computers after interaction with clients. However, this system did not work in Asia—where clerks were given this responsibility—because sales representatives were ranked hierarchically above clerks and did not expect to have to do basic data entry. To be successful, the software designers needed to alter the user interface and security rules. Globalization has brought all nations closer together in business, and anthropologists play a critical role in bridging cultural gaps.

>> The Role of Development in the World System

During the Industrial Revolution, a strong current of thought viewed industrialization as a beneficial process of organic development and progress. Many economists still assume that industrialization increases production and income. They seek to create in Third World ("developing") countries a process like the one that first occurred spontaneously in eighteenth-century Great Britain.

We have seen that Britain used the notion of a white man's burden to justify its imperialist expansion and that France claimed to be engaged in a mission civilisatrice—a civilizing mission—in its colonies. Both these ideas illustrate an **intervention philosophy,** an ideological justification for outsiders to guide native peoples in specific directions. Economic development plans also have intervention philosophies. John Bodley (2008) argues that the basic belief behind interventions—whether by colonialists, missionaries, governments, or development planners—has been the same for more than a hundred years. This belief is that industrialization, modernization, Westernization, and individualism are desirable evolutionary advances and that development schemes that promote them will bring long-term benefits to local people. In a more extreme form, intervention philosophy may pit the assumed wisdom of enlightened colonial or other First World planners against the purported conservatism, ignorance, or "obsolescence" of "inferior" or "backward" local people.

NEOLIBERALISM

One currently influential intervention philosophy, neoliberalism, encompasses a set of assumptions that have become widespread during the last thirty years. Neoliberal policies are being implemented in developing nations, including postsocialist societies (e.g., those of the former Soviet Union). **Neoliberalism** is the current form of the classic economic liberalism laid out in Adam Smith's famous capitalist manifesto, *The Wealth of Nations,* published in 1776, soon after the Industrial Revolution. Smith advocated laissez-faire (hands-off) economics as the basis of capitalism: The government should stay out of its nation's economic affairs. Free trade, Smith thought, was the best way for a nation's economy to develop. There should be no restrictions on manufacturing, no barriers to commerce, and no tariffs. This philosophy is called liberalism because it aimed at liberating, or freeing, the economy from government controls. Economic liberalism encouraged "free" enterprise and competition, with the goal of generating profits. (Note the difference between this meaning of liberal and the one that has been popularized on American talk radio, in which people use "liberal"—usually as a derogatory term—as the opposite of "conservative." Ironically, Adam Smith's liberalism is today's capitalist conservatism.)

Economic liberalism prevailed in the United States until President Franklin Roosevelt's New Deal during the 1930s. The Great Depression produced a turn to Keynesian economics, which challenged liberalism. John Maynard Keynes (1927, 1936) insisted that full employment was necessary for capitalism to grow, that governments and central banks should intervene to increase employment, and that government should promote the common good.

Especially since the fall of Communism (1989–1991), there has been a revival of economic liberalism, now known as neoliberalism, which has been spreading globally. Around the world, powerful financial institutions, such as the International Monetary Fund (IMF), the World Bank, and the Inter-American Development Bank, have imposed neoliberal policies (see Edelman and Haugerud 2004). Neoliberalism entails open (tariff- and barrier-free) international trade and investment. Profits are sought through lowering of costs, whether through improving productivity, laying off workers, or seeking workers who accept lower wages. In exchange for loans, the governments of postsocialist and developing nations have been required to accept the neoliberal premise that deregulation leads to economic growth, which will eventually benefit everyone through a process sometimes called "trickle down." Accompanying the belief in free markets and the idea of cutting costs is a tendency to impose austerity measures that cut government expenses. This can entail reduced public spending on education, health care, and other social services (Martinez and Garcia 2000).

neoliberalism Revival of Adam Smith's classic economic liberalism, the idea that governments should not regulate private enterprise and that free market forces should rule; a currently dominant intervention philosophy.

>> The Second World

The labels "First World," "Second World," and "Third World" represent a common, although ethnocentric, way of categorizing nations. The *First World* refers to the "democratic West"—traditionally conceived in opposition to a "Second World" ruled by "Communism." The *Second World* refers to the former Soviet Union and the socialist and once-socialist countries of Eastern Europe and Asia. Proceeding with this classification, the "less-developed countries" or "developing nations" make up the *Third World.*

COMMUNISM

The two meanings of communism involve how it is written, whether with a lowercase (small) or an uppercase (large) *c*. Small-*c* **communism** describes a social system in which the community owns property and people work for the common good. Large-*C* **Communism** was a political movement and doctrine seeking to overthrow capitalism and establish a form of communism such as that which prevailed in the Soviet Union (USSR) from 1917 to 1991. The heyday of Communism was a forty-year period from 1949 to 1989, when more Communist regimes existed than at any time before or after. Today only five Communist

communism Spelled with a lowercase *c*, describes a social system in which the community owns property and people work for the common good.

Communism Spelled with an uppercase *C*, describes a political movement and doctrine seeking to overthrow capitalism and to establish a form of communism such as that which prevailed in the Soviet Union (USSR) from 1917 to 1991.

states remain—China, Cuba, Laos, North Korea, and Vietnam—compared with twenty-three in 1985.

Communism, which originated with Russia's Bolshevik Revolution in 1917, and took its inspiration from Karl Marx and Friedrich Engels, was not uniform over time or among countries. All Communist systems were *authoritarian* (promoting obedience to authority rather than individual freedom). Many were *totalitarian* (banning rival parties and demanding total submission of the individual to the state). Several features distinguished Communist societies from other authoritarian regimes (e.g., Spain under Franco) and from socialism of a social democratic type. First, the Communist Party monopolized power in every Communist state. Second, relations within the party were highly centralized and strictly disciplined. Third, Communist nations had state ownership, rather than private ownership, of the means of production. Finally, all Communist regimes, with the goal of advancing communism, cultivated a sense of belonging to an international movement (Brown 2001).

Before and after Communism. Top: on May Day (May 1, 1975), large photos of Politburo members (Communist Party leaders) adorn buildings in Moscow. Bottom: A potential customer watches (then) Russian President Dmitry Medvedev (currently Russia's Prime Minister) address the nation on television sets at an electronics store in Moscow.

POSTSOCIALIST TRANSITIONS

Social scientists have tended to refer to "Second World" societies as socialist rather than Communist. Today research by anthropologists is thriving in *postsocialist* societies—those that once emphasized bureaucratic redistribution of wealth according to a central plan (Verdery 2001). In the postsocialist period, states that once had planned economies have been following the neoliberal agenda, by divesting themselves of state-owned resources in favor of privatization. Some of them have moved toward formal liberal democracy, with political parties, elections, and a balance of powers (Grekova 2001).

Neoliberal economists assumed that dismantling the Soviet Union's planned economy would raise gross domestic product (GDP) and living standards. The goal was to enhance production by substituting a decentralized market system and providing incentives through privatization. In October 1991, Boris Yeltsin, who had been elected president of Russia that June, announced a program of radical market-oriented reform, pursuing a changeover to capitalism. Yeltsin's program of "shock therapy" cut subsidies to farms and industries and ended price controls. Since then, postsocialist Russia has faced many problems. The anticipated gains in productivity did not materialize. After the fall of the Soviet Union, Russia's GDP fell by half. Life expectancy and the birth rate declined, and poverty increased, with a quarter of the population now living below the poverty line.

Got IT? Can you differentiate between socialism, communism, and Communism, drawing on recent world history for examples?

>> The World System Today

The spread of industrialization continues today, although nations have shifted their positions within the world system (see Table 10.1). By 1900, the United States had become a core nation, having overtaken Great Britain in iron, coal, and cotton production. In a few decades (1868–1900), Japan changed from a medieval handicraft economy to an industrial one, joining the semiperiphery by 1900 and moving to the core between 1945 and 1970. India and China have joined Brazil as leaders of the semiperiphery. The map on page 206 shows "The World System Today."

Twentieth-century industrialization added hundreds of new industries and millions of new jobs. Production increased, often beyond immediate demand, spurring strategies, such as advertising, to sell everything industry could churn out. Mass production gave rise to a culture of consumption, which valued acquisitiveness and conspicuous consumption.

How do things stand in the 21st century? Worldwide, young people are abandoning traditional subsistence pursuits and seeking cash. A popular song once queried "How're you gonna keep 'em down on the farm after they've seen Paree?" Nowadays most people have seen Paree—Paris, that is—along with other world capitals, maybe not in person, but in print or on-screen images. Young people today are better educated and wiser in the ways of the world than ever before. Increasingly, they are exposed to the material and cultural promises of a better life away from the farm. They seek paying jobs, but work is scarce, spurring migration within and across national boundaries. If they can't get cash legally, they seek it illegally.

Recently work has been scarce as well in the industrial world, including the United States and western Europe. As the United States struggled to emerge from the recession of 2008–2009, its stock market more than doubled between March 2009 and April 2012. In what many saw as a "jobless recovery," increasingly profitable corporations held onto their cash, rather than using it to hire new workers. The goal of capitalism, remember, is to generate profits and to maintain profitability. In a global economy, profitability doesn't necessarily result from hiring workers who are fellow citizens. Jobs continue being outsourced. Machines and information technology continue to replace people. Corporations, such as airlines and banks, offer their customers incentives to bypass humans. Even outside the industrial world, but especially within it, the Internet allows an increasing number of people to buy plane tickets, print boarding passes, rent cars, reserve hotel rooms, move money, or pay bills online. Amazon, as a virtual bookstore and, increasingly, a department store as well, threatens to send not only "mom and pop" shops but even national chains such as Sears and Radio Shack into oblivion. Borders bit the dust in 2011. Nowadays, when one does manage to speak by phone to an actual human, that person is as likely to be in Mumbai or Manila as in Minneapolis or Miami.

Did You Know ? The Chinese economy has grown considerably in the past twenty years. In 2011, the United States' trade deficit with China was $295 billion, up from $84 billion in 2000, and $6 billion in 1985. The United States imported $295 billion more in goods, resources, and materials from China than it exported to China. Over 70 percent of Walmart's goods are made in China.

TABLE 10.1

Ascent and Decline of Nations within the World System

Periphery to Semiperiphery	Semiperiphery to Core	Core to Semiperiphery
United States (1800–1860)	United States (1860–1900)	Spain (1620–1700)
Japan (1868–1900)	Japan (1945–1970)	
Taiwan (1949–1980)	Germany (1870–1900)	
S. Korea (1953–1980)		

Source: Copyright © 1996 Thomas R. Shannon. Reprinted by permission of Westview Press, a member of Perseus Book Group.

The World System Today

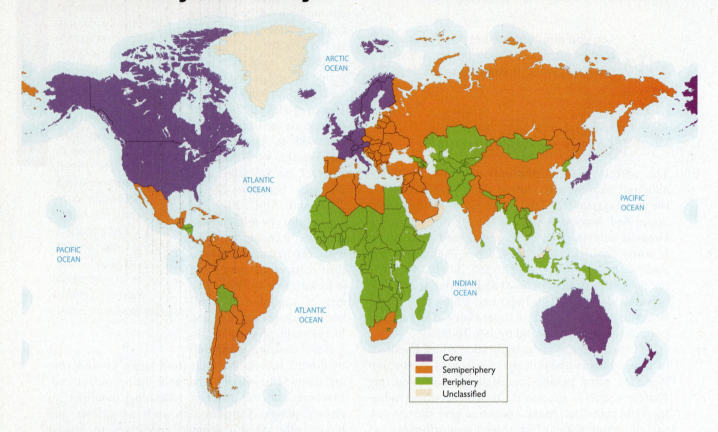

Source: From *Anthropology,* 10th ed., Fig. 23.5, p. 660, by Conrad Kottak. Reprinted by permission of The McGraw-Hill Companies.

Energy Consumption in Various Contexts

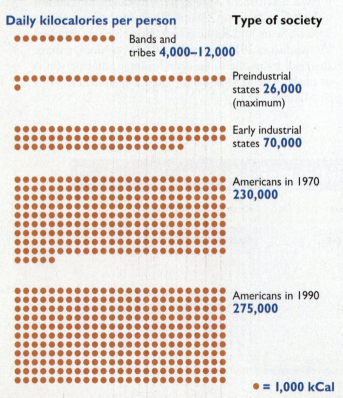

Daily kilocalories per person **Type of society**

Bands and tribes **4,000–12,000**

Preindustrial states **26,000** (maximum)

Early industrial states **70,000**

Americans in 1970 **230,000**

Americans in 1990 **275,000**

● = 1,000 kCal

Source: From *Anthropology and Contemporary Human Problems,* by John H. Bodley. Reprinted by permission of John H. Bodley.

Companies claim, with some justification, that labor unions limit their flexibility, adaptability, and profitability in the global economy. American corporations have become more ideologically opposed to unions and more aggressive in discouraging organizing drives. Unions still bring benefits to their workers. Median weekly earnings for union members—$917 in 2010—remain higher than those of nonunion workers—$717 (Greenhouse 2011). Still, union membership in the United States has fallen to its lowest point in more than seventy years. The unionized percentage of the American workforce fell to 11.9 percent in 2010, compared with 20.1 percent in 1983, and a high of 35 percent during the mid-1950s. The number of unionized private sector workers stood at 7.1 million in 2010, versus a larger share—7.6 million workers—in the public sector (Greenhouse 2011). What jobs do you know that are unionized? How likely is it that you will join a union?

ENERGY CONSUMPTION AND INDUSTRIAL DEGRADATION

Industrialization entailed a shift from reliance on renewable resources to the use of fossil fuels. Stored over millions of years, fossil fuel energy (oil, gas, coal, etc.) is being depleted rapidly to support a previously unknown level of consumption. The population of the United States is the world's foremost consumer of nonrenewable energy. The average American consumes

Energy Consumption in Selected Countries, 2012

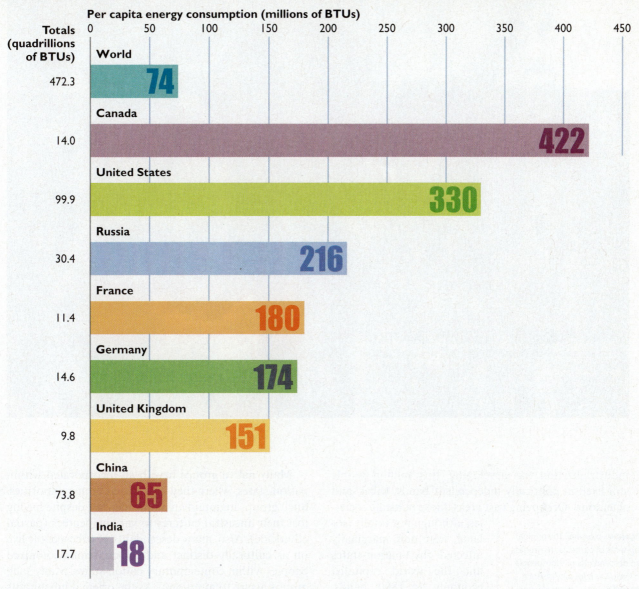

Per capita energy consumption (millions of BTUs)

Totals (quadrillions of BTUs)

Country	Total	Per capita
World	472.3	74
Canada	14.0	422
United States	99.9	330
Russia	30.4	216
France	11.4	180
Germany	14.6	174
United Kingdom	9.8	151
China	73.8	65
India	17.7	18

Source: Based on data in *Statistical Abstract of the United States,* 2012 (Table 1383), p. 864.

CULTURE THINK

The amount of energy an individual consumes is sometimes called her or his "ecological footprint." How big is your footprint? What kinds of things do you use energy for each day? How much energy went into making the food you consumed yesterday? How much of that comes from fossil fuels?

about 35 times more energy than the average forager or tribesperson (Bodley 1985, 2008).

"Energy Consumption in Selected Countries, 2012" compares energy consumption, per capita and total, in the United States and selected other countries. The United States represents 21.1 percent of the world's annual energy consumption, compared with China's 15.6 percent, but the average American consumes 6 times the energy used by the average Chinese and 21 times the energy used by the average inhabitant of India.

Industrialization and factory labor now characterize many societies in Latin America, Africa, the Pacific, and Asia. One effect of the spread of industrialization has been the destruction of indigenous economies, ecologies, and populations. Two centuries ago, as

Copsa Mica, Romania, may well be the world's most polluted city. A factory belches out smoke that leaves its mark on these boys' faces, food, and lungs.

industrialization was developing, fifty million people still lived in politically independent bands, tribes, and chiefdoms. Occupying vast areas, those nonstate societies, although not totally isolated, were only marginally affected by nation-states and the world capitalist economy. In 1800, bands, tribes, and chiefdoms controlled half the globe and 20 percent of its population (Bodley 2008). Industrialization tipped the balance in favor of states (see Hornborg and Crumley 2007).

indigenous peoples The original inhabitants of particular territories; often descendants of tribespeople who live on as culturally distinct colonized peoples, many of whom aspire to autonomy.

As industrial states have conquered, annexed, and "developed" nonstates, there has been genocide on a grand scale. *Genocide* refers to a deliberate policy of exterminating a group through warfare or murder. Examples include the Holocaust, Rwanda in 1994, and Bosnia in the early 1990s. Bodley (2008) estimates that an average of 250,000 indigenous people perished annually between 1800 and 1950. Besides warfare, the causes included foreign diseases (to which natives lacked resistance), slavery, land grabbing, and other forms of dispossession and impoverishment.

Many native groups have been incorporated within nation-states, where they now live as ethnic minorities. Such groups maintain an ethnic identity, despite having lost their ancestral cultures to varying degrees (partial ethnocide). Also, many descendants of tribespeople live on as culturally distinct and self-conscious colonized peoples within contemporary nation-states. Many such groups aspire to autonomy. As the original inhabitants of their territories, they are called **indigenous peoples** (see Maybury-Lewis 2002).

Globally many contemporary nations are repeating—at an accelerated rate—the process of resource depletion that started in Europe and the United States during the Industrial Revolution. Fortunately, today's world has some environmental watchdogs that did not exist during the first centuries of the Industrial Revolution. Given national and international cooperation and sanctions, the modern world may benefit from the lessons of the past (see Hornborg, McNeill, and Martinez-Alier 2007).

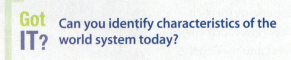

Got IT? Can you identify characteristics of the world system today?

Learn to read your dinner plate like a map of the world system. The American diet relies heavily on imports of both goods and labor. Supplementing information on the source of a particular food item (packaging often identifies sources) with Internet research, use the food you eat to gain information on global capitalism and global inequality. For example, let's say your grapes came from California. Hondurans who migrated across Mexico to work on farms in California may have harvested your grapes. Although working for extremely low wages, Honduran migrant workers manage collectively to send huge remittances in U.S. dollars back to Honduras. Who in the United States might benefit from this and how? Who in Honduras might benefit? Given these facts, what would you suspect is Honduras' position of economic power in the world system?

FOR REVIEW

EXPERIENCING CULTURE

TO ACCESS THESE VIDEOS ON YOUR COMPUTER, VISIT

www.mhhe.com/gezonqr

10-1

I. When and why did the world system develop, and what is it like today?

- A global system of economic and political relations emerged in the fifteenth century, as Europeans established transoceanic trade with other peoples, who then entered Europe's sphere of influence. Over the next several hundred years, an exchange of people, resources, products, ideas, and diseases linked the Old and the New Worlds. By the eighteenth century, European industrialization, fed by capital from transoceanic trade, hastened the separation of workers from the means of production. Today's capitalistic world economy maintains the contrast between owners and workers, but a partial shift in power to the masses has reduced the polarization. Currently, world stratification features a contrast between both capitalists and workers in the core nations and workers on the periphery. Industrialization is implicated in the destruction of indigenous economies, ecologies, and populations and an accelerated rate of resource depletion.

II. When and how did European colonialism develop, and how is its legacy expressed in postcolonial studies?

- The first phase of European colonialism began with the exploration and exploitation of the Americas after Columbus. In the nineteenth century, the search for new markets led European nations to take and hold foreign colonies. During this new phase of colonialism (1875–1914), Britain and France promoted their commercial interests in their respective colonies and sought to "civilize" native peoples. Colonizers constructed whole countries and divisions within them. *Postcolonial* refers to the lasting effects of European colonization and the study of the period after it. The settler, nonsettler, and mixed countries that were former colonies had different colonial experiences. The United States, although colonized, usually isn't perceived as postcolonial because of its current world power position, its treatment of Native Americans, and its annexation of foreign territories.

III. How do colonialism, development, industrialization, neoliberalism, and Communism exemplify intervention philosophies?

- These ideologies and historical developments have been shaped by justifications for guiding native peoples in specific directions. Colonial powers have engaged in political, social, economic, and cultural domination. Paternalistic views of non-Western peoples'"backwardness" helped colonial powers to legitimize imperialist expansion. Development plans assume that retracing the "First World's" path among "developing" countries will promote long-term benefits for them. Powerful financial institutions impose neoliberal policies, entailing open trade and investment, cost control, and austerity measures that cut government aid for social services. Communism has promoted obedience to authority and often demanded total submission of individuals to the state.

Pop Quiz

Multiple Choice:

1. The modern world system is best understood as
   a. A system in which ethnic groups are increasingly isolated from nation-states.
   b. A system of social class stratification mirroring Karl Marx's theory of class conflict.
   c. A global system in which nations are economically and politically interdependent.
   d. A system whose major contrast pits capitalists against workers in core nations.

2. Which of the following statements about world-system theory is false?
   a. The three different positions of economic and political power are core, semiperiphery, and periphery.
   b. The theory sees society as consisting of inter-related parts.
   c. The theory claims that a set of economic and political relations has characterized much of the globe since the Old World and New World established regular contact.
   d. The theory applies mainly to economic and political relations among Western nations.

3. Marx argued that class consciousness results from
   a. the intersection of ethnic and national identities with social class identity.
   b. recognizing collective economic interests and identifying with a group sharing those interests.
   c. a growing distinction among religions.
   d. the extension of notions of kinship beyond the boundaries of actual biological relations.

4. Imperialism refers to extending rule of a country or empire over foreign nations and holding foreign colonies, while colonialism refers specifically to
   a. the political, social, economic, and cultural domination of a territory and its people by a foreign power for an extended time.
   b. imperial influence that disappears when former colonies gain independence.

   c. european domination of a territory.
   d. efforts to civilize the world by implanting European languages.

5. Although Communism was not uniform over time or among countries that adopted it,
   a. all Communist systems have been authoritarian.
   b. few Communist systems have been totalitarian.
   c. all Communist nations mix state ownership with private ownership of means of production.
   d. few Communist regimes have stressed identification with the international movement.

6. Which of the following statements does *not* characterize the modern world system?
   a. Twentieth-century industrialization added hundreds of new industries and millions of new jobs.
   b. Mass production has given rise to a culture of consumption.
   c. The U.S. lags behind India and China in total energy consumption.
   d. Industrialization has caused the destruction of indigenous economies, ecologies, and populations.

Fill in the Blank:

1. _____ refers to wealth or resources invested in business with the intent of producing a profit.
2. Karl Marx's two opposed socioeconomic classes were the _____ and the _____.
3. Britain used the notion of a white man's burden to justify its imperialist expansion. France claimed to be engaged in a civilizing mission in its colonies. These, together with some forms of economic development plans, illustrate an _____, an ideological justification for outsiders to guide native peoples in specific directions.
4. The term _____ is used to describe the relations between European countries and their former colonies in the second half of the 20th century.

1. (c), 2. (d), 3. (b), 4. (a), 5. (a), 6. (c)

1. Capital; 2. bourgeoisie, proletariat; 3. intervention philosophy; 4. *postcolonial*

11

ETHNICITY AND RACE

UNDERSTANDING OURSELVES

How do you imagine human "diversity"? Maybe you associate that word with "race" or "ethnicity." Perhaps you think of differences—like skin or eye color, hair form, or height—that can be observed by the naked eye. In fact, human biological diversity encompasses much more than observable physical differences. It includes, for example, our variable abilities to digest various foods and our innate resistance or susceptibility to particular diseases.

Meeting every day in contemporary North America are people whose ancestors lived in many lands. The first (Native) Americans had to cross a land bridge that once linked Siberia to North America. For later immigrants, perhaps including your own parents or grandparents, the voyage may have been across the sea, or overland from nations to the south. They came for many reasons; some came voluntarily, while others were brought in chains. The scale of migration in today's world is so vast that millions of people routinely cross national borders or live far from the homelands of their grandparents. The American population includes millions of people whose biological features reflect adaptations to environments other than the ones they now inhabit.

Diversity also includes the various identities that the same person may hold in different situations. Part of human adaptive flexibility is our ability to consciously (and sometimes subconsciously) shift self presentation in response to context. Italians, for example, maintain separate sets of clothing to be worn inside and outside the home. They invest much more in their outside wardrobe—thus supporting a vibrant Italian fashion industry—and what it says about their public persona than in indoor garb, which is for family and intimates to see. Both behavior and identities can change with context. One person can be both black and Hispanic, or a father and a ballplayer. One identity is claimed or perceived in certain settings, another in different ones. Among African Americans a "Hispanic" baseball player might be black; among Hispanics, Hispanic. When asked "who are you?" what first comes to mind? How might that vary according to situation?

>> Ethnic Groups and Ethnicity

As with any culture, members of an **ethnic group** share certain beliefs, values, habits, customs, and norms because of their common background. They define themselves as different and special because of cultural features. This distinction may arise from language, religion, historical experience, geographic placement, kinship, or "race" (see Spickard 2012). Markers of an ethnic group may include a collective name, belief in common descent, a sense

ethnic group Group distinguished by cultural similarities (shared among members of that group) and differences (between that group and others); ethnic group members share beliefs, values, habits, customs, and norms, and a common language, religion, history, geography, kinship, and/or race.

ethnicity Identification with, and feeling part of, an ethnic group and exclusion from certain other groups because of this affiliation.

CULTURE THINK

What identities other than ethnicity do people negotiate depending on the situation they are in? Hint: Think about social class, religion, relationship status, etc.

of solidarity, and an association with a specific territory, which the group may or may not hold (Ryan 1990, pp. xiii, xiv). The graphic "Racial/Ethnic Identification in the United States, 2010" lists American ethnic groups, as reported in the 2010 U. S. census.

According to Fredrik Barth (1969), ethnicity can be said to exist when people claim a certain ethnic identity for themselves and are defined by others as having that identity. **Ethnicity** means identification with, and feeling part of, an ethnic group and exclusion from certain other groups because of this affiliation. Ethnic feelings and associated behavior vary in intensity within ethnic groups and countries and over time. A change in the degree of importance attached to an ethnic identity may reflect political changes (Soviet rule ends—ethnic feeling rises) or individual life-cycle changes (young people relinquish, or old people reclaim, an ethnic background).

Cultural differences may be associated with ethnicity, class, region, or religion. Individuals often have more than one group identity. People may be loyal (depending on circumstances) to their neighborhood, school, town, state or province, region, nation, continent, religion, ethnic group, or interest group (Ryan 1990, p. xxii). In a complex society such as the United States or Canada, people constantly negotiate their social identities. All of us "wear different hats," presenting ourselves sometimes as one thing, sometimes as another.

TABLE 11.1

Racial/Ethnic Identification in the United States, 2010 (as reported by U.S. Census Bureau from the 2010 Census)

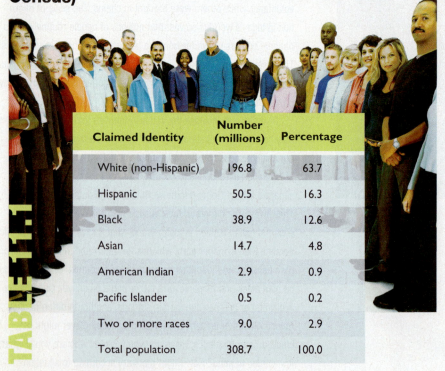

Claimed Identity	Number (millions)	Percentage
White (non-Hispanic)	196.8	63.7
Hispanic	50.5	16.3
Black	38.9	12.6
Asian	14.7	4.8
American Indian	2.9	0.9
Pacific Islander	0.5	0.2
Two or more races	9.0	2.9
Total population	308.7	100.0

Source: U.S. Census Bureau, decennial census data, 2010.

STATUS SHIFTING

Sometimes our identities (aka social statuses) are mutually exclusive. It's hard to be both black and white or male and female. Sometimes, assuming an identity or joining a group requires a conversion experience, acquiring a new and overwhelming primary identity, such as becoming a born-again Christian.

Some statuses aren't mutually exclusive, but contextual. A person can be both black and Hispanic or both a mother and a senator. One identity is used in certain settings, another in different ones. We call this the *situational negotiation of social identity* (Leman 2001). Hispanics, for example, may shift ethnic affiliations as they negotiate their identities. "Hispanic" is a category based mainly on language. It includes whites, blacks, and "racially" mixed Spanish speakers and their ethnically conscious descendants. (There also are Native

CULTURETHINK

After Barack Obama's election to the presidency in 2008, some claimed this as evidence that we live in a "postracial" world, where race is no longer a barrier to success. Do you agree?

American and even Asian Hispanics.) "Hispanics," the fastest-growing ethnic group in the United States, lumps together people of diverse geographic origin— Puerto Rico, Mexico, Cuba, El Salvador, Guatemala, the Dominican Republic, and other Spanish-speaking countries of Central and South America and the Caribbean. "Latino" is a broader category, which also can include Brazilians (who speak Portuguese). National origins are shown in the graph "American Hispanics/Latinos, 2009" (which excludes Brazilians).

Mexican Americans (Chicanos), Cuban Americans, and Puerto Ricans may mobilize to promote general Hispanic issues (e.g., opposition to English-only laws) but act as three separate interest groups in other contexts. Cuban Americans are richer on average than Chicanos and Puerto Ricans are, and their class interests and voting patterns differ. Cubans often vote Republican, but Puerto Ricans and Chicanos are more likely to favor Democrats. Some Mexican Americans whose families have lived in the United States for generations have little in common with new Hispanic immigrants, such as those from Central America. Many Americans (especially those fluent in English) claim Hispanic ethnicity in some contexts but shift to a general "American" identity in others.

In many societies a racial, ethnic, or caste status is associated with a position in the social-political hierarchy. Certain groups, called **minority groups,** are subordinate. They have inferior power and less secure access to resources than do **majority groups** (which are superordinate, dominant, or controlling). Often ethnic groups are minorities. When an ethnic group is assumed to have a biological basis (distinctively shared "blood" or genes), it is called a **race.** Discrimination against such a group

> **minority groups** Subordinate groups in a social-political hierarchy, with inferior power and less secure access to resources than majority groups have.
>
> **majority groups** Superordinate, dominant, or controlling groups in a social-political hierarchy.
>
> **race** An ethnic group assumed to have a biological basis.

American Hispanics/ Latinos, 2009

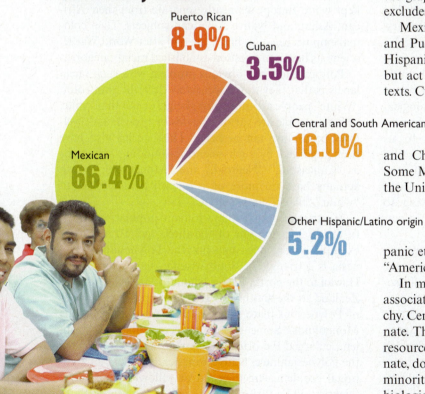

Puerto Rican
8.9%

Cuban
3.5%

Central and South American
16.0%

Other Hispanic/Latino origin
5.2%

Mexican
66.4%

Source: Statistical Abstract of the United States, 2012, Table 37, p. 42.

is called **racism** (Cohen 1998; Montagu 1997; Scupin 2003; Shanklin 1995; Wade 2002).

 Got IT? Can you define "ethnic group" and identify what it means to shift and negotiate ethnic identities depending on context?

>> Human Biological Diversity and the Race Concept

The photos in this book offer only a glimpse of the range of human biological variation. Additional illustration comes from your own experience. Look around you in your classroom or library, or at the mall or multiplex. Inevitably you'll see people whose ancestors lived in many lands. Physical diversity within such nations as the United States and Canada is evident to anyone. Anthropology's job is to explain these contrasts.

racism Discrimination against an ethnic group assumed to have a biological basis.

racial classification The attempt to assign humans to discrete categories (purportedly) based on common ancestry.

Historically, scientists have approached the study of human biological diversity in two main ways: (1) racial classification (now largely abandoned) versus (2) the current explanatory approach, which focuses on understanding specific differences. First we'll consider problems with **racial classification**—the attempt to assign humans to discrete categories (purportedly) based on common ancestry. Then we'll offer some explanations for specific aspects of human biological diversity (in this case, light versus dark skin color). Biological differences are real, important, and apparent to us all. Modern scientists find it most productive to seek explanations for this diversity, rather than trying to pigeonhole people into categories called races.

What is race anyway? In theory, a biological race would be a geographically isolated subdivision of a species. (A species is a population whose members can interbreed to produce offspring that can live and reproduce.) Such a subspecies would be capable of interbreeding with other subspecies of the same species, but it would not actually do so because of its geographic isolation. Some biologists also use "race" to refer to "breeds," as of dogs or roses. Thus, a pit bull and a Chihuahua would be different races of dogs. Such domesticated "races" have been bred by humans for generations. Humanity (*Homo sapiens*) lacks such races because human populations have not been isolated enough from one another to develop into such discrete groups. Nor have humans experienced controlled breeding like that which has created the various kinds of dogs and roses.

A race is supposed to reflect shared genetic material (inherited from a common ancestor), but early scholars instead used phenotypical traits (usually skin color) for human racial classification. Phenotype refers to an organism's evident traits, its "manifest biology"—anatomy and physiology. Humans display hundreds of evident (detectable) physical traits. They range from skin color, hair form, eye color, and facial features (which are visible) to blood groups and enzyme production (which become evident through testing).

Racial classifications based on phenotype raise the problem of deciding which traits are most important. Should races be defined by height, weight, body shape, facial features, teeth, skull form, or skin color? Like their fellow citizens, early European and American scientists gave priority to skin color. Many school books and encyclopedias still proclaim the existence of three great races: the white, the black, and the yellow. This overly simplistic classification was compatible with the political use of race during the colonial period of the late nineteenth and early twentieth centuries. Such a tripartite scheme kept white Europeans neatly separate from their African, Asian, and Native American subjects. Then colonial empires began to break up, and after World War II, scientists began to question established racial categories.

Politics aside, one obvious problem with such racial labels is that they don't accurately describe skin color. "White" people are more pink, beige, or tan than white. "Black" people are various shades of brown, and "yellow" people are tan or beige. These terms also have been dignified by such scientific-sounding synonyms as "Caucasoid," "Negroid," and "Mongoloid," which actually have no more of a scientific basis than do "white," "black," and "yellow."

It's true also that many human populations don't fit neatly into any one of the three "great races." For example, where does one put the Polynesians? Polynesia is a triangle of South Pacific islands formed by Hawaii to the north, Easter Island to the east, and New Zealand to the southwest. Does the bronze skin color of Polynesians place them with the Caucasoids or the Mongoloids? Some scientists, recognizing this problem, enlarged the original tripartite scheme to include the Polynesian race. Native Americans present an additional problem. Are they red or yellow? Again, some scientists add a fifth race—the red, or Amerindian—to the major racial groups.

Photos, from left to right: an Aymaran from Bolivia; a Samburu woman from Kenya; a woman from Guangzhou province, People's Republic of China; and England's Prince Harry.

Many people in southern India have dark skins, but scientists have been reluctant to classify them with black Africans because of their Caucasoid facial features and hair form. Some, therefore, have created a separate race for these people. What about the Australian aborigines, hunters and gatherers native to the most isolated continent? By skin color, one might place some Native Australians in the same race as tropical Africans. However, similarities to Europeans in hair color (light or reddish) and facial features have led some scientists to classify them as Caucasoids. But there is no evidence that Australians are closer genetically or historically to either of these groups than they are to Asians. Recognizing this problem, scientists often regard Native Australians as a separate race.

Finally, consider the San ("Bushmen") of the Kalahari Desert in southern Africa. Scientists have perceived their skin color as varying from brown to yellow. Those who regard San skin as yellow have placed them in the same category as Asians. In theory, people of the same race share more recent common ancestry with each other than they do with any others; but there is no evidence for recent common ancestry between San and Asians. More reasonably, the San are classified as members of the Capoid (from the Cape of Good Hope) race, which is seen as being different from other groups inhabiting tropical Africa.

Similar problems arise when any single trait is used as a basis for racial classification. An attempt to use facial features, height, weight, or any other phenotypical trait

CULTURE THINK

Try to identify the people shown in these photos using traditional racial categories: Race typically is assigned based on a combination of ancestry and appearance. Without knowing their ancestry, can you identify their "race"? How accurate are traditional racial categories for identifying people?

Answers: (left to right): Polynesian, southern Indian, Native Australian, San (southern Africa).

CULTURE THINK

The fact that race lacks a biological basis does not make it irrelevant. How is race an issue for many people today?

is fraught with difficulties. For example, consider the Nilotes, natives of the upper Nile region of Uganda and Sudan. Nilotes tend to be tall and to have long, narrow noses. Certain Scandinavians also are tall, with similar noses. Given the distance between their homelands, to classify them as members of the same race makes little sense. There is no reason to assume that Nilotes and Scandinavians are more closely related to each other than either is to shorter (and nearer) populations with different kinds of noses.

Would it be better to base racial classifications on a combination of physical traits? This would avoid some of the problems just discussed, but others would arise. First, skin color, stature, skull form, and facial features (nose form, eye shape, lip thickness) don't go together as a unit. For example, people with dark skin may be tall or short and have hair ranging from straight to very curly. Dark-haired populations may have light or dark skin, along with various skull forms, facial features, and body sizes and shapes. The number of combinations is very large, and the amount that heredity (versus environment) contributes to such phenotypical traits is often unclear.

There is a final objection to racial classification based on phenotype. The phenotypical characteristics on which races are based supposedly reflect genetic material that is shared and that has stayed the same for long periods. But phenotypical similarities and differences don't necessarily have a genetic basis. Because of changes in the environment that affect individuals

during growth and development, the range of phenotypes characteristic of a population may change without any genetic change. There are several examples. In the early twentieth century, the anthropologist Franz Boas (1940/1966) described changes in skull form among the children of Europeans who had migrated to the United States. The reason for this wasn't a change in genes, since the European immigrants tended to marry among themselves. Some of their children had been born in Europe and merely raised in the United States. Something in the new environment, probably in the diet, was producing this change. We know now that changes in average height and weight produced by dietary differences in a few generations are common and have nothing to do with race or genetics.

 Got IT? Can you identify and evaluate the reasons why scientists have largely discredited race as a biological category?

EXPLAINING SKIN COLOR

Traditional racial classification assumed that biological characteristics were determined by heredity and were stable (immutable) over long periods. We know now that a biological similarity doesn't necessarily indicate recent common ancestry. Dark skin color, for example, can be shared by tropical Africans and Native Australians for reasons other than common ancestry. It is not possible to define human races biologically. Still, scientists have made much progress in explaining variation in skin color, along with many other expressions of human biological diversity. We shift now from classification to explanation, in which natural selection plays a key role.

First recognized by Charles Darwin and Alfred Russel Wallace, natural selection is the process by which the forms most fit to survive and reproduce in a given environment—such as the tropics—do so in greater numbers than others in the same population do. Over the years, the less fit organisms die out and the favored types survive by producing more offspring. The role of natural selection in producing variation in skin color illustrates the explanatory approach to human biological diversity. Comparable explanations have been provided for many other aspects of human biological variation.

Melanin, the primary determinant of human skin color, is a chemical substance manufactured in the epidermis, or outer skin layer. The melanin cells of darker-skinned people produce more and larger granules of melanin than do those of lighter-skinned people. By screening out ultraviolet (UV) radiation from the sun, melanin offers protection against a variety of maladies, including sunburn and skin cancer.

Before the sixteenth century, most of the world's very dark-skinned populations lived in the tropics, a belt extending about 23 degrees north and south of the

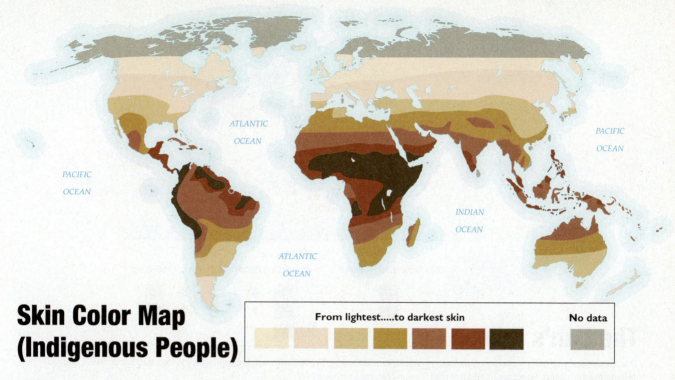

Skin Color Map (Indigenous People)

From lightest.....to darkest skin   **No data**

Before the sixteenth century, most of the world's very dark-skinned populations lived in the tropics, a belt extending about 23 degrees north and south of the equator. Outside the tropics, skin color tends to be lighter.

Source: G. Chaplin, "Geographic Distribution of Environmental Factors Influencing Human Skin Coloration," *American Journal of Physical Anthropology* 125:292–302, 2004; map updated in 2007.

equator, between the Tropic of Cancer and the Tropic of Capricorn. The association between dark skin color and a tropical habitat existed throughout the Old World, where humans and their ancestors have lived for millions of years. The darkest populations of Africa evolved not in shady equatorial forests but in sunny open grassland, or savanna, country.

Outside the tropics, skin color tends to be lighter. Moving north in Africa, for example, there is a gradual transition from dark brown to medium brown. Average skin color continues to lighten as one moves through the Middle East, into southern Europe, through central Europe, and to the north. South of the tropics skin color also is lighter. In the Americas, by contrast, tropical populations don't have very dark skin. This is because the settlement of the New World, by light-skinned Asian ancestors of Native Americans, was relatively recent, probably dating back no more than eighteen thousand years.

How, aside from migrations, can we explain the geographic distribution of human skin color? Natural selection provides an answer. In the tropics, intense UV radiation poses a series of threats that make light skin color an adaptive disadvantage. First, UV radiation can cause severe sunburn, which aside from discomfort can lead to vulnerabilities in the body. By damaging sweat glands, sunburn reduces the body's ability to perspire and thus to regulate its own temperature (thermoregulation). Sunburn also can increase susceptibility to

disease. Yet another disadvantage of having light skin color in the tropics is that exposure to UV radiation can cause skin cancer (Blum 1961). Melanin, nature's own sunscreen, confers a selective advantage (i.e., a better chance to survive and reproduce) on darker-skinned people living in the tropics because it helps protect them from sunburn and skin cancer.

Another selective factor in the geographic distribution of human skin color relates to the manufacture (synthesis) of vitamin D in the body. Years ago, W. F. Loomis (1967) focused on the role of UV radiation in stimulating the manufacture of vitamin D by the human body. The unclothed human body can produce its own vitamin D when exposed to sufficient sunlight. However, in a cloudy environment that also is so cold that people have to dress themselves much of the year (such as northern Europe, where very light skin color evolved), clothing interferes with the body's manufacture of vitamin D. The ensuing shortage of vitamin D diminishes the absorption of calcium in the intestines. A nutritional disease known as rickets, which softens and deforms the bones, may develop. In women, deformation of the pelvic bones from rickets can interfere with childbirth. In cold northern areas, light skin color maximizes the absorption of UV radiation and the synthesis of vitamin D by the few parts of the body that are exposed to direct sunlight. There has been selection against dark skin color in northern areas because melanin screens out UV radiation.

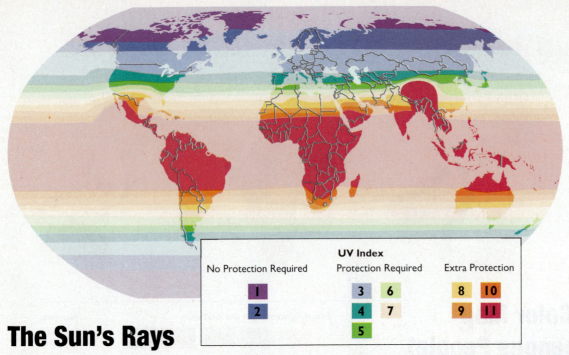

The Sun's Rays

UV Index

No Protection Required
1
2

Protection Required
3
4
5
6
7

Extra Protection
8
9
10
11

This color-coded map of the world shows the mean annual UV radiation level in 2003, with purple designating the lowest radiation levels, and red designating the highest. How does this data fit with the skin color map on page 219?

This natural selection continues today: East Asians who have migrated recently from India and Pakistan to northern areas of the United Kingdom have a higher incidence of rickets and osteoporosis (also related to vitamin D and calcium deficiency) than the general British population. A related illustration involves Eskimos (Inuit) and other indigenous inhabitants of northern Alaska and northern Canada. According to Nina Jablonski (quoted in Iqbal 2002), "Looking at Alaska, one would think that the native people should be pale as ghosts." One reason they aren't is that they haven't inhabited this region very long in terms of geological time. Even more important, their traditional diet, which is rich in seafood, including fish oils, supplies sufficient vitamin D so as to make a reduction in pigmentation unnecessary. However, and again illustrating natural selection at work today, "when these people don't eat their aboriginal diets of fish and marine mammals, they suffer tremendously high rates of vitamin D-deficiency diseases such as rickets in children and osteoporosis in adults" (Jablonski quoted in Iqbal 2002). Far from being immutable, skin color can become an evolutionary liability very quickly.

According to Jablonski and George Chaplin (2000), another key factor explaining the geographic distribution of skin color involves the effects of UV radiation on folate, an essential nutrient that the human body manufactures from folic acid. Folate is needed for cell division and the production of new DNA. Pregnant women require large amounts of folate to support rapid cell division in the embryo, and there is a direct connection between folate and individual reproductive success. Folate deficiency causes neural tube defects (NTDs) in human embryos. NTDs are marked by the incomplete closure of the neural tube, so the spine and spinal cord fail to develop completely. One NTD, anencephaly (with the brain an exposed mass), results in stillbirth or death soon after delivery. With spina bifida, another NTD, survival rates are higher, but babies have severe disabilities, including paralysis. NTDs are the second most common human birth defect after cardiac abnormalities. Today, women of reproductive age are advised to take folate supplements to prevent serious birth defects such as spina bifida.

Natural sunlight and UV radiation destroy folate in the human body. Because melanin, as we have seen, protects against UV hazards, such as sunburn and its consequences, dark skin coloration is adaptive in the tropics. Now we see that melanin also is adaptive because it conserves folate in the human body and thus protects against NTDs, which are much more common in light-skinned than in darker-skinned populations (Jablonski and Chaplin 2000). Studies confirm that Africans and

Did You Know?

Before the 1930s, when milk first was fortified with vitamin D, rickets was a major health concern in the United States. The National Institutes of Health directly linked vitamin D deficiency with low sun exposure. You could say that fortifying milk is a cultural adaptation to the environmental stress of low sun exposure.

African Americans have a low incidence of severe folate deficiency, even among individuals with marginal nutritional status. Folate also plays a role in another process that is central to reproduction: spermatogenesis, the production of sperm. In mice and rats, folate deficiency can cause male sterility; it may well play a similar role in humans.

Today, of course, cultural alternatives to biological adaptation permit light-skinned people to survive in the tropics and darker-skinned people to live in the far north. People can clothe themselves and seek shelter from the sun; they can use artificial sunscreens if they lack the natural protection that melanin provides. Dark-skinned people living in the north can, indeed must, get vitamin D from their diet or take supplements. Today, pregnant women are routinely advised to take folic acid or folate supplements as a hedge against NTDs. Even so, light skin color still is correlated with a higher incidence of spina bifida. Jablonski and Chaplin (2000) explain variation in human skin color as resulting from a balancing act between the evolutionary needs to (1) protect against all UV hazards (favoring dark skin in the tropics) and (2) have an adequate supply of vitamin D (favoring lighter skin outside the tropics).

This discussion of skin color shows that common ancestry, the presumed basis of race, is not the only reason for biological similarities. Natural selection, still at work today, makes a major contribution to variations in human skin color, as well as to many other human biological differences and similarities.

[**Got IT?** Can you explain how scientists understand human biological diversity based on natural selection?

>> Race and Ethnicity

Race, like ethnicity in general, is a cultural category rather than a biological reality. That is, ethnic groups, including "races," derive from contrasts perceived and perpetuated in particular societies, rather than from scientific classifications based on common genes (see Wade 2002).

Rickets, based on a significant vitamin D deficiency, can lead to softening of the bones, which may result in bow legs as illustrated by the child shown in this nineteenth-century photo.

Human races cannot be defined biologically. Only cultural constructions of race are possible—even though the average person conceptualizes "race" in biological terms. The belief that human races exist and are important is much more common among the public than it is among scientists. Most Americans, for example, believe that their population includes biologically based races to which various labels have been applied. These labels include "white," "black," "yellow," "red," "Caucasoid," "Negroid," "Mongoloid," "Amerindian," "Euro-American," "African American," "Asian American," and "Native American."

We hear the words "ethnicity" and "race" frequently, but American culture doesn't draw a very clear line between them. Consider a *New York Times* article published on May 29, 1992. Discussing the changing ethnic composition of the United States, the article explained (correctly) that Hispanics "can be of any race" (Barringer 1992, p. A12). In other words, "Hispanic" is an ethnic category that crosscuts racial contrasts such as that between "black" and "white." Another *Times* article published that same day reported that during the Los Angeles riots in spring 1992, "hundreds of Hispanic residents were interrogated about their immigration status on the basis of their race alone [emphasis added]" (Mydans 1992a, p. A8). Use of "race" here seems inappropriate because "Hispanic" usually is perceived as referring to a linguistically based (Spanish-speaking) ethnic group, rather than a biologically based race. Since these Los Angeles residents were being interrogated because they were Hispanic, the article is actually reporting on ethnic, not racial, discrimination.

In a more recent case, consider a speech delivered by then Appeals Court Judge Sonia Sotomayor, newly nominated (in May 2009; confirmed in August 2009) for the U.S. Supreme Court by President Barack Obama. In a 2001 lecture titled "A Latina Judge's Voice," delivered as the "Judge Mario G. Olmos Memorial Lecture" at the University of California, Berkeley, School of Law, Sotomayor declared (as part of a much longer speech): "I would hope that a wise Latina woman with the richness of her experiences would more often than not reach a better conclusion than a white male who hasn't lived that life" (Sotomayor 2001/2009).

"Hispanic" and "Latino" are ethnic categories that cross-cut "racial" contrasts such as between "black" and "white." Note the physical diversity among these children in Trinidad, Cuba.

Conservatives, including former House speaker Newt Gingrich and radio talk show host Rush Limbaugh, seized on this declaration as evidence that Sotomayor was a "racist" or a "reverse racist." Again, however, "Latina" is an ethnic (and gendered-female) rather than a racial category. I suspect that Sotomayor also was using "white male" as an ethnic-gender category, to refer to nonminority men. These examples from our everyday experience illustrate difficulties in drawing a precise distinction between race and ethnicity. It probably is better to use the term "ethnic group" rather than "race" to describe any such social group, for example, African Americans, Asian Americans, Anglo Americans, Hispanics, Latinos, Latinas, and even non-Hispanic whites.

>> The Social Construction of Race

Races are ethnic groups assumed (by members of a particular culture) to have a biological basis, but actually race is socially constructed. The "races" we hear about every day are cultural, or social, rather than biological categories. Many Americans mistakenly assume that whites and blacks, for example, are biologically distinct and that these terms stand for discrete races. But these labels, like racial terms used in other societies, really designate culturally perceived rather than biologically based groups.

HYPODESCENT: RACE IN THE UNITED STATES

How is race culturally constructed in the United States? In American culture, one acquires his or her racial identity at birth, as an ascribed status, but race isn't based on biology or on simple ancestry. Take the case of the child of a "racially mixed" marriage involving one black and one white parent. We know that 50 percent of the child's genes come from one parent and 50 percent from the other. Still, American culture overlooks heredity and classifies this child as black. This rule is arbitrary. On the basis of genotype (genetic composition), it would be just as logical to classify the child as white.

American rules for assigning racial status can be even more arbitrary. In some states, anyone known to have any black ancestor, no matter how remote, is classified as a member of the black race. This is a rule of **descent** (it assigns social identity on the basis of ancestry), but of a sort that is rare outside the contemporary United States. It is called **hypodescent** (Harris and Kottak 1963) because it automatically places the children of a union between members of different groups in the minority group (*hypo* means "lower"). Hypodescent

CULTURETHINK

Based on your own experiences, think of several ways in which skin color and ethnicity affect judgments and evaluations of people.

A biracial American, Halle Berry, with her mother. What is Halle Berry's race?

divides American society into groups that have been unequal in their access to wealth, power, and prestige.

The rule of hypodescent affects blacks, Asians, Native Americans, and Hispanics differently (see Hunter 2005). Native American or Hispanic identity is easier to negotiate than black identity. The ascription rule isn't as definite, and the assumption of a biological basis isn't as strong.

> **descent** Rule assigning social identity on the basis of some aspect of one's ancestry.
>
> **hypodescent** A rule that automatically places the children of a union or mating between members of different socioeconomic groups in the less privileged group.

To be considered Native American, one ancestor out of eight (great-grandparents) or out of four (grandparents) may suffice. This depends on whether the assignment is by federal or state law or by an Indian tribal council. The child of a Hispanic may (or may not, depending on context) claim Hispanic identity. Many Americans with an Indian or Latino grandparent consider themselves white and lay no claim to minority group status.

Questions on Race and Hispanic Origin from Census 2010

5. Is this person of Hispanic, Latino, or Spanish origin?

☐ No, not of Hispanic, Latino, or Spanish origin
☐ Yes, Mexican, Mexican Am., Chicano
☐ Yes, Puerto Rican
☐ Yes, Cuban
☐ Yes, another Hispanic, Latino, or Spanish origin — *Print origin, for example, Argentinean, Colombian, Dominican, Nicaraguan, Salvadoran, Spaniard, and so on.*

[ ]

6. What is this person's race? *Mark* ☒ *one or more boxes.*

☐ White
☐ Black, African Am., or Negro
☐ American Indian or Alaska Native — *Print name of enrolled or principal tribe.*

[ ]

☐ Asian Indian ☐ Japanese ☐ Native Hawaiian
☐ Chinese ☐ Korean ☐ Guamanian or Chamorro
☐ Filipino ☐ Vietnamese ☐ Samoan
☐ Other Asian — *Print race, for example, Hmong, Laotian, Thai, Pakistani, Cambodian, and so on.* ☐ Other Pacific Islander — *Print race, for example, Fijian, Tongan, and so on.*

[ ]

☐ Some other race — *Print race.*

[ ]

Source: U.S. Census Bureau, Census 2010 questionnaire.

RACE IN THE U.S. CENSUS

The U.S. Census Bureau has gathered data by race since 1790. The racial categories included in the 1990 census were "White," "Black or Negro," "Indian (American)," "Eskimo," "Aleut or Pacific Islander," and "Other." A separate question was asked about Spanish-Hispanic heritage. Check out the reproduction of the questionnaire on racial categories in the 2010 census.

Attempts to add a "multiracial" census category have been opposed by the National Association for the Advancement of Colored People (NAACP) and the National

Visible Minority Population of Canada, 2006 Census

100.0% Total population: 31,241,030

Percent

4.0%	South Asian	1,262,865
3.9%	Chinese	1,216,515
2.5%	Black	783,795
1.3%	Filipino	410,695
1.2%	Arab/West Asian	374,835
1.0%	Latin American	304,245
0.8%	Southeast Asian	239,935
0.5%	Korean	141,890
0.3%	Japanese	83,300
0.4%	Other visible minority	116,895
0.4%	Multiple visible minority	133,120
16.2%	**Total visible minority population:**	**5,068,090**

83.8%
Not visible minority (i.e. majority):
26,172,940

Source: From Statistics Canada, 2006 Census, http://www12.statcan.ca/english/census06/data/highlights/ethnic.

CULTURETHINK

Imagine you are on a panel to debate whether or not to add a "multiracial" census category. What would be your arguments for and against?

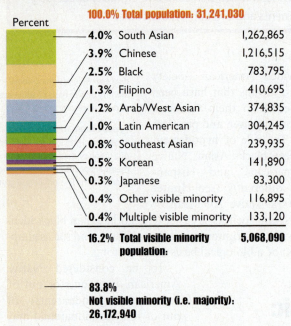

Council of La Raza (a Hispanic advocacy group). Racial classification is a political issue (Goldberg 2002) involving access to resources, including jobs, voting districts, and federal funding of programs aimed at minorities. The hypodescent rule results in all the population growth being attributed to the minority category. Minorities fear their political clout will decline if their numbers go down.

But things are changing. Choice of "some other race" in the U.S. Census tripled from 1980 (6.8 million) to 2010 (over 19 million)—suggesting imprecision in and dissatisfaction with the existing categories. In the 2000 census, 2.4 percent of Americans chose a first-ever option of identifying themselves as belonging to more than one race. That figure rose to 2.9 percent in the 2010 census. The number of interracial marriages and children is increasing, with implications for the traditional system of American racial classification. "Interracial," "biracial," or "multiracial" children undoubtedly identify with qualities of both parents. It is troubling for many of them to have so important an identity as race dictated by the arbitrary rule of hypodescent. It may be especially discordant when racial identity doesn't parallel gender identity, for instance, a boy with a white father and a black mother, or a girl with a white mother and a black father.

How does the Canadian census compare with the American census in its treatment of race? Rather than race, the Canadian census asks about "visible minorities." That country's Employment Equity Act defines such groups as "persons, other than Aboriginal peoples [aka First Nations in Canada], who are non-Caucasian in race or non-white in colour" (Statistics Canada 2001). The figure on this page shows that "South Asian" and "Chinese" are Canada's largest visible minorities. Note that Canada's total visible minority population of 16.2 percent in 2006 (up from 11.2 percent in 1996) contrasts with a figure of about 25 percent for the United States in the 2000 census, rising to 36 percent in the 2010 census. In particular, Canada's black population of 2.5 percent contrasts with the American figure of 12.6 percent (2010) for African Americans, while Canada's Asian population is significantly higher than the U.S. figure of 4.8 percent (2010) on a percentage basis. Only a tiny fraction of the Canadian population (0.4 percent) claimed multiple visible minority affiliation, compared with 2.9 percent claiming more than one race in the United States in 2010.

Canada's visible minority population has been increasing steadily. In 1981, visible minorities accounted for just 4.7 percent of the population, versus 16.2 percent in 2006 (the most recent census data avalable as of this writing). Visible minorities are growing much faster than is Canada's overall population. Between 2001 and 2006, the total population increased 5 percent, while visible minorities rose 27 percent. If recent immigration trends continue, visible minorities will soon account for 20 percent of Canada's population.

"NOT US": RACE IN JAPAN

American culture ignores considerable diversity in biology, language, and geographic origin as it socially constructs race in the United States. North Americans also overlook diversity by seeing Japan as a nation that is homogeneous in race, ethnicity, language, and culture—an image the Japanese themselves cultivate.

Scholars estimate that 10 percent of Japan's national population are minorities of various sorts. These include aboriginal Ainu, annexed Okinawans, outcast *burakumin,* children of mixed marriages, and immigrant nationalities, especially Koreans, who number more than seven hundred thousand (De Vos, Wetherall, and Stearman 1983; Lie 2001; Ryang and Lee 2009).

How is race culturally constructed in Japan? The (majority) Japanese define themselves by opposition to others, whether minority groups in their own nation or outsiders—anyone who is "not us." The "not us" should stay that way; assimilation generally is discouraged. Cultural mechanisms, especially residential segregation and taboos on "interracial" marriage, work to keep minorities "in their place."

In its construction of race, Japanese culture regards certain ethnic groups as having a biological basis, when there is no evidence that they do. The best example is the *burakumin,* a stigmatized group of at least four million outcasts, sometimes compared to India's untouchables. The burakumin are physically and genetically indistinguishable from other Japanese. Many of them "pass" as (and marry) majority Japanese, but a deceptive marriage can end in divorce if burakumin identity is discovered (Aoki and Dardess, eds. 1981).

Burakumin are perceived as standing apart from majority Japanese. Through ancestry, descent (and thus, it is assumed, "blood," or genetics) burakumin are "not us." Majority Japanese try to keep their lineage pure by discouraging mixing. The burakumin are residentially segregated in neighborhoods (rural or urban) called *buraku,* from which the racial label is derived. Compared with majority Japanese, the burakumin are less likely to attend high school and college. When burakumin attend the same schools as majority Japanese, they face discrimination. Majority children and teachers may refuse to eat with them because burakumin are considered unclean.

In applying for university admission or a job and in dealing with the government, Japanese must list their address, which becomes part of a household or family registry. This list makes residence in a buraku, and likely burakumin social status, evident. Schools and companies use this information to discriminate. (The best way to pass is to move so often that the buraku address eventually disappears from the registry.) Majority Japanese also limit "race" mixture by hiring marriage mediators to check out the family histories of prospective spouses. They are especially careful to check for burakumin ancestry (De Vos et al. 1983).

The origin of the burakumin lies in a historical tiered system of stratification dating to the Tokugawa period (1603-1868). The top four ranked categories were warrior-administrators (*samurai*), farmers, artisans, and merchants. The ancestors of the burakumin were below this hierarchy, an outcast group who did unclean jobs such as animal slaughter and disposal of the dead. Burakumin still do similar jobs, including work with leather and other animal products. The burakumin are more likely than majority Japanese to do manual labor (including farm work) and to belong to the national lower class. Burakumin and other Japanese minorities

Japan's stigmatized burakumin are physically and genetically indistinguishable from other Japanese. In response to burakumin political mobilization, Japan has dismantled the legal structure of discrimination against burakumin. This Sports Day for burakumin children is one kind of mobilization.

also are more likely to have careers in crime, prostitution, entertainment, and sports (De Vos et al. 1983).

Like blacks in the United States, the burakumin are class-stratified. Because certain jobs are reserved for the burakumin, people who are successful in those occupations (e.g., shoe factory owners) can be wealthy. Burakumin also have found jobs as government bureaucrats. Financially successful burakumin can temporarily escape their stigmatized status by travel, including foreign travel.

Discrimination against the burakumin is strikingly like the discrimination that blacks have experienced in the United States. The burakumin often live in villages and neighborhoods with poor housing and sanitation. They have limited access to education, jobs, amenities, and health facilities. In response to burakumin political mobilization, Japan has dismantled the legal structure of discrimination against burakumin and has worked to improve conditions in the buraku. (The website http://blhrri.org/index_e.htm is sponsored by the Buraku Liberation and Human Rights Research Institute and includes the most recent information about the Buraku liberation movement.) Still Japan has yet to institute American-style affirmative action programs for education and jobs. Discrimination against nonmajority Japanese is still the rule in companies. Some employers say that hiring burakumin would give their company an unclean image and thus create a disadvantage in competing with other businesses (De Vos et al. 1983).

PHENOTYPE AND FLUIDITY: RACE IN BRAZIL

There are more flexible, less exclusionary ways of socially constructing race than those used in the United States and Japan. Along with the rest of Latin America, Brazil has less exclusionary categories, which permit individuals to change their racial classification. Brazil shares a history of slavery with the United States, but it lacks the hypodescent rule.

Brazilians use many more racial labels—over five hundred were once reported (Harris 1970)—than Americans or Japanese do. In northeastern Brazil, Conrad Kottak found forty different racial terms in use in Arembepe, then a village of only seven hundred and fifty people (Kottak 2006). Through their traditional classification system Brazilians recognize and attempt to describe the physical variation that exists in their population. The system used in the United States, by recognizing only three or four races, blinds Americans to an equivalent range of evident physical contrasts. The system Brazilians use to construct social race has other special features. In the United States one's race is an ascribed status; it is assigned automatically by hypodescent and usually doesn't change. In Brazil racial identity is more flexible, more of an achieved status.

These photos, taken in Brazil by Conrad Kottak in 2003 and 2004, give just a glimpse of the spectrum of phenotypical diversity encountered among contemporary Brazilians.

CULTURE THINK

How are the Brazilian and Japanese racial labels similar to and different from those of the United States?

Brazilian racial classification pays attention to phenotype. **Phenotype** refers to an organism's evident traits, its "manifest biology"—physiology and anatomy, including skin color, hair form, facial features, and eye color. A Brazilian's phenotype and racial label may change because of environmental factors, such as the tanning rays of the sun or the effects of humidity on the hair.

As physical characteristics change (sunlight alters skin color, humidity affects hair form), so do racial terms. Furthermore, racial differences may be so insignificant in structuring community life that people may forget the terms they have applied to others. Sometimes they even forget the ones they've used for themselves. In Arembepe, Kottak made it a habit to ask the same person on different days to tell him the races of others in the village (and his own). In the United States he is "white" or "Euro-American," but in Arembepe he was given several terms besides *branco* ("white"). He could be *claro* ("light"), *louro* ("blond"), *sarará* ("light-skinned redhead"), *mulato claro* ("light mulatto"), or *mulato* ("mulatto"). The racial term used to describe Kottak or anyone else varied from person to person, week to week, even day to day. His best informant, a man with very dark skin color, changed the term he used for himself all the time—from *escuro* ("dark") to *preto* ("black") to *moreno escuro* ("dark brunet").

For centuries the United States and Brazil have had mixed populations, with ancestors from Native America, Europe, Africa, and Asia. Although races have mixed in both countries, Brazilian and American cultures have constructed the results differently. The historical reasons for this contrast lie mainly in the different characteristics of the settlers of the two countries. The mainly English early settlers of the United States came as women, men, and families, but Brazil's Portuguese colonizers were mainly men—merchants and adventurers. Many of these Portuguese men married Native American women and recognized their racially mixed children as their heirs. Like their North American counterparts, Brazilian plantation owners had sexual relations with their slaves. But the Brazilian landlords more often freed the children that resulted—for demographic and economic reasons. (Sometimes these were their only children.) Freed offspring of master and slave became plantation overseers and foremen and filled many intermediate positions in the emerging Brazilian economy. They were not classed with the slaves, but were allowed to join a new intermediate category. No hypo-descent rule developed in Brazil to ensure that whites and blacks remained separate (see Degler 1970; Harris 1964).

In today's world system, Brazil's system of racial classification is changing in the context of international identity politics and rights movements. Just as more and more Brazilians claim indigenous (Native Brazilian) identities, an increasing number now assert their blackness and self-conscious membership in the African diaspora. Particularly in such northeastern Brazilian states as Bahia, where African demographic and cultural influence is strong, public universities have instituted affirmative action programs aimed at indigenous peoples and especially at blacks. Racial identities firm up in the context of international (e.g., pan-African and pan-Indian) mobilization and access to strategic resources based on race.

phenotype An organism's evident traits, its "manifest biology"— anatomy and physiology.

Got IT? Can you describe how race is socially constructed in the United States, Japan, and Brazil?

>> Ethnic Groups, Nations, and Nationalities

The term *nation* once was synonymous with *tribe* or *ethnic group*. All three of these terms have been used to refer to a single culture sharing a single language, religion, history, territory, ancestry, and kinship. Thus one could speak interchangeably of the Seneca (American

Indian) nation, tribe, or ethnic group. Now *nation* has come to mean *state*—an independent, centrally organized political unit, or a government. *Nation* and *state* have become synonymous. Combined in **nation-state** they refer to an autonomous political entity, a country—like the United States, "one nation, indivisible" (see Farner 2004; Gellner 1997; Hastings 1997).

Because of migration, conquest, and colonialism, most nation-states are not ethnically homogeneous. A 2003 study by Fearon found that about 70 percent of all countries have an ethnic group that forms an absolute majority of the population, and the average population share of such groups is 65 percent. The average size of the *second*-largest group, or largest ethnic minority, is 17 percent. Only 18 percent of all countries have a single ethnic group that accounts for 90 percent or more of its population.

NATIONALITIES AND IMAGINED COMMUNITIES

Ethnic groups that once had, or wish to have or regain, autonomous political status (their own country) are called **nationalities.** In the words of Benedict Anderson (1991), they are "imagined communities." Even when they become nation-states, they remain imagined communities because most of their members, though feeling comradeship, will never meet (Anderson 1991, pp. 6–10). They can only imagine they all participate in the same unit.

Anderson traces Western European nationalism, which arose in imperial powers such as England, France, and Spain, back to the eighteenth century. He stresses that language and print played a crucial role in the growth of European national consciousness. The novel and the newspaper were "two forms of imagining" communities (consisting of all the people who read the same sources and thus witnessed the same events) that flowered in the eighteenth century (Anderson 1991, pp. 24–25).

CULTURE THINK

In what ways is the United States an imagined community? What role does the media play in this community creation?

Over time, political upheavals, wars, and migration have divided many imagined national communities that arose in the eighteenth and nineteenth centuries. The German and Korean homelands were artificially divided after wars, according to communist and capitalist ideologies. World War I split the Kurds, who remain an imagined community, forming a majority in no state. Kurds are a minority group in Turkey, Iran, Iraq, and Syria.

In creating multitribal and multiethnic states, colonialism often erected boundaries that corresponded poorly with preexisting cultural divisions. But colonial institutions also helped create new "imagined communities" beyond nations. An example is the idea of *négritude* ("black identity") developed by African intellectuals in Francophone (French-speaking) West Africa. Négritude can be traced to the association and common experience in colonial times of youths from Guinea, Mali, Ivory Coast, and Senegal at the William Ponty school in Dakar, Senegal (Anderson 1991, pp. 123–124).

 Got IT? Can you evaluate the relationship between ethnicity and political status today and with reference to colonial history?

>> Ethnic Tolerance and Accommodation

Ethnic diversity may be associated with positive group interaction and coexistence or with conflict (discussed shortly). There are nation-states, including some less developed countries, in which multiple cultural groups live together in reasonable harmony.

ASSIMILATION

The process of change that a minority ethnic group may experience when its members move to a country where another culture dominates is known as **assimilation.** By assimilating, the minority adopts the patterns and norms of its host culture. It is incorporated into the dominant culture to the point that it no longer exists as a separate cultural unit. Some countries, such as Brazil, are more assimilationist than others. Germans, Italians, Japanese, Middle Easterners, and East Europeans started migrating to Brazil late in the nineteenth century. These immigrants have assimilated to a common Brazilian culture, which has Portuguese, African, and Native American roots. The descendants of these immigrants speak the national language (Portuguese) and participate in the national culture. (During World War II, Brazil, which was on the Allied side, forced assimilation by banning instruction in any language other than Portuguese—especially in German.)

THE PLURAL SOCIETY

Assimilation isn't inevitable, and ethnic harmony can exist without it. Ethnic distinctions can persist despite generations of interethnic contact. Through a study of three ethnic groups in Swat, Pakistan, Fredrik Barth (1958/1968) challenged an old idea that interaction always leads to assimilation. He showed that ethnic groups can be in contact for generations without assimilating.

Barth (1958/1968, p. 324) defines **plural society** (an idea he extended from Pakistan to the entire Middle East) as a society combining ethnic contrasts, ecological specialization (i.e., use of different environmental resources by each ethnic group), and the economic interdependence of those groups. In Barth's view, ethnic boundaries are most stable and enduring when the groups occupy different ecological niches. That is, they make their living in different ways and don't compete. Ideally, they should depend on one another's activities and exchange with one another. When different ethnic groups exploit the *same* ecological niche, the militarily more powerful group will normally replace the weaker one. If they exploit more or less the same niche, but the weaker group is better able to use marginal environments, they also may coexist (Barth 1958/1968, p. 331). Given niche specialization, ethnic boundaries and interdependence can be maintained, although the specific cultural features of each group may change. By shifting the analytic focus from individual cultures or ethnic groups to *relationships* between cultures or ethnic groups, Barth (1958/1968, 1969) has made important contributions to ethnic studies.

MULTICULTURALISM AND ETHNIC IDENTITY

The view of cultural diversity in a country as something good and desirable is called **multiculturalism** (see Kottak and Kozaitis 2012). The multicultural model is the opposite of the assimilationist model, in which minorities are expected to abandon their cultural traditions and values, replacing them with those of the majority population. The multicultural view encourages the practice of cultural-ethnic traditions. A multicultural society socializes individuals not only into the dominant (national) culture but also into an ethnic culture. Thus in the United States millions of people speak both English and another language, eat both "American" (apple pie, steak, hamburgers) and "ethnic" foods, and celebrate both national (July 4, Thanksgiving) and ethnic-religious holidays.

In the United States and Canada multiculturalism is of growing importance. This reflects an awareness that the number and size of ethnic groups have grown dramatically in recent years. If this trend continues, the ethnic composition of the United States will change dramatically (see "Ethnic Composition of the United States" on p. 230).

> **plural society** A society that combines ethnic contrasts, ecological specialization (i.e., use of different environmental resources by each ethnic group), and the economic interdependence of those groups.
>
> **multiculturalism** The view of cultural diversity in a country as something good and desirable; a multicultural society socializes individuals not only into the dominant (national) culture, but also into an ethnic culture.

The United States is increasingly a multicultural society. It features growing ethnic enclaves such as New York's Chinatown, shown here, often located right next to others, such as Little Italy in the same city.

Several states, including Arizona, Alabama, and Georgia, have passed laws giving law enforcement agents the right to require people to provide evidence of their citizenship status whether or not they are suspected of committing a crime. There have been unintended negative consequences: in Georgia in 2011, farmers lost 40% of their labor force and $140 million in revenues when undocumented immigrants left the state. Hoping to avoid a comparable labor shortage in 2012, state officials sent prisoners to harvest fruits and vegetables.

http://www.forbes.com/ sites/realspin/2012/05/17/ the-law-of-unintended-consequences-georgias-immigration-law-backfires/

Even now, because of immigration and differential population growth, whites are outnumbered by minorities in many urban areas. For example, of the 8,302,659 people living in New York City in 2009, 25 percent were black, 27 percent Hispanic, 12 percent Asian, and 36 percent other—including non-Hispanic whites. The comparable figures for Los Angeles county in 2010 were 9 percent black, 48 percent Hispanic, 12 percent Asian, and 29 percent other, including non-Hispanic whites (U.S. Census Bureau 2010).

In October 2006, the population of the United States reached 300 million people, just 39 years after reaching 200 million and 91 years after reaching the 100 million mark (in 1915). The country's ethnic composition has changed dramatically in the past 40 years. The 1970 census, the first to attempt an official count of Hispanics, found they represented no more than 4.7 percent of the American population. By the 2010 census this figure had risen to 16.3 percent–over 50 million Hispanics. The number of African Americans grew from 11.1 percent in 1967 to 12.6 percent in 2010, while (non-Hispanic) whites ("Anglos") declined from 83 to 63.7 percent. In 1967 fewer than 10 million people in the United States (5 percent of the population) had been born elsewhere, compared with more than 38 million foreign born today (12.5 percent– all data from U.S. Census Bureau 2010). In 2011, for the first time in American history, minorities (including Hispanics, blacks, Asians, Native Americans, and those of mixed race) accounted for more than half (50.4 percent) of all births in the United States (Tavernise 2012). In 1973, 78 percent of the students in American public schools were white, and 22 percent were minorities: blacks, Hispanics, Asians, Pacific Islanders, and "others." By 2004, 57 percent of public school students were white, and 43 percent were minorities. If current trends continue, minority students will outnumber (non-Hispanic) white students by 2015. They

Ethnic Composition of the United States

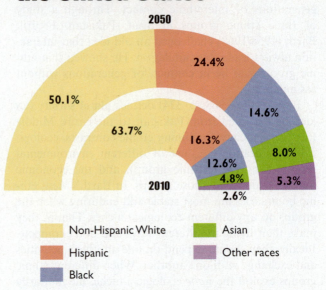

The proportion of the American population that is white and non-Hispanic is declining. The projection for 2050 shown here comes from a 2008 U.S. Census Bureau report. Note especially the dramatic rise in the Hispanic portion of the American population between 2010 and 2050.

Source: Based on 2010 data from U.S. Census Bureau, decennial census, and a 2008 projection by the U.S. Census Bureau, http://www.census.gov/population/www/projections/analyticaldocument09.pdf, Table 1, p. 17.

already do in California, Hawaii, Mississippi, New Mexico, and Texas (Dillon 2006).

Immigration, mainly from southern and eastern Europe, had a similar effect on classroom diversity, at least in the largest American cities, a century ago. A study of American public schools in 1908–1909 found that 42 percent of those urban students were native-born, while 58 percent were immigrants. In a very different (multicultural now versus assimilationist then) context, today's American classrooms have regained the ethnic diversity they demonstrated in the early 1900s, when author Conrad Kottak's German-speaking Austro-Hungarian-born father and grandparents immigrated to the United States.

One response to ethnic diversification and awareness has been for many whites to reclaim ethnic identities (Italian, Albanian, Serbian, Lithuanian, etc.) and to join ethnic associations (clubs, gangs). Some such groups are new. Others have existed for decades, although they lost members during the assimilationist years of the 1920s through the 1950s.

Multiculturalism seeks ways for people to understand and interact that depend not on sameness but rather on respect for differences. Multiculturalism stresses the interaction of ethnic groups and their contribution to the country. It assumes that each group has something to offer to and learn from the others. Several forces have propelled North America away from the assimilationist model toward multiculturalism. First, multiculturalism reflects the fact of recent large-scale migration, particularly from the "less developed countries" to the "developed" nations of North America and Western Europe. The global scale of modern migration introduces unparalleled ethnic variety to host nations. Multiculturalism is related to globalization: People use modern means of transportation to migrate to nations whose lifestyles they learn about through the media and from tourists who increasingly visit their own countries (see Inda and Rosaldo, eds. 2008).

Migration also is fueled by rapid population growth, coupled with insufficient jobs (for both educated and uneducated people), in the less developed countries. As traditional rural economies decline or mechanize, displaced farmers move to cities, where they and their children often are unable to find jobs. As people in the less developed countries get better educations, they seek more skilled employment. They hope to partake of an international culture of consumption that includes such modern amenities as refrigerators, televisions, and automobiles (Ahmed 2004).

In the face of globalization, much of the world, including Europe and North America, is experiencing an ethnic revival. The new assertiveness of long-resident ethnic groups extends to the Basques and Catalans in

Spain, the Bretons and Corsicans in France, and the Welsh and Scots in the United Kingdom. The United States and Canada are becoming increasingly multicultural, focusing on their internal diversity (see Laguerre 1999). "Melting pots" no longer, they are better described as ethnic "salads" (each ingredient remains distinct, although in the same bowl, with the same dressing).

Got IT? Can you assess the conditions under which multiple cultural groups tend to live together in reasonable harmony?

>> Roots of Ethnic Conflict

Ethnicity, based on perceived cultural similarities and differences in a society or nation, can be expressed in peaceful multiculturalism or in discrimination or violent interethnic confrontation. The roots of ethnic differentiation—and therefore, potentially, of ethnic conflict—can be political, economic, religious, linguistic, cultural, or racial (see Kuper 2006). Why do ethnic differences often lead to conflict and violence? The causes include a sense of injustice because of resource distribution, economic or political competition, and reaction to discrimination, prejudice, and other expressions of devalued identity (see Friedman, ed. 2003; Ryan 1990, p. xxvii).

In Iraq, under the dictator Saddam Hussein, one Muslim group (Sunnis) discriminated against others (Shiites and Kurds). Sunnis, although a numeric minority within Iraq's population, enjoyed privileged access to power, prestige, and position. After the 2005 elections, which many Sunnis chose to boycott, Shiites gained political control. A civil war developed out of *sectarian violence* (conflicts among sects of the same religion). Sunnis (and their foreign supporters) fueled an insurgency against the new government and its foreign supporters, including the United States. Shiites retaliated against Sunni attacks and a history of Sunni privilege and perceived discrimination against Shiites, as Shiite militias engaged in ethnic (sectarian) cleansing of their own.

> **prejudice** Devaluing (looking down on) a group because of its assumed behavior, values, capabilities, or attributes.
>
> **stereotypes** Fixed ideas—often unfavorable—about what members of a group are like.

PREJUDICE AND DISCRIMINATION

Ethnic conflict often arises in reaction to prejudice (attitudes and judgments) or discrimination (action). **Prejudice** means devaluing (looking down on) a group because of its assumed behavior, values, capabilities, or attributes. People are prejudiced when they hold stereotypes about groups and apply them to individuals. (**Stereotypes** are fixed

ANTHROPOLOGY WORKS

Billy Willey is making a career change to become a community police officer. In his interview for this position, he was asked about how he would interact with people from different cultural backgrounds. He felt well prepared for this because of the time he spent in his anthropology classes reflecting on cultural difference and his own ethnocentricities. After Billy was hired, he was told that having such a "well-rounded" education would be invaluable in the diverse situations and settings he might encounter in a single night as a police officer on patrol. Later, during his formal training at the police academy, an instructor talked to Billy's class about how quickly local communities are becoming increasingly diverse in race, culture, and ethnicity. A background in anthropology prepares people well for any job that requires community interactions.

discrimination Policies and practices that harm a group and its members.

genocide Policies aimed at, and/or resulting in, the physical extinction (through mass murder) of a people perceived as a racial group, that is, as sharing defining physical, genetic, or other biological characteristics.

ethnocide Destruction by a dominant group of the culture of an ethnic group.

refugees People who have been forced (involuntary refugees) or who have chosen (voluntary refugees) to flee a country, to escape persecution or war.

cultural colonialism Within a nation or empire, domination by one ethnic group or nationality and its culture/ideology over others—e.g., the dominance of Russian people, language, and culture in the former Soviet Union.

ideas—often unfavorable—about what the members of a group are like.) Prejudiced people assume that members of the group will act as they are "supposed to act" (according to the stereotype) and interpret a wide range of individual behaviors as evidence of the stereotype. They use this behavior to confirm their stereotype (and low opinion) of the group.

Discrimination refers to policies and practices that harm a group and its members. Discrimination may be *de facto* (practiced, but not legally sanctioned) or *de jure* (part of the law). An example of de facto discrimination is the harsher treatment that American minorities (compared with other Americans) tend to get from the police and the judicial system. This unequal treatment isn't legal, but it happens anyway. Segregation in the southern United States and *apartheid* in South Africa provide two examples of de jure discrimination, which no longer are in existence. In both systems, by law, blacks and whites had different rights and privileges. Their social interaction ("mixing") was legally curtailed.

CHIPS IN THE MOSAIC

Although the multicultural model is increasingly prominent in North America, ethnic competition and conflict also are evident. There is conflict between newer arrivals—for instance, Central Americans and Koreans—and longer-established ethnic groups, such as African Americans. Ethnic antagonism flared in South-Central Los Angeles in spring 1992 in rioting that followed the acquittal of four white police officers who were tried for the videotaped beating of Rodney King (see Abelmann and Lie 1995).

Angry blacks attacked whites, Koreans, and Latinos. This violence expressed frustration by African Americans about their prospects in an increasingly multicultural society. A *New York Times* CBS News poll conducted just after the Los Angeles riots found that blacks had a bleaker outlook than whites about the effects of immigration on their lives. Only 23 percent of the blacks felt they had more opportunities than recent immigrants, compared with twice that many whites (Toner 1992).

AFTERMATHS OF OPPRESSION

Fueling ethnic conflict are such forms of discrimination as genocide, forced assimilation, ethnocide, and cultural colonialism. The most extreme form of ethnic discrimination is **genocide,** the deliberate elimination of a group (such as Jews in Nazi Germany, Muslims in Bosnia, or Tutsi in Rwanda) through mass murder. A dominant group may try to destroy the cultures of certain ethnic groups (**ethnocide**) or force them to adopt the dominant culture (*forced assimilation*). Many countries have penalized or banned the language and customs of an ethnic group (including its religious observances). One example of forced assimilation is the anti-Basque campaign that the dictator Francisco

Discrimination *refers to policies and practices that harm a group and its members. This protest sign, hoisted in New Orleans' Lower 9th Ward, shows that at least some community residents see ethnic and racial bias.*

Franco (who ruled between 1939 and 1975) waged in Spain. Franco banned Basque books, journals, newspapers, signs, sermons, and tombstones and imposed fines for using the Basque language in schools (Ryan 1990). His policies led to the formation of a Basque terrorist group and spurred strong nationalist sentiment in the Basque region.

A policy of *ethnic expulsion* aims at removing culturally different groups from a country. There are many examples, including Bosnia-Herzegovina in the 1990s. Uganda expelled 74,000 Asians in 1972. The neofascist parties of contemporary Western Europe advocate repatriation (expulsion) of immigrant workers (West Indians in England, Algerians in France, and Turks in Germany) (see Friedman, ed. 2003; Ryan 1990, p. 9). A policy of expulsion may create **refugees**—people who have been forced (involuntary refugees) or who have chosen (voluntary refugees) to flee a country, to escape persecution or war.

In many countries, colonial nation-building left ethnic strife in its wake. Thus, over a million Hindus and Muslims were killed in the violence that accompanied the division of the Indian subcontinent into India and Pakistan. Problems between Arabs and Jews in Palestine began during the British mandate period.

Multiculturalism may be growing in the United States and Canada, but the opposite is happening in the former Soviet Union, where ethnic groups (nationalities) want their own nation-states. The flowering of ethnic feeling and conflict as the Soviet empire disintegrated illustrates that years of political repression and ideology provide insufficient common ground for lasting unity. **Cultural colonialism** refers to internal domination by one group and its culture or ideology over others. One example is the domination over the former Soviet empire by Russian people, language, and culture, and by communist ideology. The dominant culture makes itself the official culture. This is reflected in schools,

Two faces of ethnic difference in the former Soviet empire. The propaganda poster on the left portrays a happy mix of nationalities that make up the population of Kyrgyzstan, Central Asia. The photo on the right, taken in May 2010 in Kyrgyzstan, shows Kyrgyz soldiers guarding a university following an attempt to storm that campus during a period of ethnic violence between Kyrgyz mobs and minority Uzbeks.

the media, and public interaction. Under Soviet rule ethnic minorities had very limited self-rule in republics and regions controlled by Moscow. All the republics and their peoples were to be united by the oneness of "socialist internationalism." One common technique in cultural colonialism is to flood ethnic areas with members of the dominant ethnic group. Thus, in the former Soviet Union, ethnic Russian colonists were sent to many areas, to diminish the cohesion and clout of the local people.

The Commonwealth of Independent States (CIS), founded in 1991 and headquartered in Minsk, Belarus, is what remains of the once-powerful Soviet Union

(see Yurchak 2005). In Russia and other formerly Soviet nations, ethnic groups (nationalities) have sought, and continue to seek, to forge separate and viable nation-states based on cultural boundaries. This celebration of ethnic autonomy is part of an ethnic flowering that—as surely as globalization and transnationalism—is a trend of the late twentieth and early twenty-first centuries.

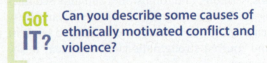

Got IT? Can you describe some causes of ethnically motivated conflict and violence?

get**involved!**

Test your stereotypes about ethnicity and "race" in sports. What ethnicity do you assume to be especially common among players in each of the following: hockey, baseball, football, and basketball? Pick a city near you with a professional sports team or a college or university sports program you know well. Find rosters of players, then use photos of the players and their family names to help you ascertain ethnic backgrounds. Watch a game in each sport and see who plays the most. How do your stereotypes accord with the rosters and the players you see in the games?

Might players of a particular ethnic background excel in or even dominate certain sports? If so, what roles do you think society's ethnic stereotypes, players' early enculturation, and their families' regional and social class backgrounds might play in this dominance? Take the interactive sports quiz that is part of the American Anthropological Association's project on race: http://www.understandingrace.org/lived/sports/index.html.

FOR REVIEW

I. How are race and ethnicity socially constructed?

- Both ethnic groups and "races" derive from contrasts perceived and perpetuated in particular societies. Race is a problematic scientific concept because humans do not fit neatly into any racial classifications. Contemporary anthropology uses a much more fruitful approach to human biological diversity than pigeonholing humans into racial categories. Anthropologists today focus on specific biological differences, such as skin color, and use the concept of natural selection to explain them. Members of an ethnic group define themselves through a common language, religion, historical experience, geographic placement, kinship, and/or "race." Ethnic group markers may include a collective name, belief in common descent, sense of solidarity, and association with a territory, real or imagined. Race is an ethnic group that is assumed to have a biological basis. Racial labels designate *culturally* perceived groups.

II. How does racial classification differ in three contemporary nations: the United States, Japan, and Brazil?

- In the United States, race is assumed to have a biological basis and racial status is ascribed. American culture assigns racial status arbitrarily. Children of a union between members of different groups are assigned the status of the minority group. Traditional American racial categories are changing as biracial and multiracial children begin to resist having the hypodescent rule dictate their identity. In Japan, a perceived racial difference is sufficient reason to value one person less than another. Offspring of marriages between "pure" majority Japanese and members of a minority are stigmatized. In Brazil, classification is more flexible and racial identity is more of an achieved status. If a Brazilian's phenotype changes because of environmental factors, racial labels change accordingly.

III. What are the negative and positive aspects of ethnicity?

- Ethnic diversity may be associated both with conflict and with positive group interaction and coexistence. The assimilation of an ethnic minority group may be expected or even forced. Although multiculturalism seeks ways for different groups to interact with and learn from one other, it does not necessarily end conflict. Unequal access to resources, economic or political competition, prejudice, and discrimination may lead to conflict and violence. Genocide is the deliberate elimination of a group. Ethnocide, forced expulsion, and cultural colonialism also endanger ethnic groups and fuel conflict. Ethnicity may be the basis for mobilizing group members to self-help and dealing with discrimination. It also may be the basis for seeking to forge separate nation-states.

Pop Quiz

Multiple Choice:

1. Which of the following expresses scientists' preference for explaining biological differences among humans rather than pigeonholing humans into racial classifications?

    a. Skin color presents a useful basis for assigning humans to racial classifications.

    b. All human populations fit neatly into one or other of the so-called great races.

    c. Scientists who have used four to five or so physical traits to classify races find that these traits always go together as a unit in a population.

    d. Natural selection, such as that against the concentration of melanin in skin in northern regions, contributes to differences in human skin color.

2. Which of the following statements would apply to both ethnicity and race?

    a. Both terms describe a minority group.

    b. Both terms are cultural rather than biological categories.

    c. American culture defines these terms in a way that sharply distinguishes one from the other.

    d. The basis of both of these terms is biological.

3. The rule or principle that automatically places the children of a union between members of different socioeconomic groups in the minority group is called

    a. Hypodescent

    b. Natural descent

    c. Racial mixing

    d. Achieved status

4. What distinguishes racial classification in Brazil from that in the United States?

    a. Race in Brazil is ascribed.

    b. Brazilians have created a profusion of racial labels that often leads to mislabeling a person's race.

    c. Brazilian racial identity is flexible, more of an achieved status.

    d. A Brazilian's phenotype remains fixed.

5. Which of the following is *not* true about minority groups that move to a country where another culture dominates?

    a. They usually assimilate by the second or, at latest, the third generation.

    b. Their members may continue to speak their own languages and practice their ways yet still live in ethnic harmony with the dominant culture.

    c. If they maintain their ethnicity and use environmental resources different from those used by other groups, they may live in a state of ecological interdependence with those groups.

    d. The boundaries between ethnic groups are most stable and enduring when the groups occupy different ecological niches.

6. What is the term for a dominant group's attempt to destroy the cultures of certain ethnic groups or attempt to force them to adopt the dominant culture?

    a. Colonialism

    b. Genocide

    c. Ethnocide

    d. Ethnic expulsion

Fill in the Blank:

1. Given the lack of distinction between race and ethnicity, this chapter suggests using the term _____ instead of *race* to describe any such social group.

2. _____ refers to an organism's evident traits, its "manifest biology."

3. _____ is the view of cultural diversity as valuable and worth maintaining.

4. _____ refers to the devaluing of a group because of its assumed behavior, values, abilities, or attributes.

1. (d), 2. (b), 3. (a), 4. (c), 5. (a), 6. (c)

1. *ethnic group*; 2. Phenotype; 3. Multiculturalism; 4. Prejudice

12

APPLYING ANTHROPOLOGY

UNDERSTANDING OURSELVES

Is change always good? The idea that innovation is inherently desirable is axiomatic in American culture, especially in advertising. "New and improved" is a slogan we hear all the time—a lot more often than "old reliable." Which do you think is best—change or the status quo? That "new" isn't always "improved" is a painful lesson learned by the Coca-Cola Company (TCCC) in 1985 when it changed the formula of its premier soft drink and introduced "New Coke." After hordes of customers protested, TCCC brought back old, familiar, reliable Coke under the name "Coca-Cola Classic," which thrives today. New Coke, now history, offers a classic case of how not to treat consumers. TCCC tried a *top-down change* (a change initiated at the top of a hierarchy rather than inspired by the people most affected by the change). Customers didn't ask TCCC to change its product; executives made that decision.

The field of market research, which employs a good number of anthropologists, is based on the need to appreciate what actual and potential customers do, think, and want. Smart planners study and listen to people to try to determine *locally based demand*. What changes do the people—and which people—want? How can conflicting wishes and needs be accommodated? Applied anthropologists help answer these questions, which are crucial in understanding whether change is needed and how it will work.

Innovation succeeds best when it is culturally appropriate. This axiom of applied anthropology is a useful guide for international programs aimed at social and economic change as well as for businesses. Each time an organization expands to a new nation, it must devise a culturally appropriate strategy for fitting into the new setting. In their international expansion, companies and organizations have learned that more money, and more progress, can be made by fitting in with, rather than trying to Americanize, local habits.

>> What Is Applied Anthropology?

As we learned in Chapter 1, applied anthropology is the use of anthropological data, perspectives, theory, and methods to identify, assess, and solve contemporary problems (see Ervin 2005). Applied anthropologists help make anthropology relevant and useful to the world beyond anthropology. Medical anthropologists, for example, have worked as cultural interpreters in public health programs, helping such programs fit into local culture. Development anthropologists work for or with international development agencies, such as the World Bank and the U.S. Agency for International Development (USAID). The findings of garbology, the archaeological study of waste, are relevant to the Environmental Protection Agency, the paper industry, and packaging and trade associations. Archaeology also is applied in cultural resource management and historic preservation. Biological anthropologists apply their expertise in programs aimed at public health, nutrition, genetic counseling, aging, substance abuse, and mental health. Forensic anthropologists work with the police, medical examiners, the courts, and international organizations to identify victims of crimes, accidents, wars, and terrorism. Linguistic anthropologists study physician-patient communication and show how dialect differences influence classroom learning. Most applied anthropologists seek humane and effective ways of helping local people (Table 12.1 gives examples of applied anthropology in all four subfields).

The ethnographic method is a particularly valuable tool in applying anthropology. Remember that ethnographers study societies firsthand, living with, observing, and learning from ordinary people. Nonanthropologists working in social-change programs often are content to converse with officials, read reports, and copy statistics. However, the applied anthropologist's likely early request is some variant of "take me to the local people." Anthropologists know that people must play an active role in the changes that affect them and that "the people" have information that "the experts" lack.

Anthropological *theory,* the body of findings and generalizations of the four subfields, also guides applied anthropology. Just as theory aids practice, application fuels theory (see Rylko-Bauer, Singer, and Van Willigen 2006). As we compare social-change programs, our

TABLE 12.1

The Four Subfields and Two Dimensions of Anthropology

Anthropology's Subfields (Academic Anthropology)	Examples of Application (Applied Anthropology)
Cultural anthropology	Development anthropology
Archaeological anthropology	Cultural resource management (CRM)
Biological or physical anthropology	Forensic anthropology
Linguistic anthropology	Study of linguistic diversity in classrooms

understanding of cause and effect increases. We add new generalizations about culture change to those discovered in traditional and ancient cultures.

>> The Role of the Applied Anthropologist

EARLY APPLICATIONS

Application was a central concern of early anthropology in Great Britain (in the context of colonialism) and the United States (in the context of Native American policy). Before turning to the new, we should consider some dangers of the old. For the British empire, specifically its African colonies, Malinowski (1929) proposed that "practical anthropology" (his term for colonial applied anthropology) should focus on **Westernization**—the diffusion of European culture into tribal societies. Malinowski questioned neither the legitimacy of colonialism nor the anthropologist's role in making it work. He saw nothing wrong with aiding colonial regimes by studying land tenure and land use in order to recommend how much of their land local people should be allowed to keep and how much Europeans should get. Malinowski's views exemplify a historical association between early anthropology, particularly in Europe (especially England, France, and Portugal), and colonialism (see also Duffield and Hewitt, eds. 2009; Lange 2009; Maquet 1964; Rylko-Bauer, Singer, and Van Willigen 2006).

During World War II, American anthropologists studied Japanese and German "culture at a distance" in an attempt to predict the behavior of the enemies of the United States. After that war, applied anthropologists worked on Pacific islands to promote local-level cooperation with American policies in various trust territories. The American Anthropological Association (AAA) has raised strong ethical objections to applying anthropology in war zones and for military intelligence. Such concerns were voiced during the Vietnam War. More recently they have emerged in criticisms of anthropologists' participation in the Human Terrain System (HTS) project in Iraq and Afghanistan, as discussed in Chapter 3. Anthropological research should not be applied to the potential detriment of the people anthropologists study.

ACADEMIC AND APPLIED ANTHROPOLOGY

After World War II, the baby boom, which began in 1946 and peaked in 1957, fueled a tremendous expansion of the American educational system. New junior, community, and four-year colleges opened, and anthropology became a standard part of the college curriculum. During the 1950s and 1960s, most American anthropologists were college professors, although some still worked in agencies and museums.

The growth of academic anthropology continued through the early 1970s. Especially during the Vietnam War, undergraduates flocked to anthropology classes to learn about other cultures. Students were especially interested in Southeast Asia, whose indigenous societies were being disrupted by war. Many anthropologists protested the superpowers' apparent disregard for non-Western lives, values, customs, and social systems.

> **Westernization** The diffusion of European cultures into tribal societies.

Most anthropologists still worked in colleges and museums during the 1970s and 1980s. However, an increasing number of anthropologists were employed by international organizations, governments, businesses, hospitals, and schools. The AAA estimates that nowadays more than half of anthropology Ph.D.s seek nonacademic employment. This shift toward application has benefited the profession. It has forced anthropologists to consider the wider social value and implications of their research.

APPLIED ANTHROPOLOGY TODAY

Most contemporary applied anthropologists see their work as radically removed from the colonial enterprise. Modern applied anthropology usually is seen as a helping profession, devoted to assisting local people, as anthropologists speak up for the disenfranchised.

During the Vietnam War, many anthropologists protested the superpowers' disregard for the values, customs, social systems, and lives of indigenous peoples. Several anthropologists attended this all-night Columbia University teach-in about the war in 1965.

However, applied anthropologists also have clients that are neither poor nor powerless. An applied anthropologist working as a market researcher for a business is concerned with discovering how to expand profits for his or her employer or client. Such goals can pose ethical dilemmas, as can work in cultural resource management (CRM). The CRM anthropologist helps decide how to preserve significant remains when sites are threatened by development or public works. A CRM firm typically is hired by someone seeking to build a road or a factory. That client may have a strong interest in an outcome in which no sites are found that need protecting.

Even if they don't work for colonial powers or the military, applied anthropologists still face ethical questions: To whom does the researcher owe loyalty? What problems are involved in holding firm to the truth? What happens when applied anthropologists don't make the policies they are required to implement? How does one criticize programs in which one has participated (see Escobar 1991, 1994)? Anthropology's professional organizations have addressed such questions by establishing codes of ethics and ethics committees. As Karen Tice (1997) notes, attention to ethical issues has become paramount in the teaching of applied anthropology today.

Anthropologists are experts on human problems and social change who study, understand, and respect diverse cultural values. Given this background, anthropologists are highly qualified to suggest, plan, and implement social policy affecting people. Proper roles for applied anthropologists include (1) identifying needs for change that local people perceive, (2) working with those people to design culturally appropriate and socially sensitive change, and (3) protecting local people from harmful policies and projects that may threaten them.

Supervised by archaeologists from India, with funding from the United Nations, these workers are cleaning and restoring the front façade of Cambodia's historical Angkor Wat temple. To decide what needs saving, and to preserve significant information about the past even when sites cannot be saved, is the work of cultural resource management (CRM).

>> Development Anthropology

The branch of applied anthropology that focuses on social issues in, and the cultural dimension of, economic development is called **development anthropology.** Development anthropologists don't just carry out development policies planned by others; they also plan and guide policy. (For more detailed discussions of issues in development anthropology, see Edelman and Haugerud 2004; Escobar 1995; Ferguson 1995; Nolan 2002; and Robertson 1995.)

Still, ethical dilemmas often confront development anthropologists (Escobar 1991, 1995). Foreign aid usually doesn't go where the need and suffering are greatest. It is spent on political, economic, and strategic priorities as international donors, political leaders, and powerful interest groups perceive them. Planners' interests don't always coincide with the best interests of the local people. Although the aim of most development projects is to enhance the quality of life, living standards often decline in the target area (Bodley 1988).

EQUITY

A commonly stated goal of recent development policy is to promote equity. **Increased equity** means reduced poverty and a more even distribution of wealth. If projects are to increase equity, however, they must have the support of reform-minded governments. Wealthy and powerful people typically resist projects that threaten their vested interests.

Some development projects actually widen wealth disparities; that is, they have a negative equity impact. An initial uneven distribution of resources often becomes the basis for even greater socioeconomic inequality after the project. In Bahia, Brazil (Kottak 2006), for example, sailboat owners (but not nonowners) received loans to buy motors for their boats. To repay the loans, the owners increased the percentage of the catch they took from the men who fished in their boats. Over the years, they used their rising profits to buy larger and more expensive boats. The result was stratification—the creation of a group of wealthy people within a formerly egalitarian community. These events hampered individual initiative and interfered with further development of the fishing industry. With new boats so expensive, ambitious young men who once would have sought careers in fishing no longer had any way to obtain their own boats. They sought wage labor on land instead. To avoid such results, credit-granting agencies must seek out enterprising young fishers rather than giving loans only to owners and established businesspeople.

>> Strategies for Innovation

Development anthropologists should work closely with local people to assess, and help them realize, their own wishes and needs for change. Funding development projects in area A that are inappropriate there but needed in area B, or that are unnecessary anywhere, is a waste of money when so many true local needs cry out for a solution. Development anthropology can help sort out the needs of the As and Bs and fit projects accordingly. Projects that put people first by consulting with them and responding to their expressed needs must be identified (Cernea, ed. 1991). Thereafter, development anthropologists can work to ensure socially compatible ways of implementing a good project.

CULTURE THINK

What's the difference between equity and equality? (*Equality* means that each person or group would be treated the same and receive the same benefits.) What are the challenges in striving for equality as a development goal?

development anthropology The branch of applied anthropology that focuses on social issues in, and the cultural dimension of, economic development.

equity, increased A reduction in absolute poverty and a fairer (more even) distribution of wealth.

Fishing boats in Mui Ne Harbor, Vietnam. A boat owner receives a loan to buy a motor. To repay the loan, he increases the share of the catch he takes from his crew. Later, he uses his rising profits to buy a more expensive boat and takes even more from his crew. Is this fair?

In a comparative study of sixty-eight rural development projects from around the world, Conrad Kottak found the *culturally compatible* economic development projects to be twice as successful financially as the incompatible ones (Kottak 1990b, 1991). This finding shows that using anthropological expertise in planning to ensure cultural compatibility is cost effective. To maximize social and economic benefits, projects must (1) be culturally compatible, (2) respond to locally perceived needs, (3) involve men and women in planning and carrying out the changes that affect them, (4) harness traditional organizations, and (5) be flexible.

overinnovation Characteristic of development projects that require major changes in people's daily lives, especially ones that interfere with customary subsistence pursuits.

OVERINNOVATION

In Kottak's comparative study, the compatible and successful projects avoided the fallacy of **overinnovation** (too much change). We would expect people to resist development projects that require major changes in their daily lives. People usually want to change just enough to keep what they have. Motives for modifying behavior come from the traditional culture and the small concerns of ordinary life. Peasants' values are not such abstract ones as "learning a better way," "progressing," "increasing technical know-how," "improving efficiency," or "adopting modern techniques." (Those phrases exemplify intervention philosophy.)

Instead, people's objectives are down-to-earth and specific ones. They want to improve yields in a rice field, amass resources for a ceremony, get a child through school, or have enough cash to pay the tax bill. The goals and values of subsistence producers differ from those of people who produce for cash, just as they differ from the intervention philosophy of development planners. Different value systems must be considered during planning.

Development projects that fail usually are either economically or culturally incompatible (or both). For example, one South Asian project promoted the cultivation of onions and peppers, expecting this practice to fit into a preexisting labor-intensive system of rice growing. Cultivation of these cash crops wasn't traditional in the area. It conflicted with existing crop priorities and other interests of farmers. Also, the labor peaks for pepper and onion production coincided with those for rice, to which the farmers gave priority.

Another naive and incompatible project was an overinnovative scheme in Ethiopia. Its major fallacy was to try to convert nomadic herders into sedentary cultivators. It ignored traditional land rights. Outsiders—commercial farmers—were to get much of the herders' territory. The pastoralists were expected to settle down and start farming. This project helped wealthy outsiders instead of the local people. The planners naively expected free-ranging herders to give up a generations-old way of life to work three times harder growing rice and picking cotton for bosses.

CULTURETHINK

The concept of under-differentiation shows us that paying attention to local culture is important when trying to bring about economic change. A study in Zimbabwe determined that a solution to wood shortages was to plant trees in communally owned woodlots. Would communally owned lots work in your community? Why or why not?

UNDERDIFFERENTIATION

The fallacy of **underdifferentiation** is the tendency to view the "less developed countries" as more alike than they are. Development agencies have often ignored cultural diversity (e.g., between Brazil and Burundi) and adopted a uniform approach to deal with very different sets of people. Neglecting cultural diversity, many projects also have tried to impose incompatible property notions and social units. Most often, the faulty social design assumes either (1) individualistic productive units that are privately owned by an individual or couple and worked by a nuclear family, or (2) cooperatives that are at least partially based on models from the former Eastern bloc and Socialist countries.

One example of faulty Euro-American models (the individual and the nuclear family) was a West African project designed for an area where the extended family was the basic social unit. The project succeeded despite its faulty social design because the participants used their traditional extended family networks to attract additional settlers. Eventually, twice as many people as planned benefited, as extended family members flocked to the project area. Here, settlers used the principles of their traditional society to modify the project design that had been imposed on them.

The second dubious foreign social model that is common in development strategy is the cooperative. In the comparative study of rural development projects, new cooperatives fared badly. Cooperatives succeeded only when they harnessed preexisting local-level communal institutions. This is a corollary of a more general rule: *Participants' groups are most effective when they are based on traditional social organization or on a socioeconomic similarity among members.*

An alternative to such foreign models is needed: greater use of indigenous social models in economic development. These are traditional social units, such as the clans, lineages, and other extended kin groups of Africa, Oceania, and many other nations, with their communally held estates and resources. *The most humane and productive strategy for change is to base the social design for innovation on traditional social forms in each target area.*

> **underdifferentiation** Planning fallacy of viewing less developed countries as an undifferentiated group; ignoring cultural diversity and adopting a uniform approach (often ethnocentric) for very different types of project beneficiaries.

INDIGENOUS MODELS

Many governments are not genuinely, or realistically, committed to improving the lives of their citizens. Interference by major powers also has kept governments from enacting needed reforms. In some nations, however, the government acts more as an agent of the people. Madagascar provides an example. The people of Madagascar, the Malagasy, had been organized into descent groups before the origin of the state. The Merina, creators of the major precolonial state of Madagascar, wove descent groups into its structure, making members of important groups advisers to the king and

To maximize benefits, development projects should respond to locally perceived needs. Shown here (foreground) is the president of a Nicaraguan cooperative that makes and markets hammocks. This cooperative has been assisted by a nongovernmental organization (NGO) whose goals include increasing the benefits that women derive from economic development.

thus giving them authority in government. The Merina state made provisions for the people it ruled. It collected taxes and organized labor for public works projects. In return, it redistributed resources to peasants in need. It also granted them some protection against war and slave raids and allowed them to cultivate their rice fields in peace. The government maintained the water works for rice cultivation. It opened to ambitious peasant boys the chance of becoming, through hard work and study, state bureaucrats.

Throughout the history of the Merina state—and continuing in modern Madagascar—there have been strong relationships between the individual, the descent group, and the state. Local Malagasy communities, where residence is based on descent, are more cohesive and homogeneous than are communities in Latin America or North America. Madagascar gained political independence from France in 1960. Although it still was economically dependent on France when Conrad Kottak first did research there in 1966–1967, the new government had an economic development policy aimed at increasing the ability of the Malagasy to feed themselves. Government policy emphasized increased production of rice, a subsistence crop, rather than cash crops. Furthermore, local communities, with their traditional cooperative patterns and solidarity based on kinship and descent, were treated as partners in, not obstacles to, the development process.

anthropology and education
Anthropological research in classrooms, homes, and neighborhoods, viewing students as total cultural creatures whose enculturation and attitudes toward education belong to a larger context that includes family, peers, and society.

In a sense, the descent group is preadapted to equitable national development. In Madagascar, members of local descent groups have customarily pooled their resources to educate their ambitious members. Once educated, these men and women gain economically secure positions in the nation. They then share the advantages of their new positions with their kin. For example, they give room and board to rural cousins attending school and help them find jobs.

This Madagascar example suggests that when government officials are of "the people" (rather than the elites) and have strong personal ties to common folk, they are more likely to promote democratic economic development. In Latin America, by contrast, leaders and followers too often have been from different socioeconomic strata, with no connections based on kinship, descent, marriage, or common background. When elites rule, elites usually prosper. Recently, however, Latin America has elected some nonelite leaders. Brazil's lower class (indeed the entire nation) benefited socioeconomically when one of its own was elected president. Luis Inácio da Silva, aka Lula, a former factory worker with only a fourth-grade education, served two terms (ending in 2011) as one of the Western Hemisphere's most popular leaders.

Realistic development policies promote change but not overinnovation. Many changes are possible if the aim is to preserve things while making them work better. Successful economic development projects respect, or at least don't attack, local cultural patterns. Effective development draws on indigenous cultural practices and social structures. As nations become more tied to the world capitalist economy, it is not inevitable that indigenous forms of social organization will break down into nuclear family organization, impersonality, and alienation. Descent groups, with their traditional communalism and solidarity, have important roles to play in economic development.

Got IT? Can you evaluate how the fallacies of overinnovation and underdifferentiation lead to failed development projects? Can you identify a better approach?

>> Anthropology and Education

Attention to culture also is fundamental to **anthropology and education,** involving research that extends from classrooms into homes, neighborhoods, and communities (see Spindler 2000, 2005). In classrooms, anthropologists have observed interactions among teachers, students, parents, and visitors. Jules Henry's classic account of the American elementary school classroom (1955) shows how students learn to conform to and compete with their peers. Anthropologists view children as total cultural creatures whose enculturation and attitudes toward education belong to a context that includes family and peers.

Sociolinguists and cultural anthropologists have worked side by side in education research. In one classic study of Puerto Rican

Afghan girls attend a lesson at the secondary school in Sarkani village, Kunar Province, eastern Afghanistan. What do you see here that differs from classrooms in your country?

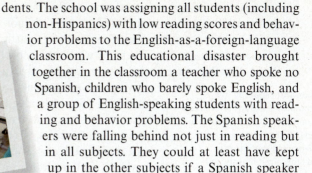

bilingual teachers to work with Spanish-speaking students. The school was assigning all students (including non-Hispanics) with low reading scores and behavior problems to the English-as-a-foreign-language classroom. This educational disaster brought together in the classroom a teacher who spoke no Spanish, children who barely spoke English, and a group of English-speaking students with reading and behavior problems. The Spanish speakers were falling behind not just in reading but in all subjects. They could at least have kept up in the other subjects if a Spanish speaker had been teaching them science, social studies, and math until they were ready for English-language instruction in those areas.

seventh-graders in the urban Midwest (Hill-Burnett 1978), anthropologists uncovered some misconceptions held by teachers. The teachers mistakenly had assumed that Puerto Rican parents valued education less than did non-Hispanics, but in-depth interviews revealed that the Puerto Rican parents valued it more.

The anthropologists also identified certain practices that were preventing Hispanics from being adequately educated. For example, the teachers' union and the board of education had agreed to teach "English as a foreign language." However, they had provided no

>> Urban Anthropology

For centuries, cities have been influenced by global forces, including world capitalism and colonialism (Smart and Smart 2003). However, the roles of cities in the world system have changed recently because of the time-space compression made possible by modern transportation and communication systems. That is, everything appears closer today because contact and movement are so much easier.

In the context of globalization, the mass media have joined local factors in guiding people's routines,

One-sixth of Earth's population lives in urban slums. Roçinha (shown here) is a populous shantytown within the city of Rio de Janeiro, Brazil. How might anthropologists study slums?

dreams, and aspirations. Although people live in particular places, their imaginations are not locally confined (Appadurai 1996). Media-transmitted images and information help draw people to cities. People migrate partly for economic reasons, but also to be where the action is. Rural Brazilians routinely cite *movimento,* urban activity and excitement, as something to be valued. International migrants tend to settle in large cities, where a lot is going on, and where they can feel at home in ethnic enclaves. Consider Canada, which, after Australia, is the country with the highest percentage of foreign-born population: Seventy-one percent of immigrants to Canada settle in Toronto, Vancouver, or Montreal. Nearly half of Toronto's citizens were born outside Canada (Smart and Smart 2003).

urban anthropology The anthropological study of life in and around world cities, including the study of urban social problems, differences between urban and other environments, and adaptation to city life.

Urban living has increased steadily since the Industrial Revolution. The percentage of the world's population living in cities surpassed 50 percent for the first time in 2008 and is projected to rise to 70 percent by 2050 (Handwerk 2008). Only about 3 percent of people were city dwellers in 1800, compared with 13 percent in 1900, over 40 percent in 1980, and over 50 percent today (see Handwerk 2008; Smart and Smart 2003). The more developed countries (MDCs) were 76 percent urbanized in 1999, compared with 39 percent for the less developed countries (LDCs). However, the urbanization growth rate is much faster in the LDCs (Smart and Smart 2003). In Africa and Asia alone, a million people a week migrate to cities (Handwerk 2008). The world had only 16 cities with more than a million people in 1900, versus 314 such cities in 2005 (Butler 2005; Stevens 1992).

One billion people now live in urban slums, mostly without reliable water, sanitation, and public services (Handwerk 2008; Vidal 2003). If current trends continue, urban population increase and the concentration of people in slums will be accompanied by rising rates of crime, along with water, air, and noise pollution. These problems will be most severe in the LDCs.

As industrialization and urbanization spread globally, anthropologists increasingly study these processes and the social problems they create. **Urban anthropology,** which has theoretical (basic research) and applied dimensions, is the cross-cultural and ethnographic study of global urbanization and life in cities (see Gmelch and Zenner, eds. 2002; Smart and Smart 2003; Stevenson 2003). The United States and Canada have become popular arenas for urban anthropological research on topics such as immigration, ethnicity, poverty, class, and urban violence (Vigil 2003, 2010).

URBAN VERSUS RURAL

An early student of urbanization, the anthropologist Robert Redfield, contrasted rural communities, whose social relations are on a face-to-face basis, with cities, where impersonality characterizes many aspects of life. Redfield (1941) proposed that urbanization be studied along a rural-urban continuum. He described differences in values and social relations in four sites that spanned such a continuum. In Mexico's Yucatán peninsula, Redfield compared an isolated Maya-speaking Indian community, a rural peasant village, a small provincial city, and a large capital. Several studies in Africa (Little 1971) and Asia were influenced by Redfield's view that cities are centers through which cultural innovations spread to rural and tribal areas.

In any nation, urban and rural represent different social systems. However, cultural diffusion or borrowing occurs as people, products, images, and messages move from one to the other. Migrants bring rural practices and beliefs to cities and take urban patterns back home. The experiences and social forms of the rural area affect adaptation to city life. City folk also develop new institutions to meet specific urban needs (Mitchell 1966).

An applied anthropology approach to urban planning starts by identifying key social groups in specific urban contexts—avoiding the fallacy of underdifferentiation. After identifying those groups, the anthropologist might elicit their wishes for change, convey those needs to funding agencies, and work with agencies and local people to realize those goals. In Africa relevant groups might include ethnic associations, occupational groups, social clubs, religious groups, and burial societies. Through membership in such groups, urban Africans maintain wide networks of personal contacts and support. The groups provide cash support and urban lodging for their rural relatives. Sometimes such groups think of themselves as a gigantic kin group, a clan that includes urban and rural members. Members may call one another "brother" and "sister." As in an extended family, richer members help their poorer relatives. A member's improper behavior, however, can lead to expulsion—an unhappy fate for a migrant in a large, ethnically heterogeneous city.

One role for the urban applied anthropologist is to help relevant social groups deal with urban institutions, such as legal and social services, with which recent migrants may be unfamiliar. In certain North American cities, as in Africa, kin-based ethnic associations are relevant urban groups. One example comes from Los Angeles, which has the largest Samoan immigrant community (over twelve thousand people) in the United States. Samoans in Los Angeles draw on their traditional system of *matai* (*matai* means "chief"; the matai system

> ## "I must admit that I personally measure success in terms of the contributions an individual makes to her or his fellow human beings."
>
> Margaret Mead

now refers to respect for elders) to deal with modern urban problems. One example: In 1992, a white police officer shot and killed two unarmed Samoan brothers. When a judge dismissed charges against the officer, local leaders used the matai system to calm angry youths (who have formed gangs, like other ethnic groups in the Los Angeles area). Clan leaders and elders organized a well-attended community meeting, in which they urged young members to be patient. The Samoans then used the American judicial system. They brought a civil case against the officer in question and pressed the U.S. Justice Department to initiate a civil rights case in the matter (Mydans 1992b). Not all conflicts involving gangs and law enforcement end so peacefully.

James Vigil (2003, 2010) examines gang violence in the context of large-scale immigrant adaptation to American cities. He notes that before the 1970s most gangs were located in white ethnic enclaves in eastern and midwestern cities. Back then, gang incidents typically were brawls involving fists, sticks, and knives. Today, gangs more often are composed of nonwhite ethnic groups, and handguns have replaced the less lethal weapons of the past. Gangs still consist mostly of male adolescents who have grown up together, usually in a low-income neighborhood, where it's estimated that about 10 percent of young men join gangs. Female gang members are much rarer—from 4 to 15 percent of gang members. With gangs organized hierarchically by age, older members push younger ones (usually fourteen- to eighteen-year-olds) to carry out violent acts against rivals (Vigil 2003, 2010).

The populations that include most of today's gang members settled originally in poorer urban areas. On the East Coast these usually were run-down neighborhoods where a criminal lifestyle already was present. Around Los Angeles, urban migrants created squatter-like settlements in previously empty spaces. Immigrants tend to reside in neighborhoods apart from middle-class people, thus limiting their opportunities for integration. Confined in this manner, and facing residential overcrowding, poor people often experience frustration, which can lead to aggressive acts (Vigil 2003). In addition, many industries and jobs have moved from inner cities to distant suburbs and foreign nations. Given their limited access to entry-level jobs, many urban minority youth pursue informal and illegal economic arrangements, of which drug trafficking in particular has heightened gang violence (Singer 2008; Vigil 2003, 2010). How might an applied anthropologist approach the problem of urban violence? Which groups would need to be involved in the study?

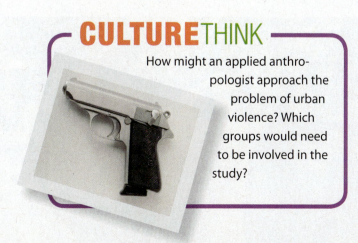

CULTURE THINK

How might an applied anthropologist approach the problem of urban violence? Which groups would need to be involved in the study?

>> Medical Anthropology

Medical anthropology is both academic and applied/practical and includes anthropologists from all four subfields (see Anderson 1996; Briggs 2005; Brown and Barrett 2010; Dressler et al. 2005; Joralemon 2010; Singer and Baer 2007; Trevathan, Smith, and McKenna, eds. 2008). Medical anthropologists examine such questions as which diseases and health conditions affect particular populations (and why) and how illness is socially constructed, diagnosed, managed, and treated in various societies.

medical anthropology Field that unites biological and cultural anthropologists in the study of disease, health problems, health care systems, and theories about illness in different cultures and ethnic groups.

disease An etic, or scientifically identified, health threat caused by a bacterium, virus, fungus, parasite, or other pathogen.

illness An emic condition of poor health felt by the individual.

Disease refers to a scientifically identified health threat caused genetically or by a bacterium, virus, fungus, parasite, or other pathogen. **Illness** is a condition of poor health perceived or felt by an individual (Inhorn and Brown 1990). Perceptions of good and bad health, along with health threats and problems, are culturally constructed. Various ethnic groups and cultures recognize different illnesses, symptoms, and causes and have developed different health care systems and treatment strategies.

The incidence and severity of *disease* vary as well (see Baer, Singer, and Susser 2003; Barnes 2005). Group differences are evident in the United States. Keppel, Pearch, and Wagener (2002) examined data between 1990 and 1998 using ten health status indicators in relation to racial and ethnic categories from the U.S. census: non-Hispanic white, non-Hispanic black, Hispanic, American Indian or Alaska Native, and Asian or Pacific Islander. Black Americans' rates for six measures (total mortality, heart disease, lung cancer, breast cancer, stroke, and homicide) exceeded those of other groups by a factor ranging from 2.5 to almost 10. Other ethnic groups had higher rates for suicide (white Americans) and motor vehicle accidents (American Indians and Alaska Natives). Overall, Asians had the longest life spans (see Dressler et al. 2005).

Hurtado and colleagues (2005) note the prevalence of poor health and unusually high rates of

early mortality among indigenous populations in South America. Life expectancy at birth is at least twenty years shorter among indigenous groups compared with other South Americans. In 2000, the life expectancy of indigenous peoples in Brazil and Venezuela was lower than that in Sierra Leone, which had the lowest reported national life expectancy in the world (Hurtado et al. 2005).

How can applied anthropologists help ameliorate the large health disparity between indigenous peoples and other populations? Hurtado and colleagues (2005) suggest three steps: (1) Identify the most pressing health problems that indigenous communities face; (2) gather information on solutions to those problems; and (3) implement solutions in partnership with the agencies and organizations in charge of public health programs for indigenous populations.

In many areas, the world system and colonialism worsened the health of indigenous peoples by spreading diseases, warfare, servitude, and other stressors. Traditionally and in ancient times, hunter-gatherers, because of their small numbers, mobility, and relative isolation from other groups, lacked most of the epidemic infectious diseases that affect agrarian and urban societies (Cohen and Armelagos, eds. 1984; Inhorn and Brown 1990). Epidemic diseases such as cholera, typhoid, and bubonic plague thrive in dense populations, and thus among farmers and city dwellers. The spread of malaria has been linked to population growth and deforestation associated with food production.

Certain diseases, and physical conditions such as obesity, have spread with economic development and globalization (Ulijaszek and Lofink 2006). *Schistosomiasis,* or bilharzia (blood and liver flukes), is probably the fastest-spreading and most dangerous parasitic infection

treat illness differently. Health standards are cultural constructions that vary in time and space (Martin 1992). Still, all societies have what George Foster and Barbara Anderson call "disease-theory systems" to identify, classify, and explain illness. Foster and Anderson (1978) identified three basic theories about the causes of illness: personalistic, naturalistic, and emotionalistic. *Personalistic disease theories* blame illness on agents, such as sorcerers, witches, ghosts, or ancestral spirits. *Naturalistic disease theories* explain illness in impersonal terms. One example is Western medicine, or *biomedicine,* which aims to link illness to scientifically demonstrated agents that bear no personal malice toward their victims. Thus Western medicine attributes illness to organisms (e.g., bacteria, viruses, fungi, or parasites), accidents, toxic materials, or genes.

Other naturalistic ethnomedical systems blame poor health on unbalanced body fluids. Many Latin societies classify food, drink, and environmental conditions as "hot" or "cold." People believe their health suffers when they eat or drink hot or cold substances together or under inappropriate conditions. For example, one shouldn't drink something cold after a hot bath or eat a pineapple (a "cold" fruit) when one is menstruating (a "hot" condition).

> **health care systems** Beliefs, customs, and specialists concerned with ensuring health and preventing and curing illness; a cultural universal.

Emotionalistic disease theories assume that emotional experiences cause illness. For example, Latin Americans may develop *susto,* an illness caused by anxiety or fright (Bolton 1981; Finkler 1985). Its symptoms (lethargy, vagueness, distraction) are similar to those of "soul loss," a diagnosis of similar symptoms made by people in Madagascar. Modern psychoanalysis also focuses on the role of the emotions in physical and psychological well-being.

All societies have **health care systems** consisting of beliefs, customs, specialists, and techniques aimed at ensuring health and at preventing, diagnosing, and

now known. It is propagated by snails that live in ponds, lakes, and waterways, usually those created by irrigation projects. A study done in a Nile Delta village in Egypt (Farooq 1966) illustrated the role of culture (religion) in the spread of schistosomiasis. The disease was more common among Muslims than among Christians because of an Islamic practice called *wudu*—ritual ablution (bathing) before prayer. The applied anthropology approach to reducing such diseases is to see if local people perceive a connection between the vector (e.g., snails in the water) and the disease. If not, such information may be provided by enlisting active local groups, schools, and the media.

The highest global rates of HIV infection and AIDS-related deaths are in Africa, especially southern Africa. As it kills productive adults, AIDS leaves behind children and seniors who have difficulty replacing the lost labor force (Baro and Deubel 2006). In southern and eastern Africa, AIDS and other sexually transmitted diseases (STDs) have spread along highways, via encounters between male truckers and female prostitutes. STDs also are spread through prostitution, as young men from rural areas seek wage work in cities, labor camps, and mines. When the men return to their natal villages, they infect their wives (Larson 1989; Miller and Rockwell, eds. 1988). Cities also are prime sites of STD transmission in Europe, Asia, and North and South America (see Baer, Singer, and Susser 2003; French 2002). Cultural factors also affect the spread of HIV, which is less likely to be transmitted when men are circumcised than when they are not.

The kinds of and incidence of disease vary among societies, and cultures perceive and

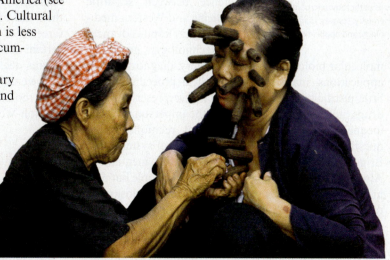

A traditional healer at work in Malaysia. Shown here, mugwort, a small, spongy herb, is burned to facilitate healing. The healer lights one end of a moxa stick, roughly the shape and size of a cigar, and attaches it, or holds it close, to the area being treated for several minutes until the area turns red. The purpose of moxibustion is to strengthen the blood, stimulate spiritual energy, and maintain general health.

Strengths of Western use of biomedicine are (1) effective drugs, (2) preventive health care, and (3) safe surgical procedures.

Weaknesses are (1) overprescription of drugs, (2) opposition between mind and body, (3) unnecessary surgery, and (4) distant physician–patient relationships.

curing illness. A society's illness-causation theory influences treatment. When illness has a personalistic cause, magicoreligious specialists may be good curers. They draw on varied techniques (occult and practical) that are part of their special expertise. A shaman may cure soul loss by enticing the spirit back into the body. Shamans may ease difficult childbirths by asking spirits to travel up the birth canal to guide the baby out (Lévi-Strauss 1967). A shaman may cure a cough by counteracting a curse or removing a substance introduced by a sorcerer.

If there is a "world's oldest profession" besides hunter and gatherer, it is **curer,** often a shaman. The curer's role has some universal features (Foster and Anderson 1978). Thus curers emerge through a culturally defined process of selection (parental prodding, inheritance, visions, dream instructions) and training (apprentice shamanship, medical school). Eventually, the curer is certified by older practitioners and acquires a professional image. Patients believe in the skills of the curer, whom they consult and compensate.

We should not lose sight, ethnocentrically, of the difference between **scientific medicine** and Western medicine per se. Despite advances in technology, genomics, molecular biology, pathology, surgery, diagnostics, and applications, many Western medical procedures have little justification in logic or fact. Overprescription of drugs, unnecessary surgery, and the impersonality and inequality of the physician-patient relationship are questionable features of Western medical systems (see Briggs 2005 for linguistic aspects of this inequality). Also, overuse of antibiotics, not just for people but also in animal feed, seems to be triggering an explosion of resistant microorganisms, which may pose a long-term global public health hazard.

Still, biomedicine surpasses tribal treatment in many ways. Although medicines such as quinine, coca, opium,

curer Specialized role acquired through a culturally appropriate process of selection, training, certification, and acquisition of a professional image; the curer is consulted by patients, who believe in his or her special powers, and receives some form of special consideration; a cultural universal.

scientific medicine As distinguished from Western medicine, a health care system based on scientific knowledge and procedures, encompassing such fields as pathology, microbiology, biochemistry, surgery, diagnostic technology, and applications.

ephedrine, and rauwolfia were discovered in nonindustrial societies, thousands of effective drugs are available today to treat myriad diseases. Preventive health care improved during the twentieth century. Today's surgical procedures are much safer and more effective than those of traditional societies.

But industrialization and globalization have spawned their own health problems. Modern stressors include poor nutrition, dangerous machinery, impersonal work, isolation, poverty, homelessness, substance abuse, and noise, air, and water pollution (see McElroy and Townsend 2003). Health problems in industrial nations are caused as much by economic, social, political, and cultural factors as by pathogens. In modern North America, for example, poverty contributes to many illnesses, including arthritis, heart conditions, back problems, and hearing and vision impairment (see Bailey 2000). Poverty also is a factor in the differential spread of infectious diseases.

In the United States and other developed countries today, good health has become something of an ethical imperative (Foucault 1990). Individuals are expected to regulate their behavior and shape themselves in keeping with new medical knowledge. Those who do so acquire the status of sanitary citizens—people with modern understanding of the body, health, and illness, who practice hygiene and depend on doctors and nurses when they are sick. People who act differently (e.g., smokers, overeaters, those who avoid doctors) are stigmatized as unsanitary and blamed for their own health problems (Briggs 2005; Foucault 1990).

Even getting an epidemic disease such as cholera may be interpreted today as a moral failure. It's assumed that people who act rationally can avoid "preventable" diseases. Individuals are expected to follow scientifically based imperatives (e.g., "boil water," "don't smoke"). People (e.g., gay men, smokers, veterans) can become objects of avoidance and discrimination simply by belonging to a group seen as having a greater risk of disease or poor health (Briggs 2005).

Health interventions always have to fit into local cultures and be accepted by local people. When Western medicine is introduced, people usually retain many of their old methods while also accepting new ones (see Green 1987/1992). Native curers may continue to treat certain conditions (e.g., spirit possession), while physicians deal with others. When patients are cured, the native curer and the physician share the credit.

A more personal treatment of illness that emulates the non-Western curer-patient-community relationship

CULTURETHINK

Consider one of the controversial health issues listed on pp. 250–253. What do you think, for example, of life-prolonging medical treatments and assisted suicide for terminal patients?

could probably benefit Western systems. Western medicine tends to draw a rigid line between biological and psychological causation. Non-Western theories usually lack this sharp distinction, recognizing that poor health has intertwined physical, emotional, and social causes. The mind-body opposition is part of Western folk taxonomy, not of science (see also Brown and Barrett 2010; Helman 2001; Joralemon 2010; Strathern and Stewart 2010).

Medical anthropology also considers the impact of new scientific and medical techniques on ideas about life, death, and *personhood* (what it means to be a person). For decades, disagreements about personhood—such as when life begins and ends—have been part of political and religious discussions of contraception, abortion, assisted suicide, and euthanasia (mercy killing). More recent additions to such discussions include stem cells, "harvested" embryos, assisted reproduction, genetic screening, cloning, and life-prolonging medical treatments. How long should a human body be kept alive if there is no hope of recovery?

Kaufman and Morgan (2005) emphasize the contrast between what they call low-tech and high-tech births and deaths in today's world. A desperately poor young mother dies of AIDS in Africa while half a world away an American child of privilege is born as the result of a $50,000 in-vitro fertilization procedure. Medical anthropologists increasingly are concerned with new and contrasting conditions that allow humans to enter, live, and depart life, and with how the boundaries of life and death are being questioned and negotiated in the twenty-first century.

Got IT? Can you provide examples of how illness is culturally constructed and treated in various societies? Can you explain some ways that globalization has affected health?

>> Anthropology and Business

For decades anthropologists have used ethnography to understand business settings (Arensberg 1987; Jordan 2003). Ethnographic research in an auto factory, for example, may view workers, managers, and executives as different social categories participating in a common system. Each group has characteristic attitudes, values, and behavior patterns. These are transmitted through *microenculturation,* the process by which people learn particular roles within a limited social system. The free-ranging nature of ethnography takes the anthropologist back and forth from worker to executive. Each employee is both an individual with a personal viewpoint and a cultural creature whose perspective is, to some extent, shared with other members of his or her group. Applied anthropologists have acted as "cultural brokers," translating managers' goals or workers' concerns to the other group (see Ferraro 2010).

By studying social interactions in factories such as this one in Seattle, Washington, applied anthropologists have acted as "cultural brokers," translating managers' goals or workers' concerns to the other.

Carol Taylor (1987) emphasizes the value of an "anthropologist-in-residence" in a large, complex organization, such as a hospital or corporation. A free-ranging ethnographer can be a perceptive oddball when information and decisions typically move through a rigid hierarchy. If allowed to observe and converse freely with all types and levels of personnel, the anthropologist may acquire a unique perspective on organizational conditions and problems. Such high-tech companies as Xerox, IBM, and Apple have employed anthropologists in various roles. Closely observing how people actually use computer products, anthropologists work with engineers to design products that are more user friendly.

Key features of anthropology that are of value to business include (1) ethnography and observation as ways of gathering data, (2) a focus on diversity, and (3) cross-cultural expertise. Businesses have heard that anthropologists are specialists on cultural diversity and observing behavior in natural settings, including home and office. Hallmark Cards has hired anthropologists to observe parties, holidays, and celebrations of ethnic groups to improve its ability to design cards for targeted audiences. Applied anthropologists routinely go into people's homes to see how they actually use products (see Sunderland and Denny 2007).

Got IT? Can you explain some of the major issues that anthropologists face in the areas of education, urban issues, health, and business?

>> Careers and Anthropology

Many college students find anthropology interesting and consider majoring in it. However, their parents or friends may discourage them by asking, "What kind of job are you going to get with an anthropology major?" The first step in answering this question is to consider the more general question, "What do you do with any college major?" The answer is, "Not much, without a good bit of effort, thought, and planning." A survey of University of Michigan college graduates showed that few had jobs that were clearly linked to their majors. Medicine, law, and many other professions require advanced degrees. Although many colleges offer bachelor's degrees in engineering, business, accounting, and social work, master's degrees often are needed to get the best jobs in those fields. Anthropologists, too, need an advanced degree, almost always a Ph.D., to find gainful employment in academic, museum, or applied anthropology.

A broad college education, and even a major in anthropology, can be an excellent foundation for success in many fields. A recent survey of women executives showed that most had majored not in business but in the social sciences or humanities. Only after graduating did they study business, obtaining a master's degree in business administration. These executives felt that the breadth of their college educations had contributed to their business careers. Anthropology majors go on to medical, law, and business schools and find success in many professions that often have little explicit connection to anthropology.

Anthropology's breadth provides knowledge and an outlook on the world that are useful in many kinds of work. For example, an anthropology major combined with a master's degree in business is excellent preparation for work in international business. Breadth is

CULTURE THINK

What job(s) are you interested in having someday? How might anthropology be useful to you?

anthropology's hallmark. Anthropologists study people biologically, culturally, socially, and linguistically, across time and space, in developed and underdeveloped nations, in simple and complex settings. Most colleges have anthropology courses that compare cultures and others that focus on particular world areas, such as Latin America, Asia, and Native North America. The knowledge of foreign areas acquired in such courses can be useful in many jobs. Anthropology's comparative outlook, its longstanding Third World focus, and its appreciation of diverse lifestyles combine to provide an excellent foundation for overseas employment (see Omohundro 2001).

For work in North America, anthropology's focus on culture is increasingly relevant. Every day we hear about cultural differences and about social problems whose solutions require a multicultural viewpoint—an ability to recognize and reconcile ethnic differences. Government, schools, hospitals, and businesses constantly deal with people from different social classes, ethnic groups, and cultural backgrounds. Physicians, attorneys, social workers, police officers, judges, teachers, and students can all do a better job if they understand social differences in a part of the world such as ours that is one of the most ethnically diverse in history.

Knowledge of the traditions and beliefs of the groups that make up a modern nation is important in planning and carrying out programs that affect those groups. Experience in planned social change—whether community organization in North America or economic development overseas—shows that a proper social study should be done before a project or policy is implemented. When local people want the change and it fits their lifestyle and traditions, it has a better chance of being successful, beneficial, and cost effective.

People with anthropology backgrounds are doing well in many fields. Even if one's job has little or nothing to do with anthropology in a formal or obvious sense, a background in anthropology provides a useful orientation when we work with our fellow human beings. For most of us, this means every day of our lives.

Got IT? Can you identify skills and career opportunities that an anthropology degree provides?

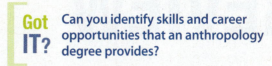

Talk with three fellow students of various cultural backgrounds (different ethnicity, religion, or region). Explain that you are investigating how different groups perceive and respond to illness and its treatment. Ask each student the following questions about their last illness:

- What symptoms did you note?
- What causes did you suspect?
- Does your group have any specific beliefs about the illness, its causes, and its treatment?
- Did you consult a physician or other health care practitioner? If so, what was the diagnosis and the recommended treatment? Did you find the diagnosis acceptable and the treatment, if you tried it, effective? (If you did not consult a practitioner, explain how you attempted to manage your illness.)
- Describe your level of comfort with the setting in which you received diagnosis and treatment.

From these cases, what conclusions can you draw about how cultural background influences our experience of illness, disease, and treatment?

FOR REVIEW

EXPERIENCING CULTURE

TO ACCESS THESE VIDEOS
ON YOUR COMPUTER, VISIT
www.mhhe.com/gezonqr

12-1

12-2

12-3

I. How can change be bad?

- Applied anthropology recognizes that designs for social or economic change may have unforeseen negative consequences. When foreign aid goes to the developmental priorities as seen by powerful interests rather than to where the need is greatest, the living standards of the needy may actually decline. Channeling inputs through the rich may severely widen economic disparities. Development projects that begin with an uneven distribution of resources often create greater skewing after the project. Projects not implemented by culturally compatible means, failing to use indigenous social models, are less likely to benefit the targeted area.

II. How can anthropology be applied to education, medicine, and business?

- Anthropology and education researchers study the various settings relevant to education. Researchers may identify problematic school practices, misconceptions held by teachers, and problems in interaction among teachers, students, and parents. Researchers then make policy recommendations. Medical anthropologists consider different societies' divergent health care systems and the cultural construction of health and illness. Medical anthropologists serve as cultural interpreters in public health programs and help ensure that interventions fit into local cultures. In businesses and other organizations, ethnographers develop a unique perspective on organizational conditions. They help resolve issues of cultural diversity, study how consumers use products, and translate managers' goals and workers' concerns to the other group.

III. How does the study of anthropology fit into a career path?

- Anthropology's comparative perspective, four-field breadth, and multicultural outlook provide a basis for working in international business and in careers in government, schools, medicine, or private firms, or with interest groups that require the ability to recognize and reconcile ethnic differences and understand social problems. Anthropologists with advanced degrees can find employment in academic, museum, or applied anthropology. A background in anthropology can aid and enrich our work with people regardless of the type of employment.

Pop Quiz

Multiple Choice:

1. According to the text, what is the most valuable and distinctive tool of the applied anthropologist?
   a. Knowledge of genetics
   b. Familiarity with environmental problems
   c. Statistical expertise
   d. The ethnographic method

2. An applied anthropologist today would most likely do which of the following?
   a. Supply information to help colonial regimes
   b. Offer assistance to local people who lack a voice in the international political arena
   c. Use survey research to solve economic problems for clients able to pay them
   d. Supervise the controlled flooding of archaeological sites for underwater archaeology

3. Which of the following would *not* be a goal of an applied anthropological approach to urban programs?
   a. Work with the target community to ensure that a proposed change is implemented effectively
   b. Create a universal policy to be applied to all urban communities
   c. Identify key social groups in the urban context
   d. Elicit needs and desires from the target community and translate them to funding agencies

4. Which of the following best describes medical anthropology?
   a. It studies how indigenous peoples maintain their traditional treatments in societies that offer technologically advanced health care.
   b. It studies how traditional health knowledge can best be incorporated within the Western medical system.
   c. It is the academic study and application of Western medicine to solve health problems around the world.
   d. It studies how illness and its diagnosis and treatment are socially constructed and managed in different societies.

5. Why would a business or other complex organization hire an anthropologist?
   a. To gain access to the unique, ethnographic perspective on organizational problems
   b. To learn about the Code of Ethics of the American Anthropological Association
   c. To ensure that workers' concerns remain those of the workers, and are not translated to managers
   d. Because anthropologists are cheaper than sociologists and tend to be more presentable

6. Which of the following points about anthropology and careers is false?
   a. Anthropology offers broad knowledge about human life that is useful in many kinds of work.
   b. The knowledge of foreign cultures acquired in anthropology courses can serve as preparation for work in international business.
   c. Anthropology's focus on culture and its diversity is valuable to any career in which solutions require a multicultural viewpoint.
   d. To gain employment in academic, applied, or museum anthropology, students of anthropology rarely need an advanced degree.

Fill in the Blank:

1. _____ examines the sociocultural dimensions of economic development.

2. The term _____ describes the consequence of development programs that try to achieve too much change.

3. Increased _____ describes the goal of reducing absolute poverty, with a more even distribution of wealth.

4. Medical anthropologists use the term _____ to refer to a scientifically identified health threat caused by a known pathogen, while the term _____ refers to a condition of poor health perceived or felt by an individual.

1. (d), 2. (b), 3. (b), 4. (d), 5. (a), 6. (d)

1. Development anthropology; 2. overinnovation; 3. equity; 4. *disease, illness*

This chapter applies an anthropological perspective to contemporary global issues. We begin by considering different meanings of the term *globalization*. The fact that certain risks now have global implications leads to a discussion of climate change, aka global warming. Next, we return to issues of development, this time alongside an intervention philosophy that seeks to impose global ecological morality without due attention to cultural variation and autonomy. Also considered is the threat that deforestation poses to global biodiversity. The second half of this chapter turns from ecology to the contemporary flows of people, technology, finance, information, images, and ideology that contribute to a global culture of consumption. Globalization promotes intercultural communication, through the media, travel, and migration, which bring people from different societies into direct contact. Finally, we'll consider how such contacts and external linkages influence indigenous peoples, and how those groups have organized to confront and deal with national and global issues, including their mobilization to promote human, cultural, and political rights.

Note that it would be impossible in a single chapter to discuss all or even most of the global issues that are salient today and that anthropologists have studied. Some such issues (e.g., war, displacement, terrorism, NGOs) have been considered in previous chapters. For timely anthropological analysis of a range of global issues, see recent books by John H. Bodley (2008a, 2008b) and Richard H. Robbins (2008). The current global issues these anthropologists consider include, but are not limited to, hunger, international interventions, peacekeeping, global health, and sanitation.

>> Globalization: Its Meaning and Its Nature

Chapter 2 characterized globalization as a series of processes that promote change in a world in which nations and people are increasingly interlinked and mutually dependent. Its forces include international manufacture, commerce, and finance; travel and tourism; transnational migration; the media, the Internet, and other high-tech information flows. Globalization deserves a closer look in this final chapter.

Mark Smith and Michele Doyle (2002) distinguish between two meanings of globalization:

1. *Globalization as fact:* the spread and connectedness of production, communication, and technologies across the world. This meaning is like the one described above and in Chapter 2.

2. *Globalization as ideology and policy:* efforts by the International Monetary Fund (IMF), the World Bank, and other international financial powers to create a global free market for goods and services.

In this second sense, for neoliberal economists, globalization is the way the world should go. For their opponents—anti-neoliberals—it is the way the world should not go (Lewellen 2010). It is this neoliberal view of globalization that has generated the protests described in Chapter 2.

The first meaning is more neutral. Globalization as *systemic connectedness* reflects the relentless and ongoing growth of the world system. In its current form, that system, which has existed for centuries, has some radical new aspects. Three are especially noteworthy: the *speed* of global communication, the *scale* (complexity and size) of global networks, and the sheer *volume* of international transactions.

With the fall of the Soviet Union in 1989–90, the "Second World" opened to world capitalism. Once that happened a truly global economy could emerge (Lewellen 2010). According to Manuel Castells (2001), three key features of this new economy are as follows: (1) It is based on knowledge and information; (2) its networks of financing, production, management, and exchange are transnational; and (3) its core activities, even if dispersed, can proceed as a unit in real time.

The Internet has made possible the rapid, often instantaneous, transmission of information and resources distributed across the globe. Activities that are spatially dispersed can now be coordinated in real time. Activities that once involved face-to-face contact are now conducted impersonally and often across vast distances. For example, when you order something from the Internet, the only human being you might speak to is the delivery driver (Smith and Doyle 2002).

UNDERSTANDING OURSELVES

Modern technology makes it easier than ever for us to perceive the Earth as both a planet and our world. Ethnographers can use Google Earth to locate communities they have studied in remote corners of the world. Anthropologists have even used space images to choose communities to study on Earth. Interested in the causes of deforestation in Madagascar, for example, Lisa Gezon, Conrad Kottak and their colleagues examined a series of satellite images taken in successive years to determine areas where the forest cover had diminished significantly. Then they traveled to Madagascar to study those areas on the ground.

It's interesting to imagine what an extraterrestrial might "see" in similar images. If space aliens were interested in studying life on earth, rather than conquering or controlling its inhabitants, they would have a lot to interpret. The electric grids of Earth's megacities can be seen from space, as can the power outages caused by extreme weather events that may reflect global climate change. Intensifying global trends include reliance on fossil fuels and increased fossil-fuel emissions, human population increase, and the shift from subsistence to cash economies. These trends promote agricultural intensification, resource depletion (from deforestation to oil spills), and emigration from rural areas to cities and across national boundaries.

Such transnational migration, in turn, increases cultural diversity in the United States, Canada, and western Europe. Small towns throughout America now have Chinese restaurants and stores that sell sushi. Pizza and tacos are as American as apple pie. Your McDonald's outlet sells burritos and lattes, along with that familiar sandwich whose prototype originated in Hamburg, Germany. Every day you encounter not just products, but people whose ancestral countries and cultures have been studied by anthropologists for generations—making cultural anthropology all the more relevant to our daily lives in an increasingly interconnected world.

This chapter applies an anthropological perspective to contemporary global issues. We begin by considering different meanings of the term *globalization*. The fact that certain risks now have global implications leads to a discussion of climate change, aka global warming. Next, we return to issues of development, this time alongside an intervention philosophy that seeks to impose global ecological morality without due attention to cultural variation and autonomy. Also considered is the threat that deforestation poses to global biodiversity. The second half of this chapter turns from ecology to the contemporary flows of people, technology, finance, information, images, and ideology that contribute to a global culture of consumption. Globalization promotes intercultural communication, through the media, travel, and migration, which bring people from different societies into direct contact. Finally, we'll consider how such contacts and external linkages influence indigenous peoples, and how those groups have organized to confront and deal with national and global issues, including their mobilization to promote human, cultural, and political rights.

Note that it would be impossible in a single chapter to discuss all or even most of the global issues that are salient today and that anthropologists have studied. Some such issues (e.g., war, displacement, terrorism, NGOs) have been considered in previous chapters. For timely anthropological analysis of a range of global issues, see recent books by John H. Bodley (2008a, 2008b) and Richard H. Robbins (2008). The current global issues these anthropologists consider include, but are not limited to, hunger, international interventions, peacekeeping, global health, and sanitation.

>> Globalization: Its Meaning and Its Nature

Chapter 2 characterized globalization as a series of processes that promote change in a world in which nations and people are increasingly interlinked and mutually dependent. Its forces include international manufacture, commerce, and finance; travel and tourism; transnational migration; the media, the Internet, and other high-tech information flows. Globalization deserves a closer look in this final chapter.

Mark Smith and Michele Doyle (2002) distinguish between two meanings of globalization:

1. *Globalization as fact:* the spread and connectedness of production, communication, and technologies across the world. This meaning is like the one described above and in Chapter 2.
2. *Globalization as ideology and policy:* efforts by the International Monetary Fund (IMF), the World Bank, and other international financial powers to create a global free market for goods and services.

In this second sense, for neoliberal economists, globalization is the way the world should go. For their opponents—anti-neoliberals—it is the way the world should not go (Lewellen 2010). It is this neoliberal view of globalization that has generated the protests described in Chapter 2.

The first meaning is more neutral. Globalization as *systemic connectedness* reflects the relentless and ongoing growth of the world system. In its current form, that system, which has existed for centuries, has some radical new aspects. Three are especially noteworthy: the *speed* of global communication, the *scale* (complexity and size) of global networks, and the sheer *volume* of international transactions.

With the fall of the Soviet Union in 1989–90, the "Second World" opened to world capitalism. Once that happened a truly global economy could emerge (Lewellen 2010). According to Manuel Castells (2001), three key features of this new economy are as follows: (1) It is based on knowledge and information; (2) its networks of financing, production, management, and exchange are transnational; and (3) its core activities, even if dispersed, can proceed as a unit in real time.

The Internet has made possible the rapid, often instantaneous, transmission of information and resources distributed across the globe. Activities that are spatially dispersed can now be coordinated in real time. Activities that once involved face-to-face contact are now conducted impersonally and often across vast distances. For example, when you order something from the Internet, the only human being you might speak to is the delivery driver (Smith and Doyle 2002).

Pop Quiz

Multiple Choice:

1. According to the text, what is the most valuable and distinctive tool of the applied anthropologist?

   a. Knowledge of genetics

   b. Familiarity with environmental problems

   c. Statistical expertise

   d. The ethnographic method

2. An applied anthropologist today would most likely do which of the following?

   a. Supply information to help colonial regimes

   b. Offer assistance to local people who lack a voice in the international political arena

   c. Use survey research to solve economic problems for clients able to pay them

   d. Supervise the controlled flooding of archaeological sites for underwater archaeology

3. Which of the following would *not* be a goal of an applied anthropological approach to urban programs?

   a. Work with the target community to ensure that a proposed change is implemented effectively

   b. Create a universal policy to be applied to all urban communities

   c. Identify key social groups in the urban context

   d. Elicit needs and desires from the target community and translate them to funding agencies

4. Which of the following best describes medical anthropology?

   a. It studies how indigenous peoples maintain their traditional treatments in societies that offer technologically advanced health care.

   b. It studies how traditional health knowledge can best be incorporated within the Western medical system.

   c. It is the academic study and application of Western medicine to solve health problems around the world.

   d. It studies how illness and its diagnosis and treatment are socially constructed and managed in different societies.

5. Why would a business or other complex organization hire an anthropologist?

   a. To gain access to the unique, ethnographic perspective on organizational problems

   b. To learn about the Code of Ethics of the American Anthropological Association

   c. To ensure that workers' concerns remain those of the workers, and are not translated to managers

   d. Because anthropologists are cheaper than sociologists and tend to be more presentable

6. Which of the following points about anthropology and careers is false?

   a. Anthropology offers broad knowledge about human life that is useful in many kinds of work.

   b. The knowledge of foreign cultures acquired in anthropology courses can serve as preparation for work in international business.

   c. Anthropology's focus on culture and its diversity is valuable to any career in which solutions require a multicultural viewpoint.

   d. To gain employment in academic, applied, or museum anthropology, students of anthropology rarely need an advanced degree.

Fill in the Blank:

1. _____ examines the sociocultural dimensions of economic development.

2. The term _____ describes the consequence of development programs that try to achieve too much change.

3. Increased _____ describes the goal of reducing absolute poverty, with a more even distribution of wealth.

4. Medical anthropologists use the term _____ to refer to a scientifically identified health threat caused by a known pathogen, while the term _____ refers to a condition of poor health perceived or felt by an individual.

1. (d), 2. (b), 3. (b), 4. (d), 5. (a), 6. (d)

1. Development anthropology; 2. overinnovation; 3. equity; 4. disease, illness

13

ANTHROPOLOGY'S ROLE IN A GLOBALIZING WORLD

The computers that take and process your order from Amazon can be on different continents, and the products you order can come from a warehouse anywhere in the world.

Commenting on studies of commodities and globalization (e.g., Haugerud, Stone, and Little, eds. 2000), Ted Lewellen (2010) notes that the average food product now travels 1,300 miles and changes hands a dozen times before it reaches the American consumer. He suggests that for contemporary anthropologists who wish to develop a good "system awareness," local fieldwork isn't enough. They also need to follow networks of production, processing, advertising, distribution, and consumption.

Michael Burawoy suggests that researchers shift "from studying 'sites' to studying 'fields,' that is, the relations *between sites*" (Burawoy 2000, p. xii). He observes that people increasingly live their lives across borders, maintaining social, financial, cultural, and political connections with either a "home" country or multiple countries. Such "multiplaced" folk would include business and intellectual leaders, development workers, and members of multinational corporations, as well as migratory domestic, agricultural, and construction workers (see Lewellen 2010).

By the beginning of the 21st century, multinational corporations accounted for a third of global output, and two-thirds of world trade (Gray 1999, p. 62). Profit-seeking multinationals move production, sales, and services to areas where labor and materials are cheap. This globalization of labor creates unemployment "back home" as industries relocate and outsource abroad.

Multinationals also seek out new markets, striving to create new needs among different target groups, especially the youth market. Young people increasingly construct their identities and relationships around consumption, especially of brand-name products. Successful multinationals, including Nike, Apple, Coca-Cola, and McDonald's, invest huge sums in promoting their brands. The goal is to make a particular brand an integral part of the way people see themselves. Savvy branders try to "get them young" (Klein 2000; Smith and Doyle 2002).

Multinational companies (e.g., General Motors) increasingly influence national policy and attempt to forge beneficial alliances with politicians and government officials, especially those who are most concerned with world trade. The influence of multinationals extends to key transnational players, such as the European Union and the World Bank. With the globalization of financial markets, nations have less control over their own economies. Such institutions as the World Bank, the International Monetary Fund, the European Union, and the European Central Bank routinely constrain and dictate national economic policy.

As capitalism has spread globally, the gap between rich and poor has widened both within and between nations. The widening gap in the United States was discussed in the chapter "The World System and Colonialism." David Landes (1999) calculated the difference in per capita income between the world's richest nation (he cited Switzerland) and the poorest nation (Mozambique) as 400 to 1, versus around 5 to 1 when the Industrial Revolution began. The key role of knowledge in today's global economy has accelerated this gap, because knowledge tends to be concentrated in core countries and certain areas within them. *Knowledge capitalism* describes the commercial value of generating new ideas and converting them into products and services that consumers want (Leadbeater 1999).

Another key component of globalization is the *globalization of risk* (Smith and Doyle 2002). Ecological risks have multiplied. Hazards linked to industrial production or a cyber attack can spread quickly beyond their point of origin. Climate risks also have become globalized. Each consumer of fossil fuels makes his or her own individual contribution to global climate change, to which we now turn.

Got IT? Can you describe and explain major characteristics of globalization?

>> Global Climate Change

The year 2010 tied with 2005 as the hottest ever recorded by NASA's Goddard Institute for Space Studies (GISS), whose analysis covers 131 years. Earth's surface temperatures have risen about 1.48 degrees Fahrenheit (0.78 degrees Centigrade) since the early twentieth century. About two-thirds of this increase has been since 1978 (see "Global Temperature Change"). Scientific measurements confirm that global warming is not due to increased solar radiation. The causes are mainly *anthropogenic*—caused by humans and their activities. It stands to reason that 7 billion people, along with their animals, crops, and machines, have more of an impact on the environment than the 5 million or so hunter-gatherers who lived on our planet twelve thousand years ago—before the advent of food production.

greenhouse effect Warming from trapped atmospheric gases.

Because Earth's climate changes constantly, the key question becomes this: How much climate change is due to human activities versus natural climate variability? Most scientists agree that human activities play a major role in global climate change. How can the human factor not be significant given population growth and rapidly increasing use of fossil fuels, which produce greenhouse gases in the atmosphere?

The **greenhouse effect** is a natural phenomenon that keeps the Earth's surface warm. Without greenhouse gases—water vapor (H_2O), carbon dioxide (CO_2),

Global Temperature Change

Annual global mean surface air temperature (°Celsius)

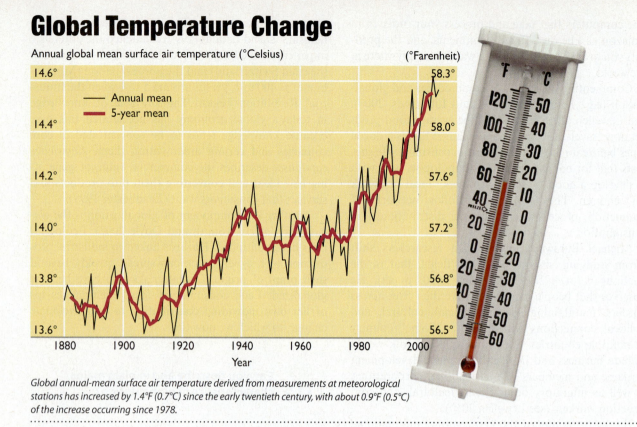

(°Farenheit)

Legend:
— Annual mean
— 5-year mean

Global annual-mean surface air temperature derived from measurements at meteorological stations has increased by 1.4°F (0.7°C) since the early twentieth century, with about 0.9°F (0.5°C) of the increase occurring since 1978.

Source: Goddard Institute for Space Studies, from "Understanding and Responding to Climate Change: Highlights of National Academies Reports," http://dels.nas.edu/basc/Climate-HIGH.pdf.

methane (CH_4), nitrous oxide (N_2O), halocarbons, and ozone (O_3)—life as we know it wouldn't exist. Like a greenhouse window, such gases allow sunlight to enter and then prevent heat from escaping the atmosphere. All those gases have increased since the Industrial Revolution. Today, the atmospheric concentration of greenhouse gases has reached its highest level in four hundred thousand years. It will continue to rise—as will global temperatures—without actions to slow it down (National Academies 2007).

How do the events in the (book and) movie The Lorax *(by Dr. Seuss) relate to global climate change?*

TABLE 13.1

What Heats, What Cools, the Earth?

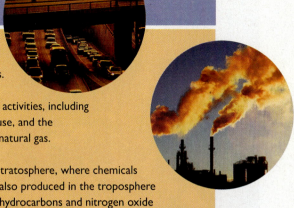

Warming	
Carbon dioxide (CO$_2$)	Has natural and human sources; levels increasing due to burning of fossil fuels.
Methane (CH$_4$)	Has risen due to an increase in human activities, including livestock raising, rice growing, landfill use, and the extraction, handling, and transport of natural gas.
Ozone (O$_3$)	Has natural sources, especially in the stratosphere, where chemicals have depleted the ozone layer; ozone also produced in the troposphere (lower part of the atmosphere) when hydrocarbons and nitrogen oxide pollutants react.
Nitrous oxide (N$_2$O)	Has been rising from agricultural and industrial sources.
Halocarbons	Include chlorofluorocarbons (CFCs), which remain from refrigerants in appliances made before CFC ban.
Aerosols	Some airborne particles and droplets warm the planet; black carbon particles (soot) produced when fossil fuels or vegetation are burned; generally have a warming effect by absorbing solar radiation.

Cooling	
Sea ice	Reflects sunlight back to space.
Tundra	Reflects sunlight back to space.
Aerosols	Some cool the planet; (SO$_4$) aerosols from burning fossil fuels reflect sunlight back to space.
Volcanic eruptions	Emit gaseous SO$_2$ which, once in the atmosphere, forms sulfate aerosol; and ash. Both reflect sunlight back to space.

Warming/Cooling	
Forests	Deforestation creates land areas that reflect more sunlight back to space (cooling); it also removes trees that absorb CO$_2$ (warming).

Scientists prefer the term **climate change** over *global warming*. The former term points out that, beyond rising temperatures, there have been changes in sea levels, precipitation, storms, and ecosystem effects. (Table 13.1 summarizes forces that work to warm and cool the Earth.) The precise effects of climate change on regional weather patterns have yet to be determined. Land areas are expected to warm more than oceans, with the greatest warming in higher latitudes, such as Canada, the northern United States, and northern Europe. Climate change may benefit these areas, offering milder winters and extended growing seasons. However, many more people worldwide probably will be harmed. Already we know that in the Arctic, temperatures have risen almost twice as much as the global average. Arctic landscapes and ecosystems are changing rapidly and perceptibly.

The U.S. National Academy of Sciences has issued several reports on climate change. Those reports are summarized in a downloadable brochure titled *Understanding and Responding to Climate Change*, 2008 edition (http://dels-old.nas .edu/dels/rpt_briefs/climate_change_2008_final.pdf), on which some of this discussion has been based (see also Crate and Nuttall 2008).

climate change Global warming, plus changing sea levels, precipitation, storms, and ecosystem effects.

Meeting global energy needs is the single greatest obstacle to slowing climate change. In the United States, about 80 percent of all energy used comes from fossil fuels. Worldwide, energy use continues to grow with economic and population expansion. China and India in particular are rapidly increasing their use of energy, mainly from fossil fuels, and consequently their emissions (see "Projected Emission of Greenhouse Gases. 2025"). Among the alternatives to fossil fuels are nuclear power and such renewable energy technologies as solar, wind, and biomass generators.

Many scientists see recent weather catastrophes as reflecting climate change. Such events might include the 2005 hurricane season featuring Katrina, the 2011 tsunami that devastated Japan, and 2012's Superstorm Sandy. Shown here, a tsunami survivor (young woman) cries amid debris in the devastated town of Natori, Miyagi prefecture, Japan. Are there weather events that you attribute to global climate change?

Projected Emission of Greenhouse Gases, 2025

Trillions of tons of carbon equivalent

	0	2	4	6	8	10	12	14	16

World — 57%
Developed — 35%
Developing — 84%

	0	.5	1	1.5	2	2.5	3

U.S. — 39%
China — 118%
EU — 19%
Former Soviet Union — 42%
India — 70%
Africa — 80%
Brazil — 68%
Japan — 26%
Mexico — 124%

■ 2000 emissions

● Projected emissions, 2025

50% Projected increase from 2000 levels

Greenhouse gasses do not include CO_2 from land use change.

In 2000, the United States was the largest emitter of CO_2 from fossil fuels. China is expected to take the lead by 2025.

Source: Baumert 2005.

CULTURE THINK

Critics of ethanol, made from corn, as an alternative fuel source, claim it raises food costs and that producing ethanol uses more energy than it yields. Others maintain that use of ethanol has significant environmental benefits. Do an online search. What's the current status of this debate?

>> Environmental Anthropology

Anthropology always has been concerned with how environmental forces influence humans and how human activities affect the biosphere and the Earth itself. The 1950s–1970s witnessed the emergence of an area of study known as *cultural ecology* or **ecological anthropology.** That field focused on how cultural beliefs and practices helped human populations adapt to their environments, and how people used elements of their culture to maintain their ecosystems.

Early ecological anthropologists showed that many indigenous groups did a reasonable job of managing their resources and preserving their ecosystems. Such groups had traditional ways of categorizing resources, regulating their use, and preserving the environment. An **ethnoecology** is any society's set of environmental practices and perceptions—that is, the society's cultural model of the environment and its relation to people and society. Indigenous ethnoecologies increasingly are being challenged, as migration, media, and

The world's most populous nations, China and India, are rapidly increasing their use of energy, mainly from fossil fuels, and consequently their emissions of CO_2. Pictured here are crowds of cars and buses moving slowly during a serious Beijing traffic jam.

commerce spread people, institutions, information, and technology. In the face of national and international incentives to exploit and degrade, ethnoecological systems that once preserved local and regional environments increasingly are ineffective or irrelevant.

Anthropologists routinely witness threats to the people they study and their environments. Among such threats are commercial logging, industrial pollution, and the imposition of external management systems on local ecosystems (see Johnston 2009). Today's ecological anthropology, aka *environmental anthropology,* attempts not only to understand but also to find solutions to environmental problems. Such problems must be tackled at the national and international levels (e.g., global warming). Even in remote places, ecosystem management now involves multiple levels. For example, author Lisa Gezon found that among the Antankarana of northern Madagascar (Gezon 2006), several levels of authority claim the right to use and regulate natural resources and local ecosystems. Actual or would-be regulators there include local communities, traditional leaders (the regional king or chief), provincial and national governments, and the WWF, the Worldwide Fund for Nature (formerly the World Wildlife Fund), an international nongovernmental organization (NGO). Local people, their landscapes, their ideas, their values, and their traditional management systems face attacks from all sides. Outsiders attempt to remake native landscapes and cultures in their own image. The aim of many agricultural development projects, for example, seems to be to make

CULTURE THINK

Do you do anything because it is "good for the globe"? What advice would you give to an environmentalist who wanted to convince people in your town or community to buy environmentally friendly goods, even if they cost more money?

ecological anthropology Study of cultural adaptations to environments.

ethnoecology A culture's set of environmental practices and perceptions.

the world as much like a midwestern American agricultural state as possible. Often there is an attempt to impose mechanized farming and nuclear family ownership, even though these institutions may be inappropriate in areas far removed from the midwestern United States. Development projects usually fail when they try to replace indigenous institutions with culturally alien concepts (Kottak 1990).

GLOBAL ASSAULTS ON LOCAL AUTONOMY

A clash of cultures related to environmental change may occur when development threatens indigenous peoples and their environments. A second clash of cultures related to environmental change may occur when external regulation aimed at conservation confronts indigenous peoples and their ethnoecologies. Like development projects, conservation schemes may ask people to change their ways in order to satisfy planners' goals rather than local goals. In places as different as Madagascar, Brazil, and the Pacific Northwest of the United States, people have been asked, told, or forced to abandon basic economic activities because to do so is good for "nature" or "the globe." "Good for the globe" doesn't play very well in Brazil, whose Amazon is a focus of international environmentalist attention. Brazilians complain that outsiders (e.g., Europeans and North Americans) promote "global needs" and "saving the Amazon" after having destroyed their own forests for economic growth. Well-intentioned conservation plans can be as insensitive as development schemes that promote radical changes without involving local people in planning

and carrying out the policies that affect them. When people are asked to give up the basis of their livelihood, they usually resist.

The spread of environmentalism may expose radically different notions about the "rights" and value of plants and animals versus humans. In Madagascar, many intellectuals and officials complain that foreigners seem more concerned about lemurs and other endangered species than about the people of Madagascar (the Malagasy). As a geographer there remarked to Conrad Kottak, "The next time you come to Madagascar, there'll be no more Malagasy. All the people will have starved to death, and a lemur will have to meet you at the airport." Most Malagasy perceive human poverty as a more pressing problem than animal and plant survival.

On the other hand, who can doubt that conservation, including the preservation of biodiversity, is a worthy goal? The challenge for applied ecological anthropology is to devise culturally appropriate strategies for achieving biodiversity conservation in the face of unrelenting population growth and commercial expansion. How does one get people to support conservation measures that may, in the short run at least, diminish their access to resources? Like development plans in general, the most effective conservation strategies pay attention to the needs and wishes of the local people.

DEFORESTATION

Deforestation is another expression of the globalization of risk. Forest loss can lead to increased greenhouse gas (CO_2) production, which contributes to global warming. Tropical forests contain at least half of Earth's species while covering just 6 percent of the planet's land surface. The ongoing destruction of tropical forests also is a major factor in the loss of global biodiversity.

A Xingu Indian man holds a seedling from ISA, a Brazilian NGO supported by several European donors. ISA manages a tree nursery for encouraging Indian communities to replant former rainforest habitats that were deforested.

Applied anthropology uses anthropological perspectives to identify and solve contemporary problems that affect humans. Deforestation is one such problem. Here women take part in a reforestation project in coastal Tanzania near Dar es Salaam.

Generations of anthropologists have studied how human economic activities (ancient and modern) affect the environment. Anthropologists know that food producers (farmers and herders) typically do more to degrade the environment than foragers do. Population increase and the need to expand farming caused deforestation in many parts of the ancient Middle East and Mesoamerica (see Hornborg and Crumley, eds. 2007). Even today, many farmers think of trees as giant weeds to be removed and replaced with productive fields.

Often, deforestation is demographically driven—caused by population pressure. For example, Madagascar's population is growing at a rate of 3 percent annually, doubling every generation. Population pressure leads to migration, including rural-urban migration. Madagascar's capital, Antananarivo, had one hundred thousand people in 1967. The population grew to about two million by 2007.

Urban growth promotes deforestation if city dwellers rely on fuel wood from the countryside, as is true in Madagascar. As forested watersheds disappear, crop productivity declines. Madagascar is known as the "great red island," after the color of its soil. On that island, the effects of soil erosion and water runoff are visible to the naked eye. From the look of its rivers, Madagascar appears to be bleeding to death. Increasing runoff of water no longer trapped by trees causes erosion of low-lying rice fields near swollen rivers as well as siltation in irrigation canals (Kottak 2007).

Causes of deforestation include demographic pressure (from births or immigration) on subsistence economies, commercial logging, road building, cash cropping, fuel wood needs associated with urban expansion, and clearing and burning associated with livestock and grazing. The fact that forest loss has several causes has a policy implication: Different deforestation scenarios require different conservation strategies.

What can be done? On this question applied anthropology weighs in (see Chapter 12), spurring policy makers to think about new conservation strategies. The traditional approach has been to restrict access to forested areas designated as parks, then employ park guards and punish violators. Modern strategies are more likely to consider the needs, wishes, and abilities of the people (often impoverished) living in and near the forest. Since effective conservation depends on the cooperation of the local people, their concerns must be addressed in devising conservation strategies.

Reasons to change behavior must make sense to local people (see Sillitoe 2007). In Madagascar, the economic value of the forest for agriculture (as an anti-erosion mechanism and reservoir of potential irrigation water) provides a much more powerful incentive against forest degradation than do such global goals as "preserving biodiversity." Most Malagasy have no idea that lemurs and other endemic species exist only in Madagascar. Nor would such knowledge provide much of an incentive for them to conserve the forests if doing so jeopardized their livelihoods.

To curb the global deforestation threat, we need conservation strategies that work. Laws and enforcement may help reduce commercially driven deforestation caused by burning and clear-cutting. But local people also use and abuse forested lands. A challenge for the environmentally oriented applied anthropologist is to find ways to make forest preservation attractive to local people and ensure their cooperation. Applied anthropologists must work to make "good for the globe" good for the people.

Following the destabilization of the government in Madagascar in 2009, illegal timber exploitation by foreign companies has increased significantly, even in protected areas.

Did You Know?

CULTURE THINK

People concerned with conservation debate which is more effective: putting up fences and hiring guards to keep people out of areas to be preserved, or engaging local people as partners and allowing limited use of endangered resources. What do you think would be the strengths and weaknesses of each approach?

Got IT? Can you identify ways in which anthropologists have been concerned with environmental issues, including global warming and deforestation?

>> Interethnic Contact

Since at least the 1920s anthropologists have investigated the changes—on both sides—that arise from contact between industrial and nonindustrial societies. Studies of "social change" and "acculturation" are abundant. British and American ethnographers, respectively, have used those terms to describe the same process. *Acculturation* refers to changes that result when groups come into continuous firsthand contact—changes in the cultural patterns of either or both groups (Redfield, Linton, and Herskovits 1936, p. 149). Acculturation differs from *diffusion,* or cultural borrowing, which can occur without firsthand contact. For example, most North Americans who eat hot dogs ("frankfurters") have never been to Frankfurt, Germany, nor have most North American Toyota owners or sushi eaters ever visited Japan. Although acculturation can be applied to any case of sustained cultural contact and change, the term most often has described **Westernization**—the influence of Western expansion on indigenous peoples and their cultures.

Westernization The influence of Western expansion on indigenous peoples and their cultures.

cultural imperialism The rapid spread or advance of one culture at the expense of others, or its imposition on other cultures, which it modifies, replaces, or destroys—usually because of differential economic or political influence.

Thus, local people who wear store-bought clothes, learn Indo-European languages, and otherwise adopt Western customs are called acculturated. Acculturation may be voluntary or forced, and there may be considerable resistance to the process.

Different degrees of destruction, domination, resistance, survival, adaptation, and modification of native cultures may follow interethnic contact. In the most destructive encounters, native and subordinate cultures face obliteration. In cases where contact between the indigenous societies and more powerful outsiders leads to destruction—a situation that is particularly characteristic of colonialist and expansionist eras—a "shock phase" often follows the initial encounter (Bodley 2008). Outsiders may attack or exploit the native people. Such exploitation may increase mortality, disrupt subsistence, fragment kin groups, damage social support systems, and inspire new religious movements, such as the cargo cults examined in the chapter "Religion" (Bodley 2008). During the shock phase, there may be civil repression backed by military force. Such factors may lead to the group's cultural collapse (*ethnocide*) or physical extinction (*genocide*).

ANTHROPOLOGY WORKS

After earning her bachelor's degree in anthropology, Stephanie Siegel completed two law enforcement academies and got a job working as a police officer in Washington, DC. She used what she had learned in her anthropology classes to communicate with people from different countries, as well as with tourists from all over the United States. On one occasion, she encountered a highly agitated Austrian man loitering near a government building. Stephanie, who speaks conversational German, was able to calm the man down and get him to explain his problem to her—he claimed to be seeing ghosts. Her supervising officer later remarked on her sensitivity and success in this case, saying that the man had refused to speak to the officers who had arrived first on the scene.

CULTURAL IMPERIALISM

Cultural imperialism refers to the spread or advance of one culture at the expense of others, or its imposition on other cultures, which it modifies, replaces, or destroys, usually because of differential economic or political influence. Thus, children in the French colonial empire learned French history, language, and culture from standard textbooks also used in France. Tahitians, Malagasy, Vietnamese, and Senegalese learned the French language by reciting from books about "our ancestors the Gauls."

To what extent do contemporary global forces propel cultural imperialism? Some commentators see the spread of modern technology, the media, and global brands as erasing cultural differences, as homogeneous products reach more people worldwide. Others note that certain innovations have allowed social groups (local cultures) to express themselves and to survive (Marcus and Fischer 1999). For example, modern radio, TV, digital media, and increasingly the Internet (e.g., YouTube) constantly bring local happenings to

In San Gimignano, Italy, boys and young men don medieval costumes and beat drums in a parade through the streets during one of the town's many pageants. Increasingly, local communities perform "traditional" ceremonies for TV and tourists.

the attention of a larger public. Susan Boyle's rendition of "I Dreamed a Dream" on a British TV show soon became an Internet sensation and made her a global star. Without YouTube, appreciation of Boyle's voice might have been confined to the United Kingdom. What have you watched lately on YouTube? Contemporary media play a role in stimulating and organizing local and community activities of many sorts. Think of ways in which this is done by YouTube, Facebook, and Twitter—global networks all.

In Brazil, local practices, celebrations, and performances have changed in the context of outside forces, including the mass media and tourism. In the town of Arembepe (Kottak 2006), TV coverage stimulated increased participation in a traditional annual performance, the Chegança. This is a fishermen's danceplay that reenacts the Portuguese discovery of Brazil. Arembepeiros have traveled to the state capital to perform the Chegança before television cameras, for a TV program featuring traditional performances from many rural communities, and cameras have come to Arembepe to record it.

In several towns along the Amazon River, annual folk ceremonies now are staged more lavishly for TV and video cameras. In the Amazon town of Parantíns, for example, boatloads of tourists arriving any time of year are shown a video recording of the town's annual Bumba Meu Boi festival. This is a costumed performance mimicking bullfighting, parts of which have been shown on national TV. This pattern, in which local communities preserve, revive, and intensify the scale of traditional ceremonies to perform for the media and tourists, is expanding. Nowadays, you can watch snippets of these annual events in Arembepe and Parantíns on YouTube!

The Brazilian mass media also have helped spread the popularity of holidays like Carnaval and Christmas (Kottak 1990a). TV has aided the national spread of Carnaval beyond its traditional

Resistance to commercial expansion and its effects: These Greenpeace environmental activists wearing tiger costumes are protesting against deforestation in front of a KFC outlet in Manila on June 2, 2012. They want KFC to ensure that it does not contribute to deforestation in Indonesia, home to the endangered Sumatran Tiger.

urban centers. Still, local reactions to the nationwide broadcasting of Carnaval and its trappings (elaborate parades, costumes, and frenzied dancing) are not simple or uniform responses to external stimuli.

Rather than direct adoption of Carnaval, local Brazilians respond in various ways. Often they don't take up Carnaval itself but modify their local festivities to fit Carnaval images. Others actively spurn Carnaval. One example is Arembepe, where Carnaval has never been important, probably because it occurs around the same time as the main local festival, which is held in February to honor Saint Francis of Assisi. In the past, villagers couldn't afford to celebrate both occasions. Now, not only do the people of Arembepe reject Carnaval; they are also increasingly hostile to their own main festival. Arembepeiros resent the fact that the Saint Francis festival has become "an outsiders' event," because it draws thousands of tourists to Arembepe each February. The villagers think that commercial interests and outsiders have appropriated Saint Francis.

In opposition to these trends, many Arembepeiros now say they like and participate more in the traditional June festivals honoring Saint John, Saint Peter, and Saint Anthony. In the past, these were observed on a much smaller scale than was the festival honoring Saint Francis. Arembepeiros celebrate them now with a new vigor and enthusiasm, as they react to outsiders and their celebrations, both televised and live. The national or the global only can become that if the local cooperates.

Got IT? Can you identify changes that arise from contact between industrial and nonindustrial societies, including diffusion, cultural imperialism, and those related to migration?

>> Making and Remaking Culture

In the process of globalization, people constantly make and remake culture as they evaluate, and assign their own meanings to, the information, images, and products they receive from outside. Those meanings reflect their cultural backgrounds and experiences.

indigenized Modified to fit the local culture.

INDIGENIZING POPULAR CULTURE

As global forces reach new communities, they are **indigenized**—modified to fit the local culture. This is true of cultural domains as different as fast food, music, movies, housing styles, science, terrorism, celebrations, and political ideas and institutions (Appadurai 1990; Fiske 1989). One classic example is how the movie *Rambo* (the first one in the series) was indigenized by Native Australians. Eric Michaels (1986, 1991) found *Rambo* to be popular among aborigines in the deserts of central Australia, who had manufactured their own meanings from the film. Their interpretation was very different from the one imagined by the movie's creators. The Native Australians saw Rambo as someone from the Third World battling white oppressors. This view expressed their resentment about white paternalism and inequitable race relations. The Native Australians also imagined that there were tribal ties and kin links between Rambo and the prisoners he was rescuing. Based on their experience, all this made sense. Native Australians are disproportionately represented

Chinese children dressed as Colonel Sanders at the opening of a KFC outlet in Beijing, China. Illustrating indigenization, KFCs in China have added egg tarts and other local favorites to the typical menu.

Foods offered in such chains as McDonald's, KFC, and Cinnabon (shown here) are now consumed internationally, though always indigenized somewhat to meet local expectations.

in Australia's jails, and their most likely savior would be someone with a personal link to them.

A GLOBAL SYSTEM OF IMAGES

All cultures express imagination—in dreams, fantasies, songs, myths, and stories. Today, however, more people in many more places imagine "a wider set of 'possible' lives than they ever did before. One important source of this change is the mass media [radio, TV, movies, video games, and the Internet], which present a rich, ever-changing store of possible lives" (Appadurai 1991, p. 197). The United States as a media center has been joined by Canada, Japan, Western Europe, Brazil, Mexico, Nigeria, Egypt, India, and Hong Kong.

Like print (see Anderson 1991), the electronic mass media can diffuse the cultures of different countries within (and sometimes beyond) their own boundaries, thus enhancing national cultural identity. For example, millions of Brazilians who used to be cut off (by geographic isolation or illiteracy) from urban, national, and international events and information now participate in a larger "mediascape" (Appadurai 1991) through the Internet and especially television (Kottak 1990a, 2009). Many Americans mistakenly think that American programs, when available abroad, inevitably triumph over local products. In fact, this usually doesn't happen when there is appealing local competition.

In Brazil the most popular network (TV Globo) relies heavily on its own productions, especially *telenovelas* (nightly serial melodramas often compared to American soap operas). Globo plays each night to the world's largest and most devoted audience (perhaps 80 million viewers throughout the nation and beyond—via satellite TV). The programs that attract this horde are made by Brazilians, for Brazilians. Thus, it is not the spread of North American culture through globalization, but a new form of pan-Brazilian national culture, that Globo is propagating. Illustrating once again the importance of cultural fit, as discussed in the previous chapter, we may generalize that programming that is culturally alien won't do very well anywhere if a quality local choice is available. Confirmation comes from many countries, including Japan, Mexico, India, and Nigeria, in all of which national productions are very popular.

The mass media also play a role in maintaining ethnic and national identities among people who lead transnational lives. Arabic-speaking Muslims, including migrants in several countries, follow the TV network Al Jazeera, based in Qatar, which helps reinforce ethnic and religious identities. As groups move, they can stay linked to one another and to their homeland through global media. **Diasporas** (People who have spread out from an original, ancestral homeland) have enlarged the markets for media, communication, brands, and travel services targeted at specific ethnic, national, or religious groups who now live in various parts of the world.

diaspora People who have spread out from an original, ancestral homeland.

A GLOBAL CULTURE OF CONSUMPTION

Besides the electronic media, another key transnational force is finance. Multinational corporations and other business interests look beyond national boundaries for places to invest and draw profits. As anthropologist Arjun Appadurai (1991, p. 194) puts it, "money, commodities, and persons unendingly chase each other around the world." Residents of many Latin American communities now depend on outside cash, remitted from international labor migration. Also, the U.S.

CULTURE THINK

One way that media help establish a national identity is to create the sense that those who are not citizens of that nation are different. What images of non-Western peoples do television and other media provide? Do you think these images represent those people fairly?

POP CULTURE

What's your favorite science fiction movie or TV show? What images of other planets stand out in your memory? Can you easily visualize *Star Wars*' Death Star, poor old Alderan, Yoda's misty world in the Dagoba system, the two suns of Tatooine? How about *Avatar*'s Pandora? Such movie images may be as familiar to you as those of real planets. Think, too, about how extraterrestrials have been portrayed in movies. On the one hand are *ET*'s harmless plant collectors and *Avatar*'s endangered Na'vi. On the other hand—and more typical—are Earth's would-be conquerors, as shown in *Independence Day, Starship Troopers, V,* and a hundred others. Still other films, most notably *The Day the Earth Stood Still* (either the 1951 or the 2008 version), feature omnipotent, omniscient guardians of interplanetary affairs. How, if at all, do the issues portrayed in such science fiction movies relate to the global issues examined in this chapter?

economy is increasingly influenced by foreign investment, especially from Britain, China, Canada, Germany, the Netherlands, and Japan (Rouse 1991). The American economy also has increased its dependence on foreign labor—through both the immigration of laborers and the export of jobs.

Globalization is driven by flows of people, technology, products, finance, information, images, and ideology (Appadurai 1990, 2001). Business, technology, and the media have increased the craving for commodities and images throughout the world (Gottdiener, ed. 2000). This has forced nation-states to accept a global culture of consumption. Almost everyone today participates in this culture. Few people have never seen a T-shirt advertising a Western product. American and English rock stars' recordings blast through the streets of Rio de Janeiro, while taxi drivers from Toronto to Madagascar play Brazilian music. Peasants and tribal people participate in the global economy not only because they have been hooked on cash, but also because their products and images are appropriated by world capitalism (Root 1996). They are commercialized by others (like the Quileute nation in the *Twilight* series). Furthermore, indigenous peoples also market their own images and products, through outlets like Cultural Survival (see Mathews 2000).

[Got IT?] Can you evaluate ways that people assign their own meanings to cultural influences they receive from the outside?

>> People in Motion

Arjun Appadurai (1990, p. 1) characterizes today's globalized world as a "translocal" "interactive system" that is "strikingly new." People appear to travel more than ever. Routinely crossing national borders are tourists, migrants, laborers, refugees, pilgrims, proselytizers, businesspeople, development workers, employees of nongovernmental organizations, politicians, terrorists, soldiers, sports figures, and media-borne images.

In previous chapters, we saw that foragers and herders are typically seminomadic or nomadic. Today, the scale of human movement has expanded dramatically. So important is transnational migration that many Mexican villagers find "their most important kin and friends are as likely to be living hundreds or thousands of miles away as immediately around them" (Rouse 1991). Most migrants maintain their ties with their native land (phoning, emailing, visiting, sending money, watching "ethnic TV"). In a sense, they live multilocally—in different places at once. Dominicans in New York City, for example, have been characterized as living "between two islands": Manhattan and the Dominican Republic (Grasmuck and Pessar 1991). Many Dominicans—like migrants from other countries—migrate to the United States temporarily, seeking cash to transform their lifestyles when they return to the Caribbean.

With so many people "in motion," the unit of anthropological study expands from the local community to the diaspora. As anthropologists, we increasingly follow descendants of the villages we have studied as they move from rural to urban areas and across national boundaries.

Postmodernity describes today's world in flux, with people on the move who have learned to manage multiple identities depending on place and context. In its most general sense, **postmodern** refers to the blurring and breakdown of established rules, standards, categories, distinctions, and boundaries. The word is taken from **postmodernism**—a style and movement in architecture that began in the 1970s and followed modernism. Postmodern architecture rejected the rules, geometric order, and austerity of modernism. Modernist buildings were expected to have a clear and functional design. Postmodern design is "messier" and more playful. It draws on a diversity of styles from different times and places—including popular, ethnic, and non-Western cultures. Postmodernism extends "value" well beyond classic, elite, and Western cultural forms. *Postmodern* is now used to describe comparable developments in music, literature, and visual art. From this origin, *postmodernity* describes a world in which traditional standards, contrasts, groups, boundaries, and identities are opening up, reaching out, and breaking down.

New kinds of political and ethnic units have emerged. In some cases, cultures and ethnic groups have banded together in larger associations. Examples include a growing pan-Native American identity (Nagel 1996) and an international pantribal movement. Thus, in June 1992, the World Conference of Indigenous Peoples met in Rio de Janeiro concurrently with UNCED (the United Nations Conference on the Environment and Development). Along with diplomats, journalists, and environmentalists came three hundred representatives of the tribal diversity that survives in the modern world—from Lapland to Mali (Brooke 1992; see also Maybury-Lewis 2002). The meeting itself was a global forum, sponsored by the United Nations, perhaps the closest thing Earth has to a planetary council.

Got IT? Can you explain the effects of globalization on cultural boundaries and distinctions?

>> Indigenous Peoples

The term *indigenous people* entered international law with the creation in 1982 of the United Nations Working Group on Indigenous Populations (WGIP). This group, which meets annually, has members from six continents. The draft of the Declaration of Indigenous Rights, produced by the WGIP in 1989, was accepted by the UN for discussion in 1993. Convention 169, an ILO (International Labor Organization) document that supports cultural diversity and indigenous empowerment, was approved in 1989. Such documents, along with the work of the WGIP, have influenced governments, NGOs, and international agencies to adopt policies aimed at benefiting indigenous peoples. Social movements worldwide now use the term "indigenous people" as a self-identifying label in their quests for social, cultural, and political rights (Brower and Johnston 2007; de la Peña 2005).

postmodernity Condition of a world in flux, with people on the move, in which established groups, boundaries, identities, contrasts, and standards are reaching out and breaking down.

postmodern In its most general sense, describes the blurring and breakdown of established canons (rules, standards), categories, distinctions, and boundaries.

postmodernism A style and movement in architecture that followed modernism. Compared with modernism, it is less geometric, less functional, less austere, more playful, and more willing to include elements from diverse times and cultures; *postmodern* now describes comparable developments in music, literature, and visual art.

In Spanish-speaking Latin America, social scientists and politicians now favor the term *indígena* (indigenous person) over *indio* (Indian). The latter is a colonial term that European conquerors used for Native Americans, whose situation did not necessarily improve after Latin American nations gained independence from Spain and Portugal, mostly by the 1820s. For the white and *mestizo* (mixed) elites of the new nations, *indios* and their lifestyle seemed alien to (European) civilization (de la Peña 2005).

Until the mid- to late 1980s, Latin American public policy emphasized assimilation. Indians were associated with a romanticized past, but marginalized in the present, except for museums, tourism, and folkloric events. Indigenous Bolivians and Peruvians were encouraged to self-identify as *campesinos* (peasants). The last thirty years have witnessed a dramatic shift from assimilation—*mestizaje*—to cultural difference. In Ecuador, groups seen previously as Quichua-speaking peasants are classified now as indigenous communities with their own territories. Brazil has recognized thirty new indigenous communities in the northeast, a region previously seen as having lost its native population. Guatemala, Nicaragua, Brazil, Colombia, Mexico, Paraguay, Ecuador, Argentina, Bolivia, Peru, and Venezuela now are officially multicultural (Jackson and Warren 2005). Several national constitutions recognize the rights of indigenous peoples to cultural distinctiveness and political representation. In Colombia, indigenous territories have the same benefits as any local government (de la Peña 2005).

Mary Simat, with the Massi Women for Education and Economic Development from Kenya, testifies at the Indigenous Peoples' Global Summit on Climate Change in Anchorage, Alaska, in April 2009. The five-day United Nations–affiliated conference attracted about four hundred people from eighty nations.

The indigenous rights movement exists in the context of globalization, including transnational movements focusing on human rights, women's rights, and environmentalism. Transnational organizations have helped indigenous peoples to influence legislation. Since the 1980s there has been a general shift in Latin America from authoritarian to democratic rule. Still, inequality and discrimination persist, and there has been resistance

essentialism The process of viewing an identity as established, real, and frozen, so as to hide the historical processes and politics within which that identity developed.

to indigenous mobilization, including assassinations of leaders and their supporters. Guatemala, Peru, and Colombia have witnessed severe repression. There have been thousands of indigenous deaths, refugees, and internally displaced persons (Jackson and Warren 2005).

Ceuppens and Geschiere (2005) explore a recent upsurge, in multiple world areas, of the notion of *autochthony* (being native to, or formed, in the place where found), with an implicit call for excluding strangers. The terms *autochthony* and *indigenous* both go back to classical Greek history, with similar implications. Autochthony refers to self and soil. "Indigenous" literally means "born inside," with the connotation in classical Greek of being born "inside the house." Both notions stress the need to safeguard ancestral lands (patrimony) from strangers, along with the rights of first-comers to special rights and protection versus later immigrants—legal or illegal (Ceuppens and Geschiere 2005).

During the 1990s, autochthony became an issue in many parts of Africa, inspiring violent efforts to exclude (European and Asian) "strangers." Simultaneously, autochthony became a key notion in debates about immigration and multiculturalism in Europe. European majority groups have claimed the label *autochthon*. This term highlights the prominence that the exclusion of strangers has assumed in day-to-day politics worldwide (Ceuppens and Geschiere 2005). One familiar example is the United States, as represented in recent debates over illegal immigration.

Representatives of indigenous tribes and environmental activists carry out a demonstration, in Sao Paulo, on August 20, 2011, against the construction of Belo Monte dam on the Xingu River, a tributary of the Amazon in the northeastearn Brazilian state of Pará.

IDENTITY IN INDIGENOUS POLITICS

Essentialism describes the process of viewing an identity as established, real, and frozen, so as to hide the historical processes and politics within which that identity developed. Identities, emphatically, are not fixed. We saw in the chapter "Ethnicity and Race" that identities can be fluid and multiple. People seize on particular, sometimes competing, self-labels and identities. Some Peruvian groups, for instance, self-identify as mestizos but still see themselves as indigenous. Identity is a fluid, dynamic process, and there are multiple ways of being indigenous. Neither speaking an indigenous language nor wearing "native" clothing is required. Identities are asserted at particular times and places by particular individuals and groups and after various kinds of negotiations. Indigenous identity coexists with, and must be managed in the context of, other identity components, including religion, race, and gender. Identities always must be seen as (1) potentially plural, (2) emerging through a specific process, (3) ways of being someone or something in particular times and places (Jackson and Warren 2005).

world. Anthropology teaches us that the adaptive responses of humans can be more flexible than those of other species because our main adaptive means are sociocultural. However, the cultural forms, institutions, values, and customs of the past always influence subsequent adaptation, producing continued diversity and giving a certain uniqueness to the actions and reactions of different groups. With our knowledge and our awareness of our professional responsibilities, let us work to keep anthropology, the study of humankind, the most humanistic of all the sciences.

Got IT? Can you describe how the term "indigenous" has become a politically important identity marker?

Got IT? Can you identify anthropological approaches that are crucial to an understanding of globalization?

>> The Continuance of Diversity

In our globalizing world, anthropology has a crucial role to play, by promoting a more people-centered vision of social change, one that respects the value of human biological and cultural diversity. The existence of anthropology is itself a tribute to the continuing need to understand similarities and differences among human beings throughout the

FOR REVIEW

EXPERIENCING CULTURE

TO ACCESS THESE VIDEOS ON YOUR COMPUTER, VISIT

www.mhhe.com/gezonqr

13-1

13-2

13-3

I. **How is global climate change related to globalization, and how can anthropologists study both processes, along with other environmental threats?**

- Globalization has two meanings: as fact (the worldwide spread and connectedness of production, communication, and technologies) and as ideology and policy (efforts by international financial powers to create a global free market for goods and services). Modern ecological anthropology focuses on understanding and finding solutions to environmental threats that must be tackled at the national and international as well as local levels. Global climate change includes rising temperatures and changes in sea levels, precipitation, storms, and ecosystems. Human population growth and the increasing use of fossil fuels contribute to these changes. Global forces challenge indigenous peoples; outside environmental regulation confronts their ethnoecologies. Anthropologists believe that the most effective conservation strategies are those that pay attention to the needs and wishes of local people.

II. **What is cultural imperialism, and what forces work to favor and oppose it?**

- Cultural imperialism is the spread or advance of one culture at the expense of others, or its imposition on other cultures, which it modifies, replaces, or destroys. Modern mass media are alternately viewed as agents of cultural imperialism and means for allowing local cultures to express themselves. Electronic mass media can reinforce national and ethnic identities. Cultural forces entering new societies from world centers are often modified to fit the local culture. Business, technology, and mass media have increased the craving for commodities and images worldwide. Peasants and tribal peoples participate in the world system in part because world capitalism appropriates their products and images, but indigenous peoples may market their own images and products to the world.

III. **What are indigenous peoples, and how and why has their importance increased in recent years?**

- Social movements worldwide use the term *indigenous people* as a self-identifying political label that is based on past oppression but now signals a quest for social, cultural, and political rights. International law and the work of the UN's Working Group on Indigenous Populations have influenced governments, nongovernmental organizations, and international agencies to adopt policies aimed at recognizing and benefiting indigenous peoples. The indigenous rights movement exists in the global context of transnational movements that focus on human rights, women's rights, and environmentalism. Various world areas have seen an upsurge in the notion of *autochthony*, with an implicit call from native peoples to exclude strangers. Indigenous identities are fluid, multiple, and sometimes competing, asserted at particular times and places.

Pop Quiz

Multiple Choice:

1. Scientific measurements confirm that global warming isn't caused by increased solar radiation. Rather, the causes are mainly anthropogenic. This means that
   a. Humans and their activities cause global warming.
   b. The causes are indigenized.
   c. Global warming caused by normal climate fluctuations affects humans.
   d. The causes are social constructions used for political purposes.

2. Which of the following is false about changes arising from contact between local cultures and more powerful outsiders?
   a. Changes occur on just one side of the contact.
   b. Westernization is a form of acculturation involving the influence of Western expansion on indigenous peoples and their cultures.
   c. Interethnic contact may result in destruction, domination, resistance, adaptation, and modification of native cultures.
   d. Religious proselytizing can promote ethnocide.

3. The spread or advance of one culture at the expense of others, or its imposition on other cultures, which it modifies, replaces, or destroys, is most accurately called
   a. Cultural relativism
   b. Westernization
   c. Cultural imperialism
   d. Acculturation

4. When forces from world centers are modified to fit the local culture, this process is called
   a. Religious proselytizing
   b. Indigenization
   c. Acculturation
   d. Assimilation

5. Which of the following statements about mass media is true?
   a. The United States is unique among media centers in offering varied images of possible lives.
   b. Media images and ideas tend to be too general and "top-down" to help create or spread national and ethnic identities.
   c. American television programs don't necessarily triumph over local competition.
   d. Mass media can work to maintain ethnic identities only when people live inside their nation of origin.

6. In Latin America, which of the following would be an exception to the drive by indigenous peoples for indigenous identity and empowerment?
   a. Favoring of the term *indígena* over *indio* (Indian)
   b. A shift in policy from cultural difference to assimilation
   c. National constitutions' recognition of the rights of indigenous peoples to political representation
   d. Participation in transnational indigenous rights movements

Fill in the Blank:

1. Scientists prefer the term _____ to *global warming*. The former term points out that, beyond rising temperature, there have been changes in sea levels, precipitation, storms, and ecosystem effects.

2. An _____ is any society's set of environmental practices and perceptions—that is, its cultural model of the environment and its relation to people and society.

3. _____ refers to changes that result when groups come into continuous firsthand contact. _____, however, can occur without firsthand contact.

4. With so many people in motion in today's world, the unit of anthropological study expands from the local community to the _____, which is the term for the offspring of an area who have spread to many lands.

1. (a), 2. (a), 3. (c), 4. (b), 5. (c), 6. (b)

1. *climate change;* 2. *ethnoecology;* 3. Acculturation, Diffusion; 4. diaspora

A

acculturation   The exchange of cultural features that results when groups come into continuous firsthand contact; the original cultural patterns of either or both groups may be altered, but the groups remain distinct.

achieved status   Social status that comes through talents, actions, efforts, activities, and accomplishments (e.g., big man, convicted felon).

adaptation   The process by which organisms cope with environmental stresses.

agriculture   Nonindustrial system of plant cultivation characterized by continuous and intensive use of land and labor.

anthropology   The study of the human species and its immediate ancestors.

anthropology and education   Anthropological research in classrooms, homes, and neighborhoods, viewing students as total cultural creatures whose enculturation and attitudes toward education belong to a larger context that includes family, peers, and society.

applied anthropology   The application of anthropological data, perspectives, theory, and methods to identify, assess, and solve contemporary social problems.

archaeological anthropology   The branch of anthropology, commonly known as "archaeology," that reconstructs, describes, and interprets human behavior and cultural patterns through material remains; best known for the study of prehistory.

ascribed status   Social status that people have little or no choice about occupying (e.g., race, gender).

assimilation   The process of change that a minority group may experience when it moves to a country where another culture dominates; the minority is incorporated into the dominant culture to the point that it no longer exists as a separate cultural unit.

B

band   Basic unit of social organization among foragers. A band includes fewer than 100 people; it often splits up seasonally.

big man   Figure often found among tribal horticulturalists and pastoralists. The big man occupies no office but creates his reputation through entrepreneurship and generosity to others. Neither his wealth nor his position passes to his heirs.

biological anthropology   Also called *physical anthropology,* the branch of anthropology that studies human biological diversity in time and space—for instance, hominid evolution, human genetics, human biological adaptation; also includes primatology (behavior and evolution of monkeys and apes).

C

chiefdom   Form of sociopolitical organization intermediate between the tribe and the

state; kin-based with differential access to resources and a permanent political structure.

clan   Unilineal descent group based on stipulated descent.

climate change   Global warming, plus changing sea levels, precipitation, storms, and ecosystem effects.

complex societies   Nations; large and populous, with social stratification and central governments.

conflict resolution   The means by which disputes are socially regulated and settled; found in all societies, but the resolution methods tend to be more formal and effective in states than in nonstates.

core values   Key, basic, or central values that integrate a culture and help distinguish it from others.

correlation   An association between two or more variables such that when one changes (varies), the other(s) also change(s) (covaries); for example, temperature and sweating.

cultural anthropology   The study of human society and culture; describes, analyzes, interprets, and explains social and cultural similarities and differences.

cultural colonialism   Within a nation or empire, domination by one ethnic group or nationality and its culture/ideology over others—e.g., the dominance of Russian people, language, and culture in the former Soviet Union.

cultural consultant   Someone the ethnographer gets to know in the field, who teaches him or her about their society and culture (also called "informant").

cultural imperialism   The rapid spread or advance of one culture at the expense of others, or its imposition on other cultures, which it modifies, replaces, or destroys—usually because of differential economic or political influence.

cultural relativism   The position that the values and standards of cultures differ and deserve respect. Anthropology is characterized by methodological rather than moral relativism: In order to understand another culture fully, anthropologists try to understand its members' beliefs and motivations. Methodological relativism does not preclude making moral judgments or taking action.

cultural resource management (CRM)   The branch of applied archaeology aimed at preserving sites threatened by dams, highways, and other projects.

cultural rights   Doctrine that certain rights are vested not in individuals but in identifiable groups, such as religious and ethnic minorities and indigenous societies.

culture   Traditions and customs that govern behavior and beliefs; distinctly human; transmitted through learning.

curer   Specialized role acquired through a culturally appropriate process of selection, training, certification, and acquisition of a professional image; the curer is consulted by patients, who believe in his or her special powers, and receives some form of special consideration; a cultural universal.

D

descent   Rule assigning social identity on the basis of some aspect of one's ancestry.

descent group   A permanent social unit whose members claim common ancestry; fundamental to tribal society.

development anthropology   The branch of applied anthropology that focuses on social issues in, and the cultural dimension of, economic development.

diaspora   People who have spread out from an original, ancestral homeland.

differential access   Unequal access to resources; basic attribute of chiefdoms and states. *Superordinates* have favored access to such resources, while the access of *subordinates* is limited by superordinates.

diffusion   Borrowing between cultures either directly or through intermediaries.

discrimination   Policies and practices that harm a group and its members.

disease   An *etic*, or scientifically identified, health threat caused by a bacterium, virus, fungus, parasite, or other pathogen.

domestic–public dichotomy   Contrast between women's role in the home and men's role in public life, with a corresponding social devaluation of women's work and worth.

dowry   A marital exchange in which the wife's group provides substantial gifts to the husband's family.

E

ecological anthropology   Study of cultural adaptations to environments.

economy   A population's system of production, distribution, and consumption of resources.

emic   The research strategy that focuses on native explanations and criteria of significance.

enculturation   The social process by which culture is learned and transmitted across the generations.

endogamy   Marriage between people of the same social group.

equity, increased   A reduction in absolute poverty and a fairer (more even) distribution of wealth.

ethnic group   Group distinguished by cultural similarities (shared among members of that group) and differences (between that group and others); ethnic group members are thought to share beliefs, values, habits, customs, and norms, and a common language, religion, history, geography, kinship, and/or race.

ethnicity   Identification with, and feeling part of, an ethnic group, and exclusion from certain other groups because of this affiliation.

ethnocentrism   The tendency to view one's own culture as best and to judge the behavior and beliefs of culturally different people by one's own standards.

ethnocide   Destruction by a dominant group of the culture of an ethnic group.

ethnoecology   A culture's set of environmental practices and perceptions.

ethnography   Fieldwork in a particular culture.

ethnology   The theoretical, comparative study of society and culture; compares cultures in time and space.

etic   The research strategy that emphasizes the observer's rather than the natives' explanations, categories, and criteria of significance.

exogamy   Mating or marriage outside one's kin group; a cultural universal.

extended family household   Expanded household including three or more generations.

F

family   A group of people (e.g., parents, children, siblings, grandparents, grandchildren, uncles, aunts, nephews, nieces, cousins, spouses, siblings-in-law, parents-in-law, children-in-law) who are considered to be related in some way, such as by "blood" (common ancestry or descent) or marriage.

family of orientation   Nuclear family in which one is born and grows up.

family of procreation   Nuclear family established when one marries and has children.

fiscal   Pertaining to finances and taxation.

food production   Plant cultivation and animal domestication.

G

gender roles   The tasks and activities that a culture assigns to each sex.

gender stereotypes   Oversimplified but strongly held ideas about the characteristics of males and females.

gender stratification   Unequal distribution of rewards (socially valued resources, power, prestige, and personal freedom) between men and women, reflecting their different positions in a social hierarchy.

genealogical method   Procedures by which ethnographers discover and record connections of kinship, descent, and marriage, using diagrams and symbols.

general anthropology   The field of anthropology as a whole, consisting of cultural, archaeological, biological, and linguistic anthropology.

generality   Culture pattern or trait that exists in some but not all societies.

genocide   Policies aimed at, and/or resulting in, the physical extinction (through mass murder) of a people perceived as a racial group, that is, as sharing defining physical, genetic, or other biological characteristics.

globalization   A set of processes, including *diffusion, migration,* and *acculturation,* that promote change in today's interlinked world.

greenhouse effect   Warming from trapped atmospheric gases.

H

health care systems   Beliefs, customs, and specialists concerned with ensuring health and preventing and curing illness; a cultural universal.

hegemony   The internalization of a dominant ideology.

holistic   Interested in the whole of the human condition past, present, and future; biology, society, language, and culture.

hominids   Members of the zoological family that includes fossil and living humans, chimps, and gorillas.

hominins   Members of the evolutionary line leading to and including modern humans, as distinct from chimps and gorillas.

horticulture   Nonindustrial system of plant cultivation in which plots lie fallow for varying lengths of time.

human rights   Doctrine that invokes a realm of justice and morality beyond and superior to particular countries, cultures, and religions. Human rights, usually seen as vested in individuals, include the right to speak freely, to hold religious beliefs without persecution, and not to be enslaved.

hypodescent   A rule that automatically places the children of a union or mating between members of different socioeconomic groups in the less privileged group.

I

illness   An *emic* condition of poor health felt by the individual.

incest   Sexual relations with a close relative.

independent invention   Development of the same culture trait or pattern in separate cultures as a result of comparable needs and circumstances.

indigenized   Modified to fit the local culture.

informed consent   An agreement sought by ethnographers from community members to take part in research.

intellectual property rights (IPR)   Each society's cultural base—its core beliefs and principles. IPR is claimed as a group right—a cultural right, allowing indigenous groups to control who may know and use their collective knowledge and its applications.

international culture   Cultural traditions that extend beyond national boundaries.

intersex   Pertaining to a group of conditions reflecting a discrepancy between the external and the internal genitals.

interview schedule   Ethnographic tool for structuring a formal interview. A prepared form that guides interviews with households or individuals being compared systematically. This contrasts with a questionnaire because the researcher has personal contact and records people's answers.

K

key cultural consultant   An expert on a particular aspect of local life who helps the ethnographer understand that aspect.

L

law   A legal code, including trial and enforcement; characteristic of state-organized societies.

life history   Of a cultural consultant; provides a personal cultural portrait of existence or change in a culture.

lineage   Unilineal descent group based on demonstrated descent.

linguistic anthropology   The branch of anthropology that studies linguistic variation in time and space, including interrelations between language and culture; includes historical linguistics and sociolinguistics.

lobola   A customary gift before, at, or after marriage from the husband and his kin to the wife and her kin.

longitudinal research   Long-term study of a community, society, culture, or other unit, usually based on repeated visits.

M

majority groups   Superordinate, dominant, or controlling groups in a social–political hierarchy.

market principle   Profit-oriented principle of exchange that dominates in states, particularly industrial states. Goods and services are bought and sold, and values are determined by supply and demand.

matriarchy   A political system in which women play a much more prominent role than men do in social and political organization.

matrilineal descent   Unilineal descent rule in which people join the mother's group automatically at birth and stay members throughout life.

matrilocality   Customary residence with the wife's relatives after marriage, so that children grow up in their mother's community.

means (or factors) of production   Land, labor, technology, and capital—major productive resources.

medical anthropology   Discipline that unites biological and cultural anthropologists in the study of disease, health problems, health care systems, and theories about illness in different cultures and ethnic groups.

minority groups   Subordinate groups in a social–political hierarchy, with inferior power and less secure access to resources than majority groups have.

mode of production   Way of organizing production—a set of social relations through which labor is deployed to wrest energy from nature by means of tools, skills, and knowledge.

multiculturalism   The view of cultural diversity in a country as something good and desirable; a multicultural society socializes individuals not only into the dominant (national) culture, but also into an ethnic culture.

N

national culture   Cultural experiences, beliefs, learned behavior patterns, and values shared by citizens of the same nation.

nationalities   Ethnic groups that once had, or wish to have or regain, autonomous political status (their own country).

nation-state   An autonomous political entity, a country like the United States or Canada. See also *state*.

neolocality   Postmarital residence pattern in which a couple establishes a new place of residence rather than living with or near either set of parents.

nomadism, pastoral   Movement throughout the year by the whole pastoral group (men, women, and children) with their animals. More generally, such constant movement in pursuit of strategic resources.

O

office   Permanent political position.

overinnovation   Characteristic of development projects that require major changes in people's daily lives, especially ones that interfere with customary subsistence pursuits.

P

pantribal sodality   A nonkin-based group that exists throughout a tribe, spanning several villages.

participant observation   A characteristic ethnographic technique; taking part in the events one is observing, describing, and analyzing.

particularity   Distinctive or unique culture trait, pattern, or integration.

pastoralists   People who use a food-producing strategy of adaptation based on caring for herds of domesticated animals.

patriarchy   Political system ruled by men in which women have inferior social and political status, including fewer basic human rights.

patrilineal descent   Unilineal descent rule in which people join the father's group automatically at birth and stay members throughout life.

patrilineal–patrilocal complex   An interrelated constellation of patrilineality, patrilocality, warfare, and male supremacy.

patrilocality   Customary residence with the husband's relatives after marriage, so that children grow up in their father's community.

peasant   Small-scale agriculturist living in a state, with rent fund obligations.

phenotype   An organism's evident traits, its "manifest biology"—anatomy and physiology.

plural marriage   Marriage of a man to two or more women (polygyny) or marriage of a woman to two or more men (polyandry)—at the same time; see also *polygamy*.

plural society   A society that combines ethnic contrasts, ecological specialization (i.e., use of different environmental resources by each ethnic group), and the economic interdependence of those groups.

polyandry   Variety of plural marriage in which a woman has more than one husband.

polygamy   Marriage with three or more spouses, at the same time; see also *plural marriage*.

polygyny   Variety of plural marriage in which a man has more than one wife.

postmodern   In its most general sense, describes the blurring and breakdown of established canons (rules, standards), categories, distinctions, and boundaries.

postmodernism   A style and movement in architecture that followed modernism. Compared with modernism, it is less geometric, less functional, less austere, more playful, and more willing to include elements from diverse times and cultures; *postmodern* now describes comparable developments in music, literature, and visual art.

postmodernity   Condition of a world in flux, with people on the move, in which established groups, boundaries, identities, contrasts, and standards are reaching out and breaking down.

potlatch   Competitive feast among Indians on the North Pacific Coast of North America.

power   The ability to exercise one's will over others—to do what one wants; the basis of political status.

prejudice   Devaluing (looking down on) a group because of its assumed behavior, values, capabilities, or attributes.

prestige   Esteem, respect, or approval for acts, deeds, or qualities considered exemplary.

primates   Members of the zoological order that includes humans, apes, monkeys, and prosimians (e.g., lemurs).

R

racial classification   The attempt to assign humans to discrete categories (purportedly) based on common ancestry.

racism   Discrimination against an ethnic group assumed to have a biological basis.

reciprocity   One of the three principles of exchange. Governs exchange between social equals; major exchange mode in band and tribal societies.

reciprocity continuum   Regarding exchanges, a range running from generalized reciprocity (closely related/deferred return) through balanced reciprocity, to negative reciprocity (strangers/immediate return).

redistribution Flow of goods into the center, then back out; characteristic of chiefdoms, many archaic states, and some states with managed economies.

refugees People who have been forced (involuntary refugees) or who have chosen (voluntary refugees) to flee a country, to escape persecution or war.

S

sample A smaller study group chosen to represent a larger population.

science A systematic field of study or body of knowledge that aims, through experiment, observation, and deduction, to produce reliable explanations of phenomena, with reference to the material and physical world.

scientific medicine A health care system based on scientific knowledge and procedures, encompassing such fields as pathology, microbiology, biochemistry, surgery, diagnostic technology, and applications.

sexual dimorphism Marked differences, such as in height and weight, in male and female biology besides the contrasts in breasts and genitals.

sexual orientation A person's habitual sexual attraction to, and activities with, persons of the opposite sex (heterosexuality), the same sex (homosexuality), or both sexes (bisexuality); also, the lack of sexual attraction (asexuality).

social control Fields of the social system that maintain norms and resolve conflict.

sociopolitical typology Classification scheme based on the scale and complexity of social organization and the effectiveness of political regulation; includes band, tribe, chiefdom, and state.

state (nation-state) Complex sociopolitical system that administers a territory and populace with substantial contrasts in occupation, wealth, prestige, and power. An independent, centrally organized political unit, a government.

status Any position that determines where someone fits in society; may be ascribed or achieved.

stereotypes Fixed ideas—often unfavorable—about what members of a group are like.

stratification Characteristic of a system with socioeconomic strata.

subcultures Different cultural symbol-based traditions associated with subgroups in the same complex society.

subordinate The lower, or underprivileged, group in a stratified system.

superordinate The higher, or privileged, group in a stratified system.

survey research Characteristic research procedure among social scientists other than anthropologists, which studies society through sampling, statistical analysis, and impersonal data collection.

symbol Something, verbal or nonverbal, that arbitrarily and by convention stands for something else, with which it has no necessary or natural connection.

T

transgender A category of varied individuals whose gender identity contradicts their biological sex at birth and the gender identity that society assigned to them in infancy.

transhumance One of two variants of pastoralism; part of the population moves seasonally with the herds while the other part remains in home villages.

tribe Form of sociopolitical organization usually based on horticulture or pastoralism. Socioeconomic stratification and centralized rule are absent in tribes, and there is no means of enforcing political decisions.

U

underdifferentiation Planning fallacy of viewing less developed countries as an undifferentiated group; ignoring cultural diversity and adopting a uniform approach (often ethnocentric) for very different types of project beneficiaries.

unilineal descent Matrilineal or patrilineal descent.

universal Something that exists in every culture.

urban anthropology The anthropological study of life in and around world cities, including the study of urban social problems, differences between urban and other environments, and adaptation to city life.

V

variables Attributes (e.g., sex, age, height, weight) that differ from one person or case to the next.

village head Leadership position in a village (as among the Yanomami, where the head is always a man); has limited authority; leads by example and persuasion.

W

wealth All of a person's material assets, including income, land, and other types of property; the basis of economic status.

Westernization The acculturation influence of European cultures on tribal societies.

Abelmann, N., and J. Lie. 1995. *Blue Dreams: Korean Americans and the Los Angeles Riots.* Cambridge, MA: Harvard University Press.

Adherents.com. 2002. Major Religions of the World Ranked by Number of Adherents. http://www.adherents.com/Religions_By_Adherents.html.

Ahmed, A. S. 2004. *Postmodernism and Islam: Predicament and Promise.* Rev. ed. New York: Routledge.

Allegretto, S. A. 2011. The State of Working America's Wealth, Briefing Paper no. 292, Economic Policy Institute, March 23. http://www.epi.org/page/-/BriefingPaper292.pdf.

Amadiume, I. 1987. *Male Daughters, Female Husbands.* Atlantic Highlands, NJ: Zed.

———. 2007. American Anthropological Association Executive Board Statement on the Human Terrain System Project. http://www.aaanet.org/about/Policies/statements/Human-Terrain-System-Statement.cfm.

Anderson, B. 1991. *Imagined Communities: Reflections on the Origin and Spread of Nationalism.* Rev. ed. London: Verso.

Anderson, R. 1996. *Magic, Science, and Health: The Aims and Achievements of Medical Anthropology.* Fort Worth, TX: Harcourt Brace.

Aoki, M. Y., and M. B. Dardess, eds. 1981. *As the Japanese See It: Past and Present.* Honolulu: University Press of Hawaii.

Appadurai, A. 1990. Disjuncture and Difference in the Global Cultural Economy. *Public Culture* 2(2):1–24.

———. 1991. Global Ethnoscapes: Notes and Queries for a Transnational Anthropology. In *Recapturing Anthropology: Working in the Present,* R. G. Fox, ed., pp. 191–210. Santa Fe, NM: School of American Research Advanced Seminar Series.

———. 1996. *Modernity at Large. Cultural Dimensions of Globalization.* Minneapolis: University of Minnesota Press.

Appadurai, ed. 2001. *Globalization.* Durham, NC: Duke University Press.

Arensberg, C. 1987. Theoretical Contributions of Industrial and Development Studies. In *Applied Anthropology in America,* 2nd ed., E. M. Eddy and W. L. Partridge, eds. New York: Columbia University Press.

Arrighi, G. 1994. *The Long Twentieth Century; Money, Power, and the Origins of Our Times.* New York: Verso.

Asad, T. 2008 (orig. 1983). The Construction of Religion as an Anthropological Category. In *A Reader in the Anthropology of Religion,* M. Lambek, ed, pp. 110–226. Malden, MA:Blackwood.

Ashcroft, B., G. Griffiths, and H. Tiffin. 1989. *The Empire Writes Back: Theory and Practice in Post-colonial Literatures.* New York: Routledge.

Baer, H. A., M. Singer, and I. Susser. 2003. *Medical Anthropology and the World System.* Westport, CT: Praeger.

Bailey, E. J. 2000. *Medical Anthropology and African American Health.* Westport, CT: Bergin and Garvey.

Bailey, R. C. 1990. *The Behavioral Ecology of Efe Pygmy Men in the Ituri Forest, Zaire.* Ann Arbor: Anthropological Papers, Museum of Anthropology, University of Michigan, no. 86.

Bailey, R. C., G. Head, M. Jenike, B. Owen, R. Rechtman, and E. Zechenter. 1989. Hunting and Gathering in Tropical Rain Forests: Is It Possible? *American Anthropologist* 91:59–82.

Barnaby, F., ed. 1984. *Future War: Armed Conflict in the Next Decade.* London: M. Joseph.

Barnard, A., ed. 2004. *Hunter-Gatherers in History, Archaeology and Anthropology.* New York: Oxford University Press.

Barnes, E. 2005. *Diseases and Human Evolution.* Albuquerque: University of New Mexico Press.

Barnett, M. 2005. *Keeping an Eye on You.* By: Barnett, Megan, U.S. News & World Report, 00415537, 6/20/2005, Vol. 138, Issue 23.

Baro, M., and T. F. Deubel. 2006. Persistent Hunger: Perspectives on Vulnerability, Famine, and Food Security in Sub-Saharan Africa. *Annual Review of Anthropology* 35:521–538.

Barringer, F. 1992. New Census Data Show More Children Living in Poverty. *New York Times,* May 29, pp. A1, A12–A13.

Barth, F. 1968. (orig. 1958). Ecologic Relations of Ethnic Groups in Swat, North Pakistan. In *Man in Adaptation: The Cultural Present,* Yehudi Cohen, ed., pp. 324–331. Chicago: Aldine.

———. 1969. *Ethnic Groups and Boundaries: The Social Organization of Cultural Difference.* London: Allen & Unwin.

Beeman, W. 1986. *Language, Status, and Power in Iran.* Bloomington: Indiana University Press.

Behar, R. 1993. *Translated Woman: Crossing the Border with Esperanza's Story.* Boston: Beacon Press.

Bellah, R. N. 1978. Religious Evolution. In *Reader in Comparative Religion: An Anthropological Approach,* 4th ed., W. A. Lessa and E. Z. Vogt, eds., pp. 36–50. New York: Harper and Row.

Benedict, R. 1940. *Race, Science and Politics.* New York: Modern Age Books.

Benedict, R. 1946. *The Chrysanthemum and the Sword.* Boston: Houghton Mifflin.

Bennett, J. W. 1969. *Northern Plainsmen: Adaptive Strategy and Agrarian Life.* Chicago: Aldine.

Berlin, B., and P. Kay. 1969/1992. *Basic Color Terms: Their Universality and Evolution.* 2nd ed. Berkeley: University of California Press.

Bernard, H. R. 2006. *Research Methods in Anthropology: Qualitative and Quantitative Approaches.* 4th ed. Lanham, MD: AltaMira.

Bernard, H. R., ed. 1998. *Handbook of Methods in Cultural Anthropology,* Walnut Creek, CA: AltaMira.

Bicker, A., P. Sillitoe, and J. Pottier. 2004. *Investigating Local Knowledge: New Directions, New Approaches.* Burlington, VT: Ashgate.

Bird-David, N. 1992. Beyond "The Original Affluent Society": A Culturalist Reformulation. *Current Anthropology* 33(1):25–47.

Bjuremalm, H. 1997. Rattvisa kan skippas i Rwanda: Folkmordet 1994 gar att forklara och analysera pa samma satt som forintelsen av judarna. *Dagens Nyheter,* June 3, 1997, p. B3.

Blackwood, E., and S. Wieringa, eds. 1999. *Female Desires: Same-Sex Relations and Transgender Practices across Cultures.* New York: Columbia University Press.

Bloch, M., ed. 1975. *Political Language and Oratory in Traditional Societies.* London: Academic Press.

Blommaert, J. 2010. *Sociolinguistics of Globalization.* New York: Cambridge University Press.

Blum, H. F. 1961. Does the Melanin Pigment of Human Skin Have Adaptive Value? *Quarterly Review of Biology* 36: 50–63.

Boas, F. 1966 (orig. 1940). *Race, Language, and Culture.* New York: Free Press.

Bodley, J. H. 2007. *Anthropology and Contemporary Human Problems.* 5th ed. Lanham, MD: AltaMira.

———. 2008. *Victims of Progress.* 5th ed. Lanham, MD: AltaMira.

Bodley, J. H., ed. 1988. *Tribal Peoples and Development Issues: A Global Overview.* Mountain View, CA: Mayfield.

Boellstorff, T. 2007. Queer Studies in the House of Anthropology. *Annual Review of Anthropology* 36:375–389.

Bolton, R. 1981. Susto, Hostility, and Hypoglycemia. *Ethnology* 20(4): 227–258.

Bonvillain, N. 2008. *Language, Culture, and Communication: The Meaning of Messages.* 5th ed. Upper Saddle River, NJ: Prentice Hall.

———. 2012. *Language, Culture, and Communication: The Meaning of Messages,* 7th ed. Boston: Prentice Hall.

Boserup, E. 1970. *Women's Role in Economic Development.* London: Allen and Unwin.

Bourdieu, P. 1977. *Outline of a Theory of Practice.* R. Nice (trans.). Cambridge: Cambridge University Press.

———. 1982. *Ce Que Parler Veut Dire.* Paris: Fayard.

———. 1984. *Distinction: A Social Critique of the Judgment of Taste.*

Bourque, S. C., and K. B. Warren. 1987. Technology, Gender and Development. *Daedalus* 116(4):173–197.

Bowen, J. R. 2008. *Religion in Practice: An Approach to Anthropology of Religion.* 4th ed. Boston: Pearson/Allyn and Bacon.

Bowie, F. 2006. *The Anthropology of Religion: An Introduction.* Malden, MA: Blackwell.

Braudel, F. 1981. *Civilization and Capitalism, 15th–18th Century,* Vol. I, *The Structure of Everyday Life: The Limits.* S. Reynolds (trans.). New York: Harper and Row.

———. 1982. *Civilization and Capitalism, 15th–18th Century,* Vol. II, *The Wheels of Commerce.* New York: Harper and Row.

———. 1992. *Civilization and Capitalism, 15th–18th Century,* Vol. III, *The Perspective of the World.* Berkeley: University of California Press.

Bremen, J. V., and A. Shimizu, eds. 1999. *Anthropology and Colonialism in Asia and Oceania.* London: Curzon.

Brenneis, D. 1988. Language and Disputing. *Annual Review of Anthropology* 17:221–237.

Brettell, C. B., and C. F. Sargent, eds. 2009. *Gender in Cross-Cultural Perspective,* 5th ed. Upper Saddle River, NJ: Pearson/Prentice Hall.

Briggs, C. L. 2005. Communicability, Racial Discourse, and Disease. *Annual Review of Anthropology* 34:269–291.

Brooke, J. 1992. Rio's New Day in Sun Leaves Laplander Limp. *New York Times,* June 1, p. A7.

Brower, B., and B. R. Johnston 2007. *Disappearing Peoples?: Indigenous Groups and Ethnic Minorities in South and Central Asia.* Walnut Creek, CA: Left Coast Press.

Brown, A. 2001. Communism. *International Encyclopedia of the Social & Behavioral Sciences,* pp. 2323–2326. New York: Elsevier.

Brown, P. J., and R. L. Barrett. 2010. *Understanding and Applying Medical Anthropology,* 2nd ed. New York: McGraw-Hill.

Brown, R. W. 1958. *Words and Things.* Glencoe, IL: Free Press.

Buroway, M. 2000 Introduction. *Global Ethnography: Forces, Connections, and Imaginations in a Postmodern World.* Berkeley: University of California Press. City Population. http://www.mongabay.com/cities_pop_01.htm.

Buvinic, M. 1995. The Feminization of Poverty? Research and Policy Needs. In *Reducing Poverty through Labour Market Policies.* Geneva: International Institute for Labour Studies.

Carey, B. 2007. Washoe, a Chimp of Many Words Dies at 42. *New York Times,* November 1. http://www.nytimes.com.

Carneiro, R. L. 1956. Slash-and-Burn Agriculture: A Closer Look at Its Implications for Settlement Patterns. In *Men and Cultures,* Selected Papers of the Fifth International Congress of Anthropological and Ethnological Sciences, pp. 229–234. Philadelphia: University of Pennsylvania Press.

———. 1968 (orig. 1961). Slash-and-Burn Cultivation among the Kuikuru and Its Implications for Cultural Development in the Amazon Basin. In *Man in Adaptation: The Cultural Present,* Y. A. Cohen, ed., pp. 131–145. Chicago: Aldine.

———. 1970. A Theory of the Origin of the State. *Science* 69: 733–738.

Carter, J. 1988. Freed from Keepers and Cages, Chimps Come of Age on Baboon Island. *Smithsonian,* June, pp. 36–48.

Castells, M. 2001. Information Technology and Global Capitalism. In *On the Edge. Living with Global Capitalism,* W. Hutton and A. Giddens, eds. London: Vintage.

Cernea, M., ed. 1991. *Putting People First: Sociological Variables in Rural Development.* 2nd ed. New York: Oxford University Press (published for the World Bank).

Ceuppens, B., and P. Geschiere. 2005. Autochthony: Local or Global? New Modes in the Struggle over Citizenship and Belonging in Africa and Europe. *Annual Review of Anthropology* 34:385–407.

Chagnon, N. A. 1992. (orig. 1983). *Yanomamo: The Fierce People.* 4th ed. New York: Harcourt Brace.

———. 1997. *Yanomamo.* 5th ed. Fort Worth, TX: Harcourt Brace.

Chakrabarty, D. 2007. *Provincializing Europe: Postcolonial Thought and Historical Difference.* Princeton, NJ: Princeton University Press.

Chambers, E. 1987. Applied Anthropology in the Post-Vietnam Era: Anticipations and Ironies. *Annual Review of Anthropology* 16:309–337.

Chatterjee, P. 2004. *The Politics of the Governed: Reflections on Popular Politics in Most of the World.* New York: Columbia University Press.

Chiseri-Strater, E., and B. S. Sunstein. 2001. *Fieldworking: Reading and Writing Research.* 2nd ed. Upper Saddle River, NJ: Prentice Hall.

Chomsky, N. 1957. *Syntactic Structures.* The Hague: Mouton.

Clifford, J. 1982. *Person and Myth: Maurice Leenhardt in the Melanesian World.* Berkeley: University of California Press.

———. 1988. *The Predicament of Culture: Twentieth-Century Ethnography, Literature and Art.* Cambridge, MA: Harvard University Press.

Coates, J. 1986. *Women, Men, and Language.* London: Longman.

Cody, D. 1998. British Empire. http://www.stg.brown.edu/projects/hypertext/landow/victorian/history/Empire.html, May 18.

Cohen, M. 1998. *Culture of Intolerance: Chauvinism, Class, and Racism.* New Haven, CT: Yale University Press.

Cohen, M. N., and Armelagos, G., eds. 1984. *Paleopathology at the Origins of Agriculture.* New York: Academic Press.

Cohen, P. 2008. The Pentagon Enlists Social Scientists to Study Security Issues. *New York Times,* June 18.

Cohen, R. 1967. *The Kanuri of Bornu.* New York: Holt, Rinehart & Winston.

Cohen, Y. 1974. Culture as Adaptation. In *Man in Adaptation: The Cultural Present,* 2nd ed., Y. A. Cohen, ed., pp. 45–68. Chicago: Aldine.

Colson, E., and T. Scudder. 1975. New Economic Relationships between the Gwembe Valley and the Line of Rail. In *Town and Country in Central and Eastern Africa,* David Parkin, ed., pp. 190–210. London: Oxford University Press.

———. 1988. *For Prayer and Profit: The Ritual, Economic, and Social Importance of Beer in Gwembe District, Zambia, 1950–1982.* Stanford, CA: Stanford University Press.

Cooper, F., and A. L. Stoler, eds. 1997. *Tensions of Empire: Colonial Cultures in a Bourgeois World.* Berkeley: University of California Press.

Crapo, R. H. 2003. *Anthropology of Religion: The Unity and Diversity of Religions.* Boston: McGraw-Hill.

Crate, S. A., and M. Nuttall. 2008. *Anthropology and Climate Change: From Encounters to Actions.* Walnut Creek, CA: Left Coast Press.

Cresswell, T. 2006. *On the Move: Mobility in the Modern West.* New York: Routledge.

Crosby, A. W., Jr. 2003. *The Columbian Exchange: Biological and Cultural Consequences of 1492.* Westport, CT: Praeger.

Cultural Survival Quarterly. 1989. Quarterly journal. Cambridge, MA: Cultural Survival.

Cunningham, G. 1999. *Religion and Magic: Approaches and Theories.* New York: New York University Press.

DaMatta, R. 1991. *Carnivals, Rogues, and Heroes: An Interpretation of the Brazilian Dilemma.* John Drury (trans.). Notre Dame, IN: University of Notre Dame Press.

D'Andrade, R. 1984. Cultural Meaning Systems. In *Culture Theory: Essays on Mind, Self, and Emotion,* R. A. Shweder and R. A. Levine, eds., pp. 88–119. Cambridge: Cambridge University Press.

Das, V., and D. Poole, eds. 2004. *Anthropology in the Margins of the State.* Santa Fe, NM: School of American Research Press.

Degler, C. 1970. *Neither Black nor White: Slavery and Race Relations in Brazil and the United States.* New York: Macmillan.

de la Peña, G. 2005. Social and Cultural Policies toward Indigenous Peoples: Perspectives from Latin America. *Annual Review of Anthropology* 34:717–739.

DeNavas-Walt, C., B. D. Proctor, and J. C. Smith. 2010. *Income, Poverty, and Health Insurance Coverage in the United States: 2009.* U.S. Census Bureau, Current Population Reports, P60–238. U.S. Government Printing Office, Washington, DC, 2010. http://www.census.gov/prod/2010pubs/p60-238.pdf.

Dentan, R. K. 1979. *The Semai: A Nonviolent People of Malaya,* Fieldwork ed. New York: Harcourt Brace.

De Vos, G. A., W. O. Wetherall, and K. Stearman. 1983. *Japan's Minorities: Burakumin, Koreans, Ainu and Okinawans.* Report no. 3. London: Minority Rights Group.

De Waal, F. B. M. 1997. *Bonobo: The Forgotten Ape.* Berkeley: University of California Press.

Di Leonardo, M., ed. 1991. *Toward a New Anthropology of Gender.* Berkeley: University of California Press.

Diamond, J. M. 1997. *Guns, Germs, and Steel: The Fates of Human Societies.* New York: Norton.

Dicker, R. 2012 Oscars 2012: Ads Grant Marketers An Advantage Over Super Bowl Spots, An Audience With Tons Of Women. *Huffington Post,* February 25. http://www.huffingtonpost.com/2012/02/24/oscars-ads-_n_1298860.html.

Dillon, S. 2006. In Schools Across U.S., the Melting Pot Overflows. *New York Times,* August 27. http://www.nytimes.com.

Dorward, D. C., ed. 1983. *The Igbo "Women's War" of 1929: Documents Relating to the Aba Riots in Eastern Nigeria.* Wakefield, England: East Ardsley, 1983.

Dove, M. R, and C. Carpenter, eds., 2008. *Environmental Anthropology: A Historical Reader.* Malden, MA: Blackwell.

Dressler, W. W., K. S. Oths, and C. C. Gravlee. 2005. Race and Ethnicity in Public Health Research. *Annual Review of Anthropology* 34:231–252.

Duffield, M., and V. Hewitt, eds. 2009. *Empire, Development, and Colonialism: The Past in the Present.* Rochester, NY: James Currey.

Dunham, S. A. 2009. *Surviving Against the Odds: Village Industry in Indonesia.* Durham, NC: Duke University Press.

Durkheim, E. 1951 (orig. 1897). *Suicide: A Study in Sociology.* Glencoe, IL: Free Press.

———. 1961 (orig. 1912). *The Elementary Forms of the Religious Life.* New York: Collier Books.

———. 2001 (orig. 1912). *The Elementary Forms of the Religious Life.* Carol Cosman (trans.). Abridged with an introduction and notes by Mark S. Cladis. New York: Oxford University Press.

Dwyer, K. 1982. *Moroccan Dialogues: Anthropology in Question.* Baltimore: Johns Hopkins University Press.

Earle, T. K. 1987. Chiefdoms in Archaeological and Ethnohistorical Perspective. *Annual Review of Anthropology* 16:279–308.

———. 1997. *How Chiefs Come to Power: The Political Economy in Prehistory.* Stanford, CA: Stanford University Press.

Eastman, C. M. 1975. *Aspects of Language and Culture.* San Francisco: Chandler and Sharp.

Eckert, P., and S. McConnell-Ginet. 2003. *Language and Gender.* New York: Cambridge University Press.

Edelman, M., and A. Haugerud. 2004. *The Anthropology of Development and Globalization: From Classical Political Economy to Contemporary Neoliberalism.* Malden, MA: Blackwell.

———. 2005. *The Anthropology of Development and Globalization: From Classical Political Economy to Contemporary Neoliberalism.* Malden, MA: Blackwell.

Ervin, A. M. 2005. *Applied Anthropology: Tools and Perspectives for Contemporary Practice.* 2nd ed. Boston: Pearson/Allyn & Bacon.

Escobar, A. 1991. Anthropology and the Development Encounter: The Making and Marketing of Development Anthropology. *American Ethnologist* 18:658–682.

———. 1994. Welcome to Cyberia: Notes on the Anthropology of Cyberculture. *Current Anthropology* 35(3):211–231.

———. 1995. *Encountering Development: The Making and Unmaking of the Third World.* Princeton, NJ: Princeton University Press.

Eskridge, W. N., Jr. 1996. *The Case for Same-Sex Marriage: From Sexual Liberty to Civilized Commitment.* New York: Free Press.

Evans-Pritchard, E. E. 1970. Sexual Inversion among the Azande. *American Anthropologist* 72:1428–1433.

Fagan, B. M. 1998. *World Prehistory: A Brief Introduction.* 4th ed. New York: Longman.

Farner, R. F., ed. 2004. *Nationalism, Ethnicity, and Identity: Cross-National and Comparative Perspectives.* New Brunswick, NJ: Transaction Publishers.

Farooq, M. 1966. Importance of Determining Transmission Sites in Planning Bilharziasis Control: Field Observations from the Egypt-49 Project Area. *American Journal of Epidemiology* 83:603–612.

Farr, D. M. L. 1980. British Empire. *Academic American Encyclopedia,* Vol. 3, pp. 495–496. Princeton, NJ: Arete.

Fasold, R. W. 1990. *The Sociolinguistics of Language.* Oxford: Blackwell.

Ferguson, R. B. 1995. *Yanomami Warfare: A Political History.* Santa Fe, NM: School of American Research.

———. 2002. *The State, Identity, and Violence: Political Disintegration in the Post-Cold War Era.* New York: Routledge.

Ferraro, G. P. 2010. *The Cultural Dimension of International Business,* 6th ed. Upper Saddle River, NJ: Prentice Hall.

Finkler, K. 1985. *Spiritualist Healers in Mexico: Successes and Failures of Alternative Therapeutics.* South Hadley, MA: Bergin and Garvey.

Finnstrom, S. 1997. Postcoloniality and the Postcolony: Theories of the Global and the Local. http://www.stg.brown.edu/projects/hypertext/landow/post/poldiscourse/finnstrom/finnstrom1.html.

Fiske, J. 1989. *Understanding Popular Culture.* Boston: Unwin Hyman.

Fiske, S. March 2007. Providing Cultural Translation for Global Financial Services. *Anthropology News.* pp. 38–39.

Fiske, S. September 2007. Anthropologists and the Public Health Agenda. *Anthropology News.* pp. 51–52.

Fiske, S. March 2008. Defining Who Gets Counted, and How. *Anthropology News.* p. 32–33.

Fiske, S. May 2008. Community Engagement and Cultural Heritage in Fort Apache. *Anthropology News.* p. 41. FFricke, T. 1994. *Himalayan Households: Tamang Demography and Domestic Processes.* 2nd ed. New York: Columbia University Press.

Fleisher, M. L. 2000. *Kuria Cattle Raiders: Violence and Vigilantism on the Tanzania/Kenya Frontier.* Ann Arbor: University of Michigan Press.

Ford, C. S., and F. A. Beach. 1951. *Patterns of Sexual Behavior.* New York: Harper Torchbooks.

Fortes, M. 1950. Kinship and Marriage among the Ashanti. In *African Systems of Kinship and Marriage,* A. R. Radcliffe-Brown and D. Forde, eds., pp. 252–284. London: Oxford University Press.

Foster, G. M., and B. G. Anderson. 1978. *Medical Anthropology.* New York: McGraw-Hill.

Foucault, M. 1979. *Discipline and Punish: The Birth of the Prison.* A. Sheridan (trans.). New York: Vintage Books.

———. 1990. *The History of Sexuality,* Vol. 2, *The Use of Pleasure.* R. Hurley (trans.). New York: Vintage.

Fouts, R. S. 1997. *Next of Kin: What Chimpanzees Have Taught Me about Who We Are.* New York: William Morrow.

Fouts, R. S., D. H. Fouts, and T. E. Van Cantfort. 1989. The Infant Loulis Learns Signs from Cross-Fostered Chimpanzees. In *Teaching Sign Language to Chimpanzees,* R. A. Gardner, B. T. Gardner, and T. E. Van Cantfort, eds., pp. 280–292. Albany: State University of New York Press.

Freilich, M., D. Raybeck, and J. Savishinsky. 1991. *Deviance: Anthropological Perspectives.* Westport, CT: Bergin and Garvey.

French, H. W. 2002. Whistling Past the Global Graveyard. *New York Times,* July 14. http://www.nytimes.com/2002/01/14/weekinreview/14FREN.html.

Fricke, T. 1994. *Himalayan Households: Tamang Demography and Domestic Processes.* 2nd ed. New York: Columbia University Press.

Fried, M. H. 1967. *The Evolution of Political Society: An Essay in Political Anthropology.* New York: McGraw-Hill.

Friedan, B. 1963. *The Feminine Mystique.* New York: W. W. Norton.

Friedl, E. 1962. Vasilika: A Village in Modern Greece: New York: Holt, Rinehart, and Winston.

———. 1975. *Women and Men: An Anthropologist's View.* New York: Holt, Rinehart & Winston.

Friedman, J., ed. 2003. *Globalization, the State, and Violence.* Walnut Creek, CA: AltaMira.

Friedman, K. E., and J. Friedman. 2008. *The Anthropology of Global Systems.* Lanham, MD: AltaMira.

Gal, S. 1989. Language and Political Economy. *Annual Review of Anthropology* 18:345–367.

Gardner, R. A., B. T. Gardner, and T. E. Van Cantfort, eds. 1989. *Teaching Sign Language to Chimpanzees.* Albany: State University of New York Press.

Geertz, C. 1973. *The Interpretation of Cultures.* New York: Basic Books.

Geis, M. L. 1987. *The Language of Politics.* New York: Springer-Verlag.

Gellner, E. 1997. *Nationalism.* New York: New York University Press.

Gezon, L. L. 2006. *Global Visions, Local Landscapes: A Political Ecology of Conservation, Conflict, and Control in Northern Madagascar.* Lanham, MD: AltaMira.

Giddens, A. 1981. *The Class Structure of the Advanced Societies,* 2nd ed. London: Hutchinson.

Gilmore, D. D. 1987. *Aggression and Community: Paradoxes of Andalusian Culture.* New Haven, CT: Yale University Press.

———. 2001. *Misogyny: The Male Malady.* Philadelphia: University of Pennsylvania Press.

Gimpel, J. 1988. *The Medieval Machine: The Industrial Revolution of the Middle Ages,* 2nd ed. Aldershot, Hants, England: Wildwood House.

Gledhill, J. 2000. *Power and Its Disguises: Anthropological Perspectives on Politics.* Sterling, VA: Pluto Press.

Gmelch, G., and W. Zenner, eds. 2002. *Urban Life: Readings in the Anthropology of the City.* Prospect Heights, IL: Waveland.

Goldberg, D. T. 2002. *The Racial State.* Malden, MA: Blackwell.

Goleman, D. 1992. Anthropology Goes Looking for Love in All the Old Places. *New York Times,* November 24, 1992, p. B1.

Goodall, J. 1996. *My Life with the Chimpanzees.* New York: Pocket Books.

Gottdiener, M., ed. 2000. *New Forms of Consumption: Consumers, Culture, and Commodification.* Lanham, MD: Rowman & Littlefield.

Gramsci, A. 1971. *Selections from the Prison Notebooks.* Q. Hoare and G. N. Smith, ed. and trans. London: Wishart.

Grasmuck, S., and P. Pessar. 1991. *Between Two Islands: Dominican International Migration.* Berkeley: University of California Press.

Gray, J. 1999. *False Dawn. The Delusions of Global Capitalism,* London: Granta.

Greaves, T. C. 1995. Problems Facing Anthropologists: Cultural Rights and Ethnography. *General Anthropology* 1(2):1, 3–6.

Green, E. C. 1992 (orig. 1987). The Integration of Modern and Traditional Health Sectors in Swaziland. In *Applying Anthropology,* A. Podolefsky and P. J. Brown, eds., pp. 246–251. Mountain View, CA: Mayfield.

Greenhouse, S. 2011. Union Membership in U.S. Fell to a 70-Year Low Last Year. *New York Times,* January 21.

Grekova, M. 2001. Postsocialist Societies. *International Encyclopedia of the Social & Behavioral Sciences,* pp. 11877–11881. New York: Elsevier.

Gremaux, R. 1993. Woman Becomes Man in the Balkans. In *Third Sex Third Gender: Beyond Sexual Dimorphism in Culture and History,* G. Herdt, ed. Cambridge: MIT Press.

Gudeman, S., ed. 1999. *Economic Anthropology.* Northhampton, MA: E. Elgar. Gumperz, J. J., and S. C. Levinson, eds. 1996. *Rethinking Linguistic Relativity.* New York: Cambridge University Press.

Gumperz, J. J., and S. C. Levinson, eds. 1996. *Rethinking Linguistic Relativity.* New York: Cambridge University Press.

Gupta, A., and J. Ferguson. 1997a. Culture, Power, Place: Ethnography at the End of an Era. In *Culture, Power, Place: Explorations in Critical Anthropology,* A. Gupta and J. Ferguson, eds., pp. 1–29. Durham, NC: Duke University Press.

———. 1997b. Beyond "Culture": Space, Identity, and the Politics of Difference. In *Culture, Power, Place: Explorations in Critical Anthropology,* A. Gupta and J. Ferguson, eds., pp. 33–51. Durham, NC: Duke University Press.

Gupta, A., and J. Ferguson, eds. 1997c. *Anthropological Locations: Boundaries and Grounds of a Field Science.* Berkeley: University of California Press.

———. 1997d. *Culture, Power, Place: Explorations in Critical Anthropology.* Durham, NC: Duke University Press.

Guyot, J., and C. Hughes. 2007. Researchers Find Earliest Evidence for Modern Human Behavior. *Arizona State University Research Magazine.* http://researchmag.asu.edu/2008/02researchers_find_earliest_evid.html.

Hall, Edward T. 1990 (orig. 1966). *The Hidden Dimension.* New York: Anchor.

Hallowell, A. I. 1955. *Culture and Experience.* Philadelphia: University of Pennsylvania Press.

Handwerk, B. 2008. Half of Humanity Will Live in Cities by Year's End. *National Geographic News,* March 13. www.nationalgeographic.com/news/pf30472163.html.

Hansen, K. V. 2004. *Not-So-Nuclear Families: Class, Gender, and Networks of Care.* New Brunswick, NJ: Rutgers University Press.

Hansen, K. V., and A. I. Garey, eds. 1998. *Families in the U.S.: Kinship and Domestic Politics.* Philadelphia: Temple University Press.

Harding, S. 1975. Women and Words in a Spanish Village. In *Toward an Anthropology of Women,* R. Reiter, ed., pp. 283–308. New York: Monthly Review Press.

Harper, J. 2002. *Endangered Species: Health, Illness, and Death among Madagascar's People of the Forest.* Durham, NC: Carolina Academic Press.

Harris, M. 1964. *Patterns of Race in the Americas.* New York: Walker.

———. 1970. Referential Ambiguity in the Calculus of Brazilian Racial Identity. *Southwestern Journal of Anthropology* 26(1):1–14.

———. 1974. *Cows, Pigs, Wars, and Witches: The Riddles of Culture.* New York: Random House.

———. 1978. *Cannibals and Kings.* New York: Vintage Books.

———. 2001 (orig. 1968). *The Rise of Anthropological Theory.* Walnut Creek, CA: AltaMira.

Harris, M., and C. P. Kottak. 1963. The Structural Significance of Brazilian Racial Categories. *Sociologia* 25:203–209.

Harrison, G. G., W. L. Rathje, and W. W. Hughes. 1994. Food Waste Behavior in an Urban Population. In *Applying Anthropology: An Introductory Reader,* 3rd ed., A. Podolefsky and P. J. Brown, eds., pp. 107–112. Mountain View, CA: Mayfield.

Harrison, K. D. 2007. *When Languages Die: The Extinction of the World's Languages and the Erosion of Human Knowledge.* New York: Oxford University Press.

Hart, C. W. M., A. R. Pilling, and J. C. Goodale. 1988. *The Tiwi of North Australia.* 3rd ed. Fort Worth, TX: Harcourt Brace.

Harvey, D. J. 1980. French Empire. *Academic American Encyclopedia,* Vol. 8, pp. 309–310. Princeton, NJ: Arete.

Hastings, A. 1997. *The Construction of Nationhood: Ethnicity, Religion, and Nationalism.* New York: Cambridge University Press.

Haugerud, A., M. P. Stone, and P. D. Little, eds. 2011. *Commodities and Globalization: Anthropological Perspectives.* Lanham, MD: Rowman & Littlefield.

Hawkes, K., J. O'Connell, and K. Hill. 1982. Why Hunters Gather: Optimal Foraging and the Aché of Eastern Paraguay. *American Ethnologist* 9:379–398.

Helman, C. 2001. *Culture, Health, and Illness: An Introduction for Health Professionals.* 4th ed. Boston: Butterworth-Heinemann.

Henry, J. 1955. Docility, or Giving Teacher What She Wants. *Journal of Social Issues* 2:33–41.

Herskovits, M. 1937. *Life in a Haitian Valley.* New York: Knopf.

Hill, J. H. 1978. Apes and Language. *Annual Review of Anthropology* 7:89–112.

Hill, K., H. Kaplan, K. Hawkes, and A. Hurtado. 1987. Foraging Decisions among Aché Hunter-Gatherers: New Data and Implications for Optimal Foraging Models. *Ethology and Sociobiology* 8:1–36.

Hill-Burnett, J. 1978. Developing Anthropological Knowledge through Application. In *Applied Anthropology in America,* E. M. Eddy and W. L. Partridge, eds., pp. 112–128. New York: Columbia University Press.

Hobhouse, L. T. 1915. *Morals in Evolution*. Rev. ed. New York: Holt.

Hoebel, E. A. 1954. *The Law of Primitive Man*. Cambridge, MA: Harvard University Press.

———. 1968. (orig. 1954). The Eskimo: Rudimentary Law in a Primitive Anarchy. In *Studies in Social and Cultural Anthropology*, J. Middleton, ed., pp. 93–127. New York: Crowell.

Hoge, W. 2001. Kautokeino Journal; Reindeer Herders, at Home on a (Very Cold) Range. *New York Times*, March 26, late ed.—final, sec. A, p. 4.

Holden, A. 2005. *Tourism Studies and the Social Sciences*. New York: Routledge.

Hopkins, T., and I. Wallerstein. 1982. Patterns of Development of the Modern World System. In *World System Analysis: Theory and Methodology*, by T. Hopkins, I. Wallerstein, R. Bach, C. Chase-Dunn, and R. Mukherjee, eds., pp. 121–141. Thousand Oaks, CA: Sage.

Hornborg, A., and C. L. Crumley, eds. 2007. *The World System and the Earth System: Global Socioenvironmental Change and Sustainability since the Neolithic*. Walnut Creek, CA: Left Coast Press.

Huffington Post. 2009. Geneva WTO Protests 2009: Police Clash with Black Bloc Demonstrators. http://www.huffingtonpost.com/2009/11/28/geneva-wto-protests-2009-_n_372855.html.

Hunt, R. C. 2007. *Beyond Relativism: Comparability in Cultural Anthropology*. Lanham, MD: AltaMira.

Hunter, M. L. 2005. *Race, Gender, and the Politics of Skin Tone*. New York: Routledge.

Hurtado, A. M., C. A. Lambourne, P. James, K. Hill, K. Cheman, and K. Baca. 2005. Human Rights, Biomedical Science, and Infectious Diseases among South American Indigenous Groups. *Annual Review of Anthropology* 34:639–665.

Inda, J. X., and R. Rosaldo, eds. 2008. *The Anthropology of Globalization: A Reader*. Malden, MA: Blackwell.

Inhorn, M. C., and P. J. Brown. 1990. The Anthropology of Infectious Disease. *Annual Review of Anthropology* 19:89–117.

Iqbal, S. 2002. A New Light on Skin Color. *National Geographic Online Extra*. http://magma.nationalgeographic.com/ngm/0211/feature2/online_extra.html.

Jablonski, N. G., and G. Chaplin. 2000. The Evolution of Human Skin Coloration. *Journal of Human Evolution* (39):57–106.

Jackson, J., and K. B. Warren. 2005. Indigenous Movements in Latin America, 1992–2004: Controversies, Ironies, New Directions. *Annual Review of Anthropology* 34:549–573.

Jenks, C. 2005. *Culture* 2nd ed. New York: Routledge.

Johnson, A. W. 1978. *Quantification in Cultural Anthropology: An Introduction to Research Design*. Stanford, CA: Stanford University Press.

Johnson, A. W., and T. K. Earle. 2000. *The Evolution of Human Societies: From Foraging Group to Agrarian State*. 2nd ed. Stanford, CA: Stanford University Press.

Johnston, B. R. 2009. *Life and Death Matters: Human Rights, Environment, and Social Justice*. 2nd ed. Walnut Creek, CA: Left Coast Press.

Joralemon, D. 2010. *Exploring Medical Anthropology*, 3rd ed. Boston: Pearson.

Jordan, A. 2003. *Business Anthropology*. Prospect Heights, IL: Waveland.

Kan, S. 1986. The 19th-Century Tlingit Potlatch: A New Perspective. *American Ethnologist* 13:191–212.

———. 1989. *Symbolic Immortality: The Tlingit Potlatch of the Nineteenth Century*. Washington, DC: Smithsonian Institution Press.

Kaneshiro, Neil K. 2009. Intersex. *Medline Plus*. National Institutes of Health, U/S. National Library of Medicine. PERLINK "http://www.nlm.nih.gov/medlineplus/ency/article/001669.htm" http://www.nlm.nih.gov/medlineplus/ency/article/001669.htm.

Kaufman, S. R., and L. M. Morgan. 2005. The Anthropology of the Beginnings and Ends of Life. *Annual Review of Anthropology* 34:317–341.

Kearney, M. 1996. *Reconceptualizing the Peasantry: Anthropology in Global Perspective*. Boulder, CO: Westview Press.

Kellenberger, J. 2008. *Moral Relativism: A Dialogue*. Lanham, MA: Rowman and Littlefield.

Kelly, R. C. 1976. Witchcraft and Sexual Relations: An Exploration in the Social and Semantic Implications of the Structure of Belief. In *Man and Woman in the New Guinea Highlands*, P. Brown and G. Buchbinder, eds., pp. 36–53. Special Publication no. 8. Washington, DC: American Anthropological Association.

Kelly, R. L. 1995. *The Foraging Spectrum: Diversity in Hunter-Gatherer Lifeways*. Washington, DC: Smithsonian Institution Press.

Kent, S. 1992. The Current Forager Controversy: Real versus Ideal Views of Hunter-gatherers. *Man* 27:45–70.

———. 1996. *Cultural Diversity among Twentieth-Century Foragers: An African Perspective*. New York: Cambridge University Press.

———. 2002. *Ethnicity, Hunter-gatherers, and the "Other": Association or Assimilation in Africa*. Washington: Smithsonian Institution Press.

Kent, S., and H. Vierich. 1989. The Myth of Ecological Determinism: Anticipated Mobility and Site Organization of Space. In *Farmers as Hunters: The Implications of Sedentism*, S. Kent, ed., pp. 96–130. New York: Cambridge University Press.

Keppel, K. G., J. N. Pearch, and D. K. Wagener. 2002. Trends in Racial and Ethnic-Specific Rates for the Health Status Indicators: United States, 1990–98. *Healthy People Statistical Notes* No. 23. Hyattsville, MD: National Center for Health Statistics.

Keynes, J. M. 1927. *The End of Laissez-Faire*. London: L and Virginia Woolf.

———. 1936. *General Theory of Employment, Interest, and Money*. New York: Harcourt Brace.

Kimmel, M. S. 2007. *The Gendered Society*. 3rd ed. New York: Oxford University Press.

Kimmel, M. S., and M. A. Messner, eds. 2013. *Men's Lives*, 9th ed. Boston: Allyn & Bacon.

Kimmel, M. S., and R. Plante. 2004. *Sexualities: Identities, Behaviors, and Society*. New York: Oxford University Press.

Kinsey, A. C., W. B. Pomeroy, and C. E. Martin. 1948. *Sexual Behavior in the Human Male*. Philadelphia: W. B. Saunders.

Kjaerulff, J. 2010. *Internet and Change: An Ethnography of Knowledge and Flexible Work*. Walnut Creek, CA: Left Coast Press.

Klass, M. 2003. *Mind over Mind: The Anthropology and Psychology of Spirit Possession*. Lanham, MA: Rowman & Littlefield.

Klein, N. 2000. *No Logo: Taking Aim at the Brand Bullies*. New York: Picador.

Kluckhohn, C. 1944. *Mirror for Man: A Survey of Human Behavior and Social Attitudes*. Greenwich, CT: Fawcett.

Kottak, C. P. 1980. *The Past in the Present: History, Ecology, and Social Organization in Highland Madagascar*. Ann Arbor: University of Michigan Press.

———. 1990a. Culture and "Economic Development." *American Anthropologist* 93(3):723–731.

———. 1990b. *Prime-Time Society: An Anthropological Analysis of Television and Culture*. Belmont, CA: Wadsworth.

———. 2006. *Assault on Paradise: The Globalization of a Little Community in Brazil*. 4th ed. New York: McGraw-Hill.

———. 2007. Return to Madagascar: A Forty Year Retrospective. *General Anthropology: Bulletin of the General Anthropology Division of the American Anthropological Association* 14(2):1–10.

———. 2009. *Prime-Time Society: An Anthropological Analysis of Television and Culture*, updated ed. Walnut Creek, CA: Left Coast Press.

Kottak, C. P., and K. A. Kozaitis. 2008. *On Being Different: Diversity and Multiculturalism in the North American Mainstream*. 3rd ed. Boston: McGraw-Hill.

———. 2012. *On Being Different: Diversity and Multiculturalism in the North American Mainstream*, 4th ed. Boston: McGraw-Hill.

Kottak, N. C. 2002. *Stealing the Neighbor's Chicken: Social Control in Northern Mozambique.* Ph.D. dissertation. Department of Anthropology, Emory University, Atlanta, GA.

Kulick, D. 1998. *Travesti: Sex, Gender, and Culture among Brazilian Transgendered Prostitutes.* Chicago: University of Chicago Press.

Kurtz, D. V. 2001. *Political Anthropology: Power and Paradigms.* Boulder, CO: Westview Press.

Kutsche, P. 1998. *Field Ethnography: A Manual for Doing Cultural Anthropology.* Upper Saddle River, NJ: Prentice Hall.

Labov, W. 1972a. *Language in the Inner City: Studies in the Black English Vernacular.* Philadelphia: University of Pennsylvania Press.

———. 1972b. *Sociolinguistic Patterns.* Philadelphia: University of Pennsylvania Press.

Laguerre, M. 1999. *The Global Ethnopolis: Chinatown, Japantown, and Manilatown in American Society.* New York: St. Martin's Press.

Lakoff, R. T. 2004. *Language and Woman's Place.* Rev. ed. New York: Oxford University Press.

———. 2012. *On Being Different: Diversity and Multiculturalism in the North American Mainstream,* 4th ed. Boston: McGraw-Hill.

Lambek, M. 2008. *A Reader in the Anthropology of Religion.* Malden, MA: Blackwell.

Landes, D. 1999. *The Wealth and Poverty of Nations. Why Some Are So Rich and Some Are So Poor.* London: Abacus.

Lange, M. 2009. *Lineages of Despotism and Development: British Colonialism and State Power.* Chicago: University of Chicago Press.

Larson, A. 1989. Social Context of Human Immunodeficiency Virus Transmission in Africa: Historical and Cultural Bases of East and Central African Sexual Relations. *Review of Infectious Diseases* 11:716–731.

Lassiter, L. E. 1998. *The Power of Kiowa Song: A Collaborative Ethnography.* Tucson: University of Arizona Press.

Leach, E. R. 1955. Polyandry, Inheritance and the Definition of Marriage. *Man* 55:182–186.

———. 1961. *Rethinking Anthropology.* London: Athlone Press.

Leadbeater, C. 1999. *Europe's New Economy.* London: Centre for European Reform.

Lee, R. B. 1979. *The !Kung San: Men, Women, and Work in a Foraging Society.* New York: Cambridge University Press.

———. 1984. *The Dobe !Kung.* New York: Harcourt Brace.

———. 2003. *The Dobe Jul'hoansi.* 3rd ed. Belmont, CA: Wadsworth.

Lee, R. B., and R. H. Daly. 1999. *The Cambridge Encyclopedia of Hunters and Gatherers.* New York: Cambridge University Press.

Leman, J. 2001. *The Dynamics of Emerging Ethnicities: Immigrant and Indigenous Ethnogenesis in Confrontation.* New York: Peter Lang.

Lenski, G. 1966. *Power and Privilege: A Theory of Social Stratification.* New York: McGraw-Hill.

Levine, N. E. 2008. Alternative Kinship, Marriage, and Reproduction. *Annual Review of Anthropology* 37:17–35.

Lèvi-Strauss, C. 1963. *Totemism.* R. Needham (trans.). Boston: Beacon Press.

———. 1967. *Structural Anthropology.* New York: Doubleday.

Levy, J. E., with B. Pepper. 1992. *Orayvi Revisited: Social Stratification in an "Egalitarian" Society.* Santa Fe, NM: School of American Research Press, and Seattle: University of Washington Press.

Lewellen, T. C. 2003. *Political Anthropology: An Introduction.* 3rd ed. Westport, CT: Praeger.

———. 2010. Groping toward Globalization: In Search of Anthropology Without Boundaries. *Reviews in Anthropology* 31(1):73–89

Lie, J. 2001. *Multiethnic Japan.* Cambridge, MA: Harvard University Press.

Lindenbaum, S. 1972. Sorcerers, Ghosts, and Polluting Women: An Analysis of Religious Belief and Population Control. *Ethnology* 11:241–253.

Linton, R. 1943. Nativistic Movements. *American Anthropologist* 45:230–240.

Little, K. 1971. *Some Aspects of African Urbanization South of the Sahara.* Reading, MA: Addison-Wesley, McCaleb Modules in Anthropology.

Lockwood, W. G. 1975. *European Moslems: Economy and Ethnicity in Western Bosnia.* New York: Academic Press.

Loomis, W. F. 1967. Skin-Pigmented Regulation of Vitamin-D Biosynthesis in Man. *Science* 157: 501–506.

Lowie, R. H. 1961 (orig. 1920). *Primitive Society.* New York: Harper & Brothers.

Malinowski, B. 1927. *Sex and Repression in Savage Society.* London and New York: International Library of Psychology, Philosophy and Scientific Method.

———. 1929. Practical Anthropology. *Africa* 2:23–38.

———. 1961 (orig. 1922). *Argonauts of the Western Pacific.* New York: Dutton.

———. 1978 (orig. 1931). The Role of Magic and Religion. In *Reader in Comparative Religion: An Anthropological Approach,* 4th ed., W. A. Lessa and E. Z. Vogt, eds., pp. 37–46. New York: Harper and Row.

Malkki, Liisa H. 1995. *Purity and Exile: Violence, Memory, and National Cosmology among Hutu Refugees in Tanzania.* Chicago: University of Chicago Press.

Maquet, J. 1964. Objectivity in Anthropology. *Current Anthropology* 5:47–55.

Marcus, G. E., and D. Cushman. 1982. Ethnographies as Texts. *Annual Review of Anthropology* 11:25–69.

Marcus, G. E., and M. M. J. Fischer. 1986. *Anthropology as Cultural Critique: An Experimental Moment in the Human Sciences.* Chicago: University of Chicago Press.

———. 1999. *Anthropology as Cultural Critique: An Experimental Moment in the Human Sciences.* 2nd ed. Chicago: University of Chicago Press.

Margolis, M. L. 1984. *Mothers and Such: American Views of Women and How They Changed.* Berkeley: University of California Press.

———. 2000. *True to Her Nature: Changing Advice to American Women.* Prospect Heights, IL: Waveland.

Marshall, R. C., ed. 2011. *Cooperation in Economy and Society.* Lanham, MD: Rowman & Littlefield.

Martin, E. 1992. The End of the Body? *American Ethnologist* 19:121–140.

Martin, K., and B. Voorhies. 1975. *Female of the Species.* New York: Columbia University Press.

Martin, S. M. 1988. *Palm Oil and Protest: An Economic History of the Ngwa Region, South-Eastern Nigeria, 1800–1980.* New York: Cambridge University Press.

Martinez, E., and A. Garcia. 2000. What Is "Neo-Liberalism"? A Brief Definition. http://www. globalexchange.org/campaigns/econ101/neoliberalDefined.html.pdf.

Marx, K., and F. Engels. 1976 (orig. 1948). *Communist Manifesto.* New York: Pantheon.

Mascia-Lees, F., and N. J. Black. 2000. *Gender and Anthropology.* Prospect Heights, IL: Waveland.

Mathews, G. 2000. *Global Culture/Individual Identity: Searching for Home in the Cultural Supermarket.* New York: Routledge.

Maugh, T. H., III. 2007. One Language Disappears Every 14 Days; about Half of the World's Distinct Tongues Could Vanish This Century, Researchers Say. *Los Angeles Times,* September 19.

Maybury-Lewis, D. 2002. *Indigenous Peoples, Ethnic Groups, and the State.* 2nd ed. Boston: Allyn & Bacon.

Mayell, H. 2003. Orangutans Show Signs of Culture, Study Says. National Geographic News, January 3. http://news.nationalgeographic.com/news/2002/12/1220_021226_orangutan.html.

Mba, N. E. 1982. *Nigerian Women Mobilized: Women's Political Activity in Southern Nigeria, 1900–1965.* Berkeley: University of California Press, 1982.

McElroy, A., and P. K. Townsend. 2003. *Medical Anthropology in Ecological Perspective.* 4th ed. Boulder, CO: Westview Press.

McKinnon, S. 2005. On Kinship and Marriage: A Critique of the Genetic and Gender Calculus of Evolutionary Psychology. In *Complexities: Beyond Nature and Nurture,* S. McKinnon and S. Silverman, eds., pp. 106–131. Chicago: The University of Chicago Press.

Mead, M. 1937. *Cooperation and Competition among Primitive Peoples.* New York: McGraw-Hill.

Meigs, A., and K. Barlow. 2002. Beyond the Taboo: Imagining Incest. *American Anthropologist* 104(1):38–49.

Mead, M. 1937. *Cooperation and Competition among Primitive Peoples.* New York: McGraw-Hill.

Merry, S. E. 2006. Anthropology and International Law. *Annual Review of Anthropology* 35:99–116.

Michaels, E. 1986. Aboriginal Content. Paper presented at the meeting of the Australian Screen Studies Association, December, Sydney.

———. 1991. Aboriginal Content: Who's Got It–Who Needs It? *Visual Anthropology* 4: 277–300.

Miles, H. L. 1983. Apes and Language: The Search for Communicative Competence. In *Language in Primates,* J. de Luce and H. T. Wilder, eds., pp. 43–62. New York: Springer Verlag.

Miller, B. D. 1997. *The Endangered Sex: Neglect of Female Children in Rural North India.* New York: Oxford University Press.

Miller, N., and R. C. Rockwell, eds. 1988. *AIDS in Africa: The Social and Policy Impact.* Lewiston, NY: Edwin Mellen.

Mintz, S. 1985. *Sweetness and Power: The Place of Sugar in Modern History.* New York: Viking Penguin.

Mitani, J. C., and D. P. Watts. 1999. Demographic Influences on the Hunting Behavior of Chimpanzees. *American Journal of Physical Anthropology* 109:439–454.

Mitchell, J. C. 1966. Theoretical Orientations in African Urban Studies. In *The Social Anthropology of Complex Societies,* M. Banton, ed., pp. 37–68. London: Tavistock.

Montagu, A., ed. 1997. *Man's Most Dangerous Myth: The Fallacy of Race.* Walnut Creek, CA: AltaMira.

Mooney, A. 2011. *Language, Society, and Power.* New York: Routledge.

Moro, P. A. and J. E. Meyers, eds. 2010. *Magic, Witchcraft, and Religion: A Reader in the Anthropology of Religion.* 8th ed. New York: McGraw-Hill.

Morrill, C., D. A. Snow, and C. White. 2005. *Together Alone: Personal Relationships in Public Places.* Berkeley: University of California Press.

Motseta, S. 2006. Botswana Gives Bushmen Tough Conditions. *Tulsa World,* December 14.

Murdock, G. P. 1957. World Ethnographic Sample. *American Anthropologist* 59:664–687.

Murray, S. O., and W. Roscoe, eds. 1998. *Boy-wives and Female Husbands: Studies in African Homosexualities.* New York: St. Martin's Press.

Mydans, S. 1992a. Criticism Grows over Aliens Seized during Riots. *New York Times,* May 29, p. A8.

Nadeem, S. 2011. *Dead Ringers: How Outsourcing Is Changing the Way Indians Understand Themselves.* Princeton, NJ: Princeton University Press.

Nagel, J. 1996. *American Indian Ethnic Renewal: Red Power and the Resurgence of Identity and Culture.* New York: Oxford University Press.

Nanda, S. Nadeem, S. 2011. *Dead Ringers: How Outsourcing Is Changing the Way Indians Understand Themselves.* Princeton, NJ: Princeton University Press.

———. 2000. *Gender Diversity: Crosscultural Variations.* Prospect Heights, IL: Waveland.

National Academies. 2007. Understanding and Responding to Climate Change: Highlights of National Academies Reports. http://dels.nas.edu/basc/Climate-HIGH.pdf.

Naylor, L. L. 1996. *Culture and Change: An Introduction.* Westport, CT: Bergin and Garvey.

Nazarea, V. D. 2006. Local Knowledge and Memory in Biodiversity Conservation. *Annual Review of Anthropology* 35:317–335.

Nolan, R. W. 2002. *Development Anthropology: Encounters in the Real World.* Boulder, CO: Westview Press.

Nordstrom, C. 2004. *Shadows of War: Violence, Power, and International Profiteering in the Twenty-First Century.* Berkeley: University of California Press.

Nugent, D., and J. Vincent, eds. 2004. *A Companion to the Anthropology of Politics.* Malden, MA: Blackwell.

O'Leary, C. 2002. *Class Formation, Diet and Economic Transformation in Two Brazilian Fishing Communities.* Unpublished Ph.D. dissertation, University of Michigan, Ann Arbor.

Omohundro, J. T. 2001. *Careers in Anthropology.* 2nd ed. Boston: McGraw-Hill.

Ong, A. 1987. *Spirits of Resistance and Capitalist Discipline: Factory Women in Malaysia.* Albany: State University of New York Press.

———. 1989. Center, Periphery, and Hierarchy: Gender in Southeast Asia. In *Gender and Anthropology: Critical Reviews for Research and Teaching,* S. Morgen, ed., pp. 294–312. Washington, DC: American Anthropological Association.

Ong, A., and S. J. Collier, eds. 2005. *Global Assemblages: Technology, Politics, and Ethics as Anthropological Problems.* Malden, MA: Blackwell.

Ontario Consultants on Religious Tolerance. 2001. *Religions of the World:* Number of Adherents; Rates of Growth. http://www.religioustolerance.org/worldrel.htm.

———. 2002. *Religions of the World:* Number of Adherents; Rates of growth. http://www.religioustolerance.org/worldrel.htm.

Oriji, J. N. 2000. Igbo Women From 1929–1960. *West Africa Review:* 2:1.

Ortner, S. B. 1984. Theory in Anthropology Since the Sixties. *Comparative Studies in Society and History* 126(1):126–166.

Paine, R. 2009. *Camps of the Tundra : Politics Through Reindeer among Saami Pastoralists.* Oslo : Instituttet for sammenlignende kulturforskning.

Palmer, S. 2001. The Rael Deal. *Religion in the News* 4:2. Hartford, CT: Trinity College, The Leonard E. Greenberg Center for the Study of Religion in Public Life. http://www.trincoll.edu/depts/csrpl/RINVol4No2/Rael.htm.

Patterson, F. 1978. Conversations with a Gorilla. *National Geographic,* October, pp. 438–465.

Paulson, T. E. 2005. Chimp, Human DNA Comparison Finds Vast Similarities, Key Differences. *Seattle Post-Intelligencer Reporter,* September 1. http://seattlepi.nwsource.com/local/238852_chimp01.html.

Peletz, M. 1988. *A Share of the Harvest: Kinship, Property, and Social History among the Malays of Rembau.* Berkeley: University of California Press.

Pelto, P. 1973. *The Snowmobile Revolution: Technology and Social Change in the Arctic.* Menlo Park, CA: Cummings.

Petraglia-Bahri, D. 1996. Introduction to Postcolonial Studies. http://www.emory.edu/ENGLISH/Bahri/.

Piddocke, S. 1969. The Potlatch System of the Southern Kwakiutl: A New Perspective. In *Environment and Cultural Behavior,* A. P. Vayda, ed., pp. 130–156. Garden City, NY: Natural History Press.

Plattner, S., ed. 1989. *Economic Anthropology.* Stanford, CA: Stanford University Press.

Podolefsky, A., and P. J. Brown, eds. 1992. *Applying Anthropology: An Introductory Reader.* 2nd ed. Mountain View, CA: Mayfield.

Pospisil, L. 1963. *The Kapauku Papuans of West New Guinea.* New York: Holt, Rinehart & Winston.

Potash, B., ed. 1986. *Widows in African Societies: Choices and Constraints.* Stanford, CA: Stanford University Press.

Price, R., ed. 1973. *Maroon Societies.* New York: Anchor Press/Doubleday.

Radcliffe-Brown, A. R. 1952 (orig. 1924). The Mother's Brother in South Africa. In A. R. Radcliffe-Brown, *Structure and Function in Primitive Society,* pp. 15–31. London: Routledge & Kegan Paul.

———. 1965 (orig. 1962). *Structure and Function in Primitive Society.* New York: Free Press.

Ramos, A. R. 1995. *Sanumá Memories: Yanomami Ethnography in Times of Crisis.* Madison, WI: University of Wisconsin Press.

Ranger, T. O. 1996. Postscript. In *Postcolonial Identities,* R. Werbner and T. O. Ranger, eds. London: Zed.

Rappaport, R. A. 1974. Obvious Aspects of Ritual. *Cambridge Anthropology* 2:2–60.

———. 1999. *Holiness and Humanity: Ritual in the Making of Religious Life.* New York: Cambridge University Press.

Rathje, W. L., and C. Murphy. 2001. *Rubbish!: The Archaeology of Garbage.* Tucson: University of Arizona Press.

Rathus, S. A., J. S. Nevid, and J. Fichner-Rathus. 2013. *Human Sexuality in a World of Diversity.* 9th ed. Boston: Allyn & Bacon.

Redfield, R. 1941. *The Folk Culture of Yucatan.* Chicago: University of Chicago Press.

Redfield, R., R. Linton, and M. Herskovits. 1936. Memorandum on the Study of Acculturation. *American Anthropologist* 38:149–152.

Reese, W. L. 1999. *Dictionary of Philosophy and Religion: Eastern and Western Thought.* Amherst, NY: Humanities Books.

Robbins, R. 2011. *Global Problems and the Culture of Capitalism,* 5th ed. Boston: Pearson/Allyn & Bacon.

Roberts, S., A. Sabar, B. Goodman, and M. Balleza. 2007. 51% of Women Are Now Living without Spouse. *New York Times,* January 16. http://www.nytimes.com.

Robertson, A. F. 1995. *The Big Catch: A Practical Introduction to Development.* Boulder, CO: Westview Press.

Rodseth, L., R. W. Wrangham, A. M. Harrigan, and B. Smuts. 1991. The Human Community as a Primate Society. *Current Anthropology* 32:221–254.

Romaine, S. 1999. *Communicating Gender.* Mahwah, NJ: Erlbaum.

———. 2000. *Language in Society: An Introduction to Sociolinguistics.* 2nd ed. New York: Oxford University Press.

Root, D. 1996. *Cannibal Culture: Art, Appropriation, and the Commodification of Difference.* Boulder, CO: Westview Press.

Rosaldo, M. Z. 1980a. *Knowledge and Passion: Notions of Self and Social Life.* Stanford, CA: Stanford University Press.

Roscoe, W. 1991. *The Zuni Man-Woman.* Albuquerque: University of New Mexico Press.

———. 1998. *Changing Ones: Third and Fourth Genders in Native North America.* New York: St. Martin's Press.

Rouse, R. 1991. Mexican Migration and the Social Space of Postmodernism. *Diaspora* 1(1):8–23.

Royal Anthropological Institute. 1951. *Notes and Queries on Anthropology.* 6th ed. London: Routledge and Kegan Paul.

Ryan, S. 1990. *Ethnic Conflict and International Relations.* Brookfield, MA: Dartmouth.

Ryang, S., and J. Lie 2009. *Diaspora Without Homeland: Being Korean in Japan.* Berkeley: University of California Press.

Rylko-Bauer, B., M. Singer, and J. Van Willigen. 2006. Reclaiming Applied Anthropology: Its Past, Present, and Future. *American Anthropologist* 108(1) 178–190.

Sabloff, J. A. 2008. *Archaeology Matters: Action Archaeology in the Modern World.* Walnut Creek, CA: Left Coast Press.

Sahlins, M. D. 1968. *Tribesmen.* Englewood Cliffs, NJ: Prentice Hall.

———. 2004. *Stone Age Economics.* New York: Routledge.

Salzman, P. C. 1974. Political Organization among Nomadic Peoples. In *Man in Adaptation: The Cultural Present,* 2nd ed., Y. A. Cohen, ed., pp. 267–284. Chicago: Aldine.

———. 2008. *Culture and Conflict in the Middle East.* Amherst, NY: Humanity Books.

Salzmann, Z., J. M. Stanlaw, and N. Adachi. 2012. *Language, Culture, and Society: An Introduction to Linguistic Anthropology,* 5th ed. Boulder, CO: Westview Press.

Sanday, P. R. 1974. Female Status in the Public Domain. In *Woman, Culture, and Society,* M. Z. Rosaldo and L. Lamphere, eds., pp. 189–206. Stanford, CA: Stanford University Press.

———. 2002. *Women at the Center: Life in a Modern Matriarchy.* Ithaca, NY: Cornell University Press.

Sapir, E. 1931. Conceptual Categories in Primitive Languages. *Science* 74:578–584.

———. 1956 (orig. 1928). The Meaning of Religion. In E. Sapir, *Culture, Language and Personality: Selected Essays.* Berkeley: University of California Press.

Scheidel, W. 1997. Brother-Sister Marriage in Roman Egypt. *Journal of Biosocial Science* 29(3):361–371.

Scheinman, M. 1980. Imperialism. *Academic American Encyclopedia,* Vol. 11, pp. 61–62. Princeton, NJ: Arete.

Schneider, D. M. 1967. Kinship and Culture: Descent and Filiation as Cultural Constructs. *Southwestern Journal of Anthropology* 23:65–73.

Scholte, J. A. 2000. *Globalization: A Critical Introduction.* New York: St. Martin's Press.

Schroeder, Rick. 1999. *Shady Practices: Agroforestry and Gender Politics in The Gambia.* University of California Press.

Scott, J. C. 1985. *Weapons of the Weak.* New Haven, CT: Yale University Press.

———. 1990. *Domination and the Arts of Resistance.* New Haven, CT: Yale University Press.

Scudder, T., and E. Colson. 1980. *Secondary Education and the Formation of an Elite: The Impact of Education on Gwembe District, Zambia.* London: Academic Press.

Scupin, R. 2003. *Race and Ethnicity: An Anthropological Focus on the United States and the World.* Upper Saddle River, NJ: Prentice Hall.

Sebeok, T. A., and J. Umiker-Sebeok, eds. 1980. *Speaking of Apes: A Critical Anthropology of Two-Way Communication with Man.* New York: Plenum.

Service, E. R. 1962. *Primitive Social Organization: An Evolutionary Perspective.* New York: McGraw-Hill.

———. 1966. *The Hunters.* Englewood Cliffs, NJ: Prentice Hall.

Shaffer, M. S., ed. 2008 *Public Culture: Diversity, Democracy, and Community in the United States.* Philadelphia: University of Pennsylvania Press.

Shanklin, E. 1995. *Anthropology and Race.* Belmont, CA: Wadsworth.

Shannon, T. R. 1996. *An Introduction to the World-System Perspective.* 2nd ed. Boulder, CO: Westview Press.

Sharma, A., and A. Gupta, eds. 2006. *The Anthropology of the State: A Reader.* Malden, MA: Blackwell.

Shostak, M. 1981. *Nisa: The Life and Words of a !Kung Woman.* Cambridge, MA: Harvard University Press.

Silberbauer, G. 1981. *Hunter and Habitat in the Central Kalahari Desert.* New York: Cambridge University Press.

Singer, M. 2008. *Drugging the Poor: Legal and Illegal Drugs and Social Inequality.* Long Grove, IL: Waveland.

Singer, M., and H. Bauer. 2007. *Introducing Medical Anthropology: A Discipline in Action.* Lanham, MD: AltaMira.

Smart, A., and J. Smart. 2003. Urbanization and the Global Perspective. *Annual Review of Anthropology.* 32:263–285.

Smith, A. 2008 (orig. 1776). *An Inquiry Into the Nature and Causes of the Wealth of Nations: A Selected Edition.* New York: Oxford University Press.

Smith, A. T. 2003. *The Political Landscape: Constellations of Authority in Early Complex Polities.* Westport, CT: Praeger.

Smith, M. K., and M. E. Doyle. 2002. 'Globalization' *The Encyclopedia of Informal Education.* http://www.infed.org/biblio/globalization,.htmhttp://www.infed.org/biblio/globalization.htm.

Solway, J., and R. Lee. 1990. Foragers, Genuine and Spurious: Situating the Kalahari San in History (with CA treatment). *Current Anthropology* 31(2):109–146.

Sotomayor, S. 2009. A Latina Judge's Voice. The Judge Mario G. Olmos Memorial Lecture, delivered at the University of California, Berkeley, School of Law in 2001; published in the spring 2002 issue of the *Berkeley La Raza Law Journal,* republished by the *New York Times* on May 14, 2009.

Spencer, E. T. 2010. *Sociolinguistics.* Hauppauge, NY: Nova Science Publishers.

Spickard, P., ed. 2004. *Race and Nation: Ethnic Systems in the Modern World.* New York: Routledge.

———. *Race and Immigration in the United States: New Histories.* New York; Routledge.

Spindler, G. D. 2005. *New Horizons in the Anthropology of Education.* Mahwah, NJ: Erlbaum.

Spindler, G. D., ed. 2000. *Fifty Years of Anthropology and Education, 1950–2000: A Spindler Anthology.* Mahwah, NJ: Erlbaum.

Srivastava, J., N. J. H. Smith, and D. A. Forno. 1998. *Integrating Biodiversity in Agricultural Intensification: Toward Sound Practices.* Washington, DC: World Bank.

Stack, C. B. 1975. *All Our Kin: Strategies for Survival in a Black Community.* New York: Harper Torchbooks.

Statistical Abstract of the United States. Washington, DC: U.S. Bureau of the Census, U.S. Government Printing Office. 2012 *Statistical Abstract of the United States,* 2012. http://www.census.gov/prod/www/statistical-abstract.html.

Statistics Canada. 2001. *1996 Census.* National Tables. http://www.statcan.ca/english/census96/nation.htm.

Stein, R. L., and P. L. Stein. 2011. *The Anthropology of Religion, Magic, and Witchcraft,* 3rd ed. Upper Saddle River, NJ: Pearson Prentice Hall.

Stevens, W. K. 1992. Humanity Confronts Its Handiwork: An Altered Planet. *New York Times,* May 5, pp. B5–B7.

Stevenson, D. 2003. *Cities and Urban Cultures.* Philadelphia: Open University Press.

Stoler, A. 1977. Class Structure and Female Autonomy in Rural Java. *Signs* 3:74–89.

Stone, L. S. 2004. Gay Marriage and Anthropology. *Anthropology News* 45(5). http://www.aaanet.org/press/an/0405if-comm4.htm.

———. 1999. *Curing and Healing: Medical Anthropology in Global Perspective.* Durham, NC: Carolina Academic Press.

Strathern, A., and P. J. Stewart. 2010. *Kinship in Action: Self and Group.* Boston: Prentice Hall.

Sunderland, P. L., and R. M. Denny. 2007. *Doing Anthropology in Consumer Research.* Walnut Creek, CA: Left Coast Press.

Suttles, W. 1960. Affinal Ties, Subsistence, and Prestige among the Coast Salish. *American Anthropologist* 62:296–305.

Swift, M. 1963. Men and Women in Malay Society. In *Women in the New Asia,* B. Ward, ed., pp. 268–286. Paris: UNESCO.

Tanaka, J. 1980. *The San Hunter-Gatherers of the Kalahari.* Tokyo: University of Tokyo Press.

Tannen, D. 1990. *You Just Don't Understand: Women and Men in Conversation.* New York: Ballantine Books.

———. 2005. *Conversational Style: Analyzing Talk Among Friends,* new ed. New York: Oxford University Press.

Tannen, D., ed. 1993. *Gender and Conversational Interaction.* New York: Oxford University Press.

Tannen, D., S. Kendall, and C. Gordon., eds. 2007. *Family Talk: Discourse and Identity in Four American Families.* New York: Oxford University Press.

Taylor, C. 1987. Anthropologist-in-Residence. In *Applied Anthropology in America,* 2nd ed., E. M. Eddy and W. L. Partridge, eds. New York: Columbia University Press.

Terrace, H. S. 1979. *Nim.* New York: Knopf.

Thistlewaite, Susan Brooks. 2010. *USAID's New Approach: CAP Talks with Afeefa Syeed.* Center for American Progress. http://www.americanprogress.org/issues/security/news/2010/04/13/7565/usaids-new-approach/

Thomas, L., and S. Wareing, eds. 2004. *Language, Society, and Power: An Introduction.* New York: Routledge.

Thompson, W. 1983. Introduction: World System with and without the Hyphen. In *Contending Approaches to World System Analysis,* W. Thompson, ed., pp. 7–26. Thousand Oaks, CA: Sage.

Tice, K. 1997. Reflections on Teaching Anthropology for Use in the Public and Private Sector. In *The Teaching of Anthropology: Problems, Issues, and Decisions,* C. P. Kottak, J. J. White, R. H. Furlow, and P. C. Rice, eds., pp. 273–284. Mountain View, CA: Mayfield.

Tishkov, V. A. 2004. *Chechnya: Life in a War-Torn Society.* Berkeley: University of California Press.

Titiev, M. 1992. *Old Oraibi: A Study of the Hopi Indians of Third Mesa.* Albuquerque: University of New Mexico Press.

Toner, R. 1992. Los Angeles Riots Are a Warning, Americans Fear. *New York Times,* May 11, pp. A1, A11.

Trivedi, B. P. 2001. Scientists Identify a Language Gene. *National Geographic News,* October 4. http://news.nationalgeographic.com/news/2001/10/1004_Tvlanguagegene.html.

Trudgill, P. 2000. *Sociolinguistics: An Introduction to Language and Society.* 4th ed. New York: Penguin Books.

Trudgill, P. 2010. *Investigations in Sociohistorical Linguistics: Stories of Colonisation and Contact.* New York: Cambridge University Press.

Turnbull, C. 1965. *Wayward Servants: The Two Worlds of the African Pygmies.* Garden City, NY: Natural History Press.

Turner, V. W. 1974 (orig. 1967). *The Ritual Process.* Harmondsworth, England: Penguin Books.

———. 1995 (orig. 1969). *The Ritual Process.* Hawthorne, NY: Aldine de Gruyter.

Tylor, E. B. 1958 (orig. 1871). *Primitive Culture.* New York: Harper Torchbooks.

Ulijaszek, S. J., and H. Lofink. 2006. Obesity in Biocultural Perspective. *Annual Review of Anthropology* 35:337–360.

U. S. Census Bureau. 2010. Decennial census. http://2010.census.gov/2010census/data/

———. 2012. Profile America, Facts for Figures, Valentine's Day 2012: February 14. http://www.census.gov/newsroom/releases/archives/facts_for_features_special_editions/cb12-ff02.html.

Van Allen, J. 1971. *"Aba Riots" or "Women's War"?: British Ideology and Eastern Nigerian Women's Political Activism.* Waltham, MA: African Studies Association.

Van Cantfort, T. E., and J. B. Rimpau. 1982. Sign Language Studies with Children and Chimpanzees. *Sign Language Studies* 34:15–72.

Vayda, A. P. 1968 (orig. 1961). Economic Systems in Ecological Perspective: The Case of the Northwest Coast. In *Readings in Anthropology,* 2nd ed., Vol. 2, M. H. Fried, ed., pp. 172–178. New York: Crowell.

Veblen, T. 1934. *The Theory of the Leisure Class: An Economic Study of Institutions.* New York: Modern Library.

Verdery, K. 2001. Socialist Societies: Anthropological Aspects. *International Encyclopedia of the Social & Behavioral Sciences,* pp. 14496–14500. New York: Elsevier.

Vidal, J. 2003. Every Third Person Will Be a Slum Dweller within 30 Years, UN Agency Warns: Biggest Study of World's Cities Finds 940 Million Already Living in Squalor. *The Guardian,* October 4. http://www.guardian.co.uk/international/story/0,3604,1055785,00.html.

Vigil, J. D. 2003. Urban Violence and Street Gangs. *Annual Review of Anthropology* 32:225–242.

———. 2010. *Gang Redux: A Balanced Anti-Gang Strategy.* Long Grove, IL: Waveland.

Wade, N. 2005. For Gay Men, Different Scent of Attraction. *New York Times,* May 10, late ed.—final, p. A1.

Wade, P. 2002. *Race, Nature, and Culture: An Anthropological Perspective.* Sterling, VA: Pluto Press.

Wallace, A. F. C. 1956. Revitalization Movements. *American Anthropologist* 58:264–281.

———. 1966. *Religion: An Anthropological View.* New York: McGraw-Hill.

———. 1969. *The Death and Rebirth of the Seneca.* New York: Knopf.

Wallerstein, I. M. 1982. The Rise and Future Demise of the World Capitalist System: Concepts for Comparative Analysis. In *Introduction to the Sociology of "Developing Societies,"* H. Alavi and T. Shanin, eds., pp. 29–53. New York: Monthly Review Press.

———. 2004b. *World-Systems Analysis: An Introduction.* Durham, NC: Duke University Press.

Ward, M. C., and M. Edelstein. 2009. *A World Full of Women,* 5th ed. Needham Heights, MA: Allyn & Bacon.

Warms, R., J. Garber, and R. J. McGee, eds. 2009. *Sacred Realms: Readings in the Anthropology of Religion.* 2nd ed. New York: Oxford University Press.

Weber, M. 1958 (orig. 1904). *The Protestant Ethic and the Spirit of Capitalism.* New York: Scribner.

———. 1968 (orig. 1922). *Economy and Society.* E. Fischoff et al. (trans.). New York: Bedminster Press.

Webster's New World Encyclopedia. 1993. College Edition. Englewood Cliffs, NJ: Prentice Hall.

Weston, K. 1991. *Families We Choose: Lesbians, Gays, Kinship.* New York: Columbia University Press.

White, L. A. 1959. *The Evolution of Culture: The Development of Civilization to the Fall of Rome.* New York: McGraw-Hill.

Whorf, B. L. 1956. A Linguistic Consideration of Thinking in Primitive Communities. In *Language, Thought, and Reality: Selected Writings of Benjamin Lee Whorf,* J. B. Carroll, ed., pp. 65–86. Cambridge, MA: MIT Press.

Wilford, J. N. 2007. *Archaeologists Find Signs of Early Chimps' Tool Use.* New York Times. February 13. http://www.nytimes.com/2007/02/13/science/13chim.html?pagewanted=print.

Wilk, R. R., and L. Cliggett. 2007. *Economies and Culture: Foundations of Economic Anthropology.* Boulder, CO: Westview.

Williams, L. M., and D. Finkelhor. 1995. Paternal Caregiving and Incest: Test of a Biosocial Model. *American Journal of Orthopsychiatry* 65(1):101–113.

Wilmsen, E. N. 1989. *Land Filled with Flies: A Political Economy of the Kalahari.* Chicago: University of Chicago Press.

Wilson, R., ed. 1996. *Human Rights: Culture and Context: Anthropological Perspectives.* Chicago: Pluto Press.

Winter, R. 2001. Religions of the World: Number of Adherents; Names of Houses of Worship; Names of Leaders; Rates of Growth. http://www.religioustolerance.org/worldrel.htm.

Wolcott, H. F. 2008. *Ethnography: A Way of Seeing.* 2nd ed. Lanham, MD: AltaMira.

Wolf, E. R. 1966. *Peasants.* Englewood Cliffs, NJ: Prentice Hall.

———. 1982. *Europe and the People without History.* Berkeley: University of California Press.

Wolf, E. R., with S. Silverman. 2001. *Pathways of Power: Building an Anthropology of the Modern World.* Berkeley: University of California Press.

Worsley, P. 1985 (orig. 1959). Cargo Cults. In *Readings in Anthropology* 85/86. Guilford, CT: Dushkin.

Young, A. 2000. *Women Who Become Men: Albanian Sworn Virgins.* New York: Berg.

Yurchak, A. 2005. *Everything Was Forever until It Was No More: The Last Soviet Generation.* Princeton, NJ: Princeton University Press.

Zeitzen, M. K. 2008. *Polygamy: A Cross-Cultural Analysis.* New York: Berg.

Zimmer-Tamakoshi, L. 1997. The Last Big Man: Development and Men's Discontents in the Papua New Guinea Highlands. *Oceania* 68(2):107–122.

Front Matter

Page i: © Rubberball/Punchstock RF

Brief Contents

Page iii(top): © Allan Shoemake/Stockbyte/Getty Images RF; p. iii(center left): © Kimberly White/Corbis; p. iii(center): © Paul Bucknall/Alamy; p. iii(bottom): © Santokh Kochar/Getty Images RF.

Table of Contents

Page v: © Robin Utrecht/Fotografie/HillCreek Pictures/Corbis; p. vi: © James L. Stanfield/National Geographic Stock; p. vii(left): © Doranne Jacobson/International Images; p. vii(right): © Olivier Martel/Corbis; p. viii: © Anders Blomqvist/Lonely Planet Images/Getty Images; p. ix: © Thanassis Stavrakis/AP/Wide World Photos; p. x: © Valdrin Xhemaj/epa/Corbis; p. xi(left): © Drew Crawford/The Image Works; p. xi(right): © Steve McCurry/Magnum Photos; p. xii: © Philippe Lissac/Godong/Corbis; p. xiii: © Monika Graff/The Image Works; p. xiv: © Frans Lemmens/Getty Images; p. xv: © Frans Lanting/Corbis.

Chapter 1

Opener: © Robin Utrecht/Fotografie/HillCreek Pictures/Corbis; p. 2(top left): © Jia Dequan/Panorama/The Image Works; p. 2(top center): © Randy Olson/Aurora Photos; p. 2(top right): © Bruce Avera Hunter/National Geographic Stock; p. 2(bottom): © Ron Gilling/Lineair/Robert Harding; p. 3: © Jia Dequan/Panorama/The Image Works; p. 4(left): © David Bathgate/Corbis; p. 4(right): © BananaStock/Jupiterimages RF; p. 5(top): © David Samuel Robbins/Getty Images; p. 5(bottom): © Alfredo Dagli Orti/The Art Archive/Corbis; p. 6: © National Anthropological Archives. Neg.#906-B; p. 7(top): © Mike Zens/Corbis; p. 7(bottom): © AP Photo/Obama Presidential Campaign; p. 8(top left): © iStock photo.com/Ollo; p. 8(top right): © iStockphoto.com/Malerapaso; p. 9:© Randy Olson/Aurora Photos; p.10(top left): © Digital Vision/Getty Images RF; p. 10(top center): © Eric Martin/Iconotec.com RF; p. 10(top right): © S. Nicolas/Iconotec.com RF; p. 10(bottom): © Emma Wood/Alamy; p. 12(top): © Bruce Avera Hunter/National Geographic Stock; p.12(bottom)Kobak Collection/Lucasfilm/Paramount Pictures/Art Resource; p. 13: © Image Source/Getty Images RF.

Chapter 2

Opener: © James L. Stanfield/National Geographic Stock; p. 18(top left): © Neil Emmerson/Robert Harding World Imagery/Corbis; p. 18(top center): © Hideo Haga/The Image Works; p. 18(top right): © Monica Stevenson Photography/Getty Images; p. 18(bottom): © Ferdinando Scianna/Magnum Photos; p. 19(top): © LWA/Dann Tardif/Blend Images/Corbis; p. 19(center): © Jetta Productions/Blend Images/Corbis; p. 19(bottom): © Ryan McVay/Getty Images RF; p. 20(top left): © Jenny Matthews/Alamy; p. 20(center): © Mary Evans Picture Library/The Image Works; p. 20(top right): © Neil Emmerson/Robert Harding World Imagery/Corbis; p. 21(top): © Imaginechina via AP Images; p. 21(bottom): © Kristin Callahan/Everett Collection/Newscom; p. 22: © Ariadne Van Zandbergen/Alamy; p. 23(top): © Corbis RF; p. 23(bottom): © OSF/Clive Bromhall; p. 24(center): © iStockphoto.com/Eric Isselée; p. 24(bottom): © Justine Evans/Alamy; p. 26(left): © Hideo Haga/The Image Works; p. 26(right): © Carl D. Walsh/Aurora Photos; p. 28(top left): © Bob Rowan/Corbis; p. 28(top right): © Robert Holmes/Corbis; p. 28(bottom): © Ryan McVay/Getty Images RF; p. 29(top): © Marilyn Humphries/The Image Works; p. 29(center): © Jasper Juinen/Getty Images; p. 29(bottom): © iStockphoto.com/Vasko Miokovic; p. 30: © Frans Lemmens/Getty Images; p. 31: © Monica Stevenson Photography/Getty Images; p. 32: © Anders Ryman/Corbis; p. 33: © Tom Salyer/Alamy; p. 34(top): © Bill Bachmann/Alamy; p. 34(bottom): © SuperStock RF.

Chapter 3

Opener: © Doranne Jacobson/International Images; p. 40(top left): © Melvin Konner/Anthro-Photo; p. 40(top center): © Richard Lord/PhotoEdit; p. 40(top right): Courtesy of Lisa Gezon; p. 40(bottom): © AP Photo; p. 41: © Melvin Konner/Anthro-Photo; p. 42: © Sylvain Leser/Le Desk/Alamy; p. 43: Courtesy of Lisa Gezon; p. 44: © Richard Lord/PhotoEdit; p. 45: © Historical Picture Archive/Corbis; p. 46(top): © Mary Evans Picture Library/The Image Works; p. 46(center): © BEAWIHARTA/Reuters/Corbis; p. 46(bottom): © Athar Hussain/Reuters/Corbis; p. 48: Conrad P. Kottak; p. 49: © TRBfoto/Getty Images RF; p. 50(top left): © Peggy & Yoran Kahana/Shooting Star; p. 50(top right): © Janine Wiedel Photolibrary/Alamy; p. 50(bottom): © Bob Daemmrich/The Image Works; p. 51: © Brand X Pictures/PunchStock RF; p. 52: © 20th Century Fox. All rights reserved/Everett Collection; p. 53: © The McGraw-Hill Companies, Inc./Ken Cavanagh, photographer; p.53(bottom) © St Petersburg Times/Cherie Diez/The Image Works.

Chapter 4

Opener: © Olivier Martel/Corbis; p. 58(top left): © Sandro Vannini/Corbis; p. 58(top center): © Keijiro Komine/Getty Images; p. 58(top right): © Allan Shoemake/Stockbyte/Getty Images RF; p. 58(bottom): © Donald Pye/Alamy; p. 59(top): © Jason Leer/Reuters/Corbis; p. 59(bottom): © Michael Nichols/National Geographic Stock; p. 61(top left): © Pixtal/age fotostock RF; p. 61(top right): © EPA/Julian Smith/Corbis; p. 61(center): © Per-Anders Pettersson/Getty Images; p. 61(bottom): © Sandro Vannini/Corbis; p. 62(top): © Martin Thomas Photography/Alamy; p. 62(bottom left): © Pixtal/age fotostock RF; p. 62(bottom right): © Bloom Productions/Getty Images RF; p. 63(both): © Noel Hendrickson/Getty Images RF; p. 65(top): © Lonny Shavelson; p. 65(bottom): © AP Photo/Activision; p. 66(top): © Keijiro Komine/Getty Images; p. 66(bottom): © Steven Kazlowski/Alaska Stock/National Geographic Stock; p. 67(top): © Dirk Shadd/St. Petersburg Times/Zuma Press; p. 67(bottom): © Allan Shoemake/Stockbyte/Getty Images RF; p. 68(top): © Jeff Greenberg/age fotostock; p. 68(bottom): © Andrew G Hobbs/Getty Images; p. 69: © Jon Arnold/JA/Corbis; p. 70(top): © Michael Siluk/The Image Works; p. 70(bottom): © AP Photo/The News & Observer, Shawn Rocco; p. 71: © Kevin Winter/Getty Images; p. 73: © Brand X/JupiterImages/Getty Images RF.

Chapter 5

Opener: © Anders Blomqvist/Lonely Planet Images/Getty Images; p. 78(top left): © Earl & Nazima Kowall/Corbis; p. 78(top center): © Carl D. Walsh/Aurora Photos; p. 78(top right): © John Eastcott/Yva Momatiuk/Woodfin Camp & Associates; p. 78(bottom): © BrianIndia/Alamy; p. 81(top): © Danita Delimont/Getty Images; p. 81(bottom): © Arco/W. Dolder/age fotostock; p. 82: © Earl & Nazima Kowall/Corbis; p. 83: © Santokh Kochar/Getty Images RF; p. 85(left): © MedioImages/Getty Images RF; p. 85(center left): © iStockphoto.com/Morley Read; p. 85(center): © Kent Knudson/PhotoLink/Getty Images RF; p. 85(center right): © Getty Images RF; p. 85(right): © Steve Allen/Brand X Pictures RF; p. 86: © Carl D. Walsh/Aurora Photos; p. 87: © BananaStock/PunchStock RF; p. 88: © AP Photo/Imaginechina; p. 89(top): © Gideon Mendel/Corbis; p. 89(bottom): © Jupiter Images RF; p. 90: © Burke/Triolo Productions/Getty Images RF; p. 91: © Blend Images/Alamy RF; p. 92(top): © John Eastcott/Yva Momatiuk/Woodfin Camp & Associates; p. 92(bottom): © AP Photo/PRNewsfoto; p. 94(top): © Elbridge W. Merrill Collection Photograph Collection/Alaska State Library and Archives [P57-028]; p. 94(bottom): © Jesse Grant/WireImage/Getty Images.

Chapter 6

Opener: © AP Photo/Thanassis Stavrakis; p. 100(top left): © Joy Tessman/National Geographic Stock; p. 100(top center): © Burt Glinn/Magnum Photos; p. 100(top right): © Gamal Noman/AFP/Getty Images; p. 100(bottom): © AP Photo/Andres Kudacki; p. 102: © Joy Tessman/National Geographic Stock; p. 104: © Spencer Grant/age fotostock; p. 105: © Peer Grimm/epa/Corbis; p. 106: © Burt Glinn/Magnum Photos; p. 107(top): © Amos Morgan/Getty Images RF; p. 107(bottom): © Daniel Berehulak/Getty Images; p. 108(top): © Douglas Kirkland; p. 108(bottom): © Walt Disney Studios Motion Pictures Photographer: Zade Rosenthal/Photofest; p. 111: © Peter Adams/Getty Images RF; p. 112(top): © Gamal Noman/AFP/Getty Images; p. 112(bottom): © Anders Ryman/Corbis; p. 113: © David W. Hamilton/Getty Images; p. 114(left): © Martin Harvey/Corbis; p. 114(center left): © Brand X Pictures/PunchStock RF; p. 114(center right): © Frederic Soltan/Corbis; p. 114(right): © Corbis RF; p. 115: © Michael Siluk/The Image Works; p. 116(top): © AP Photo/Felipe Dana; p. 116(bottom): ©Masterfile RF; p. 118: © AP Photo/Sunday Alamba; p.119: © Areil Skelly/Getty Images RF.

Chapter 7

Opener: © Valdrin Xhemaj/epa/Corbis; p. 124(top left): © Ami Vitale/Alamy; p. 124(top center): © Francis Dean/Dean Pictures/The Image Works; p. 124(top right): © Behrouz Mehri/AFP/Getty Images; p. 124(bottom): © Peter Menzel/Menzel Photography; p. 125: © Hill Street Studios/Blend Images RF; p. 126: © Brenninger/Sueddeutsche Zeitung Photo/The Image Works; p. 127 (top): © ABC/Photofest © ABC/Photographer: Bob D'Amico; p. 127(bottom): © Monica Lau/Getty Images RF; p. 129(top): © Digital Vision/Getty Images RF; p. 129(bottom): © Katja Heinemann/Aurora Photos; p. 132(left): © Ami Vitale/Alamy; p. 132(right): © John Eastcott/Yva Momatiuk/Stock Boston; p. 133 (top): © Peter M. Fisher/Corbis; p. 133(bottom): © Francis Dean/Dean Pictures/The Image Works; p. 136: © Kimberly White/Corbis; p. 137: © Robert Galbraith/Reuters/Corbis; p. 138: © Geri Engberg/The Image Works; p. 139: © Behrouz Mehri/AFP/Getty Images; p. 140: © AP Photo/Mike Hutchings; p. 141(top): © Stan Honda/AFP/Getty Images; p. 141(bottom): © Alan Collins/Alamy.

Chapter 8

Opener: © Drew Crawford/The Image Works; p. 146(left): © Wojciech Dabrowski RF; p. 146(center): © Lindsay Hebberd/Corbis; p. 146(right): © AP Photo/Kevin Frayer; p. 147(top): © Gregory Wrona/Alamy; p. 147(bottom): © Lionsgate/Photo by Murray Close/Photofest; p. 148(left): © Connie Coleman/Getty Images RF; p. 148(center): © Henri Conodul/Iconotech.com RF; p. 148(right): Wojciech Dabrowski RF; p. 149(top left): © Jeffrey Rotman/Corbis; p. 149(top right): © iStockphoto.com/David Liu; p. 149(bottom): © istockphoto.com/JackJelly; p. 150(top left): © Louise Gubb/Corbis; p. 150(top right): © Corbis RF; p. 150(bottom): © Stockbyte RF; p. 151: © Getty Images RF; p. 152(top): © Chris Stowers/Panos Pictures; p. 152(bottom): © Paul Nicklen/National Geographic Stock; p. 153: © Lindsay Hebberd/Corbis; p. 154: © George Holton/Photo Researchers; p. 155: Courtesy Lindsay Meyer; p. 156: © National Archives; p. 157: © iStockphoto.com/Pixhook; p. 158: © Bjanka Kadic/Alamy; p. 162(top): © AP Photo/Kevin Frayer; p. 162(bottom): © Ricardo Gomes/Globo via Getty Images; p. 165: © Viviane Moos/Corbis.

Chapter 9

Opener: © Steve McCurry/Magnum Photos; p. 170(left): © Peter Essick/Aurora Photos; p. 170(center): © Getty Images RF; p. 170 (right): © Ted Spiegel/Corbis; p. 172(top): © Gianni Dagli Orti/Corbis; p. 172(bottom): © Roger De La Harpe/Gallo Images/Corbis; p. 173: © Peter Essick/Aurora Photos; p. 174: © Ingram Publishing/Alamy RF; p. 175(left): © Getty Images RF; p. 175(right): © ERproductions Ltd./Getty Images RF; p. 176(top left): © Thierry Secretan/COSMOS/Woodfin Camp & Associates; p. 176(top right): © Bob Krist/Corbis; p. 176(bottom): © Jeff Haynes/Reuters/Corbis; p. 177(top): © Image Source RF; p. 177(bottom): © Ted Spiegel/Corbis; p. 178: © AP Photo/Jessica Kourkounis; p. 179: © Paul Kane/Getty Images; p. 181: Showtime Networks/Photofest; p. 182: © Kal Muller/Woodfin Camp & Associates; p. 183: © Raul Spinasse/Agencia a Tarde/AE/Corbis; p. 184: © BananaStock/PunchStock RF; p. 185: © Roberto Herrett/Alamy.

Chapter 10

Opener: © Philippe Lissac/Godong/Corbis; p. 190(left): © Vicky Kasala/Getty Images; p. 190(center): © Hulton Archive/Getty Images; p. 190(right): © Vincent Leloup; p. 191: © Luciopix/Alamy; p. 192 (top): © Romeo Gacad/Getty Images; p. 192(bottom): © Vicky Kasala/Getty Images; p. 193(top): © ARPL/Topham/The Image Works; p. 193(bottom): © Ingram Publishing/SuperStock RF; p. 195(top): National Archives and Records Division. NAIL Control Number: NWDNS-102-LH-488; p. 195(bottom): © The Art Archive/Karl Marx Museum Trier/Alfredo Dagli Orti; p. 197: © Culver Pictures; p. 198(top): © Hulton Archive/Getty Images; p. 198(bottom): © Bonnie Kamin/PhotoEdit; p. 201: © Lions Gate/The Kobal Collection/Art Resource; p. 204(top): © Bettmann/Corbis; p. 204(bottom): © Andrey Smirnov/AFP/Getty Images; p. 207: © Nancy Honey/Getty Images RF; p. 208: © Vincent Leloup; p. 209: © George Rose/Getty Images.

Chapter 11

Opener: © Monika Graff/The Image Works; p. 214(top left): © Paul Bucknall/Alamy; p. 214(top center): © PJ. Griffiths/Magnum Photos; p. 214(top right): AP Photo/Zarip Toroyev; p. 214(bottom): © Ryan McVay/Getty Images RF; © p. 215(top): © Leon/Retna/Corbis; p. 215(bottom): © Jack Hollingsworth/Getty Images RF; p. 217 (top left): © Hubert Stadler/Corbis; p. 217(top right): © AP Photo/Express Newspapers; p. 217(center left): © Nigel Pavitt/JAI/Corbis; p. 217(center right): © Ed George/National Geographic Stock; p. 217(bottom left): © Blickwinkel/Alamy; p. 217(bottom center left): © dbimages/Alamy; p. 217(bottom center right): © David Levenson/Alamy; p. 217(bottom right): © Ariadne Van Zandbergen/Africa Media Online/The Image Works; p. 221: © SSPL/The Image Works; p. 222(top): © Paul Bucknall/Alamy; p. 222(bottom): © Fox-TV/The Kobal Collection/Art Resource; p. 223: © Albert L. Ortega/WireImage/Getty Images; p. 224: © Rob Melnychuk/Brand X/Corbis RF; p. 225: © PJ. Griffiths/Magnum Photos; p. 226(all): Courtesy, Conrad P. Kottak; p. 229: © Alan Schein/Alamy RF; p. 231: © Photostock/Dieter Heinemann/Alamy RF; p. 233: © Tyrone Turner/National Geographic Stock; p. 234(left): © Bradley Mayhew/Lonely Planet Images/Getty Images; p. 234(right): © AP Photo/Zarip Toroyev; p. 235: © Jim McIsaac/Getty Images.

Chapter 12

Opener: © Frans Lemmens/Getty Images; p. 240(top left): © Mike Yamashita/Woodfin Camp & Associates; p. 240(top center): © Anders Blomqvist/Getty Images; p. 240(top right): © Antonio Scorza/AFP/Getty Images; p. 240(bottom left): © Ron Nickel/Design Pics/Corbis; p. 240(bottom center left): © Boris Roessler/dpa/Corbis; p. 240(bottom center right): © Adam Gault/Getty Images RF; p. 240(bottom right): © Digital Vision/Getty Images RF; p. 242(top): © Charles Harbutt/Actuality, Inc.; p. 242(bottom): © Mike Yamashita/Woodfin Camp & Associates; p. 243: © Andrew Aitchison/In Pictures/Corbis; p. 244(top): © Anders Blomqvist/Getty Images; p. 244(bottom): © Alexander Joe/AFP/Getty Images; p. 245: © Betty Press/Woodfin Camp & Associates; p. 246: © Oleg Popov/Reuters/Corbis; p. 247(top): © Ron Nickel/Design Pics/Getty Images RF; p. 247(bottom): © Antonio Scorza/AFP/

Chapter 13

Bibliography

MAP ATLAS

CONTENTS

MAP 1

Annual Percent of World Forest Loss, 1990–2000

Deforestation is a major environmental problem. In the tropics, large corporations clear forests seeking hardwoods for the global market in furniture and fine woods. As well, the agriculturally driven clearing of the great rain forests of the Amazon Basin, west and central Africa, Middle America, and Southeast Asia has drawn public attention. Reduced forest cover means the world's vegetation system will absorb less carbon dioxide, resulting in global warming. Of concern, too, is the loss of biodiversity (large numbers of plants and animals), the destruction of soil systems, and disruptions in water supply that accompany clearing.

QUESTIONS

Look at Map 1, "Annual Percent of World Forest Loss, 1990–2000."

1. On what continents do you find stable or increased forest cover?

2. Are there areas of Africa with stable or increased forest cover? Where are they? What might the reasons be for this lack of deforestation?

3. How does deforestation in India compare with the area to its east, which includes mainland and insular Southeast Asia?

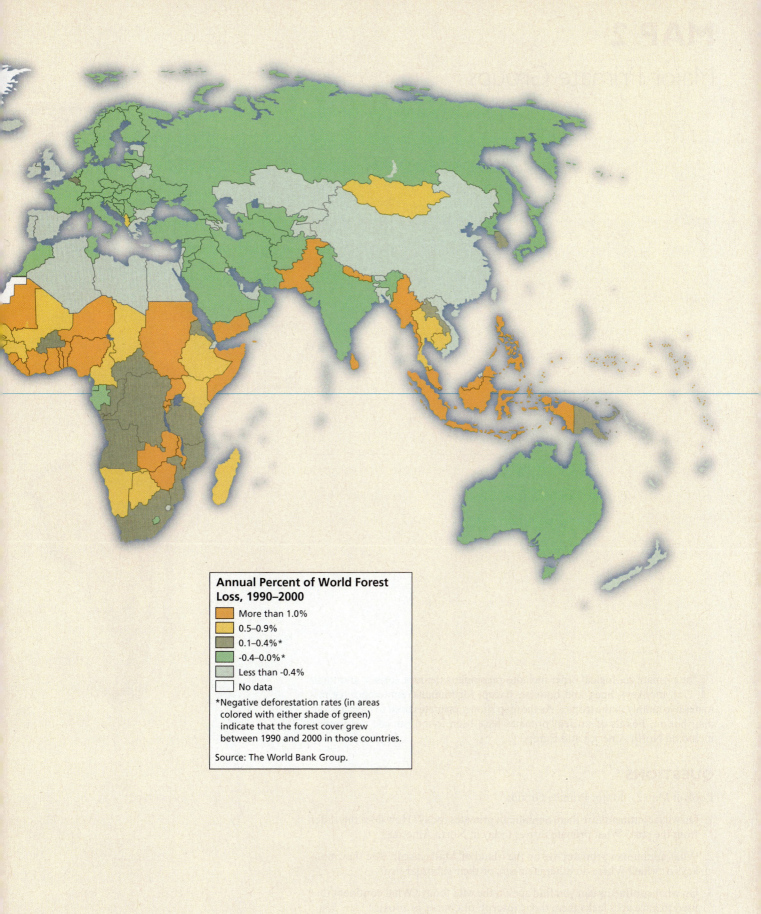

Annual Percent of World Forest Loss, 1990–2000

- More than 1.0%
- 0.5–0.9%
- 0.1–0.4%*
- -0.4–0.0%*
- Less than -0.4%
- No data

*Negative deforestation rates (in areas colored with either shade of green) indicate that the forest cover grew between 1990 and 2000 in those countries.

Source: The World Bank Group.

MAP 2
Major Primate Groups

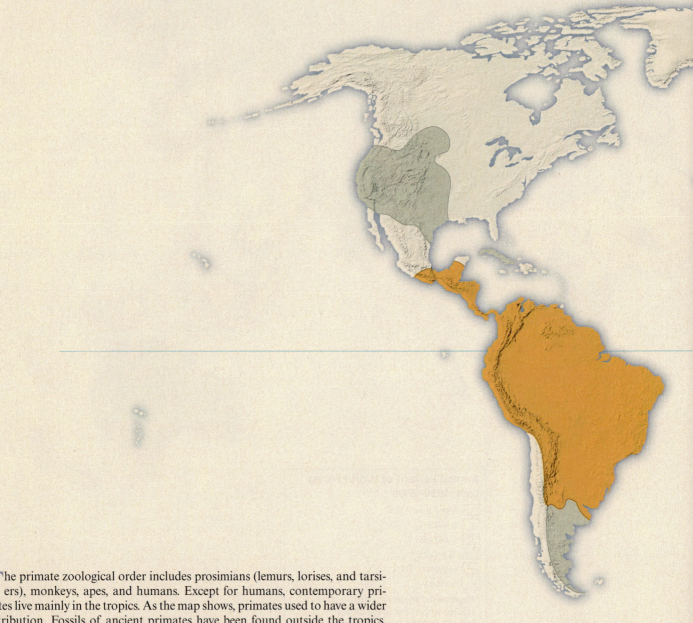

The primate zoological order includes prosimians (lemurs, lorises, and tarsiers), monkeys, apes, and humans. Except for humans, contemporary primates live mainly in the tropics. As the map shows, primates used to have a wider distribution. Fossils of ancient primates have been found outside the tropics, including North America and Europe.

QUESTIONS

Look at Map 2, "Major Primate Groups."

1. On what continents are there nonhuman primates today? How does this differ from the past? What primate thrives today in North America?

2. What nonhuman primates live on the island of Madagascar? Are they monkeys or what? Where do other members of their suborder live?

3. On what continents can you find apes in the wild today? What continent that used to have apes lacks them today (except, of course, in zoos).

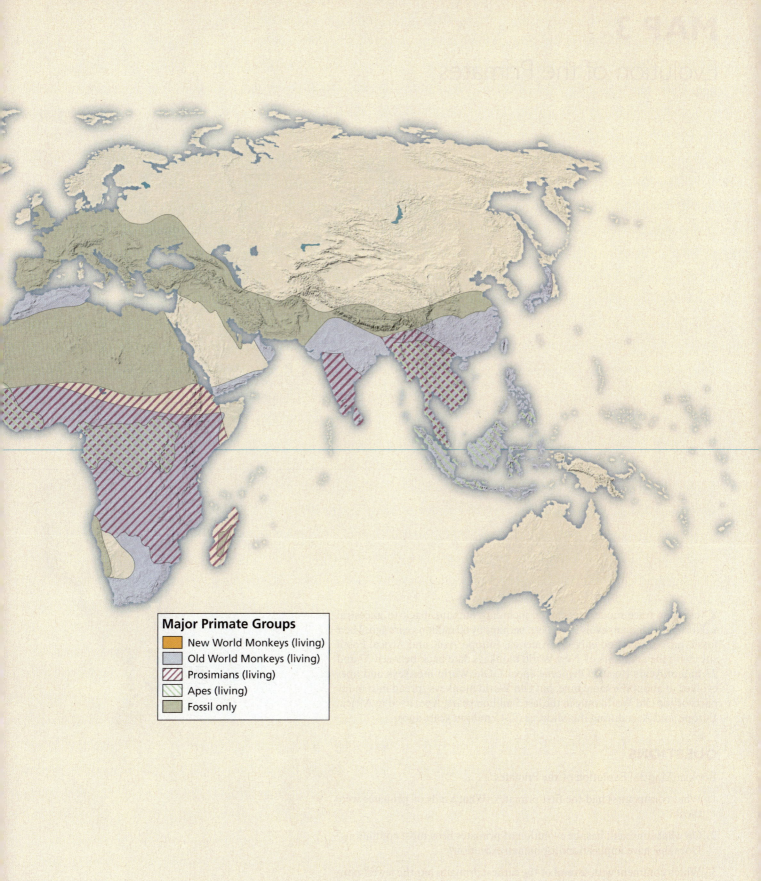

Major Primate Groups

- New World Monkeys (living)
- Old World Monkeys (living)
- Prosimians (living)
- Apes (living)
- Fossil only

MAP 3
Evolution of the Primates

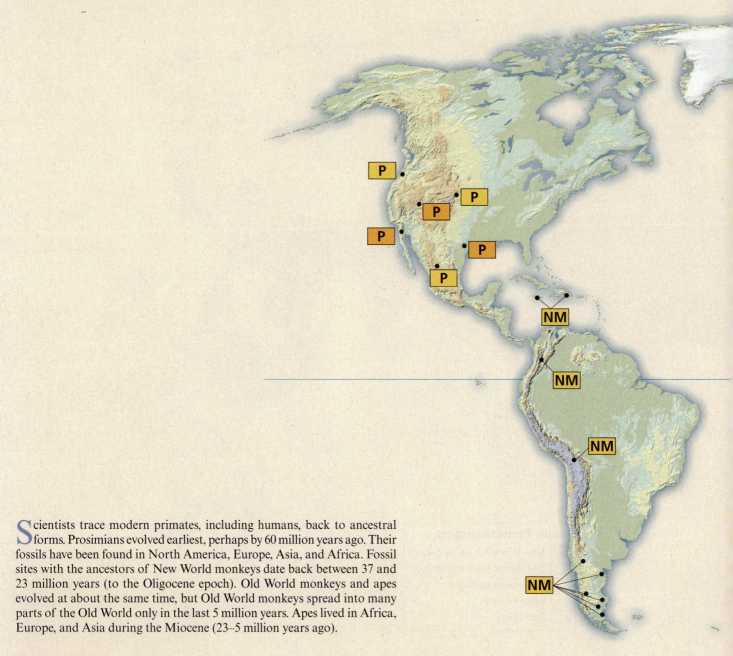

Scientists trace modern primates, including humans, back to ancestral forms. Prosimians evolved earliest, perhaps by 60 million years ago. Their fossils have been found in North America, Europe, Asia, and Africa. Fossil sites with the ancestors of New World monkeys date back between 37 and 23 million years (to the Oligocene epoch). Old World monkeys and apes evolved at about the same time, but Old World monkeys spread into many parts of the Old World only in the last 5 million years. Apes lived in Africa, Europe, and Asia during the Miocene (23–5 million years ago).

QUESTIONS

Look at Map 3, "Evolution of the Primates."

1. What continent(s) had the first primates? What kinds of primates were those?

2. On what continent has the evolution of primates been most continuous? Does this have implications for human evolution?

3. Which continent with several of the earliest primates has the fewest non-human primates today?

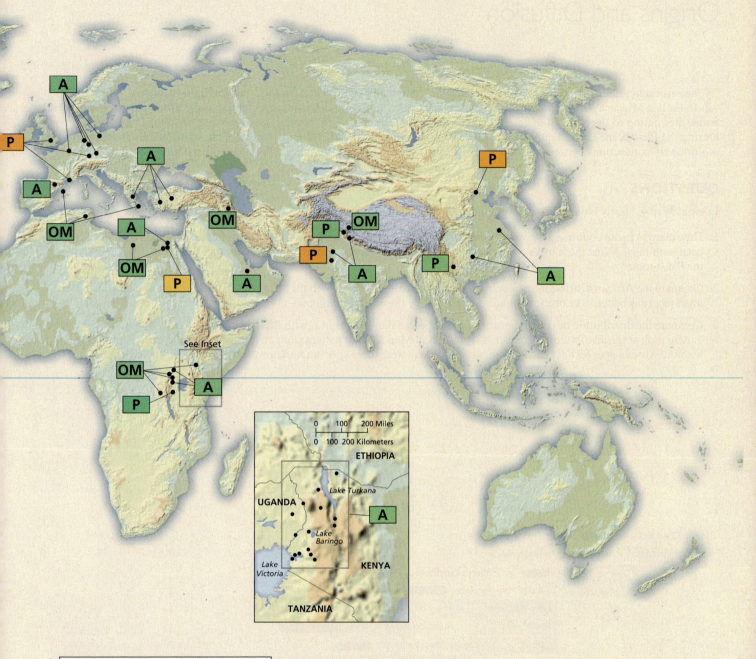

A
P
A
A
OM
A
OM
P
OM
P
OM
P
A
P
A
A
P
A
See Inset
OM
A
P
0 100 200 Miles
0 100 200 Kilometers
ETHIOPIA
Lake Turkana
UGANDA
A
Lake Baringo
Lake Victoria
KENYA
TANZANIA
Evolution of the Primates
Eocene: 57–37 million years ago
Oligocene: 37–23 million years ago
Miocene: 23–5 million years ago
OM Old World monkeys
NM New World monkeys
P Prosimians
A Apes

MAP 4
Early Hominins (and Hominids): Origins and Diffusion

The earliest hominins, including the ancestors of modern humans, evolved in Africa around 6 million years ago. Many sites date to the late Miocene (8–5 million years ago) when the lines leading to modern humans, chimps, and gorillas may have separated. Some sites dating to the end of the Pliocene epoch (5–1.8 million years ago) contain fossil remains of human ancestors, *Homo*. During the Pleistocene Era (1.8 million–11,000 years ago), humans spread all over the world. Scholars don't always agree on the evolutionary connections between the different fossils, as indicated in the question marks and broken lines on the time line.

QUESTIONS

Look at Map 4, "Early Hominins (and Hominids): Origins and Diffusion."

1. How many African countries have early hominin or hominid sites? Which countries contain sites of hominids that may not have been hominins? Name those two sites. How many African countries have sites from the Miocene? From the Pliocene? And from the Pleistocene?

2. Compare the African distribution of nonhuman primate fossils in Map 3 with the distribution of early hominins in Map 4. Which fossil record is better—the one for nonhuman primates or the one for hominins?

3. Compare the distribution of contemporary African apes, as shown in Map 2, with the distribution of early hominin sites in Map 4. Also look at the distribution of extinct African apes in Map 3. What patterns do you notice? Where did early hominins overlap with the African apes (extinct and contemporary)? Where were there apes but no known early hominins, and vice versa?

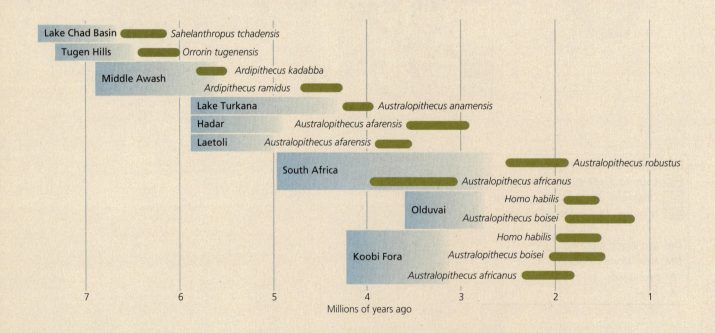

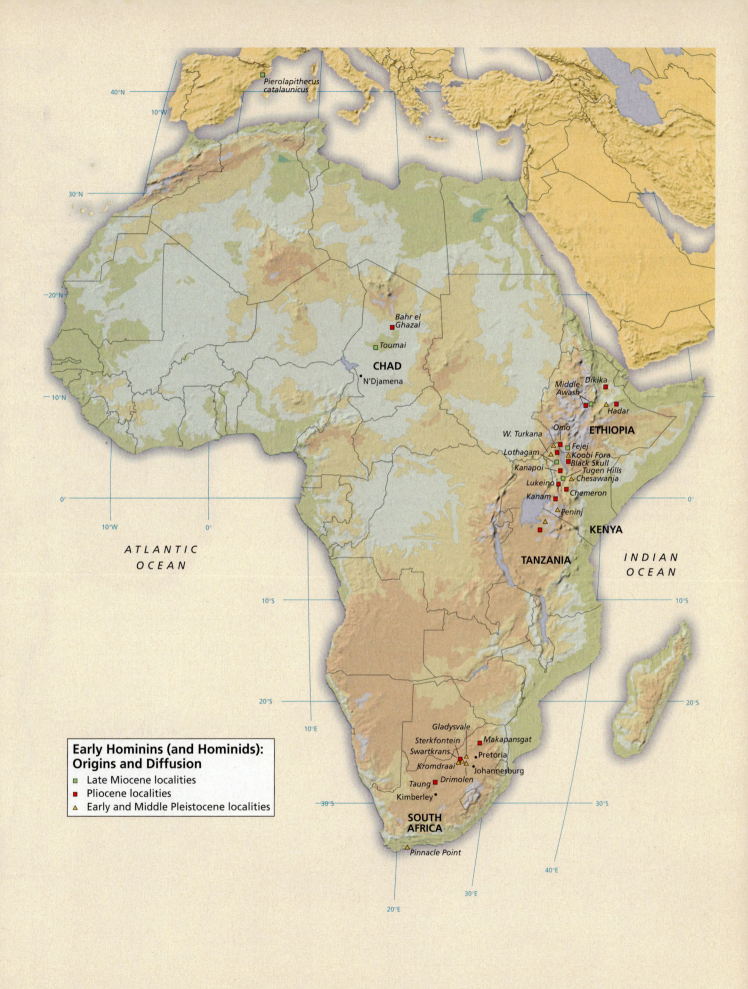

Early Hominins (and Hominids): Origins and Diffusion

- ■ Late Miocene localities
- ■ Pliocene localities
- ▲ Early and Middle Pleistocene localities

Pierolapithecus catalaunicus

Bahr el Ghazal
Toumai
CHAD
• N'Djamena

Middle Awash
Dikika
Hadar
W. Turkana
Omo
ETHIOPIA
Fejej
Lothagam
Koobi Fora
Black Skull
Kanapoi
Tugen Hills
Chesawanja
Lukeino
Kanam
Chemeron
Peninj
KENYA

TANZANIA

INDIAN OCEAN

ATLANTIC OCEAN

Gladysvale
Sterkfontein
Makapansgat
Swartkrans
Pretoria
Kromdraai
Johannesburg
Taung
Drimolen
Kimberley •
SOUTH AFRICA
Pinnacle Point

MAP 5

The Emergence of Modern Humans

Early forms of *Homo (H.) erectus,* sometimes called *H. ergaster,* have been found in East Africa and the former Soviet Georgia. By 1.7 million years ago, *H. erectus* had spread from Africa into Asia, including Indonesia, and eventually Europe. The *H. erectus* period may have lasted until 300,000 years ago. Other archaic forms of *Homo,* including fossils sometimes called *H. antecessor* and *H. heidelbergensis,* have been found in various parts of the Old World.

QUESTIONS

Look at Map 5, "The Emergence of Modern Humans."

1. Locate the site of Dmanisi (Georgia). Locate the site of Nariokotome (East Turkana, Kenya). These are sites where similarly dated early remains of *Homo erectus* (or *Homo ergaster*) have been found. Find two additional sites where hominins with similar dates (1.8–1.6 m.y.a.) have been found.

2. Considering Africa and Asia, name five sites (other than Dmanisi and Nariokotome) where *Homo erectus* fossils have been found.

3. Locate Heidelberg (Mauer) and Ceprano. What kinds of hominin fossils have been found there?

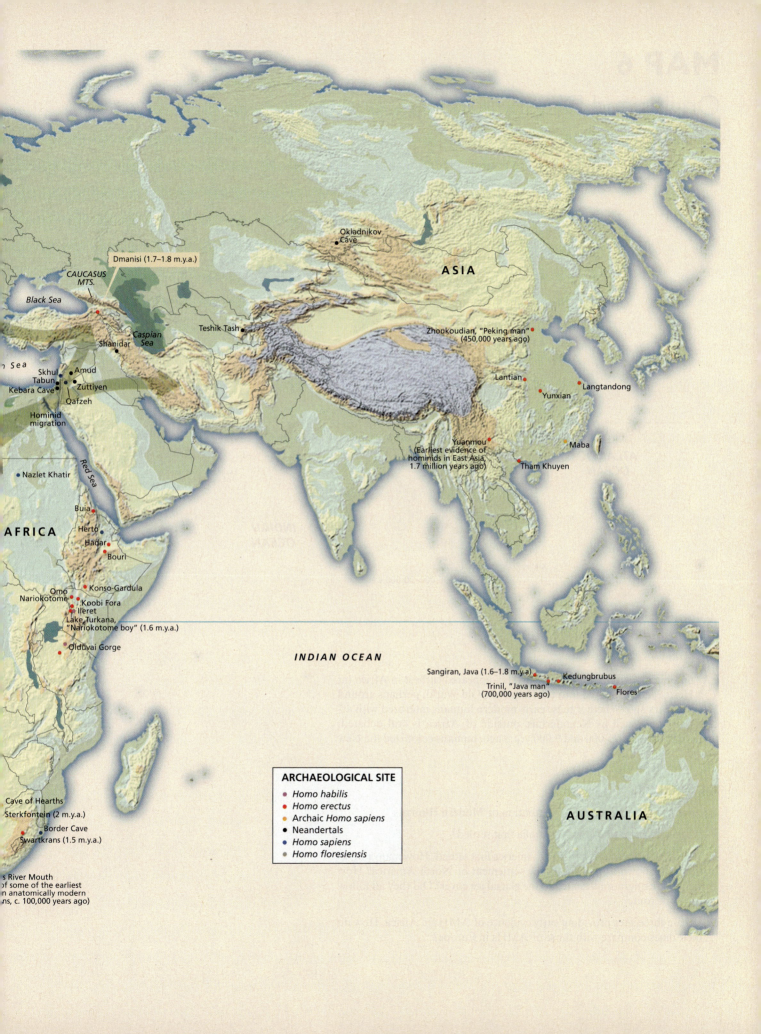

Okladnikov
Cave

ASIA

Dmanisi (1.7–1.8 m.y.a.)

CAUCASUS
MTS.

Black Sea

Zhoukoudian, "Peking man"
(450,000 years ago)

Teshik Tash

Caspian
Sea

Shanidar

Lantian

Langtandong

Yunxian

Skhul
Tabun
Amud
Zuttiyen
Kebara Cave
Qafzeh

n Sea

Hominid
migration

Maba

Red Sea

Yuanmou
(Earliest evidence of
hominids in East Asia,
1.7 million years ago)

Tham Khuyen

• Nazlet Khatir

Buia

AFRICA

Herto

Hadar

Bouri

Konso-Gardula

Omo
Nariokotome
Koobi Fora
Ileret
Lake Turkana,
"Nariokotome boy" (1.6 m.y.a.)

Olduvai Gorge

INDIAN OCEAN

Sangiran, Java (1.6–1.8 m.y.a)
Kedungbrubus

Trinil, "Java man"
(700,000 years ago)

Flores

Cave of Hearths
Sterkfontein (2 m.y.a.)

Border Cave
Swartkrans (1.5 m.y.a.)

AUSTRALIA

s River Mouth
of some of the earliest
n anatomically modern
ns, c. 100,000 years ago)

ARCHAEOLOGICAL SITE

● *Homo habilis*
● *Homo erectus*
● Archaic *Homo sapiens*
● Neandertals
● *Homo sapiens*
● *Homo floresiensis*

MAP 6

Origins and Distribution of Modern Humans

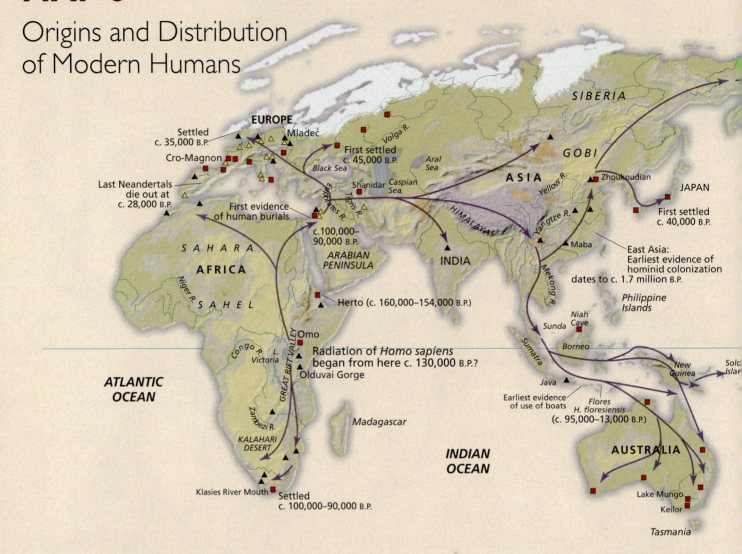

Labels on map:

SIBERIA

EUROPE
Settled c. 35,000 B.P.
Mladeč
Cro-Magnon
Last Neandertals die out at c. 28,000 B.P.
First evidence of human burials
First settled c. 45,000 B.P.
Black Sea
Volga R.
Aral Sea
Caspian Sea
Shanidar
Euphrates R.
Tigris R.
c.100,000–90,000 B.P.
ARABIAN PENINSULA
SAHARA
AFRICA
SAHEL
Niger R.
INDIA
HIMALAYAS
ASIA
GOBI
Yellow R.
Zhoukoudian
JAPAN
First settled c. 40,000 B.P.
Maba
Yangtze R.
East Asia: Earliest evidence of hominid colonization dates to c. 1.7 million B.P.
Mekong R.
Herto (c. 160,000–154,000 B.P.)
Omo
Congo R.
L. Victoria
GREAT RIFT VALLEY
Radiation of *Homo sapiens* began from here c. 130,000 B.P.?
Olduvai Gorge
Philippine Islands
Niah Cave
Sunda
Borneo
Sumatra
New Guinea
Solo Island
Java
Earliest evidence of use of boats
Flores *H. floresiensis* (c. 95,000–13,000 B.P.)
ATLANTIC OCEAN
Zambezi R.
KALAHARI DESERT
Madagascar
INDIAN OCEAN
AUSTRALIA
Lake Mungo
Keilor
Tasmania
Klasies River Mouth
Settled c. 100,000–90,000 B.P.

Anatomically modern humans (AMHs), appeared earliest in Africa (at Herto?) and migrated into the rest of the Old World, perhaps around 130,000 years ago. Whether these early modern humans interbred with archaic humans, such as Neandertals, outside of Africa is still debated. Sometime between 25,000 and 9,000 years ago, humans colonized the New World.

QUESTIONS

Look at Map 6, "Origins and Distribution of Modern Humans."

1. When and from where was Australia first settled?

2. When and from where was North America first settled? How many migrations are shown as figuring in the settlement of North America? How were these migrations related to the glacial ice cover? Did they all follow the same route?

3. Locate three sites providing early evidence of AMHs in Africa. How do their dates compare with those of AMHs in Europe?

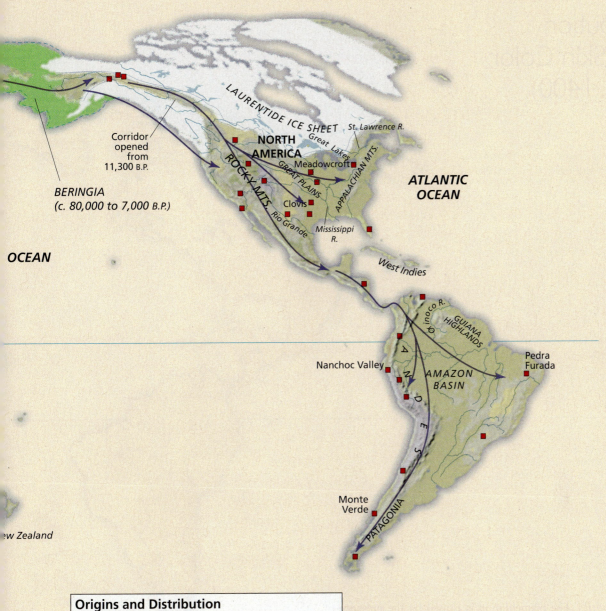

LAURENTIDE ICE SHEET

St. Lawrence R.

Great Lakes

NORTH
AMERICA

Meadowcroft

ATLANTIC
OCEAN

Corridor
opened
from
11,300 B.P.

ROCKY MTS.

GREAT PLAINS

APPALACHIAN MTS.

Clovis

Rio Grande

Mississippi
R.

West Indies

BERINGIA
(c. 80,000 to 7,000 B.P.)

OCEAN

inoco R.

GUIANA
HIGHLANDS

Pedra
Furada

Nanchoc Valley

A
N
D
E
S

AMAZON
BASIN

Monte
Verde

PATAGONIA

New Zealand

Origins and Distribution of Modern Humans

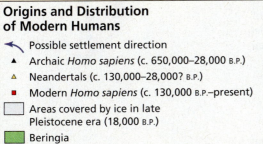

- Possible settlement direction
- ▲ Archaic *Homo sapiens* (c. 650,000–28,000 B.P.)
- △ Neandertals (c. 130,000–28,000? B.P.)
- ■ Modern *Homo sapiens* (c. 130,000 B.P.–present)
- ▢ Areas covered by ice in late Pleistocene era (18,000 B.P.)
- ▢ Beringia

MAP 7

The Distribution of Human Skin Color (Before C.E. 1400)

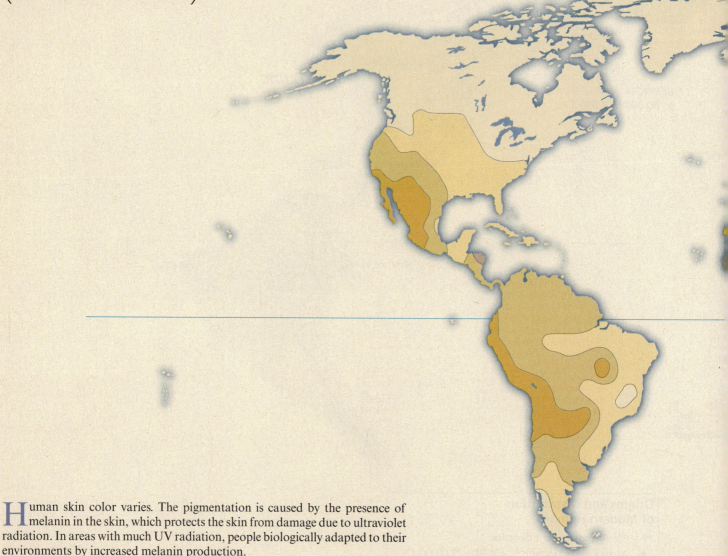

Human skin color varies. The pigmentation is caused by the presence of melanin in the skin, which protects the skin from damage due to ultraviolet radiation. In areas with much UV radiation, people biologically adapted to their environments by increased melanin production.

QUESTIONS

Look at Map 7, "The Distribution of Human Skin Color (Before C.E. 1400)."

1. Where are the Native Americans with the darkest skin color located? What factors help explain this distribution?

2. In both western and eastern hemispheres, is the lightest skin color found in the north or the south? Outside Asia, where do you find skin color closest to northern Asian skin color? Is this surprising given what you have read about migrations and settlement history?

3. Where are skin colors darkest? How might you explain this distribution?

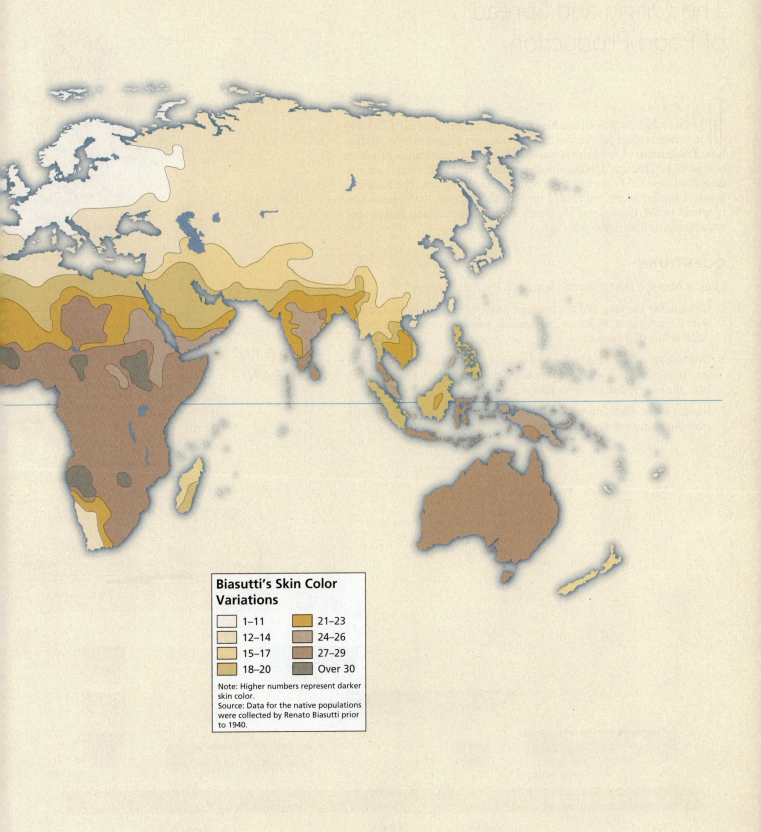

Biasutti's Skin Color Variations

☐ 1–11	☐ 21–23
☐ 12–14	☐ 24–26
☐ 15–17	☐ 27–29
☐ 18–20	☐ Over 30

Note: Higher numbers represent darker skin color.

Source: Data for the native populations were collected by Renato Biasutti prior to 1940.

MAP 8

The Origin and Spread of Food Production

The Neolithic, or New Stone Age, refers to the period of early farming settlements when people who had been foragers shifted to food production. This pattern of subsistence was based on the domestication of plants and animals. Through domestication, people transformed plants and animals from their wild state to a form more useful to humans. The Neolithic began in the fertile crescent area of the Middle East over 10,000 years ago. It spread to the Levant and Mediterranean, finally reaching Britain and Scandinavia around 5,000 years ago.

QUESTIONS

Look at Map 8, "The Origin and Spread of Food Production."

1. Considering the map and the timeline, name three regions where cattle were domesticated. Based on the timeline, what animals were domesticated in North America?

2. Did Ireland receive Middle Eastern domesticates? What is the origin of the "Irish potato," or white potato (see the timeline), which became, much later, the caloric basis of Irish subsistence?

3. Besides cattle, what animals were domesticated more than once? Where were those areas of domestication?

ATLANTIC OCEAN

Seine R.
Loire R.
Douro R.
Tagus R.
Ebro R.
Guadalquivir R.

Dog

N

0   250   500 Miles
0   250   500 Kilometers

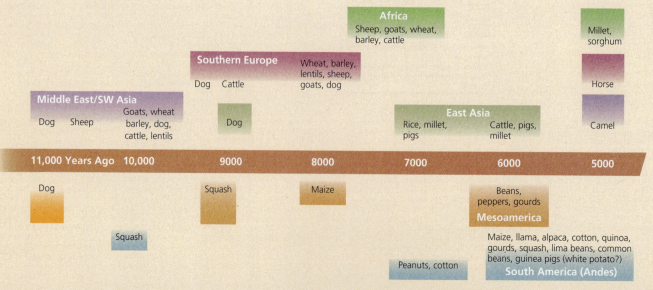

		Africa		Millet, sorghum
		Sheep, goats, wheat, barley, cattle		
	Southern Europe			
		Wheat, barley, lentils, sheep, goats, dog		Horse
	Dog Cattle			
Middle East/SW Asia			East Asia	
	Goats, wheat barley, dog, cattle, lentils	Dog	Rice, millet, pigs Cattle, pigs, millet	Camel
Dog Sheep				

11,000 Years Ago   10,000   9000   8000   7000   6000   5000

Dog	Squash	Maize		Beans, peppers, gourds	
				Mesoamerica	
Squash				Maize, llama, alpaca, cotton, quinoa, gourds, squash, lima beans, common beans, guinea pigs (white potato?)	
		Peanuts, cotton		South America (Andes)	

Early Neolithic Sites of the Middle East and Europe

Settlement region and date
Settlement sites
Possible migration routes
Areas of domestication

Lake Ladoga

Lake Peipus

Baltic Sea

Aral Sea

Elbe R.

Goose

Oder R.

Bug R.

Vistula R.

Dniester R.

Dnieper R.

Horse

Sea of Azov

Ural R.

Volga R.

Caspian Sea

Danube R.

Po R.

Sava R. 7,500

7,700

Danube R.

7,800

Black Sea

7,700

7,800 9,000

8,000

Cattle

8,400

9,000

8,900

9,400?

9,600

9,800

10,300

Pig

Cattle

Sheep

Tigris R.

Euphrates R.

Goat

Goat

Persian Gulf

Adriatic Sea

Mediterranean Sea

Dromedary

10,300

Ass
Honey Bee
Cat

Yam, oil palm

Cat (Egypt)

Chickens (south-central Asia)

| 4000 | 3000 | 2000 | 1000 Years Ago |

Marsh elder
Sunflower
Squash

Lamb's quarters

Maize

North America

White potato

Mediterranean Domestication

Barley	Dates	Grapes
Cattle	Garlic	Lentils
Celery	Goat	Lettuce
		Olives

Southwest Asia Domestication

Barley	Duck	Melons
Beans	Fruits (seed	Oats
Beets	and stone)	Oil seeds
Camel (Bactrian)	Goat	Onions
Carrots	Grapes	Rye
Cattle	Hemp	Sheep
Dog	Horse	Wheat

MAP 9

Ancient Civilizations of the Old World

Kumbi Saleh

Ghana
A.D. 800–1076

Songhay/Songhai
A.D. 1325–1550

Mali
A.D. 1230–1500

Jenne-jeno
2200 B.P.–
1000 B.P. (A.D. 1000)

ATLANTIC OCEAN

North Sea

Medit

Archaic states developed in many parts of the Old World at different periods. The earliest civilizations, such as Mesopotamia, Egypt, and the Indus Valley, are generally placed at about 5500 B.P. States developed later in Asia, Africa, and the Americas (see Map 13).

QUESTIONS

Look at Map 9, "Ancient Civilizations of the Old World."

1. What contemporary nations would you have to visit if you wanted to see all the places where ancient civilizations developed in the Old World? Would some countries be off limits for political reasons? How do you think such limitations have affected the archaeological record?

2. Of the ancient states shown on Map 9, which developed latest? Why do you think the first states developed when and where they did?

3. In which of the ancient states shown on Map 9 were Middle Eastern domesticates basic to the economy? In which states shown on Map 9 were other domesticates basic to the economy?

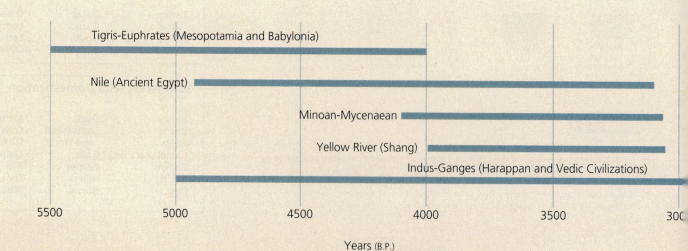

Tigris-Euphrates (Mesopotamia and Babylonia)

Nile (Ancient Egypt)

Minoan-Mycenaean

Yellow River (Shang)

Indus-Ganges (Harappan and Vedic Civilizations)

| 5500 | 5000 | 4500 | 4000 | 3500 | 300 |

Years (B.P.)

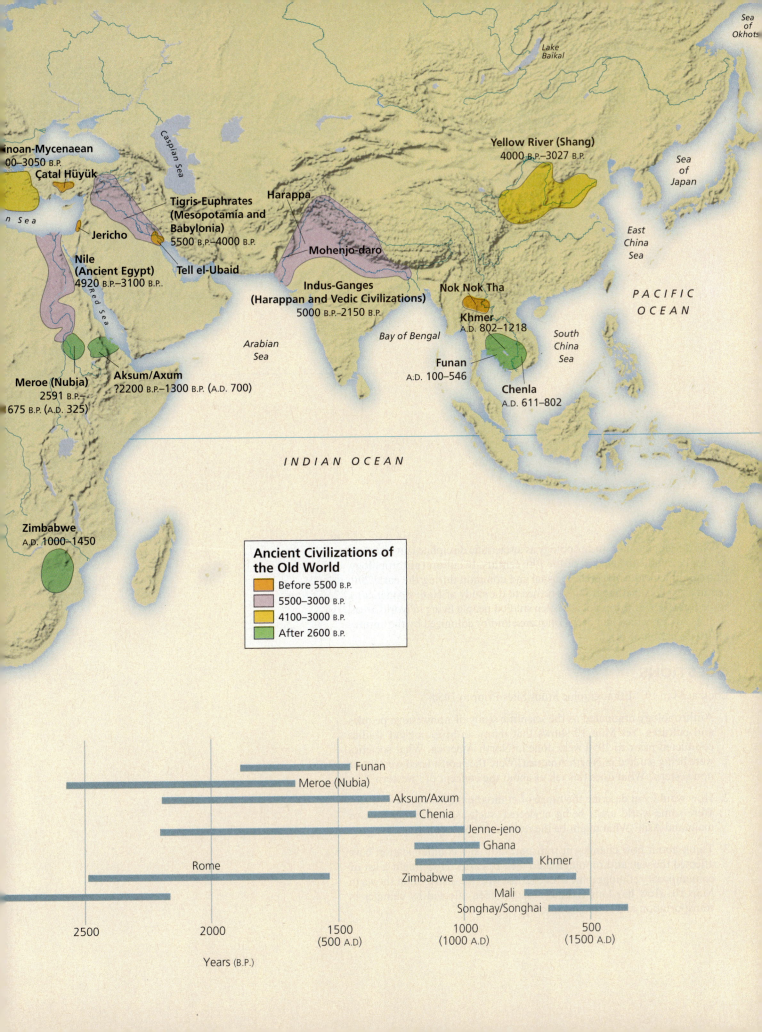

Minoan-Mycenaean
00–3050 B.P.

Çatal Hüyük

Jericho

**Tigris-Euphrates
(Mesopotamia and
Babylonia)**
5500 B.P.–4000 B.P.

Tell el-Ubaid

**Nile
(Ancient Egypt)**
4920 B.P.–3100 B.P.

Harappa

Mohenjo-daro

**Indus-Ganges
(Harappan and Vedic Civilizations)**
5000 B.P.–2150 B.P.

Yellow River (Shang)
4000 B.P.–3027 B.P.

Nok Nok Tha

Khmer
A.D. 802–1218

Funan
A.D. 100–546

Chenla
A.D. 611–802

Meroe (Nubia)
2591 B.P.–
675 B.P. (A.D. 325)

Aksum/Axum
?2200 B.P.–1300 B.P. (A.D. 700)

Zimbabwe
A.D. 1000–1450

Caspian Sea

n Sea

Red Sea

*Arabian
Sea*

Bay of Bengal

*South
China
Sea*

*East
China
Sea*

*Sea
of
Japan*

*Sea
of
Okhots*

*Lake
Baikal*

*PACIFIC
OCEAN*

INDIAN OCEAN

Ancient Civilizations of the Old World

■ (orange)	Before 5500 B.P.
■ (pink)	5500–3000 B.P.
■ (yellow)	4100–3000 B.P.
■ (green)	After 2600 B.P.

Funan
Meroe (Nubia)
Aksum/Axum
Chenia
Jenne-jeno
Ghana
Khmer
Zimbabwe
Mali
Songhay/Songhai
Rome

2500   2000   1500
(500 A.D)   1000
(1000 A.D)   500
(1500 A.D)

Years (B.P.)

MAP 10
Ethnographic Study Sites Prior to 1950

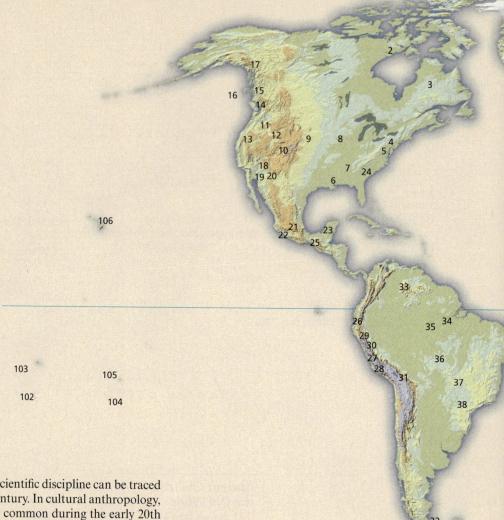

The development of anthropology as a scientific discipline can be traced to the middle to late part of the 19th century. In cultural anthropology, ethnographic field work became usual and common during the early 20th century. American ethnographers turned to the study of Native Americans, while European anthropologists often studied people living in world areas, such as Africa, which had been conquered and/or colonized by the anthropologist's nation of origin.

QUESTIONS

Look at Map 10, "Ethnographic Study Sites Prior to 1950."

1. Anthropology originated as the scientific study of nonwestern peoples and cultures. Yet Map 10 shows that many anthropological studies conducted prior to 1950 were done in North America. What societies were being studied in North America? Were they considered western or nonwestern? What does this tell us about the concept of "western"?

2. How would you describe the range of ethnographic sites prior to 1950? Were some world areas being neglected, such as the Middle East or mainland Asia? What might be the reasons for such omissions?

3. Think about how changes in transportation and communication have affected the way anthropologists do their research. How might a list of contemporary ethnographic sites contrast with the distribution shown in Map 10. How has longitudinal research been affected by changes in transportation and communication?

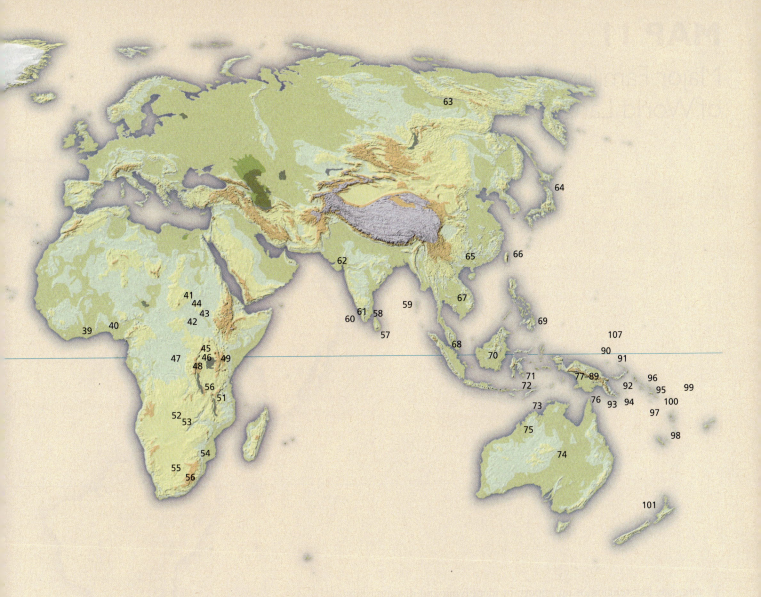

Ethnographic Study Sites Prior to 1950

North America
1. Eastern Eskimo
2. Central Eskimo
3. Naskapi
4. Iroquois
5. Delaware
6. Natchez
7. Shawnee
8. Kickapoo
9. Sioux
10. Crow
11. Nez Percé
12. Shoshone
13. Paviotso
14. Kwakiutl
15. Tsimshian
16. Haida
17. Tlingit
18. Navajo
19. Hopi
20. Zuñi
21. Aztec
22. Tzintzuntzan and Cuanajo
23. Maya
24. Cherokee
25. San Pedro

South America
Ecuador
26. Jívaro
Peru
27. Inca
28. Machiguenga
29. Achuara
30. Campa
Bolivia
31. Aymara
Chile
32. Yahgan
Venezuela
33. Yanomamö
Brazil
34. Tapirapé
35. Mundurucu
36. Mehinacu
37. Kuikuru
38. Caingang

Africa
Ghana
39. Ashanti
Nigeria
40. Kadar

Sudan
41. Fur
42. Dinka
43. Nuer
44. Azande
Uganda
45. Bunyoro
46. Ganda
Dem. Rep. of Congo
47. Mbuti
Rwanda
48. Watusi
Kenya
49. Masai
Tanzania
50. Nyakyusa
51. Lovedu
Zambia
52. Ndembu
53. Barotse
Mozambique
54. Bathonga
South Africa
55. !Kung Bushmen
56. Zulu

Asia
Sri Lanka
57. Vedda
58. Sinhalese
India
59. Andaman
60. Nayar
61. Tamil
62. Rajput
Siberia
63. Tungus
Japan
64. Ainu
China
65. Luts'un village
Taiwan
66. Taiwan Chinese
Vietnam
67. Mnong-Gar
Malaya
68. Semai

Pacific
Philippines
69. Tasaday
Indonesia Area
70. Dyaks
71. Alorese
72. Tetum
Australia
73. Tiwi
74. Arunta
75. Murngin
76. Saibai Islanders
New Guinea
77. Arapesh
78. Dani
79. Gururumba
80. Kai
81. Kapauku
82. Mae Enga
83. Kuma
84. Mundugumor
85. Tchambuli
86. Tsembaga Maring
87. Tavade
88. Foré
89. Etoro

Melanesian Islands
90. Manus Islands
91. New Hanover Islanders
92. Trobriand Islanders
93. Dobuans
94. Rossel Islanders
95. Kaoka
96. Malaita Islanders
97. Espiritu Santo Islanders
98. Tana Islanders
99. Tikopia
100. Sivai

Polynesian Islands
101. Maori
102. Tongans
103. Samoans
104. Mangians
105. Tahitians
106. Hawaiians

Micronesian Islands
107. Truk

MAP 11
Major Families
of World Languages

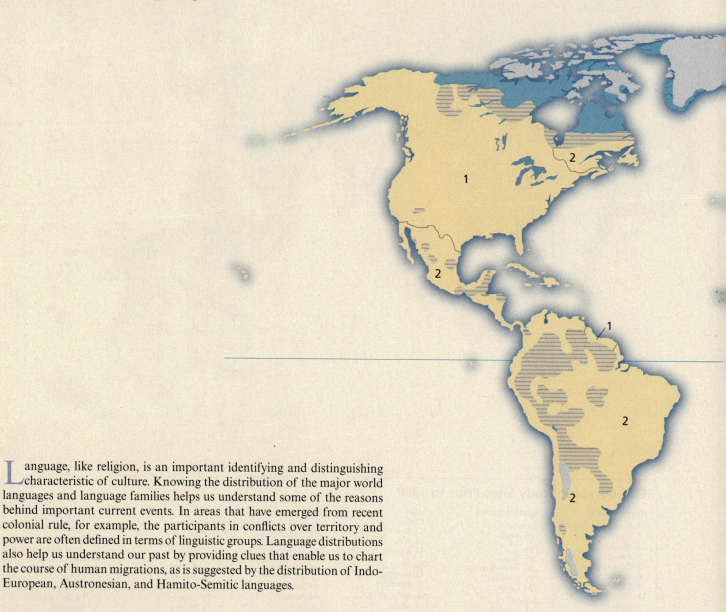

Language, like religion, is an important identifying and distinguishing characteristic of culture. Knowing the distribution of the major world languages and language families helps us understand some of the reasons behind important current events. In areas that have emerged from recent colonial rule, for example, the participants in conflicts over territory and power are often defined in terms of linguistic groups. Language distributions also help us understand our past by providing clues that enable us to chart the course of human migrations, as is suggested by the distribution of Indo-European, Austronesian, and Hamito-Semitic languages.

QUESTIONS

Look at Map 11, "Major Families of World Languages."

1. Name three language families or subfamilies that are spoken on more than one continent. How do you explain this distribution?

2. Where are the Austronesian languages spoken? How might one explain this distribution?

3. What language families are spoken on the African continent? Locate the Niger-Congo language family, of which the Bantu languages comprise a subfamily.

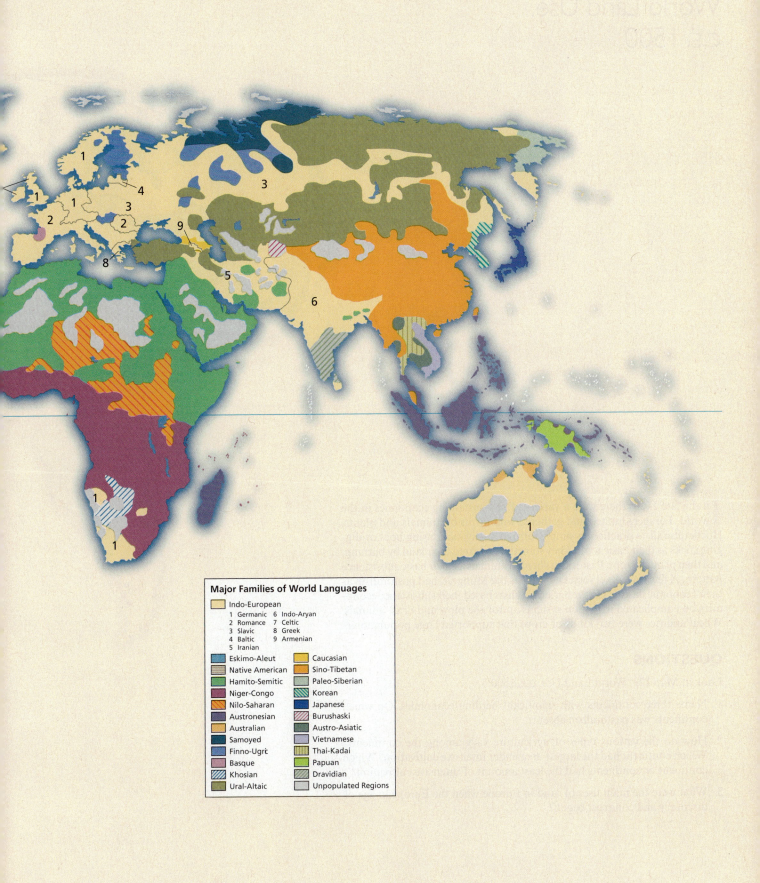

Major Families of World Languages

Indo-European
1 Germanic	6 Indo-Aryan
2 Romance	7 Celtic
3 Slavic	8 Greek
4 Baltic	9 Armenian
5 Iranian	

Eskimo-Aleut
Native American
Hamito-Semitic
Niger-Congo
Nilo-Saharan
Austronesian
Australian
Samoyed
Finno-Ugric
Basque
Khosian
Ural-Altaic

Caucasian
Sino-Tibetan
Paleo-Siberian
Korean
Japanese
Burushaski
Austro-Asiatic
Vietnamese
Thai-Kadai
Papuan
Dravidian
Unpopulated Regions

MAP 12
World Land Use,
c.e. 1500

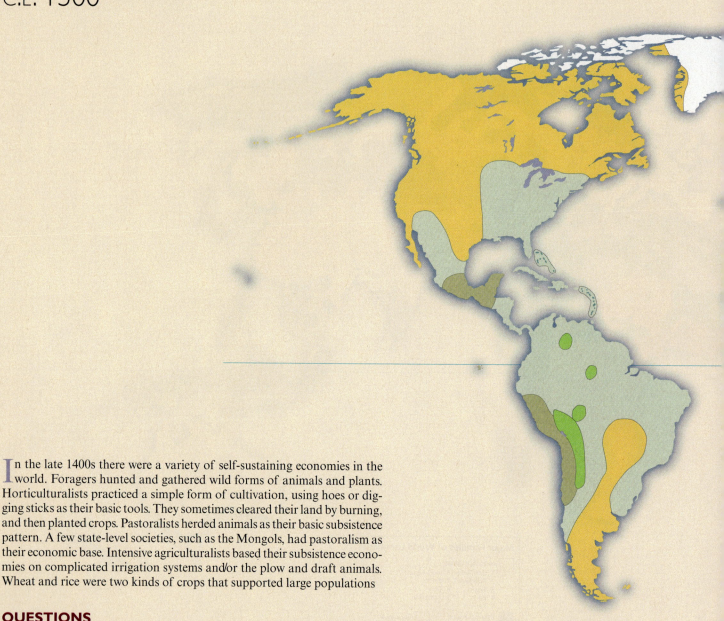

In the late 1400s there were a variety of self-sustaining economies in the world. Foragers hunted and gathered wild forms of animals and plants. Horticulturalists practiced a simple form of cultivation, using hoes or digging sticks as their basic tools. They sometimes cleared their land by burning, and then planted crops. Pastoralists herded animals as their basic subsistence pattern. A few state-level societies, such as the Mongols, had pastoralism as their economic base. Intensive agriculturalists based their subsistence economies on complicated irrigation systems and/or the plow and draft animals. Wheat and rice were two kinds of crops that supported large populations

QUESTIONS

Look at Map 12, "World Land Use, c.e. 1500."

1. Name three continents with significant herding economies. On which continents was pastoralism absent?

2. How do the various types of agriculture vary among the continents? Which continent had the largest area under intensive cultivation? Which continent or continents had the least amount of intensive cultivation?

3. What were the main uses of land in Europe when the European age of discovery and conquest began?

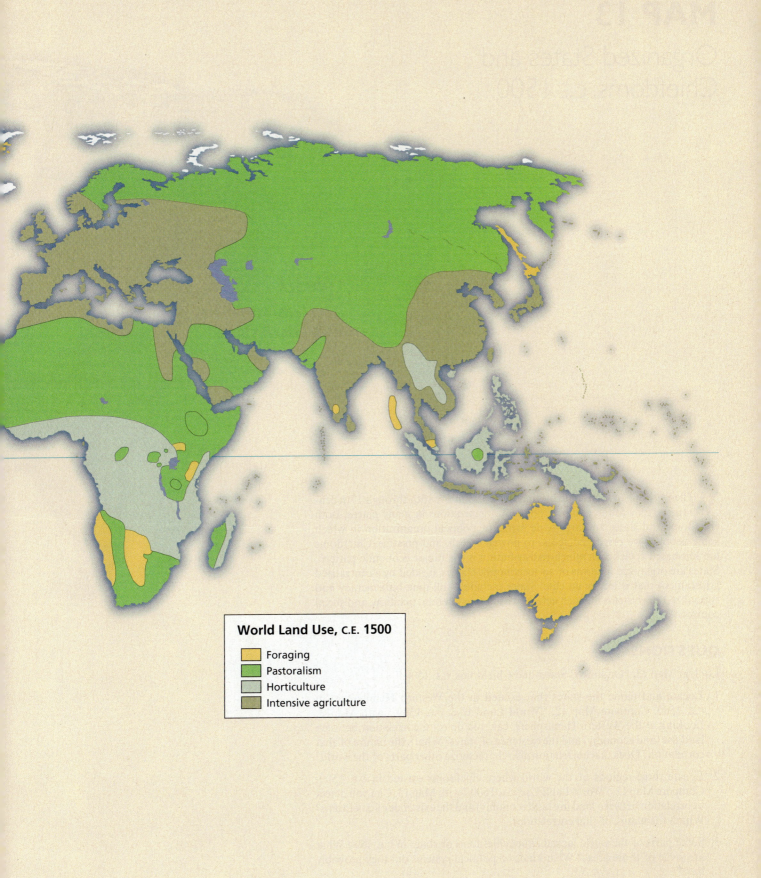

World Land Use, C.E. 1500

- Foraging
- Pastoralism
- Horticulture
- Intensive agriculture

MAP 13

Organized States and Chiefdoms, C.E. 1500

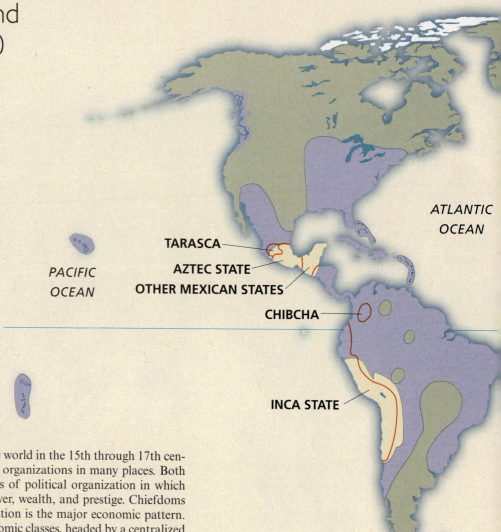

ATLANTIC
OCEAN

PACIFIC
OCEAN

TARASCA

AZTEC STATE

OTHER MEXICAN STATES

CHIBCHA

INCA STATE

When Europeans started exploring the world in the 15th through 17th centuries, they found complex political organizations in many places. Both chiefdoms and states are large-scale forms of political organization in which some people have privileged access to power, wealth, and prestige. Chiefdoms are kin-based societies in which redistribution is the major economic pattern. States are organized in terms of socioeconomic classes, headed by a centralized government that is led by an elite. States include a full-time bureaucracy and specialized subsystems for such activities as military action, taxation, and social control.

QUESTIONS

Look at Map 13, "Organized States and Chiefdoms, C.E. 1500."

1. Locate and name the states that existed in the Western Hemisphere in C.E. 1500. Compare Map 12, "World Land Use: C.E. 1500," with Map 13. Looking at the Western Hemisphere, can you detect a correlation between land use (and economy) and the existence of states? What's the nature of that correlation? Does that correlation also characterize other parts of the world?

2. Locate three regions of the world where chiefdoms existed in C.E. 1500. Compare Map 12, "World Land Use: C.E. 1500," with Map 13. Can you detect a correlation between land use (and economy) and the existence of chiefdoms? What's the nature of that correlation?

3. Some parts of the world lacked either chiefdoms or states in C.E. 1500. What are some of those areas? What kinds of political systems did they probably have?

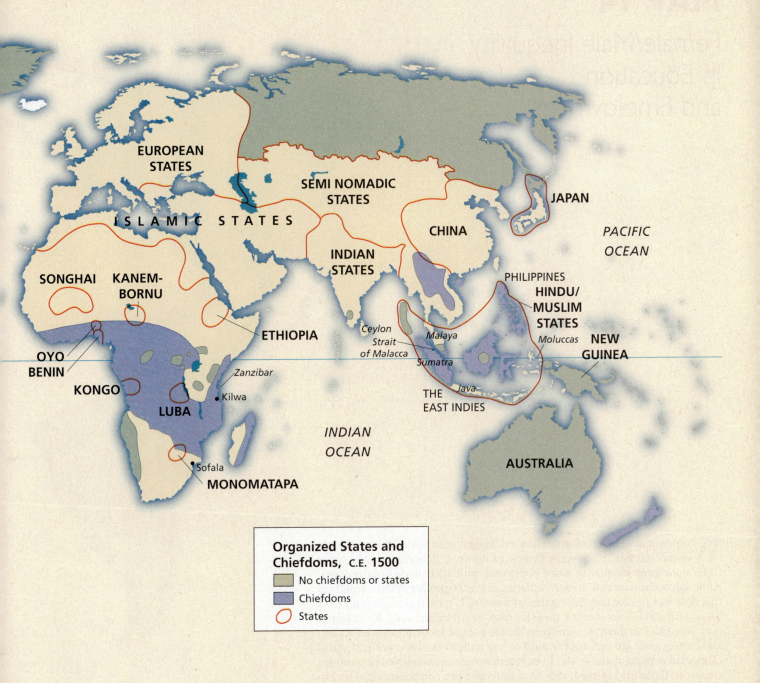

EUROPEAN
STATES

SEMI NOMADIC
STATES

JAPAN

ISLAMIC STATES

CHINA

PACIFIC
OCEAN

INDIAN
STATES

SONGHAI

KANEM-
BORNU

PHILIPPINES

HINDU/
MUSLIM
STATES

NEW
GUINEA

ETHIOPIA

Ceylon
Strait
of Malacca

Malaya

Moluccas

OYO
BENIN

Sumatra

KONGO

Zanzibar

THE
EAST INDIES

Java

LUBA

Kilwa

INDIAN
OCEAN

MONOMATAPA

Sofala

AUSTRALIA

**Organized States and
Chiefdoms,** C.E. **1500**

No chiefdoms or states

Chiefdoms

States

MAP 14

Female/Male Inequality in Education and Employment

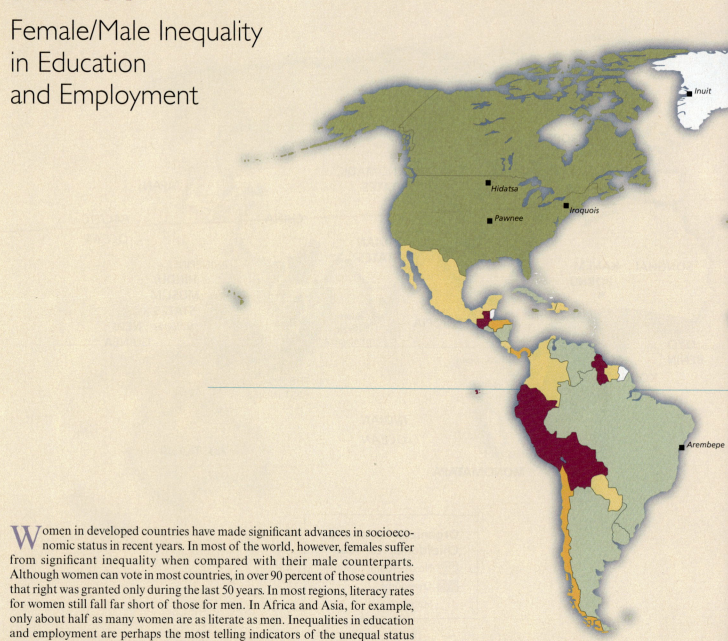

Women in developed countries have made significant advances in socioeconomic status in recent years. In most of the world, however, females suffer from significant inequality when compared with their male counterparts. Although women can vote in most countries, in over 90 percent of those countries that right was granted only during the last 50 years. In most regions, literacy rates for women still fall far short of those for men. In Africa and Asia, for example, only about half as many women are as literate as men. Inequalities in education and employment are perhaps the most telling indicators of the unequal status of women in most of the world. Even where women are employed in positions similar to those held by men, they tend to receive less compensation. The gap between rich and poor involves not only a clear geographic differentiation, but a clear gender differentiation as well.

QUESTIONS

Look at Map 14 "Female/Male Inequality in Education and Employment."

1. Locate and name three Third World countries with the same degree of gender-based inequality as the United States and Canada.

2. Two of the world's largest developing nations are coded as having "less inequality." What are they?

3. Most European countries are coded as having "least inequality." Which western European countries are exceptions?

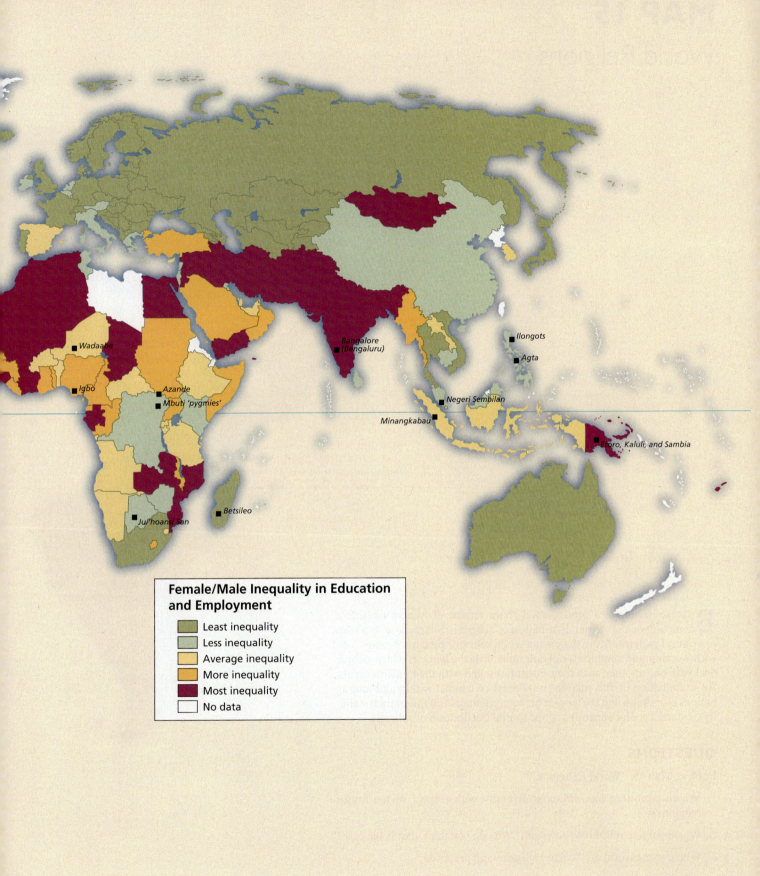

Female/Male Inequality in Education and Employment

- Least inequality
- Less inequality
- Average inequality
- More inequality
- Most inequality
- No data

Wadaabe

Igbo

Azande

Mbuti 'pygmies'

Ju/'hoansi San

Betsileo

Bangalore (Bengaluru)

Minangkabau

Negeri Sembilan

Ilongots

Agta

Etoro, Kaluli, and Sambia

MAP 15
World Religions

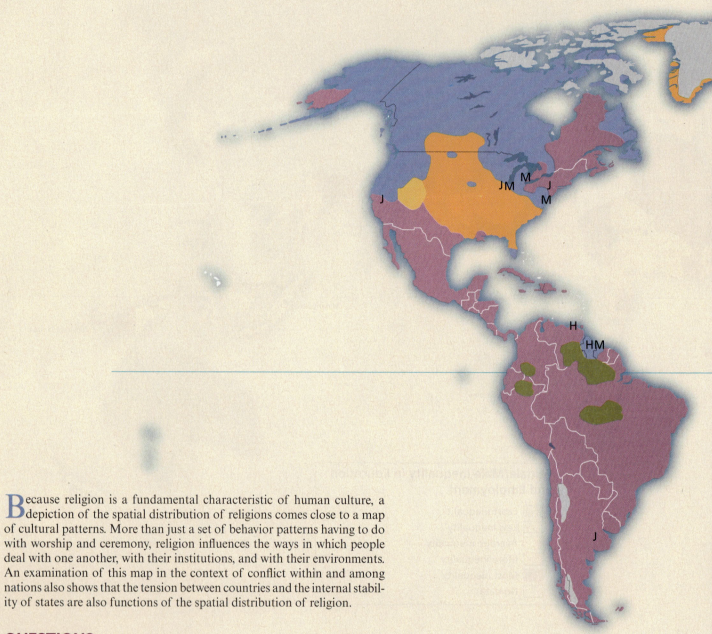

Because religion is a fundamental characteristic of human culture, a depiction of the spatial distribution of religions comes close to a map of cultural patterns. More than just a set of behavior patterns having to do with worship and ceremony, religion influences the ways in which people deal with one another, with their institutions, and with their environments. An examination of this map in the context of conflict within and among nations also shows that the tension between countries and the internal stability of states are also functions of the spatial distribution of religion.

QUESTIONS

Look at Map 15, "World Religions."

1. Which continent has the most diversity with respect to the major religions?

2. Which continent is most Protestant? Why do you think that is the case?

3. Where in the world are "tribal" religions still practiced?

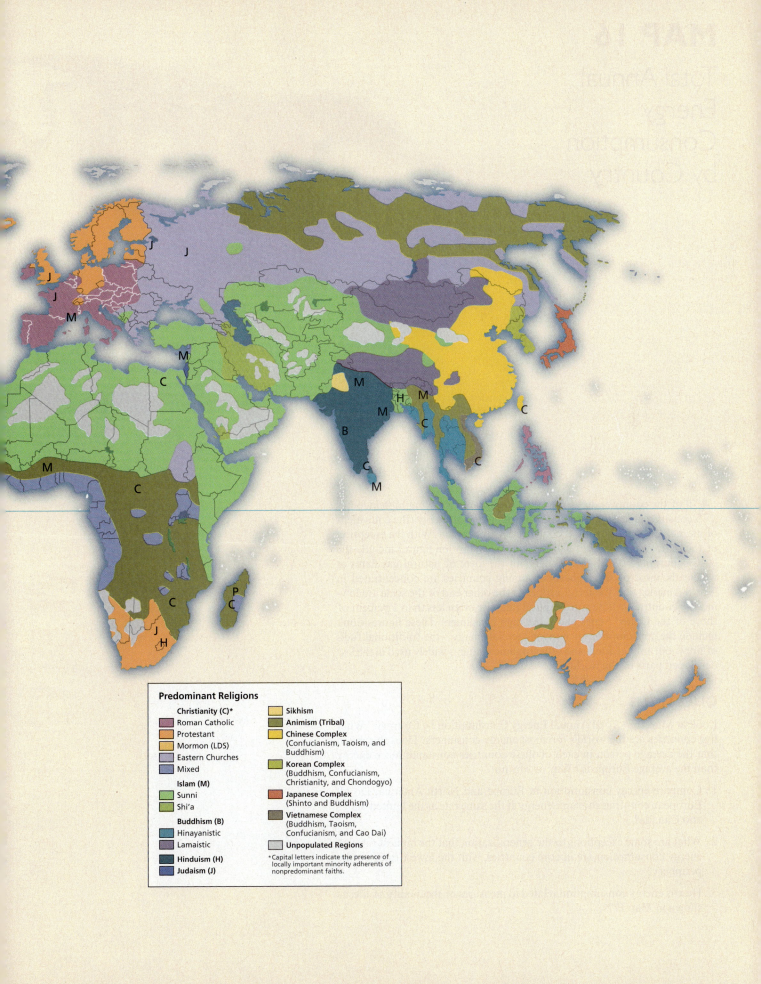

Predominant Religions

Christianity (C)*
- Roman Catholic
- Protestant
- Mormon (LDS)
- Eastern Churches
- Mixed

Islam (M)
- Sunni
- Shi'a

Buddhism (B)
- Hinayanistic
- Lamaistic

Hinduism (H)

Judaism (J)

- Sikhism
- Animism (Tribal)
- Chinese Complex
(Confucianism, Taoism, and Buddhism)
- Korean Complex
(Buddhism, Confucianism, Christianity, and Chondogyo)
- Japanese Complex
(Shinto and Buddhism)
- Vietnamese Complex
(Buddhism, Taoism, Confucianism, and Cao Dai)
- Unpopulated Regions

*Capital letters indicate the presence of locally important minority adherents of nonpredominant faiths.

MAP 16

Total Annual Energy Consumption by Country

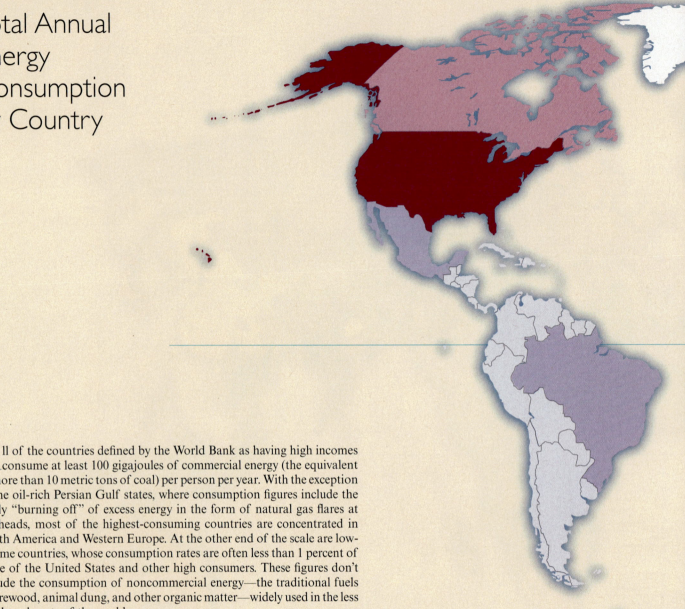

All of the countries defined by the World Bank as having high incomes consume at least 100 gigajoules of commercial energy (the equivalent of more than 10 metric tons of coal) per person per year. With the exception of the oil-rich Persian Gulf states, where consumption figures include the costly "burning off" of excess energy in the form of natural gas flares at wellheads, most of the highest-consuming countries are concentrated in North America and Western Europe. At the other end of the scale are low-income countries, whose consumption rates are often less than 1 percent of those of the United States and other high consumers. These figures don't include the consumption of noncommercial energy—the traditional fuels of firewood, animal dung, and other organic matter—widely used in the less developed parts of the world.

QUESTIONS

Look at Map 16, " Total Annual Energy Consumption by Country." What five countries are the world's foremost energy consumers? Does this mean that the average person in each of these countries consumes more energy than the average European? Why or why not?

1. Compare energy consumption in Europe and North America. Do all European countries consume energy at the same rate as the United States and Canada?

2. What are some exceptions to the generalization that the highest rates of energy consumption are in core countries, with the lowest rates on the periphery?

3. How is energy consumption related to measures of the quality of life, as shown in Map 17?

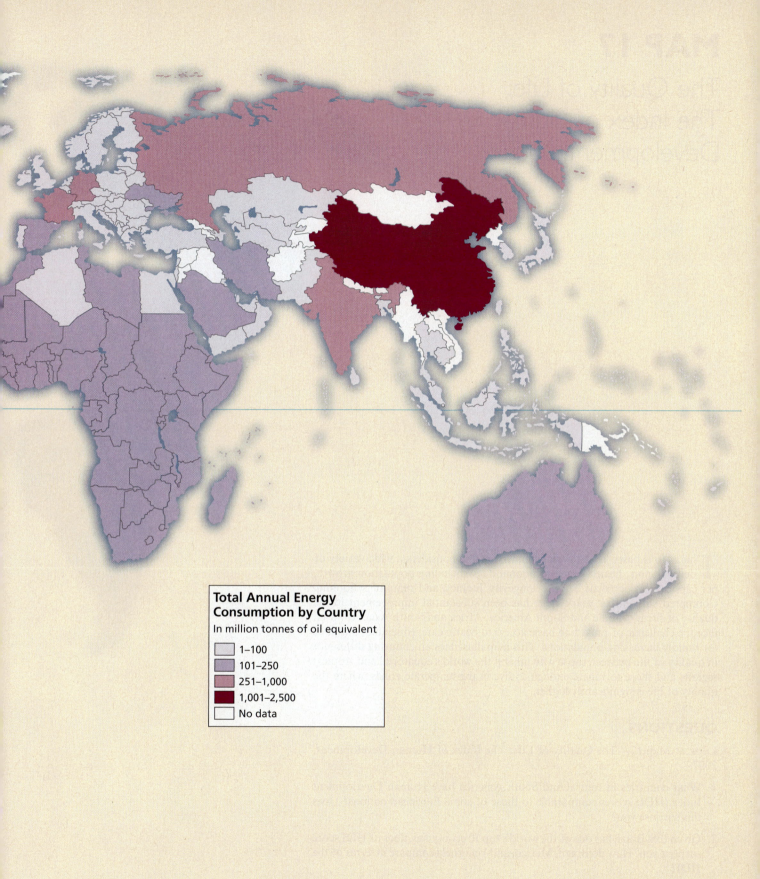

Total Annual Energy Consumption by Country

In million tonnes of oil equivalent

- 1–100
- 101–250
- 251–1,000
- 1,001–2,500
- No data

MAP 17

The Quality of Life: The Index of Human Development, 2007

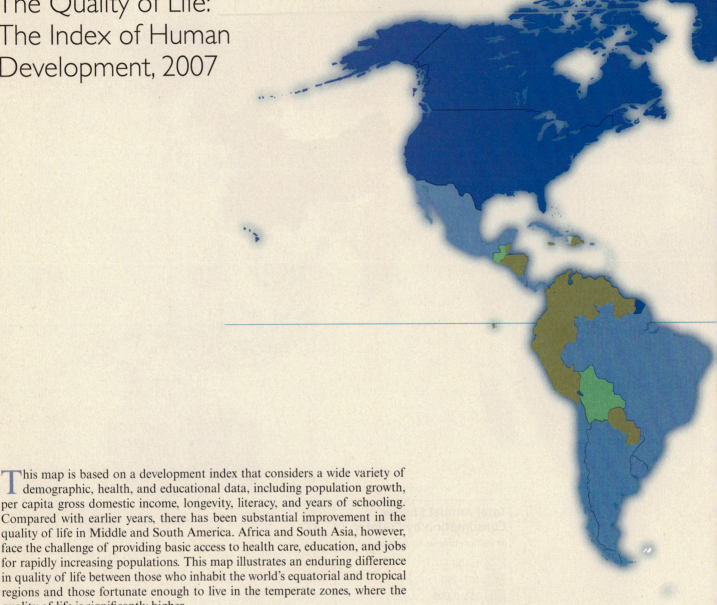

This map is based on a development index that considers a wide variety of demographic, health, and educational data, including population growth, per capita gross domestic income, longevity, literacy, and years of schooling. Compared with earlier years, there has been substantial improvement in the quality of life in Middle and South America. Africa and South Asia, however, face the challenge of providing basic access to health care, education, and jobs for rapidly increasing populations. This map illustrates an enduring difference in quality of life between those who inhabit the world's equatorial and tropical regions and those fortunate enough to live in the temperate zones, where the quality of life is significantly higher.

QUESTIONS

Look at Map 17, "The Quality of Life: The Index of Human Development, 2007."

1. What countries in central and South America have Human Development Index (HDI) scores comparable to those of some European nations? Does this surprise you?

2. Given that Brazil has one of the world's top 10 economies, does its HDI score surprise you? How do Brazil, Mexico, and Venezuela compare in terms of the HDI?

3. Do you notice a correlation between deforestation (Map 1) and quality of life? Does India fit this correlation?

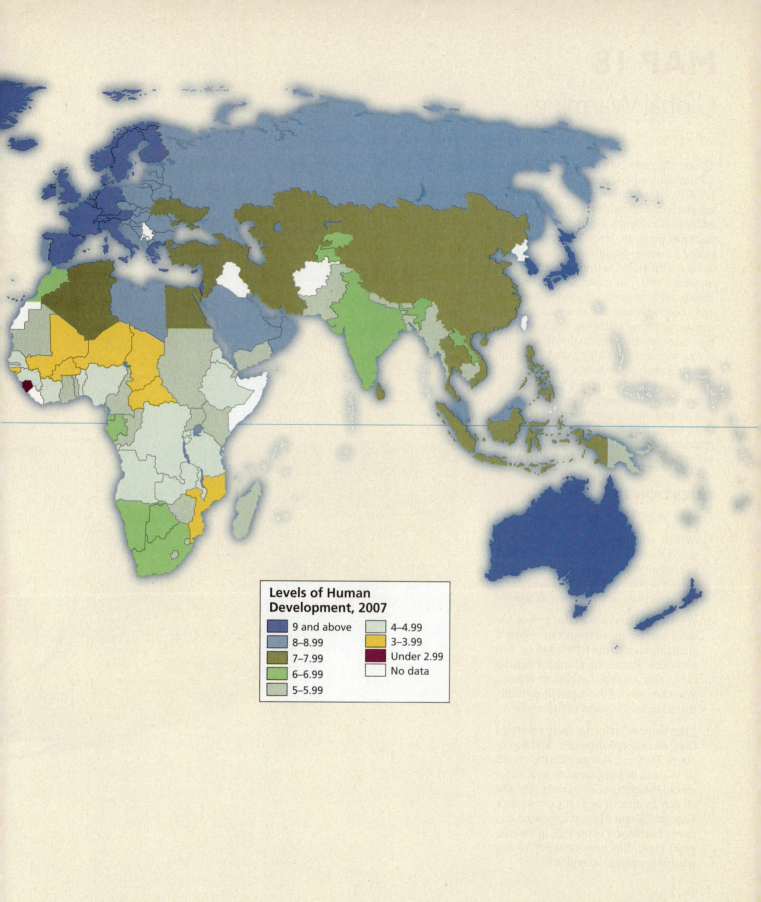

Levels of Human Development, 2007

- 9 and above
- 8–8.99
- 7–7.99
- 6–6.99
- 5–5.99
- 4–4.99
- 3–3.99
- Under 2.99
- No data

MAP 18
Global Warming

Since the early 20th century, the Earth's surface temperatures have risen about 1.4° F (0.7° C). Rising temperatures, shrinking glaciers, and melting polar ice provide additional evidence for global warming. Scientists prefer the term climate change to *global warming*. Scientific measurements confirm that global warming is not due to increased solar radiation, but rather are mainly *anthropogenic*—caused by humans and their activities. Because our planet's climate is always changing, the key question becomes: How much global warming is due to human activities versus natural climate variability. Most scientists agree that human activities play a major role in global climate change. Given population growth and rapidly increasing use of fossil fuels, the human factor is significant. The map represents the relative impact of global warming in different regions of the world.

QUESTIONS

Look at Map 18, "Global Warming."

1. Which geographical regions of the world show noticeable effects of global warming? Which show the least? What about the polar regions? Why are certain major sections of the oceans affected?

2. Widespread and long-term trends toward warmer global temperatures and a changing climate are referred to as "fingerprints." Researchers look for them to detect and confirm that climate change. What are some of the recent fingerprints that have been covered in the media?

3. "Harbingers" refer to such events as fires, exceptional droughts, and downpours. They can also include the spread of disease-bearing insects and widespread bleaching of coral reefs. Any and all may be directly or partly caused by a warmer climate. Have you noticed any recent harbingers in the U.S. in the past year? Have they been confined to any specific geographical regions?

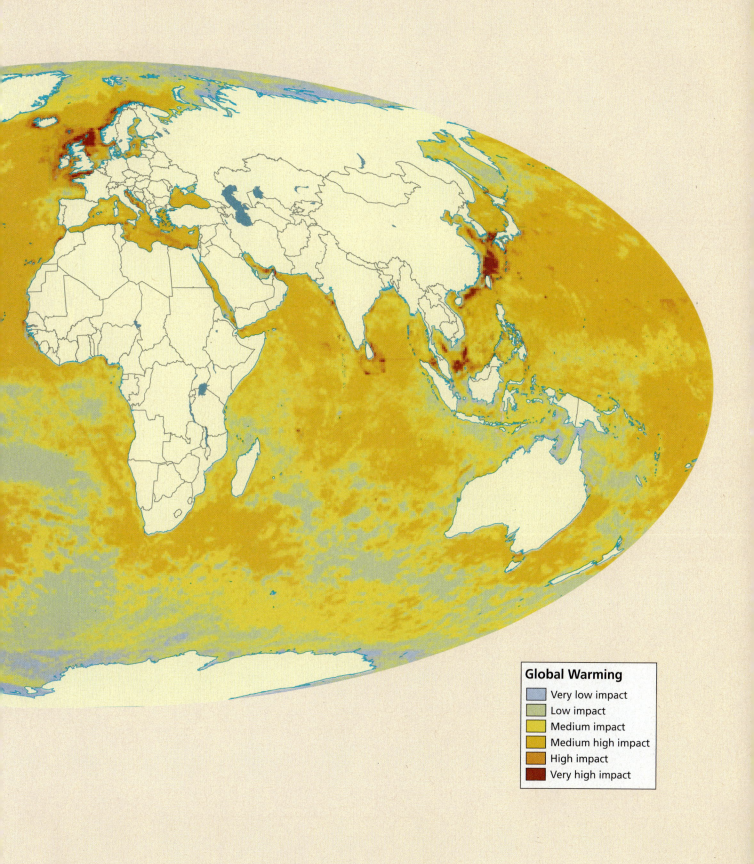

Global Warming
- Very low impact
- Low impact
- Medium impact
- Medium high impact
- High impact
- Very high impact